The Church as a Social Institution

The Church
as a
Social Institution

The Sociology of American Religion

Second Edition

David O. Moberg

BAKER BOOK HOUSE

Grand Rapids, Michigan 49506

Preface to the First Edition

The sociological interpretation of religion is like a pattern in a kaleidoscope. When the instrument is turned a bit to get the historical perspective, a different pattern emerges, although the basic elements are the same. Similarly, the composition varies when viewed from the perspective of anthropology, psychology, philosophy, theology, and other disciplines.

As a survey of the sociology of American religion, this book deals with those aspects of the church which can be observed and interpreted by sociological methodology. It deliberately minimizes discussions of primitive religions, church history, the philosophy of religion, and tangential topics except as they are needed to understand social aspects of contemporary religion. Built around the sociological framework of the American church as a social institution, it emphasizes the roles of Protestantism, Catholicism, and Judaism with occasional references to other religions and to such nonreligious phenomena as are linked with or relevant to the church.

The sources of the materials included are not exclusively sociological. Pertinent information has been drawn from anthropology, political science, church history, psychology, social psychology, education, theology, and social work. Materials from these diverse disciplines are woven into an integrated picture of the church in America.

This attempt to present a balanced picture of the church as a social institution may be disliked by some, since it exposes findings which the convinced churchman would prefer to keep secret, while at the same time it recognizes strengths and virtues which critics of the church would prefer to overlook. Scientific integrity demands recognition of both. This book is written neither to lampoon nor to laud the church, but rather to serve as a systematic compendium of sociological data about American religion.

The Church as a Social Institution is designed for a broad audience. As a survey of factual material about the church in American society, it will be useful in theological seminaries and among clergymen. It will help laymen understand the church and its relationships with other parts of society. It will serve as a textbook, with or without collateral reading assignments, in pertinent college courses. As a survey which includes references to numerous

71347

research studies, it will be useful to social scientists, scholars in other disciplines, and students. Hopefully, the numerous questions it implicitly raises
and the resources it supplies will stimulate further research and thus contribute to increased knowledge about the church.

Those who have contributed to this book directly or indirectly are legion.
They include my parents, friends, instructors, colleagues, pastors, and other
church workers who have increased my insights of practical church life.
Outstanding among them is Professor Herbert Blumer whose suggestions
have greatly improved the quality of the work.

Lastly, I wish to express my thanks to my wife, to my father-in-law, John
Heitzman, to Paul, Lynette, Jonathan, and Philip who have missed their
father's companionship, and to students and colleagues at Bethel College
and Seminary and at the State University of Groningen, The Netherlands,
who helped sharpen my thinking, identify significant problems, disclose subjects needing attention, and discover sources of information which contribute
to a more balanced and complete picture of the church as a social institution.

Preface to the Second Edition

Reviews and critiques of the first edition of this book
described it as "the finest existing compilation and synthesis of studies
on the sociology of the church," "a goldmine of reference material,"
"probably the most comprehensive review of the data pertaining to contemporary American church life," and yet an impressive and convincing
panoramic review of church attributes and functions pointing to the
church's "inescapable involvement in the total human scene." Its "en-
cyclopedic quality" has served me well in my own teaching and research,
for it summarizes or refers to almost everything published in the sociology
of American religion up to 1961. The detailed index has facilitated making
cross-references, stimulated seminal thoughts, and led to resources for
in-depth study.

The book was especially appreciated by Christians who were coping
with the issues it discussed and who felt that most current texts were
unfairly critical of their values. They intuitively sensed that the author
was a Christian and a churchman who had experienced their own dilemmas, joys, and sorrows and hence wrote from the interpretive sociological
perspective of a *verstehende* engagement rather than an aloof, unfeeling,
empirical detachment.

Widely adopted as a textbook in colleges, universities, and theological

seminaries and frequently cited in the literature of the sociology of religion, religious research, and other fields, the book nevertheless fell on
hard times as "the movement" with its strong anti-institutional bias tainted
academia and the rest of society in the late 1960's and much of the 1970's,
influencing the original publisher to decide against a revision. To revise
it today along the same comprehensive lines as the first edition would
require at least two or three additional volumes of equal length, for there
has been a vast explosion of knowledge related to religion. Indeed, just
an annotated bibliography of all the books, monographs, and articles published on the subject since 1960 could easily equal or exceed the length
of this book. Many additional religious groups have been studied; a few
new concepts have been added; new scholars and researchers have made
contributions; some new theoretical models, especially from ethnomethodological and structural perspectives, have been constructed.

Yet Charles Lemert's critique of recent theoretical paradigms in sociology seems to apply to much sociology of religion as well: "All were
synthetic works and all relied heavily on rather classical ideas. . . . It is
possible that what really took place was marginal diversification within a
traditional paradigm."[1] Therefore this book is still very useful as a reference tool, as an interpretation, and even as a text. The generalizations
and principles presented in it have stood the test of time and still are
valid. It can be used either by itself or as a steppingstone from which
more recent data can be examined through further reading, lectures, and
research projects. Such study will not supplant or contradict its contents
but will reinforce and extend them. Since its publication, the first edition
has required only the updating of its findings and the filling in of details
of outlines, which confirms the validity and reliability of its summaries.

No single theoretical orientation dominates this sociological analysis of
American religion. Even though its focus is organizational, centering
around both micro- and macro-sociological views of the church, attention
is given to personal and non-institutionalized religious behavior as well.
Sociologists will find that symbolic interactionism, structural functionalism, conflict sociology, and exchange theory are clearly evident, as well
as elements of other theoretical schools. The social facts, behavior, and
definition paradigms are all reflected, as are the perspectives of sociology
as one of the humanities, even though a "scientific" orientation is
dominant.

This theoretical synthesis or eclecticism reflects my opinion that theories, like methods, are tools for analysis. They ought not to become ideological "gods" restricting our vision to some narrow, particularized set
of data or delimited range of interpretations. This is not to deny, of course,
that a consistent, in-depth application of any given theoretical model can

---

[1] Charles C. Lemert, *Sociology and the Twilight of Man* (Carbondale: Southern Illinois
University Press, 1979), pp. 4–5.

throw much light on any subject we study, but it is to insist that all human knowledge is fragmentary and delimited, never absolute and complete.

This edition updates the statistical data in several passages, most notably Chapter 2, and adds Chapter 19 on selected new developments in the sociology of American religion. Many recent references have been added at the ends of chapters and in footnotes. Readers can learn much from them as well as from the index. It was not feasible to change the many passages in which *man* and male pronouns refer to any human being, male or female.

I am grateful, of course, to all who have contributed in some way or another to this second edition. They include family members, students and colleagues who have stimulated my thinking, sociologists and others who recommended bringing this book back into print, researchers and scholars of religion who have produced such rich material that it was difficult to write less than a lengthy book for Chapter 19, and our efficient secretaries, Elizabeth Schuman and Claudine Gorlick, who have typed the manuscript changes and additions. Most of all I am grateful to Allan Fisher, Douglas Polinder, and Dan Van't Kerkhoff, editors at Baker Book House, who proposed this new edition, explored its feasibility, and gave oversight during the revision and production process. I know that it will be a useful tool for my own continuing teaching, consultation, research, and writing, and I hope it will be of help to thousands of others as well.

Contents

Part One: *Introduction*

♨ Chapter 1

The Sociology of American Religion

The church is a major social institution in America. It consists of all organizations which directly seek to kindle, renew, and guide the religious life of people. It includes the roles and statuses of the persons in such groups, their ideological values, goals, and group-related activities, and all the social structures and processes related to religious worship, prayer, association, and other activities in ecclesiastical organizations. "The church" is therefore synonymous with "organized religion."

More memberships of Americans are in churches than in any other type of voluntary organization. A large part of the population participate in church activities every week and believe the doctrines propagated in them. The Bible is the only book that consistently remains a best seller decade after decade. Billions of dollars are invested in church property. Church budgets annually consume millions of dollars of the national income. Other social institutions, such as the family, school, and business, are all influenced by the church and simultaneously exert their influence upon it.

Symbolic expressions of organized religion surround Americans. Communications are dated by the Christian calendar. Religious holidays are regularly celebrated. Coins and many postage stamps bear the slogan, "In God We Trust." Political and legal oaths are sworn upon the Bible and in the name of God. Religious and quasi-religious music and art are a significant part of the environment. Over a thousand places bear biblical names. "There is scarcely a sphere of man's life that is left untouched by the conditioning effect of religious ideas." [1] From the cradle to the grave Americans are influenced directly or indirectly by organized religion in nearly all their activities. It is impossible to understand American society without understanding the church.

By the same token, it is not possible to understand the church without understanding its relationships with the rest of society. Regardless of its doctrinal beliefs, organization, and practices, every church is in the world and cannot ignore it. It operates in a social environment which exerts various pressures upon it, subjects it to many limitations, and provides a framework of general conditions for its formation, development, and survival. Society outside the church provides the people, economic resources, means of communication, and freedom without which it could not exist. Effective churchmanship requires knowledge of this cultural milieu.

America today is vastly different from any society of the past, and there are numerous indications that major changes are still taking place. Among these are the rapid growth of population in metropolitan areas, especially in the suburbs, and the accompanying decline in many rural areas. Shifts in places of residence bring together people from widely divergent backgrounds. Other developments with complex social and religious implications include continuing industrialization, accompanied by impersonal relationships between workers and by the socioeconomic problems associated with increasing automation; expansion of the duties and power of centralized national government and the possibility that strong international government may emerge within a generation; mounting pressures on sub-cultures to discontinue racial and ethnic discrimination; increasing speed and scope of transportation and communication; the ever-rising level of both formal and informal education in the general public; the all-pervading scope of modern mass communications like newspapers, radio, and television; rapid advancements in science and technology, affecting not only the development of atomic power and space missiles but also the customs of daily life and even conventional interpretations of scripture; the breaking down of traditional values and time-honored means of controlling individual behavior; growth of a mass society in which institutions become bureaucratic and, on the surface, seem less closely related to each other than in the past and more competitive for the time and loyalty of people and for the right to be recognized as the performers of certain essential tasks; and the prevalence of such reflections of personal alienation as suicide, mental illness, delinquency, and anxiety among people who have become mere faces in "the lonely crowd." All indications are that change will continue to be rapid in America.

---

[1] Ray H. Abrams in Foreword to "Organized Religion in the United States," *Annals of the American Academy of Political and Social Science*, 256 (March 1948), vii.

The church must adjust to these changes. If it ignores them and continues a purely traditional program, it will soon lose its influence and decay. What ought to be the reaction of a rural church when its members move to cities, or when they remain in the community but attend a town church that may be less than ten minutes away by modern means of transportation? How should the church react when scientific discoveries contradict established interpretations of the Bible? How can the church help its members face their personal problems when they are confronted daily with neighbors of different cultural backgrounds? How can the church adjust its educational programs to meet the needs of youth and adults who will live tomorrow in a different world from that of today? How can the clergy make the basic doctrines and tenets of their faith relevant to the demands of people living in the twentieth century? For what problems of society does the church have a realistic, even if incomplete, answer? How can its leaders guide the church so that it will be an effective institution in a fluid society?

Sociological study of these and hundreds of other problems faced by the church is essential if adequate solutions are to be reached. This book does not profess to give specific answers to such questions, but it provides a background of knowledge and understanding upon which the answers must be based to be constructive. Painstaking study of the church's relationships to its environment is not only advisable; in our generation it is essential for its meaningful survival. The sociological study of religion provides a body of knowledge on the church and its relation to society which is necessary if the church is to fulfill its mission effectively and efficiently in an ever-new social environment.

The Social Nature of Religion and the Church

Religion may be seen and studied from many different points of view. This book approaches it in terms of its social dimension and character. Numerous definitions of *religion* are available. Most social scientists would agree that one or more of the following must be present in order to have religious groups and religious behavior: (1) Belief in supernatural power, force, or beings, accompanied by attempts to get and remain in a relationship believed to be favorable. (2) Belief in values thought to transcend immediate social situations and hence to be worthy of allegiance, together with the organizations and symbolic activities for promoting these values. (3) Systematized beliefs and values used to explain the mysterious and the unknown or to answer teleological questions; these become organized into a social institution in which emotional attitudes dominate.[2]

---

[2] For a discussion of some of the classical anthropological and sociological definitions of religion see Clifford Kirkpatrick, *Religion in Human Affairs* (New

American religion hence includes such diverse categories as Roman Catholicism, Protestantism, Judaism, Mormonism, Buddhism, Ethical Culture, Peyotism, Moral Re-Armament, Theosophy, Jehovah's Witnesses, Christian Science, Islam, Rastafarians, and the Unification Church.

The religious life of any people is profoundly social. Vital religious devotion, piety, or worship is a personal experience, but even when a person is alone his religious behavior rests upon values and sentiments shared with other people. Personal religious beliefs and actions are largely a product of a process of learning from others; they are significantly influenced by past social experiences. This fact, of course, does not demand a belief that all religious phenomena are solely social in nature. "Faith and concern are social phenomena, to be treated as such, but they cannot be reduced, in their deepest roots and highest peaks, to the level of social relations." [3]

In any religious body individuals worship together, engage in common rituals, and share religious beliefs. They learn or acquire religious doctrines and practices from one another and secure support for such beliefs and activities through association with each other. Their basic ideas of God, religious observance, religious duty, and the nature of the universe are largely a result of communication in social settings. Clergymen and other religious leaders convey their messages in efforts to kindle and rekindle religious feelings and to inspire deeds of devotion. Religious values are used to organize personal lives and to guide relationships with others. The desire for fellowship and personal recognition in human groups, tribulations and anxieties, the need to explain the universe and man's place in it, and the search for security, all lead men to partake of a common fund of religious experience and to associate with others in religious groups. These few observations, which will be expanded and clarified in this book, make it clear that religion involves communication and interaction among men as well as with God.

Churches arise and exist in this social fabric of communication and human interaction. They consist of the association and organization of people on behalf of religious sentiments and values. Each church is a primary medium for fostering, preserving, renewing, and expressing religious experience. To perform such functions, a church necessarily becomes *an organized body* of human beings, as evidenced by numerous features. It has, for example, a structure based upon the division of labor between

York: John Wiley and Sons, 1929), pp. 13-56. See also Walter Houston Clark, "How Do Social Scientists Define Religion?" *Journal of Social Psychology,* 47 (Feb. 1948), 143-47; and Purnell H. Benson, *Religion in Contemporary Culture* (New York: Harper and Brothers, 1960), pp. 124-63.

[3] Nels F. S. Ferré, *Christian Faith and Higher Education* (New York: Harper and Brothers, 1954), p. 191. Reprinted by permission. See R. Lofton Hudson, "The Social Context of Religion," *Sociology and Social Research,* 31 (Sept.-Oct. 1946), 43-47.

leaders, officials, and members, the sets of different tasks to be performed, and the apparatus for performing them. A church has an organized round of life which focuses upon its meetings, ceremonies, and rituals. It has a shared body of beliefs and values in the form of creeds, doctrines, and tenets; it has sets of rules and regulations to guide the activities of people within it. Members have a sense of identity, a feeling that theirs is a religious organization distinct from other churches and groups. A church acts to preserve itself and to protect and advance its interests. Such features are found in every religious group, whether it is a simple primitive sect or a huge, complex denomination. They signify that the church by its very being is a social organization.

A church in its development and functioning is subject to the play of social processes which operate in all social institutions. As an operating organization, each church develops a structure, forms a body of beliefs and values to which it is committed, creates sets of rules and operating procedures, forms conceptions of its mission, faces tasks and problems set by the world in which it operates, and devises policies and procedures to deal with those tasks and problems. In meeting these requirements of its life, a church, like other social institutions, must be recognized as an organization made, and continually remade, by men. The inner structure which is formed, the rules and regulations which are established, the means which are fashioned to nurture and sustain religious beliefs, the purposes and goals which are cultivated, the policies and procedures which are devised, and the sense of identity which is developed are all products of collective effort by the people who comprise the church. Much of this effort is deliberate and far-sighted, but much of it is a haphazard product of the process of meeting emergencies. The results of earlier endeavor provide the framework for later efforts; the hands of the past always rest on the present.

The church takes many different forms and varies greatly in size and complexity. It may take the form of a religious cult in a primitive society, a rural evangelistic sect, a "store-front church," a house church, or a huge city church. It may also take the form of a religious order, a national denomination like the United Presbyterian Church, a large international organization like the Roman Catholic Church, or a federation like the National Council of the Churches of Christ in the United States. Accordingly, a church may be small or large, simple or complex, loosely organized or highly bureaucratic. In every case, the key to understanding it is organization—the fact that human beings are acting together in diverse ways on behalf of religious interests. The term "church" is used in this book as a general concept to refer to this fact of organization. Hence it covers all instances in which people have established some form of functioning and continuing organization to serve their religious needs and purposes.

Every religious organization has some degree of formalism or institutionalization. This is true even of groups that claim to be "merely a fellowship, not a denomination," and of those so informally and loosely organized that they claim to lack organization altogether.

> Those most critical of what they consider the institutionalism of the church themselves exhibit it. Sects, for example, like the Primitive Baptist, representing extreme anti-ecclesiastical attitudes, maintaining the utmost simplicity and freedom in worship and an unpaid ministry, are genuinely shocked by the excesses of the Holy Rollers as the latter appear in mountain communities. Yet the truth is that the mountain preacher who most loudly proclaims that he receives his sermon by direct inspiration of God is asserting a highly-developed religious convention. Even in the most informal intercourse of his group he is subject to the dead hand of social ritualism. . . . Peculiar religious diction and intonation are universally employed in primitive religious services to signify the inter-communion between the human and the divine members of a common society. One who has witnessed the "speaking with tongues" of the wilder religions is sure to have been impressed by the imitative manner of vocalization. Institutionalization, then, has no exclusive connection with prayer-books or a sacerdotal order of clergy.
>
> Moreover, in religious groups whose ecclesiasticism is least developed, formalized group judgments defining and evaluating the person are more frequent and burdensome than in the ritualistic churches. . . . Even in the freest churches prayer becomes stereotyped. Testimony repeats old patterns. The religious originality of the first generation slips down into the institutionalized custom of succeeding ones. The ecclesiasticism of the sect is a different sort from that of the established church, but it is not a whit less institutionalized.
>
> The attempt, then, to conceive of a non-institutionalized religion for modern man is sociologically infantile. It is an attack on rationality and ethical stability themselves. Religion cannot have currency without developing some generalized form, and generalized form implies habits resistant to change which are the essence of institutionalization.[4]

The church, then, is a social structure. In the pursuit of its goals it functions as a social entity in a social world. This means that, like other institutions, it is subject to the play of social forces in both its formation and its operation. This book is devoted to the study and analysis of these forces and the manner in which the church in American society responds to them.

The cardinal aspects of the church can be and have been studied from many different points of view. The historian's perspective focuses upon unique or distinctive factors in the case of a specific church or set of churches. The psychologist's viewpoint stresses the operation of psycholog-

[4] H. Paul Douglass and Edmund deS. Brunner, *The Protestant Church as a Social Institution* (New York: Institute of Social and Religious Research, 1935), pp. 13-15. Reprinted by permission. Cf. Charles H. Cooley, *Social Organization* (New York: Charles Scribner's Sons, 1909), pp. 374-75.

ical processes in the experience of individuals who comprise the church. The philosopher's approach seeks through reflection and deduction to interpret philosophical principles related to the life and career of the church. The theologian analyzes questions about the attributes of God, His relations to man, the church's values, and the basic nature of the universe. The sociological approach, dominating this book, falls in the area conventionally designated "the sociology of religion."

The Sociology of Religion

Sociology is the social science that deals with the development, organization, and behavior of human groups. One of its central subjects is social interaction—the reciprocal actions of people as they influence each other. Sociological study of religion is based on the recognition that both religious life and the church as its institutional expression are profoundly social. Religion is a major aspect of human society and justly occupies an eminent position alongside such other areas as economic life, politics, education, family life, recreation, and welfare. The church correspondingly may be studied with as much profit as business, government, schools, the family and other institutions. Such study leads to richer understanding of a vital area of group life and more intelligent control of problems that arise within it. And the sociology of religion brings the same sociological perspective, methods of inquiry, and schemes of analysis to bear on religion as sociology brings to its study of other aspects of human society.

The unique character of religion does not prevent such study. Even though religion is distinctively sacred and involves divine relationships, it is a part of human group life. The feelings, values, and beliefs which set it apart from other areas of life arise in the context of human association and are fashioned and sustained by the character of this context. In turn, such feelings, values, and beliefs play upon and enter into other areas of human experience, affecting the conceptions, values, and practices of people in them.

The above remarks indicate the broad interests of the sociology of religion. It is concerned, for example, with such questions as the following. What social conditions are conducive to the formation of a religious outlook on life? What social conditions sustain or undermine such an outlook? What kinds of group processes nurture and strengthen sacred feelings of devotion and consecration, and what kinds destroy and diminish these feelings? How are religious values affected by the general mode of life of people, such as that in a simple pastoral society, a prosperous agricultural community, a complex urban civilization, an enslaved state, or a politically dominant nation? How are religious beliefs formed and modified under divergent varieties of group experience? What processes and social influences are related to such religious changes as the passage from primitive animism to the conception of a single deity? Under what conditions do religious feelings, values, and beliefs flow readily into other areas of group life, and under what conditions is their sway over such areas limited or hindered? How does religion affect such social complexes as imperial government, modern capitalism, a caste system, feudalism, or democracy? This sample of questions illustrates the kinds of concern included in the sociology of religion. Anyone with knowledge of the numerous and diverse forms of organized religion in the history of man will readily recognize the validity and importance of such questions.

Sincere study of such problems does not eliminate or weaken genuine religious emotions and spiritual values. Such feelings and ideals are rooted in the collective experiences of people; they are not the product of the scholars who analyze the experiences. In showing how such feelings and values are sustained or hindered, how they are formed and transformed, and how they influence the rest of group life, scholars contribute to increased understanding and appreciation of the nature, and important role, of religion.

The church as a social institution is a major subject in the sociology of religion. The church is a peculiarly appropriate object for sociological study because it is a collective undertaking, an association of people organized to act together. As such, the church is subject to the play of all the basic social processes operating in human societies. Organizations come into existence through the actions of human beings, whatever the original motives which inspire their actions may be. The character of each organization is affected by the conditions out of which it originates. It must develop some kind of structure on behalf of its mission or objective. This structure involves separation of people into different *roles*—the patterns of rights, privileges, duties, and responsibilities which are expected or required of those who occupy certain social positions within the group. The diverse activities that comprise the on-going life of the organization give status to its members, providing each with a relative position of prestige, privilege, and authority on the basis of his roles. This entire organizational structure is peculiarly subject to the play of such sociological processes as formalization or institutionalization, bureaucratization, conflict, and integration. As a consciously functioning enterprise with an identity recognized by its membership, it is confronted by the surrounding world in which it must operate. The institution must deal with this world; it devises policies and practices to meet the problems and requirements that flow from its efforts to exist and operate in its own specific social setting. It tries to protect or advance its particular interests and values. All of the matters mentioned in this paragraph are conditions and needs that confront every human organization. They are subjects sociologists study, and the methods and concepts used in analyzing them can be applied effectively to the study of churches.

The Sociological Study of the Church

Sociological analysis of the church pertains to many of its general features. Obviously, churches come into being, undergo development, seek to realize purposes, elaborate interests, form an inner organization, and develop activities. No church accomplishes this in a vacuum. It is lodged in a social setting which consists of all the institutions, customs, and traditions and the entire round of life of its society. Interaction between the church and its surrounding social world necessarily results; other institutions act on the church, and the church in its turn acts on them. In addition, because the church is an organization of human beings, it is subject to the interaction which occurs among its members. Their patterns of working relationships with each other, their disagreements and conflicts, their forms of adjustment and cooperation, and their efforts to act together on behalf of common interests contribute to the internal life and organizational patterns of the church. All of these facets of the life of a church signify the importance of social influences and processes in its formation and functioning, and as such are suitable objects of sociological study.

A multitude of phenomena may be studied sociologically in analyzing the origin, development, structure, and functions of churches. These range from minor matters to those of very great significance. Some of the major concerns in such study are the social conditions which favor the rise and development of churches, the social forces which influence and shape them, the social functions performed in society by them, the social processes which operate within them to shape their organization and their modes of confronting the world, the kinds of internal structures which formally and informally develop within them, the ways in which these organizational forms affect their efforts to attain objectives, the church's control over activities of the people who collectively comprise it, the fundamental forms of religious organization, and the social values which give direction to church activities and provide an ideological hub for its entire program.

Just as scholarly analysis of religion contributes knowledge which increases its vitality as an important human experience, sociological study of the church offers means of making it a more effective social institution. Insights yielded by such study also contribute to intelligent awareness of the conditions which impair its effective growth and operation.

The sociological study of the church has at least three distinctive characteristics. First of all, it rests on the recognition that the church is a collective or social undertaking. As we have seen, each church is an *organi-*

zation of human beings interacting with one another, influencing one another, affecting each other's feelings, thoughts, and behavior. Since it must confront and deal with its surrounding world, it interacts with other institutions and with non-religious phases of group life. This social interaction, occurring both within the church and between it and its social milieu, must be studied in its own right. It cannot be reduced to psychological traits of individuals; it cannot be fully understood in psychological terms alone. Social factors are of utmost significance, for instance, in such characteristic differences as the solemnity of religious ceremonies in one church compared to the ecstatic frenzy in the services of another, the tight system of theocratic control in one and the loose system of voluntary cooperation in another, the high prestige the clergy enjoy at one period of time and their lesser prestige later, and the recruitment of members of a given church from one social segment rather than from others.

A second distinguishing feature of the sociological approach is that it stresses what is common to many phenomena, rather than what is unique to one given instance. Sociological study seeks to understand processes and conditions which are characteristic of churches in general. Hence it is concerned with such universal matters as the process by which churches develop formal and rigid structures, become encased in a framework of tradition, develop a bureaucratic administration, or form an association with high morale or great zeal. In its concern with general processes, sociological analysis relies heavily on comparative and conceptual study with the goal of improving the quality of human life. Sociology hence is one of the humanities, not just a science.

Finally, sociological study of the church is scientific. This means assembling large bodies of reliable and verifiable facts—facts that are open to the scrutiny and testing of more than one person. It means studying under rules which assure honest and careful observation and using investigative techniques which protect against bias and unwitting errors. It means imaginative, yet disciplined, analysis resulting in knowledge that is both new and tested. It implies study for the sake of scientific truth and not solely to promote one special faith, group, or doctrine. Description of some of the basic features of science will clarify the sociological approach to the analysis of the church.

The Scientific Method

The man who classifies facts of any kind, sees their mutual relationships, and describes their sequences is applying the scientific method. The unity of science does not reside in the material that is studied by it but solely in its method. *Science* is basically a method, but it also refers to the organization of men, equipment, and facilities for the application of that method, any body of knowledge accumulated by that method, and any discipline which uses that method. Failure to recognize the dependence

of all sciences upon a basic concept of scientific methodology has sometimes led to misunderstanding among scientists, as well as to the failure of
laymen to appreciate their work.

The goal of the scientific method is to develop new and dependable
knowledge by discovering facts and relationships between them in any
given area of scientific interest. In doing this it is forced to go beyond conventional or folk knowledge and to concern itself with what is vague, concealed, or inadequately known. By identifying genuine facts and establishing verifiable relations between them, science pushes back the walls of
ignorance and broadens man's knowledge, insight, and understanding.

Many methodological techniques are used in science, but all of them
are empirical, that is, based upon man's experience and observation,
especially through the use of his senses. Nevertheless, scientific knowledge may properly include certain conclusions based upon subjective experiences if these experiences are shared with one another and "spirit
bears witness with spirit." In the behavioral sciences strictly empirical
methods are supplemented by insight (*Verstehen*) which aids the evaluation of subjective meanings and beliefs that can be only partly apparent
to the senses. The scientist is less concerned with the ultimate truth or
falsity of these beliefs than with their implications for behavior; he realizes that if men believe their ideas to be true, whether they conform to
reality or not, the consequences of the ideas are real indeed. The definitions and explanations men attach to situations in which they find themselves are of great importance to their conduct.

The scientific method has limitations. It is based upon a set of unproven
postulates. It is restricted to that which is verifiable and accordingly observable; science cannot either affirm or deny the truth of propositions
which lie beyond these limits. Science as such does not control the new
knowledge that results from its efforts. The application of such knowledge
on occasions creates or points up problems which can be solved only
through implementing moral or religious ideals.

This picture of science can now be projected onto the subject of religion. Scientific study can advance the interests of both churchmen and
social scientists by replacing inadequate understanding with reliable
knowledge in those areas to which the scientific method can be applied.
Those who fear that such knowledge will undermine or eliminate religion
misunderstand the nature of both religion and science. With its emphasis
upon empirical facts, science necessarily sees religion as a natural and
vital part of human experience; religion is obviously grounded in group
life as a natural phenomenon and not as an occurrence which results from
some artificial, non-social force.

Science can neither prove nor disprove the supernatural elements of
religion, but it can help free religion from restraints of ignorance, erroneous information, and false notions. It can thus give religious groups new

horizons of action and a new perspective of their tasks and opportunities. This is especially true in the case of the church as a social institution. Most of the church's life is empirically observable and hence capable of scientific study. Accurate knowledge of church life is more necessary than ever before, for the church is caught in a new developing world—a world which introduces a new social setting, poses new problems, and makes new demands. To fulfill its mission effectively the church needs the reliable knowledge scientific study can produce.

Since beliefs are so important in religion, scientists analyzing the church must be even more involved in the study of normative behavior and group values than those who study most other segments of society. Many aspects of these beliefs cannot be understood fully by the non-believer. He is often limited in his participant observation of religious rites and ceremonies to the objective and intellectual aspects of them, and he sometimes is completely barred from participation or even observation. Lacking the emotional overtones and undertones, he is likely also to lack full understanding of the meaning of religious acts to believing participants. "Without empathy into the religious experience underlying the content of the 'official ecclesiastical sources,' the complete ideology will escape [the researcher] to a great extent and with it will escape the ability of grasping the facts." [5] Participant observation by the outsider should therefore be supplemented by the work of observing participants. Only thus can the socio-psychological meanings attached to the emotionally-tinged attitudes and values of a religious group be sufficiently appreciated.[6] The scientist who is a believer must also exercise caution in studies of his own religious groups lest he falsely assume that elements based solely upon his faith are empirically observable and part of his scientific evidence.

Qualitative aspects of religious behavior need to be distinguished from the quantitative in scientific studies. A religious minority which is ardent in its faith shows more "religious energy" or vitality than a numerically dominant majority which is apathetic. The intensity of meaning involved in the practice of religion is perhaps more important to its role as a causative variable in society than quantitative elements which usually are easier to study.[7] Because of the way it combines empirical research with experiential insight, the sociology of religion has been viewed as an art as well as a science.[8]

[5] Rudolph E. Morris, "Problems Concerning the Institutionalization of Religion," *American Catholic Sociological Review,* 17 (June 1956), 100.

[6] Clarence Marsh Case, "Toward Gestalt Sociology," in *Essays in Social Values,* Emory S. Bogardus, ed. (Los Angeles: University of Southern California, 1944), pp. 105-19.

[7] Francois A. Isambert, "Développement et Dépassement de L'Etude de la Pratique Religieuse Chez Gabriel LeBras," *Cahiers Internationaux de Sociologie,* 20 (Jan.-June 1956), 149-69.

[8] Prentiss L. Pemberton, "An Examination of Some Criticisms of Talcott Parsons' Sociology of Religion," *Journal of Religion,* 36 (Oct. 1956), 241-56. Cf. Robert

The Scientific Study of Religion

Until recently scientific study of religion and the church in America was relatively neglected by social scientists. The close association of religion with philosophy and metaphysics led some to think that the church could not be studied empirically. Others were repelled by opposition in certain church circles, and those in state-supported institutions of higher learning were discouraged by the American tradition of separation of church and state. Some in the pre-World War II era felt that the church was on the way to becoming ineffective and insignificant, hence not meriting the costs of study.[9] Other social scientists, reflecting their emotional "emancipation" from certain aspects of traditional or personal religion, revolted against any contact with it. Perhaps the most important reason for neglect of scientific study of the church, however, lay in the preoccupation of social scientists with other areas of interest and the lack of compelling or inviting reasons for directing their studies to the field of religion.

The general American resurgence of interest in religion since World War II has been accompanied by increasing scientific study of religion and the church. One reflection of this growing interest is the Society for the Scientific Study of Religion organized in 1950. Its purposes include bringing together religious scholars and social scientists, stimulating the scientific study of religion, inter-stimulating and inter-fertilizing the thinking of those who are scientifically studying religion, appraising research projects, and encouraging and facilitating joint research. The first issue of its *Journal for the Scientific Study of Religion* appeared in 1961. The Religious Research Association also has contributed much to the sociology of religion. Its *Review of Religious Research* began in 1959, and its annual H. Paul Douglass Lectures are attracting increasing attention. The Association for the Sociology of Religion publishes the quarterly *Sociological Analysis*, successor to the *American Catholic Sociological Review*, and the international *Social Compass* begun in 1953 also is helpful.

One section of each annual convention of the American Sociological Association deals with the sociology of religion. Articles on the subject in professional social science literature are increasing in number and improving in quality. Many relevant monographs and survey books are appearing. The scant, often negatively biased, treatment of religion in general sociological books before World War II also has gradually been modified. Today textbook authors generally make a serious attempt to

Redfield, "The Art of Social Science," *American Journal of Sociology,* 54 (Nov. 1948), 181-91; and Jessie Bernard, "The Art of Science: A Reply to Redfield," *ibid.,* 55 (July 1949), 1-9.

[9] Perhaps the best example is Harry Elmer Barnes, *The Twilight of Christianity* (New York: Vanguard Press, 1929), pp. 442-44. Cf. Kingsley Davis, *Human Society* (New York: The Macmillan Co., 1949), p. 536.

understand religious institutions and the functions of religion in modern society instead of ignoring or discrediting them.[10]

Sociologists have encountered much resistance and opposition within church circles when they have proposed or made scientific studies of religion. Examination of the nature and sources of this resistance sheds light on problems confronted in the study of the church as a social institution. The experience of the Institute of Social and Religious Research, which from 1922 to 1934 conducted 48 research projects published in 78 volumes, is especially instructive. Throughout its existence, the Institute's efforts were under continual suspicion and frequently aroused open opposition. The opposition was least against community or territorial studies directly concerned with local church units, especially when their results pointed out remedies for already acknowledged evils. It was greatest against studies touching on the organization and functions of the church in general or of the ministry. Four major sources of resistance were especially important.[11] The *popular* type of resistance prevailed among the masses of church members who habitually made a sharp distinction between the external aspects of the church and its spiritual aspects. They wished to devote all their efforts to spiritual work and were unimpressed by objective study of church phenomena. They charged the scientific attitude with ignoring the invisible features of the church, illicitly treating its visible part as though it were merely a cold, lifeless phenomenon, and thus being a subversive influence hindering the work of the Holy Spirit.

Professional resistance to religious studies was found among professional church personnel. Any shortcoming of the institution was interpreted as diminishing their prestige. The extreme sensitiveness with respect to objective studies among ministers did not follow denominational lines. It was discovered among "convinced high-churchmen" as well as among the "common or garden type of minister."

Doctrinal resistance was based upon the opinion that the church had failed either to live or to proclaim the gospel, and that consequently an emphasis upon existing church organization would lead to perpetuation of a decadent institution by hindering an appreciation of its basic social or spiritual needs. Teaching tricks of institutional survival and efficiency to an apostate or defiled organization would do a disservice to true religion.

---

[10] Compare Robert L. Sutherland, "Sociology," in *College Reading and Religion* (New Haven: Yale University Press, 1948), pp. 263-85; Brewton Berry, "Religion and the Sociologists," *Christian Century,* 58 (Oct. 22, 1941), 1301-03; William F. Buckley, Jr., *God and Man at Yale* (Chicago: Henry Regnery Co., 1951), pp. 199-206; and A. H. Hobbs, *The Claims of Sociology* (Harrisburg, Pa.: Stackpole Press, 1951), pp. 129-30.

[11] Douglass and Brunner, *The Protestant Church,* pp. 4-13. The professional and doctrinal ("clerical" and "theological") types of resistance to research in Catholicism are discussed in Thomas F. O'Dea, *American Catholic Dilemma* (New York: Sheed and Ward, 1958), pp. 131-33, *passim.*

Radical opposition to church research was found among those who believed it to be too conservative and behind the times. The objections of unconventional mystics who compartmentalized their religion, of doctrinal and ethical radicals, and of some who believed themselves to have a monopoly on the scientific method as applied to religion, arose because they alleged that the studies assumed, or at least did not preclude, the perpetuation of the church in its present forms.

Other common sources of opposition to scientific study of the church include the following beliefs: that objectivity presupposes indifference; that the status quo is satisfactory; that there is no need to study the church as long as all seems to be well in it; that the monetary costs of scientific study are a waste of "the Lord's money"; that enemies of the church may use the findings of research; that research results may encourage proselyting; and that scientific study is an enemy's effort to overthrow the church.

Actually, each of these arguments gives way under objective analysis. Scientific studies presuppose interest in the church rather than indifference, except when they are conducted on a purely routine basis under economic or moral compulsion. Objectivity involves honesty, careful control of the researcher's biases; to equate this with indifference is a gross error. Satisfaction with the status quo may be only superficial; it may disappear when systematic investigation clarifies facts about the church and its place in society. Furthermore, study of well-organized and integrated churches is an essential basis for understanding the problems of those that are becoming disorganized and disintegrated. Monetary costs of scientific research are repaid many times when they lead to more effective church programs. If research reveals weaknesses in organized religion, they can be corrected, thus not increasing opposition but removing some of the basis for enmity against the church. Proselyting is often opposed most effectively by possessing the truth about one's own institution. Science and theology are not basically enemies, for they involve two distinct, though overlapping, areas of thought and practice. They often investigate the same subjects, but they do so from different philosophical and methodological perspectives. While science is concerned with structure and mechanism, theology is concerned more with significance and purpose. Science is basically descriptive, while theology is basically teleological. Christianity and Judaism, America's dominant religions, have much in common with science, especially from an ethical viewpoint (Chapter 13).

With increasing recognition by churchmen of the nature and role of science and increasing appreciation by social scientists of the value of studying religion, scientific study of the church is acquiring renewed vigor. We may confidently expect rapid expansion of such study in the closing decades of the twentieth century. Out of this research will flow numerous benefits to science, the church, and society, not the least of which may be increased ability to predict the consequences of events and thus to plan the future of the church more effectively than ever before.[12]

The Nature of the Church as a Social Institution

To study the church sociologically it is necessary to have a clear working definition of what is meant by "the church" and by a "social institution."

"Church" is often used sociologically as a synonym for "organized religion." As such, any organization or association of persons striving to perpetuate or propagate some religious belief or ideal is a church. From this broad perspective, a church may be a loosely organized group of preliterate idol worshipers or a highly bureaucratic, rigidly structured institution like the Roman Catholic Church. The concept of "church" has at least seven different meanings in the context of Christianity. Most of these usages are applicable, with appropriate modifications, to other religions as well.

1. A building used for religious worship. It may be a chapel, temple, cathedral, mosque, or store-front hall. This use will appear only rarely in this book.

2. A spiritual fellowship or "communion of saints." This is an ideal or goal of religious groups more than a completely achieved reality, so it lies outside the realm of sociological observation. It can be used, however, as a normative standard to evaluate the degree to which goals are in fact achieved.

3. The invisible, incorrupt, "true," catholic, or *universal church,* consisting of all believers in Christ, past, present, and future. This theological concept is not directly susceptible to sociological analysis but is a part of the normative structure of some groups. Roman Catholics and certain others regard their ecclesiastical institution to be *the* Christian church. This sectarian use of the term appears in this book only when it is pertinent to understanding norms and inter-institutional relationships.

4. A congregation, association, community, or organization of persons with Christian beliefs who are banded together primarily or ostensibly for religious purposes. Usually such a group also possesses a building; often the meeting-place and congregation are referred to synonymously as, e.g., the First Methodist Church of Hometown, U.S.A. In some denominations the territorial area the church serves is also included as part of a single unit, the parish. This fourth concept is referred to in this book as the congregation or *local church.*

---

[12] See Carl E. Seashore, "The Functions of Science in Religion," *Religious Education,* 43 (Mar.-Apr. 1948), 103-05.

5. An organization of many congregations sharing certain beliefs and practices which carries the burden of cooperative enterprises. Usually this is called a *denomination,* but sometimes the terms sect and cult are also used. (Chapter 4 gives the distinctions drawn between these in typological analyses.) The United Methodist Church is an illustration of a denomination.

6. A *denominational family.* This is a group of similar denominations, whether in direct fellowship and cooperation with one another or not. They have common elements in their history, doctrines, or organization and therefore are often referred to as if they were an analytical unit. We may speak of the Baptist Church in this sense, although there are numerous Baptist denominations and the impression of organic unity could hence be misleading.

7. The *church as an abstract, universal institution.* Used in this way "the church" refers to a generalized symbolic conception, including any and all aspects of organized religious practice, irrespective of denominational family or type of religion. To refer to the church as an institution in this sense is much like labeling "private property" an institution. One may appropriately look upon private property as an abstract arrangement, present in most societies in the form of recognized claims of ownership surrounded by laws, courts, police agencies, insurance companies, and real estate enterprises for protecting and exchanging such property. One may similarly think of the church as an abstract arrangement in the form of an organizational structure, a normative system of beliefs, rituals, and symbols, and a complex pattern of social interrelationships among its members. This meaning does not refer to any specific church but to that which is generally characteristic of all churches and denominations.

In dealing with "the church as a social institution" we rely chiefly on the seventh definition. Such an approach is conventionally designated as *macro-institutional.* Since sociology is concerned with what is recurrent in social life, it presents generalized descriptions and interpretations of *the* church, just as it speaks of the family, the criminal, the black, the city, or the human group. In each instance, a large number of items are taken into consideration and the general picture summarizes a wide range of observable quantitative and qualitative variations and central tendencies. Generalization from such a wide range of phenomena leads, perhaps inevitably, to generic terminology. As a generic term "the church as a social institution" includes such a broad scope of human endeavor that it can be stated logically that there is, in reality, no such thing as *the* church. The concept is a scientific abstraction; it represents an artificial entity emerging out of intellectual and scientific analysis. The danger of reifying this abstraction must be guarded against; only local churches, denominations, and other religious organizations are present in concrete reality.

Whenever appropriate, the term "church" is used in this book to refer to various specific or concrete religious bodies of types 4, 5, and 6 above, but especially to local churches. This is customarily designated as the *micro-institutional* approach. When a local church is the subject of analysis, it may be viewed as (1) a legal corporation formed under the laws of the state, holding and administering property for religious purposes; (2) a super-imposed association, whenever conditions for its existence have been determined by exterior authorities like a Catholic bishop acting on behalf of the pope; (3) an institutionalized association with locally patterned relationships that are distinctive and unique; (4) a communal group in which integration of a number of people occurs primarily because of their system of religious values; (5) a cluster of numerous formal and informal sub-groupings; (6) a series of statistical categories of adherents; or (7) in numerous cases, a network of family and kinship relationships.[13]

Study of a local church can be facilitated by the objective analysis of its major type parts: (1) The common reciprocating attitudes and conventionalized behavior patterns of persons in the institution (respect, loyalty, fear, awe, devotion, etc.) can be analyzed by direct observation and by attitude scales. (2) The weight, volume, number, and monetary value of utilitarian culture traits (objects or property like the church edifice, hymnals, pews, and the parking lot) that satisfy needs can be determined relatively easily. (3) Symbolic culture traits (objects charged with sentimental meanings to which human behavior has been conditioned, as a cross, shrine, ikon, altar, or mezuzah) can be similarly enumerated, measured, weighed, and valued. (4) The code of written or oral specifications (a church constitution, creed, statement of faith, etc.), which consists of language symbols preserving the descriptions and specifying the patterns of interrelationship among the other type parts, is susceptible to legal and semantic analysis and interpretation.[14] Comparisons of churches can add analysis of historical traditions, roles and relationships among personnel, and the sociocultural setting. (See the Appendix.)

What Is a Social Institution?

The term "institution" does not enjoy a universally accepted definition in social science; hence a wide range of diverse phenomena are called institutions. They include government, the parliamentary system, monarchy, the family, marriage, Christmas, slavery, the Federal Reserve System, warfare, a large bank, a university, public education, and even comic strip characters like Li'l Abner. These many usages share the traits of being well established, enduring, and in most instances fully sanctioned

---

[13] Joseph H. Fichter, "Conceptualizations of the Urban Parish," *Social Forces,* 31 (Oct. 1952), 43-46.

[14] F. Stuart Chapin, *Contemporary American Institutions* (New York: Harper and Brothers, 1935), esp. pp. 13-16, 358-60.

in their respective societal settings. Sociologists generally apply the term *social institution* to three different kinds of structure abstracted from reality in their analyses: (1) important areas of group life, such as education, government, law, the family, and religion; (2) complex systems of social relationships and norms, such as private property, marriage, slavery, and a monetary system; and (3) a functioning organization, such as the United States Steel Corporation, the Tennessee Valley Authority, Harvard University, or the Roman Catholic Church. Since each of these three forms of usage has its proper place in sociological analysis, all three appear in our discussions, the context always indicating which one or more is applicable. Our primary concern, however, is with the church, which is defined as an institution largely on the basis of the latter two meanings. A summary of major characteristics and basic types of institutions will clarify the orientation of this book and help us understand the nature of the church as a major social institution.

Characteristics of Institutions. Applying the first two of the three definitions specified above, sociologists discern the following important features of social institutions.[15]

1. *Stability.* Institutions outlast any generation and serve as social conservators of culture traits and patterns. Their structure and function change only slowly and gradually, and most of them have developed over long periods of time. This stability is largely due to their independence from the individuals and groups through which and by which they function.

2. *Universality.* The major institutions have existed among all known groups of people. The family, organized religion, government, and education are found in some form in every society.

3. *Identification with human needs.* Many have considered the satisfaction of basic human needs, interests, wishes, or even instincts as the central characteristic, distinguishing feature, and *raison d'être* of social institutions. Some have assumed that each institution crystallized in a process of evolution around some basic need—the family around propagation and protection of the young; government around protection of the group; education around the need to socialize the child and preserve the material and nonmaterial culture; organized religion around the need to worship or to explain the unknown. Such theories have many defects. They fail to account for the extreme variability of social institutions from one culture to another. Widely divergent needs are satisfied by families within

---

[15] These are based largely upon Constantine Panunzio, *Major Social Institutions* (New York: The Macmillan Co., 1939), pp. 19-22; and Don Martindale and Elio D. Monachesi, *Elements of Sociology* (New York: Harper and Brothers, 1951), pp. 381-403; with some assistance from Florian Znaniecki, "Social Organization and Institutions," in *Twentieth Century Sociology,* Georges Gurvitch and Wilbert E. Moore, eds. (New York: Philosophical Library, 1945), pp. 172-217.

the same culture. The very "needs" that presumably led to the formation and maintenance of institutions contribute to social disorganization in periods of revolutionary change. Many needs are usually satisfied within a single institution. Circular reasoning is involved in the "proof" of such theories (e.g., religion is needed because all men have religion), and the intricate interaction of duties and privileges, rewards and punishments, demands and satisfactions makes it impossible to separate needs clearly from rewards, penalties, burdens, and obligations. Empirical analysis of the specific factors that motivate any given person, and hence a group, in any specific situation is very difficult. Basic human requirements are met in such diverse ways and so many of them are intertwined with one another that it is difficult to determine which one need, if any, is dominant. Nevertheless, social institutions collectively provide the societal framework within which man satisfies or attempts to satisfy both organically innate and socially acquired needs.

4. *Variability.* Although the basic institutions are found in all parts of the world, among all social classes, and in all types of culture, there are variations among them from one culture to another and, within a culture, from one sub-group to another and from one period of time to another.

5. *Interrelation.* All of a society's institutions are intricately interrelated. Their functions constantly mix and overlap. Major changes in any one bring about changes in all the others. They are interdependent and interpenetrative. Together they form a syndrome, constellation, or web of net-like interrelationships; when one strand of this web is influenced, the entire web shifts and concomitant modification of the relative positions of the various parts inevitably takes place. No institution can be understood in isolation from the others in its society. Changes in one necessitate changes in all the others.

6. *Systemization of positions.* The places of individuals in society are systemized by institutions. Their various positions are standardized; the roles that they play are defined. This simplifies social interaction by enabling fairly accurate prediction of people's institutionalized actions. It makes cooperative, disciplined action possible. The status or relative rank of a person is determined primarily by his roles in groups which are the concrete units of organized social action. Operationally, an institution may even be defined as a pattern of usages which define the roles of its members. These roles become so incorporated into each person's self in the process of socialization that they are imbedded in his personality. As a result, institutional behavior becomes automatic for a large proportion of man's conduct. Spontaneous and largely nondeliberate reciprocal actions therefore tend to characterize human interaction with others and with the environment. Personal interaction is to a great extent controlled by institutions whose values and action patterns have been internalized.

All six of these characteristics apply to the church. It is stable, continuing to exist even though local churches die and disappear, for others arise and replace them. The church is universally found among all major groups of people in all parts of the world. The church is identified with human needs, satisfying many of them even as it modifies them and creates additional ones. The church is variable, having many different forms and functions. It is interrelated with all other institutions, reciprocally affecting and affected by them. It cannot remain unchanged in a changing society. The church systemizes the positions of participants, and even many non-participants in it, helping to define roles and determine statuses.

Types of Social Institutions. Sociologists have classified institutions in various ways. The types they have thus developed diverge considerably because they are based on different conceptions of institutions, most of which fall under the three central usages specified above. Several of the more significant classifications help clarify the nature of the church; they are much more closely related than might appear at first glance.

Sumner distinguished between *crescive* institutions—which developed as a result of the crystallization of folkways into customs, customs into mores, and ultimately of mores into basic institutions like religion—and *enacted* institutions like local churches, which result from rational invention in high civilization.[16] *Associations,* which are groups of persons united for a specific reason and held together by approved or recognized modes of procedure, are contrasted by Ginsberg with *institutions,* which refer to forms or modes of social relationships rather than to individuals in union.[17] *Diffused-symbolic* or general institutions like the church as a social institution, which are spread over wide-flung areas and tend to be symbolic in character, are distinguished in Chapin's operational definitions from *nucleated* or specific institutions like local churches, which are definite and recognizable, possessing such tangible aspects as having a definite locus, being specific in area, and having type parts of the kinds described in the preceding section on the definition and study of the church.[18] The church as a social institution would be classified as a *compound group institution* by Znaniecki, while a local church would be called an *institutionalized group.*[19] *Traditionalistic* institutions, which result from long-established practices in the society, are separated by Martindale and Monachesi from *rationalistic* institutions, which result from deliberate choice.[20] *The* church is not an institution at all, unless reference

[16] William G. Sumner, *Folkways* (Boston: Ginn and Co., 1940), pp. 53-55, (original ed. 1906).
[17] Morris Ginsberg, "Association," *Encyclopaedia of the Social Sciences* (New York: The Macmillan Co., 1930), 2, pp. 284-86.
[18] Chapin, *Contemporary American Institutions,* pp. 13-16, 358-60.
[19] Znaniecki, "Social Organization and Institutions."
[20] Martindale and Monachesi, *Elements of Sociology,* p. 388.

is to the system of principles that underlies the activities of specific religious bodies. Since there is such tremendous diversity of churches, and no single body of rules and principles defines the relationships of all groups of church members, officers, and clergy to one another, to refer to all such groups as "the church" is to use the term as an intellectual category rather than a societal reality. Hence there is no one traditionalistic institution called "the church"; rather, there are many churches.

These types are analogous to one another, as Table 1 indicates. Although the concepts are not identical in content or scope, they are parallel. They overlap and share a common core of meaning. Both structure and function are important in these definitions, as in all institutional analysis. The main focus of this book is on the broad or general use of the term "church" which is best indicated by the second column of Table 1. Yet scientific study of the church must always be done in terms of specific local churches, denominations, and organizations which would come under definitions in the third column. In this book the context will make clear which sense of "church" is being used.

The church as a social institution refers to all of organized religion, its values, patterns of relationship between persons and groups, and accomplishments in society. It is a culturally oriented system which in reality consists of the behavior of interacting individuals in group situations. Indeed, much of its apparent orderliness results from the abstractions made by observing scientists. To treat the church apart from a recognition of the roles individual members play in it is to distort and reify it by abstracting from reality only a portion of the relevant behavior.[21]

Each local church is a human institution with a natural history, for it is a product of *institutionalization*—the process by which social functions, relationships, and values gradually or suddenly become crystallized, formalized, or stabilized so that they produce relatively uniform behavior among members and organizational groupings. This is not a denial of the theological position that the church is a divine institution established by God's command and developed under His guidance. The church as a "spiritual institution" is outside the realm of purely sociological analysis and is only indirectly included in our study.[22]

The Theoretical Framework of This Book

This book is concerned with the church and does not attempt to survey the entire field of the sociology of religion. Yet because of the closely

---

[21] Robert S. Lynd, *Knowledge For What?* (Princeton: Princeton University Press, 1939), pp. 21-50, 124-25, 152-56.

[22] Joseph H. Fichter, *Social Relations in the Urban Parish* (Chicago: University of Chicago Press, 1954), pp. 235-38.

Table 1

Analogous Concepts of Institutional Types

Source	Broad or general types	Specific or narrow types	Purpose
Wm. G. Sumner	Crescive institution	Enacted institution	To distinguish between presumed origins and established sources of institutions.
M. Ginsberg	Institution	Association	To distinguish between intangible relationships and a tangible organization.
F. Stuart Chapin	General or diffused-symbolic institutions	Specific or nucleated institutions	To afford a basis for verifiable empirical description.
F. Znaniecki	Compound group institution	Institutionalized group	To make the terminology heuristically useful.
D. Martindale and E. D. Monachesi	Traditionalistic institution	Rationalistic institution	To clarify the concept on the basis of historical development.
Illustrations:	The church as a social institution	A local church	
	The Protestant church	Bethlehem Baptist Church	

Sources: Consult text.

interwoven relationships between religion and the church, it is impossible to analyze the institution without reference to some of the more general aspects of religion. Such discussion will be concerned chiefly with showing, on one hand, the role of the church as the organized expression and bearer of religion in society and, on the other, the ways by which the church affects religious life. Our central concern will consistently be with the church as a social institution, as defined in the preceding section. Hence we will omit or treat only briefly certain important topics in the sociology of religion. Only a vast encyclopedia could cover all its subjects and summarize all its available data. References in footnotes and chapter bibliographies will assist readers to pursue special interests into a wide range of relevant topics.

In addition, we shall limit ourselves almost completely to the contemporary American church for a number of reasons. First of all, we believe that a fuller and deeper comprehension of institutional religion can be gained by concentrating on direct analysis of churches in a reasonably limited culture than by trying to spread one's treatment over the exceedingly broad subject of all churches throughout the world and over the long period of historical time. Occasional references to churches elsewhere and in the past will be sparing and are designed to illuminate the contemporary American situation. A second reason for focusing on the American church is that there is a sizable and rapidly growing body of pertinent research studies about it. Finally, we recognize that most readers of this book will be Americans with an interest in developing richer knowledge of churches with which they already are familiar.

In dealing with the contemporary American church our emphasis is placed on the kind of world which now confronts it. This emphasis gives a particular slant to our analysis. Instead of undertaking lengthy, and perhaps tedious, discussions of abstruse theoretical matters, we shall concern ourselves more with scientific conclusions about social conditions and developments that vitally affect the American church and about its functioning as an institution. Theoretical treatment of topics will not be ignored, but it will be reduced to what most helpfully clarifies the structure and action patterns of the church in its American setting.

With this objective, we shall draw upon a wide range of sources. The materials used reflect many kinds of sociological analysis which, when applied to a social institution, comprise what may be termed *institutional analysis*. At various points they include the demographic, ecological, normative, typological, natural history, case study, structural-functional, social interactionist, social disorganization, social conflict, statistical, qualitative, and logical-theoretical approaches. The observations of certain theologians, historians, psychologists, anthropologists, and other non-sociologists are included when they help to increase knowledge and critical understanding of the church as a social institution. This book is not, therefore, a particularistic interpretation; it is a survey of the subject, not a narrow monograph. Empirical data are given preference, but qualitative data based upon careful application of insight-producing procedures are included because emotions and subjective meanings involved in the practice of religion are as important to its influence as the purely quantitative aspects which are more easily studied by the scientific method.

Our discussion is in a series of logically connected and overlapping parts introduced by this chapter. Part II presents some characteristics of the American church. Demographic and ecological data are accompanied by interpretations of the current growth of American churches and the impact of population movements on the church. The normative descriptions include variations in beliefs and values among religious bodies and the impact of religious norms upon individuals. Part III is basically typological. It deals intensively with Troeltsch's church-sect typology and modifications of it that result from its application in America. Other classifications of the church are also presented, as is the natural history of churches. Mobility on the church-sect continuum, social sources of religious bodies, and the life cycle of the typical local church are included.

Social functions and dysfunctions of the American church are dealt with in Part IV. Many activities commonly considered to be "purely religious" are demonstrated to be largely social. The church's educational and missionary work is given considerable attention. Part V surveys the social processes of cooperation and opposition as they operate within the church and between the church and the rest of society. The ecumenical movement, the fundamentalist-modernist controversies, the conflict of science with religion, Protestant-Catholic and Christian-Jewish tensions, and competition with other institutions are included.

The church's relationships with the family and with government are summarized in Part VI. Part VII presents certain aspects of the social psychology of American religion. Interesting data are given about social influences on conversion, cycles of revivalism, the reasons why people join churches, and the church's part in the origin, prevention, and treatment of social problems. A chapter on the clergy (Part VIII) emphasizes social influences upon the ministry and the social roles of the church's professional leaders. The book then concludes with a summary of recent developments and a sketch of some empirical and theoretical work that remains to be done in the sociology of religion.

In short, this book surveys the sociology of American religion, blending together many of its theoretical orientations without being blinded to the virtues of any by an undiscerning commitment to one. In the framework of the institutional approach, it includes much material about Judaism, Catholicism, and Protestantism, and it contains references to many cults and minority religions. The materials included are intended to be a balanced sociological description and appraisal which neither lampoons nor

lauds the church and neither attacks nor condones everything associated
with it. When criticism of traditional institutionalized religion is implicit,
it is not intended as a blanket condemnation of any religion or church.
Constructive criticism of religion can contribute both to the development
of the sociology of religion and to improvements in the quality of work
and effectiveness of religious organizations in American society.

Selected References

For general works on the sociology of religion see the references at the end of
chapters 19 and 20.

Baum, Gregory, *Religion and Alienation*. New York: Paulist Press, 1975. A
"theological reading of sociology" which reviews and critiques significant theoretical issues.

Berger, Peter L., *The Precarious Vision*. Garden City, N.Y.: Doubleday and
Co., 1961. A critique of social fictions by which Christian faith gives an illusion
of absoluteness to one particular coloration of the societal comedy.

Berger, Peter L., *A Rumor of Angels*. Garden City, N.Y.: Anchor Books, 1970.
An interpretation of the rediscovery of supernatural "signals of transcendence"
in modern society.

Berger, Peter L., *The Sacred Canopy: Elements of a Sociological Theory of
Religion*. Garden City, N.Y.: Doubleday and Co., 1967. An essay in the sociology
of knowledge which centers around world construction and maintenance, theodicy, alienation, and secularization.

Glock, Charles Y., and Phillip E. Hammond, eds., *Beyond the Classics?: Essays
in the Scientific Study of Religion*. New York: Harper and Row, 1973. Contributions to the study of religion by Marx, Weber, Durkheim, Malinowski, Freud,
William James, and H. R. Niebuhr, subsequent work inspired by their ideas, their
present status, and anticipated future.

Hall, Richard H., *Organizations: Structure and Process*, 2nd ed. Englewood
Cliffs, N.J.: Prentice-Hall, 1977. A textbook on the nature, structure, processes,
and relationship to society of associations and institutions.

Luckmann, Thomas, *The Invisible Religion: The Problem of Religion in Modern
Society*. New York: Macmillan, 1967. An interpretation of the alleged decline of
institutionalized forms of religion and rising significance of privatized religious
representations.

Martin, David, John Orme Mills, O.P., and W. S. F. Pickering, eds., *Sociology
and Theology: Alliance and Conflict*. New York: St. Martin's Press, 1980. Diverse
perspectives on central problems of the often confused relationship between sociology and theology.

Mehl, Roger, *The Sociology of Protestantism*, trans. James H. Farley. Philadelphia: Westminster, 1970. A dialectical interpretation by a French professor
which emphasizes the doctrinal starting point of ecclesial realities.

Scherer, Ross P., ed., *American Denominational Organization: A Sociological
View*. Pasadena, Calif.: William Carey Library, 1980. Wide-ranging studies of
organizational patterns, agencies and subgroups, and the strains and change within
denominations, centered around an open systems theory.

Towler, Robert, *Homo Religiosus: Sociological Problems in the Study of Religion*. New York: St. Martin's Press, 1974. Discussions of basic questions by a
British sociologist.

Yinger, J. Milton, *Sociology Looks at Religion*. New York: Macmillan, 1961.
Essays emphasizing that the student of society must be a student of religion, and
vice versa.

Part Two: *Characteristics of American Churches*

🏛 Chapter 2

The Demography and Ecology of American Religion

Since there can be no institutions without people, one aspect of institutional analysis is the study of the make-up and distribution of the institution's membership. Such analysis is an aspect of demography, the scientific study which describes and interprets statistical aspects of the composition, movement, and vital processes of a population. It is closely related to human ecology, which concentrates on the distribution of man and his institutions and activities in space and time in relationship to his environment.

⌈To understand any institution in relation to the world in which it operates, it is essential to have information on the number, characteristics, and location of the people who comprise it.⌊ Such information is enlightening since it indicates the institution's strength, its position in the larger society, the kinds of people it serves, and certain problems of organization and operation which confront it. Membership distribution provides insights concerning the kind of milieu in which the institution operates, the types of areas in which it is strong or weak, whether it is widely dispersed or compact, and the kinds of institutional complexes to which it must adjust in its society.

A knowledge of the population composition of an institution is particularly valuable when, as in the American church, it includes a number of

27

separate organizations. Comparisons of demographic and ecological data then throw great light upon the separately functioning bodies as well as the general or abstract institution of which they are specific instances. Even more important than the knowledge yielded by cross-sectional analysis of demographic data is the knowledge that comes from viewing these data over periods of time. Such review reveals important changes and trends, such as growth or decline in membership, changes in its composition, and changes in the institution's milieu. Knowledge of these changes is of special importance in trying to understand the institution, for they point to needs of adjustment which are thrust on the institution, and they highlight organizational changes which must be made to meet these needs. Demographic and ecological data are therefore of great importance in the analysis of the contemporary American church.

Sources of American Church Statistics

Most census-taking nations include questions about religious preference or affiliation in their regular population enumerations. It becomes easy then for social scientists to study relationships between religion, and other phenomena such as fertility, occupation, migration, and education. It also makes the task of planning certain aspects of strategy much easier for religious leaders. In the United States, however, the collection of census data on religion has met obstacles. The First Amendment to the Constitution restrains Congress from making any law to establish a religion or to prohibit the free exercise thereof. This generally has been assumed to prohibit the inclusion of questions pertaining to religion in the decennial census on the grounds that asking such questions would violate the freedom of religion.

In every decade from the 1880's to 1950, information concerning the nation's religious bodies as distinct from the individual's religion was collected by the Federal Government. The permanent Census Act of 1902 provides for regular collection of data about religious affiliations. As a result, a Census of Religious Bodies was completed for the years 1906, 1916, 1926, and 1936. This census was completely separate from the regular decennial Census of Population. The data are incomplete and lack internal consistency and comparability. It is almost impossible to correlate them with other census data.[1]

Weaknesses of the Census of Religious Bodies, failure to complete the 1946 census and even to begin one in 1956, increasing appreciation of the value of census data for guiding church policies, increasing popularity of religion in America's social climate, and the success of other nations in gathering information about religion led to a strong movement to include

---

[1] U.S. Dept. of Commerce, *Appraisal of Census Programs* (Washington, D.C.: U.S. Government Printing Office, 1954), p. 55.

one or more questions about the religious preference of a sample of the population in the 1960 Census. Preliminary questioning in several localities during 1956 and a national survey in 1957 met with better cooperation than that which has been received on other questions conventionally asked by census enumerators. Nevertheless, the economic expense, the dubious value of statistics based on a broad general question, doubt about its legality as "an invasion of personal privacy and religious freedom," and especially opposition from organizations including the Baptist Joint Committee on Public Affairs and the American Civil Liberties Union led finally to the decision not to include a question on religion in 1960 and to suspend further publication of materials from the March 1957 survey on religious preference. Despite the efforts of some researchers and religious leaders, nothing on religion was included in the 1970 and 1980 Censuses of Population.

The most used source of church statistics is the *Yearbook of American and Canadian Churches*. Published intermittently since 1916 and annually since 1951 by the National Council of Churches, it compiles information submitted by religious bodies which have distinct features of denominational organization. Any defects that are present in the original denominational statistics are transferred into this compilation. Membership definitions vary; denominational statistics sometimes are incomplete; some denominations refuse to submit statistics; and the data are for different fiscal or reporting years. These and other technical details limit the reliability and completeness of the data.

The Bureau of Research and Survey of the National Council of Churches has published a Church Distribution Study which enumerates and analyzes churches and church membership by counties, states, and regions.[2] It relates church statistics for 1952 to certain aspects of the 1950 Census of Population. The number of church members included was equal to almost half of the total continental United States population. These bulletins provide valuable information for use in church extension programs, evaluations of church work, and research.

Every major denomination (with the possible exception of the Church of Christ, Scientist, whose doctrine opposes any enumeration of its membership) compiles statistics for its own needs. It is difficult, however, to use the yearbooks and reports in comparative studies because of the tremendous variability among them.

Statistics of American Religion

Recent estimates have classified less than one-fourth of the world's population as Christian (Table 2), a figure that may be diminishing under

---

[2] Bureau of Research and Survey, *Churches and Church Membership in the United States* (New York: National Council of Churches), 80 bulletins in 5 series, 1956-1958. (Distributions by denomination remain similar in the 1980s.)

Table 2

Estimated Strength of the Principal Religions of the World, 1981

Religion	Estimated "membership"	Per cent of world population
Christianity	1,028,170,300	22.0
Roman Catholic	606,793,800	13.0
Protestant	353,513,200	7.6
Eastern Orthodox	67,863,300	1.4
Islam	548,075,500	11.7
Hinduism	457,881,100	9.8
Buddhism	249,569,400	5.3
Confucianism	168,615,000	3.6
Shintoism	38,135,000	0.8
Taoism	25,000,000	0.5
Judaism	16,820,850	0.4
Zoroastrianism	257,450	0.005
Total	2,532,524,600	54.105

Source: Franklin H. Littell, "World Church Membership," *1983 Britannica Book of the Year* (Chicago: Encyclopaedia Britannica, 1983), p. 601. Percentages are based upon the United Nations estimate of 4,680,526,000 world population at mid-year 1982. Littell indicates that he omits groups like Bahai, Ch'ondokyo, the Unification Church, and Marxism, "which functions in some ways like a state church." Reports on Hinduism sometimes include Sikhs and Jains, which are omitted wherever possible from these Hindu statistics. Some earlier estimates included categories like "Primitive religions," "Spiritism," and other groups.

Table 3

Church Membership by Major Categories, United States, 1980–81

Religious group	Reporting bodies	Number of churches	Membership Inclusive membership	Per cent of total	Per cent of population
Protestant*	184	305,273	73,479,341	54.5	32.4
Roman Catholic	1	24,188	50,449,842	37.4	22.3
Jewish**	1	3,500	5,920,000	4.4	2.6
Eastern Orthodox	18	1,606	3,822,590	2.8	1.7
Old Catholic, Polish National Catholic, and Armenian	7	436	923,985	0.7	0.4
Buddhist (1975)	1	60	60,000	0.04	0.03
Miscellaneous†	6	1,218	161,185	0.12	0.07
Total	218	336,281	134,816,943	100.0	59.5

Source: Constant H. Jacquet, Jr., ed., *Yearbook of American and Canadian Churches 1982* (Nashville: Abingdon Press, 1982), p. 242. Totals are based upon current or most recent data on inclusive (not full, communicant, or confirmed) membership. Of the 218 bodies reporting, 119 (55%) have provided current (1980 or 1981) data. Population calculations are based upon the U.S. population of 226,504,825 in the 1980 Census.

*Some bodies included here are, strictly speaking, not "Protestant" in the usual sense, such as various Latter-day Saints groups and Jehovah's Witnesses.

**Includes Orthodox, Conservative, and Reform branches.

†This is a grouping of bodies which are officially non-Christian, including Spiritualists, Ethical Culture Movement, and Unitarian Universalists.

the heavier impact of the population explosion in non-Christian than in Christian areas. Other sources, however, indicate that Christianity accounted for 34.4 per cent of the world's population in 1900 and 32.8 per cent in mid-1980, despite differential fertility and the political hostility in many nations. Worldwide there are about 20,800 Christian denominations among some 8,990 peoples speaking 7,010 languages. The diversity much less reflects divisiveness than it does the adaptability of the faith to diverse circumstances.[3]

About three-fifths of the U.S. population are church members, according to the incomplete statistics in the *Yearbook of American and Canadian Churches* (Table 3). Many who participate in church life are not counted as members, including large numbers of Protestant children who are ineligible for membership until they reach a minimum age designated by their respective denominations or congregations. When asked if they are members of a church or synagogue, about seven in every ten adults answer affirmatively, and many non-members regularly attend religious gath-

Table 4
Major Groupings of Protestant Religious Bodies, 1980–81

Major group or family	Number of denominations	Number of churches	Inclusive membership
Baptist	23	96,197	26,015,364
Methodist, Wesleyan, AME, etc.	11	56,496	13,762,288
Lutheran	14	18,337	8,507,335
Presbyterian and Reformed	16	17,073	4,219,032
Pentecostal, Apostolic, and Holiness	26	24,793	3,392,412*
Latter-day Saints (Mormons)	2	8,435	3,001,087
Episcopal	3	7,320	2,794,845
Christian Churches, Disciples of Christ	5	10,045	2,256,568
Churches of God	16	18,035	1,770,809
United Church of Christ	1	6,462	1,736,244
Churches of Christ	6	14,105	1,669,865
Adventist	3	4,104	601,526
Jehovah's Witnesses	1	7,515	565,309
Salvation Army and Volunteers of America	2	1,663	453,993
Moravians and Brethren	10	3,220	429,626
Mennonite, Amish, and Hutterite	12	2,508	287.922
Congregational	4	2,370	245,356
Community Churches	1	185	190,000
Christian and Missionary Alliance	1	1,382	189,710
Friends (Quakers)	5	1,159	120,678
Independent Fundamental Churches	1	1,059	120,446

Source: Jacquet, *Yearbook of American and Canadian Churches 1982*, pp. 228-235. "Protestant" is loosely defined and my classifications were arbitrarily made without careful study of the doctrines and alliances of each denomination. Many statistics are for earlier years.

*Two Pentecostal bodies with 164 congregations gave no membership data.

---

[3] David B. Barrett, ed., *World Christian Encyclopedia* (Nairobi: Oxford University Press, 1982), pp. 4, v. (Many of its statistics for other religions also deviate from those in Table 2).

erings. Estimates of church membership are hazardous because all available statistics have limitations.

Many groups do not send data to the *Yearbook*. Melton identified 1,275 religious bodies in the U.S. in 1976, and the *World Christian Encyclopedia* reported 2,050 as of 1980. Most unreported bodies are small, but the Church of Christ, Scientist may have 250,000 members.[4] Our confusion when observing the religious scene is reduced when we note that most people are in one of several "families," and 85.4 per cent of the reported members are in Christian bodies of a million or more (Tables 3, 4, and 5).

In addition to and overlapping with church membership is a large enrollment in Sunday and Sabbath schools and related educational organizations. In 1980–81 the 193,462 schools reported by 119 religious bodies had an enrollment of 33,451,109 persons.[5] The majority of those enrolled are children, but there are many adults in Sunday schools of the Southern Baptists and other groups which emphasize religious education for people of all ages.

Table 5

Christian Religious Bodies of 1,000,000 or More Members, 1980–81

Rank	Name of organization	Inclusive membership	Year
1	Roman Catholic Church	50,449,842	1980
2	Southern Baptist Convention	13,600,126	1980
3	United Methodist Church	9,584,711	1980
4	National Baptist Convention, U.S.A. Inc.	5,500,000	1958
5	Lutheran Church in America	2,923,260	1980
6	Church of Jesus Christ of Latter-day Saints	2,811,000	1980
7	The Episcopal Church	2,786,004	1980
8	National Baptist Convention of America	2,668,799	1956
9	Lutheran Church—Missouri Synod	2,625,650	1980
10	United Presbyterian Church in the U.S.A.	2,423,601	1980
11	American Lutheran Church	2,353,229	1980
12	African Methodist Episcopal Church	2,050,000	1980
13	Greek Orthodox Archdiocese of North and South America	1,950,000	1977
14	United Church of Christ	1,736,244	1980
15	Assemblies of God	1,732,371	1980
16	American Baptist Churches in the U.S.A.	1,600,521	1979
17	Churches of Christ	1,600,000	1979
18	American Baptist Association	1,500,000	1981
19	Christian Church (Disciples of Christ)	1,177,984	1980
20	African Methodist Episcopal Zion Church	1,134,176	1980
21	Christian Churches and Churches of Christ	1,063,254	1981
22	The Orthodox Church in America	1,000,000	1978
	Total	115,186,596	

Source: Jacquet, *Yearbook of American and Canadian Churches 1982*, pp. 229–35.

4 *Ibid.*, p. 725, and J. Gordon Melton with James V. Geisendorfer, *A Directory of Religious Bodies in the United States* (New York: Garland Publishing, Inc., 1977), pp. 8-9.

5 Jacquet, *Yearbook of American and Canadian Churches 1982*, p. 236.

The average church congregation had 456 members in 1980–81, compared to 357 in 1959 and 235 in 1926, but the size varied considerably by denominational family. Roman Catholics had 2,086 per parish, but Protestants averaged only 241, Baptists 270, Methodists 244, Lutherans 464, Presbyterians 247, Pentecostalists 137, Episcopalians 382, Churches of God 98, Mennonites 115, and Friends 104. Some groups deliberately restrict congregational size, and others are largely in rural communities with a limited population pool from which to attract members.

In March 1957 the U.S. Bureau of the Census surveyed a nationwide sample of the civilian population aged 14 years and over. Answers to the question, "What is your religion? " were given on a voluntary basis. Two-thirds of these Americans regarded themselves as Protestant, one-fourth as Roman Catholic, and the remainder as having some other religion or none (Table 6). Protestant denominational self-identifications were classi-

Table 6

Religious Preference of Persons 14 Years Old and Over, U.S. Civilian Population, March 1957

Religion		Number of persons	Per cent of population
Protestant		78,952,000	66.2
Baptist	23,525,000		19.7
Methodist	16,676,000		14.0
Lutheran	8,417,000		7.1
Presbyterian	6,656,000		5.6
Other Protestant	23,678,000		19.8
Roman Catholic		30,669,000	25.7
Jewish		3,868,000	3.2
Other religion*		1,545,000	1.3
No religion†		3,195,000	2.7
Religion not reported		1,104,000	0.9
Total		119,333,000	100.0

Source: Bureau of the Census, "Religion Reported by the Civilian Population of the United States: March 1957," *Current Population Reports: Population Characteristics,* Series P-20, no. 79. February 2, 1958.

* Eastern Orthodox, Polish Catholic, Old Catholic, Buddhist, Moslem, etc.

† Includes atheists and agnostics.

fied into five categories. Baptists were the most numerous, followed by Methodists, Lutherans, and Presbyterians.

The Census survey indicated that persons with Jewish preference were somewhat older than the national average, Catholics younger, and Protestants near average. These variations reflect different birth and death rates as well as migration patterns. Jews were almost exclusively urban, nearly nine out of ten residing in cities of 250,000 or more. Eight out of ten Catholics also were urban, while over two-fifths of the Protestants were rural.

The 1979 responses to the question, "What is your religious preference . . . ?" again showed Catholics first with 28 per cent, followed by Baptists at 19 per cent, Methodists 10, Lutherans 6, Presbyterians 4, Episcopalians and Jews 2 per cent each, Mormons and Eastern Orthodox 1 per cent each, other Protestant groups 13, and 4 per cent Protestant without designation. Three per cent claimed other religious preferences and 7 per cent none.[6]

Geographic Distribution of Church Membership

A thorough study of population distribution in 1980 analyzed *adherents*—all persons who were communicant, confirmed, or full members, plus their children and the estimated number of other regular participants. Of adherents in the 111 denominations studied, 91.9 per cent were in 17 bodies with 1,000,000 or more, 6.9 per cent were in 25 bodies with 100,000 to 999,999, and 1.2 per cent were in 69 bodies of under 100,000. Unfortunately, what proportion of all Judeo-Christian adherents is represented by the study is unknown. The Conservative Jews reported only 240,097 and Reform Judaism 562,629. No data were provided on Orthodox Jews, who claimed 1,300,000 members. Four Eastern Orthodox bodies with 55,000 adherents are included; 17 are missing. Only 4 black denominations totaling 1,800,000 are in the study; 6 of the largest black bodies are omitted. Eleven other bodies in the *Yearbook* with over 100,000 members each are omitted, as are independent, community, and other religious movements and associations.[7]

Table 7 summarizes the regional distribution of adherents in those 111 denominations. The adherents totaled less than half of the population in only three regions; in at least one of those (South Atlantic) addition of the major black Baptist bodies undoubtedly would push the percentage well over half. In six regions and thirty-seven states the Catholic Church had the largest number of adherents. Southern Baptists were strongest in eleven states and three regions. The Church of Jesus Christ of Latter-day Saints had 89.7 per cent of the adherents in Utah and 51.0 per cent of those in Idaho. In only one state, West Virginia, where the United Methodist Church had 28.4 per cent of the adherents, did any other denomination rank first.[8]

Distributions by denominational families are not always the same as those for specific bodies. Baptists are so dominant among blacks that an

[6] Princeton Religion Research Center, *Religion in America 1982* (Princeton, N.J.: The Gallup Poll, 1982), pp. 22–25.

[7] Bernard Quinn et al., *Churches and Church Membership in the United States 1980* (Atlanta: Glenmary Research Center, 1982), pp. ix–xvii.

[8] *Ibid.*, pp. 5–9.

Table 7

Regional Distribution of Church Adherents in 111 Denominations and the Two Largest Religious Bodies in Each Region, 1980

Region and denomination	Members	Percentage distribution Regional Population	Percentage distribution Regional Adherents	National
New England	7,451,972	60.3	100.0	6.6
Catholic Church	5,751,857	46.6	77.2	
United Church of Christ	382,645	3.1	5.1	
Middle Atlantic	19,941,403	54.2	100.0	17.7
Catholic Church	13,097,729	35.6	65.7	
United Methodist Church	1,477,790	4.0	7.4	
East North Central	21,093,360	50.6	100.0	18.7
Catholic Church	10,347,095	24.8	49.1	
United Methodist Church	2,087,957	5.0	9.9	
West North Central	10,271,622	59.8	100.0	9.1
Catholic Church	3,363,850	19.6	32.7	
United Methodist Church	1,225,424	7.1	11.9	
South Atlantic	16,357,882	44.3	100.0	14.5
Southern Baptist Convention	5,326,963	14.4	32.6	
Catholic Church	2,973,368	8.0	18.2	
East South Central	8,097,758	55.2	100.0	7.2
Southern Baptist Convention	4,034,138	27.5	49.8	
United Methodist Church	1,243,980	8.5	15.4	
West South Central	13,233,197	55.7	100.0	11.8
Southern Baptist Convention	4,634,482	19.5	35.0	
Catholic Church	3,810,354	16.0	28.8	
Mountain	5,259,099	46.3	100.0	4.7
Catholic Church	1,766,820	15.5	33.6	
Latter-day Saints	1,567,330	13.8	29.8	
Pacific	10,832,017	34.1	100.0	9.6
Catholic Church	5,709,667	18.0	52.7	
Latter-day Saints	621,417	2.0	5.7	
Total, all regions	112,538,310	49.7	100.0	99.9

Source: Bernard Quinn et al., *Churches and Church Membership in the United States 1980* (Atlanta: Glenmary Research Center, 1982), pp. 5–9. The 99.9 per cent national total is merely a result of rounding the figures.

old saying was that "if a Negro is not a Baptist, someone has been tampering with him." Blacks' dispersal into metropolitan areas of all regions contributes to their increasing religious diversification. The same is true of Hispanics, a majority of whom are at least nominally Catholic.

The Limitations and Significance of Religious Statistics

Statistics are both subject to and the product of interpretation. As a result of misleading interpretations or failure to understand their limitations, they may become instruments of deceit.

The sources of religious statistics impose major limitations upon their use. Incomplete reporting, duplications from overlapping memberships, failure to keep records up to date, and other defects are common. Internal inconsistencies are often evident.[9]

Comparability of statistics is reduced by variations in the criteria used in reckoning membership. Certain bodies report all *baptized persons* as members. Notable among these are Roman Catholics, about one-fourth of whom are children, many Lutheran groups, Latter-day Saints, and several smaller bodies. Baptists and similar groups which practice "believer's baptism" have a considerably different age composition from those which include baptized infants as members. The latter also are less likely to drop members from their lists. Other religious bodies report as members only *communicants* (persons entitled to partake of Communion). In most of these churches communicants are at least 13 years of age and have completed an indoctrination course which culminated in the rite of confirmation. Certain groups list as members all *persons in the ethnic group*. Eastern Orthodox churches tend to enumerate as members all persons of the nationality served by each of the respective church bodies. Jewish "membership" similarly is an estimate of the number of Jews living in communities which have Jewish congregations. Only about 20 per cent of American Jews attend services in a typical week, and about 40 per cent are affiliated with a synagogue.[10] Hence 2,370,000 may be a fair estimate of Jewish "membership."

As of January 1, 1982, the Catholic Church reported a membership of 51,207,579 or 22.7 per cent of the national population. During 1981 their infant baptisms represented 26.9 per cent of the nation's live births, and Catholic statistics accounted for 21.4 per cent of all deaths and 14.5 per cent of all marriages.[11] Rules against remarriage of divorced persons with unannulled earlier marriages may keep the latter low. Most Catholic parishes now keep membership lists or take censuses which provide the main basis for national statistical compliations.

Efforts are sometimes made to eliminate the inclusion of children in statistics used to compare the strength of religious bodies, but the necessary data are often unavailable. In the 1936 Census of Religious Bodies it was found that only one major denomination, the Church of Christ, Scientist, had no children under age 13 in its membership. The Congregational and Christian Churches followed with 2.6 per cent. Others with low percentages were the Churches of Christ (3.1 per cent), Pres-

---

[9] For example, *Official Catholic Directory* reports of annual increases by converts plus infant baptisms often total less than the net gain even when deductions for deaths are ignored. (Conrad H. Moehlman, *The Wall of Separation Between Church and State* [Boston: Beacon Press, 1951], pp. 187-92.)

[10] See reports by Alan M. Fisher and Alvin Chenkin in *American Jewish Yearbook 1983* (New York: American Jewish Committee, 1982), pp. 115, 131.

[11] Calculated from data in *The Official Catholic Directory for 1982* (New York: P. J. Kenedy & Sons, 1982), "General Summary," pp. 1-4, and U.S. Bureau of the Census, *Statistical Abstract of the United States 1982–83* (Washington, D.C.: Government Printing Office, 1982), p. 60.

byterian Church, U.S.A. (3.8 per cent), Northern Baptist Convention (5.2 per cent), and Southern Baptist Convention (5.8 per cent) At the other extreme, the six major bodies with the most members under 13 were the Roman Catholic Church (27.4 per cent) the Evangelical Lutheran Synod of Missouri, Ohio, and Other States (27.3 per cent), American Lutheran Church (26.5 per cent), Norwegian Lutheran Church of America (26.1 per cent), Church of Jesus Christ of Latter-day Saints (24.9 per cent), and Evangelical Lutheran Augustana Synod of North America (23.2 per cent).[12]

Many Lutherans and some other bodies emphasize family religion and attempt to include in their membership entire families rather than individuals. In contrast, groups like the Baptists believe that joining the church is an individual rather than family act.

The limitations of quantitative data and their failure to reflect the normative goals of religion have made some scholars stress religious vitality more than numbers. The piety of church members is not indicated by their total number; the significance of a religious group in American national life has never been dependent upon size alone. The methods and degree of participation—especially in Catholicism which emphasizes the sacraments—are at least as important as the total number of persons involved. Surely 100 contributing and attending members are worth more to a church than 1,000 names on an inactive membership list! Yet most statistics of religious affiliation fail to distinguish between the various types of members. (See Chapter 15.)

In spite of such aspects of unreliability and uncertainty as those mentioned above, statistics of American religion tell much about the church. They show it to be an enormous institution embracing a significant majority of the population. Whatever be the bonds of relationship of these members to the church, the massiveness of church membership signifies that it has vast potentialities for influencing the lives of Americans. Statistics show that the religious community is grouped overwhelmingly in huge religious families and bodies. These large organizations and groupings reflect a mass society with characteristic problems referred to later. The statistics also reveal the importance of local churches; in 1981 there were over 336,000 of them. They constitute an impressive number of acting units woven into the basic fabric of American community life. Since they represent the primary source of organized religious effort, their number is in many ways more significant than the number of people professing an attachment to a religion. The American church is a vast institution deeply entrenched in American society.

The statistics presented here are little more than an introduction. The scholar who wishes further analysis of the American church or any part of it can compile relevant statistics and relate them to a host of topics.

---

[12] T. Lynn Smith, *Population Analysis* (New York: McGraw-Hill Book Co., 1948), pp. 188-89.

He may wish to compare the average size of local church membership
by geographical region, by religious faith or denomination, by rural,
urban, or suburban location, by incidence of selected social problems
like crime rates, etc. He may wish to relate figures on membership to
age composition, education, ethnic background, occupation, income, social class, or political affiliation. Such statistical studies constitute a large
and growing area of research which is still relatively undeveloped, yet
highly rewarding. Much future study of the church as a social institution will consist of such analyses; they will reveal much valuable information even if they are limited to the more formal aspects of religious
life.

Trends in American Religion

There are no dependable statistics on religious affiliation in early American history. From scanty available data it is estimated that in the colonies not more than four per cent were church members in the early
eighteenth century, nor more than ten per cent in 1800. Conditions for
membership often included property ownership, qualification as a voter,
and other limitations that prevented a majority of the population from
meeting the standards.[13]

The proportion of church members in our population has increased
considerably over the past century, as Figure 1 on the next page indicates.
The greatest increase in membership strength occurred during the 1890's
at the peak of the Moody revivals and in the post-World War II era. Growth
has not been limited to either Catholicism or Protestantism. Catholicism included only one per cent of the white population in 1790 but gained rapidly by immigration in the nineteenth and early twentieth century. In
1926 27.0 per cent of the population were Protestants and 16.0 per cent
were Catholics. Both increased at a fairly steady rate, especially after
1940, until in 1959 35.3 per cent of the population were Protestants and
23.1 per cent Catholics.[14] Judaism has also experienced a distinct "revival" since the late 1930's.[15] The widespread nature of this "revival,"
affecting all major churches and religions, indicates it to be a societal
phenomenon reflecting basic conditions of the general social system more
than conditions strictly internal to one or a few churches.[16]

---

[13] Harold A. Phelps and David Henderson, *Population in Its Human Aspects* (New
York: Appleton-Century-Crofts, 1958), p. 303, and Moehlman, *The Wall of Separation*, p. 67.

[14] Benson Y. Landis, ed., *Yearbook of American Churches for 1961*, pp. 281-82.

[15] Nathan Glazer, "The Jewish Revival in America," *Commentary*, 21 (Dec. 1955),
493-99 and 22 (Jan. 1956), 17-24.

[16] Winthrop S. Hudson believes booming church membership is largely an illusion
because the "growing edge" of most rapid increase lies largely outside the circle of "cooperative Protestantism." ("Are Churches Really Booming?" *Christian Century*, 72
[Dec. 21, 1955], 1494-96.) Although the highest percentage gains occur in small sectarian churches, growth is observable in all major bodies. In this section our concern is

Figure 1

Reported Church Membership as a Proportion of the Total U.S. Population,
1850-1980

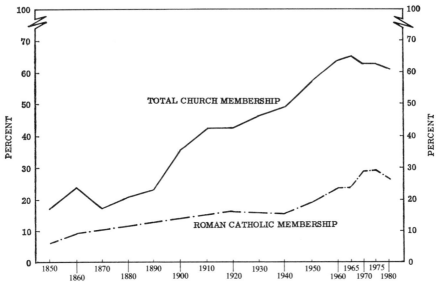

Source: Jacquet, *Yearbook of American and Canadian Churches*, various editions; earlier
editions of the *Yearbook of American Churches*, ed. Benson Y. Landis; Jean-Marie Jammes,
"Statistiques du Catholicisme Américain," *Archives de Sociologie des Religions*, 2, no. 3
(Jan.-June 1957), pp. 97-120.

Growing interest in religion is seen in many trends in society. The
decline in religious magazine articles which was observed into the 1930's
was followed by a rise of interest. By 1952 almost one-third of surveyed
newspapers had religious-news editors. Four-fifths of the best-selling
nonfiction books in 1949 were religious titles and one-third of all commercial book sales in 1976 were for religious books.[17]

It is impossible to determine what proportion of the population regularly
attended church a century ago. Two-fifths of all adults (39 to 42 per cent)
in 1939, 1950, and annually from 1969 to 1982 said they had attended
church or synagogue in the preceding seven days. The figure reached a
low of 37 per cent in 1940 and a high of 49 per cent in 1955 and 1958.
Only 28 per cent in 1981 had not attended within six months.[18] Half of

---

with the general growth. Differential growth of specific churches is discussed in Chapter 9.

[17] Hornell Hart, "Religion," *American Journal of Sociology*, 47 (May 1942), 888-97; Theodore B. Pratt, "The Church Editor in the Daily Press," *Christian Century*, 69 (June 25,
1952), 749-51; and Eugene Exman, "Reading, Writing, and Religion," *Harper's*, 206, no.
1236 (May 1953), 84-90. Some recent data and mention of the ignoring of religious titles in
best-seller lists are summarized in Jeremy Rifkin with Ted Howard, *The Emerging Order:
God in the Age of Scarcity* (New York: G. P. Putnam's Sons, 1979), p. 112. The U.S. had
3,490 religious bookstores in 1983.

[18] Princeton Center, *Religion in America 1982*, pp. 44, 101.

the 1939 sample said they attend less often than their parents did, one third about the same, and one-sixth more often.[19]

The Mid-Century "Revival of Religion"

Many believe that religious statistics reflect a revival of vital religion rather than of mere religiosity. Some believe that man has an inborn need to worship God which is now being recognized, while others think the revival is due to a sense of insecurity people feel as a result of hot and cold wars, atomic missiles, earth satellites, fear of economic insecurity, insatiable desires instilled by advertising, anxieties arising from increased information about illnesses, and other conditions of modern life. Many, however, think that factors other than a true revival of religion are responsible for current church growth. For instance, Rosenberg has suggested that four social psychology processes (the "success of the huckster," the elevation of conformity, disruption of community, and cultural discrepancy between ethics and practice) operate to bring Americans into the churches.[20]

How much speculation about the recent "revival of religion" is consistent with fact? Relatively little research has been done on the subject. Nevertheless, many indications point to the conclusion that the mid-century popularity of religion may be viewed most satisfactorily as an organic part of America's social history rather than as a "revival" that stands aloof from trends in the rest of society.[21] Social factors which help account for the increases in church membership and participation may be classified as conditions in churches and conditions in society at large.[22]

Contributing Conditions in Churches

1. Membership policies of churches may have been relaxed. It is possible that a decreasing "quality" of membership may accompany increasing numbers. It often is difficult to distinguish church members from nonmembers except when seen directly in relationship to the church itself. Increasing size of a church congregation appears to be accompanied by a

[19] Hadley Cantril, ed., *Public Opinion 1935-1946* (Princeton, N.J.: Princeton University Press, 1951), pp. 699-700.

[20] Milton J. Rosenberg, "The Social Sources of the Current Religious Revival," *Pastoral Psychology*, 8, no. 75 (June 1957), 31-36. Rosenberg recognizes that individuals may also be attracted to religion by other motives.

[21] Cf. Sydney E. Ahlstrom, "The Levels of Religious Revival," *Confluence*, 4 (Apr. 1955), 32-43; and Sydney E. Ahlstrom, "Theology and the Present-Day Revival," *Annals of the American Academy of Political and Social Science*, 332 (Nov. 1960), 20-36.

[22] Compare the various analyses in Dean R. Hoge and David A. Roozen, eds., *Understanding Church Growth and Decline 1950–1978* (New York: Pilgrim Press, 1979).

diminution of the average member's sense of obligation to work, give, and participate. As demands upon members decrease, losses from excluding marginal participants presumably decrease.

2. Overlapping church memberships may be increasingly common. As people become more mobile, moving at frequent intervals from one neighborhood or even one community to another, it is increasingly difficult for the churches to maintain up-to-date membership records. Upon joining a new church, the member often fails to notify the one in which he previously was a member; as a result he may be carried for years as a member of both. This is especially likely when membership transfers cross denominational lines (Chapter 10). Interfaith and interdenominational marriages similarly contribute to inflated statistics, for some spouses change affiliation without notifying their original church. Some local churches maintain affiliation with more than one denomination. Adding together total denominational memberships thus results in inflated figures of the strength of religion in America.

3. Children may be included as members to a greater degree than in the past. They may be no more "religious" today, but the church as a social institution may open its doors to them earlier and increase the number of persons on membership records without increasing the number of persons served. Thus in the Episcopal Church only one per cent of the members were children under age 13 in 1916, compared to 26 per cent in 1926.[23]

4. Churches are more accessible. Largely as a result of increasing urbanization and improved transportation, it is easier for people to find within reasonable distance a religious body whose doctrinal and behavioral position is similar to their own.

5. Churches have increased their functions and activities. People are attracted by leisure-time programs, the emphasis on friendliness, aesthetically pleasing architecture and appointments, church music, or pastoral counseling services. Many who join may do so less for traditional religious purposes than to secure satisfactions previously received in other social settings.

6. Churches have increased their formal promotional activities. Competitive public relations efforts to attract members have contributed to effective programs of evangelism and proselyting that have brought many people into the church who, under past conditions, would have remained outside it or only on its fringes. It is also possible that use of the media of mass communications by many religious organizations has increased their influence upon members and nonmembers who stay at home but hear, read, or see some of the church's teachings and programs.

7. Church membership is linked with nationalism: being a good Amer-

---

[23] Truman B. Douglass, "Ecological Changes and the Church," *Annals of the American Academy of Political and Social Science,* 332 (Nov. 1960), 82.

ican requires church membership. "By every realistic criterion the American Way of Life is the operative faith of the American people"; it serves as the common denominator for Catholics, Protestants, and Jews in a vague national religion.[24] Thus the current "revival" may reflect growth primarily of an American "culture religion" in which being a good citizen is the chief qualification for membership. Having "peace of mind," being on good terms with "the Man Upstairs," and believing in the United States as God's chosen nation are other major elements.[25]

Contributing Conditions in American Society

Numerous conditions in American society as a whole overlap with internal adaptations in churches to contribute to the growth or decline of church membership. Among the more significant are the following.

1. Urbanization. The growing number of religious denominations and cults, the search for primary group relationships in church when they are absent elsewhere, and problems of church discipline related to growth are all affected by increasing urbanization. As these conditions are accentuated, church membership is influenced in ways such as were indicated in the preceding section.

2. Changes in population composition. As the nation's population gradually includes proportionately more women, old people, well-educated persons, middle and upper class people, and urban residents, church membership may increase rather automatically because such persons are more likely to be church members than others.

3. Technological changes in transportation and communication. In the "horse and buggy age" it was difficult for all except those living near churches to be active in them. Since the advent of the modern automobile, increased accessibility of churches has made membership more likely. Churches have used the media of mass communications to gain wider audiences and help some who may otherwise have remained nonmembers to find churches compatible with their own interests. More important, perhaps, is the manner in which the entire "revival of religion" is centered around and is partly given its form by the mass media.

4. Economic changes. Reduction in the working hours of laborers and white-collar workers may have helped increase membership by giving increased leisure time, some of which can be occupied by church-related activities. Economic prosperity also has made it possible for many churches to employ specialized personnel to lead leisure time activities and head

---

24 Will Herberg, *Protestant – Catholic – Jew* (Garden City, N.Y.: Doubleday and Co., 1955), p. 88.

25 A. Roy Eckardt, "The New Look in American Piety," *Christian Century*, 71 (Nov. 17, 1954), 1395-97; and Thomas P. Coffey, " 'Somebody,' Anybody?," *The Reporter*, 20, no. 1, (Jan. 8, 1959), 31. See also our discussion of "The American Religion" in Chapter 3.

organizations which only recently have come to be considered a part of the church's sphere of work.

5. The search for identification. As nationality identification diminishes with assimilation into the total population, third generation persons once identified by ethnic or national backgrounds tend to transfer their loyalty from the nationality group to a religious group. When asked what he is, the typical American, according to Herberg, is believed to establish his social location by his affiliation as Protestant, Catholic, or Jew. An inner necessity compels the American to place himself in one of these categories for social identification; this constitutes an added impetus for membership.[26] (Other ideological identities now seem equally acceptable.)

6. Attitudes toward the church. The intellectual climate has changed so that it is now popular to belong to a church. Even people from intellectually elite circles that once considered themselves "emancipated" from religion find it necessary to identify themselves with a church.

Was There a True Revival of Religion?

It seems reasonable to believe that the shifting characteristics of churches and society combine with the factors contributing to the growth or decline of local churches discussed in Chapter 9 to produce changes in the relative and total membership of religious bodies. As a social institution, the church may appear to be stronger than ever before. In terms of spiritual vitality and moral power, it may have grown increasingly weak.[27]

Because of the limitations of religious statistics and especially the qualifications associated with their significance, it can be questioned whether there was a "religious revival" at all in mid-century America. Continuities in the history of religious life are indicated by rather regular patterns of church attendance, donations, seating capacity of church sanctuaries, the proportion of the population who are clergymen, and religious beliefs. These support the hypothesis that levels of American religiosity simply continue a pattern that has prevailed for at least a century.[28] Much of the discussion around this question is based upon divergent definitions and indicators of religiousness. Working within different frames of reference, scholars arrive at contradictory conclusions; "none of the work done to assess the state of religion in America currently or historically meets even the minimum standards of scientific inquiry."[29]

---

[26] Herberg, *Protestant – Catholic – Jew.*

[27] This is a major theme of Herbert W. Schneider, *Religion in Twentieth Century America* (Cambridge: Harvard University Press, 1952).

[28] Seymour M. Lipset, "Religion in America: What Religious Revival?" *Review of Religious Research,* 1 (Summer 1959), 17-24 (reprinted from *Columbia University Forum,* Winter 1959).

[29] Charles Y. Glock, "The Religious Revival in America," in *Religion and the Face of America,* Jane C. Zahn, ed. (Berkeley: University Extension, University of California, 1959), p. 41.

Population Movements and the Church

The long-range urbanization accompanying industrialization is one of the most obvious American demographic facts. Quantitatively it involves an increase in urban, and a relative decrease in rural, population. Its qualitative effects upon the lives of people and the activities of organizations are evident in nearly all areas of social life.

Rural churches reflect the impact of urbanization most noticeably. As people move from country to city, they are slow to move their church memberships. One-seventh of the members of rural churches studied by the Institute of Social and Religious Research from 1922 to 1934 were non-resident, and most of these were living in urban areas. (The proportion is often as high as one-third in contemporary rural churches.) Deaths of rural churches, especially in the open country, exceeded births of such churches by three to two.[30] Migration was a major cause. Mobility of rural people also has increased the sects and denominations competing with one another in the rural community. When new transportation facilities are developed, churches that were once separated by an hour or more of time-distance are brought into close proximity and become competitors. In one rural county, Lowry Nelson located 36 open-country churches of the same denomination, four of which were located on one five-mile stretch of country road. These four were served on a circuit basis, so none was doing a thorough job. Nationality differences kept them separate.

The inability of rural churches to attract and hold the interests of youth in an age of competition with movies, television, and commercial recreation also reflects urbanization. Inability of poorly prepared church leadership to see the needs of the countryside surrounding the small village church, pastoral inefficiency due to part-time and far-traveling pastorate systems, and the lack of opportunities for self-improvement and socioeconomic advancement in the rural pastorate are other factors that have contributed to the decline or death of many rural churches.[31]

With the trend toward an increasing ethnic and religious heterogeneity in the rural community, some religious leaders have attempted to "homogenize the parish" by listing in denominational periodicals the farms and businesses for sale near their churches in the hope that families will be retained or gained for their denomination. Use of new methods and techniques of churchmanship is increasing in rural areas. Even the airplane is now used by some pastors in their regular ministry.

---

[30] H. Paul Douglass and Edmund deS. Brunner, *The Protestant Church as a Social Institution* (New York: Institute of Social and Religious Research, 1935), pp. 38, 84.

[31] Jamieson More, "Rural Churches Dying in America," *Current History,* 25 (1926-27), 343-47, and A. T. Boisen, "Factors Which Have to Do with the Decline of the Country Church," *American Journal of Sociology,* 22 (Sept. 1916), 177-92.

City churches are located in areas where the typical rural migrant is likely to enter first, those parts of the city which have rundown housing and rundown churches. These churches are not likely to offer him an outstretched hand of welcome, even though (or because?) they are often on the verge of closing down or moving to a more fruitful location in or near the suburbs.[32] One result of their aloofness toward the newly arrived rural migrant is the emergence of new sects that draw much of their membership from such people. (See Chapter 5.) Blacks and other minorities experience similar rebuffs. As a result, intra-urban invasions may be accompanied by the establishment of new congregations.

The arrival of new people forces the city to expand both within and beyond what was once a realistic boundary. Movements of the population lead to mobility of churches; moving the church is much easier for the pastor and members than adapting to a new type of people in the old location. Some churches have moved repeatedly even during a relatively short history of less than a century. In some cases this has reflected rising land values, resulting from the invasion of business, which prevented the purchase of property needed for church expansion. Churches have thus retreated before the advance of expanding business buildings in their pursuit of shifting residential districts.[33] Sometimes a church chooses to continue its program among a new population type with a few faithful members remaining in the gradually diminishing congregation, hoping to preserve its old traditions. Occasionally one in a central location develops into a metropolitan church serving the entire city with a highly specialized ministry. An infrequent solution is to remain in the same location and attempt to adapt the program to the changing population of the neighborhood.[34]

As the nation's population has become increasingly urban in its orientation, churches have been compelled to adjust their programs to the new conditions. This adjustment was very slow during the nineteenth century among Protestants,[35] but it has recently become more rapid and realistic. Some modifications, such as the application of zoning regulations, were forced upon churches by city planners long before most church leaders would otherwise have responded to their need. Others reflected the impersonal character of much city life. The business-like, formal methods

[32] David W. Barry, "The City Church and Human Need," in E. Theodore Bachmann, *Churches and Social Welfare*, III, *The Emerging Perspective* (New York: National Council of Churches, 1956), pp. 32-35.

[33] Calvin F. Schmid, *Social Trends in Seattle* (Seattle: University of Washington Publications in the Social Sciences, 14, 1944), pp. 47-49. This frequent moving of Protestant churches was noted at least as early as 1910 (Roy S. Baker, *The Spiritual Unrest*, New York: F. A. Stokes Co., 1910).

[34] Douglass and Brunner, *The Protestant Church*, pp. 69-70; and Robert E. L. Faris, *Social Disorganization* (New York: Ronald Press Co., 1948), pp. 315-18.

[35] Aaron I. Abell, *The Urban Impact on American Protestantism, 1865-1900* (Cambridge: Harvard University Press, 1943).

adopted in many churches, so unappealing to rural migrants, simply reflected the urban way of life. The use of professional fund-raisers, the holding of multiple services, drive-in services planned so that people are able to worship on their way to a day of travel or fishing, and many other recent innovations have grown out of increasing urbanization. When a substantial proportion of wives work during the week, businesses sometimes adjust by keeping open on Sundays to make it possible for husband and wife to do their marketing together. The abandonment of Sunday evening services and other adjustments by the church are a common result.

The city church is often an evolved rural church even today. Some city churches date back to the time when the city was still a small town; they retain village-oriented traditions, trying to escape into quiet residential neighborhoods when urban problems are thrust upon them. Others have been located in villages swallowed up by suburban expansion. Some have been organized to meet the needs of incoming rural migrants while others reflect a rural orientation dominant in certain denominations, subjecting them to rural standards of "success" as they strive to remain on friendly terms with denominational leaders. In the 1920's only a minority of urban churches bore the special marks of the city; over half of them were "in the city rather than of it." [36] This persistence of a rural flavor has been due partly to the large number of rural migrants and their immediate descendants in the membership, and especially in the leadership and ministry of city churches.

Yet influence always flows in two directions. Rural churches not only influence but are also influenced by city churches. Some scholars believe that the dominant emerging values of contemporary America are neither rural nor urban but a blending of elements from both as exurbanites seek a new way of life in the suburbs.[37]

Suburban Churches. The growth of American suburbs has not been accompanied by the decline in church affiliation and participation that many once feared. Of 200 suburban people interviewed in the Minneapolis-St. Paul area, only 15 per cent reported their church participation to be less than it had been before. When they were contacted by church members or friends and were invited to attend church in the new community, they were likely to increase their church attendance over what it had previously been, but if the contact was made by the pastor of a church, it seemed to produce no change. When one mate changed the degree of church participation, the other was likely to make a similar change. The longer a person resided in the same suburban community, the greater

36 H. Paul Douglass, *One Thousand City Churches* (New York: George H. Doran Co., 1926), pp. 83-86.

37 Shirley E. Greene, "Rurbanization Faces the Church," *Christian Century,* 75 (May 7, 1958), 551-52.

was his participation in church affairs.[38] Church attendance of both Catholics and Protestants seems lower in rapidly growing suburban fringe areas, however, than in the more stable central city.[39]

Since the suburbanization of Catholics typically is a movement of second generation immigrant groups, it often is accompanied by Church losses which reflect mobility into a higher socioeconomic class, increasing property-consciousness, involvement with material luxuries, and increased assimilation resulting in estrangement from the immigrant group. Lapses of the faith are hence common.[40] The suburban Protestant church is more likely to adapt to and reflect the "suburban mind" of its parishioners than to lose them because of their upward social mobility. Rapidly adapting to the one-class suburban community, most churches have accepted the trend toward "the cafeteria-like religious services and the denomination-blurring homogenization of the suburban church." [41] Suburban Judaism is oriented less toward traditional rituals than toward the strengthening of family and ethnic units.[42]

Conclusion

It is clear that the American church is caught up in vast demographic and ecological changes. Among important current trends are the vast increase in population, significant modifications of the population's age structure, differential rates of increase in the respective portions of the population from which the various churches draw their membership, the rapid transformation from a rural to an urban and now to a suburban environment, emergence of the megalopolis, the high rate of mobility of people with an estimated one-fifth changing their residence every year, and the depopulation of some areas while population burgeons rapidly in others. These are the broad kinds of population changes in society within which churches are caught and to which they are adjusting. East-West and South-North migration patterns are reflected in the rapid growth of all churches in immigrant-receiving areas and the gradual spreading of once-regional bodies like the Southern Baptist Convention

[38] Roy G. Francis, Charles E. Ramsey, and Jacob A. Toews, "The Church in the Rural Fringe," *Minnesota Farm and Home Science,* 12, no. 2 (Feb. 1955), 8, 13.

[39] At least this is the case in the Flint, Michigan, metropolitan area. Basil G. Zimmer and Amos H. Hawley, "Suburbanization and Church Participation," *Social Forces,* 37 (May 1959), 348-54.

[40] Dennis Clark, "The Church in the Suburbs," *Social Order,* 5 (Jan. 1955), 26-29; and Francois Houtart, "A Sociological Study of the Evolution of American Catholics," *Sociaal Kompas,* 2 (Jan.-Apr. 1955), 189-216.

[41] Richard D. Lambert, "Current Trends in Religion — A Summary," *Annals of the American Academy of Political and Social Science,* 332 (Nov. 1960), 154. See also Gibson Winter, "The Church in Suburban Captivity," *Christian Century,* 72 (Sept. 28, 1955), 1112-14.

[42] Albert I. Gordon, *Jews in Suburbia* (Boston: Beacon Press, 1959).

into all parts of the nation. In Chapter 17 some concomitants of Negro migration and overseas immigration are presented. The influence of rural-urban migration upon the founding and growth of sects is discussed in Chapter 5, and various other aspects of population changes which influence the church appear in other contexts.

Every American church is in a changing world. Its demographic and ecological features are in flux. There is a constant flow of members who are moving, dying, bearing children, and changing their positions in institutional life. Every aspect of the church program must be adapted to these changes if it is to survive. The wise churchman will heed these demographic and ecological trends. The sociological student of the church will study them carefully so that he can provide helpful knowledge to those whose responsibility is the guidance of the church's destiny. The social scientist will analyze them and their implications so that he can understand society better.

Selected References

American Jewish Yearbook. New York: The American Jewish Committee, issued annually. Articles, organizations with addresses, statistics, and reports of events related to Jewish life.

Bureau of Research and Survey, *Churches and Church Membership in the United States*. New York: National Council of Churches, 1956–58. Eighty bulletins which summarize the number of churches and their membership in 114 religious bodies by counties, states, and regions as of 1952 with relationships to selected data from the 1950 Census of Population.

The Directory of Religious Organizations in the United States, 2nd ed. Falls Church, Va.: McGrath Publishing Co., Consortium Books, 1982. The purpose, work, addresses, etc., of 1,628 general organizations, other than religious bodies and religious orders, which are active in the field of religion.

Gaustad, Edwin Scott, *Historical Atlas of Religion in America*, rev. ed. New York: Harper and Row, 1976. A "religious history of America" from 1650 to 1975.

Halvorson, Peter L., and William M. Newman, *Atlas of Religious Change in America 1952–71*. Washington, D.C.: Glenmary Research Center, 1978. Time-series data from the Bureau of Research and Survey study above and similar data for 1971; includes four maps of distribution patterns and changes for 35 denominations.

Johnson, Douglas W., Paul R. Picard, and Bernard Quinn, *Churches and Church Membership in the United States, 1971*. Washington, D.C.: Glenmary Research Center, 1974. The distribution of the membership of 53 Christian denominations by counties, regions, and states.

Landis, Benson Y., "A Guide to the Literature on Statistics of Religious Affiliation with References to Related Social Studies," *Journal of the American Statistical Association*, 54 (June 1959), 335–57. A thorough bibliographic article with 206 selected references.

Melton, J. Gordon, *The Encyclopedia of American Religions*, 2 vols. Wilmington, N.C.: McGrath Publishing Co., 1978. Descriptions of about 1,200 religious bodies in 16 families of denominations, sects, and cults.

Melton, J. Gordon, with James V. Geisendorfer, *A Directory of Religious Bodies in the United States*. New York: Garland Publishing, 1977. A directory with descriptions and addresses of about 1,275 denominations, sects, and cults.

Newman, William M., and Peter L. Halvorson, *Patterns in Pluralism: A Portrait of American Religion 1952–1971*. Washington, D.C.: Glenmary Research Center, 1980. Denominational distributions by regions, the mid-century "religious revival" and other trends, and social causes of denominational patterns.

Official Catholic Directory. New York: P. J. Kenedy and Son, issued annually. Besides addresses and other information, each issue has a summary of ecclesiastical statistics of the Catholic Church in the U.S.A.

Princeton Religion Research Center, *Religion in America*. Princeton, N.J.: The Gallup Poll, issued annually. Findings on questions about religion.

U.S. Bureau of the Census, *Census of Religious Bodies*. Washington, D.C.: Government Printing Office, 1906, 1916, 1926, and 1936. Rich statistical and other data about American denominations which are useful in historical analyses, trend studies, and comparative research.

Yearbook of American and Canadian Churches. Nashville: Abingdon, issued annually. Statistics compiled from over 200 religious bodies, along with names and addresses of denominational and ecumenical organizations, church-related colleges and seminaries, interpretive articles on trends, and much more.

Chapter 3

Social Norms of the Church

The social values of an institution constitute one of its important dimensions. The term "social value" refers to what is treasured, respected, and sanctioned by people in the life they share in common. Patriotism to one's country, the sanctity of marriage, free public education, the right to private property, and impartial application of laws are examples. Values include all that people recognize as necessary or important to their mode of living, believe to be right and proper, and therefore are disposed to justify and defend.

Social values provide organizing principles for both individual and social life. They are partly ideal and abstract, including many goals which people seek to realize but do not fully attain. For the most part, however, they have a practical and tangible character, for they do in fact guide much human action. In both respects values serve as social norms, i.e., as models and rules of conduct. Values permeate every aspect of society. They provide it with philosophies of life, aims, and guiding principles. They establish general patterns for the organization of group life and furnish individuals with sanctioned goals and rules around which activities and careers are organized.

Every social institution therefore centers around a set of social values. Thus, the American family is organized around such values as monogamy, equality of husband and wife, high regard for children's well-being, and democratic relationships amongst members. In a different society values governing the family may stress plural marriage, dominance of the husband, readiness to exploit children, and autocratic paternalism. The family is a much different kind of institution in the two cases. These observations illustrate the great importance of social values in institutional life. Institutions are distinguished from each other partly by the values around which they are organized. Our task in this chapter is to analyze the American church from the standpoint of its social values or norms and to note similarities and differences in the value systems of its major branches.

Relations Between Social Values and the Church

Religion is sometimes defined as a set of values which are expressed in a creed. These values comprise a system of ultimate meanings which unite individuals into a religious group.[1] The church as the operating institution of religion is related to social values in several other important ways.

First of all, the church preserves and transmits many norms of the larger society. Many of these are the moral and ethical values basic to social life itself, such as honesty, respect for the rights of others, and brotherly love. Some other general values are private property, democratic government, public education, free enterprise, obedience to the law, and private philanthropy. Above all, the church stresses religious values which are general in the society, such as faith in God, the sacredness of certain beliefs and symbols, and the value of religious fellowship. By sanctioning and reaffirming societal values, the church performs a vital function in social life. By preserving and transmitting such values the church provides an anchorage for the social order, acting as a primary agency of stability and continuity.

Second, many churches try to change certain norms of society or of subcultures within it. Although they generally sanction societal values, churches nevertheless attempt to modify those values through education, use of the mass media of communications, and influence by their leaders in community organizations. Great variations prevail in the degree to which they sanction, condone, or condemn cultural values, as well as in the specific normative goals toward which they work as an ideal for society. These variations are related to basic theological orientations as well as to the social positions and backgrounds of their dominant members.

These first two relations to cultural values constitute a very important basis for analysis of any religious body. One may profitably seek to identify

---

[1] Cf. Pitirim A. Sorokin, *Society, Culture, and Personality* (New York: Harper and Brothers, 1947), p. 225; and Edgar S. Brightman, *A Philosophy of Religion* (Englewood Cliffs, N.J.: Prentice-Hall, Inc., 1940), p. 17.

the social values which any local church sanctions and affirms, those it opposes and condemns, those it attempts to change, and those to which it is indifferent. Such inquiry enables one to see where that church stands in relation to the society of which it is part. It indicates the extent to which that church is compliant with the society and to what extent it resists or opposes the basic social order. This analysis indicates the church's relation to other institutions, such as schools, business, and government and clarifies how that church is linked with the social class structure. It reveals how far the church is responsive to any changes in values which may occur in the wider society. Such analysis is of particular importance in contemporary America. It reveals much about the conflicts and struggles within a given church. Such conflicts often center around values disputed in society at large, such as the extension of full civil and economic rights to minority racial groups, the right of industrial workers to steady employment, or the extension of subsidized medical care to people with low incomes. Studying the church in terms of its response to the values of society is hence a major aid to understanding the church as a social institution.

Thirdly, social values are of importance in the church because they are prominent in the church's mission of developing and stabilizing the character and personality of its members. They serve as basic precepts around which individuals organize their orientations toward the universe and their fellow men. Honesty, respect, friendship, compassion for the weak, and self-integrity are among sanctioned moral values which serve as a basis for character. Obedience to the law, the sanctity of the family, sacrifice for one's children, seeking respect from neighbors, and prudence in one's conduct represent values around which personality may be formed. These values, and the associated attitudes and beliefs of members in even the most individualistic types of religion, are acquired primarily in institutional settings. The language and other symbols used in the most private and introspective personal religious meditation, prayer, and devotions have their meaning in experiences shared socially with others, usually in church-related situations. Communication and learning in the social contexts of the church and family are major influences on personal as well as institutional religious experiences.[2]

Study of this function of any church constitutes an important way in which to ascertain its vitality and effectiveness. The means used to inculcate such values may become formal and routine or they may be endowed with freshness and imagination. The values may be presented

---

[2] Goodwin Watson, "A Psychologist's View of Religious Symbols," in *Religious Symbolism,* F. Ernest Johnson, ed. (New York: Institute for Religious and Social Studies, 1955), pp. 117-27; and Floyd H. Allport, *Institutional Behavior* (Chapel Hill: University of North Carolina Press, 1933), pp. 423-42.

as abstract precepts divorced from actual life experiences, or they may be depicted in ways that facilitate meaningful application to the situations people encounter in daily life. Study of the values that a church seeks to impart and of the methods used to impart them throws much light on its character as an institution.

There is a fourth way in which social values are significant in the analysis of any church. Many fundamental differences among churches consist of variations in values which they espouse. In other words, the life of each church centers around a complex of values, some of which are given special significance. Differences between the sets of values of various churches are often minor but sometimes momentous. Investigation of how social values on the one hand unite members in a church and, on the other, distinguish them from members of other churches is of particular importance in the sociology of religion. Religious bodies obviously differ in their respective creeds, beliefs, symbols, rituals, and ceremonies. Attachment of the members of a given church to the values and normative practices that distinguish it from others is a major source of the solidarity between them and, simultaneously, is a fountainhead for the renewal of personal faith. Such attachment involves "ethnocentrism"; i.e., the members of a church tend to regard only its own values and norms to be right and proper and accordingly may view the values and norms of other churches with scorn, disdain, or even open hostility. Ethnocentrism is a basis for much of the differentiation between churches **and in its most extreme forms precipitates serious cleavages and conflicts in society. (Some scholars label it "particularism.")**

The foregoing observations suggest the fruitfulness of viewing churches in terms of their values and social norms. Understanding and recognizing the norms of a group is always necessary in order to understand the behavior of its members. Even the most extreme activities of cults make sense to the participants, for the subjectively intended meanings in their behavior are oriented toward a set of social norms. To them these norms appear consistent with reality. Demons and evil spirits feared by preliterate people may not exist in reality, but belief in them makes the consequences of demon-oriented behavior very real. The actions labeled absurd, foolish, or ridiculous by non-members of a group often are logical or even inevitable outgrowths of its system of values. The intense attachment of many people to their religion can be understood only when the normative systems to which they subscribe are recognized as a significant part of their lives. Even when religious beliefs rest entirely on faith and are not susceptible to direct observation or scientific proof, they play a significant role in the lives of men. To understand any religious group, one must view that group from the perspective of the social norms to which its members explicitly and implicitly subscribe.

Variations in the Social Norms of American Churches

Many major and minor divisions in American religion are directly related to differences in the social norms adhered to by the various groups.
This is true not only of ethical teachings and basic doctrines, but also of
church organization and administration as well as forms of worship, rites,
and ceremonies. Many differences between religious bodies can be traced
in part to differences in the socially-instilled values adhered to by constituents and especially by their founders and leaders. While the major
American churches share most of their basic doctrines with corresponding
bodies in other nations, Judaism, Catholicism, and Protestantism all reflect
the influence of the New World environment.

Americanisms in Catholicism

The Roman Catholic in America has not had his religion imposed upon
him by pressures from the general cultural environment to the same
degree and in the same manner as the Catholic in Ireland, Spain, Italy,
Colombia, or Brazil. Social condemnation is not as strong if he chooses
silently to convert to Protestantism. He tends to be more tolerant of non-
Catholic religions than his brethren in the "one-religion" nations. Religious pluralism is an obvious fact to him rather than a scandal. He does
not entertain the fantastic notions about Protestants that tend to dominate
the interfaith beliefs of his brethren in predominantly Catholic countries;
he knows too many Protestants to accept extreme statements about them
as a group. As a "good American" he would rather have his neighbors
in a Protestant or Jewish church than in no church at all. Within the
Church, he is not suspicious of and hostile toward the clergy; the anti-
clericalism so marked in some Catholic nations is slight. His religion is
an activistic one dominated by good works, moral endeavors, and doing
in general, rather than by theological considerations and contemplation.[3]

In the foreign mission field American Roman Catholics also differ
from their counterparts from other nations. They have more friendly
relationships with Protestant missionaries, partly because so many of the
latter also are from America. The common language and cultural background promotes such fellowship. Coming from a land where Protestants
are dominant, American Catholics have been forced into associations
that have increased their understanding and tolerance of the Protestant
religion.

As a result of international variations within Catholicism, concessions and
modifications in Church rules are sometimes made to meet special cultural

---

[3] L. Putz, ed., *Catholic Church, U. S. A.* (Chicago: Fides Publishers, 1957); and
Neil P. Hurley, S.J., "Of Note: The Church in America," *Commonweal,* 69 (Feb. 27,
1959), 21-22.

demands. These, in turn, increase the differences between nations within Catholicism. American individualism, which produced a pupil-centered type of Protestant religious education to replace the content-centered emphasis in instruction, has had a profound impact upon Catholicism. Its doctrine of the corporate union of the members of the parish "family" as well as its educational system has been affected by individualism and other cultural influences.[4] Democratic tendencies are discernible in parish administration, and it has been hypothesized that as one moves downward in the hierarchical Church structure toward the layman the American elements in Catholicism increase.[5]

The national differences brought by various Catholic groups to America are diminishing, although Irish and German influences remain dominant; "what remains has gradually blended with the distinctively American pattern of social behavior."[6] A new general Catholic culture is emerging in America as its ethnic elements merge and Catholics rise into the middle classes. Since the models of behavior in the American middle class have always been Protestant, the dominant religion of the United States increasingly threatens the distinctives of the Catholic religion.[7]

American Adaptations in Judaism

Judaism in America similarly differs from Judaism elsewhere. Because of its relative strength it has influenced and changed the Jewish life and ceremony of other lands. The emergence of Reform Judaism reflects maximal acceptance of change. The mediating role of Conservatism as a link between the Jewish culture of the past and the opportunities and problems of the American environment—as well as between Orthodox and Reform Judaism—have made it, especially, a distinctively American movement to which at least two-fifths of affiliated Jews belong.[8]

The influence of middle class values on Conservatism is seen in the movement of its women toward a position of equality with men, increased solemnity and decorum in worship, departure from "commercialism" in

---

[4] John D. Donovan, "The Social Structure of the Parish," in *The Sociology of the Parish*, C. J. Nuesse and Thomas J. Harte, eds. (Milwaukee: Bruce Publishing Co., 1951), pp. 75-99; and David H. Fosselman, C. S. C., "The Parish in Urban Communities," in Nuesse and Harte, p. 152.

[5] J. Milton Yinger, *Religion, Society and the Individual* (New York: The Macmillan Co., 1957), p. 286.

[6] Joseph H. Fichter, *Social Relations in the Urban Parish* (Chicago: University of Chicago Press, 1954), p. 244.

[7] Everett C. and Helen MacGill Hughes, *Where Peoples Meet: Racial and Ethnic Frontiers* (Glencoe, Ill.: The Free Press, 1952), pp. 127-29; and Philip Scharper, "What a Modern Catholic Believes," *Harper's*, 218, no. 1306 (March 1959), 40-49.

[8] Marshall Sklare, *Conservative Judaism: An American Religious Movement* (Glencoe, Ill.: The Free Press, 1955), and *Encyclopaedia Judaica* (Jerusalem: Keter Publishing House, 1971), vol. 5, p. 906.

fund-raising for the synagogue, the introduction of Friday night services which permit both Sabbath worship and nominally prohibited Saturday activities, and often the addition of a social hour after the Friday evening service. Yet radical changes in the form of services typically are not accompanied by changes in the content. Continuity with previous experience and tradition is thus guaranteed. Conservatism thus borrows from and mediates between the demands of Jewish tradition, feelings both of "alienation and nostalgia toward first and second settlement areas," and the norms of American middle class religion.[9]

The movement out of the Jewish community, narrowly defined, into suburban areas has brought many changes. Upward social mobility has been a result both of adaptation to American values and of adherence to traditional Jewish religious and socioeconomic characteristics. In spite of many changes in Jewish life and worship, however, there is evidence that Jews generally adhere to their traditional culture patterns proportionately more than most other American ethnic groups. Strong relationships between parents and children, the linkage of cultural identification and survival with religious affiliation, and pressures in American culture to belong to an established religious category all combine to maintain a continuity of cultural values, even after new forms and appurtenances have been accepted.[10] Messianism, which is at the heart of Jewish religious experience when broadly defined as a hope for the future, undoubtedly has contributed to this continuity of Jewish life and culture. Even the nonbelieving, secularistic Jew, whose hope in religious belief has been abandoned, may retain a type of messianic search for deliverance.[11] Socially derived and shared norms are thus basic to an understanding of the American Jew.

American Protestantism

Perhaps the greatest international differences of all occur within Protestantism. Although the various Protestant churches generally claim doctrinal unity in all parts of the world, unity is often absent in significant details. For instance, Baptists in the U.S. generally attempt to maintain the separation of church and state, but Baptists in Sweden accept state funds to support certain educational ventures. American Mennonites are theologically conservative, but in the Netherlands they are noted for their theological liberalism. Pentecostal church members from Sweden often react against emotional excesses in American Pentecostalism and find

---

[9] *Ibid.*, esp. Chap. 4.

[10] David G. Mandelbaum, "Change and Continuity in Jewish Life," in *The Jews: Social Patterns of an American Group,* Marshall Sklare, ed. (Glencoe, Ill.: The Free Press, 1958), pp. 509-19.

[11] Arthur A. Cohen, "Messianism and the Jew," *Commonweal,* 62 (July 15, 1959), 367-69.

themselves much more at home in evangelical Methodist or Baptist churches, especially if they include Swedish Americans.

Relationships between the church and other institutions, the cooperative and antagonistic elements in the church, and the techniques and methods used by it combine to give the pattern of organized religion in America a "new look" that is distinctive in the world's history. This entire book may be viewed as a documentation of the distinctive social features of American religion, particularly of Protestantism which is dominant.

Effects of Differences in Church Norms

Differences between the social norms (including theology and church doctrines) of Catholicism and Protestantism have been used by many scholars to explain differential participation and leadership in other institutions. Weber's famous study of the relationship between the Protestant ethic and the spirit that undergirds capitalism has been followed by many other analyses of the relationship between religious values and economic activity.[12] These studies generally have concluded that the values propounded in Protestantism are more favorable to the development of capitalism and to success in capitalistic endeavors than those of Catholicism.

Similarly, Catholics produce few scientific personnel and contribute little to national scientific production in comparison to Jews and Protestants who are much more productive in these areas. The difference has been attributed by Father Cooper to the lesser value placed upon critical rationality and utilitarianism and the higher value placed upon a teleological conception of the universe by Catholics than by most Protestants. Verbalism, formalism, authoritarianism, clericalism, moralism, and defensiveness also have impeded Catholic intellectual activity.[13]

Progress in science is hindered by the imposition of "truth" by organized, non-scientific, dogmatic authority. The canons of validity in science are highly individualistic, vested in scientists' individual consciences and judgements. The values of Jews favor empirical rationality and learning. The Protestant elevation of reason as a gift of God and of research and study as a source of better understanding God through understanding the universe in which He is believed to have revealed Himself help explain the greater

---

[12] Max Weber, *The Protestant Ethic and the Spirit of Capitalism,* translated by Talcott Parsons (London: George Allen and Unwin, 1930); R. H. Tawney, *Religion and the Rise of Capitalism* (New York: Harcourt, Brace and Co., 1926); V. A. Demant, *Religion and the Decline of Capitalism* (New York: Charles Scribner's Sons, 1952). For discussion on this topic see Chapter 7.

[13] J. M. Cooper, "Catholics and Scientific Research," *Commonweal,* 42 (1945), 147-49, and Thomas F. O'Dea, *American Catholic Dilemma* (New York: Sheed and Ward, 1958). However, differing membership definitions may produce spurious correlations; the "low productivity" of Catholics may be partly a result of the inclusion of all baptized persons in their statistics.

Protestant contribution to science.[14] Even if religious norms have become secularized to a high degree, the underlying social values of the major American religions still are reflected in the differential participation of constituents in science and other areas of social activity. As Troeltsch said, "Spiritual forces can exercise a dominant influence even where they are avowedly repudiated." [15]

To the individual Catholic or Protestant, differences between the basic norms of their religious bodies often are not directly apparent. Nevertheless, the rituals and ceremonies, the accouterments of the clergy and other church personnel, the appointments of the church structure, and other manifest differences between the major branches of Christianity may be related directly to their normative structures. The belief in church *sacraments* (outward and visible signs which confer saving merit and inward spiritual graces) in contrast to *ordinances* (symbols of the working of God in the individual's life with no inherent merit) leads to contrasting viewpoints of the significance of such rituals as baptism and communion. Beliefs about the clergy significantly influence their roles. Beliefs about the nature of the church have a profound effect upon the church's role in relationship to the individual. Differences in church architecture may be traced even more directly to variations in beliefs or norms, for contemporary architects attempt to reflect the basic spirit and doctrines of a church in its house of worship.

Differences in religious interpretations of the nature and meaning of work have had important effects upon every-day activities of the faithful; they have also significantly influenced many who have gained the relevant portions of the faith without recognizing it. The early Puritan belief that hard work is a duty, success in work is evidence of God's favor, the measure of success is money and property, and the way to success is through industry and thrift has left an imprint which is felt in contemporary America.[16] When work is viewed as God's punishment for the sinfulness of man, the spirit and the manner in which it is done differ considerably from those which accompany the belief that one's occupation is a vocation into which one has been called by God. While much of the "this-worldly asceticism" of early Protestantism has been lost, the basic attitudes toward work still differ from those of Catholicism to a degree sufficient to bring about observable differences in the economic activity of the two groups.[17]

---

[14] Bernard Barber, *Science and the Social Order* (Glencoe, Ill.: The Free Press, 1952), pp. 57-66, 136-37; Robert K. Merton, "Puritanism, Pietism and Science," in *Social Theory and Social Structure,* rev. ed. (Glencoe, Ill.: The Free Press, 1957), pp. 574-606.

[15] Quoted in Merton, *Social Theory and Social Structure,* note 28, p. 583.

[16] Delbert C. Miller and William H. Form, *Industrial Sociology* (New York: Harper and Brothers, 1951), pp. 558-63.

[17] See C. Wright Mills, *White Collar: The American Middle Classes* (New York:

Beliefs of sectarian groups have a distinct impact upon the decision-making process within them. In the Old Colony Mennonite Church it is believed that practice is preceded both in time and priority of importance by dogma. The *principle of shock insulation* makes them believe it is safer to interact with people greatly different from themselves than with persons who are similar, for the danger of assimilation into a larger population is greater when differences are slight. Hence they have closer relationships to "secular" than to Mennonite welfare agencies. The *principle of efficiency* makes them consider as best the course of action which conflicts least with previous decisions and costs the least amount of energy to decide. This contributes to the maintenance of tradition and the building up of a system of precedence in which hierarchical "experts" make major decisions on an authoritarian basis. In their efforts to "keep separate from the world," they must draw the line at some point, such as the prohibiting of rubber front tires on tractors in order to prevent their use as automobiles. Thus they apply the *principle of keeping the camel's nose out of the tent* in attempts to prevent the gradual progression of worldliness. Much change is seen as disrupting and betraying the faith of their fathers, so the *principle of perpetuation* is applied to retain youths in agriculture and to maintain the cognitive orientation that regards reality as consisting of a clearly black and white, holy and unholy dichotomy. The norms of their religious faith thus directly influence daily individual and collective action.[18]

Theological values help significantly to maintain the boundary lines which keep Protestant denominations distinct. In "Springdale," New York, all but one of the ministers nominally support local ecumenicalism and work together on such projects as joint religious services on special occasions, joint summer Bible classes, Go to Church Week, and ministerial council projects. Yet none is completely committed to ecumenicalism, for all cling to theological distinctions which they will not sacrifice. Sacraments which distinguish Episcopalianism prevent the Episcopal minister from participating in any joint activity of a sacramental nature. The Methodists and Baptists have apocalyptic attitudes which prevent cooperation in any context that implies a historical attitude toward Christ and the books of Revelation, Ezekiel, and Daniel. The Baptists distinguish themselves by adult baptism, and they together with the Congregationalists refuse to take part in any activity which appears to deny the direct, unmediated connections of each person to Christ by acknowledging a "worldly" hierarchy of religious leaders. All the ministers stress the

---

Oxford University Press, 1951), pp. 215-20, for a brief discussion of differential meanings of work. Such differences no doubt prevail also between Calvinistic and Arminian Protestants, but to the writer's knowledge no social scientist has studied them. Strong cultural forces gradually diminish the differences.

[18] Calvin Redekop, "Decision Making in a Sect," *Review of Religious Research,* 2 (Fall 1960), 79-86.

distinctions between their doctrines and those of other churches. Theology is thus "a central part of the framework of rhetoric and discussion surrounding church-centered activities," "an organizational device for holding and recruiting members and, as such, . . . a branch of administration." [19]

Value Differences as a Basis for Church Conflict

Much misunderstanding between religious groups can be traced to differences between their social norms. William James' contrast of Protestantism and Catholicism in 1902 continues to apply today: Catholicism "offers so much richer pasturage and shade to the fancy, has so many cells with so many different kinds of honey, is so indulgent in its multiform appeals to human nature, that Protestantism will always show to Catholic eyes the almshouse physiognomy. The bitter negativity of it is to the Catholic mind incomprehensible." [20] Many intellectual Catholics consider the antiquated beliefs and practices of their church to be as childish, when taken literally, as Protestants do. But to the Catholic "they are childish in the pleasing sense of 'childlike'—innocent and amiable, and worthy to be smiled on in consideration of the undeveloped condition of the dear people's intellects. To the Protestant, on the contrary, they are childish in the sense of being idiotic falsehoods" which must be stamped out with a literalness that will make the Catholic shudder.[21] Tensions between Protestants and Catholics, arising in part out of proselyting activities, thus have a normative base. Similarly the manifest differences between the numerous Protestant bodies must be attributed partly to differences in their underlying values. Although numerous other factors have operated in the fundamentalist-modernist controversies, for instance, it would be highly erroneous to assume that doctrinal differences were not important in them (Chapter 11). The oft heard admonition, "Never argue about religion," is one evidence of the attempt to remove such tension-producing and group-breaking items from general social intercourse.[22]

Opposing sides in sectarian controversies often appeal to the same body of social doctrine. Differences in the interpretation of common doctrines pertinent to such issues as prohibition, pacifism, and social integration of blacks have contributed significantly to conflicts in Protestantism. Social and regional differences often override theological considerations in

---

[19] Arthur J. Vidich and Joseph Bensman, *Small Town in Mass Society* (Princeton, N.J.: Princeton University Press, 1958), pp. 241-51, 252-56 (quotations from pp. 253 and 254).

[20] William James, *The Varieties of Religious Experience* (New York: The Modern Library ed., Random House, n.d.), p. 451.

[21] *Ibid.*

[22] Robin M. Williams, Jr., *American Society* (New York: Alfred A. Knopf, 1951), p. 425.

the practical application of Christian doctrine.[23] Two persons or groups with the same verbal statements of beliefs may be widely separated in their interpretations of the statements. They actually do not adhere to the same beliefs, even though the casual observer may at first think so.

Denominational differences in beliefs remain a source of division in Protestantism; many splinter groups that have emerged out of larger bodies in protest against certain practices or doctrines have normative considerations as their basic, and sometimes only, foundation. A Belief Index that ranks persons on a continuum from "unadjusted fundamentalism" to "a positively asserted humanism" was applied to 1,800 persons from eleven religious denominations. It revealed a direct relationship between members' denominations and the positions of their beliefs on the scale. The members of two groups that had recently divided in a Baptist schism had high, statistically significant differences in scores on the scale. The results confirmed the presence of theological differences by denomination even among lay people.[24]

The Internal Significance of Variations in Norms

Studies also have confirmed the importance of doctrinal beliefs to the nature and form of entire social systems. Mormon society, for instance, has been profoundly influenced by the belief that the Kingdom of God was being built on earth. The ecological pattern of the Mormon community, as well as the cooperatives and other institutions in it, bears the marks of Mormon doctrine and testifies to the institutionalization of Mormon values.[25]

Theologians within any denomination are usually eager to indicate that their church's polity (its system of government and administration) is consistent with and founded upon their doctrinal beliefs. Many, especially those in sect-like religious bodies, accompany praise of their own group with condemnation of the inconsistencies of others. Every institution incorporates into its structure some norms that are incompatible or potentially incompatible with each other.

The three basic forms of church polity—the episcopal, presbyterian, and congregational types—can be traced largely to doctrinal differences. The *episcopal* form—which emphasizes the role of bishops, other hierarchical personnel, and the clergy as their representatives—rests upon such beliefs as authority through apostolic succession and the supreme importance of the church as God's representative on earth. The *presby-*

---

[23] Paul A. Carter, *The Decline and Revival of the Social Gospel* (Ithaca, N.Y.: Cornell University Press, 1954), pp. 195-200, 221.

[24] C. V. Gustafson, "A Doctrinal Survey of Selected Protestant Groups in Portland, Oregon, and Vicinity," abstract of a paper read to the Society for the Scientific Study of Religion, November 10, 1956.

[25] Thomas F. O'Dea, *The Mormons* (Chicago: University of Chicago Press, 1957).

terian form stresses control of the church by a presbytery or equivalent body of clergymen. Exalting the role and often the person of the clergy-man, it can be traced back to aristocratic tendencies in the history of presbyterian bodies and to an emphasis upon theological doctrines of the sacred character and educationally developed talents of the clergy. The *congregational* type places the highest authority in church government in the hands of the local congregation. This democratic type of admin-istration, which has flowered in American society, is based ultimately upon belief in the priesthood of the believer and its attendant doctrines. In America many churches have a mixed type of polity; when modifica-tions are made in their system of government, changes are interpreted as being theologically consistent and in line with historic traditions of the church.

Religious Norms in American Society

Surveys reveal that about 94 per cent of American adults believe in God, 85 per cent believe in the divinity of Jesus Christ, 45 per cent believe the only hope for heaven is through personal faith in him, 35 per cent claim to have had a born-again experience, 33 per cent read the Bible at least weekly, and 37 per cent believe that it is the literal word of God, an additional 42 per cent believing that it is inspired by God.[26] Religious beliefs are widespread enough and of such a nature that the term "Chris-tian nation" may not be entirely a misnomer. When, however, any *one* interpretation of the meaning of belief in God, life after death, or the divinity of Christ is taken as a standard, a large proportion of such beliefs is found to fall short of that standard. To believe in God obviously does not mean the same to the fundamentalist Christian as it does to the Un-itarian or the liberal Jew. For this and other reasons Herberg has con-cluded that mounting religiosity in the United States is accompanied by pervasive secularism. The prevalent religion among contemporary Amer-icans "has lost much of its authentic Christian (or Jewish) content. Even when they are thinking, feeling, or acting religiously, their thinking, feel-ing, and acting do not bear an unequivocal relation to the faiths they profess."[27]

One concomitant of the coexistence of religious revival and mounting secularism is the tendency of Americans to identify themselves by their religious community. Protestant, Catholic, and Jew are looked upon as three diverse representations of the one great "American religion," pre-sumably standing for the same spiritual values as are represented by

---

[26] Princeton Religion Research Center, *Religion in America 1982* (Princeton, N.J.: The Gallup Poll, 1982), and earlier Gallup Poll reports, 1978–81.

[27] Will Herberg, *Protestant – Catholic – Jew* (Garden City, N.Y.: Doubleday and Co., 1955), p. 15.

American democracy. While denominational lines are neither denied nor depreciated, they are held secondary to the three great sub-communities and "an inner necessity" compels the American to place himself in one of them. As nationality lines gradually become more and more indistinct in the American melting pot, religion becomes the "differentiating element and the context of self-identification and social location." The general religious pattern is distinctly American. Dominated and defined by Protestantism, it is the one to which Catholics and Jews as well as Protestants increasingly conform.[28] In this "American religion" with its generalized ideas of doing good and upholding democracy, "God's guidance" generally consists of a few principles which often can be interpreted in terms of one's personal interests. Religious norms have thus come to play a different role from that of the past when dogmatism was more common.

The "American religion" recommends itself more for the services it performs than for the truth it teaches. It emphasizes what religion can do for the individual and tends to minimize or even to erase denominational distinctions. The instrumentalism, individualism, and non-denominationalism of American churches in general are related to the linking of religious faith, however vaguely or variously defined, with democracy and other political and even economic values. The new American piety adds to godliness the glorification of commercial success. Religious loyalty, loyalty to the democratic state, and the civic values associated with national pride are so intimately related to one another that they seem to the average American but two sides of the same coin.[29] Church and state are kept theoretically separate in the new religion, but religion and citizenship are identified. Secularism, with separation of government and church as a central theme, prevails; "the American way" is the main creed. A "passionate faith in the great whatever"[30] replaces the faith in God, His Word, His Church, or His Chosen People that predominated in the great western religions of past centuries.

Secularization in American Society

While the thesis that one single American religion is emerging is perhaps an over-simplified interpretation, there is general agreement among social scientists that the long-range trend in American society is one of increasing secularization. *Secularization* is the process by which naturalistic ex-

---

[28] *Ibid.*, pp. 31-35, 51-54, 240.
[29] Herbert W. Schneider, "The Old Theory and the New Practice of Religious Loyalty," *American Quarterly,* 5 (Winter 1953), 291-300; Arthur A. Cohen, "Religion as a Secular Ideology," *Partisan Review,* 23 (Fall 1956), 495-505.
[30] The expression is taken from a review of Edward R. Murrow's *This I Believe.* (William Lee Miller, "A Passionate Faith in the Great Whatever," *The Reporter,* 10 [April 1954], 46-48.)

planations of the universe increase at the expense of theological and mythical ones.[31] The essence of secularization, in its practical impact, consists in the neglect of religious techniques to move and control the operative powers and working causes of the world. Secularization has been observed in American culture in many ways. The changing role of religion in public education, the decline of supernatural sanctions in justice and law, subordination of the church's power to that of business, failure of religious beliefs to serve as internalized sources of authority or spurs to individuals' consciences, the tendency to make certain "by-products" of religion its chief goal, changes in the nature and interpretation of American ceremonies and other rituals, the divorce of science from religious sanctions, increasing separation of basic human experiences (birth, marriage, work, and death) from the religious context of the will of God, and the general tendency for all social and religious life to lose supernatural sanctions are some of them. Secular values of equalitarian family relationships have superseded the traditionally sacred value of the primacy of the husband-father. Religion as a primary life value that is expected to give the leading satisfactions of life is generally outranked by the values of home, career, and leisure among college students.[32]

The religious personality in pluralistic America is a segmental one that results from the divergence of sacred and secular values. It does not cut across all of life with a sacred orientation. Even in the act of joining a church, the contemporary Protestant is motivated and influenced by a large number of secular and semi-secular factors.[33] Churches typically incorporate many features which a half century ago would have been branded as "worldly." Consequently, the practical meaning and influence of religion have been radically transformed. Prayers are mechanically dispensed by telephone. Basic creeds have been rewritten, for as society changes, language changes and new statements must be made. The Scriptures also must be translated into a "new" tongue; since the King James Version in 1611 over 500 English translations of the Bible have been published. Some church programs have changed until they are unrecognizable as religious activities, and secular considerations are involved increasingly in church participation.

The typical contemporary church is so concerned with mundane affairs that it tends to lose most of its supernatural orientation. It is involved

---

[31] This is but one phase of a sociological usage that is often much broader. "Secularization" is in some ways a weasel word. It has many uses, some of which are inconsistent with each other. For instance, Roman Catholic efforts to counteract secularism may be interpreted sociologically as efforts to strengthen a bureaucracy, hence as contributing to increased secularization.

[32] W. Seward Salisbury, "Religion and Secularization," *Social Forces,* 36 (March 1958), 197-205. This does not establish a trend; perhaps it always has been the case!

[33] David O. Moberg, "Die Säkularisierung und das Wachstum der Kirchen in den Vereinigten Staaten," *Kölner Zeitschrift für Soziologie und Sozialpsychologie,* 10, no. 3 (1958), 430-38.

less in the problem of "making saints" than in "the task of recasting the ethical ideals of society. The religious adherent today is called upon not to keep himself 'unspotted from the world,' but to socialize his behavior." [34] Even many who do not accept Durkheim's theory of the origin of religion agree with his assertion that history clearly teaches us "that religion tends to embrace a smaller and smaller portion of social life. Originally, it pervades everything; everything social is religious . . . Then, little by little, political, economic, scientific functions free themselves from the religious function . . ." [35] If God continues to dominate the world at all, it is "from on high and at a distance" in ever more general and indeterminate ways, as society gradually changes from one dominated by mechanical solidarity toward one in which organic solidarity predominates.

The secularization of the Sabbath, removal of social welfare activities from the churches, and the separation of religious considerations from politics, all noted by the Lynds in their Middletown, can be observed in almost any community which one would choose to study in America. "Mass instrumentalism" tends to dominate the church as well as other institutions. The nominal stress in the church upon ends rather than means has given way by subtle psychological transfer until going to church becomes a type of life-insurance policy, an adjunct to getting ahead in society, an emotionally stabilizing agent which has left the defining of values to the leadership of other social agencies. In Middletown what a person believes has become less significant than having nominal membership in a church that is socially proper and which gives identification to the individual. [36]

It may be inevitable for a society of increasing industrialization, urbanization, and education to experience a shift away from values traditionally held sacred and toward a more secular orientation of life. As traditional religious values relative to work are dissipated by the advent of new working conditions, religious life becomes increasingly separated from man's daily existence. When religious homogeneity within a community is broken down by increasing social mobility and differentiation, toleration of "strange" beliefs becomes necessary and syncretistic sects are likely to emerge. As specialized agencies and organizations arise to perform duties which were once the task of the church, organized religion

---

[34] Constantine Panunzio, *Major Social Institutions* (New York: The Macmillan Co., 1939), pp. 308-9.

[35] Emile Durkheim, *The Division of Labor in Society,* translated by George Simpson (Glencoe, Ill.: The Free Press, 1949), p. 169.

[36] Robert S. and Helen Merrell Lynd, *Middletown in Transition* (New York: Harcourt, Brace and Co., 1937), pp. 306-7, 315-18, 462. However, the 1976–81 followup concluded that there was more continuity than change in religion during the entire century; cf. Theodore Caplow et al., *All Faithful People: Change and Continuity in Middletown's Religion* (Minneapolis: University of Minnesota Press, 1983).

loses many of its traditional tasks in society.[37] Ethics tend to replace a transcendental deity in the society's value system.

The influence of the church on the daily lives of its members may grow progressively weaker in a society of advancing secularization, even if religious institutions grow in strength. During transitional periods of increasing secularization, the person who wishes to retain some elements of a supernatural religion and accept new interpretations from the emerging modernized views of religion and society is faced with many problems. He often becomes a marginal man, emotionally and socially secure neither in the new nor the old type of faith. The lack of consistency and integration of institutions around a central core of values leads both to marginal church membership and marginal non-membership.

Church Norms and Individual Conduct

Two major problems confront the church as it tries to extend its influence into the everyday affairs of its members. One may be labeled "fractional conversion"; the other is the age-old problem of the relationship between beliefs and behavior traditionally labeled "faith and works."

Many persons who are church members, whether they have entered the church through early religious education or as a result of a profound emotional experience, are converted only in part to their church's ideals. Some deliberately refuse to accept the teachings of the church in regard to certain aspects of their behavior, while others never hear or never learn the practical significance of religious doctrines for all areas of life. Because this is true to some degree of most church members, the influence of the church is not as great as one might conclude from the fact that **about two-thirds of the American population have church affiliation.**

It is difficult to determine whether fractional conversion or the inconsistency of behavior with professed beliefs is the more significant factor in explaining the prevalence of wars, racial bigotry, economic exploitation, and other injustices in avowedly Christian nations. "Giving only lip service to the supreme injunction of Christianity, all-giving and all-forgiving love for God and man, and little practicing it, they are the victims of their own belligerency and aggressiveness, hatred, greed and lust of power, and other antisocial and antimoral traits." [38] It is one thing to have a creed; it is another to recognize and practice its implications conscientiously.

Sometimes patterns of behavior which are ultimately incompatible with the norms of the church become institutionalized in society. Since the church tends to be conservative—i.e., to conserve prevailing institutional arrangements of society—it may sanction and stabilize mundane interests

---

[37] W. Banning, "Enige Sociologische Opmerkingen over het Secularisatie-proces," *Sociologisch Bulletin*, 5, no. 3 (1951), 84-90.

[38] Pitirim A. Sorokin, *The Reconstruction of Humanity* (Boston: Beacon Press, 1948), p. 43.

of the classes that are economically or socially dominant. Protestants and Catholics alike, with few notable exceptions, tend to follow locally established patterns of race relations. Their attitudes toward war and peace generally reflect their social climate. Most churches do not look into the sources of the contributions they receive; they do not ask whether wealthy employers are taking unfair advantage of employees as long as the former contribute generously to church work; nor do they take steps to ascertain whether the offerings they receive come from dishonorable methods or types of work. Institutionalized injustices are seldom recognized as such by churches despite valiant efforts by many theologians and activists.

Tensions are sometimes generated in the religiously faithful because they observe discrepancies between actual practices and the ideals upheld by the church. These tensions are a frequent source of theological discussion. They are often involved in the mental processes accompanying assimilation and socialization into a church; one mark of spiritual maturity is recognition of such discrepancies and possession of a solution for them that enables the believer to live at peace with himself and the world. Some theological solutions to the problem of the relationship between Christ and culture emphasize the opposition of Christianity and society, and others the coincidence of them. Some consider Christ to be the fulfillment of cultural aspirations and the restorer of ideal institutions. Certain of them emphasize dual loyalties of the Christian as a citizen both on earth and in another world; others stress the need for conversion and believe that the solution to all problems lies in the regeneration of individuals and the anticipated millennial reign of Christ.[39]

The core participants in religious groups have more intense religious feelings than marginal participants. They are more attached by action as well as faith to their churches; their church participation and faith are closely related to each other. Faith is sometimes derived from belief in divine revelation, sometimes from the influence of charismatic leadership, sometimes from ritual in which one does what others do and gradually comes into "the unity of the faith" as the solidarity of the religious community increases, and sometimes from a combination of these. Whichever of these holds for a particular group affects the quality of interaction which takes place within the religious system.

When charismatic leadership plays a major part in defining the faith of a church, frequent changing of pastors may be disastrous to its growth and vigor. Members may lose security with the changes, especially if there are observable variations between the pastors' interpretations of the faith. If ritual is the chief bond holding the faithful together, parishioners may detest the pastor but still continue to be faithful to the church. The norms included in a system of beliefs tend to be a series of separate units which are in a continually shifting and re-combining configuration. Even the Roman Catholic Church is a dynamic, evolving in-

---

[39] For an excellent discussion of these socio-theological problems see H. Richard Niebuhr, *Christ and Culture* (New York: Harper and Brothers, 1951).

stitution continually adapting to the social climate of the communities in which its parishes are located. The core members of churches are attracted to them primarily by some aspect or aspects of faith.[40]

The social norms of a church are correlated to some degree with the normative patterns of its members—their ideas of right and wrong, good and bad—as we shall see from studies reported elsewhere in this book. The correlation is far from perfect; but when the practical implications of religious beliefs are clear, church members tend to live closer to the pattern defined by their church as ideal than those who do not profess by word or by such deeds as membership to adhere to these beliefs.

Religious Symbolism

Symbolic expressions of religious values emerge in the institutional development of every religion. Worship hymns reflect theological doctrines, even if the groups using them fail to accept the doctrines literally. Pagodas, mosques, cathedrals, temples, and other church buildings reflect basic concepts of religious faith and practice. Religious drama, art, literature, liturgy, and ceremonies perform similar functions in the perpetuation and propagation of the faith, but the role of symbolism goes far beyond its purely doctrinal aspects.

Many religious symbols are addressed to the question of what makes man unique in the universe. The question is answered in Christianity by rich symbolic pictures: The Lamb of God dying for sinful man, the Lord as a Good Shepherd providing all the needs of his sheep, Christ as a bridegroom and His church as the bride, and God as the Heavenly Father are but a few of them. The appeal of Christianity rests partly on "the symbolic power of a personality—so idealized and interpreted as to be in effect a system as well as a man—and partly on a changing but always elaborate structure of doctrines, ritual, polity, preaching and the like. Take away these symbols and there is nothing distinctive left." [41]

Interpretations of religious ceremonies are fluid in time and relative to person and place. Varieties of meanings are attached to the same ceremonies in different cultures; even within the same culture there may be differences from one person to another. Between religious groups the differences are often vast. Symbolic interpretations of the Lord's Supper are considerably different in fundamentalist and liberal Protestantism, and these are not the same as the equivalent ceremony in Catholicism. The liturgical Protestant and the Catholic are likely to look to formal

[40] W. Seward Salisbury, "The Structure of Religious Action in a Small City," a paper read to the American Sociological Society in Atlantic City, Sept. 4, 1952. This paragraph is based upon his findings in Oswego, N.Y.
[41] Charles H. Cooley, *Social Organization* (New York: Charles Scribner's Sons, 1909), p. 374.

ritual as a major support of their faith; the non-liturgical Protestant is more likely to have his religious feelings heightened by meditation and charismatic leadership. Among Jews family religious observances are the major support of religious faith.[42]

The outstanding social function of religious ritualism lies in its contribution to group consensus and the concomitant reinforcing of group identity. Sacred holy days, which tend to become secular holidays, organize the religious group and often the entire society in a cyclical framework of activity. The typical Protestant church year is built around such "significant days" as Labor Day, Armistice (Veteran's) Day, Thanksgiving, New Year, Memorial Day, Independence Day—sometimes even Halloween and April Fool's Day—as well as around more strictly religious holy days like Christmas, Good Friday, and Easter. Catholicism and Judaism are organized even more clearly around special days. The major events represented by special days thus serve as unifying centers for much church activity. The group is united around symbolic rites not only as members participate in them, but also as they anticipate them and look back on them with happy memories. Memorial Day is a unifying ritual that brings together some of the most diverse components of society in a symbolic ceremony elaborating upon the sacrifice of the individual for the group.[43] Easter for many is little more than a spring festival and a time for personal enjoyment and self-indulgence. In modern, dynamic society there may be emerging from it the symbolic function of affirming belief in social progress.[44]

The specific forms of religious symbols are determined primarily by environmental influences of the general culture. Fishermen have nautical symbols, while a nomadic sheep-herding people build their symbols around the shepherd, green pastures, and sheep. American pictures of Christ sometimes view him as an astute businessman or a great salesman. The economic interests and basic maintenance mores of a people profoundly influence their religion.

Most religious rituals and ceremonies may be divided into two main categories—life-cycle rituals and sustenance rites (Chapter 14). *Life-cycle rituals* are rites of passage that relate to the individual's life-cycle, especially to major events in it: birth, puberty, marriage, and death. Religious birth ceremonials include infant baptism, dedication, christening, and circumcision. They serve societal as well as religious functions, for they publicly declare the child's parenthood and once were a means of registration for census and taxation purposes. Puberty ceremonies, such as confirmation and first communion, celebrate transition from child-

---

[42] W. Seward Salisbury, "Faith, Ritualism, Charismatic Leadership and Religious Behavior," *Social Forces,* 34 (March 1956), 241-45. (These conclusions are based upon a study of 1,008 college students.)

[43] W. Lloyd Warner, *American Life: Dream and Reality* (Chicago: University of Chicago Press, 1953), pp. 1-26.

[44] James H. Barnett, "The Easter Festival: A Study in Cultural Change," *American Sociological Review,* 14 (Feb. 1949), 62-70.

hood to adolescence and often include teaching of the physical as well as the social aspects of sex. Religious sanction is given to the family by the church wedding. The religious funeral emphasizes the passage of the soul to a new life, thus helping to remove "the sting of death." [45]

Sustenance rites relate to the economic life of the group that is involved in worship. Through religious feasts God is symbolically thanked for His help and His collaboration is sought in procuring food or in averting calamities that would affect human well-being. Although such symbolism is more true of the rites of preliterate peoples, modern religious and semi-religious festivals and seasons of Thanksgiving, Christmas, New Year's, Easter, and Lent bear economic as well as religious symbolism. They are related to the material needs and desires of the group as well as to the worship of God.[46]

Creeds—the brief, precisely worded statements of faith that set forth the essential doctrines of a religion—usually are in a form that is easily memorized and repeated; thus they help to defend the faith against attacks by philosophers, skeptics, and members of other religions. They are bulwarks of the religious system, which in pre-industrialized societies is so intimately bound up with the rest of the culture that to preserve the religion often means to support and maintain the entire culture. They build group cohesion among adherents and have a significant influence upon the spread of the religion. Creeds and church ceremonies help establish feelings of cooperativeness, unanimity, filiation, and bonds of affection that contribute to worshipers a sense of security, peace and God's presence; at the same time they help to establish a feeling of common humanity and rapport that binds one worshiper to another.[47]

Like symbols in other areas of life, church symbols must always be interpreted in their figurative, allegorical, metaphorical, or emblematic context. To interpret these symbols literally and then to condemn religious people for "superstitiousness" is as fallacious as to evaluate rationally every folkway of etiquette and to condemn all that do not have obviously manifest and rational functions. Understanding of religious symbols requires an understanding of the entire religious, social, cultural, and historical setting in which they appear.

> Why is it that the symbol encroaches and persists beyond its function? Evidently just because it is external, capable of imitation and repetition without fresh thought and life, so that all that is inert and mechanical clings to it. All dull and sensual persons, all dull and sensual moods in any person, see the form and not the substance. The spirit, the idea, the sentiment, is plainly enough the reality *when one*

[45] Panunzio, *Major Social Institutions*, pp. 292-94.
[46] *Ibid.*, p. 294.
[47] *Ibid.*, pp. 290-91; and Leon Fram, "Symbol and Ceremonial as a Source of Religious Vitality," *Religious Education*, 41 (July-Aug. 1946), 203-8.

is awake to see it, but how easily we lose our hold upon it and come to think that the real is the tangible. The symbol is always at command: we can always attend church, go to mass, recite prayers, contribute money, and the like; but kindness, hope, reverence, humility, courage, have no string attached to them; they come and go as the spirit moves . . .[48]

The question of why religious groups perpetuate rituals that have originated in a philosophy or religion antithetical to their own teachings is easily answered when one considers the current functions of these ceremonies. The pagan origins of much that is associated with the celebration of Easter and Christmas are not a matter of concern to the average Christian celebrant. He is made a more loyal member of his church by active participation during these holidays that help to clarify the roles and values related to his faith. Ritual often serves mankind as a means to commonly shared goals, a tool of social organization and worship. Sometimes, especially in religions that are in the declining period of their life cycle, ritual becomes a master, an end in itself. When this is the case, ceremonies once rich in significance become forms to which only lip-service and rote performance are devoted. Dead ritual is often better for the group than no ritual at all, but it can also be very injurious if it makes slaves of the participants.

The symbolism in religious doctrines, rites, and ceremonies helps maintain the religious values of the group, contributes to social solidarity (group consensus and unity), reaffirms values of the society and of the religious subculture, and serves other social, material, and spiritual needs. Yet symbols have a tendency to live beyond their period of social and spiritual utility, to change their meanings, and to be transformed from means to ends. A major problem for the American church, as perhaps for any religion, is how to maintain a wholesome balance between the formalism that symbols promote and spontaneous religious expression. People's nonofficial religion—their subjective meanings and beliefs and their actual behavior—typically deviates from the officially prescribed and interpreted "ideal" model.[49] In small sects the discrepancies may be minor, but in large denominations they can be very great.

The variations in time and place of symbols and their meanings and in the beliefs and practices sanctioned for church members demonstrate clearly the interdependence of every church with its surrounding world. The church is a social institution irrevocably linked with and involved in the other institutions of society. Its values therefore can never be clearly distinct and completely separate from those prevalent in the larger society.

---

[48] Cooley, *Social Organization*, p. 376. Reprinted by permission.

[49] See Meredith B. McGuire, "Official and Nonofficial Religion," Chapter 4 in *Religion: The Social Context* (Belmont, Calif.: Wadsworth Publishing Co., 1981), pp. 75–104.

Selected References

Ahlstrom, Sydney E., *A Religious History of the American People*, 2 vols. New Haven, Conn.: Yale University Press, 1972. A history of American religious life in its social, political, and intellectual context from European origins to the twentieth century.

Bellah, Robert N., *The Broken Covenant: American Civil Religion in Time of Trial*. New York: Seabury, 1975. The Nixon era as the third trial period in which national cohesion via consistency with ultimate ideals was being tested.

Berger, Peter L., *The Heretical Imperative: Contemporary Possibilities of Religious Affirmation*. Garden City, N.Y.: Anchor Press, Doubleday, 1979. A stimulating analysis of religion in modern pluralistic society. (See also the Review Symposium, *Journal for the Scientific Study of Religion*, 20, no. 2 [June 1981], 181–96.)

Gaustad, Edwin Scott, *A Religious History of America*, rev. ed. New York: Harper and Row, 1974. The role of religion in American life from the Age of Exploration to the present.

Gehrig, Gail, *American Civil Religion: An Assessment*. Storrs, Conn.: Society for the Scientific Study of Religion, 1981. A well-documented analysis of the empirical and theoretical writings on civil religion.

Handy, Robert T., ed., *Religion in the American Experience: The Pluralistic Style*. New York: Harper and Row, 1972. Illustrations of the pluralism of religious life and its meaning for the American people.

Herberg, Will, *Protestant—Catholic—Jew: An Essay in American Religious Sociology*. Garden City, N.Y.: Doubleday and Co., 1955. Presents the thesis that a single tripartite American religion dominates the U.S.A.

Hill, Samuel S., Jr., et al., *Religion and the Solid South*. Nashville: Abingdon, 1972. The symbolic and functional role of religion in southern society.

Hurvitz, Nathan, "Sources of Middle-Class Values of American Jews," *Social Forces*, 37 (Dec. 1958), 117–23. The influence of American middle-class values on a socially mobile minority group.

Marty, Martin E., *A Nation of Behavers*. Chicago: University of Chicago Press, 1976. Six current types of American religion analyzed from the perspective of habits, conduct, and practice.

Robbins, Thomas, and Dick Anthony, eds., *In Gods We Trust: New Patterns of Religious Pluralism in America*. New Brunswick, N.J.: Transaction Books, 1980. Papers on the contemporary religious ferment with special attention to controversies related to the new religions.

Simmel, Georg, *Sociology of Religion*, trans. Curt Rosenthal. New York: Philosophical Library, 1959. A theoretical classic which emphasizes the role of belief in God, love, communion, symbolic values, and ceremonies in promoting unity in religious groups.

Sklare, Marshall, *America's Jews*. New York: Random House, 1971. A sociological description of Jews as an American ethnic group.

Wakin, Edward, and Father Joseph F. Scheuer, *The De-Romanization of the American Catholic Church*. New York: Macmillan, 1966. Social, cultural, economic, political, and intellectual dimensions of the church as social institution and people.

Warner, W. Lloyd, *The Living and the Dead*. New Haven: Yale University Press, 1959. A detailed socio-psychological study of sacred and secular symbols in American life.

Part Three: *Types of Churches*

🏛 Chapter 4

Church-Sect and Other Typologies

The church is so large and diversified that it is necessary to identify the different forms it typically takes. Several of the more significant classifications developed by scholars are presented here to indicate the church's variety and complexity and to show how understanding and insight is increased by using typological methods of research. The contrasting categories are what sociologists term *ideal types*. They are "ideal" in the sense that they represent patterns of organization and action which we may rationally assume would be attained if each given class of churches were to develop without interference from accidental or extraneous conditions. No ideal type will be found in pure or logically perfect form. Each is an abstract conception which singles out significant features that are entwined with numerous other traits in the case of actual churches. The ideal type must not be confused, then, with exact reality. Neither does it refer to ethical desirability; the term "ideal" refers only to the logical purity of an *idea*, not a standard of perfection or a goal to be sought.

Ideal-type methodology simplifies observation of the complex scene of reality by calling attention to central features scholars have studied. In any one typology these usually stand in clear contrast to each other. In the world of things-as-they-are, it must be remembered, the types of actual phenomena do not stand in such clearly contrasting positions. Most, if not all, fall between the extremes and may be thought of as arrayed along a continuum with innumerable intermediate categories. Ideal types hence are abstractions from reality which are conceptually pure; they are discrete only from the theoretical perspective of the rationally distinct concepts discerned by the scholar. Rightly understood and used, the ideal type is a penetrating tool for analysis of the church as a social institution.

Troeltsch's Church-Sect Typology

One of the best-known classifications of religious bodies was developed by Ernst Troeltsch, a German theologian, historian, and philosopher. His historical survey of the social teachings of Christian churches published in 1912 dealt with the development and relevance of religious doctrines and organization to society. Two main types of ecclesiastical organizations, church and sect, were distinguished from each other.[1]

The *church* type, as Troeltsch defined it, is conservative, to a certain extent accepting the secular order of society although claiming domination over it. In principle it is universal in that it desires to cover the whole life of humanity. It uses the state and the ruling classes to accomplish its goals; thus it becomes an integral part of the social order dependent upon the upper classes. The individual is born into the church and comes under its "miraculous influence" through infant baptism. It minimizes the need for subjective holiness and emphasizes objective treasures of Christ's grace and redemption, imparting the benefits of Christ's saving work to individuals through the clergy, the Word, and the Sacraments.

The contrasting type is the *sect*. Sects are comparatively small. They renounce the idea of dominating the world and tend to avoid the state and society—either by merely tolerating them or by attempting to replace other institutions with their own society. They tend to be connected with the lower classes and other elements that oppose the state and the established culture. Membership is voluntary. Believers are bound together by the fact that all have experienced the "new birth." Because direct personal intercourse with God is emphasized, the sacraments are minimized or are replaced by emphasis upon the Holy Spirit and enthusiasm. Lay leadership, service, and power dominate the sect in contrast to the church's priesthood, ecclesiastical ordination, and tradition. The sect is inclined toward asceticism and mysticism. Law is emphasized more than grace in its doctrine, and its concept of Christian order is based upon love. The Christ of the sect is the Lord, example and lawgiver of Divine authority and dignity. Though He allows His elect to pass through contempt and misery, it is believed, He will com-

[1] Ernst Troeltsch, *The Social Teaching of the Christian Churches,* trans. by Olive Wyon (London: George Allen and Unwin, 1931), 2 vols. The following discussion is based primarily upon I, pp. 331-81, and II, pp. 993-1013.

plete the work of redemption upon His return to earth and His establishment of the Kingdom of God. In contrast, the church believes the work of redemption was finished by the Atoning Death of Christ. The sect stresses literal obedience to scriptural and primitive church ideals; the church views these ideals as but the starting point for its development. Sects, besides lacking continuity, need constant renewal of their ideal and have a pronounced individualism which expects to see the world transformed by purely moral principles of love. Subjective holiness is emphasized, and many stress the "communion of the saints" as they seek to differentiate themselves from "hypocrites" and "heretics." [2]

Troeltsch presented a third type of Christian thought, *mysticism,* as emerging beside the church and sect. Mysticism depends neither upon the institution, as does the church, nor upon literal interpretation of the Law of God in the Bible, as does the sect. It is an individualism freely combining Christian ideas with other elements. Sometimes it has led to idealistic speculations and created social utopias, the first of which was Sir Thomas More's. In mysticism ideas which have hardened into formal worship and doctrine are replaced by purely personal experiences. Its groups have no permanent organization. Voluntary association with like-minded people replaces both church and sect and is equally remote from both. The Christ of Mysticism is an inward spiritual principle which was divinely incarnate in the Christ of History; He can be recognized and affirmed only in inward spiritual experience. The Kingdom of God is only within men. Redemption is a process continually being repeated that culminates in union of the soul with God. Mysticism threatens to sacrifice fellowship altogether and easily develops into relativism.

These three types of Christian religion are distinct only in the theoretical, conceptual, or logical sense. "In actual life, of course, these different types mingle and combine with each other, just as the different types of Christian fellowship also mingle and combine. But this abstract analysis makes the history of dogma much clearer and simpler." [3] These types are tools for analysis and interpretation more than descriptions of concrete reality. Their specific characteristics vary considerably in time and place. Mysticism is understandably omitted from most analyses of organized religion, for only rarely is it found in institutional form, and never as an ideal type. Only the church and the sect are distinct types of social institutions. [4]

---

[2] The characteristics of churches and sects listed here are indicative of major contrasts in doctrine, organization, and relationships to the rest of society. They are but a small fraction of Troeltsch's extensive description.

[3] Troeltsch, *The Social Teaching of the Christian Churches,* II, p. 995.

[4] Troeltsch's distinctions between the church and sect were based upon Max Weber's work published in 1906 as a supplement to his *Protestant Ethic and the Spirit of Capitalism* and elaborated upon in subsequent publications. Weber indicated

Troeltsch's church-sect typology has been acclaimed as perhaps the most important analytic tool for sociological interpretation and even prediction of the behavior of religious groups.[5] It is therefore appropriate to examine some of the work stimulated by his historical-sociological analysis.

American Modifications of the Church-Sect Typology

The concept of the church as a religious organization into which one is born, and the sect as one joined voluntarily is not easy to apply in America. These ideal types were developed in Europe where the contrasts between state churches and free churches or sects were clearly manifested. The transplanting of a state church to America did not make it an established church with an all-inclusive membership, although a few such attempts were made in colonial times. Even "churches" were voluntarily joined, and many "churches" competed with one another as well as with "sects" for membership, power, and influence. Modifications of the church-sect typology are hence necessary to analyze American religious patterns.

Giddings' analysis of modern religious cultural groups concluded that only *sectarian bodies,* which were mere denominational or partisan associations, were being created around the turn of the century. The *self-sufficing community* growing out of cultural conflicts and associated with religious ideologies was no longer emerging. The Puritan Pilgrims, Quakers, Dunkards, Moravians, Mennonites, and Mormons with concentrated membership and well-defined habitats contrasted sharply with the new dispersed sect of Christian Science which created no community group. The sect or denomination with no restricted local habitation but adherents here and there in various provinces, states, or nations and either locally concentrated or widely dispersed, appeared to be the predominant emerging form of American religion.[6]

---

that sect membership was the equivalent of a certificate of moral qualification, for only religiously qualified persons were accepted into the voluntary membership. This could not hold true of church membership, for affiliation with a church was obligatory in principle and based upon birth rather than upon the member's qualities. (Hans H. Gerth and C. Wright Mills, *From Max Weber: Essays in Sociology* [New York: Oxford University Press, 1946], pp. 287-88, 305-6, 313-19, 450 note 1.)

Troeltsch acknowledged the stimulation of Weber in developing his concepts. (*The Social Teaching of the Christian Churches,* I, p. 34 note 8; p. 433 note 164.) The two scholars were personal friends who for a while resided in the same house.

[5] J. Milton Yinger, "The Sociology of Religion of Ernst Troeltsch," in *An Introduction to the History of Sociology,* Harry Elmer Barnes, ed. (Chicago: University of Chicago Press, 1948), p. 314.

[6] Franklin H. Giddings, "Are Contradictions of Ideas and Beliefs Likely to Play an Important Group-making Role in the Future?" *American Journal of Sociology,* 13 (May 1908), 784-91.

Park and Burgess bridged the gap between the typologies of Giddings and Troeltsch. They indicated that the *sect* is at war with existing mores. In seeking to be different from the world about them, its members adopt peculiar forms of speech and dress which make them the object of scorn, derision, and eventually persecution. Persecution, in turn, tends to sanctify the external marks of the sect and hence to perpetuate them as essential to the faith. Eventually it may compel the sect to seek refuge in territorial isolation. It then becomes the dominant power within the region it occupies, assumes the form of a state, and becomes like a nationality group. The Mormons in Utah and especially Ulster in Ireland illustrate this evolutionary process. The sect originates in social unrest and follows a gradual process of institutionalization. Eventually it accommodates itself to rival organizations; when it is tolerated and tolerant, it assumes the form of a *denomination*. Thus sectarian movements of conflict groups aim to reform the mores by working upon society from within. Gradually they crystallize into denominations which are accommodation groups no longer at war with one another and with the world.[7]

Ethical Dimensions of Church and Sect

This inter-relatedness of the church and sect is emphasized by Yinger. "The sect grows out of certain aspects of the teachings of the church and, if it is to survive in the historical current, must grow again into a church." [8] This paradoxical tendency grows out of what Yinger believes to be the major dilemma of the churches, namely, the conflict between the demands of religious ideals and the claims of secular interests. Achievement of the values a religion demands necessitates some kind of power over constituents; this power is embodied in organization which in turn may defeat its original purpose through adopting secular disciplinary methods and permitting itself to be invaded by secular interests until ostensibly religious functions become weapons in mundane struggles for power. The church is forced to compromise in order to maintain its position; the sect in its refusal to compromise becomes opposed to some of the most powerful secular beliefs and groups.

Although the long-range trend of the sect is to become more church-like, sects engaged in the struggle for power typically refuse to compromise their ideal and withdraw from normal participation in the dominant social structure in order to maintain their ideal in a small, intimate community. Churches gain more formal power than sects; they

---

[7] Robert E. Park and Ernest W. Burgess, *Introduction to the Science of Sociology* (Chicago: University of Chicago Press, 1921), pp. 50, 872-74.

[8] J. Milton Yinger, *Religion in the Struggle for Power* (Durham, N.C.: Duke University Press, 1946), p. 19. The following paragraphs are based on pp. 20-26 and 219-27.

compromise their ideals by accepting the status quo and establishing themselves alongside the ruling powers in society. Hence most of their influence is not religious but is merely secular power in religious garb. They help to reduce hardships within the social structure, but they also help preserve the structure and thus add to the very abuses they are trying to soften. The church loses its opportunity to influence social change by sanctifying that which is established in society; the sect loses its influence by withdrawal and lack of an organizational principle. Concentrating on otherworldly objectives, the sect preserves its ideals in a small community of believers while operating with a sharply limited breadth of influence.

On the basis of the ethical dimension of religion (its effects on the relationships of man to man), Yinger classifies religious groups as ranging from the ideal type of the *sect,* which theoretically is completely withdrawn from the world, to the *established sect,* which is more stable, to the *universal church* and finally the *church,* which represents theoretically complete acceptance of the world. It is at the midpoint of this continuum that church and sect tendencies are hypothesized to be in balance and the ability of a religious body to control the behavior of individuals is at its theoretical maximum.

Becker's Four Types of Churches

Perhaps the most familiar of additional modifications of Troeltsch's typology was made by Howard Becker, who divided churches (defined as the creedal communions of monotheistic religions) into four main sub-varieties, the ecclesia, denomination, sect, and cult.[9] Members are born into the *ecclesia.* It is a predominantly conservative institution not in open conflict with secular aspects of social life and professedly universal in its aims. It attaches high importance to the means of grace it administers, its system of doctrine, official administration of its sacraments, and teachings of its clergy. It is closely allied with economic and national interests and is committed to adjusting its ethics to those of the secular world, for it must represent the ethical morality of the respectable majority. It may be either national, like the Lutheran and Anglican churches in Europe, or international, like the Roman Catholic Church.

The *sect* stands in sharp contrast to the ecclesia. It is relatively small, has abandoned attempts to win the whole world over to its doctrines, and is an elective body which one joins on the basis of religious expe-

---

[9] Howard Becker, *Systematic Sociology: On the Basis of the 'Beziehungslehre' and 'Gebildelehre' of Leopold Von Wiese* (Gary, Ind.: Norman Paul Press, Wisc. Ed., 1950), pp. 624-42; and *Through Values to Social Interpretation* (Durham, N.C.: Duke University Press, 1950), pp. 114-18.

rience. It often rejects an official clergy by its emphasis upon the priesthood of all believers. Frequent persecution reinforces its separatist and semi-ascetic attitude toward the world. It generally prefers isolation from the world over compromise with it. It is illustrated by such groups as the Cathari, Waldensians, and Wyckliffites before the Reformation and the Anabaptists, Mennonites, Huguenots, Presbyterians, and Baptists since. Its fervor tends to disappear by the second or third generation. Training the children of believers is problematic; the early rigid entrance requirements usually give way to compromises such as lowering the age of "adult baptism" among Baptists and the Half-Way Covenant adopted by Presbyterians in order that children, whose calling and election were not yet certain, could enter the fold. In this advanced stage of development and adjustment to each other and to the world, sects have become *denominations*. The common opposition of Protestant bodies to one another has decreased; mutual cooperation in opposition to Roman Catholicism has replaced it. Every denomination is a sect in its doctrine and historical origin.

The tendency of sects to emphasize a strictly private, personal religion finds its full fruition in the "amorphous, loose-textured, uncondensed type of social structure" which Becker calls the *cult*. Its goal is not maintenance of the social structure but purely personal ecstatic experience, salvation, comfort, and healing. One does not join a cult, but simply chooses to believe its teachings or follow its practices. Both Protestant and Catholic mystics have had marked leanings toward the cult, but clearer illustrations are Spiritualism, Theosophy, New Thought, Christian Science, Unity, Scientology, and various pseudo-Hinduisms associated with swamis and yogis. Hypothetically a cycle of development in the natural history of a religious body may change a cult into a sect, a denomination, and finally an ecclesia.[10] (See Chapter 5.)

Becker's classification of churches is sometimes modified by those who adopt its essence. Thus sects may be divided into *withdrawing sects,* such as medieval monastic orders, Plymouth Brethren, and Old Order Amish, and *militant sects* like Jehovah's Witnesses. Denominations may be one-time sects like the Methodists and Baptists that have made peace with the world, or they may be former ecclesiae like the American Episcopal and Lutheran churches, which have been forced to accept denominational status in order to survive in a society which prohibits an established church.[11]

[10] Descriptive systems of this type can be the basis for systematized qualitative analysis. Cf. Allen H. Barton and Paul F. Lazarsfeld, "Some Functions of Qualitative Analysis in Social Research," Reprint Number 181, Columbia University Bureau of Applied Social Research (from *Frankfurter Beiträge zur Soziologie,* Band 1, 1955).
[11] Elizabeth K. Nottingham, *Religion and Society* (Garden City, N.Y.: Doubleday and Co., 1954), pp. 62-67.

Ecclesiastical, Independent, and Sectarian Bodies

Wach's socio-historical study concluded that there have been three major forms of Christian religious communities. *Ecclesiastical bodies* like the Lutherans, Zwinglians, Calvinists, and Anglicans initially claim exclusiveness and have authoritatively defined doctrines, sacraments, and orders. All appeal to the ideal of the invisible, true, incorrupt church. The *independent bodies* or denominations (Brownists, Baptists, Quakers, etc.) have some form of congregational church polity, are less institutional, and have a more spiritual notion of Christian fellowship. They oppose the practices of Roman Catholic and Reformed churches, identification of the invisible church with any institution, and the notion of fellowship found among extremists. *Sectarian bodies* oppose the religious practice of all other types of church organization and are particularly sensitive to any hostility or indifference toward principles of their own fellowship. A rigid, qualitative exclusiveness distinguishes them from ecclesiastical bodies; their fellowship is based both upon sharing definite norms of faith, ritual, and order, and upon disciplined individual conduct. They trace the legitimacy of their form of Christian fellowship to the primitive church.[12]

In America the exclusive claims of sectarian groups tend gradually to give way to a relativistic position which recognizes and tolerates other viewpoints, practices, and fellowships. Thus sectarian groups like the Quakers, Disciples, Brethren, Christian Scientists, and Swedenborgians have become independent bodies. The three types are seldom found in complete purity. Groups change from one type to another, and mixed types exist which include the characteristics of two or all three.[13] This typology is essentially the same as the church-sect and ecclesia-cult classifications. It recognizes the same basic continuum of types, ranging from the ecclesia or church, which it calls the ecclesiastical body, through the denomination, to the sect and cult.

Yinger's Extension of Troeltsch's Church-Sect Typology

Yinger criticized Troeltsch's typology for failing to give "an adequate picture of the full range" of religious organizations, even when the third concept of mysticism is introduced, and for failing to specify the social and personality factors linked with the various types. He produced a refined sixfold classification in his functional interpretation of religion. The two criteria upon which his typology is based are "the degree of in-

[12] Joachim Wach, *Types of Religious Experience: Christian and Non-Christian* (Chicago: University of Chicago Press, 1951), pp. 190-96.
[13] *Ibid.*, pp. 197-98.

clusiveness of the members of a society and the degree of attention to the function of social integration as contrasted with the function of personal need." [14] His first three types may be considered collectively as the approximate equivalent of Troeltsch's church type, and the latter three as an enlargement of his sect type.

1. The *universal church,* illustrated by the thirteenth century Roman Catholic Church, is relatively successful both in supporting the integration of society and in satisfying many personality needs of individuals from all levels. In heterogeneous societies, however, the diversity of personality needs, demands by ruling groups that the social order be maintained without adjustments, and the inflexibility of the religious system itself combine to make it generally a short-lived institution.

2. The *ecclesia* also reaches out to all levels of society, but it tends to be so much adjusted to the dominant elements as it reinforces existing patterns of social integration that the needs of many adherents, especially from the lower classes, are not met. The ecclesia is thus like a universal church which has lost its "moving equilibrium" and entered into "a state of rigidification." Contemporary Scandinavian state churches illustrate this type.

3. The *class church* or *denomination* is in substantial but incomplete harmony with society's power structure. Generally it has compromised considerably with secular power, although it may retain some sectarian tendencies. There are great diversities; few are in fact limited to one class level in membership. Some, like the Congregational Churches, persistently retain sectarian tendencies; others, like Lutheranism, are more completely accommodated to the pattern of power in society.

4. The *established sect* is an outgrowth of sects and cults. Sects like the Quakers and Mennonites, whose original concern was chiefly with the evils of society, tend to develop into established sects; Methodism and Christian Science and others which are chiefly the result of attempts to reduce burdens of personal inadequacy, sin, and guilt, tend to develop into denominations. A process of self-selection operates; ethical-protest sects attract persons who believe reform of society to be the primary problem, while sects that stress individual regeneration attract those who feel most strongly the burdens of individual anxiety, doubt, and suffering. In the established sect opposition to basic patterns of society remains; in the denomination attention is given to personal needs without presenting any serious challenge to established social structures.

5. The *sect* is likely to meet undesired situations in one of three ways. Moral Re-Armament illustrates *acceptance* rather than challenge of the social pattern, because of the belief that personal sins and failings in-

---

[14] J. Milton Yinger, *Religion, Society and the Individual* (New York: The Macmillan Co., 1957), pp. 147-48. The following discussion is based on pp. 147-55.

stead of an evil society are the key difficulties. In some lower-class sects, such as the early Anabaptists, *aggression* against an evil society and an accompanying program of social reform are emphasized. The most common sectarian protest is *avoidance,* which involves devaluing the present life and world and projecting hopes into a future, perfect world; problems of the present life are allayed by entering or forming a communion of like-minded men. More indifferent than antagonistic to society, this type of sect is more likely to develop into a denomination than are those aggressively opposed to society. Avoidance is common among Holiness, Pentecostal, and Adventist groups.

6. The *cult* stands at the farthest extreme from the universal church. Its beliefs and ceremonies are far removed from those traditional in society. It therefore tends to be small, often built around a charismatic leader, and short-lived. Its concern is almost exclusively with problems of the individual rather than of the social order. Spiritualists and some Black Muslims approximate this type of "religious mutant." Many new syncretistic movements begin as cults.

Applications of the Church-Sect Typology

Contemporary classifications of American religious bodies often use church and sect as the extremes of a hypothetical continuum. Such usage often implies that a religious group may shift from one position to another upon the continuum; generally the changes are assumed to be from the sect end toward the church end of the scale. For instance, Pope states that the sect "arises as a schism from a parent ecclesiastical body . . . It then becomes a distinct and independent type of religious organization but moves, if it survives, increasingly toward the Church type." [15]

Pope contrasted more than twenty characteristics of the church and sect, thus providing an operational definition of each as well as an objective statement of changes that must occur if sects are to evolve into churches. Most sect members are propertyless; hence their church facilities and ministers' salaries reflect economic poverty. Sects are on the cultural periphery of the community, are indifferent toward or renounce the prevailing social organization, and stress a self-centered religious experience. Each sect is a moral community which is suspicious of rival sects and ready to exclude unworthy members. Sects have unspecialized, non-professional, part-time ministers. Emphasizing evangelism, conversion, and voluntary confessional joining, their chief concern is with an "adult" membership. They adhere to such strict biblical standards as tithing or

---

[15] Liston Pope, *Millhands and Preachers* (New Haven: Yale University Press, 1942), p. 118.

nonresistance and, possessing a psychology of persecution, stress a future in the next world. Congregational participation in church administration and services is at a high level. Fervor, reliance upon spontaneous guidance of the Holy Spirit, and hymns resembling contemporary folk music are characteristic of their religious services. They emphasize religion in the home and also have a comparatively large number of special religious services, so the sect assumes hegemony over large spheres of its members' time. Church-type organizations have traits antithetical to those of the sect.[16]

In Gaston County Pope ranked the denominations in a series from sect- to church-type as follows: Free-Will Baptist Holiness, Pentecostal Holiness, Church of God, Free-Will Baptist, Independent Tabernacles, Wesleyan Methodist, Baptist, Methodist, Presbyterian, Lutheran, Protestant Episcopal, Roman Catholic. Baptists had changed their position on the continuum more than any other denomination in the county during the preceding six decades. All other Protestant denominations and sects also were moving toward the church type, although at varying rates of change. Sects originated as a reaction against both economic and religious institutions and gradually forced their way into the cultural pattern, becoming firmly established there, and hence evolving into churches. This movement in turn stimulated the rise of new sects protesting against the failure of the old ones and against society's failure to distribute its benefits more impartially.[17]

A 24-item scale based upon Pope's work was developed by Dynes to define operationally the contrasting church and sect attitudes. It was applied to a randomly selected sample of 360 Protestant adults in the Columbus, Ohio, metropolitan area. Sectarian attitudes were consistently more common in the lower socioeconomic groups, and church-type attitudes were associated with high socioeconomic status. The higher the education and occupational prestige, the more emotionalism, evangelism, and other sectarian characteristics were rejected and more institutionalized, liturgical religion accepted. Even when denominational affiliation was held constant, these differences between individuals were observed.[18] Persons who had sectarian attitudes were more likely to find meaningful association and friendships in the religious group. With increasing sectarianism came increased monthly church attendance, decreased membership in organizations outside the church, and increased membership in church organizations. Increasing sectarianism was also associated with an increasing proportion of the five closest friends coming from the membership of the same church and an increasing percentage deriving

---

[16] *Ibid.,* pp. 122-24.

[17] *Ibid.,* pp. 124-40.

[18] Russell R. Dynes, "Church-Sect Typology and Socio-Economic Status," *American Sociological Review,* 20 (Oct. 1955), 555-60.

more satisfaction from the church than from other types of social participation.[19]

In another study, scale analysis of 505 local rural churches from 43 Missouri denominations found that the sub-organizations reported were part of a consistent pattern; they formed a cumulative scale. Sunday school was usually in operation, even if the church had but one sub-organization, followed by a women's organization if the church had two, then youth organizations, choir, men's clubs, young adult groups, and older adult groups, in that order. Sect type groups and small churches were much less likely to have sub-organizations. Presumably church polity and the orientation of the sect toward religion as a way of life are related to these findings.[20]

Social Relationships in Churches and Sects

The church and sect differ from one another internally in many basic ways. In the sect the chief religious leaders must maintain intimate, personal, Gemeinschaft-like relationships with parishioners. They are less professionalized and hence have more diffuse functions to perform than the priest or minister in the church, who functions according to established professional standards. Professional aloofness may characterize the church's ministry. The church leader's work has an entire set of dogma to guide his behavior; he is likely to be a traditional or legal-rational leader, while the sect leader is likely to be a charismatic leader whose authority stems more from real or supposed personal virtue, grace, or enlightenment than from formalized norms.[21]

The roles and statuses of officers and members within the sect are less predictable and more indefinite than in the church. In determining whether or not improved practices—either in the sect itself or in the daily lives of its members—shall be adopted, personal qualities of members or officials often are more important than their formal position in the organizational structure. Power in the church is more likely to be institutionalized and vested in the form of authority in certain status-roles. Dominating personalities—such as a Joseph Smith, Brigham Young, or Judge Rutherford—may establish a structure in a sect which later becomes institutionalized if the religious body moves toward the church end of the church-sect continuum.[22]

[19] Russell R. Dynes, "The Consequences of Sectarianism for Social Participation," *Social Forces,* 35 (May 1957), 331-34.

[20] C. Milton Coughenour, "An Application of Scale Analysis to the Study of Religious Groups," *Rural Sociology,* 20 (Sept.-Dec. 1955), 197-207.

[21] Charles P. Loomis and J. Allan Beegle, *Rural Sociology* (Englewood Cliffs, N.J.: Prentice-Hall, Inc., 1957), pp. 222-24.

[22] *Ibid.,* p. 224.

Sects usually hold more powerful negative and positive sanctions over their members than churches do and hence tend to control more aspects of their lives. Relationships between members are generally more intimate and all-encompassing than in the church. Primary group relationships and direct communication predominate; the denomination or church is more likely to use the mass media and formal channels of communication to disseminate special messages to members. The church is linked directly with the rest of society; the sect or cult attempts to maintain distinct spatial or social boundaries between it and the world through various devices for limiting interaction with outsiders. Taboos are rigidly enforced to prevent contamination by the world and to maintain separation from it.[23]

Church, Sect, and Society

The efforts of sect members to perpetuate old values and live in separation from and nonconformity to the world have many implications. Thus the high value placed upon farming as the preferred way of life by the Old Order Amish and Old Order Mennonites in Lancaster County, Pa., makes them pay exorbitant prices for land in the contact zone between them and others. As a result, neighbors who drive automobiles are often induced to sell their farms and move a few miles away where larger farms can be purchased with the proceeds. Boundaries of the sectarian community are thus enlarged and the membership strength of Presbyterians, Episcopalians, and other religious groups declines. Because centuries of persecution in Europe had forced them into poor farming areas, the Pennsylvania Dutch had improved farming techniques that made possible their survival in spite of adverse conditions. Farming acquired a sacred character that has perpetuated itself as the preferred occupation. Consequently, sect members in Pennsylvania are more stable farmers than church members are.[24]

Church-sect relationships affect the larger society in many other ways. In a visit to America in 1904 Max Weber observed that the question of church affiliation was often raised in social life; in business intercourse where permanent or credit relationships were involved it nearly always came up. Personal inquiries and observations made him conclude that American sect membership was a guarantee of personal moral qualities, especially those required for success in business. Weber observed a young man being baptized into a Baptist church; the man wanted to

[23] *Ibid.*, pp. 224-31.

[24] Walter M. Kollmorgen, "The Agricultural Stability of the Old Order Amish and Old Order Mennonites of Lancaster County, Pennsylvania," *American Journal of Sociology*, 49 (Nov. 1943), 233-41.

open a bank in the county seat and had to be a church member in order
to compete successfully in the business. It seemed to Weber as if
only members of Methodist, Baptist, or related sects in the community
were successful businessmen. Credit was readily advanced to sect members; if they had economic difficulties through no fault of their own,
the sect helped them even in financial affairs. Expulsion from the sect
for moral offenses meant both economic loss of credit and loss of social
status. The ethical probation and screening of candidates for membership were guarantees of character.

Even during his brief visit, however, Weber observed that "church-
mindedness" as such was rapidly dying in cities.[25] Except in rural communities, it is likely that church membership does not bear the badge of
moral worth that sect membership seems to have had prior to this
century. The major sects have become churches into which persons
are born or denominations they enter with little or no investigation of
personal character.

The ethical life of a nation is influenced by the relative strength of
its churches and sects. While both work to advance moral virtues,
they use different means. Sects emphasize the need for conversion from
the life of sin; churches stress the development of high moral standards
through religious education. In some communities the coming of sects to
minister to the lower classes decreases interclass conflict. As they find
emotional release and social recognition through sect activities, they engage in less violent behavior than previously. Thus the sheriff of Leslie
County, Kentucky, is reported to be happy when revivalists come to the
community, for revivalism channels emotional outbursts away from brawls,
knifings, and other customary violence.[26]

Evangelical religious movements (sects) in Canada have certain features that favor their alignment with conservative political forces. As they
gained social privileges that needed protection, and as they promoted
education, temperance, and Sunday observance, they were forced to cooperate with one another against common foes. Their earlier alignment
with radical political forces had resulted from opposition to the vested
denominational interests of other groups, from a separatistic emphasis
which tended to identify itself readily with political separatist movements,
from their attraction for the isolated and the economically dispossessed,
and from evangelistic messages which easily led to economic panaceas.
Conservative political emphases emerged as they became less sect-like,
began to oppose newer sects, and became more metropolitan with

---

[25] Max Weber, "The Protestant Sects and the Spirit of Capitalism," in *From Max
Weber,* Chapter 12, Gerth and Mills, pp. 302-22.
[26] T. S. Hyland, "The Fruitful Mountaineers," *Life,* 27, no. 26 (Dec. 26, 1949),
60-67.

commercially prosperous members. The mingling of radical and conservative tendencies makes it impossible to predict what specific political program the evangelical churches might support at any particular time. Politically indifferent except when their own direct interests are involved, they tend in effect to disenfranchise much of the population. Lacking clearly defined political principles, opportunism tends to determine their political action. New sects emerged when Baptist, Methodist, and other sects grew into churches. Increasing participation in politics by evangelical leaders was offset by secession of new sects that withdrew from political activity. The persistence of the sectarian spirit has made religion a dynamic force in Canadian society, especially in regard to church-state relationships.[27]

Small sects share many characteristics. Many are refuges of the poor and the disinherited. They usually stress a puritanistic type of personal morality, attract the emotionally starved, and reflect a craving for "objectivity"—for an outward rite or observance that assures the transmission of grace and blessings. Nearly all are conservative in both theology and manner of living. Bizarre and fantastic ideas, practices, and interpretations abound, but sects tend to lose their distinctive principles as they grow in size. Growth also causes increasing dependence upon money and with it increasing influence of the prosperous. Although their religious education is of very poor quality in terms of philosophy, curricular materials, and teaching methods, many sects survive and flourish, often outstripping in rate of growth the denominations that adhere to the very latest organization and principles of religious education.[28]

The rapid growth of sects has been a source of concern to many denominational leaders. Some admit that cults and sects can teach churches certain lessons. Cult members have more definite convictions concerning their faith than most church members. Oversimplification and stereotyping partly account for the difference, but the recognition that beliefs really are important and the insistence that there is a "Christian way" in life situations also undergird this trait. The need to "witness" one's faith to others, comparative indifference to public sentiments, courage to engage in unconventional behavior, maintenance of definite membership standards, effective use of printed materials, a sense of urgency related to millennialism, a high degree of lay participation, and the provision of definite techniques for receiving the values the religion offers are other characteristics which contributed to the sects' rapid growth. Some also offer healing, economic security, free religious expression, and

---

[27] S. D. Clark, "The Religious Sect in Canadian Politics," *American Journal of Sociology,* 51 (Nov. 1945), 207-16.
[28] Elmer T. Clark, *The Small Sects in America,* rev. ed. (New York: Abingdon-Cokesbury Press, 1949), pp. 218-31.

emotional release. Since conventional churches often are "class institutions" in which lower class persons cannot feel at home, sects often are a haven for the economically and socially dispossessed.[29]

In ·his analysis of the Oxford Group Movement (MRA) Eister defined the cult as the sociological type at the extreme sect end of the church-sect typology. In contrast to the sect, which is rigorously organized and whose members have chosen to "live apart" from society, cult members seek satisfactions through some form of personal religious thrill. They comprise a loosely-organized, impermanent group which does not challenge the social order, except for an occasional reaction to it on the personal, rather than institutional, level. Response to experiences in the cult tends to be emotional rather than rational; there is but slight regard for the logical consistency in the group and in its members' conduct which sects demand. This attitude plus lack of objective analysis of situations often makes cults conservative or even reactionary in society. Leadership must be strong in order to satisfy consistently the indispensable desire for thrill. The cult is an open group with fluctuating membership, each member determining for himself the extent to which he will be committed to its activities. In contrast, the sect is a closed group with rigid tests of the qualifications of prospective members and continuing disciplines for those already admitted.[30]

Scholars generally assume that sects and cults produce more emotionally unstable and mentally ill persons than denominations and churches. Many mentally ill persons indeed are found in sects, but there may be proportionately as many in churches. What appears to be a causal relationship may result only from variations in the self-selection that operates in religious bodies with voluntary membership. Although socially isolated persons may find fellowship and security in a sect and sect preachers occasionally precipitate a psychosis in persons under severe emotional stress, there is no evidence that sect membership is an indication of poor mental health.[31]

The heterogeneity of religious life may be a major cause of the vigor of American Christianity compared to that of Europe. The individual's opportunity to find a religious group he likes is much greater when there are fifty or more distinct groups to choose from than it is when an es-

---

[29] Charles S. Braden, "What Can We Learn From the Cults? " *Religion in Life,* 14 (Winter 1954-1955), 52-64; Horton Davies, Charles S. Braden, and Charles W. Ranson, "Centrifugal Christian Sects," *Religion in Life,* 25 (Summer 1956), 323-58; and J. Paul Williams, *What Americans Believe and How They Worship* (New York: Harper and Brothers, 1952), pp. 328-31, 348-49.

[30] Allan W. Eister, *Drawing-Room Conversion* (Durham, N.C.: Duke University Press, 1950), pp. 66-88, 212-16.

[31] Samuel Southard, "Sectarianism and the Psychoses," *Religion in Life,* 23 (Autumn 1954), 580-90. Additional data relevant to this topic are presented in Chapter 17.

tablished church dominates the entire religious scene. Cultural pluralism is stimulating intellectually and socially; it probably is stimulating religiously as well.[32] The individualism that is emphasized in America encourages the establishment of new cults and sects at a much higher rate than where freedom is more limited and society more traditionally oriented. If someone with leadership abilities does not like his church, it is a relatively simple matter to start his own sect.

The relationships of church and sect to society that we have mentioned indicate the complexity of the subject. Vast variations are found; not all sects and churches have the same position nor perform the same functions in society. In addition, the local branches of a body that can best be classified as a denomination or an ecclesia may be much more sectarian than churchly in their organization and activities. Broad generalizations about specific groups are often misleading.

An Evaluation of Church-Sect Typologies

Troeltsch's typology and its derivatives have been subjected to significant criticisms. Recognition of these can increase our understanding of their potential applications and the American church.[33] Religious bodies do not always change consistently from sect to church. Many have ceased to evolve altogether, and in America religious pluralism and **separation of church and state make it impossible to reach the church** end of the continuum. Immigrants' churches have moved from church toward sect. Indeed, if there is any general trend, it is the movement of all bodies toward the denominational position as each learns and borrows from others.

Certain theologians dislike use of the term "sect"; to them it implies derogation, while "church" implies approbation. Sociologically these terms are used as typological tools in research, not name-calling devices. The typology is, however, inconsistent with certain theological definitions and Christian doctrines. Certain groups called sects in the typology qualify as churches according to the biblical definition of church.[34]

As a result of the intermingling of sect and church characteristics in specific bodies, sectarian traits may be found in churches and vice

---

[32] Cf. Herbert W. Schneider, *Religion in Twentieth Century America* (Cambridge: Harvard University Press, 1952), p. 170.

[33] This section is based upon the author's more complete analysis of criticisms, including references to primary sources, entitled "Potential Uses of the Church-Sect Typology in Comparative Religious Research," *International Journal of Comparative Sociology*, 2, fasc. 1 (Mar. 1961), 47-58.

[34] Franklin H. Littell, "Church and Sect (with Special Reference to Germany)," *Ecumenical Review*, 6 (Apr. 1954), 262-76.

versa. The types are not intended to coincide in every detail with empirically observable characteristics of specific groups. They are tools for scholarly analysis which are "pure" only in the abstract, logical sense.

Omission of mysticism from applications of Troeltsch's typology leads to overlooking the inroads that spiritualizing mystics have made into American religion. Certain aspects of neo-orthodoxy and some results of existentialism have led to an interplay between mysticism and sectarianism which is glossed over by sole emphasis upon relationships between denominations and sects. The social psychology of religious faith is similarly minimized by emphasizing the more clearly institutional aspects of religion which are the typical focus for church-sect analysis.[35]

Much research centered upon hypotheses related to the church-sect typology merely illustrates it by fitting data into a pre-conceived scheme. Little if any has empirically tested the basic theory with serious efforts to find negative as well as positive evidence. Furthermore, there is no assurance that independent researchers would classify religious bodies the same way. The typologies are severely limited as research tools until reliable and valid instruments are developed for verifiable operational definition of their basic concepts. Research by Dynes, Coughenour, and Eister has made significant progress toward that goal.

Despite its potential usefulness, Troeltsch's typology may have inhibited "further innovating ideas about the nature of religious organization. There has been too much of a tendency, perhaps, to force every variety of organizational form into the typological scheme."[36] When properly utilized, however, it is a helpful source in the increased understanding of American religion.

Types of Small Sects

The great variations among bodies at the sect end of the church-sect continuum have led to additional classifications of sub-types. Elmer T. Clark studied small American sects with special emphasis upon over a hundred which are unusual and relatively unknown. He distinguished seven main categories on the basis of the types of mind to which their leading principles appeal. Many embrace several different principles, and social pressures combine with psychological factors in their formation and development, so it is often difficult to place a given sect clearly in one specific category.[37]

---

[35] Colin Campbell, "The Secret Religion of the Educated Classes," *Sociological Analysis*, 39, no. 2 (Summer 1978), 146–56, discusses Troeltsch's "Spiritual and Mystic Religion" as gradually displacing church religion among educated people.

[36] Charles Y. Glock, "The Sociology of Religion," in *Sociology Today*, Robert K. Merton, Leonard Broom, and Leonard S. Cottrell, Jr., eds. (New York: Basic Books, Inc., 1959), p. 159.

[37] Clark, *The Small Sects in America*, is the source of the seven following types.

1. *Pessimistic or adventist sects* are groups of the disinherited who see no good in the world and no hope of its improvement. They expect the imminent, catastrophic end of the present world-order which they have rejected; they expect, as the faithful, to receive prominent places in the new temporal, millennial kingdom as well as eternal bliss in heaven. Seventh-day Adventists and Jehovah's Witnesses are prominent illustrations.

2. *Perfectionist or subjectivist sects* believe that moral perfection, spiritual holiness, and total eradication of sinful desires should be the goal of all Christians. A "second blessing" sanctification is commonly sought, and strong emotional reactions are experienced. Much emphasis is placed upon guidance by the Holy Spirit through visions and spiritual endowments which often are orgiastic in character. These sects, most of which have sprung out of Methodism, include the Wesleyan and Free Methodist Churches, Church of the Nazarene, Christian and Missionary Alliance, Church of God (Anderson, Indiana), and other Holiness bodies, as well as Moral Re-Armament and Quakers.

3. *Charismatic or pentecostal sects* are similar. They are "the left-wing of the subjectivist groups." Special blessings are sought by them and they emphasize, as manifestations of these blessings, speaking in many tongues, visions, trances, dancing before the Lord, and other experiences. Apostolic, Pentecostal, Church of God, Foursquare groups, Mormons and Father Divine's Peace Mission are included in this type.

4. *Communistic sects* have withdrawn from the world into isolated colonies where the members can secure social approval and engage in economic experimentation. Community of goods (the sharing of material possessions) is sometimes extended to a community of women. There are also other extreme deviations. Most of these sects die rapidly unless they modify their socioeconomic system. The Oneida Perfectionists, Shakers, and Llano Colony are dead or almost dead. Amana Society, House of David, and the Christian Catholic Church continue in modified form.

5. *Legalistic or objectivist sects* stress certain definite, performable rules, rituals, observances, or objects, or the denial or rejection of some practice, as essential to true religion. Their rites and taboos usually are derived from some portion of the Bible; they often consider themselves to be the "true church" or the restorers of Biblical Christianity. Foot washing, peculiar dress, acceptance of only Psalms as hymns, antipathy to musical instruments or to missionary societies, rejection of Sunday schools, and emphasis upon apostolic succession of the clergy are among their traits. Included by Clark in this category are Judaism, the Eastern Orthodox Church, Old Catholic Churches, the Orthodox Presbyterian Church, Plymouth Brethren, Mennonites, Hutterites, the Amish, many Baptist sects, Dunkers, and the Churches of Christ.

6. *Egocentric or new thought sects* seek physical comfort, bodily health, freedom from pain, personal exhilaration, and relief from ennui as their primary objectives. Christian Science, Psychiana, Divine Science, and Unity School of Christianity are illustrations.

7. *Esoteric or mystical sects* are nearly all offshoots of Hinduism. Initiation is required into the doctrines they espouse. Mysteries and the occult are so emphasized that their literature is hardly understandable to the uninitiated. They claim to possess a truth unknown to ordinary mortals, which is revealed when the proper formula is applied. Some operate like correspondence schools; others have leaders who receive messages from mystical sources and conduct seances. Among these sects are the Institute of Mentalphysics, Rosicrucians, Spiritualists, Swedenborgians, and Theosophists.

It is perhaps justifiable to add another type to Clark's list, the *non-Christian religions* imported from other nations. Zoroastrianism, Buddhism, Hinduism, Jainism, Islam, Confucianism, Taoism, and Shintoism are all represented in North America. In their pure forms they do not clearly fit into any of the seven categories, although for individual proselytes they may serve similar functions.[38] Just as Christian missions in Africa and the Orient tend to be sect-type groups, these religions have sect-like features in America.

The nature of the religious motif of a sect is highly important and provides the basis for a three-fold classification. (1) *Enthusiastic* sects see their religion as an experience to be lived. Some, like Billy Sunday, other revivalists, and Pentecostal groups, try to save the world; others are pietistic, like various Holiness groups, the Salvation Army, and the Nazarenes, and try to avoid the world. (2) *Prophetic* sects have a message to be proclaimed. They may be chiliastic, like the Adventists, warning the world that the Lord is coming, or legalistic, trying like the Jehovah's Witnesses to conquer the world and establish a new order. (3) In *Gnostic* sects religion is a secret to be divulged. The world is irrelevant for all of them. Some are Oriental, like the Buddhists, bringing wisdom from the East. New Thought groups, like Rosicrucians, stress powers within the soul; Spiritists stress voices from beyond. In all cases, their attitude toward the world largely determines their inner social structure.[39]

---

[38] For an excellent bibliographic introduction to these see Paul Honigsheim, "Die nicht-christlichen Kulturreligionen in der amerikanischen Soziologie," in Karl Gustav Specht, ed., *Soziologische Forschung in Unserer Zeit* (Köln: Westdeutscher Verlag, 1951), pp. 266-76.

[39] Peter L. Berger, "The Sociological Study of Sectarianism," *Social Research*, 21 (Winter 1954), 467-85. An excellent, closely-related typology is developed by Bryan R. Wilson, "An Analysis of Sect. Development," *American Sociological Review*, 24 (Feb. 1959), 3-15. For contrasting characteristics that can serve as the basis for

Additional Classifications of Churches

Numerous other typologies have been constructed by theologians, historians, and social scientists. One of the most useful interpretations of the relationship between Christianity and culture identifies five solutions to the problem. The solutions are Christ against culture, Christ of culture, Christ above culture, Christ and culture in paradox, and Christ as the transformer of culture.[40] Religious groups and behavior patterns may be analyzed with the help of such theological categories. Some others are liturgical-nonliturgical, Calvinistic-Arminian, sacramental-nonsacramental, low church-high church, and orthodox-neoörthodox-liberal. Use of such typologies increases the social scientist's understanding of and sympathy with the "spirit" that is at the heart of religious groups. It also clarifies relationships between and consequences of religious feelings, rituals, beliefs, knowledge, and action.

On the basis of the kind of religious behavior emphasized, churches are *quietistic* if they pay greater attention to contemplation than to outward "doing" and *activistic* if they attempt to master adverse conditions or manipulate people and things. American religion, perhaps partly because of frontier influences, tends to be much more activistic than European religion which is relatively quietistic.[41]

Urban churches were classified by the Institute of Social and Religious Research on the basis of the degree to which their programs were limited to common activities or emphasized "adventurous novelties." (1) Typically developed churches had only slightly expanded the rural church program. Most of their activities consisted of preaching services, Sunday schools, ladies aid or missionary societies, and young people's organizations. Most were small. Their parishes were concentrated in local neighborhoods. (2) Under-developed and fragmentary churches had a narrow range of activities and a very limited number of organizations. Many were abortive enterprises, very young or else old and decrepit. Dominated by narrow tradition or an ultra-reactionary spirit and scattered widely over the city, members found it difficult to come together even for their limited church program. (3) Intensively developed churches established at least the outline of a complete program of ac-

typological analysis of utopian sects see Henri Desroche, *"Heavens on Earth, Micromillénarismes et communautarisme utopique en Amérique du Nord du XVIIe au XIXe siècle," Archives de Sociologie des Religions,* 2, no. 4 (July-Dec. 1957), 57-92.

[40] H. Richard Niebuhr, *Christ and Culture* (New York: Harper and Brothers, 1951).

[41] Winfred E. Garrison, "Characteristics of American Organized Religion," *Annals of the American Academy of Political and Social Science,* 256 (Mar. 1948), 14-24; and W. W. Sweet, *The American Churches* (New York: Abingdon-Cokesbury Press, 1947), pp. 8, 110-49.

tivities differentiated to meet the particular needs of each age and sex grouping. Cultural, social, and recreational activities organized around a religious core were consciously added to their programs. (4) Socially adapted churches maintained traditional church activities as the center of their program but added health, recreational, and economic aids to people who were physically, socially, or economically handicapped. (5) Erratic churches had an unusual combination of program elements. Typically very weak, they often served special ethnic groups or were home missions enterprises exalting a social ministry. Of 1,044 churches, the respective percentages in the five types were 40, 25, 18, 4, and 13.[42] The same typology could be applied today if such recent developments as church social work and counseling clinics were included. We may reasonably assume that the first two types have proportionately decreased and the third increased as total church membership has risen, as churches have grown in average size, and as economic prosperity has made specialized programs possible.

From the perspective of methods used in approaching behavior problems and trying to guide human conduct, churches may be ranged on a continuum based on their social control patterns. At one extreme is the God-centered or *eternity-centered* institution concerned chiefly with both salvation of the individual soul and ultimate rewards and penalties. At the other extreme is the morality-centered or *society-centered* church which has a this-worldly social emphasis. The appeals, basic authority, techniques, and models for character are widely divergent in the two types. Most churches, of course, fall between the two extremes.[43]

The three basic organizational forms of churches, the episcopal, presbyterian, and congregational types, roughly correspond to political monarchies, aristocracies, and democracies, respectively. *Episcopal* polity, best illustrated by the Roman Catholic Church, is dominated by an ecclesiastical hierarchy which controls appointments of the parish clergy and exercises discipline over them. Authority flows from the highest offices down to the members, so the clergy are freed from dependence upon local congregations. *Presbyterian* polity is dominated in theory by the constituent church bodies but in fact by the clergy who control the denomination's synods or presbyteries and comprise a hierarchy of ecclesiastical oligarchs. Elders in the local church tend to exercise a similar aristocratic type of control. Since the preacher must be approved by both the local church, acting through its elders, and the presbytery, he is subject to pressures from above and below. The Presbyterian Church is an example.

[42] H. Paul Douglass and Edmund deS. Brunner, *The Protestant Church as a Social Institution* (New York: Institute of Social and Religious Research, 1935), pp. 139-46. Cf. H. Paul Douglass, *1000 City Churches* (New York: George H. Doran Co., 1926).
[43] Paul H. Landis, *Social Control*, rev. ed. (Chicago: J. B. Lippincott Co., 1956), pp. 212-20.

Congregational churches, such as Baptists, are loosely organized, with members collectively as the source of authority. Local autonomy is emphasized, and democratic organization theoretically gives all members the right to propose church action. The pastor is selected by the local congregation and is subject to their good will. He serves as the democratic leader of an organization which often consists of a series of sub-organizations loosely coordinated, although subject to the parental congregation's control.[44]

As is true of other ideal types, the three polity categories do not appear in pure form. The power structures of all three are gradually changing under the influence of the American environment, including each other. Democratic tendencies are increasingly apparent in episcopal and presbyterian types, and demands for effective cooperation have increased the power of centralized authority in congregational churches. Nevertheless, as ideal types, the key characteristics are clear: In episcopal churches power flows from top levels of the denomination downward to the local church and its members, while the opposite prevails in congregational bodies. Presbyterian groups fall between the two, with authority flowing out from the middle level of elders and presbyters to both the lower level of the local church and the higher level of the denomination. The military structure of the Salvation Army and the fraternal brotherhood organization of a few minor sects are additional types of polity.

Types of Authority and Leadership

All three types of authority distinguished by Max Weber may be observed in American churches. *Traditional* authority is based upon the argument of long existence. Innovations cannot be admitted, so they are disguised under the fiction of discovering what existed in the distant past. The leader's charisma (from a Greek word for "spiritual gift") is the basis for *charismatic* authority. Personal devotion to him and his cause results from the followers' state of mind; they believe him to have exceptional or even supernatural powers. Following his death there may be either a "routinization of the charisma" as it is passed down to succeeding generations or a designation of successors; hence this tends to develop into one of the other two types. Bureaucratic leadership is based upon *legal-rational* authority, with followers accepting an impersonal rule.[45] Bureaucratic tendencies are present in all social institutions. When

---

[44] See the excellent though brief summaries in Robin M. Williams, Jr., *American Society* (New York: Alfred A. Knopf, 1951), pp. 324-25; Nottingham, *Religion and Society,* pp. 67-69; and Walter G. Muelder, "Institutional Factors Affecting Unity and Disunity," *The Ecumenical Review,* 8 (Jan. 1956), 113-26.

[45] Max Weber, *The Theory of Social and Economic Organization,* trans. A. M. Henderson and Talcott Parsons (New York: Oxford University Press, 1947), pp. 328-41, 358-86.

organizations grow in size, internal differentiation and specialization occur, and formalization of the internal structure takes place.[46]

Traditional leadership predominates in highly centralized denominations which emphasize the sanctity of traditional polity, sacramentalism, liturgical worship, or an apostolic succession through which Christian leaders are traced back to the apostles or John the Baptist.[47] These leaders often reinforce the rest of society. Ministers in Gastonia thus were a powerful sanction for the community's economic structure. They supported the status quo and did nothing to modify economic practices which caused the Loray cotton mill strike.[48] They linked traditionalism in religion with traditional patterns of economic organization.

Charismatic religious leadership is most often apparent in new sects. Father Divine's Peace Mission movement centered around the supposed deity of the founder, the "I Am" religion built around Guy Ballard until his death, and the International Church of the Foursquare Gospel founded upon charismatic qualities of the late Aimee Semple McPherson are illustrations. Many evangelists, TV–radio ministers, and faith healers have a following because their disciples believe them to possess charismatic powers.

The typical American minister is a bureaucratic leader. His roles and duties are defined either by a denominational manual or by a church constitution. His authority stems more from this legal-rational foundation than from the tradition which partly supports the written code or the charismatic qualities which churches desire, as long as they remain within bounds designated by legal-rational rules. Professionalism and specialization accompany this bureaucratic orientation. The clergyman must seek his advancement and satisfactions within a narrowing profession; the services included in his calling have been narrowed by specialization and the growth of competing "secular" professions. Overall societal integration, and even ethical standards for professional practice, tend to be by-passed in favor of developing factual knowledge and narrowly delimited professional skills.[49]

As local churches and denominations have become "big business," disciplines once designed to assist efficiency have become intrinsic values; loyalty to ideals is measured in terms of loyalty to the institution and its

[46] F. Stuart Chapin, "The Growth of Bureaucracy: An Hypothesis," *American Sociological Review,* 16 (Dec. 1951), 835-36.

[47] Even young congregationally governed denominations may be traditionally oriented, claiming that they are re-introducing or continuing true, primitive, or apostolic Christianity. A major sectarian element among Southern Baptists, for example, is the "Landmark movement" which emphasizes the apostolic succession of baptism.

[48] Pope, *Millhands and Preachers,* pp. 329-30.

[49] Walter G. Wardwell, "Social Integration, Bureaucratization, and the Professions," *Social Forces,* 33 (May 1955), 356-59; and Herbert Stroup, "Professionalism and the Christian Faith," *Lutheran Quarterly,* 8 (Feb. 1956), 33-42.

leadership. As a result, ideals are sometimes submerged in efforts to advance the organization. Institutional prosperity becomes a goal, instead of a means to the end of building up people's spiritual lives. The bureaucracy is "the tail that wags the dog," keeping the institution in operation even if it has outlived its basic functions. Yet bureaucratic organization is essential in the large-scale enterprises of urban-industrial society. Without it many a church would collapse, and much church-related work would be undone. The bureaucratic nature of the minister's leadership is obvious in his roles as administrator and organizer; it tends to dominate nearly all activities of the typical Protestant, Catholic, and Jewish clergyman. Standardization, self-perpetuation, diminished spontaneity, and specialized service to a client-public which plays passive, spectator roles hence are prominent in American churches. Powerful boards dominated by executive secretaries play a major part in the government of congregations and denominations. The drive for unity and efficiency tends to overcome anti-bureaucratic theological doctrines.[50]

Churches generally support the basic social patterns of their society, yet norms sometimes are built into their bureaucratic structures which resist such basic social tendencies as class stratification. The charismatic qualities of Jesus make him a symbol of many standards diametrically opposed to strong positive evaluations of wealth and prestige.[51] As a model for the clergy, he exemplifies the institutionalization of non-conventional norms which is necessary for a well-balanced society.

Elements of all three types of authority are found in all major denominations, even when one type predominates. Thus each Roman Catholic order meets some peculiar need and is recognized by the papacy as legitimate and relatively autonomous for that specific purpose; in the last resort, however, the Church and the Pope are always supreme and their enunciations are the ultimate truth. Hence the administrative structure of the Holy See is monarchical, but its legitimation rests upon both tradition and legal-rational bonds to the "duty of office." Church authority is impersonal, for the sacramental authority of the priest is not derived from personal qualities but from ordination.[52] Some charismatic or quasi-charismatic leaders also appear within Roman Catholicism in the form of a Father Coughlin, Bishop Sheen, or any other outstanding leader. In Oswego, New York, priests who gained the greatest respect

---

[50] Charles H. Page, "Bureaucracy and the Liberal Church," *Review of Religion,* 16 (Mar. 1952), 137-50; John R. Scotford, "The Perils of Ecclesiastical Bigness," *Christian Century,* 76 (Nov. 4, 1959), 1276-78; Solomon Sutker, "The Jewish Organizational Elite of Atlanta, Georgia," in *The Jews,* Marshall Sklare, ed. (Glencoe, Ill.: The Free Press, 1958), pp. 249-61.
[51] Werner Cohn, "Social Stratification and the Charismatic," *The Midwest Sociologist,* 21 (Dec. 1958), 12-18.
[52] V. Bachelet, "L'organisation administrative du Saint-Siège et de la Cité du Vatican," *Revue Internationale des Sciences Administratives,* 21, no. 2 (1955), 231-74.

and were rewarded with the most success in parish work excelled through personal qualities—meeting people in a friendly, democratic way and extending themselves beyond the call of duty, instead of ensconcing themselves behind their vested authority and remaining relatively aloof from the majority of parishioners.[53]

Conclusion

Each typology was developed for a distinctive purpose. Some of them clarify the interdependence of a church's theological perspective, social norms, and action patterns with the institutions, values, and activities of the surrounding culture. Others demonstrate that a church's innermost nature is influenced by the position it takes relative to its enveloping society. The forms of social control stressed in a church, its administrative organization, programs of activity, authority patterns and power structure, goal-orientations, and types of socio-psychological appeals, all help to distinguish religious bodies from one another and to explain their origins and development.

As the various types of religious bodies are understood more clearly through additional studies, and as scientific research develops new typologies to help solve practical and theoretical problems, it will become increasingly possible to predict the future of a church from knowledge of its current features, value-orientations, and trends. Each type exercises a strong but somewhat different kind of influence over its practical objectives, functioning organization, predisposing values, effects on members, and relationships with the world. The typological approach to the church is not, therefore, an abstruse exercise merely for the sake of mental discipline. It directly aids understanding of the church as a social institution. Its relevance to analysis of the rise, growth, and modification of religious bodies will become more clear in the next chapter.

Selected References

Bainbridge, William Sims, and Rodney Stark, "Cult Formation: Three Compatible Models," *Sociological Analysis*, 40, no. 4 (Winter 1979), 283–95. Models of how novel religious ideas are generated and made social with emphasis upon compensators that substitute for desired rewards and their social exchange.

Clark, Elmer T., *The Small Sects in America*, rev. ed. Nashville: Abingdon, 1949. Descriptions of hundreds of religious bodies and analysis of seven types of American sects which blends psychological, theological, sociological, and historical data.

Earle, John R., Dean D. Knudsen, and Donald W. Shriver, Jr., *Spindles and*

---

[53] W. Seward Salisbury, "The Structure of Religious Action in a Small City," paper read to the American Sociological Society, Sept. 4, 1952.

Spires. Atlanta: John Knox Press, 1976. A new study of religion and social change in Gastonia, N.C. (see Pope below).

Enroth, Ronald, et al., *A Guide to Cults and New Religions*. Downers Grove, Ill.: Inter-Varsity Press, 1983. An analysis of ten new religions with comparisons of their teachings to those of biblical Christianity.

Garrett, William R., "Maligned Mysticism: The Maledicted Career of Troeltsch's Third Type," *Sociological Analysis*, 36, no. 3 (Fall 1975), 205–23. Evidence to support the contention that Troeltsch's mysticism type has been neglected and maligned despite its enduring promise for research and theory.

Greeley, Andrew M., *The Denominational Society: A Sociological Approach to Religion in America*. Glenview, Ill.: Scott, Foresman and Co., 1972. An interpretation which views the denomination as the most distinctive feature of American religion.

Hostetler, John A., *Amish Society*, 3rd ed. Baltimore: Johns Hopkins University Press, 1980. The cultural setting, religious life, traditions, customs, and changes among the Amish.

Hostetler, John A., *Hutterite Society*. Baltimore: Johns Hopkins University Press, 1974. An ethnography and history of Hutterite religion, social structure, and lifestyle.

Melton, J. Gordon, and Robert L. Moore, *The Cult Experience: Responding to the New Religious Pluralism*. New York: Pilgrim Press, 1982. An interpretation of the historical background and psychological appeals of minority religious groups, a brief guide to several alternative religions, and the resolution on deprogramming by the Governing Board of the National Council of Churches.

Niebuhr, H. Richard, *Christ and Culture*. New York: Harper and Row, 1951. Five types of church-society relationships which grow out of the problem of relating Christianity to the culture which contains it.

Poll, Solomon, *The Hasidic Community in Williamsburg: A Study in Sociology of Religion*. New York: Schocken Books, 1969. A study of ultra-orthodox Jews in Brooklyn whose entire life is regulated by religious rules, rituals, and customs.

Pope, Liston, *Millhands and Preachers*. New Haven: Yale University Press, 1942. A near-classic study of relationships between churches and economic institutions in Gastonia, N.C., which effectively uses the church-sect typology (see Earle et al. above).

Troeltsch, Ernst, *The Social Teaching of the Christian Churches*, 2 vols., trans. Olive Wyon. Chicago: University of Chicago Press, 1981 (London: George Allen and Unwin, 1931). A classical work in the sociology of religion and the history of Christianity which develops the church-sect typology.

Wach, Joachim, *Types of Religious Experience: Christian and Non-Christian*. Chicago: Phoenix Books, 1972 (University of Chicago Press, 1951). A typological study of religious communities based upon perspectives from sociology, history, and theology.

Washington, Joseph, *Black Sects and Cults*. Garden City, N.Y.: Doubleday and Co., 1972. African roots, social meanings, and other factors in the rise and development of Black cults and sects.

Wilson, Byran R., *Religious Sects: A Sociological Study*. New York: McGraw-Hill, 1970. A well-written analysis of numerous types of sects as protests against conventional religion and as communities of love.

Yinger, J. Milton, *The Scientific Study of Religion*. New York: Macmillan, 1970. Chap. 13, "Types of Religious Organizations," elaborates Yinger's typology presented in this chapter; other passages lend it added support.

🏛 Chapter 5

The Rise and Growth of Churches

Mobility on the Church-Sect Continuum

Many scholars have described the life cycle of religious bodies as a process by which cults originate, develop into sects, and then change into denominations, perhaps finally to emerge from the process as churches. Foremost among these is Niebuhr's theory of the life history of religious bodies. According to it, children born into the families of first generation sect members begin to change the sect into a church even before they reach adulthood. With their coming the sect must become an educational and disciplinary institution in order to make the new generation conform to its ideas and customs. The second generation holds its convictions less fervently than pioneers of the sect, whose convictions were formed in the heat of conflict and sometimes at the threat of martyrdom. With each succeeding generation isolation from the world becomes more difficult. Wealth may also increase, giving sect members vested interests in the economic order. Compromise is an inevitable result; the ethics of the sect increasingly become like those of church-type bodies.[1]

In time the sect's administration also tends to become church-like. An official clergy replaces lay leadership; easily taught creeds replace

---

[1] H. Richard Niebuhr, *The Social Sources of Denominationalism* (Hamden, Conn.: Shoe String Press, 1954), pp. 19-21.

71347

the unwritten, enthusiastically held doctrines of the emergent sect. Infant baptism or dedication becomes a means of grace as children's salvation is sought. The Half-Way Covenant of New England churches and the "birthright membership" of the Friends illustrate this process. Sectarian organization theoretically can endure in pure form for only one generation.[2]

Even the sect or cult that originates as a protest against ritualism, ceremonialism, and formalism is soon likely to have its own ritual. Regular religious services make emergence of repetitive patterns inevitable. Although the group may insist that it has no liturgy or ritual, any deviation from the customary pattern may produce insecurity or a feeling that something important is left out. Even in the anti-ritualistic church, habit eventually makes "lack of form" become a form known as the "order of worship." Social interaction is simplified by such ritualism, for regular participants know what to expect and become more efficient and systematic in their collective worship.[3] The ritual brings strength and endurance to participants; it reinforces beliefs upon which the group is based. Religious faith and feeling are increased by ritualism. Reciting a creed, carrying a Bible or Testament, wearing a cross or medal, celebrating Holy Communion, saluting the Christian flag, singing hymns, listening to sermons, and many other activities in Christian worship or behavior are all symbolically associated with underlying religious beliefs. Religious practices grow out of beliefs and also contribute to their formation. Churches hence may be considered symbolic of the beliefs of their members. As ritualism formalizes expressions of faith by believers, it also contributes to mobility of the religious body from sect toward church. When its functions are ignored, forgotten, or lost, ritualism contributes to the disintegration of that very institution it once helped to perpetuate.

Christianity originated as a despised Jewish cult, grew into a persecuted sect, developed into a somewhat tolerated denomination, and suddenly at the time of Emperor Constantine I emerged as a victorious church. Perhaps each major Christian body is destined to follow a similar sequence of development with repeated splintering of smaller sects aimed at reform.

This process has operated in many religious groups. Wesleyan Methodism moved over the sect to church continuum in eighteenth and nineteenth century England.[4] John Wesley anticipated this possibility; to prevent it he instructed prosperous Christians to gain, save, and give all they can so that they would grow in grace and lay up treasures in heaven. Baptists are chang-

---

[2] *Ibid.* The contrasting types of religious bodies emphasized by Niebuhr are two only—the sect and the church à la Troeltsch as described in Chapter 4 of this book.

[3] James Bissett Pratt, *The Religious Consciousness* (New York: The Macmillan Co., 1920), pp. 267-89.

[4] J. Milton Yinger, *Religion in the Struggle for Power* (Durham, N.C.: Duke University Press, 1946), pp. 31-34.

ing similarly in America, as is evident in the decline in church discipline, in adoption of open communion and open membership, in acceptance of the community church, in the introduction of liturgical forms, in lowering the age of "believer's baptism," and in related changes.[5] Even the young Church of the Nazarene has moved observably from sect toward church. Personality factors, religious incentives, and doctrinal issues combined with the socio-economic situation to stimulate formation of a new denomination.[6] The remainder of this section summarizes findings of several studies related to the topic of mobility on the church-sect continuum.

Methodism in America has moved far along the continuum from sect toward church since the 1780's.[7] Certain church-type traits were borrowed from the Church of England, but in its most important features Methodism was a sect in its early American history. Early Methodism was dominated by a highly personalized conception of salvation and its social reform emphasis centered upon criticizing such selected social problems as slavery. It attempted to bring about general social salvation through the salvation of individuals. Its members were primarily from the lower classes, and the experience of salvation was essential for membership. Rigid discipline upheld moral standards and frequently led to expulsion of those who deviated from group norms. Primary group relationships predominated, and mutual aid was practiced extensively. Lay leadership was organized along sectarian lines, but the conference of preachers was bureaucratically organized along lines similar to those of the Church of England. Charismatic qualities of the preacher were supplemented by the charisma of office; there were no fixed educational standards, but the ministerial candidate had to be voted into the conference to receive permission to preach. Informal meetings with simple revivalistic songs were interlaced with a formal liturgy for certain rituals and services. Irregular freewill offerings supported preachers and missionaries. Simplicity characterized the places of worship; rented pews, cushions, crosses, stained-glass windows, and similar church-type accouterments were strongly opposed.

By the 1930's the Methodist Episcopal Church had moved far from the sect end of the continuum. As a dominant religious body of over seven million members, it was concerned with reforming society. Church attendance and financial support were the measures of religious achievement. Basic societal values were embraced except in such specific areas of conflict as legalized liquor, drinking, and gambling. History and tradition had become a major concern. The membership was widely dispersed; they were but little different from non-members. Discipline and expulsion

<hr>

[5] Winthrop S. Hudson, "Themes for Research in Baptist History," *The Chronicle,* 2 (Jan. 1954), 3-23; and Joseph D. Ban, "The Hungarian Baptists in the United States," *The Chronicle,* 19 (Oct. 1956), 186-92.

[6] Walter G. Muelder, "From Sect to Church," *Christendom,* 10 (Autumn 1945), 450-62.

[7] Earl D. C. Brewer, "Sect and Church in Methodism," *Social Forces,* 30 (May 1952), 400-8.

of members were rare; joining involved mere compliance with certain formalities. Groups were highly organized in an interlocking hierarchy of structure. Both lay and professional leadership were specialized; status-roles were "structured in a complex hierarchy of offices within the bureaucratic religious institution." Increased formality and more elaborate forms of ritual characterized religious services. The church and many of its members were economically prosperous; as a result, church buildings became elaborate with increasing use of the cross, vestments, and other symbols. The movement from sect to church appears to have accelerated slightly in the twentieth century.

Early Mormonism had many sectarian traits.[8] It claimed to be a restoration of the early Apostolic church. Exclusiveness and voluntary election were the basis of its membership. Withdrawal from the secular society was emphasized. Work was sanctified. Persecution increased in-group cohesion. Its early charismatic leadership became institutionalized in the leading offices as the church grew and suffered external threats. Instead of developing in the anticipated sectarian direction, however, the Mormon Church became the core of a large culture area because of the nature of its doctrines, the success of its missionary work, the failure by 1838 of its Law of Consecration which reconciled Christian socialism with private initiative, failures which necessitated four fresh starts in sixteen years and thus prevented a set routine from developing, expulsion from the Midwest, the choice of a large expanse of western land, and an authoritarian church structure which contributed to the establishment of a central government.

The Mormon Church today does not fit the definition of either sect, denomination, or church; it is an admixture of all three. Latter-day Saints have their own sub-culture and their own homeland within the larger nation. Instead of moving from sect to church in the traditional pattern, they moved from sect to what may be called an *incipient nationality*.[9]

The limitations of the church-sect typology are also seen in an analysis of the Christian Science Church.[10] From about 1872 to 1880 (after its germinal phase, 1866-1872) Christian Science was a cult. A small group gathered about their leader, Mary Baker Eddy, was identified locally as a special group, and conceived of themselves accordingly. Continuing rivalries within the circle, the first attempt at formal organization, and the first published textbook emerged during this cult period. After 1880

---

[8] Thomas F. O'Dea, "Mormonism and the Avoidance of Sectarian Stagnation: A Study of Church, Sect, and Incipient Nationality," *American Journal of Sociology,* 50 (Nov. 1954), 285-93.

[9] *Ibid.* Cf. Thomas F. O'Dea, *The Mormons* (Chicago: University of Chicago Press, 1957); and Nels Anderson, *Desert Saints* (Chicago: University of Chicago Press, 1942).

[10] Harold W. Pfautz, "The Sociology of Secularization: Religious Groups," *American Journal of Sociology,* 61 (Sept. 1955), 121-28; and "Christian Science: A Case Study of the Social Psychological Aspect of Secularization," *Social Forces,* 34 (Mar. 1956), 246-51.

the group grew and became widely diffused; secondary relationships became necessary among members. Formalization was evident in the founding of Massachusetts Metaphysical College (1881), publication of several new editions of the basic textbook (*Science and Health*), formation of a National Christian Science Association, and the appearance of the *Journal of Christian Science*.

A revolt against Mrs. Eddy's leadership in the late 1880's led to complete reorganization; from 1890 to 1930 it gradually became, like modern Quakerism and Mormonism, an *institutionalized sect*. As such, its membership is increasingly homogeneous because of selective recruitment. The rate of growth is decreasing, and there is, in its international membership, a high degree of internal differentiation of roles and statuses. As traditional membership in contrast to voluntary membership is becoming significant, the conflict with society is becoming institutionalized. The emotional orientation of members' testimonies is decreasing as traditional and rational motivations increase. The social structure is more complex than that of a sect, and the group's power and prestige have grown until it is "respectable."

The Salvation Army in Canada emerged partly out of failure of older religious bodies to use lay leadership effectively in evangelism. Its methods of winning converts grew out of urban conditions in Britain and achieved their greatest success in urban areas. Street preaching combined with brass bands and parades, the lack of stiff formality in services, the simplicity of meeting places, and freedom of the member to participate or not attracted "foot-loose" elements of the city. Its evangelical character made it a strong movement of the masses expanding through its appeal to downtrodden people when traditional churches tried to reach all population segments. As a result, class differentiation was present in the churches, while the Salvation Army included only the elect.

In time, however, the zeal involved in intense concern for saving souls was a factor in the long-range failure to become strongly established. Failure to follow up the results of evangelism lost many converts to other groups and forced withdrawal from areas where support was insufficient to maintain a local organization. Recognition of this weakness led to efforts to build up a distinctive following willing to support the Salvation Army financially. Internal conflict accompanied this change of emphasis; by 1914 the Canadian Salvation Army was no longer a movement of the masses. A professional leadership emerged which emphasized welfare work as a primary task, in contrast to the earlier emphasis upon personal salvation and purely spiritual remedies for social evils. The Salvation Army had changed in half a century or less from a sect to a church.[11]

In its early history (c.1650-1700) the Society of Friends spread its message with a fiery zeal. Severe persecution of "Preachers of the Light"

[11] S. D. Clark, *Church and Sect in Canada* (Toronto: University of Toronto Press, 1948), pp. 408-13, 418-31.

did not hinder the organization of cell-like groups which met to wait upon the Lord and experience the moving of the Spirit. The inspired voice of prophecy arising out of the silence of the meeting often caused worshipers to quake in the dreadful presence of their Lord. During the eighteenth century priestly conservators replaced prophetic creators in the leadership. The prophetic voice was still heard, but prophets were subjected to the controlling influence of other prophets. Elders appointed to advise the ministers often exerted more repression than encouragement in their successful efforts to develop a distinctive culture pattern.

The nineteenth century was a period of conflict between a prophetic emphasis upon deriving truth from deep inward insights and a priestly emphasis upon tradition, organization, and doctrine. When the elders tried to regulate the ministers on matters of belief, the mystical-evangelical synthesis that had persisted nearly two centuries as a source of power was broken; schisms resulted in three bodies of Friends. The priestly emphasis upon conventional forms of preaching, prayer, singing, and programming of meetings—with no leeway for a spontaneous prophetic message arising out of silence—came to dominate a majority of the Friends' meetings. The twentieth century demand for intellectualism has led to thoughtful, instructive, self-conscious preaching. Emphasis upon the Spirit has given way to an emphasis upon intellect. The past emphasis upon the Divine Source of all solutions for social problems is replaced by stating social problems and suggesting their solutions. The ministry of Quakerism has thus shifted from a prophetic, to a priestly, and finally to a teaching type. The movement has passed through the cult and sect stages and is now a respected denomination.[12]

The churches of Monroe County, Indiana, have followed the basic pattern anticipated by Niebuhr's theory. The Methodists, Disciples, and Baptists at first were vital groups which insisted upon first-hand religious experience. Characterized by strong emotion, they perpetuated themselves through converts' spontaneous missionary zeal. Over a period of 120 years, however, they became "respectable" as they became more prosperous and as original believers were succeeded by their children. Religious experience showed a tendency toward standardization, and the "prophetic forward movements" were "leveled down and conventionalized." Meanwhile new sects emerged in the same spontaneous, creative manner as the older bodies had a century earlier.[13]

Religious sects are especially likely to lose their "protestant" features in America, for there is no powerful, all-inclusive church against which to protest. Similarly, churches compete and acquire many sect-like traits. If

---

[12] Howard Haines Brinton, "Prophet Ministry, Being the Dudleian Lecture for the Academic Year 1948-1949, Harvard University," *Official Register of Harvard University: Harvard Divinity School Bulletin,* 47 (Apr. 1950), 23-36.

[13] Anton T. Boisen, "Divided Protestantism in a Midwest County: A Study in the Natural History of Organized Religion," *Journal of Religion,* 20 (Oct. 1940), 359-81.

the trend toward increasing merger of denominations continues until some large united body dominates American religion, these tendencies may be reversed.

Social Sources of New Religious Bodies

If religious groups indeed begin their existence as loosely-organized, amorphous cults and gradually develop into sects, denominations, and perhaps finally churches, what is their source? Why do they arise at all? What forces give birth to them? Some have attributed their rise to psychotic aberrations separate from the facts of common life; others have considered cults to be isolated phenomena of an especially stupid class of people. Examination indicates, however, that the deviant behavior associated with emerging cults reflects the continuous existence of a people and is closely connected with normal social life.[14] Some of the major sources of new religious bodies are listed and discussed in this section. All of them are interrelated and together form a complex, interacting syndrome which may be considered the source of new religious bodies.

Migration and Transplantation

The transplanting of religious bodies from one nation to another has been especially notable in America, which has served as a haven of refuge for many minority groups.[15] The early Pilgrims and Puritans were forerunners of multitudes of immigrants who established sects in the New World, even when copying European state churches. Migrants brought with them old world forms of ecclesiastical organization and worship. As a result many American denominations are primarily ethnic religions continuing to reflect civil and social patterns which were prevalent where they first developed.[16]

Churches of immigrants have been a major rallying center of ethnic groups. Among Swedes in America, for instance, churches were the major source of ethnic unity.[17] Immigrants commonly combined Old World reli-

---

[14] Gilbert Seldes, *The Stammering Century* (New York: The John Day Co., 1928), pp. xiii-xiv, *passim*.

[15] For one sociological account of the way in which religious values were at the center of many phases in the early social and economic life of a migrant group, see the account of Seventh-Day German Baptists in Pennsylvania by Eugene E. Doll, "Social and Economic Organization in Two Pennsylvania German Religious Communities," *American Journal of Sociology*, 57 (Sept. 1951), 168-77.

[16] Frederick Hertz, *Nationality in History and Politics* (New York: Oxford University Press), 1944, pp. 98-145; and R. E. E. Harkness, "The Rise of Denominations," *Crozer Quarterly*, 8 (Oct. 1931), 456-67.

[17] George M. Stephenson, *The Religious Aspects of Swedish Immigration* (Minneapolis: University of Minnesota Press, 1932).

gious and cultural values. Preserving the old language, religion, traditions, and customs protected ethnic groups from social disorganization and cushioned the shock of adjustment to the new culture. In addition, new religious groups springing up in a community hastened the process of adjustment, defended the interests, and met many needs of members. The social purpose of new sects may thus be viewed as a defense of the needs and interests of marginal population segments.

The membership and relative strength of Roman Catholicism in America directly reflect immigration patterns. Before the Irish migration during the first half of the nineteenth century, Catholics were a negligible part of the population. With successive migrations of Catholics from Germany, Italy, and the Slavic nations, both the relative strength and internal composition of Catholicism changed significantly.

Rural migrants in large cities are often ill at ease in the relatively large, impersonal city churches. Failing to find their needs met even in churches of their own denomination, they may drop out of organized church life completely, join a sect, or help establish a new one. In a sect they may find an intimate, primary-group atmosphere like that of the rural church, and they may gain social recognition in their new environment. "By preserving important rural attitudes and values, the sects softened the impact of the strange urban world upon their members. Urban evangelical expansion may thus be viewed as a stage in the urbanization of rural people with a strong fundamentalist background." [18] The same loss of socio-religious values may be experienced when city church members move from one area to another; churches reflect the communities in which they are located and may vary widely from one region to another even in the same denomination.

The rural person migrating into the city must face the "cultural shock" of liberation from former group associations, relaxation of social controls, impersonalized social relationships, increased mobility, decreased stability, isolation, and almost complete disruption of personal and vocational habits and status. Established city churches may even become a symbol of the migrant's isolation in the new, strange, unfriendly society. As a result, he may drop all church participation or join a small sect or cult.[19] However, Dynes' study of sectarianism in an urban population does not support the hypothesis that rural migrants cushion "cultural shock" by joining sects. Persons reared in rural areas indeed were slightly more apt to have sectarian attitudes, but the sectarian was not typically a recent migrant and showed no greater residential mobility during the past five years than others. Rurality and migration are important in sectarianism only insofar

---

[18] William E. Mann, *Sect, Cult, and Church in Alberta* (Toronto: University of Toronto Press, 1955), p. 154.

[19] John B. Holt, "Holiness Religion: Cultural Shock and Social Reorganization." *American Sociological Review,* 5 (Oct. 1940), 740-47.

as they reflect lower socioeconomic status.[20] Although movement from the farm to the city tends to reduce the frequency of church attendance,[21] a probability sample of 1,887 nonfarm adults revealed that farm-reared Protestants attend church slightly more regularly than other Protestants. Adults reared on farms tend to be in the lower educational and economic classes, and are consequently less active participants than other adults in politics and non-church organizations.[22]

Migration contributes to the emergence of new religious bodies in two ways. First by transplanting them from one culture to another, and second, by stimulating those conditions in society which cause the emergence of new sects.

Social Disorganization

Historians have found that "a multiplicity of sects is common in every country where some special circumstances disturb the traditional values of its civilization." [23] The church may depend upon social stability, for when it is absent sects flourish. Perhaps this is why the sect thrives under frontier conditions and grows into a denomination as society becomes better organized.

When disorganization is present in society, many seek a new, stable, organizing influence. A few kindred spirits may unite to correct what they conceive to be some error in society or in a church. Group consciousness among members attracts others; rapid growth may occur as outsiders who are similar in temperament and interests join the group. Conflict with others in society unites sect members, contributes to a degree of social, if not spatial, isolation, and leads to feelings and actions of exclusiveness. This early period is typically succeeded by a more peaceful stage of increasing conformity to the outside world. Ultimately the sect disappears as a separate conflict group. It is a denomination, likely to be divided again by the formation of new sectarian splinter groups.[24]

Accompanying changes occur in every stage of development in members' temperaments and reflect changes in the degree of social disorgani-

[20] Russell R. Dynes, "Rurality, Migration, and Sectarianism," *Rural Sociology,* 21 (Mar. 1956), 25-33.

[21] Howard Beers and Catherine Heflin, "The Urban Status of Rural Migrants," *Social Forces,* 23 (Oct. 1944), 32-37.

[22] Ronald and Deborah Freedman, "Farm-Reared Elements in the Nonfarm Population," *Rural Sociology,* 21 (Mar. 1956), 50-61.

[23] Harold J. Laski, *The American Democracy* (New York: The Viking Press, 1948), p. 292. A large number and variety of new sects is emerging in Indonesia as profound social disorganization accompanies rapid political and socioeconomic change. Cf. Justus M. van der Kroef, "The Changing Class Structure of Indonesia," *American Sociological Review,* 21 (Apr. 1956), 138-48.

[24] Ellsworth Faris, "The Sect and the Sectarian," *American Journal of Sociology,* 60, no. 6, part 2 (May 1955), 75-89.

zation. The "combative, exclusive nonconformist" becomes the patriotic citizen. Perhaps the new convert enters the sect less because he is of like mind than because he changes his mind, desiring it to be different. As the group of which he is a member changes, changing group relationships produce changes in members' temperaments. The new existence of the sectarian involves a rebirth; he is made over into a new creature.[25]

Economic and social maladjustments more often result in "religious quickening" than in widespread increases in mental illness. The economically distressed share similar experiences and face the same problems; as a result, common interests and predispositions draw them to one another. Trying to understand their problems and to gain a perspective pertinent to ultimate realities, they are drawn into groups with a sense of earnestness and urgency that makes their religion supreme reality and an all-important source of power.[26] Their common philosophy of life thus grows out of their common social condition. By meeting needs that arise from disorganization, new sects are often "safety valves" providing disoriented people opportunity for reorientation within a new religious system that meets their peculiar social and spiritual needs. In their new-found groups, members are likely to have an intensity of religious feeling and belongingness that leads to a much higher degree of loyalty and more giving of time, service, and money than is found in older religious bodies.[27]

Occasionally new sects emerge because communication systems within existent sects disintegrate. Thus among the Doukhobors a secret language led to a "jungle of private meanings." Compromises by the sect such as accepting governmental demands, seeking schooling, and obtaining employment outside of the communities caused the formation of numerous splinter groups among the Sons of Freedom sect of the Doukhobors.[28]

Because political and religious sectarianism are related to social disorganization, both tend to arise together. The founder of Oneida Community, John Noyes, recognized the connection between revivalism, which often gives rise to new sects, and communitarian movements; periods of revival ran parallel to and only slightly in advance of periods of socialism. The great idea of revivalism was regeneration of the soul; the socialists' great idea was regeneration of society. Since the latter is the environment of the soul, the two ideas belong together and complement each other.[29] In times of social disorganization this relationship is particularly apparent;

---

[25] *Ibid.*

[26] Anton T. Boisen, *Problems in Religion and Life* (New York: Abingdon-Cokesbury Press, 1946), pp. 121-22.

[27] W. Seward Salisbury, "The 'New Churches' in a Small City," *Religious Education*, 49 (May-June 1954), 211-17.

[28] Harry B. Hawthorn, "A Test of Simmel on the Secret Society: The Doukhobors of British Columbia," *American Journal of Sociology*, 62 (July 1956), 1-7.

[29] Arthur Eugene Bestor, Jr., *Backwoods Utopias* (Philadelphia: University of Pennsylvania Press, 1950), pp. 5-6.

some people turn to economic and political innovations in order to solve the problems of mankind, while others turn to religious ones. Isolated utopian communitarian societies combined these elements in attempts to reach perfection through both individual and social regeneration.[30] Similarly, a major contribution of the evangelical sects in Alberta has been the social reorganization accomplished under their leadership. Marginal groups were incorporated into socio-religious communities, rural migrants' problems of urbanization were alleviated, needs of the economically underprivileged and the isolated were partially met, and revolutionary impulses were channelled off in non-destructive directions.[31]

The contribution of social disorganization to the rise and growth of cults and sects is evident in the Oxford Group Movement, also known as Buchmanism or Moral Re-Armament (MRA). The movement originated in unstable world conditions surrounding World War I. Dr. Frank N. Buchman, a Lutheran minister, received a personal vision which produced a "change" in his life. After confessing his faults to people against whom he held grudges, he set out to change others. Buchman realized that fear, greed, ambition, and hatred were present despite the termination of the "war to end war" and the 1921 Disarmament Conference. MRA resulted from his belief in the need for changed persons. Each changed person was to achieve absolute purity, honesty, love, and unselfishness by giving in to God during a daily quiet time, listening to His directions, recording them in writing, verifying guidance by sharing directions with another "Grouper," making restitution to others, and sharing sins in group confessions. "Soul surgery" of individuals would bring about changed society.[32]

Rising out of reaction to world problems, MRA has been viewed as a "colossal drive of escapism from the full force of the difficulty in detail of responsible living in the world."[33] It appeals to persons who need relaxation and quiet amid the high pressures of modern living and the hectic daily whirl that is common to urbanized civilization. The daily quiet time supplies serenity and relaxation; MRA provides an authority which becomes an easy refuge from the despair and mental confusion that often accompany life in a complex, non-authoritarian society. Even though the "surrender to God" may at best be obedience only to "the authority of the individual's own deepest insights," the moral imperative produced by it often satisfies the individual's need for direction.[34]

---

[30] *Ibid.,* pp. 5-10.

[31] Mann, *Sect, Cult, and Church in Alberta,* pp. 156-57.

[32] Hadley Cantril, *The Psychology of Social Movements* (New York: John Wiley and Sons, 1941), pp. 144-54.

[33] The Social and Industrial Council of the Church Assembly, *Moral Re-Armament* (Westminster, South Wales: Church Information Board of the Church Assembly, 1955), p. 5.

[34] Walter H. Clark, *The Oxford Group* (New York: Bookman Associates, 1951), pp. 244-46.

By re-establishing God as an entity entirely outside the individual, the Buchmanite is able to get external sanctions for his own wishes. He attributes to God directions and commands that are essentially his own fancies and desires. . . . And when the individual listens, the specific directions he obtains in his Quiet Time are inevitably based on his own standards of judgment and his own wishes no matter how unconscious they may be. In this way God, who exists outside the individual, gives him sanction and authority to do as he wants. God's values become his values because he has himself projected them into the symbol of God.[35]

Social disorganization as one source of MRA also is reflected in the escapism apparent in its approach to social problems. The assumption that nations and institutions can be good only when persons comprising them are good enabled it to transfer all problems to God and thus relieve the individual of social responsibility. It is perhaps for this reason that most Buchmanites have a vested interest in the status quo and normally would avoid any gospel that pointed out social responsibilities for less fortunate men. The belief that they are working for God gives members with much leisure and little personal resourcefulness a purpose for existence, even if such work pertains only to petty details of everday life. In the ultimate sense the movement is anti-democratic in its individualism and in its refusal to consider the social context within which social disorganization arises. It probably fluctuates directly with economic conditions, gaining many newcomers in periods of social crisis and indecision, and few newcomers when social stability is restored.[36]

Social Change

Rapid social change, combined with the disturbance of value-systems that accompanies it, has contributed to the genesis of numerous sects. Social change is a potent source of sects even when changes occur gradually with few major disruptions in the social order. Tensions associated with the urbanization of society, as we have seen, are modified or cushioned by religious sects. Sectarian preachers, reiterating "old-fashioned" beliefs, strengthen traditional symbols and encourage listeners to endure the crises associated with change. Simple explanations of life's difficulties provide rationalizations for problems. The emotional fervor of certain sects is often a reaction to personal strains and social crises induced by economic distress and other problems associated with change.[37]

When sect members are associated in a true community, group adjustment to social change often spares individuals much misery and mental

[35] Cantrill, *The Psychology of Social Movements,* p. 167. Reprinted by permission.
[36] *Ibid.,* pp. 154, 165-68; and Allan W. Eister, *Drawing Room Conversion* (Durham, N.C.: Duke University Press, 1950), pp. 161-202.
[37] Mann, *Sect, Cult, and Church in Alberta,* pp. 155-57; and Anton T. Boisen, *Religion in Crisis and Custom* (New York: Harper and Brothers, 1945), p. 8.

agony that might otherwise result from their marginal position in society. Thus Manitoba Mennonites have changed in many ways from a religious to an ethnic group. Group acceptance of cultural changes has given social and psychological security to members and has enabled them to change gradually with a minimum of personal maladjustment.[38]

The atomization, normlessness, or anomie of modern society, in which the individual is isolated in the midst of multitudes of strangers, is a product of far-reaching changes associated with industrialization and urbanization. Group control over the individual is so minimized that he is exposed to a variety of competing ethical standards. This contributes to the rise of cults. Some spring up rapidly, flourish briefly, and then pass away almost as suddenly as they came. Others move along the sect-church continuum to become established sects and ultimately respected denominations. The "fly-by-night" cults in slum areas recruit members mainly from ethnic minorities and underprivileged groups, while successful cults like Bahai, I Am, Psychiana, Spiritualism, Theosophy, and Unity appeal more to the middle classes, often using modern mass persuasion in their promotional programs.[39] Anomie has contributed to the growth of the Jehovah's Witnesses. They reflect material insecurity, the lack of spiritual cohesion in society, and a widespread feeling that social disputes no longer can be arbitrated through a common governmental institution. Members live *in* the world, but, rejecting it, they clearly are not *of* the general world society.[40] Some sects exchange an individual sense of isolation for isolation and solutions to problems shared by the entire group. Reassurance is provided members by the group's ideology.[41] Churches of immigrants to some extent share this nature.

This sense of isolation also contributes to the Oxford Group. Through sharing in small group interaction the individual becomes an accepted member of a closed microcosm—a little world with its own norms and behavior patterns. As an in-group member of a highly select gathering, he has knowledge that others lack. As a participant in the process of life-changing and soul surgery, his status is enhanced. Repetition of confessions brings relief, status, and sometimes an erotic pleasure as a substitute gratification for sin. Through sharing confessions, excitement and thrill are provided vicariously. Sharing a common goal binds members together and

---

[38] E. K. Francis, *In Search of Utopia: The Mennonites in Manitoba* (Glencoe, Ill.: The Free Press, 1955).

[39] Elizabeth K. Nottingham, *Religion and Society* (Garden City: Doubleday and Co., 1954), pp. 66-67; and Wayne E. Oates, *Religious Factors in Mental Illness* (New York: Association Press, 1955), pp. 76-77.

[40] Werner Cohn, "Jehovah's Witnesses as a Proletarian Movement," *The American Scholar*, 24 (Summer 1955), 281-98; and Joseph Bram, "Jehovah's Witnesses and the Values of American Culture," *Transactions of the New York Academy of Sciences*, 19 (1956), 47-54.

[41] Oates, *Religious Factors in Mental Illness*, p. 77

provides many a bewildered youth in a changing world with an aim in life (working for God) that might otherwise have been entirely missing.[42]

If a society does not satisfy men, its dominant religions will not satisfy either. New religions therefore tend to spring up among persons uprooted by social change. Cult-proneness is especially prominent among "seekers" who are institutionally alienated but religiously intense. When a cult leader comes to town, they are among the first and most frequent attenders. Their initially favorable reactions become even more favorable through exposure to cultist claims; the opposite is true of curious observers with initial skepticism.[43] Even after prophetic claims are unfulfilled, cult members may retain and even strengthen their faith. They find rationalizations for the prophecy's failure, or they reinterpret such details as the date for its eventual fulfillment.[44]

The predominantly feminine membership in most cults may grow out of changing family conditions. Husbands may have lost interest in home life, identifying themselves with a more "modern" age than their families and wandering away from them. Wives then seek comfort in cult beliefs and activities.[45]

Conflict

A large proportion of new sects and cults are organized as protest groups. The protest may be against conditions in society, in churches, or even in a sect that only recently split off from another religious body as a protest group. When opposition comes from the rest of society, the group is strengthened in its deviant position. The role of conflict in the formation of new religious bodies is discussed in Chapter 11.

Socioeconomic Differentiation

Social class distinctions contribute to the rise and growth of new sects through the social barriers they create between groups, through the divergent values of the respective classes, and through the compensatory mechanisms associated with class discrimination and other socioeconomic distinctions. (Further references to this topic appear in numerous scattered passages elsewhere.)

---

[42] Cantrill, *The Psychology of Social Movements,* pp. 161-64, 168; Clark, *The Oxford Group,* pp. 237-47; and Eister, *Drawing Room Conversion,* pp. 125-60.

[43] William R. Catton, Jr., "What Kind of People Does a Religious Cult Attract? " *American Sociological Review,* 22 (Oct. 1957), 561-66.

[44] Leon Festinger, Henry W. Riecken, and Stanley Schachter, *When Prophecy Fails* (Minneapolis: University of Minnesota Press, 1956).

[45] Arthur Huff Fauset, *Black Gods of the Metropolis* (Philadelphia: University of Pennsylvania Press, 1944), p. 82, note 6.

The division of major Protestant bodies into northern and southern branches in the pre-Civil War era and recent protestations by white splinter groups against integration in large denominations reflect black-white relationships. Blacks' desires to have their own free social organizations in a society in which they were a social, psychological, and statistical minority contributed to the genesis and growth of black churches. During the time of slavery the majority group believed that the Christian church would make blacks better servants. Black churches became instruments of, by, and for blacks. Freer self-expression was possible than when they worshiped with whites. Christian teachings of the physical brotherhood of all mankind and the spiritual brotherhood of all believers could be freely promulgated. The church took up the slack in educational, economic, and political leadership that resulted from the lack of other black institutions.[46] Religious services were partly a protest against white domination. They brought blacks together in a physical group, provided centers of communication, and allowed for exchange of opinion. The content of sermons and music promoted and reflected group feeling.

Black churches have more recently provided many with an escapist philosophy and perhaps thus helped divert black protest, but they also have strongly promoted black group identification by providing race leadership through their clergy, by fostering ideas of equality and brotherhood, and by providing a building in which black groups can gather to discuss problems and organize programs for the welfare of the race.[47]

Black churches, welcoming all who come regardless of their position in the world, have provided a sense of belonging for many lower class blacks. This has not prevented the emergence of subtle class lines between the black churches, however. Some emphasize a formal theology which gradually alienates lower class persons, while others have been extremely emotional, repelling upper class blacks who wish to belong to churches similar to the major white congregations.[48]

Through study of five prominent black cults, Fauset concluded that the factors which attract communicants are, in order of importance: the leader's personality, the desire to get closer to God, a racial or nationalistic urge, a miraculous cure, dissatisfaction with Christianity, disdain of orthodox churches, mental relief, the urge for leadership and participation, aid to business, disdain of ministers, instruction within the cult, and a

---

[46] Fauset, *Black Gods of the Metropolis*, pp. 5-6, 88, 107.
[47] Arnold M. Rose, *The Negro's Morale* (Minneapolis: University of Minnesota Press, 1949), pp. 13-14, 98-100.
[48] Robert L. Sutherland, *Color, Class, and Personality* (Washington, D.C.: American Council on Education, 1942), pp. 116-18.

common bond of friendliness and understanding.[49] Many of these are related to the migration of blacks from the rural South into the urban North and to their desire to enter a religious group similar to their original home church. Black cult members often seek reassurance through a special emotional experience of sanctification. Intense devotion to their religious faith and practices is, undoubtedly, partly due to their lack of opportunity to participate in many enriching experiences of white Americans. Cultural barrenness, as among many southern and border state whites, contributes to new cults and sects. The cults promise heaven to a disadvantaged group. They provide an atmosphere where imaginative leaders can experiment in business, politics, social reform, and social expression. Musical cadences become a compelling force that carries many a convert into the cult through "spirit possession." Intensity of esoteric feeling and a high degree of friendliness among members also helps to entice converts into the group.[50]

Garvey's Universal Negro Improvement Association was designed as a protest against injustice. Essentially it "took the form of a complete rejection of the white world through an escapist program of chauvinistic Negro nationalism." [51] However, it was not merely a nationalistic program to colonize Africa with American blacks; it was in many respects a religious cult that involved a belief that God is black and that Jesus had such dark skin that if he were to visit New York he would be expected to live in Harlem. Garvey helped organize the African Orthodox Church in 1921. Its concept of a black God was a shrewd move reflecting keen awareness of social psychological principles.[52]

Extremist movements like the Garveyites and Father Divine's Peace Mission reject the possibility of attaining their goals within the general framework of American values and institutions. They grow most rapidly and have greatest influence during periods of acute distress and crisis. Basically urban, but also attracting rural migrants, they are at odds with one another and are essentially authoritarian. The movement of members in and out of such cults may reflect the fluctuating social status of individuals.[53] The members typically react against the white stereotype of the black and sometimes modify their behavior in the direction of increased personal stability. Even in such extreme groups as the "Black Jews," who claim to have a set of new and distinctive religious practices, the essential character of their worship and theology does not deviate greatly from that

---

[49] Fauset, *Black Gods of the Metropolis,* esp. p. 121.

[50] *Ibid.,* pp. 76-86, 107-8.

[51] Edmund David Cronon, *Black Moses: The Story of Marcus Garvey and the Universal Negro Improvement Association* (Madison: University of Wisconsin Press, 1955), p. xii.

[52] *Ibid.,* pp. 177-83.

[53] Wilson Record, "Extremist Movements Among American Negroes," *Phylon,* 17 (No. 1, 1956), 17-23.

which was familiar to members in their childhood. The members (as in most groups) profess to feel superior to those who have not accepted their social and religious views.[54]

Minority group sects tend to respond to the social pattern with either acceptance, avoidance, or aggression. The total cultural tradition of the group, the degree to which secular movements drain off or channelize aggressive tendencies, the degree of acculturation to values of the dominant societal group, the leadership in the sect, personality tendencies of members, and the amount of hope for improved status (in conjunction with the amount of power to change it) all combine to determine the predominant type of sect response. The American Indian Ghost Dance illustrates the interaction of all these influences.[55]

Charismatic Leadership

Some sects are largely an outgrowth and projection of the influence of their respective founders. This leader is believed to have unique powers, divinely imparted grace, or special prophetic abilities. Such groups originate in conditions of the kinds discussed previously; the founder capitalizes upon or crystallizes the sentiments which make the group possible. Most cult leaders create grandiose illusions of perfection, economic justice, physical or spiritual happiness, and power. They have sought salvation through these illusions, rejecting the more commonly trod "paths to salvation." Having persuaded themselves of their superiority, these leaders have procured followers who have copied their lives, thus fortifying the leaders' faith in themselves and multiplying their personalities.[56] Beliefs like a distrust of secular society or a vivid faith in the literal, imminent, dated, second coming of Christ solidify the membership of many sects around their leaders; they even make some become utopian communitarian societies.[57]

One of the best known cults built around a charismatic leader is the Kingdom of Father Divine. The followers are provided with a meaning for life. They escape from material hardships and from the mental confusion caused by the complexity of conflicting circumstances. An increase in social status and self-respect accompanies joining the movement. Although most members work outside the Kingdom, compromise with the outside world is impossible. They are expected to think of the "all-powerful Father" even while working. Rigid taboos on smoking, drinking, sexual cohabitation, and signs of bodily affliction like the use of glasses, trusses,

---

[54] Howard M. Brotz, "Black Jews in the United States," Abstract of paper presented to the Committee for the Scientific Study of Religion, October 13, 1952 (mimeographed).

[55] J. Milton Yinger, *Religion, Society and the Individual* (New York: The Macmillan Co., 1957), pp. 174-82.

[56] Seldes, *The Stammering Century*, p. xiii.

[57] Bestor, *Backwoods Utopias*, pp. 6-7.

and crutches help to submerge personal identity and provide a new frame of reference centering upon the concrete symbol of Father. Praise of Father, his mysterious movements, and the power of suggestibility at his appearance after meals (when fatigued members have full stomachs) combine to increase a feeling of oneness with God and to break down ego identities. The Kingdom can be viewed as a self-contained microcosm bound together by a set of norms emphasizing that Father Divine is God.[58]

In his most extreme form, the charismatic leader may be considered a messiah by followers. Oppressed minority groups are particularly likely to long for, seek, or expect a divine deliverer. The history of messianic movements manifests a consistent pattern that cuts across political, religious, ethical, and social lines. Yet the messianic concepts of each people have been expressed uniquely, for they have been modified to conform to prevailing culture patterns. The types of Hebrew messianism have hence been similar to those of American Indians, Moslems, and aborigines in New Zealand and Africa, yet each has been distinct.[59]

Evaluation

Various theories advanced to account for the appearance of new sects were tested in Gaston County, North Carolina. The belief that instability of residence and membership explained their emergence was not found valid; all but two percent of the members of one sect group had lived in the community more than five years.[60] The theory that the "cultural shock" involved in the transition from a rural to an urban setting leads migrants to organize or join new churches that seem to defend his former standards of behavior seems plausible.[61] Yet this theory does not account for the rise and growth of new sects in villages and rural areas which are not receiving migrants and it also errs in assuming that sects preserve in some unique manner the traits of rural religion.[62]

Other theories seemed more adequate. The failure of older churches to meet religious needs of certain people was verified by the large proportion of religiously disgruntled members in sects like the Church of God. At least 80 percent of its members had come from other churches; most of the churches were Baptist. Sectarians often ridicule the exclusiveness and pride of the older churches and condemn the "coldness" of their services.

---

[58] Cantril, *The Psychology of Social Movements,* pp. 123-43.

[59] Wilson D. Wallis, *Messiahs: Their Role in Civilization* (Washington, D.C.: American Council on Public Affairs, 1943).

[60] Liston Pope, *Millhands and Preachers* (New Haven: Yale University Press, 1942), p. 133.

[61] Holt, "Holiness Religion," and Grace G. Leybourne, "Urban Adjustments of Migrants from the Southern Appalachian Plateaus," *Social Forces,* 16 (Dec. 1937), 238-46.

[62] Pope, *Millhands and Preachers,* p. 134.

The theory that economic conditions help account for the rise of sects which provide other-worldly compensation for poverty seems verified by the rapid growth of young sects during the Great Depression. Qualitative evidence in Gaston County indicated that release from psychological repressions, opportunities for self-expression, and identification of self with a greater power through phrenetic religious services are partial explanations of sect growth. In addition, the low educational level of sect leaders and part-time work by many of them brings them much closer to the level of the cotton mill laborer than the ministers of older churches. The rigid religious teachings of sects, which demand such great investment of time and devotion that members remain interested and become propagandists for their religion, also contribute to their relative strength among the lower classes.[63]

When part of a population are on the economic, political, educational, psychological, religious, or social periphery of society, they are likely to establish sects which comprise their own society. They thus protest against real or imagined injustices experienced in other institutions. New religious bodies are always the result of a complex combination of many factors. We can expect them to continue emerging in the future, for they are the product of conditions natural to society.

The Life Cycle of the Church [64]

As an institution develops, it creates an informal and a formal structure; a set of traditions, values, goals, and objectives; policies and rules; a division of labor; expectations and hopes; collective feelings (*esprit de corps*) and morale among members.[65] All these are progressively modified in the institution's evolution by processes operating within it. If it survives, it tends increasingly to impose formal rules upon members, in time producing a conformity that is no longer a product of primarily voluntary interaction. This bureaucratic growth tends to increase efficiency. Ultimately, however, a vicious circle of increasing formalization may impair effectiveness; the institution may collapse, unless renewal occurs through relaxation of formal rules, increased stress upon informal relations, or other changes.[66] Informal, unofficial relationships, practices, and organiza-

---

63 *Ibid.*, pp. 133-36.

64 Except as otherwise noted, this section is adapted from J. O. Hertzler, *Social Institutions* (Lincoln: University of Nebraska Press, 1946), pp. 79-82; Robert E. L. Faris, *Social Disorganization* (New York: Ronald Press Co., 1948), pp. 305-29. and Carl A. Dawson and Warner E. Gettys, *An Introduction to Sociology,* 3rd. ed. (New York: Ronald Press Co., 1948), pp. 689-709.

65 Cf. Herbert Blumer, "Social Movements," in *Principles of Sociology,* 2d ed.. Alfred M. Lee, ed. (New York: Barnes and Noble, Inc., 1955), pp. 199-220.

66 Alvin W. Gouldner, "Organizational Analysis," in *Sociology Today,* Robert K Merton, Leonard Broom, and Leonard S. Cottrell, Jr., eds. (New York: Basic

tion are of as great importance as the formal and official in an institution's life.

The process by which an institution develops may be called its natural history. Study of many churches reveals a typical pattern through which they pass as they emerge, grow, decline, and ultimately die. Each recurrent growth cycle of stability, experimentation, and integration[67] may be described as involving five stages. Out of the last may come reorganization or repetition of a similar cycle either within the same church or in another that arises out of its ruins.

1. The stage of *incipient organization* is usually one of unrest and dissatisfaction with existing churches. The uneasiness may be generally diffused, or it may be limited to one segment of the population, often the lower classes who complain about the "corruption" of privileged groups and the churches' complacency with their departure from traditional folkways and mores. The social unrest may arise out of a crisis which the church has failed to meet satisfactorily. It may be a reaction against ritualism that replaces personal spontaneity and devotion, against the church's involvement with "secular" affairs, or against the clergy's lack of certain spiritual or moral qualifications. When leadership arises, a new cult or sect emerges, typically as a reform movement within the parental body.

Many emerging sects have a high degree of collective excitement. Unplanned and uncontrolled emotions in crowd situations may lead to a sense of bodily possession by the Holy Spirit or by Satan that produces intense joy or fear. Physical reactions that identified such groups as the Quakers, Shakers, and "Holy Rollers" are a common result. New beliefs that deviate from those previously held may appear to upset the balance of members' personalities and subject them to the suspicion of insanity.[68] The charismatic, authoritarian, prophetic leader is characteristic of this stage. Yet in sects that emerge as a result of gradually changing mores or rational planning, leadership is apt to be so diffused that historians have a difficult time designating a "founder."

2. A period of *formal organization* closely follows the rise of leadership. An attempt is made to develop a sense of union and of common interests. Followers are asked to commit themselves by formally joining the new group, which now separates itself completely from the parental church. Goals are formulated and publicized to attract additional mem-

---

Books, Inc., 1959), pp. 400-28; and Philip Selznick, "An Approach to a Theory of Bureaucracy," *American Sociological Review*, 8 (Feb. 1943), 47-54.

[67] F. Stuart Chapin, *Contemporary American Institutions* (New York: Harper and Brothers, 1935), pp. 58-62, 294-300; and F. Stuart Chapin, *Cultural Change* (New York: D. Appleton-Century Co., 1928).

[68] Anton T. Boisen, "The Development and Validation of Religious Faith," *Psychiatry*, 14 (Nov. 1951), 455-62. George Fox and Reformation leaders illustrate this tendency.

bers, who may either object to the established society and its churches or seek to bring about the perfection of society, religion, or individuals. A creed is developed to preserve and propagate orthodoxy. Great emphasis is placed upon symbolic expressions of the difference between the new sect and worldly non-members. The symbols may seem trivial or foolish to the outsider, but to the sect member they are of utmost importance. Some center upon slogans that reflect the group's theological orientation ("saved by the blood," "baptized in the Holy Ghost," "Jesus only," etc.); others emphasize behavior that deviates from society's folkways. The use of automobiles, neckties, tobacco, instrumental music, cosmetics, or wedding rings may be considered sinful; card playing, movie attendance, dancing, or military service may be tabooed. Thus codes of behavior are developed and enforced; these distinguish members from others and often draw persecution or ridicule that increases in-group feelings and strength. Agitational forms of leadership gradually diminish as the next stage is approached.

3. In the stage of *maximum efficiency* leadership has a much less emotional emphasis and is dominated by statesmen. Effectively voicing group convictions, they lead to an increasingly rational organization that replaces charismatic leadership. Historians and apologists emerge. Propaganda is prominent; the mass media are used to publicize activities and aims of the sect. Programs of action are formulated by rational consideration of relevant facts; intellectuals repelled by the previous display of emotion may give their approval or even transfer allegiance to it. It has moved psychologically from the position of a despised sect to one of near-equality with previously recognized denominations. Hostility toward others diminishes; with it the fanatical resolution to maintain sharply different ways relaxes, for the first generation of converts usually has died by this time.

The group's formal structure rapidly develops as new committees, boards, and executives are appointed to meet the needs of the growing organization. Official leaders perform their duties enthusiastically and efficiently; the rituals and procedures in worship and in administration are still viewed as means rather than as ends in themselves. The institution is at its stage of maximum vitality or "youthful vigor";[69] its growth may be very rapid. (For social factors influencing growth see Chapter 9.) This growth is likely to be uneven, each period of rapid growth being followed by one in which new members are integrated. If such integration is not successfully accomplished, diverse purposes, interpretations of doctrines and creeds, and social interests may lead to internal dissension; new splinter groups may arise, or the sect may even disintegrate. The Assemblies of God appear to be at this stage. The gradual acceptance of

---

[69] Chapin, *Contemporary American Institutions,* pp. 200-4.

Seventh-day Adventists into fundamentalist circles illustrates movement into denominational status in this period.

4. During the *institutional* stage, formalism saps the group's vitality. Its leadership is dominated by an established bureaucracy more concerned with perpetuating its own interests than with maintaining the distinctives that helped bring the group into existence.[70] Administration centers in boards and committees that tend to become self-perpetuating. Dominated by a small group the organization may become "like boss-ridden parties. . . . The very ones who, because of the position they hold, should be most ready and anxious to make the Christian ministry a real Brotherhood *talk* one thing and *practice* another."[71] Mechanisms of the group's structure have largely become an end in themselves. The church has become a bureaucracy. Creeds become little more than venerated relics from the past. Organized worship gradually develops into a ritual which by this stage is a nearly or wholly empty formality to most "worshipers." Religious symbolism encroaches and persists beyond its usefulness because it is capable of repetition without fresh thought and always at command, in striking contrast to internal, personal devotion.[72] The institution has become the master of its members instead of their servant, making many demands upon them, suppressing personalities, and directing energies into serving the "organization church."

By this stage conflict with the outside world has been replaced completely by toleration. Conformity to societal folkways and mores is typical even on issues clearly in conflict with implications of the church's official dogma. Ulterior motives of "respectability" are often involved in joining; membership standards are relaxed as the church tries to gain all socially respectable people. Increased membership is correlated with increased heterogeneity of sentiments, interests, and dedication. Feelings of intimacy in the group decline. Membership becomes passive and remote from leadership. Interests and activities once considered secular become major attractions as the church attempts to become a center of community activity through sponsoring cultural events, scout troops, athletic organizations, counseling bureaus, and camping programs. Sermons become topical lectures dealing with social issues, rather than fervent discourses on sin, salvation, and church dogma. Many major denominations are in at least the beginning phases of this stage; many of their local churches are far into it.

---

[70] That the abatement of forces producing an organization does not necessarily dissolve it has been demonstrated in analysis of the Townsend movement. Sheldon L. Messinger, "Organizational Transformation: A Case Study of a Declining Social Movement," *American Sociological Review,* 20 (Feb. 1955), 3-10.

[71] David E. Lindstrom, *American Foundations of Religious Liberty* (Champaign, Ill.: Garrard Press, 1950), pp. 93-94.

[72] Charles H. Cooley, *Social Organization* (New York: Charles Scribner's Sons, 1909), pp. 376-77.

5. With overinstitutionalism *disintegration* sets in. "Diseases" of formalism, indifferentism, obsolescence, absolutism, red tape, patronage, and corruption are common symptoms of disintegration.[73] Lack of responsiveness by the institutional machine to the personal and social needs of constituents causes loss of their confidence. Many withdraw into new sects or drift without any formal church connections. Those who nominally continue to embrace the church ignore it in practice, or they conform to its teachings only half-heartedly, supporting it because they feel it is not consistent or logical to change their attitudes even after losing all belief in their value. Leadership with a vested interest in the institution, and followers who are emotionally attached to it, attempt to preserve it. As a result, an internal reform movement may restore the church to a position of vitality and usefulness. However, the church's strength may be gradually sapped by waning membership or by the growth of new sects until complete collapse occurs.[74]

Frequently the death of a Protestant church involves three stages. First, as a result of diminishing financial support, it is vacated by the pastor. Second, finding it difficult to secure a full-time successor, the church secures a part-time pastor either by yoking itself with another church, by hiring a lay minister who has a source of independent income, or by securing a retired or student pastor. The program of the church is attenuated. As a result, membership dwindles, some seeking a more active church. When the relatively inactive church has become so small that attempts to continue seem futile, the third stage is reached: the church "dies" by complete abandonment or by merger into another group.[75]

Of 62 closed rural Pa. churches, 28 per cent had closed for a lack of available membership, although 38 per cent of the latter were in areas of increasing population. At the time of closing they had an average of 28 members and 21 persons attending services. Shifts of population which brought persons of other faiths into the community led to the closing of 22 per cent of the churches. Overchurching, with its accompanying competition for status and survival, was the chief factor in the closing of 13 per cent of them. Congregational disputes, arising most often out of personality clashes, caused 13 per cent to close, and 11 per cent were closed because of unsatisfactory professional leadership. Financial difficulties were the chief cause in 8 per cent, changes in transportation in 3 per cent, and destruction of the church building by fire was the precipitating factor in

---

[73] Edward A. Ross, "The Diseases of Social Structures," *American Journal of Sociology*, 24 (Sept. 1918), 139-58.

[74] Insofar as sects result from weaknesses and failures of churches, the proliferation of sects is a judgment on the churches. (Editorial, "The Judges and the Judged," *Christian Century*, 74 [May 1, 1957], 551-52.)

[75] W. F. Kumlien, *The Social Problem of the Church in South Dakota* (Brookings, S.D.: A. E. S. Bulletin 294, May 1935), pp. 35-36. Cf. Samuel C. Kincheloe, "Behavior Sequence of a Dying Church," *Religious Education*, 24 (April 1929), 329-45.

one church. When the churches were closed by administrative action of denominational agencies, the after-feelings of people in the community were more often harmonious than when the churches closed "on their own." In addition, denominational closing occurred about two decades sooner; members were much more likely to establish connections with another church and continue active religious associations than when the churches had died slowly.[76]

The stage of disintegration is apparent in many churches. Abandoned church buildings are a witness to its past operation. Part-time pastors with meager salaries, poorly attended churches maintained largely by endowment funds, and churches with declining memberships, though located in areas of increasing population, often reflect the process of disintegration.

The five stages in the church's life cycle overlap. Not all religious institutions pass through all five, but a cult tends to arise in the first stage and develop into a sect in the second, a denomination in the third, and a church in the fourth. Reaction sets in at the fifth stage, and reorganization or death of the religious body is the usual result. Many are arrested at one stage or another. Some skip certain stages in a sequence of rapid development. The entire process may be completed in little more than a generation, or it may take hundreds of years for the sect to enter the denominational stage. The process may be reversed; it is not inevitable. It grows out of natural patterns of cause and effect relationships that as yet have been explored only superficially.

As institutions come under increased rational control, the result may be continuous adjusting and adapting rather than progression into the stage of disintegration with its pathological effects.[77] When churches change with the changing conditions of their environments, they may remain in a stage of constant reorganization instead of degenerating pathologically. Social institutions of the past, however, seem to have followed distinct patterns of growth and decline. U. S. religious census data for three periods of time indicate that, from 1890 to 1906, 13.8 per cent of denominations that were listed became defunct compared to 8.8 per cent in 1906-1916, and 15.3 per cent in 1916-1926. These dissolutions and other data suggested to Sorokin that the broad rivers of the great religions flow for a long time, the rivulets of denominations and sects for a short time, and small organizations within a given church appear and disappear even more quickly.[78] Variables apparently related to churches' longevity include the rapidity of the organization's creation and development, its optimum size, the balance of homogeneity and heterogeneity in its membership, its

---

[76] Theodore C. Scheifele and William G. Mather, *Closed Rural Pennsylvania Churches* (State College, Pa.: A. E. S. Bulletin 512, May 1949).

[77] John F. Cuber, "The Measurement and Significance of Institutional Disorganization," *American Journal of Sociology,* 44 (Nov. 1938), 408-14.

[78] Pitirim A. Sorokin, "Life-Span, Age-Composition, and Mortality of Social Organizations," *Mens en Maatschappij,* 9 (Jan. 1933), 69-85.

rigidity and elasticity, its willingness to accept new members, the degree to which members' talents are used, and the environmental forces in operation.[79]

Occasionally entire religious systems die. Of sixteen historical religions which had millions of adherents, only ten survive, and two of these are no longer located in the land of their origin. Some died as a result of violence from outside sources, others as a result of internal decadence.[80] Some that died appear to have been succeeded by religions which bear a new name in a changed social order.

> Doctrines, devitalized institutions, and forms die: but the religion of a people does not die, for our religion, the world over, is just the way we orient ourselves to cosmic realities in the interests of our larger life. A growing religion adjusts itself to the new social order and the new world-view and the old name carries on. So Christianity and Buddhism have, in the past, died that they might live.[81]

Certain self-corrective processes that lead to recuperation in time of disintegration operate in social institutions. Even without the benefit of specific planning, there is a natural, often unconscious, tendency of disintegrating churches to move toward an equilibrium of adjustment.[82] The adjustment may rejuvenate the institution, or it may involve emergence of a new organization out of the ruins of the old. The optimum size of a church's membership in relation to its sub-organizations appears to be a balance between the growth impulse and pressures for integration exerted by the social structure.[83]

Conclusion

Our discussion has minimized psychological theories of the sources of religious bodies, except as they are related to the basic social forces which are our chief concern. Explanations of the medieval Roman Catholic Church as originating in fearful dependence of men in the face of unknown forces, mental conflict due to guilt feelings, and the vicarious satis-

---

[79] *Ibid.*

[80] James Bissett Pratt, "Unsolved Problems: Why Do Religions Die?" *Journal of Religion*, 1 (Jan. 1921), 76-78. Cf. the thirty-five basic reasons identified by Hollis L. Green, *Why Churches Die* (Minneapolis: Bethany Fellowship, 1972).

[81] A. Eustace Haydon, "Why Do Religions Die?—A Reply," *Journal of Religion*, 1 (Mar. 1921), 196. Copyright 1921 by the University of Chicago. Reprinted by permission.

[82] F. Stuart Chapin, "Social Participation and Social Intelligence," *American Sociological Review*, 4 (April 1939), 157-66; and Faith Coxe Bailey, "Dead Churches Live Again," *Moody Monthly*, 59, no. 6 (Feb. 1959), 64-70.

[83] F. Stuart Chapin, "The Optimum Size of Institutions: A Theory of the Large Group," *American Journal of Sociology*, 62 (Mar. 1957), 449-60.

faction of thwarted desires[84] seem barren to the social scientist, for he recognizes the tremendous complexity of social institutions. As we have seen, social conditions of many kinds contribute to the rise, growth, and decline of religious groups. The state of mind that is a major factor in the establishment of new sects and cults is itself traceable to economic, social, political, and ideational conditions in society. Above all, the cultural setting that makes possible the emergence of new religious groups must be emphasized. The voluntary principle of church membership which has dominated church-state relationships, the tremendous streams of immigration that brought people from nearly every culture area of the world, and other conditions associated with national historical development have played a major part in producing the complex pattern of heterogeneous religious groups in the U.S.[85]

The emergence of sects reacting against established churches reminds the latter of their uncritical accommodation to existing social conditions. It emphasizes the importance of individual conviction in religion, and it helps to counterbalance a system of collective dogma and authority which in its extreme institutionalized form is considered evil by most churchmen.[86] That as many new cults are presently being formed as were formed in the past is doubtful despite a much larger population and rapid urbanization. Increasing homogeneity of the population and general economic prosperity hinder the emergence of large numbers of new cults designed to save the universe. The personal needs once focused upon new religious cults may now be focused more often upon socioeconomic reforms led by political parties, labor unions, and various pressure groups.[87]

The factors contributing to the life cycle of emergence, growth, and decline of religious bodies are all interrelated. They can be treated as separate items only in the abstract work of the scholar or scientist. In "real life" they combine with one another to form a complex network of interacting circumstances which operate together to produce new cults and sects. Thus it was not only Father Divine, a charismatic leader, who produced his Kingdom, but Father Divine plus a host of interrelated social forces which made emergence of his cult almost inevitable. Social disorganization, social change, conflict with and within society, race and class distinctions, and migration were all involved in the rise of his cult. Similar social factors are reciprocally involved in the life cycle of every sect and denomination.

---

[84] Daniel Katz and Richard L. Schanck, *Social Psychology* (New York: John Wiley and Sons, 1938), pp. 196-98.

[85] Cf. Sidney E. Mead, "Denominationalism: The Shape of Protestantism in America," *Church History*, 23 (Dec. 1954), 291-320.

[86] H. Richard Niebuhr, "Sects," *Encyclopaedia of the Social Sciences*, 13 (New York: The Macmillan Co., 1934), pp. 624-30.

[87] Albert Lauterbach, *Man, Motives, and Money* (Ithaca, N.Y.: Cornell University Press, 1954), pp. 172-73.

126 TYPES OF CHURCHES

Selected References

Cantril, Hadley, *The Psychology of Social Movements*. Melbourne, Fla.: Krieger, 1973 (New York: Wiley, 1941). Chapters 5 and 6 describe and interpret the rise and growth of Father Divine's "Kingdom" and the Oxford Group.

Chaffee, Grace E., "The Isolated Religious Sect as an Object for Social Research," *American Journal of Sociology*, 35 (Jan. 1930), 618–30. The early stages of the life history of Amana Society.

Clear, Val, "The Church of God: A Study in Social Adaptation," *Review of Religious Research*, 2 (Winter 1961), 129–33. Eight stages of development in the history of the Church of God (Anderson, Ind.) which have transformed it from a protest group (sect) to an accommodation group (denomination).

Eister, Allan W., *Drawing Room Conversion*. Durham, N.C.: Duke University Press, 1950. A sociological account of the Oxford Group Movement using cult-sect distinctions.

Harrison, Paul M., *Authority and Power in the Free Church Tradition*. Princeton, N.J.: Princeton University Press, 1959. A socio-historical analysis of the growth of bureaucracy in the American Baptist Convention which emphasizes types of authority.

Hoge, Dean R., and David A. Roozen, eds., *Understanding Church Growth and Decline 1950–1978*. New York: Pilgrim Press, 1979. Empirical and interpretive studies of factors which influence the growth and decline of Christian churches.

Kelley, Dean M., *Why Conservative Churches are Growing*, rev. ed. New York: Harper and Row, 1977. Evidence to support the thesis that growing churches are strong because they strictly demand a high level of commitment from members (critiqued and tested in Hoge and Roozen, 1979).

Niebuhr, H. Richard, *The Social Sources of Denominationalism*. Magnolia, Mass.: Peter Smith, and many other reprints (New York: Henry Holt, 1929). A seminal interpretation of the emergence, growth, and changes in new religious bodies.

Swatos, William, Jr., *Into Denominationalism: The Anglican Metamorphosis*. Storrs, Conn.: Society for the Scientific Study of Religion, 1979. A study of the transformation of the Church of England from a church to a denomination in England and colonial America.

Towns, Elmer L., *Is the Day of the Denomination Dead?* Nashville: Thomas Nelson, 1973. A Christian college administrator's interpretation of historical and sociological data, including the sociological cycle of church growth.

Treece, James W., Jr., "Theories on Religious Communal Development," *Social Compass*, 18, no. 1 (1971), 85–100. Histories of five religious groups test several theories; confirms the stages of the natural history life cycle.

Whitley, Oliver Read, *Trumpet Call to Reformation*. St. Louis: Bethany Press, 1959. An account of the transformation of the Disciples of Christ from sect to denomination.

Young, Frank W., "Adaptation and Pattern Integration of a California Sect," *Review of Religious Research*, 1, no. 3 (Spring 1960), 137–50. Adjustment of certain California Pentecostal groups as they changed from sect to denomination.

Zablocki, Benjamin, *The Joyful Community: An Account of the Bruderhof*. Chicago: University of Chicago Press, 1980. A study of a communal movement now in its third generation.

Part Four: *Social Functions and Dysfunctions of the Church*

🏛 Chapter **6**

Social Functions of the Church

A major way in which contemporary sociologists study institutions is by analyzing the consequences of their organization and operations. These effects are not limited to what leaders and spokesmen declare them to be. They may believe the institution accomplishes certain goals when investigation would show the true consequences to be greatly different, perhaps even directly contradictory to stated objectives. Study of the broad, persistent effects of social action is labeled "functional analysis."

Functional analysis involves determining the objective consequences, both direct and indirect, of social action. It rests upon recognition that organizational activities have many effects upon the larger social system of which they are a part. This larger system to which the analysis is oriented may be either the total society or a larger institution of which the specific activity or organization is a part. Thus the John Smith family is part of the family as a social institution; actions of its members have consequences for the John Smith family, for the family as a social institution, and for all society. If a patriarchal family system predominates in a given society, the father holds the reins of authority in most of its families. Similarly, the functions of the church are, in the final analysis, the collective effects of what specific churches and their sub-organizations do.

Any social system has certain basic *functional requirements*. These are needs which must be fulfilled if it is to continue to exist. In order for a social system, like the church in general or American society as a whole, to operate, the persons and subgroups which comprise units within the system must learn appropriate patterns of behavior and maintain suitable attitudes. Emotional tensions must be relieved; strained relationships which occur whenever people interact must be resolved in order to carry on effectively the work of the institution or society. Adaptations must be made to the environment either by adjusting to it or controlling it. Essential tasks are shared through a division of labor (role differentiation) which allows specialization of knowledge and duties, and thus presumably increases the average skill of persons and groups in the larger social system. Goals are established by rational, deliberate planning or by gradual accretion of objectives through a selective long-term process of accumulating and developing folkways and mores, rules and regulations. These goals provide guiding principles for allocating scarce resources, distributing tasks among members, and adapting to the environment. The parts of the system also must be integrated effectively. Various social arrangements for settling disputes and for dealing with violations of the norms which regulate the system must be standardized. A hierarchy of authority is developed to make basic decisions; social control devices support this authority so that the group will continue to function as an integrated system of interrelated units. If an institution or society does not solve these problems of pattern maintenance, tension management, adaptation, goal attainment, and integration, it will collapse and disappear as a distinct entity. They are therefore basic functional requirements in any social system.

Functional analysis studies the parts of a social system to determine whether they are contributing to its functional requirements. The parts include subgroups, roles, values, and specific rules or norms that regulate the subgroups and roles. Each of these units may be examined to discover whether some need of the larger system would be unfulfilled, not as well filled, or better filled without this part. If the need would be better filled without it, the part is dysfunctional; otherwise it is functional. *Functions* hence are observable consequences that constructively contribute to adjustment, adaptation, or integration of the society or institution under study. *Dysfunctions* are the consequences that decrease adaptation, stimulate maladjustment, or have disintegrative and destructive results. Some consequences, of course, are hypothetically nonfunctional, contributing neither to adjustment nor maladjustment; and many are mixed, having both positive and negative implications. Some functions and dysfunctions are *manifest* (intended, deliberately sought, and recognized by participants), while others are *latent* (unintended, unanticipated, concealed, or not recognized).

Functional analysis in its strictest sense determines consequences of the parts of a social system for the larger system, especially society as a whole, but it also includes study of the extent to which goals of the sub-system are achieved. To analyze *goal achievement* it is necessary to specify the explicit and implicit purposes, intentions, or goals and to determine whether or not the social structure and action actually achieve them. American society and most of its churches share the principle that institutions, organizations, and even society itself exist for the welfare of individuals. Assessment of goal attainment in American institutions must therefore include determination of whether indeed the common welfare and the welfare of persons is served by the institution. Functional analysis of the American church therefore studies the functional and dysfunctional effects of church-related activities, norms, roles, subgroups, organizational patterns, etc. for American society, for the church in general, for the specific church of which the activities, roles, etc. are a part, and for persons affected by them. An item that is functional for one of these may be dysfunctional for another; consequently functional analysis is complex and difficult.[1]

Intentions, deeds, and consequences are interwoven in a complex mass of organization and procedure. Part of the sociologist's task is to unravel these in order to determine the effects of specific units in the social system. The three chief methods used in arriving at knowledge concerning functional and dysfunctional contributions of the parts to the social system include (1) the mental experiment of "thinking away" the part and judging what would happen to the larger system if it were absent, (2) comparison of social systems which are similar to each other except for differences in the part one is analyzing, and (3) analysis of deviations which occur when normal social patterns are disrupted. The emphasis in functional analysis is thus upon *effects,* but these can be interpreted properly only in relation to the other aspects of the system.

A major contribution of sociology to the understanding of social life is its revelation of effects of social structures and actions which are not easily perceived by institutional leaders. These latent consequences may occur in areas of social life remote from the leaders, may have delayed results which differ from those that are obvious and immediate, or may be discernible only through special procedures of observation not used by the leaders. Latent functions must therefore receive special attention from the social scientist; he helps make latent effects of social action become manifest; latent and manifest are relative rather than absolute concepts. As a result of functional analysis, proposals for change can rest upon a realistic appraisal that sees beyond immediate consequences to long range implications of the patterns of social structure and action.[2]

---

[1] Robert K. Merton, *Social Theory and Social Structure,* rev. ed. (Glencoe, Ill.: The Free Press, 1957), pp. 21-84; and Harry C. Bredemeier, "The Methodology of Functionalism," *American Sociological Review,* 20 (Apr. 1955), 173-80.
[2] In this introduction to functional analysis of the church I have drawn most heavily upon Merton, *Social Theory and Social Structure,* and Harry M. Johnson, *Sociology: A Systematic Introduction* (New York: Harcourt, Brace and Co., 1960),

This chapter is concerned primarily with social functions of the church for American society as a whole. Attention is hence devoted less to what the church does to and for itself than to its influence upon the entire social order. Yet the impact of the units of church structure and action upon the church itself is a portion of such effects, for the church is a part of society. In addition, the church's functions and dysfunctions cannot be dealt with in isolation from other institutions in its society. While its main emphasis is upon activities and goals conventionally designated as "religious," it has many social functions which in and of themselves might be considered more pertinent to other institutions. This is true in spite of the fact that American society is "secular" in the sense that most of its institutions and practices are organically separate from the church. Except for the church-related educational system, nearly all schools are independent of direct church control. Law, government, business, art, science, social welfare, and even the family operate independently of the church. Non-religious scientific rules are applied as a basis of evaluation in several areas once traditionally considered to be within the church's sphere of privilege. Philosophy and the humanities have been secularized so that religious considerations are not a dominant concern, and church-dictated postulates are not accepted as their basis. Laws dealing with marriage, divorce, parental responsibilities, and education are based upon secular rather than religious considerations. Church membership is voluntary, with free competition between the churches. Tension between the domains of the church and of secular society creates a shifting religious-secular equilibrium analogous to that of the political parties in a bipartisan political system.[3]

Yet, in spite of this formal separation of the American church from the

pp. 48-79. Johnson's survey of structural-functional sociology is based upon the theoretical and empirical work of Parsons, Weber, Bales, Shils, Levy, Homans, and others.

The traditional anthropological interpretations of "functionalism" developed by Radcliffe-Brown, Malinowski, and Kluckhohn are somewhat narrower than the one presented here. They emphasize functional consequences of every institutional part and practice to the integration or functional unity of society as a whole or to the continuity and existence of society more than to the adjustment of individuals and the satisfaction of their needs. They have postulated that only those cultural forms which constitute some vital adjustive or adaptive response survive.

Later functional interpretations of religion by Goode, Hoult, Yinger, and others include broader interpretations which recognize functions for society, for religious and other institutions, and for individual persons. They are based upon a century of theoretical development. Cf. J. Milton Yinger, "The Influence of Anthropology on Sociological Theories of Religion," *American Anthropologist*, 60 (June 1958), 487-96.

Functional analysis is so broad and diverse that it has been referred to as little more nor less than sociological analysis itself. Cf. Kingsley Davis, "The Myth of Functional Analysis as a Special Method in Sociology and Anthropology," *American Sociological Review*, 24 (Dec. 1959), 757-72.

[3] Talcott Parsons, "Réflexions sur les Organisations Religieuses aux États-Unis,' *Archives de Sociologie des Religions*, 2, no. 3 (Jan.-June 1957), pp. 21-36.

rest of society, its functions are interrelated with those of all other institutions. In one sense all of the church's functions are social, just as in another they are all religious (Chapters 3 and 7). They are social in origin, for they are based upon the interrelationships and interaction of human beings, and they are social in effects. Certain church activities which are of particular importance to the total society are presented in this chapter.

The Church as an Agent of Socialization

"Socialization" refers to the entire process wherein a person acquires the culture patterns of the society in which he is reared and learns to conform to its standards, traditions, folkways, and mores. It includes learning how to get along with other people, making the aims and goals of the group his own, and discovering how to adjust in the give-and-take aspect of life. This process takes place chiefly within the family, play group, and school, but the church also helps socialize a large proportion of the population through its teaching and character-forming influence. It thus contributes to the on-going operation and integration of the total society.

The church provides an organized group background that aids in the social development of those who are "brought up in the church." It gives opportunity to learn and perform certain social roles and to relate them to the roles of others within its framework. It charts an ideal course of life which guides many persons. The personalities and character of many Americans have been influenced by self-conceptions fostered and nourished in the church and by definitions of social situations provided by it. Rewards and punishments are offered by the church to sanction various types of behavior. Outlets for social frustrations and psychological tensions are provided by it. These devices help to mold personalities into conformity with, or occasionally violation of, cultural values and patterns. Each person is taught obligations to institutionalized functionaries; thus he is taught in Sunday school to obey his parents and to keep the laws of his land. He is given reference groups after which to pattern his behavior and others to which he "must not be conformed." His self-identification as a Christian, Jew, Catholic, or Baptist is thus a product of both deliberate and unplanned influences in the church. His religious orientation has a direct bearing upon his roles as a member of society.

The need a person feels for religion and the kind of religion he feels he "needs" are closely related to the extent and nature of religious influences in his upbringing.[4] As the person grows toward maturity, his aspirations

---

[4] Gordon Allport, James Gillespie, and Jacqueline Young, "The Religion of the Post-War College Student," *The Journal of Psychology*, 25 (Jan. 1948), 3-33.

for the future are influenced by his religious orientation. Jewish adolescents, for instance, have a greater tendency than Protestants and Catholics to be long range planners.[5] Thus both religious and secular aspects of life are clearly influenced by socialization in the church.

Although churches deliberately conduct character-training programs, they do not always attain the goals of these programs. The moral values they uphold are sometimes violated. Practical implications of their messages are frequently not clarified. As a result, a 1956 national survey revealed that three-fourths of youths ages 17–22 believed the church had failed to help them solve the problems of adult life. Perhaps because of such opinions, only 25 per cent of teenagers in 1979 had a great deal of confidence in organized religion and 31 per cent quite a lot, compared to 40 and 25 per cent of adults.[6]

The Church as a Status-Giving Agency

Social identification is provided sect members through their religion, as we saw in Chapter 5. The social position or standing of many others in society also reflects their church affiliation. In certain communities a political candidate has almost no chance of being elected to public office unless he is a member of the "right" religious body, be it Baptist, Mormon, Jewish, Catholic, or some other. One criterion by which others identify one as of high or low status is his religion. The church becomes a reference group for its members. It enables others to identify them in terms of social class, ethnic, or other criteria besides religious values. All these factors are important to achievement and interaction in the larger societal structure. One's relative status within a church also is connected with his status in the total community structure and in society. Each reflects the other. The chairman of the board of a city's largest Protestant church is given that position partly by virtue of his status in other institutions. Having that position in turn makes it more likely that additional prestigious leadership roles in the community will be assigned to him. Numerous studies have found a close relationship between religious affiliation and the general social class structure of a community.

The generalized status of the person is also affected by the long range impact of the church's message. Christianity was a powerful influence changing the social status of the child when it denunciated the exposure of infants and established foundling asylums as one of its earliest formal

---

[5] Orville G. Brim, Jr., and Raymond Forer, "A Note on the Relation of Values and Social Structure to Life Planning," *Sociometry,* 19 (Mar. 1956), 54-60. Initial differences observed between Protestants and Catholics were not statistically significant after socioeconomic status was controlled. Lower class persons are less likely to be long range planners.

[6] Jack Stewart, "Are the Churches Failing Our Young People?" *This Week* (Oct. 21, 1956), 33-35; Princeton Religion Research Center, *Religion in America 1979–80* (Princeton, N.J.: The Gallup Poll, n. d.), pp. 22, 66–67.

welfare activities. The religious basis for protecting the interests of the child prepared the way for the moral and social basis that now predominates.[7]

Emphasis upon the sanctity of the individual in western nations stems partly from Judeo-Christian values which hold that every soul is precious in the sight of God and from the Protestant doctrine of the priesthood of the believer.[8] However, it is also true that many churches have retarded the movement toward equalization of the sexes by their insistence upon male superiority. In lowering the rights of women, they also lowered the respect accorded to them.[9] Both the general status of certain categories of people and the status of specific persons in society are thus influenced by the church. Further discussion of its functional effects for individual status appears in Chapters 15 and 17.

The Church Provides Social Fellowship

Contemporary church leaders deliberately use the desire for intimate face-to-face interaction with others of similar interests as a means of evangelism and of increasing church membership. Most Americans like "friendly" organizations; they wish to be recognized as individual persons and not as mere functionaries that serve as minor cogs in a huge machine. When these desires are not satisfied in other institutions, people may turn to the church. The most rapidly growing churches appear to be those providing the most opportunity for informal social fellowship among members.

Public worship involves fellowship; few people can get the full benefit of a service of public worship through radio or television. The evangelistic nature of Christianity encourages the social interaction involved in the process of sharing the blessings of religious experience. The appeal of Moral Re-Armament comes largely from its emphasis upon sharing personal confessions and the resulting catharsis for both the confessor and confessee. The old fashioned testimony meeting and intimate prayer meeting, still prominent in certain denominations, gain much of their appeal from the same desire to share joy and sorrow, bane and blessing, pain and pleasure. "Extending the right hand of fellowship" is a ritual of many churches by which new members are formally welcomed into the recognized community of believers.

As society becomes increasingly secularized, the demands of people for primary group relationships may be met increasingly in and by the

---

[7] Cecil C. North, *Social Differentiation* (Chapel Hill: University of North Carolina Press, 1926), p. 67.

[8] A. D. Lindsay, "Individualism," *Encyclopaedia of the Social Sciences,* 7 (New York: The Macmillan Co., 1932), pp. 674-80.

[9] North, *Social Differentiation,* pp. 99-103.

church and its organizations.[10] This may indeed be a core function of the contemporary American church.[11] This gregarious appeal is not new; it appears in the New Testament. Jesus promised that whenever two or three are gathered together in His name and agree about what they ask of God, it will be done (Mat. 18:19-20). The Apostle Paul told Christian converts to regard themselves as members of the body of Christ, thus mystically symbolizing the fellowship of faith, the cooperative inter-dependencies of all Christians, and their mutual problems, accomplishments, and aspirations (Rom. 12:3-8; I Cor. 12, and Eph. 2:11-22). A major function the twentieth-century church provides society and individuals is this *koinonia* or fellowship. Scattered references to it appear throughout this book.

The Church Promotes Social Solidarity

Religion simultaneously creates and expresses the unity of primitive society and many modern groups.[12] Doctrinal differences, though they tend to divide groups from one another, tend to unite the members within each; religious doctrine is at the same time positive, integrating, or cohesive and negative, disintegrating, or destructive. Worship similarly divides, but its chief sociological function is to form, integrate, and develop religious groups of all who share in it, for it tends to bind together and unite those who share the same central experience. This includes the sharing of theological concepts as well as social activities.[13]

Some of the most persistent and cohesive groups have grown out of religion. Common faith, a common set of values, common worship, common efforts to propagate or perpetuate the faith, common sentiments, and common religious experiences—especially if accompanied by persecution or opposition—have bound believers together into clans, cults, sects, utopian societies, and other groups that vary in size from two members, comprising one sect discovered in a sociological survey, to millions that are members of the major world religions. These groups may become the rallying point for their members; sometimes they have been identified with political, class, racial, or economic interests more than

[10] Empirical evidence is given in David O. Moberg, "Die Säkularisierung und das Wachstum der Kirchen in den Vereinigten Staaten," *Kölner Zeitschrift für Soziologie und Sozialpsychologie,* 10, no. 3 (1958), 430-38.

[11] Wayland F. Vaughan, *Social Psychology* (New York: Odyssey Press, 1948), pp. 845-46; and Wesner Fallaw, *Toward Spiritual Security* (Philadelphia: Westminster Press, 1952). Fallaw believes the clue to a revitalized church lies in making it an intimate primary group fellowship; he suggests why and how this may be done.

[12] Goode, *Religion Among the Primitives,* esp. p. 223.

[13] Joachim Wach, *Sociology of Religion* (Chicago: University of Chicago Press, 1944), pp. 34-44; and Heinrich H. Maurer, "Consciousness of Kind of a Fundamentalist Group," *American Journal of Sociology,* 31 (Jan. 1926), 485-506.

with their religious functions.[14] For example, during the frontier era in Utah, Mormon religious institutions often held people to their community when physical conditions made it very difficult to remain.[15] The only utopian communities that have long survived are those with a religious base. Religion is a basic source of social solidarity in many family, nationality, and status groups in rural communities, especially at the neighborhood level.[16] The black church has been a major integrative force among a people shorn of their cultural heritage and suffering discrimination in an alien society. The spontaneity, expressiveness, excitement, rhythm, interest in the dramatic, and love of magic apparent in much black religion provide emotional release and escape, but they also mold the group together into an integral whole.[17]

The church may contribute to even wider societal cohesion. Christianity has had a significant bearing upon the unification of the West. During the middle ages the relative universality of Christianity and strength of Roman Catholicism helped break down localisms and enlarge the groups of those who were at peace with one another. As Jews transcended the ethnocentrism of their Palestinian background, Judaism may have been even more powerful in this respect. As a result, Jews have been abhorred and persecuted by authoritarian, nationalistic states in all ages.[18]

The religion of a culture or subculture tends to support emotional patterns that exist in believers and disbelievers alike, no matter how little credence is given to the dogmas of the religion. Anxieties and hostilities related to the whole system of self-validation and social control, the criteria of success in the society, the virtues that are praised and the vices condemned, are all significantly related to religion as a socially cohesive force[19] American religion thus tends to undergird and reinforce the values necessary for successful functioning of all institutions in society, as we note in greater detail elsewhere. It does so both as a direct participant in community programs and as an influence over church members, encouraging them to practice their religion in all circumstances of life. It sanctions the democratic form of government. It supports contracts, property rights, and legal procedures. The blessing of God is invoked upon Congress and other legislative bodies. Semi-religious oaths are used

---

[14] J. O. Hertzler, "Religious Institutions," *Annals of the American Academy of Political and Social Science,* 256 (Mar. 1948), 7-19.

[15] Lowry Nelson, *The Mormon Village* (Salt Lake City: University of Utah Press, 1952), Chapter 14, "Religion as a Stabilizing Force on the Frontier."

[16] Louis Bultena, "Rural and Community Integration," *Rural Sociology,* 9 (Sept. 1944), 257-64; and Harold Hoffsommer, "The Relation of the Rural Church to Other Rural Organizations," *Social Forces,* 20 (Dec. 1941), 224-32.

[17] E. T. Krueger, "Negro Religious Expression," *American Journal of Sociology,* 38 (Jul. 1932), 22-31.

[18] Constantine Panunzio, *Major Social Institutions* (New York: The Macmillan Co., 1939), p. 319.

[19] Abram Kardiner, *The Psychological Frontiers of Society* (New York: Columbia University Press, 1945), pp. 410-11.

to swear the President, jury members, and others into office. Education is encouraged by most churches. Religion is brought into nearly every major phase of the family cycle. Much recreation, art, and philanthropy bear the imprint of religious influences in their historical development. The Christian emphasis upon work as a vocation to which one is called by God gives religious sanction to economic enterprises. Many secular institutions have emerged from the church, which earlier performed their functions, and all of the basic ones are to a high degree supported and sanctioned by religious and ethical principles it expounds.

Dependence upon supernatural or nonnatural powers is clarified and strengthened in much religious activity. This dependence is so significant in man's religious behavior that it has been used as the basis for defining religion itself.[20] This shared dependence, a major source of group integration, is strengthened by religious rituals. The Catholic modernist who no longer believes in the truth of the Roman Catholic articles of faith can continue to receive a "religious thrill" through participation in the Mass. The Protestant liberal, by contrast, who through the same exercise of reason and application of the scientific method to the study of religion has lost faith in the doctrines of his church, lacks the ritual to hold him to it and is likely to drop out of it entirely instead of continuing participation with a reinterpreted content of belief. Thus ritual is a strong conserving force binding the members of a religious system together firmly, even when they have widely divergent normative orientations toward the basic beliefs of which the ritual is a mechanical support.[21] Ritual often includes the teaching of sacrifice, thus psychologically processing people for the sacrifices demanded by community living.[22]

The religious system provides a significant framework for handling fundamental problems of social organization—reducing uncertainty and anxiety, increasing coherence of human relationships, assigning meaning to human endeavor, and providing justification for moral obligation. Solutions to the problems of social organization which are symbolic and rest upon nonempirical foundations are essential for the existence of human society.[23]

The Church as a Social Stabilizer

Together with other institutions, the church usually helps to conserve values and practices that have been found beneficial through trial and

20 John R. Everett, *Religion in Human Experience* (London: George Allen and Unwin, Ltd., 1952), pp. 42-43.

21 Luther S. Cressman, "Ritual the Conserver," *American Journal of Sociology*, 35 (Jan. 1930), 564-72.

22 Jessie Bernard, *American Community Behavior* (New York: Dryden Press, 1949), p. 125.

23 Raymond Firth, *Elements of Social Organization* (London: Watts and Co., 1951), p. 250.

error experience. Its sustaining and reinforcing work is most evident in its role as an agency of social control, as an educational institution, as an upholder and modifier of ethical principles, and as an integrating, sanctioning, and vindicating agency that helps sustain other institutions.

Religious faith, or a substitute quasi-religion like intense nationalism or communism, provides man with a transcendent interpretation of life that sustains and undergirds his existence in society. Traditional religion fails to do this effectively when it insists upon the use of outmoded and technical language that is unintelligible to the uninitiated, when it abdicates to other "theologies" that are louder, more glamorous, or more consistent with contemporary cultural conditions than its own, or when it becomes so identified with society that it speaks as its defender rather than as a representative of higher loyalties. Even the church's criticisms of society are an aspect of its stabilizing influence, for in its reformative efforts, it helps to modify existing practices gradually, so that they will remain viable and not need replacement through revolutionary change. The church tends to be neither completely conservative nor radically in favor of eliminating the status quo; it is rather a "profound appreciator of the world's value, as revealed to it through the eyes of its faith, against shallowness and despair."[24] At best it transcends sharp divisions between conservative and liberal, reactionary and radical, preserver and reformer of society by its orientation toward God and overall values higher than the myopic viewpoints of those selfishly engaged in partisan strife. It thus operates as both a critic and a sustainer of culture, fostering what it considers to be worthy values in the social order. It may be viewed sometimes as radical because of its efforts to modify society and sometimes as conservative because of its efforts to retain elements in it. During certain periods of history one or the other of these functions clearly predominates, but in both cases the church acts to preserve that which it considers to be good.[25]

Even in America where there is such heterogeneity of religious beliefs and practices, religion helps stabilize society. Collective activities of churches reaffirm the ultimate values and solidarity of society or of segments of the social order that are allied with them in competitive struggles.[26] When they affirm values related to the status quo, churches prevent the challenge to society's goals which is essential if they are to be the prophetic "conscience of society." By uncritically approving the values which are relative in time and place, some churches indirectly promote the very sins they nominally condemn.[27] The struggle for consistency in

---

[24] Robert Lynn, Kenneth Underwood, and associates, "Christian Faith and the Protestant Churches," *Social Action*, 18, no. 6 (May 1952), p. 39.

[25] *Ibid.*, pp. 34-40.

[26] Logan Wilson and William L. Kolb, *Sociological Analysis* (New York: Harcourt, Brace and Co., 1949), p. 651.

[27] James Luther Adams, "Religion and the Ideologies," *Confluence*, 4 (Apr. 1955), 72-84.

the culture as a whole leads to an inconsistency within churches that is "explained" away by rationalizations that leaders provide the faithful.

Dissenting sects and cults that work for the disruption or drastic change of society provide emotional release for the dissatisfied and thus serve as a safety valve that helps preserve the very society they are trying to revolutionize. The stabilizing effects of organized religion are considered by many functionalists to be the basic topic for functional analysis. Thus Hoult states that "sociologically considered, the most important common denominator of all religion, regardless of time or culture, is its attempt to sanctify behaviors and beliefs associated with the most permanent survival, materially or spiritually conceived." [28] Nevertheless, there are times when the church becomes a source of social instability. This usually occurs during periods of drastic change or revolution for the culture as a whole, or in times of intense competition between religious bodies struggling for power. Churches generally promote societal stability, but whenever they cause strife or play a prophetic role in society, they encourage change.

The church's integrative function in society is at a maximum when it is itself integrated and united, not divided by numerous schismatic, non-cooperating sects. It operates most effectively when social change, mobility, and differentiation are at their lowest levels. When outside pressures produce divisions in society and when the established social and psychological expectancies of people are frustrated, the church is less likely to have a manifest integrating effect.[29]

The Church as an Agent of Social Control

The church's regulation of human behavior has been so significant that some have considered *the* function of religion to be control of the environment or the provision of a theory of environmental control.[30] Although such a monolithic view is unjustifiable, one major social function of religion is that of teaching, persuading, and compelling individuals to conform to the usages and life-values of the group. The Judeo-Christian concept of God as a just, all-powerful Being interested in man's welfare because of His love has contributed to a search for truth and righteousness by the believer.[31]

The church controls the training of its leaders and members; its in-

[28] Thomas F. Hoult, "A Functional Theory of Religion," *Sociology and Social Research,* 41 (Mar.-Apr. 1957), 277-79.

[29] J. Milton Yinger, *Religion, Society and the Individual* (New York: The Macmillan Co., 1957), pp. 60-72.

[30] E.g., L. L. Bernard, *Social Control in Its Sociological Aspects* (New York: The Macmillan Co., 1939), p. 474.

[31] Alvin Good in Joseph S. Roucek et al., *Social Control* (New York: D. Van Nostrand Co., 1947), p. 107.

direct influence is also apparent in public schools. In a sample of school teachers from 232 communities in 34 states about 10 per cent reported pressures to attend Sunday school, 9 per cent to teach, and 10 per cent to participate in other church activities.[32]

Control by the church over physical and mental health is not limited to primitive religion with its medicine men and magicians. Most American churches encourage members to use modern medical services, but a few teach that this is sinful and that the ill ought to turn instead solely to God through a faith healer or religious practitioner. Many support medical institutions, especially in foreign lands where they are used in evangelistic proselyting. Churches often influence attitudes toward alcohol, tobacco, certain types of food, and cosmetics. They provide therapeutic and preventive treatment for mental illness and sponsor health-conducive recreational and social activities. Their controlling effect on the family and government is discussed in Chapter 14. They have played an active role in such political and economic issues as child labor, women's rights, wage-hour legislation, and social security. That this role has not been unified and consistent does not refute the fact that the church is an agency of social control in politics and economics.

The church conserves moral and ethical values (Chapter 7). Social obligations are made religious obligations; religion thus becomes a societal brake, especially in times of stress, conflict, uncertainty, and crisis. Its theology becomes a weapon used during political upheaval. By resisting change it protects the cultural heritage, but it sometimes becomes a tool that is used by exploiting classes to make people content and obedient.[33]

Social control techniques used by the church cover the entire range of methods used by institutions. The appeals are both inhibitory and positive. The former emphasize fear—fear of personal torment in Hell, loss of salvation, excommunication, retribution for wrong-doing by God or His representatives. Positive appeals predominate in American churches. Love of God as the heavenly Father and love of other believers and of mankind as a whole are major themes in church ritual, prayers, hymnology, and scriptures. The Christian faith offers a solace for believers' oppression, worldly limitations, and inferiorities. Its teaching of Christ's vicarious atonement offers a ready opportunity for placing on another one's sense of guilt and worthlessness, letting the sinner go morally free without closing his eyes to his sinfulness. Church opportunities for

---

[32] Mary Lichliter, "Social Obligations and Restrictions on Teachers," *School Review,* 54 (Jan. 1946), 14-23.

[33] An excellent portrayal of the manner in which and the bureaucratic leadership through which social control was exercised by the medieval church is given in Daniel Katz and Richard L. Schank, "The Roman Church of the Middle Ages as an Example of an Institution," *Social Psychology* (New York: John Wiley and Sons, 1938), pp. 196-210.

sociability in the brotherhood of faith have a positive control effect upon many.[34]

One of the most famous instruments of control used by the Roman Catholic Church has been its *Index Librorum Prohibitorum,* first issued in 1559 and revised periodically. It is an illustrative list of publications condemned by the Church. The 1948 issue listed 4,126 works, including publications by Comte, Descartes, Rousseau, Voltaire, and John Stuart Mill. About nine-tenths of the prohibited books deal with theology, dogma, ritual, or church history. The rate of additions to the *Index* apparently is slowing: 1,354 works were condemned in the nineteenth century, but only 255 in the first half of the twentieth. Rapid improvements in communication may have made the Church's control more difficult than in the past.[35] To what extent the *Index* has limited the expression of American scholars is unknown. Christian Scientists and many Protestant groups occasionally have had effective programs of censorship. Parochial schools and Christian day schools represent current efforts to shelter children from facts and theories that might stimulate thinking along non-approved religious, scientific, or intellectual lines. Such religious isolationism is a form of attempted censorship. Efforts to censor movies, television, magazines, books, and other media of mass communications are common among Protestants as well as Catholics. The Catholic Legion of Decency is perhaps the best-known agency involved in these activities.[36]

Many religious rituals serve as social control instruments. Their concern with man's situation symbolically asserts dominant attitudes. Thus the religious funeral emphasizes the importance of living in terms of the church's value system and often indirectly appeals to the authority of the deceased over survivors by indicating, "This is what he would have wished." [37] Closed communion, practiced especially in some small Protestant groups, honors believers and identifies them with one another and the church. It helps prevent acts which would exclude members from the communion service. The religious wedding ceremony is sometimes refused persons who are not church members, have been divorced, or have shown some defect of character; it hence is a means of social control. Dedication of infants and baptism likewise serve in varying degree as techniques of control over those who value them, while confession and penance release tensions and reduce friction between persons and groups, thus contributing to order in society.

---

34 Floyd H. Allport, *Social Psychology* (Boston: Houghton Mifflin Co., 1924), pp. 404-7.

35 William Albig, *Modern Public Opinion* (New York: McGraw-Hill Book Co., 1956), pp. 246-51. Publication of the *Index* was discontinued in 1966.

36 On control of movies by religious organizations, see Ruth A. Inglis, *Freedom of the Movies* (Chicago: University of Chicago Press, 1947), esp. pp. 120-25.

37 Talcott Parsons, *The Social System* (Glencoe, Ill.: The Free Press, 1951), p. 304; and Bernard, *Social Control,* pp. 468-69.

Published literature of the church often is used to publicize its desires for members' conduct. Radio and television, pastoral counseling, sermons, retreats, camps, and the entire educational program are oriented toward social control, directing members how to behave in varying types of situations. The ethical and moral codes of society are thus given religious sanction.

The power of excommunication is a potential means of control used over secular as well as ecclesiastical leaders by Roman Catholic and Greek Orthodox churches even in recent history.[38] Most Protestant church constitutions provide for the exclusion of members who violate their Christian obligations, do not attend or financially support the church, and fail to repent after attempts to restore them to the "path of Christian duty." Denominations can revoke ordination vows of ministers. Thus in 1955 the Northwest Synod of the United Lutheran Church held a formal heresy trial for the Rev. George Crist, Jr., and suspended him from the ministry.[39] Churches also have served as courts of law for their communities. In colonial America established churches exercised jurisdiction of a quasi-legal type on the basis of I Cor. 6:1-6.[40] Modern legal institutions and many of the laws related to ethics and morals which they uphold are closely linked with religion.[41]

Persecution, even to the extent of martyrdom, has been used both by and against the church. A sense of solidarity develops among the persecuted, making them even more zealous in their propagation of "the truth." "The blood of the martyrs is the seed of the church." Martyrs in early Christianity were able to meet the crisis of dying for their faith largely because they were members of societies with effective social bonds; the group had control over the martyrs; the martyrs in turn influenced the group.[42] Some contemporary American missionaries and their converts have faced similar experiences.

Organized religion also controls individual and group behavior by magical attempts to manipulate the supernatural for the detection and punishment of offenses against the mores. Canonization of saints in Catholicism and other religions stimulates some persons to live so they, too, may be canonized. Spirit possession, supernatural visions, and taboos have been used as control mechanisms. Even belief in the omnipresence and omniscience of God controls conduct, for the believer's conscience convinces

---

[38] President Perón of Argentina was excommunicated in 1955. Another striking case is described in Panunzio, *Major Social Institutions,* pp. 463-64.

[39] "Lutheran Heresy," *Time,* 66, no. 6 (Aug. 8, 1955), 62-63.

[40] Emil Oberholzer, Jr., *Delinquent Saints: Disciplinary Action in the Early Congregational Churches of Massachusetts* (New York: Columbia University Press, 1956), pp. 200-15.

[41] Nicholas S. Timasheff, *An Introduction to the Sociology of Law* (Cambridge: Harvard University Committee on Research in the Social Sciences, 1939), *passim.*

[42] Donald W. Riddle, *The Martyrs: A Study in Social Control* (Chicago: University of Chicago Press, 1931).

him of the rightness and wrongness of certain types of contemplated behavior.[43]

Control over the individual is effected by the contemporary church chiefly through the internalization of values. Cultural emphases and religious norms are so incorporated into the minds of persons that the controls, when effective, operate from internal desires, interests, and attitudes, rather than by external pressures and constraints. Members of society perhaps are less anxiety-ridden and less filled with mutual hostility and distrust when such controls operate than when control is largely a function of the police.[44] When the perspectives of a reference group are so much a part of an individual that he acts "of his own free will," social controls are more likely to operate effectively than when he is under compulsion to act in accord with external pressures contrary to his inward desires.

The effectiveness of the social control of the church varies with many conditions. Obviously, the extent to which adherents accept its teachings as valid and authoritative is a determinant of the degree to which they will follow its precepts. If they believe that religious teachings and practices are absolute truth, the authoritative revelation of God's will, behavior is much more likely to be in accord with them than if they doubt whether there is a God and are convinced that, even if there is, He would not have revealed His will in the conventionally accepted manner.

The church's relationship to other institutions is also a significant determinant of its power as an agent of social control. When it cooperates with political authority, as in the case of a State Church, each institution reinforces the other. Even under American separation of church and state, they cooperate to control such problems as divorce, each using its own methods. Each may control activities the other ignores, or one may sanction activities prohibited by the other, as in the case of certain conscientious objectors who refuse for religious reasons to serve in the armed forces. Social, economic, and political conditions make church controls operate more effectively at some times than at others. Religious controls may be especially strong in times of conflict, uncertainty, and crisis.[45] When a church is arrayed against other institutions, it can do much less than when all the forces in society are consistent with each other. When it is identified with decadent elements of society, it tends to lose its influence if a revolution occurs, its effectiveness as a control agency waning until it becomes impotent.

Most observers agree that there has been a trend away from social control appeals to the absolute, ultimate values epitomized in supernatu-

---

[43] Bernard, *Social Control*, pp. 451-79.
[44] Kardiner, *The Psychological Frontiers of Society*, p. 416.
[45] Panunzio, *Major Social Institutions*, p. 318.

ralistic religion, and toward appeals to social and temporal values. This has encouraged many to turn away from religion to science as the basic source of moral and ethical values.[46] Explanations of the universe have shifted from eternal verities to naturalistic determinisms; people have increasingly devalued religious controls over their mundane lives. Some even hold that scientism is the religion of the present generation and that science is the "sacred cow" at whose shrine men worship.[47]

The typical Protestant church no longer has sufficient authority to dictate specific rules of conduct or even to enforce outward virtue on men who are inwardly self-seeking. It succeeds or fails as a control agent largely in relation to the degree to which it changes inward attitudes and desires. More than in the past, each person must determine his own pattern of conduct. Hence there is confusion and disagreement in Christian circles about various issues of social morality.[48] Some believe, for instance, that a form of socialism is the only answer to social injustices; others believe with the libertarians that the less governmental action there is, the more Christian society will be.

The church's control is especially strong over the believer who is committed to religious faith by active membership. It also extends far beyond these believers through its indirect effects and influences the lives of everyone in society. While such indirect influence is manifestly less today than in medieval Europe, it is a gross error to assume that it is completely absent. Various aspects and illustrations of social control may be found in nearly every chapter of this book.

The Church as an Agent of Social Reform

Even though reform movements have gradually lost their religious associations, Christianity has paved the way for much social progress. The religious attitude has helped people identify themselves with each other and thus meet their own needs.[49] It has contributed to many social reform movements, as we shall see in later chapters. Yet in all honesty we must recognize that the churches have seldom taken a united stand on social issues. Some struggled against others in persistent efforts to maintain the institution of slavery, keep women subordinate, sustain privileges of propertied classes to the detriment of laborers, maintain severe retributive

---

[46] Paul H. Landis, *Social Control* (Chicago: J. B. Lippincott Co., 1939), pp. 250-51; and Bernard, *Social Control,* pp. 473-78.

[47] Anthony Standen, *Science is a Sacred Cow* (New York: E. P. Dutton Co., 1950).

[48] John M. Clark, *Social Control of Business,* second ed. (New York: McGraw-Hill Book Co., 1939), pp. 233-34.

[49] George H. Mead, *Mind, Self and Society* (Chicago: University of Chicago Press, 1934), pp. 275, 289-98.

punishment of prisoners, and uphold war. Christians today are similarly divided on many social issues. Some, supporting or rationalizing their viewpoints by appeals to the Christian scriptures, strive to maintain racial segregation while others oppose it; some are socialists and others libertarians; some are pro-capital and others pro-labor; some are strongly nationalistic and others world-minded; some support strong armed force while others are pacifists. The majority of Christians, falling somewhere between these extremes, perhaps are influenced more by the church and its teachings than are those who have already taken a dogmatic stand.

Theological interpretations of the church's social action typically view reforms as an outgrowth of ideological change. The church is seen as the specialized means through which God comes into an intellectual and spiritual relationship with man. This relationship leads to reform both as an explicit part of the church program and as a natural outgrowth of the development of man-God relationships.[50] This interpretation appears superficially to contradict the sanctifying function of the church which helps preserve the status quo, making certain aspects of it holy, and causing resistance to change. Insofar as selectivity is involved in both its reforming and stabilizing work, the combination of resistance to and encouragement of change can be highly functional for society, the individual, and the church. The complex relationship of the church to social reform is perhaps best seen in the social gospel movement.

The social gospel movement was the best articulated effort at social reform in the history of American Protestantism.[51] It "marked the emancipation of the Protestant denominations from the religious individualism that was the natural accompaniment of the pioneer period into a social consciousness that was required by an industrial society." [52] It arose in the post-Civil War period and reached its peak in the decade 1907-1917. It resulted from the problems associated with a rapidly changing society and from a growing recognition by Christians that the evils incidental to these changes had to be met by a gospel involving something more than simply individual repentance and salvation. This "something more" was defined by one of its leaders, Shailer Mathews, as the application of Jesus' teachings and the message of salvation to society, economic life, and social institutions as well as to individuals.[53] Although the movement grew out of contemporary social, economic, and political conditions, it

---

[50] Roy C. Buck, "The Contribution of the Church to the Total Community," *Town and Country Church,* 138 (Dec. 1958), 5-7.

[51] Liston Pope, "Religion as a Social Force in America," *Social Action,* 19, no. 6 (May 1953), 2-15.

[52] Harry F. Ward, "Organized Religion, the State, and the Economic Order," *Annals of the American Academy of Political and Social Science,* 256 (Mar. 1948), 72-83; quotation from p. 76.

[53] Charles H. Hopkins, *The Rise of the Social Gospel in American Protestantism, 1865-1915* (New Haven: Yale University Press, 1940), p. 3.

was based philosophically, theologically, historically, and sociologically upon the entire heritage of the Christian religion. Declarations of the Hebrew prophets, ethical teachings of the New Testament, social concerns of the Christian church from its very inception, reform movements of the Reconstruction period, and political activities of radicals, socialists, and progressivists stimulated and nourished the growth of the social gospel.[54]

The outstanding leader of the movement at its peak was Walter Rauschenbusch. As a German Baptist pastor in New York City he recognized that conventional pietism did not completely meet the needs of the poverty-stricken men of his congregation. His ideas were developed in various publications and during his professorship at Rochester Theological Seminary (1897-1918). His central concept was the kingdom of God, a collective conception involving the entire social life of man. He held up human rights as more important than material wealth and property rights. He taught that mutual service and cooperation rather than economic profit and competition should dominate economic affairs. As a champion of the working classes, and as an example of a type of Christian socialism, he stressed religious regeneration in the salvation of society and set positive religious faith against a materialistic philosophy.[55]

Rauschenbusch's writing and speaking dealt with tangible problems of society—problems of the family, the working classes, vice, immorality, and others. He persistently emphasized the need for complete regeneration of individuals so that they would reevaluate social values and let the spirit of Christ work through them to regenerate society. Christians collectively, by casting off the rationalizations protecting social evils, repenting of the sins of society, believing in a higher social order, and realizing in themselves "a new type of Christian manhood . . . which seeks to overcome the evil in the present world" instead of withdrawing from it, would revolutionize the world.[56] The entire movement was basically religious and evangelical.[57]

The social gospel was opposed by big business and was weak in churches dominated by the upper classes. Revivalistic groups considered the church's chief work to be delivering individual persons from sin. They believed society could be reformed only by winning souls to Christ. In effect they thus denied the social nature of man's problems and ignored the fact of collective sin. There can be no *social* gospel, they said, for the New Testament message is to persons. Nations, groups, and committees

---

[54] Maurice C. Latta, "The Background for the Social Gospel in American Protestantism," *Church History,* 5 (Sept. 1936), 256-70; and Justin Wroe Nixon, "The Status and Prospects of the Social Gospel," *Journal of Religion,* 22 (Oct. 1942), 346-58.

[55] Hopkins, *The Rise of the Social Gospel,* pp. 215-32.

[56] Walter Rauschenbusch, *Christianity and the Social Crisis* (New York: The Macmillan Co., 1907), pp. 345-50, 412.

[57] Hopkins, *The Rise of the Social Gospel,* p. 321.

cannot repent; only individuals can. Quietistic churches, especially those of Lutheran and German background, also opposed the social gospel. They had brought to America the typical European view that the world must learn to shift for itself without church interference. The strength of the movement was concentrated chiefly in the great evangelical denominations, notably Methodists, Northern Baptists, Congregationalists, Presbyterians, and Disciples of Christ.[58]

Many social gospel leaders made mistakes that alienated them from potential followers, other religious leaders, especially fundamentalists, and scholars. Some made the error which Rauschenbusch warned of when he said that preachers who begin to speak on social questions often fly off on a tangent, forgetting either to appeal to the individual soul for repentance or to comfort the sorrowing.[59] Occasionally statistics were so used that they became examples in college classes of the misuse of statistics. The complexity of society and its problems was often unrecognized.[60] Many people became overenthusiastic, expecting the New Era to be established in the short span of a few years. The expected results were replaced by two world wars, a major depression, the nazification of Germany, and other world-wide problems. Finally, when the "noble experiment" of prohibition failed to accomplish expected ends, many became disillusioned and tended to adopt a "futilitarian point of view." [61] The persistence of mores and of social institutions was overlooked. The movement can be interpreted partly as a middle class effort to conserve and extend American political and ecclesiastical institutions, thus identifying the kingdom of God with democracy.[62]

In spite of its failures, many positive contributions resulted from the movement. It increased the recognition that the church has a responsibility to modify and reconstruct society, that the group, and its decisions and values are significant in human life, and that the individual personality is developed in a process of social interaction and reflects the groups in which socialization takes place. It influenced many social welfare and reform movements and increased the permeation of the social viewpoint into the thinking of Christians of all major theological varieties. An "uneasy conscience" has developed even among fundamentalists. They have begun to recognize their frequent failure to apply Biblical teachings to practical societal problems and to admit their tendency to be divorced

58 William Warren Sweet, *The American Churches: An Interpretation* (New York: Abingdon-Cokesbury Press, 1948), pp. 147-48.

59 Rauschenbusch, *Christianity and the Social Crisis*, pp. 365-67.

60 Clifford Kirkpatrick, *Religion in Human Affairs* (New York: John Wiley and Sons, 1929), pp. 441-44.

61 William C. Smith, "Sociology and the Social Gospel," *Sociology and Social Research*, 32 (Nov.-Dec. 1947), 607-15.

62 H. Richard Niebuhr, *The Kingdom of God in America* (New York: Harper Torchbooks, 1959), pp. 183-84.

from the social passion that characterized the prophets, Jesus, and the early church fathers.[63]

The social gospel had begun to decline by the 1920's, but social passion has remained vital in most major Protestant denominations. As a distinct movement the social gospel has passed, but its emphasis has become an integral part of the thought and action of most churches. Many of its principles have been incorporated into official denominational statements. All Protestant bodies of a million or more members have set up national organizations and staffs to foster it. The larger the membership of a denomination, the more apt it is to look with favor upon a social action program; the smaller a denomination, the more likely its emphasis is to be chiefly upon evangelism, frowning upon efforts by the church as such to change social conditions.

How effective are reform efforts by churches? The church often seems stuck in a rut of its own methods and hence fails to reach the world with an effective program of corporate social action. In spite of official denominational attitudes open to reform, most church programs have not developed into a potent force. Resolutions on social evils and committee recommendations often seem ineffective.[64] Stubborn resistance to change, mental limitations of leaders and followers, the tendency to be comfortable with the status quo, and exhaustion of leaders with other responsibilities all help to limit its social outreach.[65]

Since World War II there has been vigorous opposition to social action even in some denominations historically most concerned with developing and expounding social policy. Denominational leaders usually are supported by conventions in their attempts to secure the endorsement of strong statements about social issues, but often laymen in local churches give little or no heed to these statements or even openly oppose them.[66] The problem is due partly to the unrepresentative nature of denominational conferences. The clergy are overrepresented and laymen underrepresented. Laymen who attend are those able to leave their work without serious financial injury and those held in sufficient esteem to be elected delegates by fellow members. Protestant lay delegates hence have better

---

[63] Carl F. H. Henry, *The Uneasy Conscience of Modern Fundamentalism* (Grand Rapids, Mich.: William B. Eerdmans Publishing Co., 1947); Eric Edwin Paulson, "Social Justice and Evangelical Christianity," *United Evangelical Action,* 14 (Mar. 1, 1955), 6, 8, 10; and D. Ivan Dykstra, "Evangelic Christianity and Social Concern," *Religion in Life,* 24 (Spring 1955), 269-77.

[64] Judson T. Landis, "Social Action in American Protestant Churches," *American Journal of Sociology,* 52 (May 1947), 517-22.

[65] Douglas W. Thompson, "Roadbound," *World Dominion and the World Today,* 29 (May-June 1951), 165-69.

[66] These problems are present in interdenominational bodies also; e.g., see J. Howard Pew, "The Chairman's Final Report to the National Lay Committee of the National Council of the Churches of Christ in the United States of America," Philadelphia, Dec. 15, 1955.

than average educational backgrounds and are well above the median economic level of their churches. They are much more likely than the general membership to understand the basic underlying dislocations of society. Hence, they favor integration, support the UN, desire fair play in labor-management relations, favor FEPC legislation, and uphold social welfare.[67] The majority of lay members "back home," failing to understand the basic problems of society, lean toward a purely individualistic approach to them and reflect their general social environment.

A study of 75 chairmen of church boards of trustees, selected as a random sample from churches in Chicago, found that only about 10 per cent had any personal acquaintance with major resolutions passed in their denominational assembly; less than 3 per cent knew of any effort that had been made to inform the congregation about them. The gap between the quality of many Protestant social pronouncements and their support by members is due to at least six major barriers to social effectiveness: (1) The right to believe and worship according to one's own convictions is protected. This freedom *for* something is often construed as freedom *from* the claims of the gospel. Separatism with regard to social issues results. (2) American individualism has carried over into a personal emphasis on presenting the gospel and often has prevented social teachings from taking root. (3) The idea of community, a sense of fellowship and one-ness in the church, has only recently begun to develop as a theological concept. (4) Because of the dominance of business, economics, and technology, any criticism of the underlying philosophy of American business seems to bite the hand that feeds everyone. Many social issues are therefore considered to be matters of business or technical skill rather than of morals. (5) Clergymen often unwittingly endorse the status quo because they lack a solid grounding in the social sciences and in some of the more demanding disciplines of religion. (6) The tremendous complexity of American society has eroded the sense of competence to remedy its ills. Instead of confidence that all evils will give way before the sheer determination that righteousness should prevail, there is now a tendency to leave things to the "experts" or to let them work themselves out.[68]

Although entire communities in rural America have in the past been socially transformed as a result of church activities,[69] it is doubtful whether the church can bring about similar change in metropolitan areas. The majority of laymen now appear to be influenced more in their stand on social issues by their position in the socioeconomic structure than by their church affiliation.[70] The role of "social critic" or "community re-

---

[67] Victor Obenhaus, "Protestant Social Policy: Why Isn't It More Effective?" *The Nation*, 177 (Aug. 1, 1953), 91-93.

[68] *Ibid.*

[69] C. O. Gill, "Social Control: Rural Religion," *Publications of the American Sociological Society*, 11 (Mar. 1917), 106-12.

[70] F. Ernest Johnson, "Protestant Social Policy," *Nation*, 177 (July 25, 1953), 66-68.

former" also no longer seems to be significant in the American ministry.[71] In the Little Rock crisis over school desegregation, institutional pressures compelled ministers to give peace within the church precedence over social reform.[72] Nevertheless, as theologians and other church leaders stress the importance of the prophetic ministry of the church, there is a possibility that its influence as a social reform agency will increase. The church affects the social actions of people who believe in God to the extent that it can know, can express, and can implement:

> What God thinks
> What God wants
> How God feels
> What God hates
> What God opposes
> What God supports and therefore,
> How God is related to the specific issues
> of our own particular day.[73]

The Church as a Welfare Institution

The church's social welfare work is evident in pertinent recommendations made by religious bodies, commissions to study social problems, lobbying for welfare purposes, occasional direct participation in politics, and alms-giving that has accompanied church work for centuries and persists in "institutions of mercy" and other charitable activities under church sponsorship. In its 48 projects the Institute of Social and Religious Research found that church interest in social welfare was expressed in five ways: (1) In its local congregations in the partial care of their own poor; (2) in a wide variety of specialized agencies; (3) in interpreting and teaching Christian social relationships and enforcing ethical obligations among people and social classes; (4) in training and inspiring members of welfare activities through non-church channels and for constructive community leadership; and (5) in directly backing and supporting community welfare agencies.[74]

Social welfare was prominent in the work of 505 rural Missouri churches. All but 14.5 per cent reported such services to members as sending flowers

---

[71] Samuel W. Blizzard, "The Minister's Dilemma," *Christian Century,* 73 (Apr. 25, 1956), 508-10.

[72] Ernest Q. Campbell and Thomas F. Pettigrew, "Racial and Moral Crisis: The Role of Little Rock Ministers," *American Journal of Sociology,* 64 (Mar. 1959), 509-16.

[73] Roy Pearson, "The Prophetic Voice of the Church," *Religion in Life,* 27 (Spring 1958), 208-23.

[74] H. Paul Douglass and Edmund deS. Brunner, *The Protestant Church as a Social Institution* (New York: Institute of Social and Religious Research, 1935), p. 184.

to the sick and to funerals, visiting the sick and aged, sending Thanksgiving and Christmas baskets, and providing medical aid (in order of frequency). Two-thirds of the churches also supported orphanages, homes for the aged, hospitals, needy individuals and families, community organizations, and such international social services as CARE and CROP.[75]

Churches generally are more interested in philanthropic welfare than in social reform to remove the underlying problems that create the needs for philanthropy. This may be interpreted as a natural outgrowth of the basic nature and typical role of the church in society. Religious values create a spirit of generosity within the framework of a social system; church leadership lacks the astuteness or vigor to condemn the system itself in the name of a higher justice. The Christian church also is pessimistic as to the possibilities of saving the world. It often is indifferent toward the needy, believing that God ordained that there should be poverty. Preoccupied with the motives underlying ethical action, the church seldom rises to the higher level of trying to deal with an entire social system. Social comfort tends to be regarded as the reward of virtue; poverty and other social needs are seen as the product of vice and laziness. Religious impulses are therefore expressed in philanthropy more than in social justice or reform.[76]

The Church's Relationship to Professional Social Work. In its concern with social welfare the church overlaps in many activities with the social work profession. Sometimes this leads to competition and professional jealousies, but more often cooperation between religious leaders and social workers results.

Professional social work grew out of activities in churches designed to alleviate certain social needs. Its broader rationale is that of Judeo-Christian ethics. This strong moral component remains as a backdrop to the entire program of social work, although many social work teachings contradict orthodox theological concepts.[77] Religion helps create a conscience than understands social needs and is ready to move toward their alleviation. It has pioneered in many fields of social work and is a resource for the social worker in dealing with specific cases.[78]

A special U.S. census report in 1903 indicated that one-third of the

---

[75] Milton Coughenour and Lawrence M. Hepple, *The Church in Rural Missouri, Part II, Religious Groups in Rural Missouri* (Columbia, Mo.: A. E. S. Research Bulletin 633B, Sept. 1957), pp. 110-17.

[76] Reinhold Niebuhr, *The Contribution of Religion to Social Work* (New York: Columbia University Press, 1932), pp. 18-33.

[77] Kimball Young, "Social Psychology and Social Casework," *American Sociological Review,* 16 (Feb. 1951), 54-61; and Alan Keith-Lucas, "Some Notes on Theology and Social Work," *Social Casework,* 41 (Feb. 1960), 87-91.

[78] Niebuhr, *The Contribution of Religion to Social Work,* pp. 1-17, 34-75; and Sue W. Spenser, "Religious and Spiritual Values in Social Casework Practice," *Social Casework,* 38 (Dec. 1957), 519-26, reprinted in *Journal of Pastoral Care,* 13. no. 1 (Spring 1959), 13-23.

nation's benevolent institutions were church-connected.[79] The proportion that is now church-related is smaller because of the rapid growth of public welfare. This decrease in proportionate strength has been referred to as the "secularization of social welfare." In 34 urban areas in 1940 96 per cent of all funds in relief and family welfare and 90 per cent of those for health and welfare came from public funds.[80] Protestant, Catholic, and Jewish groups still sponsor a large number of health and welfare agencies; at least 2,783 were related to 37 Protestant bodies in 1955. In 1983 Catholics had 710 hospitals, 121 nurses schools, 560 homes for the aged, and 190 orphanages, and a list of Jewish federations, welfare funds, and community councils required 15 pages.[81] Church-sponsored community centers, day-care and other programs for children and the aging, food and shelter services, and world relief projects use thousands of volunteers besides professional workers.[82]

Child welfare work can be traced largely to church influence. The church has made major contributions to prison reform and provides chaplains who help considerably in the rehabilitation of inmates.[83] The Salvation Army and other groups provide many social and religious services in jails and prisons and help restore criminals, alcoholics, and other deviants to useful places in society.[84] Church-sponsored work on the skidrow through rescue missions, clubs that help meet the needs of older adults, and dozens of other programs flow out of the same religious motivations.

Many foreign missionary projects include welfare work. About 40 per cent of the work of 5,300 missionaries from the U.S. in Latin America during 1952 was concerned primarily with general education, health, agriculture, and social service programs. This number of missionaries would have been equivalent to 2,100 non-missionary workers had the work been under the direction of 66 agencies that sponsor technical assistance programs. Missionary efforts represented contributions equivalent to eight to ten million dollars per year for that purpose.[85]

---

[79] Edmund H. Oliver, *The Social Achievements of the Christian Church* (Toronto: Ryerson Press, 1930), p. 147.

[80] Arthur L. Swift, Jr., "The Church and Human Welfare," in *Religion and Social Work*, F. Ernest Johnson, ed. (New York: Institute for Religious and Social Studies, 1956), pp. 1-15.

[81] Horace R. Cayton and Setsuko M. Nishi, *The Changing Scene: Current Trends and Issues* (*Churches and Social Welfare*, II) (New York: National Council of Churches, 1955); Felician A. Foy, O.F.M., and Rose M. Avato, eds., *1983 Catholic Almanac* (Huntington, Ind.: Our Sunday Visitor, 1983), pp. 572–90, and *American Jewish Year Book 1983* (New York: American Jewish Committee, 1983), pp. 328–42.

[82] *Ibid.*

[83] Lee M. and Evelyn C. Brooks, *Adventuring in Adoption* (Chapel Hill: University of North Carolina Press, 1939), pp. 93-110; and J. Arthur Hoyles, *Religion in Prison* (New York: Philosophical Library, 1955).

[84] Louis N. Robinson, *Jails* (Philadelphia: The John C. Winston Co., 1944), pp. 238, 267.

[85] James G. Maddox, *Technical Assistance by Religious Agencies in Latin America*

Religious motivations are often significant in the choice of social work as a vocation, and professional education for it includes indoctrination into a code of ethics that has much in common with basic teachings of the Judeo-Christian religion. Both emphasize the dignity of the individual, his right to self-determination, the motivation of love, and the value of helping others to become whole. Current growing interest of the church in social work as a profession seems matched by an equivalent interest among social workers with the place of religion in their work.[86] Social workers now move back and forth between religious and nonsectarian agencies with little difficulty. A small minority of the church-related agencies rebel against secular professional standards; out of intense religious convictions, they rely primarily upon prayer and personal conversion as means of opposing social evils.

The greater the conscious distinctiveness of a religious body, the more likely it is to maintain its own social services. The Amish, Hutterites, Mormons, and Quakers have little need for public welfare services as long as they remain relatively isolated and provide for the needs of their own people. The numerical predominance of Protestantism in Amercia, especially among those who bear the major burden of economic support for social services, tends to bring into nonsectarian social work the ideals and purposes held by Protestants. The demand for a distinctively Protestant social work is therefore less than demands of other groups for their own agencies.[87]

Some activities of the clergy overlap with those of social workers. This is particularly true of family counseling and the assistance given to persons with financial, emotional, or social problems. A sample survey of Protestant clergymen found that some ministers are distrustful of non-church-related social welfare. They feel that social workers are antireligious or irreligious and may draw clients away from the church, that God can solve any problem without human intervention, and that only prayer is needed for those who have problems. They also believe that ministers are better qualified to help people than non-Christian social workers, and that the agencies are not doing a good job because they do not take instructions from the church. More ministers are favorable toward social work agencies, believing that since the church and

---

(Chicago: University of Chicago Press, 1956), pp. 19-26. An appraisal of the objectives, efficiency, and quality of these programs is given by Maddox on pp. 100-24.

[86] Frank J. Bruno, *Trends in Social Work* (New York: Columbia University Press, 1948), pp. 281-82; Shelby M. Harrison, "Religion and Social Work: Perspectives and Common Denominators," in National Conference of Social Work, *Social Work in the Current Scene* (New York: Columbia University Press, 1950); Harold J. Belgum, "Religious Faith and the Helping Process," *Minnesota Welfare*, 11, no. 3 (Fall 1959), 13-18, 48.

[87] F. Ernest Johnson, "Protestant Social Work," *Social Work Year Book, 1941* (New York: Russell Sage Foundation, 1941), p. 404.

agencies work on the same problems, they should supplement and complement one another; that because the minister's time is so limited, he should use every means at his disposal to minister to all areas of people's lives; that social agencies sometimes send new prospects for membership to the church; that as an occasional agency board member, the minister must be cooperative or his influence on the board will be lost, and so forth. Relationships between the professions reflect varying educational backgrounds, vested interests, divergent philosophical and theoretical orientations of the two professions, semantic problems which hinder communication and understanding, and an anti-clericalism on the part of social workers together with an anti-secularism on the part of the clergy that increases misunderstanding and competition between them.[88]

Limitations on the church's role in social welfare. Sometimes the church has reflected the interests of dominant social classes to such an extent that it has served as a tool to keep working people "in their place." The manner in which some of its welfare activities—especially those connected with alms-giving and charity—were conducted has created professional paupers and inflicted mental injuries upon some givers and recipients.[89] Sectarianism adds to the complexities of planning and coordinating welfare programs, contributes to gaps in community services, prevents effective financial support for some community programs, and prevents public expansion in needed services.[90]

That the church is far from doing a complete job of meeting welfare needs is evident from Porterfield's studies. "Social well-being" was measured by various indices of economic welfare, education, culture, living conditions, voting, medical facilities, and health. Religion was reflected by a church score based upon the number of ministers and churches per 100,000 people and the proportion of church members among persons over age 13. A negative correlation between church scores and social well-being was discovered. Neither rural-urban variations nor racial composition of the population fully accounted for the observed differences.[91]

The scope of social welfare activities and related work of the church is so extensive, when it is functioning effectively, that it may be conceived of as a social agency *per se.* Its normal group life is a strong character-building force. Pastoral and fraternal assistance to members operates both preventively and remedially. During the pre-depression era fully one-third of all American welfare funds were used to support

---

[88] David O. Moberg and Russell H. Voight, "The Minister and Social Work," *Midwest Sociologist,* 19, no. 1 (Dec. 1956), 38-44.

[89] Harlan W. Gilmore, *The Beggar* (Chapel Hill: University of North Carolina Press, 1940), pp. 9-17, 23-25, 74, 196-209.

[90] "Sectarian Harm to Social Welfare Work," *The Standard* (American Ethical Union), 40 (Jan.-Feb. 1954), 17-19.

[91] Austin L. Porterfield, "The Church and Social Well-Being: A Statistical Analysis," *Sociology and Social Research,* 31 (Jan.-Feb. 1947), 213-19.

character-building and leisure-time programs that paralleled the normal activities of organized groups in the church. Often without general consciousness that it is exercising a social ministry, the church makes a major contribution to welfare as a by-product of its spiritual ministry.[92]

The Church as a Philanthropic Institution

Church work requires large sums of money annually. About half of all philanthropic giving (giving for purposes that are "allowable contributions" for income tax purposes) goes to churches and agencies under religious auspices.[93] Over half of all philanthropic giving comes from low-income groups. Families in the lowest income categories give the highest percentage of their income to the church. After retirement they continue giving at about the same rate they gave previously.[94]

Proportionate to income, Jewish and Catholic philanthropic giving exceeds that of Protestants. In Judaism philanthropy is not sharply distinguished from welfare contributions to nonsectarian agencies, for charity is considered a religious duty. Roman Catholics closely identify almsgiving with the Church and its doctrines. Hospitals, Catholic welfare, parochial schools, and other charities are part of its work. Giving is not considered to mean giving up anything; it is an exchange of temporal for spiritual wealth and a source of such rewards as the prayers of monks, nuns, and priests. Protestants are more content to let their feeling of responsibility for the welfare of fellow men be discharged through secular agencies or government. Hence one cannot arbitrarily draw a sharp distinction between the religious and secular philanthropic giving of any of the three major religious groups.[95] "Religion is the mother of philanthropy." [96] Religious motivations and attitudes perhaps underlie a major proportion of all individual philanthropy in America. Yet some giving—even to the church itself—is done out of ulterior motives, because of social pressures, to gain publicity, to ease a guilty conscience, to secure income tax deductions, and for other morally questionable or amoral reasons.

The contributions for all purposes reported by 40 American religious bodies during 1980 totaled $8,781,927,572, a per capita rate of $196.25 for the inclusive membership. Of this amount, 20.2 per cent was for benev-

---

[92] Douglass and Brunner, *The Protestant Church*, pp. 184-89; and Herbert W. Schneider, *Religion in 20th Century America* (Cambridge: Harvard University Press, 1952), pp. 60-89.

[93] F. Emerson Andrews, *Attitudes Toward Giving* (New York: Russell Sage Foundation, 1953), p. 85.

[94] F. Emerson Andrews, *Philanthropic Giving* (New York: Russell Sage Foundation, 1950), p. 56; and Helen H. Lamale and Joseph A. Clority, Jr., "City Families as Givers," *Monthly Labor Review*, 82 (Dec. 1959), 1303-11.

[95] *Ibid.*, pp. 174-75.

[96] Andrews, *Attitudes Toward Giving*, p. 85.

olences. Comparable figures for 22 Canadian bodies were $438,970,257, a per capita rate of $116.58.[97] Long-term trends in giving to churches follow general trends in personal income and consumption expenditures. Yet giving to religious bodies did not increase proportionately to the increase in disposable personal income during and since World War II. Increased per member giving has been accompanied by declining purchasing power of the dollar; the real value of religious contributions today is less than it was a generation ago.[98] However, government and other institutions are now performing functions once cared for through the church, so some expenditures for taxes and other purposes may be social substitutes for previous religious contributions. Parachurch ministries with religious and social service goals also attract much giving.

The smaller a church, the greater is the average "cost" of membership. Churches with fewer than 25 members often pay more per member to sustain a meager program of monthly or semi-monthly meetings and to keep their one-room building in repair than it costs the average member of a city or village church to have a resident minister, a much more adequate building, and a program of religious education, recreation, and community service.[99] The smaller the number of persons sharing fixed expenses, the higher the costs per member are. Beyond a certain minimum size—which may vary by denomination and community—a substantial proportion of the giving of a local church can go to missions and benevolences without weakening, and perhaps actually strengthening, its work. Up to that point, high percentage contributions for non-local purposes are impossible.

Such denominational and interdenominational organizations as the Church World Service, American Friends Service Committee, Mennonite Central Committee, National Catholic Welfare Conference War Relief Service, and Lutheran World Relief have made significant contributions of food, clothing, and other supplies, as well as huge monetary gifts, for needs in foreign nations. Church contributions for foreign relief are estimated to have been about $300,000,000 in 1957.[100] Most religious bodies support missionary activities which include similar benevolences.

The sums involved in religious philanthropic giving may seem large, but when analyzed in relationship to other expenditures a different impression emerges. In 1981 all philanthropic giving in the U.S. amounted

---

[97] Constant H. Jacquet, Jr., ed., *Yearbook of American and Canadian Churches 1982* (Nashville: Abingdon Press, 1982), pp. 250-51.

[98] Andrews, *Philanthropic Giving*, pp. 180-81. Cf. Benson Y. Landis, ed., *Yearbook of American Churches for 1955* (New York: National Council of Churches, 1954), pp. 286-87. (This remained true as of 1980.)

[99] Douglass and Brunner, *The Protestant Church*, pp. 210-11.

[100] *Giving USA* (New York: American Association of Fund-Raising Counsel, 1959 ed.), p. 31. (Recent statistics are unavailable.)

to 53.6 billion dollars, of which 44.5 came from individuals and 24.9 were allocated to religion. Yet expenditures for alcoholic beverages totaled 46.2 billion dollars and those for tobacco products 23.1. Estimates of the 1949 Christmas expenditures suggest that people give presents to each other which equal three times as much as they give to all religious causes during the entire year.[101] Is this a measure of the values most significant to Americans?

The traditional tithe for religious purposes, usually reckoned as ten per cent of one's income, has influenced some persons even outside the church to think their philanthropic giving ought to equal about ten per cent of their incomes.[102] Religious duties of giving and the increasing consciousness of churches' social responsibilities have undoubtedly affected charitable giving to secular as well as religious welfare. The functions of the church as a philanthropic institution extend far beyond the limitations of its own direct activities.

Conclusion

This discussion of important functions of church structure and action in American society brings out several points of major significance. First, the church contributes to the unity and maintenance of society. By imparting and affirming social norms and values of the larger society, it contributes to social stability and solidarity. In performing this function the American churches do not speak as with a single voice nor act as a united body. Yet we may validly conclude that churches contribute significantly to the integration and adaptation of society.

Second, the functions the church performs in and for American society have been changing. Change is evident particularly in the shift toward increased emphasis on public social welfare and greater stress on the social well-being of people, instead of exclusive attention to individual salvation. Functional alternatives, substitutes, and equivalents readily fill the gap when prevailing institutional patterns in society fail to meet social needs.

Third, the functions of the church are intricately intertwined with other major institutions, such as business, education, government, and the family. In general the church supports and reinforces the functions of other basic institutions.

Fourth, there are wide variations in the functional consequences of

[101] U.S. Bureau of the Census, *Statistical Abstract of the United States 1982* (Washington, D.C.: Government Printing Office, 1982), pp. 346, 422; Andrews, *Philanthropic Giving*, pp. 72, 187. Some of the giving to such other causes as health and hospitals ($7.3 billion in 1981), education ($7.4 billion), and social welfare ($5.3 billion) undoubtedly is interpreted by donors as being for religious causes.

[102] Andrews, *Attitudes Toward Giving*, pp. 13, 93-95.

specific churches and denominations. The functions of any given church are, of course, affected by its system of faith, which imposes normative limitations that modify its practices, and by its organizational structure, which may make it either more adaptable to changing conditions or less susceptible to modification when confronted with sudden needs. Relationships with other churches contribute to variations among them. Leaders' resources of knowledge, economic advantages, and available time vary widely. The states impose different patterns of limitations through their demands for safety, restrictions upon property holding, zoning, and other regulations. Variations in churches' opportunities and limitations help explain the wide variability observable in their functions and dysfunctions. Since the consequences of church action are a tangled mass of opposing effects which are simultaneously present and can be referred to in surveys like this only in terms of general tendencies, generalizations about them should not be applied to any local church or denomination without study of that organization and appropriate qualification as to time, place, and other specifics. We must avoid the "ecological fallacy."

Functionalists in sociology and anthropology have concentrated mainly upon the latent functions of religion, while debunkers and reformers have emphasized latent dysfunctions.[103] We have included both. The predominance in this chapter of manifest rather than of latent functions, and of functions rather than of dysfunctions, reflects the difficulties of discovering consequences which are not purposefully introduced or maintained, the paucity of objective discussions of dysfunctions, and the dearth of empirical studies. Most of the observations therefore must be considered tentative, incomplete, and suggestive rather than conclusive and exhaustive. We shall now go on to further analysis of goal-orientations, functional achievements, and dysfunctional effects of churches in American society.

Selected References

Churches and Social Welfare, 3 vols. New York: National Council of Churches, 1955–56. Historical and theological analysis of trends, issues, and responses related to the Protestant churches' concern for social welfare needs.

Cressman, Luther S., "Ritual the Conserver," *American Journal of Sociology*, 35 (Jan. 1930), 564–72. A functional analysis of religious ritual.

Dunlap, Knight, *Religion: Its Functions in Human Life*. Westport, Conn.: Greenwood, 1977 (McGraw-Hill, 1946). Psychological functionalism: religion as a product of conscious psychological processes related to personal needs.

Eister, Allan W., "Religious Institutions in Complex Societies: Difficulties in the Theoretic Specification of Functions," *American Sociological Review*, 22 (Aug. 1957), 387–91. Theoretical and practical problems in the functional analysis of the church.

---

[103] William J. Goode, *Religion Among the Primitives* (Glencoe, Ill.: The Free Press, 1951), pp. 32–35.

Hunt, Chester L., "Religious Ideology as a Means of Social Control," *Sociology and Social Research*, 33 (Jan.-Feb. 1949), 180–87. The Protestant church in Nazi Germany as one of the few institutions not prostituted to the totalitarian state.

Klapp, Orrin E., *Ritual and Cult: A Sociological Interpretation*. Washington, D.C.: Public Affairs Press, 1956. An analysis of the social significance and functions of rituals and ceremonies.

Mathews, Shailer, *Jesus on Social Institutions*, ed. with an introduction by Kenneth Cauthen. Philadelphia: Fortress Press, 1971. A reprint of the 1928 interpretation by a social gospel leader, a biographic essay on his life and thought, and a bibliography.

Merton, Robert K., *Social Theory and Social Structure*, rev. ed. New York: Free Press, 1957. The leading source on functionalism and theories of the middle range in sociology.

Moberg, David O., ed., *Spiritual Well-Being: Sociological Perspectives*. Washington, D.C.: University Press of America, 1979. Essays and research reports by 27 authors from five continents on various aspects of spiritual growth, maturity, health, and illness.

Mol, Hans, ed., *Identity and Religion: International, Cross-Cultural Approaches*. Beverly Hills, Calif.: Sage Publications, 1978. Sociological essays related to Mol's theory analyzing a wide range of religions around the world.

Mol, Hans, *Identity and the Sacred: A Sketch for a New Social-Scientific Theory of Religion*. Agincourt, Ontario: Book Society of Canada Ltd., 1976 (New York: Free Press). Integrates anthropological, historical, psychological, and sociological approaches to religion around the concept that "religion is the sacralization of identity and that the mechanisms of sacralization consist of objectification, commitment, ritual, and myth."

Mol, Hans, *Meaning and Place: An Introduction to the Social Scientific Study of Religion*. New York: Pilgrim Press, 1983. An introduction to sociology of religion centered around the question of what religion does for the individual, group, and society.

O'Dea, Thomas F., and Janet O'Dea Aviad, *The Sociology of Religion*, 2nd ed. Englewood Cliffs, N.J.: Prentice-Hall, 1983. A functionalist approach to the sociology of religion.

Parsons, Talcott, *Essays in Sociological Theory, Pure and Applied*. New York: Free Press, 1949. Pp. 52–66 gives the historical development of the structural-functional approach in the sociology of religion.

Schneider, Louis, and Sanford M. Dornbusch, *Popular Religion: Inspirational Books in America*. Chicago: University of Chicago Press, 1958. Themes, trends, contexts, and functions of American inspirational religious literature based upon content analysis of 46 best sellers published from 1875 to 1955.

Williams, Melvin D., *Community in a Black Pentecostal Church: An Anthropological Study*. Pittsburgh, Pa.: University of Pittsburgh Press, 1974. The church as a symbolic expression and reinforcer of a sense of community in the context of alienation and anomie.

Ziff, Larzer, "The Social Bond of Church Covenant," *American Quarterly*, 10 (Winter 1958), 454–62. The colonial Puritan church covenant as a basis for integration of public and political life.

🏛   Chapter 7

Functions and Dysfunctions
of Church Activities

Every institution overlaps and must be integrated with every other institution if society is to operate efficiently. To whatever degree there are internal inconsistencies and contradictions, society's existence is threatened. Yet the checks and balances built into the social system are part of a total pattern combining innovation (which prevents stagnation) and stability (which prevents radical revolution that could cause collapse of the social system itself).

As indicated in the introduction to Chapter 6, functional analysis of churches evaluates the consequences of their various units of structure and action. Consequences for society at large were emphasized in Chapter 6. In addition, church units have functional effects felt by the local church, the church as a general social institution, and—by virtue of the functional requirement that the institution achieve its goals—by individuals. Analysis of these must recognize what churches do, how and why they do it, and above all the manifest and latent effects of their acts. Church activities are related to religious aims. In America these aims center upon facilitating individual religious experience, even if only indirectly by drawing persons into social situations and groups through which they later will receive religious assistance. The basic goal implicit in Protestant, Catholic, and Jewish churches is the salvation and sanctification of souls.[1] The chief object of functional analysis is to discover

---

[1] This goal is expressed in a wide variety of specific concepts and interpretations.

159

what actually happens as a result of church organization and operation, not simply to list the claims of leaders, although these are a relevant part of the larger investigation.

Church activities have many social, recreational, esthetic, economic, ethical, educational, and political functions; they contribute to the maintenance of values and practices necessary for effective action in these "secular" areas of social life. In so doing, they help support the other institutions as well as the total social system. On the other hand, some church programs and practices have dysfunctional effects for themselves, other institutions, the total society, or individuals they profess to serve. Some of these functions and dysfunctions will be summarized in this chapter. It will often be difficult to discern which are manifest (intended and recognized by institutional personnel) and which are latent (unintended, unknown, or unrecognized). What is latent to one churchman or observer is manifest to another. When latent consequences are discerned by the social scientist, they may become manifest to leaders who previously have neither intended nor deliberately sought their effects.

Social Functions of Religious Activities

Perhaps the most clearly religious of all church activities is *worship*. The word is derived from two Old English words which mean worthship. In other words, worship involves attitudes and actions of reverence that declare the worth of whatever is worshiped.[2] At least four attitudes, all of which are significantly influenced by social experiences, are involved in worship: contemplation, or meditation on the divine; revelation, or insight into truth believed to be divinely imparted; communion, or the consciousness of a personal relation to God; and fruition, the new life which grows out of the experience.[3] Theologically Christian worship involves a fellowship with men and with God which is an outward, visible expression of the believer's inward, invisible communion.[4] The church encourages individual worship and, more important to the social scientist, provides for corporate worship through ritual, ceremony, and

For a Roman Catholic statement about the purpose of the Church see the Foreword by Samuel Cardinal Stritch, Archbishop of Chicago, in *The Sociology of the Parish,* C. J. Nuesse and Thomas J. Harte, eds. (Milwaukee: Bruce Publishing Co., 1951), p. vii.

[2] Clarence L. Barnhart, ed., *The American College Dictionary* (New York: Harper and Brothers, 1951), pp. 1407-8; and George Hedley, *Christian Worship* (New York: The Macmillan Co., 1953), pp. 1-3.

[3] Edgar S. Brightman, *A Philosophy of Religion* (Englewood Cliffs, N.J.: Prentice-Hall, Inc., 1940), p. 71.

[4] Frederick C. Grant, "The Function of the Church in the Modern World," *Journal of Religion,* 16 (Apr. 1936), 136-39.

religious services. Public worship is the basis and center of organized religious life. Without it or a functional equivalent the church could not exist.[5] As we saw in Chapter 3, man's most private religious devotions are a product of group experiences.

In Judaism and Christianity, God is worshiped, yet the very concept of God includes anthropomorphic, anthropocentric, and anthroposocial elements. Even the gods of preliterate peoples are perceptive, socialized beings with social personalities and an interest in the general welfare of the group; various concepts of the Judeo-Christian God emerge from the changing backgrounds and cultural aspirations reflected in the Bible.[6] Patterns of worship emerge out of and reinforce the collective behavior and sacred values of the group which develops them. Thus Christianity's most sacred writings, the New Testament, helped produce Christianity, but they were to an even greater extent produced by it. Behind the Scriptures stand persons who were members of a religious sect writing to serve the Christian cause amid the activities of living groups.[7] Worship helps define and integrate the group even as it helps separate one group from another. Non-liturgical churches sometimes refuse to cooperate with the liturgical, and vice versa; each thinks the other has perverted true worship.

Religious services of praise to God and associated rituals declare the worth of God, expressing reverence and obedience to Him, but they also have mundane ends that are inseparably interrelated with the divine. God is often worshiped in the hope or faith that man's needs will therefore be met more easily and surely, that the lot of man on earth will be lightened, that his prospect in the present and future life will be bright. In the Lord's Prayer, statements of worship ("Hallowed be Thy name") are followed by material requests ("Give us this day our daily bread, and forgive us our debts . . ."). Worship for many people is partly or wholly homocentric. We worship God to serve human needs; we implore Deity to shape our own ends; we seek guidance in human affairs; we beseech God to give us peace and security amid the uncertainties of life; we seek immortality when life seems broken by death. In theory worship is theocentric; in practice it involves many homocentric goals and motivations. As an institution *in* the world, the church in many respects is of necessity also *of* the world; it is a human institution.[8] The self-fulfilling prophecy operating

---

[5] Ernst Troeltsch, *The Social Teaching of the Christian Churches,* trans. by Olive Wyon (London: George Allen and Unwin, Ltd., 1931), 2, pp. 1006-7.

[6] William J. Goode, *Religion Among the Primitives* (Glencoe: The Free Press, 1951), pp. 43-45, 315n.; Thomas F. Hoult, *The Sociology of Religion* (New York: Dryden Press, 1958), pp. 20-26; and Bernard Heller, "Anti-Semitic Stereotypes of God," *The Humanist,* 10 (Aug. 1950), 142-47.

[7] Shirley Jackson Case, *The Social Origins of Christianity* (Chicago: University of Chicago Press, 1923), pp. 23-24.

[8] Constantine Panunzio, *Major Social Institutions* (New York: The Macmillan Co.,

in it contributes to the attainment of many of these mundane expectations.

Public religious rituals may symbolically reflect the church's position on controversial social issues. The "prayers for peace" of the community prayer meeting in Little Rock on Columbus Day, 1957, in effect provided a ritualistic termination of attempts by the clergy to guide events in the school desegregation crisis. The prayers satisfied personal and social demands that the ministers act; they could remain silent in subsequent events.[9]

Collective worship is sometimes dysfunctional for the individual in so far as it tends to impose arbitrary images of the Deity and the way to approach Him. These may break down individual spontaneity and become a barrier between the person and God.[10]

A second religious function of the church is that of *facilitating individual religious experience*. Christianity is essentially a personal religion. Protestants emphasize personal religious experience in the belief that the group exists for the benefit of the individual. When the biblical theme of the universal church is emphasized, it usually reflects interest in the persons in that church, but when this universal church is equated directly with an institution on earth, the church is given priority over the individual. In Judaism the "chosen people" concept reflects the importance of the eternal life of the nation more than that of the person.[11] In many ways the religious experiences of persons are facilitated by the church, which is a basic means of "inducing, formulating, expressing, enhancing, implementing, and perpetuating man's deepest experience, the religious." [12] These ways include the following:

1. The church helps persons discover the nature, will, and operations of God. It does this through its example as it seeks to discover the will of God in its practical affairs and through its teaching and preaching ministries. In helping persons to see the concrete practices and principles of motivation which are interpreted as God's will, the church is an agency of social control, a reinforcer of other institutions, the "conscience" of society, and a molder of people's consciences.

2. The church helps individuals experience a sense of fellowship with God. Man generally wants to feel that he has something outside of and

---

1939), p. 292; and Duncan Howlett, *Man Against the Church* (Boston: Beacon Press, 1954), pp. 65-73.

[9] Ernest Q. Campbell and Thomas F. Pettigrew, "Racial and Moral Crisis: The Role of Little Rock Ministers," *American Journal of Sociology,* 64 (Mar. 1959), 509-16.

[10] Floyd H. Allport, *Institutional Behavior* (Chapel Hill: University of North Carolina Press, 1933), pp. 423-30.

[11] John R. Everett, *Religion in Human Experience* (London: George Allen and Unwin, 1952), p. 309.

[12] J. O. Hertzler, "Religious Institutions," *Annals of the American Academy of Political and Social Science,* 256 (Mar. 1948), 5.

beyond himself and his kind to which or to whom to go. Prayer and worship facilitate the sensing of communion with the supernatural. The church member is encouraged to feel that, as a popular sacred song puts it, "My God and I, we walk the fields together." Yet when he depends entirely upon formal church rites and ceremonies, the institution may impair personal devotion.

3. The church gives the believer a sense of security. It teaches that the universe is a safe home, for God is watching over him making all things work together for good. "God's in His heaven, All's well with the world," is the attitude of the person completely committed to the will of God even in an age of atomic warfare. The church helps instill and sustain a sense of eternal security in the man who identifies himself as "abiding in God." However, a sense of sinfulness for real or imagined offenses may be implanted in others, and feelings of guilt or damnation with either a justifiable or unwarranted basis may result.

4. The church provides meaning for life. It gives believers an explanation of the universe as well as of seemingly inconsistent problem-events in man's experience. It explains why there is death, sickness, injustice and suffering in spite of—or even because of!—God's love for all mankind and His omniscience, omipresence, and omnipotence. This sometimes is considered the central function of religion around which all others revolve.[13] Each religion develops theodicies to explain problems.

Belief in immortality has helped innumerable persons to live fuller, more secure, and more serene lives than otherwise would have been possible. It provides a bond of union between the living and the dead which contributes to social equilibrium and cohesion. It sometimes has dysfunctional by-products, such as causing men to take too careless a view of their own or others' lives, but its general impact has been to reduce anxiety, make life more tolerable, and inspire thoughts of service to others so that one may live on in memory after death, secure eternal happiness, or escape everlasting punishment. Belief in immortality is a socially-derived need. It is a significant source of social discipline and provides motivations for living that otherwise would be lacking.[14]

5. The church helps develop personalities. It furnishes opportunities for social interaction and provides goals of faith and character. It aids social and psychological adjustment by providing security in an insecure world, meaning in a universe of mystery, and other values already mentioned. Religion "summates, epitomizes, relates, and conserves all the highest ideals and values—ethical, aesthetic, and religious—of man found in his culture."[15] It contributes to a sense of integrity in the individual,

---

[13] Talcott Parsons, "Réflexions sur les Organisations Religieuses aux États-Unis," *Archives de Sociologie des Religions,* 2, no. 3 (Jan.-June 1957), 21-36.

[14] Ashley Montagu, *Immortality* (New York: Grove Press, 1955), pp. 31-67.

[15] Hertzler, "Religious Institutions," p. 6.

helping him to resolve the conflicts presented by life and accept himself realistically as part of God's creation. It provides ideals to guide, inspire, and challenge in character building and gives certainty and stability in a rapidly-changing world.[16]

6. The church largely determines the kind and quality of religious life of its members. Most people lack the philosophic capacity, intellectual training, and spiritual audacity to think out seriously for themselves a philosophy of life and accompanying patterns of conduct. They tend instead to accept the beliefs and routines offered by an organized religious body.[17] They hence share many characteristics with other members of their church. The degree to which churches strive to structure constituents' lives varies. Some are highly authoritarian, like the Pharisees at the time of Jesus, but others are democratic, giving only basic principles of life and leaving the individual much freedom to interpret these principles for himself in the situations that confront him. All recommend ideal patterns of conduct to members. To whatever degree persons accept its standards, the church helps determine the nature and quality of their lives.

A third function is closely related to facilitating religious experience. The church *provides religious therapy for disturbed persons.* Its work as a "healer of souls" is complemented by that of psychiatrists, consulting psychologists, psychiatric social workers, and others in the "helping professions." Most people who have mental and emotional problems do not go to a psychiatrist; they either cannot afford the financial costs or have biases against psychiatry. The church helps many such persons solve their problems, sometimes singling out for specialized treatment those who have particularly serious needs. Clergymen are now trained to perform this function, to know their limitations, and to refer problem cases to others who can help (Chapters 17 and 18).

The personal guidance given by the church aids many confused persons even if they do not fully believe in the supernatural postulates upon which the guidance is based. It provides personal and social security that has a stabilizing effect upon the mind; in the midst of confusion, distress, and uncertainties a sense of continuity or meaning assists in the prevention and treatment of mental illness.

Individual deficiencies, failures, and inferiority feelings are compensated for by communion with the Creator of the universe, by assurance that one is "a child of the King," by sympathetic fellowship with others who share the same faith, by opportunities in religious service for fruitful use of one's energy, and by the opportunity to give vent to one's

[16] Helen L. Witmer and Ruth Kotinsky, eds., *Personality in the Making* (New York: Harper and Brothers, 1952), pp. 159-62. This is the report of the Midcentury White House Conference on Children and Youth.

[17] Hertzler, "Religious Institutions," p. 11.

emotions in religious gatherings. Dysfunctional effects upon the mental health of those who revolt against church teachings or who "take them too seriously" are more than counterbalanced by wholesome effects in the lives of countless others. So pronounced is the role of the church in alleviating suffering that it has been interpreted as "that institution which furnishes the salvation from suffering to other institutions." [18]

The church also serves, then, as *a therapeutic agency in society*. As we have seen, it helps build stable, integrated personalities that can withstand the pressures that contribute to maladjustment. It provides opportunity for emotional release through exaltation, praise, and service. Religious rituals reflect a fear of innovation and a mass compulsion to overcome anxiety. The stereotyped repetition in them is a defense mechanism in a search for security by the worshiping group.[19]

In times of societal travail, tragedy, and crisis, the church provides solace and often gives tangible help. When natural catastrophe, war, depression, or rioting causes men to suffer, individuals and groups receive assurance through church teachings that nothing can separate them from the love of God. In times of rapid social change when all on earth seems chaotic and uncertain, there is refuge in "the everlasting arms" of a God who is "the same yesterday, today, and forever."

The strain of adjusting to the great changes in social position involved in child-bearing, puberty, marriage, and death is partly alleviated by church rituals, ceremonies, and ordinances. Cathartic release from tensions accompanying the consciousness of wrong-doing occurs through confession, repentance, penance, prayer, and ceremonies performed in times of crisis. The church and its message provide opportunities for sublimating or compensating for the disappointments, ills, and discouragements of life. The downtrodden are given important roles in the church and the promise that in a future life "the last shall be first, and the first last."

Religious functions most clearly distinguish the church from other social institutions. At least in theory all its activities are related to religious aims and goals; in democratic America they all center theoretically and theologically upon facilitating individual religious experience. These goals are often attained, but the church serves society as well as individuals. It acts as a therapeutic institution, helps integrate society, symbolizes social unity, reinforces the group's collective life, builds social values, guides individual and social conduct, and performs other social functions—all this as it promotes individual and corporate worship and engages in other "sacred" activities.

---

[18] James K. Feibleman, *The Institutions of Society* (London: George Allen and Unwin, 1956), pp. 222-24.

[19] Jean Cazeneuve, "Le Principe de Répétition dan le Rite," *Cahiers Internautionaux de Sociologie,* 23 (July-Dec. 1957), 42-62.

Recreational Functions of the Church

Church activities have always had manifest and latent recreational consequences for individuals and society. Religious art, ritual, and pageantry, church music, symbolic pictures in the scriptures, messages by fluent preachers, literature in church publications, church-related social gatherings, fraternizing before and after church services, and even inquisitions against the enemies of religion have provided recreational gratifications to church members. Old-fashioned pie suppers, folk games, ice cream socials, box auctions, singing schools, and informal recreational activities have been supplemented or replaced by new functional equivalents.[20]

Many large churches have comprehensive recreational programs under paid professional leadership. The modern urban or suburban church plant is likely to include a gymnasium as well as a kitchen, lounge, social hall, and other social-recreational facilities. Drama, clubs, parties ("socials"), Sunday school contests, craft programs, visual aids, religious radio and television, athletic leagues, and numerous other church activities provide recreation for participants and observers. Symbolic of the growth of specialized recreational activities is the continuing expansion of Boy Scout, Girl Scout, Sky Pilot, Awana, Boys Brigade, and other youth clubs sponsored by churches. As of December 31, 1982, 64,087 Boy Scout troops, Cub packs, and Explorer posts, almost half (48.4 per cent) of all units, were sponsored by religious organizations.[21] In addition, numerous socio-religious recreational activities are provided by organizations like the YMCA, YWCA, YMHA, Catholic Youth Centers, Bible conferences, summer camps, and children's clubs loosely associated with churches.[22] Social changes have led to formalization of church activities and shifts in institutional roles.

Some religious groups have condemned recreational behavior as a form of idleness or some other kind of sin. When they have successfully

---

[20] Church suppers and picnics are still prominent activities in many rural areas. Cf. Milton Coughenour and Lawrence M. Hepple, *The Church in Rural Missouri, Part II, Religious Groups in Rural Missouri* (Columbia, Missouri: A.E.S. Research Bulletin 633B, Sept. 1957), pp. 107-10. For religious groups' attitudes toward leisure and recreation see Max Kaplan, *Leisure in America* (New York: John Wiley and Sons. 1960), pp. 148-67.

[21] Statistical Service, *1980 Through 1982 Local Council Index* (Dallas: Boy Scouts of America, 1983), p. xiv.

[22] These organizations are sometimes criticized because they have grown into self-perpetuating institutions which operate almost as ends in themselves, forgetful of their initial objectives. E.g., changed goals of the YMCA are denounced in Editorial, "Will the 'Y' Recover Its Gospel?" *Christianity Today,* 2, no. 3 (Nov. 11, 1957), 20-21; and Everet R. Johnson, "The Confusing 'C' in YMCA," *ibid.,* 2, no. 14 (April 14, 1958), 5-8.

blocked the satisfying of recreational impulses through other organizations, their church programs have become functional substitutes for recreational agencies.

Superficial investigation of historic trends conveys the impression that social and recreational programs have expanded in churches as emphasis upon prayer meetings, worship services, and other "spiritual" aspects of their ministry has declined. Most criticisms of this increased "secularization" fail to recognize that the prayer meeting, testimony service, and other displaced "sacred" activities included distinctly recreational functions which sociologically were not greatly different from those of the ladies sewing circle or quilting party. Formal recognition of recreational elements in the church program changes only the outward appearance. Social functions of the church may be performed in a different pattern of social interaction, but the consequences of the new pattern for individuals, society, and the church itself are similar to those of the old. Pressures resulting from basic social changes have increased the formality of many activities and modified institutional patterns of behavior. Thus committee meetings replace some of the friendly interaction that occurred a century ago in neighborly visiting, and men's brotherhoods replace the work bee called periodically in the past to repair church property, cut wood for its fuel, or give the church building an annual "housecleaning."

It is difficult to draw a line between the recreational and the nonrecreational in the church program, for recreational consequences are an intimate result of most church activities. The pastor whose sermons are not interesting and church organizations that do not have "stimulating" programs tend to lose members. "Religious literature" covers a broad range of materials; a substantial proportion is basically recreational.[23] Even strictly "religious" writings include humorous anecdotes and colorful descriptions with latent recreational functions. Most participation in church activities occurs during "leisure time"; from this perspective church attendance itself is a "recreational activity." Yet most churches do not provide members a majority of their personal recreational experiences.

Today the American church is perhaps relatively less important as a recreational agency than a century ago because so many specialized organizations have sprung up to meet recreational needs. During the period of increasing competition from emerging recreational agencies, church pressures against roller skating, bowling, movies, Sunday golf, weekend fishing and vacation trips, and the desecration of Sunday by

---

23 Of 1,572 books listed in the catalog of one large denominational publishing house, only 182 were religious (Bibles, everyday inspiration, and "fine religious references") while 1,390 were secular (history, science, homemaking, sports, etiquette, children's stories, etc.). Cf. A. Roy Eckardt, "The Pulsation of Religion," *Christian Century*, 75 (Dec. 17, 1958), 1458-60.

commercial recreation in general has gradually diminished; some churches have not only adapted to the change but tacitly or overtly encourage forms of commercialism which they formerly condemned. Variations in attitudes toward recreation provide part of the basis for much religious conflict (Chapters 11-13). Recreational functions of the church overlap considerably with its esthetic functions.

Esthetic Functions of the Church

Church ritual and liturgy, pageantry, drama, architecture, and furnishings provide many esthetic gratifications for participants and even passers-by. Attitudes of awe, reverence, joy, fear, and relaxation, which often result from esthetic elements in the church, contribute to collective worship, social fellowship, group solidarity, educational objectives, and tension management. Hence increased attention is being given to symbolism in church architecture, the contribution of various lighting and color combinations to worship, and other esthetic factors which help the church minister more effectively to "the whole person" and society. The church's esthetic functions have not been wholly lost to secular enterprises like the opera, movies, art museums, public pageants, and community art activities as Barnes has contended.[24]

Religious drama as a means of ministering to spiritual needs has regained prominence during this century, and its professional quality has gradually increased. Many Christian colleges, denominational agencies, and parachurch organizations sponsor touring players, and Christian theater companies are now found in most large metropolitan areas. At its best, Christian theater is both thoroughly professional and relevant to human needs in contemporary society. One study of 364 midwestern churches revealed that 322 had produced 947 plays during one year, 60 per cent in connection with regular services. The dominant motivations expressed (from most to least mentioned) were inspiration of the audience, education of the players, fund raising, and entertainment.[25]

Educators who teach the values, uses, and techniques of religious drama emphasize its appropriateness as an expression of worship and artistic impulses, a source of broadened sympathies, understandings, and solutions to problems, and a contributor to cooperation in church endeavors. At its best it influences basic decisions of life, develops a

---

[24] Harry Elmer Barnes, *Social Institutions* (Englewood Cliffs, N.J.: Prentice-Hall, 1942), p. 705.

[25] Jean Star Williams, "A Study of Religious Drama in Certain Churches of Six Protestant Denominations in the United States," as reported in Fred Eastman and Louis Wilson, *Drama in the Church*, rev. ed. (New York: Samuel French, 1942), pp. 4-5. Cf. Harold Ehrensperger and Stanley Lehrer, *Religious Drama: Ends and Means* (Westport, Conn.: Greenwood, 1977), and Hugh Steadman Williams, *A New Stage* (Richmond, Va.: MRA Books, n.d. [ca. 1982]).

missionary spirit, makes truth concrete, and makes Bible passages realistic. Participants gain friends, make decisions, find meaning for life, secure a deepened sense of the church's value, find wholesome attitudes for daily living, and develop their personalities. Specialists claim that it helps individuals toward the goal of life, cultivates right motives, and elevates the soul by its beauty. Producers, participants, and observers gain increased esthetic appreciation and other benefits from well-produced dramas in the church.[26]

Yet artistic elements in church life may have dysfunctional effects. Most church drama is of low quality. Amateur performers, meager and inadequate equipment, facilities poorly adapted to drama, and badly written plays make many religious productions fail spiritually, esthetically, and educationally. Although television and the movies undoubtedly have stimulated efforts to produce religious plays and have made the public adopt higher standards of success, the effects of badly written and poorly produced church plays may be disintegrative for the institution, if not for persons affected by them.

Economic Functions of the Church

Scholars have discerned many relationships between the church and the economic order. Each performs certain functions for the other. Marxists have theorized that religion evolved chiefly as a means whereby man believed he could acquire power over the environment and make the material world bend to his wishes.[27] Such economic interpretations of religion generally are avoided in capitalistic America.

The church's role in the distribution and consumption of wealth is significant. The payment of salaries to employees, purchase of supplies, possession of property, collection and dispensation of funds, erection of buildings, support of social welfare, sponsorship of recreational and missionary activities, and nearly every aspect of the work of the church involve the distribution of economic goods. In 1930 church property in the U.S. was worth a third more than the total value of all public property used for school purposes. Larson and Lowell estimate that the value of the tax-exempt church property in the nation exceeds 10 per cent of all that is taxable. New church construction reached record levels from 1922 through 1930 and again during the 1950's and 1960's. In 1958 the church construction of $863,000,000 accounted for one dollar in every

---

[26] Floy Merwyn Barnard, *Drama in the Churches* (Nashville: Broadman Press, 1950), pp. 8-14; and Florence A. and J. Edward Moseley, *Using Drama in the Church* (St. Louis: Bethany Press, 1939), pp. 13-14. These conclusions must be regarded scientifically as hypotheses, for they are not based upon systematic research.

[27] E.g., see V. F. Calverton, *The Passing of the Gods* (New York: Charles Scribner's Sons, 1934).

forty spent on privately financed construction, and another $567,000,000 was spent for buildings of non-public schools and colleges, most of which are church related. In 1980 $1,614,000,000, an all-time high, was spent on new church construction, but its real value was only about two-thirds of the $931,000,000 spent for that purpose a decade earlier.[28]

Churches use various methods to acquire their necessary finances. Some sponsor bingo parties, pie suppers, bazaars, rummage sales, and chicken dinners to make money. These activities often contribute more to social solidarity of the group than to its financial coffers. Some churches self-righteously condemn such practices as bringing commercialism into the church and emphasize the collection of free-will offerings or of tithes (one-tenth of the income) as the only proper means of financing church programs. Social scientists suspect that socially generated and sustained ulterior motives are involved in Scripture interpretations that make the tithe obligatory to the Christian, whose theology states he has been made "free from the law." [29] Controversies over finances have both group-making and group-breaking effects.

The typical church operates like a business on an annual budget. Systematic giving by members is encouraged by contribution envelopes and various adaptations of the "every member canvass." Expanding concepts and increased specialization of the church program necessitate an expensive multicelled building. This in turn creates a functional need for systematic solicitation of financial support, which is increasingly met by professional fund raisers.[30] Functional influences of modern business, private welfare, and especially the public relations profession are evident in the change to business-like methods of church finance.

The church influences individual economic behavior. It has stimulated patterns of consumption by individuals and families, even if that has not been its intent. Thanksgiving, Christmas, Hanukkah, and Easter are religious holidays which make material consumption a virtue. Church crusades agaist the commercialization of holy days are rare; when they do occur, they are not basically against consumption itself. American churches have done much to help people enjoy the American standard of living.[31] They are part of the total set of social mechanisms that maintain and reinforce basic societal values.

---

[28] Martin A. Larson and C. Stanley Lowell, *The Religious Empire* (Washington, D.C.: Robert B. Luce Co., 1976); Constant H. Jacquet, Jr., ed., *Yearbook of American and Canadian Churches 1982* (Nashville: Abingdon Press, 1982), p. 278; "Construction Level Is Still High," *Christian Century*, 76 (Jan. 28, 1959), 101.

[29] Cf. Hiley H. Ward, "Is Tithing Christian? " *Christian Century*, 74 (Feb. 13, 1957), 193-94; and Editorial, "Is Anti-Tithing Un-Christian? " *ibid.*, 74 (Mar. 13, 1957), 319-20.

[30] William H. Leach, "Financing the Local Church," *Annals of the American Academy of Political and Social Science,* 332 (Nov. 1960), 70-79.

[31] Hugh Dalziel Duncan, *Language and Literature in Society* (Chicago: University of Chicago Press, 1953), p. 32.

To whatever extent personal virtues of honesty, keeping one's word, and similar ethical standards essential in economic life are fostered by the church, it supports the national economy. Traditionally the major emphasis of most Protestant churches has been upon changing individuals, often in the assumption that through personal conversion social ills will be eliminated. Pope found no evidence in Gastonia, North Carolina, that reliance upon changed individuals in this manner is decisive either for the transformation of economic practices or for the emancipation of churches from their subservience to economic institutions.[32] Yet many lives have been radically transformed by religious conversion. It is partly because these persons are a minority and more because religion tends to be subordinate to practical economic considerations and basic social conditions that conversions have not significantly changed economic institutions.

The Protestant concept of "the calling" is a major ideological dividing line between the ancient-medieval and modern modes of thinking. Its focus was less upon business activity than productive toil; hence it was less a part of capitalistic than of industrial ethics. It played a major role in the emergence of the modern economic system.[33] The current revival of vocation, considering one's occupation as a task to which he is called by God, potentially can contribute to the economic order. When people consider their daily work to have spiritual significance, it becomes more than simply a means to an end.[34] Yet it is doubtful whether this viewpoint will ever become so widespread that it radically changes the outlook on life of workers in general.

Some persons participate in church activities for ulterior economic motives. Certain churches teach that God's special blessing rests upon those who participate generously in the church; they lead members to think that the road to economic success is tithing or giving a double tithe. Economic institutions and aspirations may hence affect religious activities ordinarily not considered to have any economic implications.[35]

The church influences the basic economic order. Religious sanctions support much of the economic system. Economic policies of government,

---

[32] Liston Pope, *Millhands and Preachers* (New Haven: Yale University Press, 1942), p. 334.

[33] Charles and Katherine George, "Protestantism and Capitalism in Pre-Revolutionary England," *Church History,* 27 (Dec. 1958), 351-71.

[34] Whiting Williams, "The Church in Relation to the Worker," *Annals of the American Academy of Political and Social Science,* 165 (Jan. 1933), 57-63; Elton Trueblood, *Your Other Vocation* (New York: Harper and Brothers, 1952); John Oliver Nelson, ed., *Work and Vocation* (New York: Harper and Brothers, 1954); and Richard G. Belcher, "The Church as Vocational Counselor," *Pastoral Psychology,* 9, no. 89 (Dec. 1958), 45-50.

[35] Little evidence of this was found in a study of unemployed laborers. Their religious practices remained basically the same as when employed. Cf. E. Wight Bakke, *The Unemployed Worker* (New Haven: Yale University Press, 1940), pp. 152-53, 277-78.

individuals, and corporations are rooted in justice and righteousness, so as the church promotes what is right, it reinforces the economic policies directly or indirectly involved. This was especially obvious in the social gospel movement (Chapter 6) with its concern for economic and social well-being. Churches sometimes help give proposed changes in the economic order an ethical justification, but they also impart sacredness to the status quo. Libertarians in churches have revolted against denominational social action groups that deal with socioeconomic issues, for they fear these groups are "dedicated to hastening the advent of the welfare state and a planned economy." [36] Although it is likely that churches generally have made a positive contribution to national economic well-being, they have made errors on socioeconomic matters, which are more difficult and complex than many ministers recognize. Over-simplification of problems and solutions has forced retreat of many religious leaders from their positions and led to a decline of church prestige. It also has encouraged some churches to retreat to the extreme of complete aloofness from all socioeconomic issues, leading people to think the church is not concerned with such aspects of man's welfare. Dysfunctional and functional consequences are thus intermingled in church activities pertinent to the economic order.

Sometimes religion is an "opiate of the people," a mask for socioeconomic privilege. More often than not it sanctions the existent economic structure. This reflects both the economic involvements of churches, which give them a vested interest in the status quo, and the strength of the middle and upper classes in church membership and leadership. Only newer sects not yet established securely are likely to be at odds with the basic institutions of society. Most churches in Gastonia were both a source of economic change and a product of prior economic changes. They sanctioned the prevailing economic organization and culture and yet were antagonists of them. The relation between religious and economic institutions was symbiotic or reciprocal in character.[37]

Organized religion contributes to social control over economic matters (Chapter 6). This influence cannot operate formally in America but must be internalized in individuals. It thus affects the professional and ethical codes that regulate business activities and other socioeconomic behavior.[38] This influence is emphasized in Max Weber's classical study of relationships between attitudes in Calvinistic Christianity and capitalistic viewpoints toward property, profits, labor, etc. Weber showed how prosperity in this life became evidence for the Calvinist, who was not

---

[36] Edmund A. Opitz, "Laymen's Revolt in the Churches," *The Freeman*, 4, no. 10 (Feb. 8, 1954), 338-39.

[37] Pope, *Millhands and Preachers*, pp. vii-viii, 331-32.

[38] John M. Clark, *Social Control of Business*, 2nd ed. (New York: McGraw-Hill Book Co., 1939), pp. 201, 233-34; and Frank Knight and Thornton W. Merriam, *The Economic Order and Religion* (New York: Harper and Brothers, 1945).

sure of salvation, that he had been elected by God to enjoy eternal life in glory, for only the righteous are blessed by Him. Although Weber's thesis has been widely discussed and often criticized, it is generally agreed that modern capitalism emerged in an atmosphere which was religiously favorable to it. Lenski's thorough statistical studies growing out of Weber's theory demonstrate the subtle, continuing, and pervasive influence of the dominant socio-religious groups on many areas of economic life.[39] Such latent functions of religion are easily overlooked by social scientists.

Empirical evidence indicates that Catholic as well as Protestant workers share in patterns of social mobility and aspirations for the future generally considered to be aspects of "the Protestant ethic." American Catholics generally rank lower than Protestants in the social class structure, but they are rising into the middle and even upper classes just as Protestant immigrant groups did before them. All religious traditions are represented among leading capitalists, and in many nations Calvinism has declined as capitalism advanced.[40]

The higher inventive productivity in Protestant than Catholic nations, Protestant opposition to gambling, and Protestant encouragement of a one-price business system result from religious values and associated personality traits. Much inventiveness in Catholic nations was the work of persons with Protestant backgrounds.[41] After the Protestant Reformation churches abdicated from areas of economic conduct and social theory that had long been claimed as their province. A new scale of ethical values was generally accepted; it turned the desire for pecuniary profit from a frailty of man into the mainspring of society. A dualism arose; the church took the individual soul as its province, and secular institutions took the province of business activities and affairs of society. The Christian church thus came to sanction covetousness and "the idolatry of wealth," which Tawney believes to be the practical religion of capitalistic societies.[42]

Religious value systems sometimes condition the entire socioeconomic

[39] Max Weber, *The Protestant Ethic and the Spirit of Capitalism*, translated by Talcott Parsons (London: George Allen and Unwin, 1930), and Gerhard Lenski, *The Religious Factor* (Garden City, N.Y.: Doubleday and Co., 1961).

[40] Raymond W. Mack, Raymond J. Murphy, and Seymour Yellin, "The Protestant Ethic, Level of Aspiration, and Social Mobility: An Empirical Test," *American Sociological Review*, 21 (June 1956), 295-300; and Bosco D. Costello, "Catholics in American Commerce and Industry, 1925-1945," *American Catholic Sociological Review*, 17 (Oct. 1956), 219-33.

[41] Isidor Thorner, "Ascetic Protestantism and the Development of Science and Technology," *American Journal of Sociology*, 58 (July 1952), 25-33; and "Ascetic Protestantism, Gambling, and the One-Price System," *American Journal of Economics and Sociology*, 15 (Jan. 1956), 161-72.

[42] R. H. Tawney, *Religion and the Rise of Capitalism* (New York: Harcourt, Brace and Co., 1926). Cf. V. A. Demant, *Religion and the Decline of Capitalism* (New York: Charles Scribner's Sons, 1952), and Winthrop S. Hudson, "The Weber Thesis Reexamined," *Church History*, 30 (Mar. 1961), 88-99.

development of an emerging or growing community. This applies most clearly, but not solely, to utopian societies founded on the basis of religiously-oriented values. Comparison of "Homestead" and "Rimrock," both located in the same natural environment, revealed marked differences in the social systems. The stress upon cooperative community action in Rimrock was traced largely to the influence of Mormonism. In contrast, the lack of a dominant religion in Homestead, where competitive denominationalism was strong, strengthened commitment to a highly individualistic value-orientation. Even differences between the irrigation pattern of farming in Rimrock, with its associated compact village settlement, and the dry-land, isolated-farm pattern of Homestead were traced partly to differences in the religious value systems.[43]

Religious pluralism in America is a concomitant of a pluralist economy which nominally stresses the free market. Both realms share a process of decision-making in which private judgment is dominant. Decentralized decisions prevail in religion, politics, and the economic order.[44] Each reinforces the other and helps solidify society.

Complex reciprocal relationships prevail between religion and the economic order. The diverse conclusions of studies related to Weber's famous inquiry reflect this complexity.[45] The reciprocal interdependence of the church and economic institutions is most clearly evident in times of crisis. The Great Depression of the 1930's had profound effects upon the activities, message, clergy, and membership as well as the finances of churches.[46] Whether it intends and wishes so or not, the church has many economic functions and dysfunctions. When it abdicates its role in economic affairs, it easily swings into a position that unwittingly condones what is evil according to its own definitions and thus indirectly supports social structures and actions which are nominally condemned by its own normative code.

Ethical-Moral Functions of the Church

The importance of the church in establishing, enforcing, and sustaining ethical and moral standards has been noted in Chapter 6. This function is

---

[43] Evon Z. Vogt and Thomas F. O'Dea, "A Comparative Study of the Role of Values in Social Action in Two Southwestern Communities," *American Sociological Review*, 18 (Dec. 1953), 645-54.

[44] Max Lerner, *America as a Civilization* (New York: Simon and Schuster, 1957), pp. 716-17.

[45] Cf. K. Boulding, "Religious Foundations of Economic Progress," *Harvard Business Review*, 30 (May-June 1952), 33-40; S. D. Clark, "Religion and Economic Backward Areas," *American Economic Review*, 4 (May 1951), 258-65; and J. Milton Yinger, *Religion, Society and the Individual* (New York: The Macmillan Co., 1957), pp. 214-23, 516-42.

[46] Samuel C. Kincheloe, *Research Memorandum on Religion in the Depression* (New York: Social Science Research Council, Bulletin No. 33, 1937).

evident in its tasks pertinent to social control, social solidarity, social welfare, education, and even economic and political affairs. The central themes of the basic American moral code have been derived from Judeo-Christian ethics.[47] The church helps define personal goals, is a critic of society, elevates social standards, guards cultural mores, and helps integrate group values. There is great overlapping between this and other church functions; in this area it is largely a reinforcer of other institutions.

1. The church helps people define life goals and purposes. It encourages good will, unselfishness, and kindness toward others as a manifestation of religious motives. The will of God is presented as the nucleus for all life values and as the focus of the conscience. The sanctions used to help determine life purposes have been modified in recent history. Appeal to a supernatural authority was gradually changed to command by the Deity's representative. The representative then grew less and less infallible and more and more secular. With increasing freedom and emphasis upon rational explanation of social conventions, the individual began to govern his attitudes and behavior by principles more than by subservience to arbitrary injunctions; religious conduct was gradually changed into largely rational systems. Ethical principles became a system separate from religion, enforced by government, public opinion, professional codes, etc.[48] In spite of this change, the church still helps many people shape their philosophy of life.

2. The church is a critic of society. As the "conscience of society," it judges cultural institutions and practices by its ethical standards. Worship of and service to God provide it in theory with a normative reference outside the culture. The social gospel movement, vocational discussion groups, and social action committees illustrate the church's attempt to make religion relevant to contemporary life and to direct its criticism at the basic structures and functions of society.[49]

The church's prophetic ministry as God's representative has problems and dangers. The prophetic institution or its spokesmen easily become self-righteous. Negativistic judgments create a sense of guilt, which sometimes makes it difficult for the church to exercise its role as a healer of souls. As part of society, the church may simply reflect the general culture pattern in passing judgment; it then is less a spokesman for God than a solidifier sanctioning social values of a nation, denomination, social class, or other finite group. The resulting disunity makes churches

---

[47] Robin M. Williams, Jr., *American Society* (New York: Alfred A. Knopf, 1951), p. 398.

[48] Charles H. Judd, *The Psychology of Social Institutions* (New York: The Macmillan Co., 1926), pp. 267-69.

[49] Robert Lynn, Kenneth Underwood, Edwin Becker, and William Miller, "Christian Faith and the Protestant Churches," *Social Action,* 18, no. 6 (May 1952), 29-34; and Herbert W. Schneider, *Religion in Twentieth Century America* (Cambridge, Mass.: Harvard University Press, 1952), pp. 60-89.

weak. The habit of viewing things from the public relations standpoint, giving more concern to what the world will think about its judgments and their effect upon growth in membership than to God's will, also hinders this task. Rationalizations to save face are a common result—after all, God wants all men to come to knowledge of the truth (interpreted pragmatically as joining one's church), so the more members a church gains, the more effectively it is serving God! In spite of limitations and problems, the conscience of society occasionally pricks a little here and there to produce gradual modification of the social order, as individuals are made sensitive to God's message. The Word of God is "the sharp sword of truth in the prophetic individual, the penetrating moral insight that cuts through the shams and excuses of even the best-organized society." [50] The church must be separate from government and other institutions in order to criticize constructively and objectively.

3. The church influences social standards. Playing its prophetic role, it helps many raise their standards of life to a higher ethical plane, thus influencing the normative patterns of society. Hertzler has called religious institutions "a great social lighthouse" because of their past role in setting up such magnificent and beneficent conceptions as the Golden Rule, love as a universal social agent, the brotherhood of man, and high principles related to beauty, goodness, and justice. Through its sanctions the church is a socializing agent that enforces socially approved values through codes, creeds, and rituals. American normative values are channelized from the core of the Judeo-Christian ethic and ideology of freedom to flow outward into nearly every aspect of community life.[51]

4. The church guards the mores of society. The support religion gives moral ideals is often presented as its greatest social significance. All religions are ethical in the sense that they support some sort of moral conduct. Social obligations tend to become religious obligations; religion thus conserves customs and habits believed beneficial to society. The taboos of the dominant social class tend to become those of religion. This socially conservative tendency is generally beneficial to society, but it also has been a chief source of the abuses of religion.[52]

Sanctions involving supernatural rewards and punishments enter early into the consciousness of the young; God is invoked to enforce proper conduct. The content of the moral code varies, but in all churches the particular code of the group is considered the will of God. For example, Puritan values which included prohibition of alcoholic beverages char-

---

[50] Kenneth E. Boulding, *The Organizational Revolution* (New York: Harper and Brothers, 1953), pp. 220-21. Cf. John C. Bennett, "The Church as Prophetic Critic," *Christian Century,* 71 (Jan. 6, 1954), 9-11.

[51] Hertzler, "Religious Institutions," and Roy C. Buck, "The Contribution of the Church to the Total Community," *Town and Country Church,* 138 (Dec. 1958), 5-7.

[52] Charles A. Ellwood, "Religion and Social Control," *Scientific Monthly,* 7 (1918), 339-41.

acterized a majority of lower class adults in a small New Brunswick city. Active participation in church clubs was associated with opposition to drinking. Denominational differences in attitudes toward the use of alcohol were also observed; 72 per cent of the Roman Catholics, 64 per cent of the Anglicans and United Church members, and 35 per cent of the Baptists accepted the custom of serving alcoholic beverages to guests.[53] These variations are at least partly the effects of religious differences. Religion is also related to the use of tobacco, certain groups considering it sinful. A carefully controlled comparison of Seventh-day Adventists, for whom tobacco use is taboo, and non-Adventists was made by Dr. Ernest L. Wynder of the Sloan-Kettering Institute. He found significant differences between the health of the matched groups, with the Adventists in a clearly advantageous position.[54] If mounting research evidence about the injurious effects of tobacco is not traced eventually to other factors, sectarian opposition to it may be justified scientifically. Minority religious sects sometimes help to modify certain aspects of society's moral code; they then are attackers, not guardians as churches tend to be, of conventional mores.

5. The church helps integrate society's values. It usually does not indiscriminately adopt the values of dominant groups. It subjects them to the scrutiny of comparison with scripture and religious traditions. It may thus unearth inconsistencies that must be ironed out and integrated into a unified, consistent system. The ideals it establishes as goals tend to be higher than can be fully attained. Complete integration of the religious value system with realistic conditions of action hence is empirically impossible. Institutionalized expectations fall short of institutionalized ideals.[55] Reconciliation of the two leads to systems of theology which incorporate basic ideals and values of society into a consistent pattern. When organized religion runs through all phases of life and one religion dominates, as in certain isolated societies, the entire ethical code forms a unitary normative system of legal, practical, esthetic, and moral rules by which individual conduct is regulated; no aspect of the system can then be considered apart from the system as a whole.[56] In America numerous and diverse religious groups, striving for consistency in dealing with moral values, help integrate values and help persons find a central focus for their plans and actions. While most churches no longer dictate an authoritative morality detail for

[53] Douglas R. Pullman, "Some Social Correlates of Attitudes toward the Use of Alcoholic Beverages," *Quarterly Journal of Studies on Alcohol,* 19 (Dec. 1958), 623-35.

[54] Lois Mattox Miller, "The Case of the Wise Abstainers," *Reader's Digest,* 37, no. 8 (Aug. 1958), 67-71.

[55] Cf. Talcott Parsons, *The Social System* (Glencoe, Ill.: The Free Press, 1951), pp. 163-67.

[56] Joachim Wach, *Sociology of Religion* (Chicago: University of Chicago Press, 1944), p. 50.

detail, they still contribute much to the consciousness of good and evil, the promulgation of social ethics, and the emergence and support of new details in society's moral code.

The church's influence on social standards is limited by the social conservatism of churches preoccupied with individual rather than group behavior, by the tendency of institutional religion to be so identified and coextensive with the community that its faults become those of the church, and by the loss in crusading power that accompanies growth and diversification of church membership. F. Ernest Johnson believes prophetic concern groups and vocational groups within churches are the most fruitful resolution of this dilemma. He thinks churches have raised the nation's moral level in at least four ways. (1) They create moral awareness by focusing attention on imperfections of human behavior, thus producing widespread recognition of harmful consequences of habitual actions. (2) They create an atmosphere that calls forth a response to universal imperatives. Many churches appeal to the *middle axiom,* an ethical proposition definite enough to avoid being "smothered in generalities" but so universal that it is not "strangled by particular practical or technical difficulties." (An illustration is the insistence on a living wage and a just share in the product for the worker in industry and agriculture.) (3) Churches raise the general moral level by their internal discipline. Their "searchlight" function is effective when internal discipline corresponds to external testimony. Thus the church does not eliminate the evils of racial segregation as long as it rigidly insists on segregation at 11:00 A.M. Sunday; it promotes integration only when it sets an example in deed as well as in word. (4) The church implements social convictions. Its emphasis on Christian vocation helps constituents implement its moral pronouncements. Some of its crusading and lobbying, especially when truly representative of members' attitudes, has helped bring about certain political developments connected with social welfare.[57]

Dysfunctional Influences of the Church

Any consideration of the church as a social institution would be very imbalanced if it considered only the positive contributions made by the church to society and its members. The church has often had a baneful effect and created serious difficulties in society. We have noted many of these dysfunctions in preceding sections; others are suggested in scattered passages throughout this book. We shall now survey briefly some dys-

[57] F. Ernest Johnson, "Do Churches Exert Significant Influence on Public Morality?" *Annals of the American Academy of Political and Social Science,* 280 (Mar. 1952), 125-32. The middle axiom is analogous to Robert K. Merton's "theories of the middle range"

functions of the church that are related to the basic social order, to individuals, and to the church's own institutional life.

Dysfunctional Influences on Society

A prominent criticism of the church is that it is too conservative. As a guardian of societal mores, it sometimes is used by dominant social classes to maintain a social system which has become a stumbling block to progress. This conservative side of religion probably is the major cause of the traditional enmity of science toward religion (Chapter 13). Opposition by the church to studies of the origin of man and his institutions; of the use of anesthetics; of mental illness and the phenomena of demonism, witchcraft, and evil spirits, and a host of other subjects demonstrates the stabilizing influence of the church but also reveals its role as an agency of reaction. It tends to endow prevailing customs and doctrines with divine sanctions and to repress new ideas and usages almost as if its primary task is to prevent change.[58] Rational solutions of technical problems have been hindered by the church. How many inventions have been withheld and how many innovators have been so discouraged by the church that they did not even try to produce desirable changes is unknown. Both directly and indirectly the church has prevented much change that would have been beneficial to all except those with strong vested interests in the status quo.

The conservatism of religion has often resulted in reactionary opposition to advancing liberty. The narrow spirit of those Pharisees in Jesus' day who were so concerned with the letter of the law that they missed its spirit has been common among fundamentalists of all times, places, and religions. "Too often through its well-meaning but be-nighted representatives, religion has mocked the findings of careful and conscientious scholars, stood with the representatives of arrant wrong against those who in love of the truth have battled for the rights of the people." [59] The church may become so enamored of the status quo that it hinders social changes which are more consistent with its theology than the current social structures and functions which it protects by supporting the powerful at the expense of the weak.[60]

The church sometimes becomes a disruptive, divisive force in society. This is most likely to be the case when religious loyalties are divided as

---

[58] Cf. Panunzio, *Major Social Institutions*, pp. 314-16; and F. B. Julian, "The Influence of Religion on the Progress of Medicine," *The Hibbert Journal*, 51 (Apr. 1953), 254-61.

[59] John L. Gillin and John P. Gillin, *Cultural Sociology* (New York: The Macmillan Co., 1948), p. 473.

[60] Cf. the discussion of Southern Baptist censorship of *The Long Bridge* by its author, Phyllis Woodruff Sapp, "It Happened to One Book," *Christian Century*, 75 (Apr. 9, 1958), 432-33.

in pluralistic America. On the basis of wide studies North concluded that only language differences are more disruptive in a group than differences in religion. Religion has been involved in some of the bloodiest wars of mankind and has been a major factor in many political and economic revolutions.[61] The destructive influence results largely from the bigotry characteristic of zealous believers. Religious zeal often turns love into hatred; it justifies the hatred in the mind of the believer who "contends for the faith." Hatred is rationalized as an expression of "righteous indignation." It is almost always returned to its giver in accentuated form, establishing a self-perpetuating vicious circle. Religious values believed essential for humanity result in proselyting that sometimes leads to conflict, for "genuine belief is always intolerant." [62] When zealots of one religion are confronted by those of another, however minute their differences in doctrine and practice, bigoted attitudes, unkind deeds, and overt conflicts often result. The historic records of the torture of heretics, tormenting of Jews, Protestant-Catholic controversies, and medieval crusades against the Moslems illustrate this tendency.

Certain groups in society have used the church to uphold their privileges. The "divine right of kings," the tendency of American churches to reflect middle-class virtues, and the vested interests of bureaucrats in theoretically democratic religious bodies are illustrations. A few churches crusade on behalf of the oppressed, but most use religious sanctions to support the status quo. Thus some used the Bible to support the enfranchisement of women while others used it to prove their inferiority. Semi-religious groups still oppose child labor laws, graduated income taxes, social security, and similar measures that protect the lower classes, and religious beliefs and customs often hinder modern sanitation practices.[63]

American religion has an individualistic emphasis. Much Protestant teaching has been exclusively concerned with the virtues, activities, attitudes, and relationships of individuals rather than of groups and institutions. By emphasizing a future personal salvation it has forgotten the society of Christian brethren on earth and hence has failed to modify society, except insofar as fortification in individuals of such cultural values as honesty and love contributes to that goal. It has tended to forget that it is through group relationships in institutions that one develops into the kind of person he is. Its major emphasis has been on primary group relationships (such as those within the family) and controls over individual behavior rather than upon relationships of secondary groups.

---

[61] Cecil C. North, *Social Differentiation* (Chapel Hill: University of North Carolina Press, 1926), pp. 41-43; and John W. Dykstra, "Problems of a Religiously Pluralistic Society," *Sociology and Social Research,* 45 (July 1961), 401-6.

[62] Howard Becker and Leopold Von Wiese, *Systematic Sociology* (Gary, Indiana: Norman Paul Press, Wisconsin edition, 1950), p. 616.

[63] Benjamin D. Paul, "The Role of Beliefs and Customs in Sanitation Programs," *American Journal of Public Health,* 48 (Nov. 1958), 1502-6.

Although the controls of secondary groups usually operate through smaller primary subgroups, there is an ever-present tendency for this emphasis to prevent the extension of religious interpretations to the world of impersonal derivative experiences. This shortcoming of religion is illustrated by a priest's protection of a U.S. Senator, when he was involved in political corruption, on the basis of his personal virtues as a model husband, loving father, and helpful neighbor. Obviously perfection in primary group relationships (being a model husband-father-neighbor) is not the same as perfection in secondary group relationships (being a good citizen-politician).[64] Religion has often failed to meet the moral demands of society by failure to recognize that personal virtues are not necessarily nor consistently correlated with the social virtues necessary for the smooth functioning of a complex, urbanized society.

Dysfunctional Influences on Individuals

Religion contributes to mental illness (Chapter 17). It may be an "escape from freedom" for the neurotic personality. It sometimes contributes to arrested intellectual development and self-deception. Closely related is the part religion plays as a narcotic, "the opiate of the people." As a refuge from the stark realities of life and an outlet for discontent, it has supported servility in the working classes. Otherworldliness, one manifestation of this, has often hindered social progress. The person whose major concern is with the future life or who believes the world will get worse and worse in spite of all men's efforts, will not work for social progress.

The church tends to determine the kind and quality of religious life for most persons. They accept ready-made beliefs and routines; even if they break away, they are likely to do so by adopting the beliefs and routines of another church. The religious needs of persons who object to accepting a pre-cast form of faith but are socially compelled to choose one are therefore not met satisfactorily. Many Americans accept their religious faiths with considerable mental reservation. Churches often insist on ancient (and therefore holy!) forms of social customs, architecture, music, language, and other social patterns. This insistence on the familiar, the established, and the archaic is often a source of personal dissatisfaction and maladjustment.[65]

Church leaders sometimes overemphasize deviation from societal norms. Clergymen who have had some clinical training may accentuate trivial eccentricities of parishioners and think nearly all to be mentally ill. They

[64] L. L. Bernard as quoted in Paul H. Landis, *Social Control* (Chicago: J. B. Lippincott Co., 1939), pp. 173-74. See also Wesner Fallaw, *Toward Spiritual Security* (Philadelphia: Westminster Press, 1952), pp. 158-72.
[65] Hertzler, "Religious Institutions," pp. 11-12; and Panunzio, *Major Social Institutions,* p. 315.

may prescribe for conditions that should be referred to psychiatrists or fail to provide in their ministry anything that will not minister directly to personal mental and spiritual health.[66] Closely related is the oversimplification of human problems by many clergymen. The writer has known pastors whose only help in time of trouble is "Let's pray about it." While prayer unquestionably is proper for believers in the sovereignty of God, it fails to satisfy the man who feels that more tangible help could be given in his time of need. Recognizing that "faith without works is dead, being alone" (James 2:26), he expects more from the church than sirupy words offered as an excuse for not giving tangible assistance.

Dysfunctional Elements Within the Church

The church suffers from flaws in its structure and functions. One of these, as in any organization, is over-institutionalization. When dead routine and a highly bureaucratized leadership have become ends in themselves instead of means toward ends, the church often loses its influence for good upon individuals and society. Many sects arise as reactions against intolerance and artificiality which come from an emphasis upon standardized forms, creeds, or theologies or from making souls fit into a rigid pattern. Over-institutionalization is usually followed by reform, schism, or death of the organization (Chapter 5). Much evidence supports Fallaw's belief that the Christian church generally has been so caught up by this "institutionalism" that organizational strength rather than personal spiritual growth has become its goal. The clutter of denominational machinery is overemphasized to the detriment of spiritual values.[67]

Extreme competition between churches has prevented them from taking a united stand against evils. Each has feared that others might get the credit, that people may lose sight of "sharp and important" differences between churches, or that a compromise of religious convictions is involved in cooperation with a church of different faith. Selfish vested interests of churches weaken their moral recommendations and teachings.

Another weakening element is hypocrisy on the part of members and leaders. Materialism and externalism have crept into much church attendance and leadership; many an Easter "worship service" is primarily an occasion to show off new clothing, and similar motivations apply at other times.[68] Hypocrisy is evident, too, in rationalizations and apologies made for the church. Its defenders tend to justify it on the basis of expediency. Religion is considered a means of weathering the storms of life, enriching spiritual experience, preserving the social order, or fending

---

[66] Vaughan, *Social Psychology,* p. 850.

[67] Fallaw, *Toward Spiritual Security,* pp. 126-27, 176-77. Cf. Robert Lee, "The Organizational Dilemma in American Protestantism," *Union Seminary Quarterly Review,* 16 (Nov. 1960), 9-19.

[68] Paul Brinkman, Jr., "A Goddess in Protestant Worship?" *Lutheran Quarterly,* 7 (Feb. 1955), 50-52.

off anxieties rather than as "a transcendent revelation of the nature of man and the world." [69] It is made homocentric rather than theocentric; the old beliefs become so hollow and empty that "peace of mind" cults and other innovations centered on man rather than on God replace them.

Every institution incorporates some dysfunctional tendencies. Dogmatism that assumes intrinsic self-worth makes it become an end in itself. Opportunism, which uses any means at hand to promote its goals, contributes to a materialistic resort to inappropriate or tainted means that presume the intrinsic worth of some single phase of life. The result of intermingling conservatism and liberalism to find means more in keeping with basic ends is schism; this leads to social reform and "redemption" of the institution.[70] Dysfunctions are a natural part of institutional structures and processes.

Changes in Church Functions

The church has changed considerably during its history, adding some functions and losing others as society has changed. Many formerly informal and incidental functions have become formalized, institutionalized, and professionalized. Some functions have shifted to other institutions. These changes are natural results of industrialization and other basic trends in a fluid society.

So many functions have shifted away from the church that Barnes believes its chief remaining field of operation is the mass organization of group sentiments in support of basic principles of kindness, sympathy, honesty, right, justice, decency, and beauty. Religion would thus become a mere adjunct to the social sciences and esthetics, serving as their public propaganda agency.[71] It is doubtful whether organized religion on a large scale could exist without a sense of mystery and a recognition of higher loyalties than those representing only man himself, even at his best.

The church was once, but is no longer, the repository of all knowledge, the center of culture and learning. It has shifted so often in modern society that for a while it seemed to have no final resting place, no task other than to proclaim a kind of quietistic, pietistic, personal communion with God that ignores the major phases of life and society. An inferiority complex characterized many churchmen as a result.[72] The church is no

---

[69] Leo Lowenthal and Norbert Guterman, *Prophets of Deceit* (New York: Harper and Brothers, 1949), p. 18.

[70] Alfred H. Lloyd, "The Institution and Some of Its Original Sins," *American Journal of Sociology*, 13 (Jan. 1908), 523-40.

[71] Barnes, *Social Institutions*, p. 706.

[72] William H. Fineshriber, "Functions of the Church," *Annals of the American Academy of Political and Social Science*, 165 (Jan. 1933), 64-71. Cf. Joseph Van Vleck, Jr., *Our Changing Churches* (New York: Association Press, 1937), pp. 114-51.

longer the center or hub of philanthropy and social welfare, but only one spoke on a wheel. It once had power over material penalties as a major formal agency of social control, but formal functions of control have shifted to government; the church's power is moral rather than material. Because it has become easier to change one's church than his business, the church's control is often less compelling than the opinions of professional associates. Ethical values that once were upheld almost exclusively by the church have almost become an independent social institution. Until recent times only the church was concerned with the "cure of souls," a task now shared with many types of psychotherapists and social workers. Physical healing has been abdicated almost entirely to the medical profession. The church once dominated international relations and played a major role in political life; today it is largely separate from government even in countries that retain an official church. Marriage has been secularized; the contract is more a civil than an ecclesiastical one.

Differential response to change contributes to the great diversity of contemporary churches. The primary emphasis in most is upon developing personal habits and attitudes; social pressures and inner compulsions are used toward this end.

The loss of church functions to other institutions is not entirely a one-way exchange. Churches have been deeply concerned with weekday religious education, formal recreation programs, psychotherapeutic training of the clergy, efforts to break down the sacred-secular dichotomy in order to emphasize the sacredness of every legitimate task, sponsorship of welfare agencies, and application of religious principles to socioeconomic and political problems. It is possible that the loss of certain functions has been counterbalanced to a high degree by gain and that, according to American values, there is as much good as evil in the changes. All major institutions are more differentiated internally than they were a century or two ago. As a more specialized institution, the church may direct the spiritual welfare of mankind more effectively than when it was expected to be the direct agent of society in numerous realms of life.

Changes in the church which accompany changes in its environment demonstrate clearly its interdependence with the rest of society. The church may be functionally regarded as an instrument promoting or retarding change; it may also be viewed as a product of cumulative changes. When social changes occur, the church may change radically, or it may remain close to its traditional faith and ritual while adjusting its organization and activities to the modified social climate. Programs that are highly effective and functional in one time and place may be ineffective and dysfunctional in another. In rapidly changing society, the church's methods and program cannot remain static if it is to implement its goals. American society consists of many subcultures; each of these varies in time. This complex pattern of groups must be recognized by church leaders to serve the needs of their generation effectively. Application of social research to evaluate church effectiveness can prevent many latent dysfunctions and promote latent as well as manifest functions for individuals, society, and the church.

Conclusion

It is evident from the samples of functions and dysfunctions presented here and in Chapter 6 that there is great variation between churches in the specific consequences of their programs. There also are differential effects of the same units of institutional structure and action. Some are highly functional from the perspective of maintaining the institution but dysfunctional for society or for individuals. Separating effects into those for society, for the church as a social institution, for the local church, and for the individual involves an artificial abstracting from reality which is imposed upon the data by the social researcher.

The long-range effects of certain changes may be strikingly different from immediate results. Thus radical changes have occurred in churches when they have shifted from unpaid lay ministers to professional clergymen, and the movement of a religious body on the church-sect continuum (Chapter 5) has profound implications for its functions relative to the social order. The church's functions are not the same at all times and places. A change either in society or in a church necessitates re-assessment of the social consequences of the church's units of structure and action. Changes affect subgroups in the church or society more than they affect the totality either of churches as a general institution or of society. Disintegration of an ineffective local church may be functional from the perspective of religion as a social institution, while it usually is dysfunctional from the perspective of the denomination of which it is a part or of its immediate members.

The overlapping functions of churches and other institutions reflect the presence of functional equivalents, alternatives, and substitutes. The same socio-psychological or societal need may be met in alternative ways; the same effects can be produced by the actions of different institutions. Furthermore, dysfunctional consequences of each institution in a social order are to some extent counterbalanced by the functions of others. The exact pattern of institutional roles hence fluctuates as equilibrium is sought but never fully attained in dynamic society.

Overlapping of the "strictly religious" and other functions of the church is so pronounced that there is a tendency to confuse its ends (as theologically defined) with the means of its program. The church tends to become an instrument of society more than an institution transcending all that is secular. From the perspective of Christian ideology, religion fills its proper place in society only when it is fitted into society as something not fitting society! That is, religious activities ideally are not adjusted to social activities when doing so involves compromising religious doctrines. When this idealistic goal is attained, religious activities are transcendent over culture and modify societal forms and practices toward those advocated by the church. Symbols provided by the church then stand above and give meaning to the values of society. Religion thus becomes both a part of society and transcendent of it.[73]

Functional and dysfunctional consequences in each area of church action are inseparable. To have the former, it usually is necessary to tolerate some of the latter. Increased understanding of both the sources and the varying consequences of alternative action patterns oriented toward similar goals can come through social science research. Latent functions and dysfunctions are difficult to discern, but they are especially important. They may not only impede effectiveness but may directly contradict the very goals the church professes to achieve. With adequate knowledge, functions can be increased and dysfunctions reduced by careful planning which discerns the long-term latent dysfunctions, as well as the immediate manifest functions, of each possible alternative.

The functions and dysfunctions of the church in American society will become increasingly clear as we examine other aspects of the church in discussions of education, evangelism and missions, relationships of the church with other institutions, the social psychology of religion, and the roles of the clergy. Although functional concepts are not the basic framework of succeeding chapters, much of their content relates directly to functions and dysfunctions of the American church.

Selected References: Macro-sociological Studies

Demant, V. A., *Religion and the Decline of Capitalism*. New York: Scribner's, 1952. A philosophical-historical study revealing latent consequences of the dissociation of economics from religious and ethical norms.

Eisenstadt, S. N., ed., *The Protestant Ethic and Modernization: A Comparative View*. New York: Basic Books, 1968. Discussions of Weber's views on relationships between religion, capitalism, and societal modernization.

Greeley, Andrew M., "The Protestant Ethic: Time for a Moratorium," *Sociological Analysis*, 25, no. 1 (Spring 1964), 20–33. Argues that simplistic views of the Weberian theory applied to contemporary society reflect a misunderstanding of Weber, ignorance of the pluralism of Catholicism, oversimplification of history, and refusal to be persuaded by contradictory empirical data.

---

[73] Robert N. Bellah, "The Place of Religion in Human Action," *Review of Religion*, 22 (Mar. 1958), 137-54; John L. Thomas, "Religion in American Society II," *Social Order*, 6 (Sept. 1956), 312-18; Rudolph E. Morris, "Problems Concerning the Institutionalizing of Religion," *American Catholic Sociological Review*, 17 (June 1956), 98-108.

Green, Robert W., ed., *Protestantism and Capitalism: The Weber Thesis and Its Critics*. Boston: Heath, 1959. Critiques of Weber's perspectives on interrelationships between capitalism and Protestantism.

Hall, Thomas Cuming, *The Religious Background of American Culture*. Boston: Little, Brown and Co., 1930. Historical analysis of religious influences in the development of America.

Hooykaas, Reijer, *Religion and the Rise of Modern Science*. Grand Rapids: Eerdmans, 1972. Analysis of the important role played by religion in the development of science.

Marshall, Gordon, *In Search of the Spirit of Capitalism: An Essay on Max Weber's Protestant Ethic Thesis*. New York: Columbia University Press, 1982. An introduction to Weber's thesis and scholarly debates it triggered.

Nelson, Benjamin, "Weber's Protestant Ethic: Its Origins, Wanderings, and Foreseeable Futures," in *Beyond the Classics*, Charles Y. Glock and Phillip E. Hammond, eds. New York: Harper and Row, 1973, pp. 71–130.

Samuelsson, Kurt, *Religion and Economic Action*. New York: Harper and Row, 1964. A summary and critique of the Weber thesis.

Scheler, Max, "The Thomist Ethic and the Spirit of Capitalism," trans. Gertrude Neuwirth, *Sociological Analysis*, 25, no. 1 (Spring 1964), 4–19. Analysis of contradictions between Weber and Sombart on the role of morality and religion in the genesis of capitalism; concludes that "the religious-metaphysical despair of modern man is everywhere the root and origin of the endless drive to work."

Sombart, Werner, *The Jews and Modern Capitalism*, trans. M. Epstein. New Brunswick, N.J.: Transaction Books, 1982 (1913). A provocative study of Jewish contributions to modern economic life, aptitude for capitalism, and its origin in race problems and historical experiences.

Tawney, R. H., *Religion and the Rise of Capitalism*. Magnolia, Mass.: Peter Smith, 1962 (Harcourt, Brace, 1926). A socio-historical study of reciprocal relationships between economic expansion and religious thought in England.

Wax, Murray, "Ancient Judaism and the Protestant Ethic," *American Journal of Sociology*, 65 (Mar. 1960), 449–55. Developments precursive to the Protestant ethic in ancient Judaism.

Weber, Max, *The Protestant Ethic and the Spirit of Capitalism*, trans. Talcott Parsons. New York: Scribner's, 1958. A classic study on relationships between the attitudes implicit in Calvinistic Protestantism and the value foundations of modern capitalism.

Yinger, J. Milton, *Religion in the Struggle for Power*. New York: Arno, 1980 (Duke University Press, 1946). Analysis of the dilemma of churches as religious values and loyalties compete with other powerful human interests.

Chapter 8

The American Church as an Educational Institution

To a very large extent the church is an educational institution. Some churches confine their objectives to a narrow set of what they believe to be solely religious goals, but they must nevertheless use educational procedures. As a church widens its program to deal with larger areas of individual experience and group life, it is forced to extend its reliance on educational efforts. In order to understand the church, one must be aware of its educational work.

This chapter is devoted to educational activities in the church. The discussion is primarily informational rather than analytical or theoretical. However, the information presented throws a great deal of light on the nature of the American church, suggesting certain conditions it must face and revealing interesting additions to and adaptations of its organizations and practices which arise out of efforts to adjust to these conditions.

The Inevitability of Education in the Church

Since the church seeks to affect the lives of people and relies, accordingly, on communication, it necessarily becomes committed in principle and in fact to a variety of educational efforts. We can readily see this if we first of all consider the contribution of religious education to the basic objectives of all church work. Lengthy studies of Christian church members and leaders indicate that eight goals of religious education stand out above others: (1) To develop a consciousness of God as a reality in human experience and a sense of personal relationship to Him. (2) To develop an understanding and appreciation of Jesus' personality, life, and teachings that will lead to experiencing Him as Savior and Lord and loyalty to Him and His cause. (3) To develop Christ-like character. (4) To develop the ability and disposition to participate constructively in a world-wide social order which embodies the ideals of the fatherhood of God and the brotherhood of man. (5) To develop the ability and disposition to participate in the church. (6) To develop appreciation of the meaning and importance of the Christian family and the ability and desire to contribute constructively to its life. (7) To offer a Christian interpretation of life and the universe, to develop an ability to see God's purpose in it, and to build a philosophy of life on that interpretation. (8) To make man's best religious experience, especially that recorded in the Bible, an effective internalized guide for students' present experience.[1] This summary of educational goals overlaps with every objective of the typical Christian church; it clearly reveals that each presupposes some form of education and instruction. This observation applies equally well to the aims of Jewish and other church groups.

The obvious kinds of educational work which the church performs provide further evidence of how naturally and pervasively educational activities enter into the church's life. At least eight forms of such work may be readily identified.

1. The church supplements public education. It reinforces the character education program, sharing similar goals for the development of moral standards and well-adjusted personalities. It gives religious training that is not offered in the schools through programs referred to later. With the growing belief by school administrators that education is incomplete unless it covers all areas of life, their cooperation with churches has increased. The church also supplements public education by sponsoring private school systems. This augments freedom by giving increased opportunity for choice of schools. The vocational guidance program of schools is complemented by church work. In addition to emphasizing the need for personnel in church-related professions, many young people's programs, Sunday school lessons, and religious publications include suggestions for vocational choice. The indirect influence of seeing professional church workers in action and of being exposed to teachings about stewardship and religious motivations also is relevant to vocational guidance.

---

[1] Jesse H. Ziegler, "Is Religious Education Fulfilling Its Function? " *Religious Education,* 45 (Nov.-Dec. 1950), 357-62. Ziegler believes that on all eight objectives the church falls far short of the task it ought to accomplish.

2. The church teaches members what to believe. By teaching its doctrines, the church helps them develop a philosophy of life and a system of faith. The effectiveness of its work varies so much that some members "don't know what they believe" or, more realistically, do not know what they are expected to believe in order to be members in good standing, while other members are almost theologians in interest and knowledge.

3. The church gives believers support for their faith. Members are taught *why* they believe church doctrines. In some groups the basic authority is the Bible, in others science, and in the case of Roman Catholicism the Church and its tradition. As evidences are brought from these authorities and linked with other relevant sources of knowledge, members are "strengthened in their faith," although the evidences may seem naïve to nonmembers. When the source and data of appeal seem inconsistent with scientific knowledge or modern philosophies, the believer's faith is sorely tried. He may then give up his faith, modify it, adopt rationalizations that support it, or rigidly cling to it insisting that supernatural revelation cannot be in error.

4. The church teaches constituents how to live. Both individual and social ethics are emphasized, although fundamentalists minimize and almost exclude the latter and some liberals belittle the former.

5. The church educates leaders. Leadership training occurs in special institutes and institutions as well as in most local churches. As the child develops into the adult, he may be given positions of leadership in his Sunday school class, in a youth group, or in other church organizations. Gradually increased responsibilities cultivate leadership abilities and make him capable of taking an active part in the church, in the community, and in business and fraternal associations. Although not yet empirically demonstrated, there is perhaps at least a partial cause-and-effect relationship in the observed correlation of church membership with leadership in community organizations (Chapter 15).

The Bible Institute movement grew largely out of a sensed need for trained lay workers in churches. Church-related colleges deliberately recruit lay and professional church workers. Conferences that include training sessions for church workers also contribute to the education of church leaders and indirectly to the training of leadership for other social institutions.

6. The church disseminates information about its work. Most churches publish a weekly bulletin announcing church activities. Many use the local newspaper for advertisements and news items about church activities. Church publications and promotional representatives inform members about missionary work and other denominational projects.

7. The church informs adherents about social problems. As it opposes social evils, it helps to broaden the social vision of members. Increasing emphasis in theological education upon practical problems

and needs of people will very likely increase future church activities in this area. By warning people against what it considers to be sins or vices and supporting crusades against them, the church educates people about these conditions. As a latent effect, youths who have been so sheltered from vice that their first knowledge of it comes through the church may be tempted to do things that had never before entered their minds. The church tends to overemphasize the problematic nature of the "sin" against which it crusades and to fail to see indirect benefits that may be present in the situation. A corresponding lack of reality in facing undesirable consequences of proposed reforms may also be present.

8. The church supplies information about people and problems in other parts of the world. Promotion of foreign missionary work makes adherents aware of nations, regions, and groups of people about which they had not heard before. Clothing drives and other world relief programs help develop a sense of brotherhood on the part of church members toward those elsewhere on earth. These educational activities usually are very unbalanced, giving fragmentary and distorted accounts of the lives of recipients of the missionary message and developing false attitudes of superiority. Nevertheless, education of a sort does take place, both directly and indirectly, through promotional activities associated with missionary and relief programs.

It should be clear from the above discussion that almost every activity of the church involves some form of education. Let us turn, then, to a survey of the educational programs and agencies of the American church.

Educational Agencies and Programs of the Church

Colonial Protestant education emphasized sermons and religious teaching in the family. In formal education, general and religious teaching were united in schools on all levels. From 1787 to about 1847 increasing secularization of life in general occurred. Religious materials were withdrawn from the school curriculum, tax support for private and church schools was withdrawn, and many religious controls over public schools were eliminated. From 1847 to 1889, the year of the first World Sunday School Convention, the public school, family, and parochial school were ruled out as the chief basis for religious education, and Sunday schools developed. Since 1889 we have been passing through a period of reorientation and experimentation, during which religious education arose as a profession.[2]

---

[2] Lewis J. Sherrill, "A Historical Study of the Religious Education Movement," in *Orientation in Religious Education,* Philip H. Lotz, ed. (New York: Abingdon-Cokesbury Press, 1950), pp. 19-24.

It is likely in the give-and-take of democratic society that no crystallized pattern will emerge in the present generation and experimentation with one form of religious education after another, some of it involving public education, will continue. Meanwhile, the outstanding program of religious education is the Sunday school.

Sunday, Sabbath, or Church Schools

There were 193,462 Sunday and Sabbath schools enrolling 33,451,109 persons in the 119 religious bodies that gave current data for the 1982 *Yearbook*. Of these, 10,302 schools (5.3 per cent) with 8,082,993 pupils (24.2 per cent) were in the Roman Catholic Church.[3] The number of teachers and officers and the age distribution of pupils were not reported, but in 1958 there was one staff person for each 12.3 pupils, and over one-third of the Protestant pupils were age 24 or older.

Catholics and Jews in many communities have followed the Protestant example of establishing such schools. The Jewish Sunday school is a result of pressures from the surrounding environment. Among second and third generation Jews it sometimes involves conflict between adult-centered and child-centered orientations; some desire it to be a basis for adult observance of Jewish customs, and others wish its primary task to be teaching children the history and meaning of those customs without pressure to engage in the practices. Where Jews are a small minority in the middle-class suburb, the "secular" child-oriented approach is likely to take precedence over the establishment of adult-oriented religious-cultural acitivities.[4]

Sunday schools have been criticized for contributing to the widespread idea that the family no longer has the primary responsibility of supplying religious nurture for its members, and that in one hour a week miracles can be performed by providing an entire phase of education not available elsewhere. Amerman has called Sunday schools "a living symbol of the sublime irrelevance of Christ" and has condemned the fraternity of specialists and the jargon they foster. The religious training they offer is often by poorly qualified, relatively untrained teachers in a poorly organized curricular program. As a result Sunday school has been labeled the "most wasted hour of the week." [5]

---

[3] Constant H. Jacquet, Jr., ed., *Yearbook of American and Canadian Churches 1982* (Nashville: Abingdon Press, 1982), pp. 229–36. No Jewish data were reported.

[4] Herbert J. Gans, "The Origin and Growth of a Jewish Community in the Suburbs: A Study of the Jews of Park Forest," in *The Jews,* Marshall Sklare, ed. (Glencoe, Ill.: The Free Press, 1958), pp. 205-48. Perhaps the largest Jewish program of Sunday religious education is in the Jewish Community Center of White Plains, N.Y.; it is described in Theodore Frankel, "Suburban Jewish Sunday School: A Report," *Commentary,* 25 (June 1958), 481-91.

[5] Lockhart Amerman, "The Menace of the Sunday School," *Christian Century*

Improvement of the Sunday schools can be expected to result from the rising level of American education, increasing emphasis upon teacher-training programs, improved leadership training in seminaries and professional religious education, revived interest in interdenominational cooperation through Sunday school conventions, gradual modifications in lessons and curricula as recommended by denominational agencies, and the growing tendency to integrate the entire educational program of the local church into a unified whole.

The Sunday school is a relatively more important part of the church program in rural than in urban areas, for in marginal churches it is often the only weekly activity of the church. The Institute of Social and Religious Research found that one-eighth of all rural church members served as teachers or officers in the Sunday school.[6] Studies in Montana, Oklahoma, and Pennsylvania have found that the more rural a church is, the higher is its Sunday school attendance or enrollment as a percentage of church membership. Urban churches are generally larger and have more subsidiary organizations competing with their Sunday schools. Sunday school attendance as a percentage of church membership is inversely related to the size of the church. Rural families also have higher fertility and hence more children to enlarge the Sunday school rolls.[7]

Parochial and Christian Day Schools

Some churches sponsor functional equivalents of public schools. In fall 1980 privately controlled schools enrolled 11.7 per cent of America's elementary and 9.4 per cent of its secondary pupils.[8] Almost two-thirds (63.4 per cent) were in those sponsored by Catholics, followed in rank order by non-church-related schools (16.0 per cent) and those of Baptists, Lutherans, Christians, Jews, Seventh-day Adventists, Episcopalians, and other religious groups. During the 1970s private schools increased slightly and their enrollments decreased less than those of public schools.[9]

The Christian day school movement is supported by certain Protestants who believe it will perpetuate their faith in the younger generation, make all aspects of knowledge fit into the Christian framework, prevent

---

61 (Feb. 9, 1944), 173-75 (Letters to the Editor, 61 [Mar. 8, 1944], 307-8); and Wesley Shrader, "Our Troubled Sunday Schools," *Life*, 42, no. 6 (Feb. 11, 1957), 100-14. Typical of dozens of replies to Shrader is Virgil E. Foster, "The Most Wasted Hour?" *Church Management*, 33, no. 7 (Apr. 1957), 15-18.

6 H. Paul Douglass and Edmund deS. Brunner, *The Protestant Church as a Social Institution* (New York: Institute of Social and Religious Research, 1935), p. 159.

7 A'Delbert Samson, *Church Groups in Four Agricultural Settings in Montana* (Bozeman, Mont.: A.E.S. Bulletin 538, Mar. 1958), pp. 22-23.

8 W. Vance Grant and Leo J. Eiden, *Digest of Education Statistics 1982* (Washington, D.C.: National Center for Education Statistics, U.S. Dept. of Education, 1982), pp. 6-7.

9 *Ibid.*, p. 48.

juvenile delinquency, assist children to study the Word of God systematically for more than the weekly hour provided by Sunday school, and
train Christian leadership.[10] Many of them also are dissatisfied with the
"secular humanism" of the "Godless public school system."

The religious school movement is deplored by those who believe that
its success could seriously impair public schools. They charge that it
contributes to the splintering of communities, dividing children and parents into hostile competing groups and tempting many to try to secure
tax funds for sectarian purposes.[11] Other critics fear that the personality
developed in the sheltered atmosphere of the parochial or Christian day
school will not be able to cope with the problems of the world when
they have to be faced in their stark reality.

A comparison of Catholic parochial school pupils with Catholics enrolled in a public school in the same midwestern urban parish found
more similarities than differences in the students, except in areas directly related to religion. Half of the parochial pupils chose fellow-
Catholics for their three best friends, compared to only 2 per cent of the
public school Catholics. All three chosen were non-Catholic for 3.5 per
cent of the parochial pupils, while 37 per cent of the public school pupils
listed only non-Catholics. Parochial school children had attitudes more
favorable toward Negroes, refugees, and foreign aid. They were more
orderly, subject to stricter discipline, and very unlikely to get into trouble
with juvenile court authorities. Supernatural motivations in civic affairs
and religious interpretations of historical events were more evident in the
thinking of parochial pupils. Sunday school was held for Catholics attending public school. Those enrolled in it tended to be categorized as
"second class parishioners" because they did not fit into the regular pattern of parochial school training, were "outsiders" to most experiences of
Catholic children in the parish, and were not as well informed about
their religion. Educational and religious reasons were given by parents
for sending children to the parochial school; comfort and convenience
were leading reasons for sending them to the public school. It was concluded that the parochial school serves the total community by saving
public funds, training citizens with high moral and social norms, ex-
emplifying successful voluntary association and primary group cooperation, and contributing to middle class mores.[12]

---

[10] Mark Fakkema, "The Case for the Christian Day School," *United Evangelical
Action,* 13 (June 15, 1954), 220-22.

[11] Nevin C. Harner, "Crucial Challenges to Present Day Religious Education,"
Religious Education, 45 (May-June 1950), 161-62.

[12] Joseph H. Fichter, S.J., *Parochial School: A Sociological Study* (Notre Dame.
Indiana: University of Notre Dame Press, 1958). Cf. Miller M. Cragon, Jr., "The
Religious Influence of the Parochial School," *Religious Education* 56 (May-June
1961), 180-84; and Gerhard Lenski, *The Religious Factor* (Garden City, N.Y.:
Doubleday and Co., 1961), pp. 240-53.

Vacation Church Schools, Camps, and Conferences

Many churches conduct vacation church schools for one or two weeks during the summer school vacation. A phenomenon of this century, they are designed to give concentrated teaching that is not possible in the Sunday school. They are used evangelistically to reach new members as well as to educate those already in the church. In 108,124 such schools using 1,158,585 teachers and officers, 7,598,940 pupils were enrolled in 1958.[13]

Growing out of the nineteenth century camp meeting, organized camping and summer conference programs have developed rapidly, especially for children and youth. As part of the larger program of religious education, camping ideally provides a laboratory for the application of religious principles on a round-the-clock basis. It opens doors to wholesome interests and lifelong hobbies that help promote awareness of God's creative power. It offers experiences away from home that help develop self-reliance and dependability and it provides a means for expanding friendships and experiencing democratic living in small groups. Churches are only beginning to take advantage of the unique opportunities presented by an organized camping program. All too often they have simply carried methods and materials of the Sunday school into the new setting instead of using the special resources of the camping environment.[14]

Weekday Church Schools

Increased awareness of the limitations of Sunday schools and a growing conviction among educational leaders that the teaching of religion is a serious aspect of total education have led many public school systems to develop a policy of releasing children from the school schedule upon parental request for the study of religion. Teachers and facilities are provided by the churches.[15]

Many programs have failed because churches were unprepared to do a good job of teaching or because they placed too much emphasis upon controversial doctrines.[16] The released-time experiment in religious education is indicted by Moehlman on more than fifteen counts, the most

---

[13] Hunt, "Religion and Education." (Recent data are unavailable.)

[14] Elizabeth Brown, "Camps and Summer Conferences," in Lotz, *Orientation in Religious Education*, pp. 338-51; and Fred D. Wentzel, "The Summer Camp Comes of Age," *Religious Education*, 41 (May-June 1946), 147-52.

[15] Erwin L. Shaver, "The Weekday Church School," in Lotz, *Orientation in Religious Education*, pp. 274-86; and Lois V. McClure, "Weekday Religious Education at the High School Level," *Religious Education*, 46 (Nov.-Dec. 1951), 345-63.

[16] Arthur C. and David H. Bining, *Teaching the Social Studies in Secondary Schools*, third ed. (New York: McGraw-Hill Book Co., 1952), p. 38.

serious of which is that it "is deceived in regard to its own value, misinterprets the religious values found in public education, and is promoting the disintegration of public educational programs which provide the only valid general approach to religion in the American way of life." [17] He believes that it promotes disunity among Protestants as well as between Protestants, Jews, and Catholics, that its promoters are not united in the goals they seek, that it is seen as a confession of churches' weakness and failure, that it helps disintegrate the democracy of the public school, that its teachers and supervisors are not qualified for their tasks, and that it is illegal.[18]

Since any program has shortcomings, many believe that it or a similar "dismissed time" program is the best practicable way yet discovered to supplement public school and church education. The released-time program is a link between the church and home, brings religion into the framework of the pupil's formal education, provides an opportunity for evangelistic outreach to the nonchurched, contributes to Protestant ecumenism, and strengthens interfaith cooperation and understanding.[19]

In the famous McCollum case in 1948 the U.S. Supreme Court decided that released-time religious education programs conducted in public, tax-supported buildings and using the school system's compulsory machinery to assist sectarian groups in disseminating their faith were invalid under the First and Fourteenth Amendments to the Constitution. Four years later in the Zorach case it upheld a New York statute providing for released-time classes during public school hours but away from public school buildings.[20] Released-time programs hence continue in school systems in all parts of the nation within the limitations indicated by these decisions.

The Church and Public Schools

The Protestant ideal of universal literacy has emphasized that the Scriptures contain all that is necessary for salvation and that people are

---

[17] Conrad H. Moehlman, *The Church as Educator* (New York: Hinds, Hayden and Eldredge, Inc., 1947), p. 126.

[18] *Ibid.*, pp. 103-28. See also Howard A. Waterhouse, "Is Released Time Worth While?" *Christian Century*, 74 (Oct. 2, 1957), 1164-66. Public school educators are divided on the question of the program's desirability. See Jordan L. Larson and Robert B. Tapp, "Released Time for Religious Education," *NEA Journal*, 47 (Nov. 1958), 572-74.

[19] Walter D. Cavert, "Six Values in 'Released Time'," *Christian Century*, 74 (Dec. 4, 1957), 1445-46. A detailed study of 152 systems in 27 states and Hawaii, and reports from Catholic and Jewish educators, are included in a symposium in *Religious Education*, 51 (Jan.-Feb. 1956), 18-58. A refutation of arguments favoring various types of religion in public education is given in *Religion in Public Education* (New York: American Jewish Committee, 1957).

[20] Clark Spurlock, *Education and the Supreme Court* (Urbana: University of Illinois Press, 1955), pp. 116-33.

capable of understanding these essentials. During the colonial period, "the Protestant Bible was easily foremost in its moral and cultural influences upon the plain people of English speech. This is the basis of the public school." [21] Even today the balance of power in most communities is in Protestant Christianity. Indirect, subtle religious controls often place nonreligious, Catholic, and Jewish teachers under attack even though outright sectarianism is forbidden.[22]

Great variations in religious practices in the public schools prevail between states and between communities within states. In Minnesota during 1958, distribution of Gideon Bibles was permitted in 42 per cent of the public school systems and forbidden in 56 per cent. Religious holidays like Christmas and Easter were commemorated through school activities in 74 per cent of the systems; 87 per cent conducted baccalaureate services at graduation time, although opposition from certain religious denominations was decreasing the practice, and 84 per cent cooperated with churches in programs of religious instruction, mostly on a released-time basis for one hour a week.[23] A Michigan survey of religion in the public schools in 1957 found religious activities (prayers, Bible reading, hymns, celebration of religious festivals) in many classrooms, religious material in classroom study (church history, hymns in choral classes, the place of religion in American culture, special character and moral training programs), and use of many school facilities by religious groups outside of school time (church recreational programs, Sunday school, Sunday worship hour, after-school religious instruction). About 10 per cent of the 1,036 schools reporting were involved in a released-time program.[24] Religious elements in the public school system have been a source of conflict in many communities and a battlefront for many of the struggles pertinent to church-state relationships. The desire of many Catholics to receive public support for parochial schools also has contributed to political struggles and especially to defeat of school budget bills in state and federal politics.[25]

The most common contemporary proposals for allocating responsibility for religious teaching are (1) that things be left as they are (because

[21] William W. Sweet, "The Protestant Churches," *Annals of the American Academy of Political and Social Science,* 256 (Mar. 1948), 48. See Henry W. Holmes, "Our Debt to the Devil: How the Puritan Belief in Satan Helped to Establish Public Education in America," *School and Society,* 67 (Mar. 27, 1948), 232-34.

[22] Cf. Howard K. Beale, "Freedom for the School Teacher," *Annals of the American Academy of Political and Social Science,* 200 (Nov. 1938), 119-43.

[23] "Religion Class Plans Reported in 84% of Schools," Minneapolis *Star,* November 22, 1958, p. 7-A. The study was by Richard B. Dierenfield of Macalester College.

[24] Robert T. Anderson, "Religion in the Michigan Public Schools," *School and Society,* 87 (May 9, 1959), 227-29. Cf. Ernst C. Helmreich, *Religion and the Maine Schools* (Brunswick, Me.: Bureau for Research in Municipal Govt., 1960).

[25] See Neil G. McCluskey, *Catholic Viewpoint on Education* (New York: Hanover House, 1959).

schools otherwise may fall under sectarian control, traditional religions would be encouraged at the cost of other modes of thinking, Protestants control the schools already, or religion belongs in the home and church); (2) that nonsectarian spiritual values be indoctrinated in the schools; (3) that religion be taught objectively in descriptive, non-evaluative courses; (4) that the core of the traditional American religions (Protestantism, Catholicism, Judaism) be indoctrinated; (5) that church-controlled schools be publicly supported, and (6) that released-time religious instruction be offered by churches in cooperation with the schools.[26] The conflict between "secularizers" and those who wish to have religious instruction in or correlated with the public school program continues the legal struggle that has characterized so much American history in dealing with this problem. Interpretations of the separation of church and state may be modified to emphasize the separation of *sectarian* religion from public schools rather than elimination of all religion.[27] One compromise suggested is that a check-and-balance system analogous to that in American government be established in education. The system would recognize that three institutions are involved in educating children (family, state, and church) and that none should have a monopoly limiting the others.[28]

The Church and Higher Education

Protestantism also laid the foundation for higher education in America. All of the nine colonial colleges were founded by Protestant churches. Of the 182 colleges and universities founded prior to the Civil War, 150 were established by Protestant churches, 13 by Roman Catholics, and only 19 by the states. The basic purpose of church-related colleges was training the ministry. Of the 40,000 graduates of American colleges up to 1855, 10,000 had entered the Protestant ministry.[29] Most early presidents of state universities were clergymen; various provisions were made to include religion on their campuses. The insistence upon complete separation of church and state arose from opposition to sectarianism rather than from indifference to religion. Many charters of state uni-

[26] J. Paul Williams, "The Relation of Religion and Public Education," in Lotz, *Orientation in Religious Education,* pp. 494-500.

[27] See Joshua A. Fishman et al., "Subsidized Pluralism in American Education," *School and Society,* 87 (May 23, 1959), 245-68; and Nicholas C. Brown, ed.; *The Study of Religion in the Public Schools: An Appraisal* (Washington, D.C.: American Council on Education, 1958).

[28] C. Emanuel Carlson, "Religion in Public Education," *Eternity,* 9, no. 12 (Dec. 1958), 20-22, 44-45.

[29] Sweet, "The Protestant Churches," pp. 48-49.

versities and colleges include an expression of faith in God, and many began as church-related institutions. These include the Universities of California, Delaware, Kentucky, and New Jersey (Rutgers).[30]

The early friendly attitude toward religion has become more hostile in the last 100 years. Bitter interdenominational rivalry made many fear that sectarian strife might erupt into the nation's educational life. Churches, fearing that a competing denomination might gain an advantage, believed it would be better to have no religious instruction on the campus than to risk the possibility that it would strengthen a rival church. The poor quality of religious instruction and the tendency to indoctrinate rather than to enlighten caused religion to lose intellectual respectability. The emergence of scientism brought a naturalistic emphasis that excluded subjective and non-empirical knowledge.[31]

One reaction against increasing secularism in higher education and advancing modernism and the social gospel in religion was the establishment of Bible institutes by interdenominational fundamentalist groups. The movement was pioneered by A. B. Simpson who established his first school (Nyack Missionary Training Institute) in 1882 and Dwight L. Moody whose school (Moody Bible Institute) was founded four years later. The Bible was central in the curriculum. Practical application of classroom learning through regular service assignments was integrated into the curriculum. Similar schools sprang up over the entire nation, some short-lived and of little statistical importance, while others had enrollments in the hundreds. One of the largest lists 2,700 active missionaries among its alumni. Many evolved into Bible colleges. The Bible college is self-limited to a single major field, the Bible, in which a minimum of thirty semester hours is needed for graduation from accredited programs. Other courses are in liberal arts subjects, but always with an attempt to correlate and organically integrate the entire curriculum with the central subject. The dichotomy between the sacred and secular is renounced in the belief that all truth is of God.[32]

Since World War II there has been an increasingly favorable attitude toward religion in public higher education. Events in Nazi Germany, opposition to atheistic Communism, recognition of the religious basis of morality, the identification of democracy with the Judeo-Christian emphasis on the worth and dignity of man, fear of nuclear warfare, and a

---

[30] Guy E. Snavely, *The Church and the Four-Year College* (New York: Harper and Brothers, 1955), pp. 137-75, and Raymond A. Withey, Jr., "The Role of Religion in Higher Education," *School and Society,* 76 (Oct. 25, 1952), 257-61.

[31] *Ibid.,* and Robert Elliot Fitch, "Why Is Protestantism in Disrepute with American Colleges and Universities?", *Religious Education,* 45 (July-Aug. 1950), 234-38.

[32] Harold W. Boon, "The Bible Institute Movement," *Alliance Weekly,* June 20, 1956, pp. 3-4; and Frank E. Gaebelein, "The Bible College in American Education Today," *School and Society,* 87 (May 9, 1959), 223-25.

belief that man must have some kind of faith have cultivated this new interest.[33] Modified views of churchmen also helped make universities more open to religion. The substitution of partnership of science and religion for their earlier controversy profoundly affected the place of religion in higher education.[34]

The growth of professional religious education with its emphasis upon teaching the whole man, and a theory of education resembling that of the colleges made a similar contribution. Simultaneous recognition of the failure of traditional types of religious teaching and of the need to supplement the meager knowledge of religion even among students reared in a religious atmosphere made churches more open to college religion. The social gospel's emphasis upon every area of life encouraged colleges to add religion to their curricula, and the ecumenical movement helped to minimize frictions and increase cooperation of the churches. Recent theological thinking, especially in liberalism and neo-orthodoxy, has paralleled certain forms of educational analysis and made educators more open toward religion. Voluntary cooperative student religious movements helped underline the importance of religion for students and the concern of churches for them. Concurrently the interest of students in religious questions, their growing favorableness toward religious attitudes, and their ignorance about even basic teachings of religion helped open the doors of public higher education to curricular and co-curricular religious training and activities.[35] From 1920 to 1945 there was only a slight increase in the percentage of college students taking elective courses in religion,[36] but it is likely that the period since 1945 has seen an increase, if for no other reason than the increased opportunity to take such courses, especially in public colleges and universities.

In fall 1980 21.8 per cent of all college students were studying in private institutions, most of which are church-related. Rapid growth of public institutions is gradually reducing this proportion. During the twentieth century the increase of Protestant colleges has been negligible, but 91 Roman Catholic colleges out of the total of 208 were established from 1920 to 1959.[37] In theory church-related institutions look to revelation to

---

[33] Withey, "The Role of Religion in Higher Education." For attitudes of university students and the general population in the State of Washington see David O. Moberg, "Religious Instruction in State Institutions of Higher Learning," *Religious Education*, 45 (July-Aug. 1950), 229-33.

[34] Merrimon Cuninggim, *The College Seeks Religion* (New Haven: Yale University Press, 1947), pp. 33-35.

[35] *Ibid.*, pp. 33-48.

[36] Charles S. Braden, "Enrollment Trends in Religion Courses," *Religious Education*, 43 (Nov.-Dec. 1948), 337-42.

[37] Hubert C. Noble, "Protestants and Higher Education," *Christian Century*, 76 (Apr. 1, 1959), 384-85.

solve questions of ultimate values, but in reality many have "the same infirmity of purpose and secular tone as nonsectarian schools; they appear as prone to cater to popular whims, indulge in expedient practices, and accept lower standards [of religious dedication]."[38] Their spiritual leadership in educational life has been jeopardized so much by increasing secularism that some doubt they can regain it, believing the university is more likely than they to lead the way in the discussion of searching questions about religion and "the highest good" in an atmosphere where truth rather than power is the goal.[39]

Various church groups have attempted to control public higher education. Even Baptists, with all their emphasis upon soul liberty and the separation of church and state, have not been free of such efforts.[40] Instruction has been limited by anti-evolution laws. Academic freedom of professors to deal with the history, philosophy, and psychology of certain religious groups has been restricted. Incidents involving discrimination or constraint centering on religious matters have occurred on many campuses.[41] Because of such pressures, the separation of church and state is often interpreted to mean that no reference to religion may be made in classes of publicly supported schools except those so general that they are almost meaningless. Court cases have helped define the relationships of church and state in education, but no fixed pattern has yet emerged.

Since 1910 most major denominations have sponsored student religious foundations. Among these are the Wesley Foundation (Methodist), Roger Williams clubs (Baptist), National Newman Club Federation (Catholic), and B'nai B'rith Hillel Foundation (Jewish). They help students cultivate their religious faith, lead them to think about the application of religion to student life and their future careers, conduct evangelistic programs, sponsor practical service projects as they seek to direct students' idealism, give training in churchmanship, and practice worldmindedness, often encouraging ecumenical enterprises.[42] Faculty Christian organizations also have been formed on many campuses. Many educa-

---

[38] Richard Hofstadter and C. DeWitt Hardy, *The Development and Scope of Higher Education in the United States* (New York: Columbia University Press, 1952), pp. 235-36.

[39] *Ibid.*, pp. 236-39.

[40] Baptists tried to gain control of the University of Georgia. Cf. E. Merton Coulter, *College Life in the Old South,* second ed. (Athens: University of Georgia Press, 1951), pp. 149-65.

[41] Paul F. Lazarsfeld and Wagner Thielens, Jr., *The Academic Mind* (Glencoe: The Free Press, 1958), pp. 62-63, 70, 198; and Theodore Caplow and Reece J. McGee, *The Academic Marketplace* (New York: Basic Books, 1958), p. 226.

[42] H. D. Bollinger, "The Contribution of Protestant Foundations to Higher Education," *Religious Education,* 48 (July-Aug. 1953), 226-30; Thomas A. Carlin, "The Nature, Significance, and Function of the National Newman Club Federation," *ibid.,* pp. 231-35; and Alfred Jospe, "The B'nai B'rith Hillel Foundations," *ibid.,* pp. 236-41.

tors sense the positive contributions religion can make as an integrating factor in general education and feel a need for positive values to counteract threats of atheism and extreme secularism. The Faculty Christian Fellowship during the 1950's, numerous evangelical associations for the respective disciplinary specialties founded during the 1970's, and the Association of Christian Scholars established in the 1980's encourage examination of their vocation in the light of Christian faith. They help many develop a clear understanding of their Christian faith, find mutual help in personal religion, discover a Christian approach to educational problems, and relate religion to their academic disciplines. They help remove the sense of isolation Christian faculty members have often had and thus tend, both directly and indirectly, to increase their Christian influence. They manifest "both the current theological renaissance and the revolution of our time."[43]

Most public universities now encourage religious organizations to work on the campus or among their students. Some employ directors or coordinators of religious activities, and others hire chaplains. Chapels, religious centers, and religious councils—in addition to courses in various aspects of religion—are increasingly common on university and college campuses.[44] Questions pertinent to the separation of church and state are avoided or resolved by refraining from partisanship toward any particular faith or denomination or, in some cases, by private financing of the religious program.

In addition to church-related colleges and theological seminaries, churches have established professional schools of many types. Among these are medical schools and schools for nurses' and teacher training. These schools often have a different impact upon students from that of corresponding nonsectarian institutions. For instance, students in religious nurses' training schools tend to retain traditional Christian-humanitarian attitudes toward their work, while those in nonsectarian schools are more inclined to accept modern professional values that include diminished emphasis on bedside contact with patients, acceptance of administrative responsibilities, and a positive evaluation of the specialization and increased technical knowledge in advanced formal education. Nurses from church-related schools are more likely to emphasize emotional and spiritual functions they can perform for the patient.[45]

[43] J. Edward Dirks, "The Editor's Preface," *The Christian Scholar,* 36 (Dec. 1953), 257; and Phillips P. Moulton, "The Emerging Faculty Christian Movement," *Religious Education,* 50 (Jan.-Feb. 1955), 64-67.

[44] Seymour A. Smith, *Religious Cooperation in State Universities: An Historical Sketch* (Ann Arbor: University of Michigan, 1957).

[45] Irwin Deutscher and Ann Montague, "Professional Education and Conflicting Value Systems: The Role of Religious Schools in the Educational Aspirations of Nursing Students," *Social Forces,* 35 (Dec. 1956), 126-31.

Other Religious Education Programs

A large number of church-related organizations extend the church's educational influence. In some education is incidental to other objectives; others are directly and specifically educational. Youth groups, men's and women's organizations, adult discussion and other special interest groups, as well as the mass media of communications are used to influence both church members and nonmembers. The content of religious education increasingly expands beyond the learning of creeds and catechisms, memorization of Bible verses, and "temperance" lessons to include nearly everything involved in character building and personality development.[46]

The Department of Education of the National Catholic Welfare Conference is the medium through which the independent Catholic diocesan school systems exchange viewpoints, educational materials, and coordinate local, state, and national movements for the improvement of both Catholic and public education. Other branches of the National Catholic Welfare Conference engaged in educational activities include the Lay Organizations, Youth, Legal, Social Action, and Press Departments. The Confraternity of Christian Doctrine has played a major part in developing the vacation church school movement among Catholics. It promotes religious instruction to public school students and religious discussion clubs for adults.

The Jewish tradition of lifelong learning as a sacred obligation has stimulated adult education as well as scholarship among children and youth. Each synagogue is a house of learning as well as a house of prayer. Jewish organizations which stimulate research and disseminate information include the American Jewish Congress, B'nai B'rith, the Commission on Jewish Education of the Union of American Hebrew Congregations, National Academy for Adult Jewish Studies, National Council of Jewish Women, and National Jewish Welfare Board. Persecution of Jews in Nazi Germany stimulated American-Jewish efforts to develop wholesome intergroup relations and to study the sources, contributing causes, and treatment of problems associated with racial and religious discrimination.

Numerous interdenominational Protestant organizations are engaged in educational work. Some have a very broad scope of activity; others are organized for narrow, specific objectives. Many city and state councils of churches sponsor such programs as released-time classes in public

---

[46] This is true even among fundamentalists. See the report of a special committee of the National Association of Evangelicals appointed to study the philosophy and practice of Christian education: Frank E. Gaebelein, *Christian Education in a Democracy* (New York: Oxford University Press, 1951).

schools. The International Council of Religious Education, organized in 1922 as a merger of two older groups, was succeeded by the Division of Christian Education when the National Council of the Churches of Christ in the U.S.A. was formed. It serves as an agency for cooperation of member churches in promoting Sunday school work, Bible study, and evangelism. It guides community enterprises in Christian education through services to constituents, works to develop a climate favorable to religious education in general, has sponsored the Revised Standard Version translation of the Bible, and published the *International Journal of Religious Education*, re-titled *Spectrum* before its demise in the 1970's.

The Religious Education Association was established in 1903 as a voluntary interfaith fellowship of people interested in improving moral and religious education. It emphasizes the integration of religion and education, cooperation between religious groups, the social responsibility of religion, the philosophy of sound education as a unifying process for the individual and church, the need for scientific research to study the effectiveness of religious education, and a functional approach which makes education include citizenship and character training. Its bimonthly journal, *Religious Education,* is a major outlet for papers on scientific studies, current trends, teaching methods, and the philosophy of religious education. It has been the stronghold of the progressive education movement in religious education.

The World Council of Christian Education emerged out of a series of world-wide conventions, the first in London in 1889. It has sponsored field visitation to strengthen Christian education organizations, developed audio-visual aids, and helped indigenous preparation of curricular materials, training of teachers, research, and administration of children's and youth work. Its conventions have promoted Christian education and laid foundations for further ecumenical cooperation. The World YWCA, the World Alliance of YMCA's, and the World's Student Christian Federation are parallel ecumenical bodies which include much religious education work.

A number of educational organizations are associated with the National Association of Evangelicals. Its Commission on Higher Education maintains a teacher-placement service for liberal arts colleges, theological seminaries, Bible institutes, Bible colleges, and secondary schools. It led to establishment of the North American Association of Bible Schools and Bible Colleges, which encourages cooperative fellowship of such schools, establishes standards to facilitate interchange of credits by transferring students, and maintains records of administrators and teachers. The National Association of Christian Schools created in 1947 promotes Christian day schools and provides for them a unified voice. The **American Association of Bible Colleges founded in 1947 had 77 accredited members, 12 candidates, and 34 applicants in fall 1980. The Evangeli-**

cal Theological Society serves as a medium for the exchange of thought and research in theological disciplines. Founded in 1949, it strengthens and promotes belief in the inerrancy of the Bible and encourages reverent study of it and related subjects. The Inter-Varsity Christian Fellowship is an interdenominational organization on college and university campuses which emphasizes daily prayer and Bible reading, soul-winning, and Christian witnessing.[47]

Two strong agencies in fundamentalism are Child Evangelism and Youth For Christ. Child Evangelism International aims to win child converts through Bible classes in which flannelgraph and other visual aids are used to teach Bible stories. Youth For Christ International similarly stands for "the fundamentals of the faith." Its weekly, bi-weekly, or monthly rallies with striking personalities, color, drama, and emotional appeals have effectively reached many youth who did not attend church and had little background religious training. The techniques and educational philosophy of these groups have been criticized severely.[48]

The Effectiveness of the Church's Education

The church also educates indirectly. The ringing church bell, the sight of a church on the corner, its advertisements and news in the newspaper, religious radio programs one might hear, and other influences impinge upon all. A study in the Detroit area indicated that an average of 18 to 37 per cent of those attending 18 worship services in four churches were nonmembers. Nonmembers who did not attend church at all manifested many traditional moral and doctrinal views of churches and were favorable to them as institutions. Cuber concluded that no distinct line can be drawn between church and nonchurch people, that the social control of the church extends beyond the limits of formal membership and attendance, and that the problem of church influence is so complex that even approximate measures of real participation in the church culture cannot be secured.[49] Both formally and informally, directly and indirectly, the church's educational influence extends into practically every aspect of American culture.

To evaluate the broad scope and wide variation of these educational

---

[47] "Evangelical Educators United for Action," *United Evangelical Action,* 14 (June 15, 1955), 232, 251; and David Ong, "Campus Evangelism: How IVCF Works," *United Evangelical Action,* 12, no. 8 (June 15, 1953), 13, 15.

[48] The development of these movements and weaknesses in them are presented in Mel Larson, *Youth For Christ* (Grand Rapids, Mich.: Zondervan Publishing House, 1947); and Roger Heidelberg, "Let's Stop Cashing in on Our Converts," *Moody Monthly,* 54, no. 1 (Sept. 1953), 9-10, 70.

[49] John F. Cuber, "Marginal Church Participants," *Sociology and Social Research,* 25 (Sept.-Oct. 1940), 57-62.

influences is not easy, but a few general observations may be made. The church is clearly an important agency in shaping the conscience of individual members and influencing the values of society. It helps broaden the horizons of the mind even though, paradoxically, it frequently makes these horizons more parochial. It educates about selected social problems, but often it proposes narrow and inadequate solutions to them. It teaches about other religions but tends to brand them as false and thus helps to close minds against fair evaluations of them. It educates about other peoples, but it may stereotype them as "heathen" and thus hinder appreciative understanding of them. It educates individuals in the teachings of the scriptures, but it tends to restrict its teachings on controversial subjects to doctrines that support only its own position, thus blinding faithful constituents to different views. Relatively little evaluative work has been done on the church's education. Such evaluation generally has consisted of philosophical and theological analysis or personal impressions rather than of careful scientific study.[50]

Protestant and Catholic laymen generally lag behind their churches' teachings with respect to economic and social issues, following instead the general tendencies of their socioeconomic segments of the general population.[51] This lag presents a major challenge to educational leaders in the church. It is a significant source of criticisms that the church is ineffective in society.

Most church leaders are reluctant to have their educational programs evaluated objectively. Some are subconsciously suspicious of what results would reveal. An antireligious bias by many social researchers makes ministers fear that their studies or reports will be slanted in a direction unfavorable to the church. Furthermore, some say, "the results should be left in the hands of God. We sow the seed and cultivate it, but it is by God's Spirit that the increase comes. We must labor for Him regardless of the results." The social scientist's answer is that the labor could be more efficient and effective if research studies were made and their findings applied. Thus a study of the graduates of a Protestant released-time program revealed that the family and church were much more important influences upon later religious behavior than the weekday church school had been.[52] Such findings can increase caution in predicting results of educational programs and suggest modifications to make church influences through the family more significant. Chapters 14, 15, 16, and

[50] For example, see the criticisms of Ernest M. Ligon's Character Research Project in Kendig Brubaker Cully, "Is Character Education Christian?" *Christian Century,* 74 (Sept. 25, 1957), 1136-37.

[51] See Camillus Ellspermann, "Knowledge of Catholic Social Teaching Among 45 Catholic Industrial Workers," *American Catholic Sociological Review,* 17 (Mar. 1956), 10-23; "Papal Principles and Social Inertia," *Information Service,* 37, no. 8 (Apr. 19, 1958), 4-5, and relevant sections elsewhere in this book.

[52] David O. Moberg and Norris A. Magnuson, "A Follow-up Study of Weekday Church School Graduates," *Religious Education,* 51 (Jan.-Feb. 1956), 59-63.

17 include references to studies evaluating the effectiveness of the church in developing moral character and producing converts.

Conclusions

Many consider religious education to be *the* central unifying force in the church. All of its subsidiary organizations are assumed to exert a character-building influence on members and are intimately associated with the cultivation of personal religious life. Education is involved in all activities conducted by the church. It is necessary for effective, meaningful accomplishment in worship, evangelism, counseling, promotion of missions, and social action in the community.[53] As it is carried forward on a coordinated basis, it can help all groups within the church to see their symbiotic relationships to one another.

No attempt has been made here to distinguish between education and indoctrination. The two are so closely related that it is difficult to separate them except in principle. The propagandist seeking to indoctrinate has the purpose of influencing others to act or think as he acts or thinks, while the educational purist supposedly imparts knowledge without an intention of promoting any particular cause. The educator presumably offers "both sides" of the subjects he teaches and seeks after "truth"; the propagandist advocates some cause and presents one side of the subject in a much more favorable light than the other, for he thinks he has discovered the truth which must be followed. In reality, however, educators indoctrinate both consciously and unconsciously, and it is difficult in many instances to discover where education ends and indoctrination begins.

Much of what we have included under the educational activities of the church involves more indoctrination than education in the purest sense of these terms. The church indoctrinates when it teaches its doctrines and tries to get people to believe them, when it informs about its missionary program in order to gain financial and moral support, when it tries to develop wholesome characters, and when it trains leaders to uphold its traditions. Yet the same can be said about a major proportion of the teaching in public schools and even universities. If the term "education" must be removed from "religious education" because of its propagandistic qualities, most other institutions and programs of learning should not be called "educational" either.

We have not surveyed the specific problems churches encounter in the teaching process, including teacher recruitment, curriculum planning, administration, and teacher-pupil relationships. These are similar to the problems of other educational agencies, with the outstanding qualification that much of the church's staff consists of nonpaid volunteers (Chap-

---

[53] Walter L. Holcomb, "The Contributions of Religious Education to the Total Church Program," *Religious Education*, 50 (Jan.-Feb. 1955), 45-50.

ter 15). The field of religious education is devoted to the study and solution of these practical problems.

Evangelistic and missionary church programs, examined in the next chapter, are highly educational in their direct and indirect goals, achievements, and consequences.

Selected References

Brekke, Milo, *How Different Are People Who Attended Lutheran Schools*. St. Louis, Mo.: Concordia Publishing House, 1974. Research data from a nationwide survey of Lutherans aged 15–65.

Cavert, Walter D., "When Parochial Schools Failed," *Christian Century*, 74 (Nov. 13, 1957), 1349–50. Why the Presbyterian experiment from 1846 to 1870 was discontinued.

Fee, Joan L., Andrew M. Greeley, William C. McCready, and Teresa A. Sullivan, *Young Catholics: A Report to the Knights of Columbus*. New York: William H. Sadlier, 1981. An extensive analysis of the beliefs and practices of Catholic and formerly Catholic youth aged 14–29 in the U.S. and Canada.

Fichter, Joseph H., *Parochial School: A Sociological Study*. Notre Dame, Ind.: University of Notre Dame Press, 1958. Excellent pre-Vatican II research on a Catholic school in a midwestern urban parish.

Greeley, Andrew M., William C. McCready, and Kathleen McCourt, *Catholic Schools in a Declining Church*. Kansas City: Sheed and Ward, 1976. A study of the educational effects of Catholic schools.

Greeley, Andrew M., and Peter H. Rossi, *The Education of Catholic Americans*. Chicago: Aldine, 1966. Survey research showing the reinforcing effect on religious beliefs and performance of education in Catholic schools.

Hoge, Dean R., *Commitment on Campus: Changes in Religion and Values over Five Decades*. Philadelphia: Westminster, 1974. A masterful summary of findings and trends on religious attitudes and behavior of college students, centered around 13 replication studies.

Johnstone, Ronald L., *The Effectiveness of Lutheran Elementary and Secondary Schools as Agencies of Christian Education*. St. Louis: Concordia Seminary Research Center, 1966. Research revealing the reinforcing effect of parochial schools on adolescents from religiously committed families and the markedly greater impact on the religious knowledge and participation of those from marginal Lutheran families.

Kraybill, Donald B., *Ethnic Education: The Impact of Mennonite Schooling*. San Francisco: R and E Research Associates, 1977. Research on the influence of Mennonite schools on beliefs and behavior.

NCRPE Bulletin. News, commentaries, reviews, and reports of events related to religion and public education published by the National Council on Religion and Public Education (University of Kansas, Lawrence, KS 66045).

Religious Education. Quarterly journal of the interfaith Religious Education Association and the Association of Professors and Researchers in Religious Education; carries interpretive, descriptive, applied, and research articles and reviews.

"Religious Education: A Jewish Perspective," *Religious Education*, 78, no. 2 (Spring 1983), 148–216. Five articles and an editorial on the historical dilemma of day schools in Reform Judaism, other topics related to Jewish schools in American society, Jewish confirmation, Jewish education and dying, and perplexities of Jews at interfaith gatherings.

ma   Chapter 9

The Church as a Missionary
Institution at Home and Abroad

The social functions of the church are intimately related to its growth. On one hand, expansion of the church reflects
success in performing a variety of functions; on the other, its growth
reacts in turn on the character and performance of those functions. Many
aspects of this reciprocal influence between institutional functions and
growth are treated at different points in this book. This chapter is concerned primarily with the general factors affecting growth of the American church. This growth includes both that which occurs at home and
that which is experienced through activities abroad. It is due both to
general conditions which are independent of the church and to churches'
deliberate efforts to increase membership and influence.

With the exception of some relatively minor subgroups, Christianity is
a missionary religion attempting to extend itself into all the world in
obedience to Christ's Great Commission (Matthew 28:18-20). The
"world" obviously includes every community, but Americans tend to
think of missionary work as limited to distant lands. Thus Christians in
Springdale, New York, had active programs of missions to non-Christians
far away but ignored non-church goers in their own community.[1] Many
churches now discourage such attitudes by a "world missions" program
that seeks converts in the home community and nation as well as abroad.

---

[1] Arthur J. Vidich and Joseph Bensman, *Small Town in Mass Society* (Princeton,
N.J.: Princeton University Press, 1958), pp. 251-52.

All efforts to enlarge the church may be considered sociologically as missionary work, hence evangelism is included here as an aspect of missions. Current American missionary work is primarily that of the Christian churches, although the development of Israel may in some respects be considered a missionary enterprise in Judaism. Reform Judaism seems increasingly open to receiving gentile converts, and there are some other indications that Judaism may again become a missionary religion.[2] Since American foreign missions and evangelism are almost entirely Christian phenomena, our discussion will pertain primarily to Christianity.

Home Missions

An outstanding activity in missionary work in the homeland is evangelism, the promulgation of the church's message with a special emphasis upon winning converts. Evangelism is closely related to religious education (Chapter 8), but this fact is easily overlooked and even becomes, at times, a basis for conflict within the church. Most evangelistic efforts of American churches are basically educational. They educate church members for the work of evangelism and instruct potential converts and prospective members. Even in the past, the most effective evangelists were good teachers. The significance of repentance, public confession of Christ, surrender of one's life to God, and church membership was clarified in terms of church doctrines. "Those who heard were given a clear interpretation as to what they were to be saved from and to. The contrasts between the life of Christian discipleship and the non-Christian life were detailed. The spiritual resources and . . . ethical responsibilities of the Christian were pointed out."[3] Educational processes are involved in every major type and phase of evangelism.[4]

The interrelationship and interdependence of religious education and evangelism is often unrecognized. Educators criticize evangelists for emphasizing a momentary conversion decision without adequate regard for the life processes essential before and after that decision to make it significant. They tend to identify evangelism with mere verbal response to an appeal rather than with surrender to the will of God. They criticize techniques that reduce evangelism to a type of super-salesmanship and

---

[2] "Jewish Proselyters," *Time*, 71, no. 8 (Feb. 24, 1958), 43. In 1960 the Jewish Information Society began publishing its quarterly, *Jewish Information*, to explain Judaism as a way of life and to make its message a more significant and potent force in the contemporary world.

[3] Harry C. Munro, *Fellowship Evangelism Through Church Groups* (St. Louis: Bethany Press, 1951), p. 125.

[4] Wilfred E. Powell, "What Educational Processes Are Involved in Evangelism?" *Religious Education*, 43 (July-Aug. 1948), 239-43; and T. Franklin Miller, "An Examination of the Educative Processes in Evangelism," *ibid.*, pp. 244-46.

THE CHURCH AS A MISSIONARY INSTITUTION

make some evangelists more interested in quantitative results than in qualitative changes of people's lives. They accuse evangelists of ignoring psychological principles of growth, readiness for certain types of learning, and individual differences. They say that evangelistic terminology is superficial or is used as magic or a patent medicine, and that the symbolic language of evangelistic songs lacks the realism of practical relationship to everyday living.[5] Meanwhile, evangelists criticize religious educators for inadequate conceptions of God, the nature of man, the lordship and saviorhood of Christ, the reality and power of the Holy Spirit, and the church. They reproach educators for having a superficial romantic faith in education and for inadequately recognizing the significance of life's crises and certain decisions. They say educators lack the sense of urgency that comes to those who feel that without Christ men are lost and are so absorbed in minor, immediate problems that they lose a sense of their ultimate meanings.[6]

One solution to the conflict between evangelists and educators may be found in the synthesis and interaction of both approaches in "educational evangelism." It assumes that the processes of Christian redemption and growth are correlated, recognizes both crisis moments and gradual development, allows for the interfusion of intellectual comprehension and emotional appreciation, and realizes that the greatest enrichment of Christian experience comes when people are "seekers." [7]

Evangelistic techniques vary widely. In Protestantism they traditionally have emphasized the revival with its mass meetings, enthusiasm, and colorful preaching (Chapter 16). Bible comic books, recorded telephone messages, motion pictures, printed tracts, contests, quiz programs, magical tricks, and even top spinning have been used to entice children and adults to religious services. Visitation evangelism and other forms of evangelizing by laymen are increasingly emphasized in the larger denominations.

Preoccupation with the ends of evangelism has sometimes blinded sincere religious leaders to implications of the means they use. Propagandistic techniques of suppression; distortion by selected proof texts, quotations without references, misquotations, and unfair comparisons; diversion from reality; and fabrication have been used as church leaders shuttled back and forth between contradictory bases of knowledge in science and revelation, in effect assuming that their ends justified the means they used.[8] Psychological trickery, which has brought superficial and unrealistic "decisions," and various forms of "bait" to attract potential converts have been used in the work of "fishing for men." Acceptance of the evangelist's gospel has been made to seem dependent upon the lures used

[5] Harry H. Kalas, "Educational Evangelism," in Philip H. Lotz, editor, *Orientation in Religious Education* (New York: Abingdon-Cokesbury Press, 1950), pp. 75-77.

[6] *Ibid.,* pp. 78-79.

[7] *Ibid.,* pp. 79-80.

[8] Frederick E. Lumley, *The Propaganda Menace* (New York: The Century Co., 1933), pp. 330-62.

and has contributed to enslavement rather than liberation of men.[9] On the cover of one nationally-distributed Christian tract no fewer than 15 logical fallacies were discernible in the approximately 50 "well-chosen" words. Such "diabolical use of the half-truth" in the religious press and pulpit is obviously inconsistent with the ethical teachings of Christianity.[10] Ethical inconsistencies are evident in many other aspects of evangelistic outreach, including advertisements in church periodicals.[11]

The Growth of Churches

Important as evangelism is in the growth of any church, to assume that growth is related solely to its evangelistic program would be a gross error. In Chapter 2 we have seen that many features of churches and society contributed to the growth of national church membership. The growth of a specific church depends also upon a complex set of interacting factors which make some grow rapidly while others barely hold their own, decline in size, or even die (Chapter 5). Certain characteristics of churches and their environments help explain differential growth.[12]

Internal Characteristics of Growing Churches. The following leading features of churches which grow are all interrelated, but each expresses a somewhat distinct characteristic. By implication, other things being equal, the opposite traits characterize those which decline. They probably, but not necessarily, are among the causes of church success as indicated by the criterion of growth in size.

1. The use of methods and techniques of churchmanship which are in tune with the times.

2. The presence of a "grass roots movement" among members which emphasizes evangelism by all and not only by formal leaders. This is often associated with a zeal and fervor linked with theological doctrines giving members a sense of urgency.

3. Adaptability to meet changing needs of constituents and the community. Rural churches that promote soil conservation practices, land ownership, health clinics, and other community improvements are likely to prosper.[13]

---

[9] David W. Baker, "Did Jesus Use Bait?" *Christianity Today,* 2, no. 7 (Jan. 6, 1958), 10-11.

[10] Richard K. Curtis, "Our Christian Obligation for Accuracy," *Providence* (Providence-Barrington Bible College), 16, no. 3 (Aug. 1954), 3, 5, 7.

[11] Robert G. Hoyt, "Ads in the Catholic Press," *The Commonweal,* 49 (Feb. 20, 1959), 538-40.

[12] This discussion is based primarily upon empirical studies of churches summarized in H. Paul Douglass and Edmund deS. Brunner, *The Protestant Church as a Social Institution* (New York: Institute of Social and Religious Research, 1935), pp. 100-2, 49, 65, 210-11, 237-56.

[13] Ralph A. Felton, *A New Gospel of the Soil* (Madison, N.J.: Drew Theological Seminary), 1952. (Or are these results, rather than causes, of success?)

4. Good timing of the church program. Scheduling of activities must be adjusted to the specific community and population it serves. Church timing varies with the size, influence, location, and values of the congregation. The church that relies upon tradition and the loyalty of its people may operate a schedule that is relatively independent of or segregated from the rhythms of activities in other institutions, but the church with a small congregation including many laborers will have to adapt to the dominant timing systems of the community, those of the major places of employment.[14] In homogeneous rural communities the church is more likely to be dominant, and hence independent in timing its program, than in the city. Nevertheless, significant variations among different types of farming areas must be recognized in scheduling evening, afternoon, seasonal, and other activities if the church program is to succeed.

5. Leadership which fits into the local situation and meets its needs. This implies training that enables leaders to perceive the needs and meet them constructively. Part-time, inexperienced, poorly-educated, or senescent pastors often contribute to the decline of a church. (They also may be considered a symptom of decline in a church which previously had strong leadership.)

6. Clear standards for membership. Churches with well-defined requirements for membership generally are growing faster than those with lax, undemanding standards. Thus one reason for the rapid growth of nineteenth century Methodism was that it did not build ecclesiastical or theological fences to keep men out. It had no distinctive theology. "There was but one condition of membership to Methodist societies—the desire to flee from the wrath to come. Wesley took pride in the fact that no doctrinal tests were ever laid down." [15]

7. A high degree of loyalty and optimum social solidarity among members. Primary group relationships and a tendency to regard participation as an end in itself seem to contribute to this.[16] When social solidarity is so strong, however, that members form a clique into which new members are admitted only slowly and begrudgingly, growth is hindered.

8. Numerous church services and diverse activities. Montana churches offering three or four services weekly grew more than those with five or more, but those with two or fewer barely held their own in membership or declined. Up to what may be called a point of diminishing returns (four services weekly in Montana), offering more activities results in increased growth appeal. Similarly, churches offering the most auxiliary

[14] Gladys Engel-Frisch, "Some Neglected Temporal Aspects of Human Ecology," *Social Forces*, 22 (Oct. 1943), 43-47.

[15] William W. Sweet, *The American Churches* (New York: Abingdon-Cokesbury Press, 1947), pp. 45-46. See Dean M. Kelley, *Why Conservative Churches Are Growing*, rev. ed. (New York: Harper and Row, 1977).

[16] John E. Tsouderos, "Organizational Change in Terms of a Series of Selected Variables," *American Sociological Review*, 20 (Apr. 1955), 206-10. Tsouderos notes that formalization and contraction operate as a vicious circle.

organizations (men's, women's, and youth groups, missionary societies, choirs, scouts, etc.) show the greatest membership increases.[17]

9. Adequate financial support. Financial support of a church is directly related both to attendance and the economic level of its community. Per member costs are highest in churches with few members, for certain minimum expenditures are necessary for ministerial leadership and church facilities whether there are ten members or a hundred.

10. Systematic budgeting of church finances. Montana churches which systematically budgeted had membership gains two and one-half times as great as those which did not. It is possible that systematic evangelization accompanies systematic budgeting, or that churches with additions necessitated by growth must keep systematic records to qualify for mortgages.[18]

11. An optimum of competition. When a large number of churches with similar doctrine and programs compete within a community of limited population, all suffer. Study of 1,400 churches in 140 agricultural villages revealed that "As competition increased, the averages for church-membership, Sunday-school enrollment, attendance at the principal service and expenditures of all kinds, showed a marked and consistent decline, as did the proportion of churches gaining in the year preceding the survey." [19] Indiana with nearly 5,000 rural churches has one church for every 350 rural residents.[20] When a population is stable or even declining, growth of any church is likely to be accompanied by decline of others. No competition at all also depresses total membership.

Environmental Characteristics of Growing Churches. The following interrelated characteristics of church environments contribute to church growth and strength:

1. Population growth. Total population growth or growth of a population category that is especially attracted to a specific church, such as migrants from a nationality or ethnic group with similar religious background, is related to church growth. Most recent Protestant increases reflect suburban expansion.

---

[17] A'Delbert Samson, *Church Groups in Four Agricultural Settings,* (Bozeman, Mont.: A.E.S. Bulletin 538, Mar. 1958), pp. 21, 24.

[18] *Ibid.,* pp. 27-28.

[19] Edmund DeS. Brunner, *Village Communities* (New York: George H. Doran Co., 1927), p. 73. It was also found, however, that the larger the number of churches in a community in proportion to population, the larger the per cent of the population enrolled in church membership and Sunday schools, the larger the number of resident ministers per 1,000 population, the higher the ratio of population in average church attendance, and the higher the local expenditures by churches per inhabitant. No efforts were made to measure spiritual effects of overchurching, but in competitive situations religious differences often prevented unified action in community programs.

[20] J. E. Losey, *The Rural Church Situation in Indiana* (Lafayette, Ind.: Purdue University A.E.S. EC-153, Sept. 1957), p. 6.

2. A high birth rate among members.

3. A relatively stable type of population. In communities of mobile people, churches tend to be weak. When home ownership is high, church membership also tends to be high. (Midwestern farm tenants, however, are not significantly different from owners in their religious behavior.)

4. A low sex ratio (more women than men) in the general population. The relationship between the distribution of the sexes and the proportion of the population who are church members is discussed in Chapters 2 and 15.

5. Rising educational levels in the population. With a few regional exceptions, notably in the "Bible Belt" of the rural South, the higher the educational level of a population the larger the proportion who are church members.

6. Homogeneity of the population. When a large number of different nationality, occupational, and other groups are found in a small community, it is difficult for any one church to gain a substantial number of people as members.

7. Economic prosperity. A higher proportion of middle and upper class people are church members than are those from the lower class. Rural communities with the highest farm values and incomes have the largest percentage of church members. In areas of depleted soil, church membership tends to be at a low level; "soil erosion means soul erosion." [21] As the economic base of a community is strengthened, the material prosperity of its churches increases.[22] Yet this relationship is not invariable. Only about 15 per cent of the regional variations in total functioning of rural Missouri churches was statistically related to classifications of soil types. The rate of farm tenancy and the level-of-living index had little or no influence on religious group action scores.[23]

Dependence of the Church Upon the Community. The success of a church and, in Protestantism, of its pastor, is significantly influenced by the community in which it is located. If it is in an "ecclesiastical catch-basin" which draws the kind of people attracted to it, it will grow. The "successful church" is not only one that gives much to causes like missions because of its relative prosperity; it typically is also one to which other churches have contributed a majority of the members.[24] The larger a

---

[21] Emerson Hynes, "The Parish in the Rural Community," in C. J. Nuesse and Thomas J. Harte, eds., *The Sociology of the Parish* (Milwaukee: Bruce Publishing Co., 1951), p. 126.

[22] Harold F. Kaufman, *Religious Organization in Kentucky* (Lexington, Ky.: A.E.S. Bulletin 524, Aug. 1948), p. 27, and Liston Pope, *Millhands and Preachers* (New Haven: Yale University Press, 1942), pp. 36-48.

[23] John S. Holik and Lawrence M. Hepple, *The Church in Rural Missouri, Part IV, Index of Religious Group Action* (Columbia, Mo.: A.E.S. Research Bulletin 633D, Jan. 1959), pp. 270-75.

[24] Arthur E. Holt, "The Ecological Approach to the Church," *American Journal of Sociology*, 33 (July 1927), 72-79.

community's population, the larger is the average membership of its churches. Church membership as a percentage of the population also increases with the size of the community.[25]

The relationships between environment and church growth are so strong that if one church in a community is growing, the others usually are also. "As goes the neighborhood, so goes the church"; "like environment, like church." [26] Exceptions appear, however, especially when a church is not truly identified with the neighborhood surrounding it and draws selectively upon an exceptional population type scattered over a wider area, or when it has exceptional sources of internal strength that enable it to rise above an adverse environment. In addition, the deterioration of a community may prove a disadvantage to one group and an advantage for another. This is particularly noticeable in the case of black congregations in urban areas previously occupied by whites.

Specific studies help to clarify the intricate interrelationships between community characteristics and church strength. Four of the "twelve greatest churches" located by a *Christian Century* survey were rural. The community of each had a homogeneous population, adequate land base, and unified culture which was strongly religious.[27] Half of 149 American Baptist Convention churches in western small towns and rural areas had a membership growth exceeding that of the community population. The stronger and more comprehensive the total church program, the more effective was the evangelistic outreach and the higher the per capita giving. Over half of the baptisms (55.7 per cent) were a result of the work of their church schools. Youth organizations also were an effective source of church members, and the most effective churches had men's organizations.[28] Successful churches in the famous St. Louis Church Survey lacked physical isolation or limitations and had neighborly feelings resulting from inter-communication, common institutions, frequent congregating within the neighborhood, homogeneity, and habits of conscious cooperation among neighborhood residents.[29] Fewer than 13 per cent of 2,000 Protestant city churches deviated from expected patterns of environmental influence. The ones that were out of line had internal characteristics that contributed to their divergence. The church has a strong tendency to be like the community it serves.[30]

---

[25] Lawrence M. Hepple, *The Church in Rural Missouri, Part V, Rural-Urban Churches Compared* (Columbia, Mo.: A.E.S. Research Bulletin 633E, July 1959), 287-90, and Samson, *Church Groups in Four Agricultural Settings,* pp. 13-15.

[26] Douglass and Brunner, *The Protestant Church,* pp. 252-55.

[27] Thomas A. Tripp. "Making 'Great' Rural Churches," *Christian Century,* 68 (Jan. 24, 1951), 109-10.

[28] Clayton A. Pepper, "Evangelistic Effectiveness in Rural Churches," (based on a thesis by William Kastning), *Town and Country Church,* 109 (Oct. 1955), 7-8.

[29] H. Paul Douglass, *The St. Louis Church Survey* (New York: George H. Doran Co., 1924), pp. 148-50.

[30] Ross W. Sanderson, "Measuring the Progress of White Protestant Churches,"

Among churches that deviate from the pattern of expected growth is a rural midwestern Catholic parish. From 1912 to 1949 its membership grew faster than the general population because of the stability of its families, the formation of new member units through intraparochial marriages, nearly one-fifth of which were with converts, and a slight advantage in religious mobility (i.e., more Catholic families moved into than out of the parish). Long-lapsed Catholics were not included in the parochial criteria of membership, although they frequently were recognized as Catholics in the community.[31]

A study of 1,950 churches in large cities measured progress by membership growth, Sunday school enrollment, total church expenditures, and general community conditions. Population growth or loss and changes in population elements most likely to affiliate with white Protestant churches were used to rank church territories into the best, above average, below average, and worst types. The changes considered included the economic status of residents, the desirability of residence in the area, unstable population elements, dependency rates, juvenile delinquency, and health. A clear relationship emerged between progress and type of territory, the greatest progress occurring in the best areas and the least in the worst areas. Some churches, however, were exceptions. Analysis of these indicated that successful churches in poor territories had more complex programs than unsuccessful ones. They also had a larger staff (pastor, assistant pastor, religious education director, church secretary, children's worker, etc.) than the average church in better territory. Unsuccessful churches in good territory had less complex programs and smaller staffs. The lack of such favorable qualities as adaptability, group solidarity, leadership, and a varied program are major sources of failure for churches; their presence accounts to a great extent for success.[32]

Studies have shown a relationship between compactness of the urban parish, as measured by the distribution of members' residences, and the rate of church growth. The closer members live to a church, the higher its rate of growth. Compact parishes tend to be located near the outer edges of the city and in territory which is superior according to various socioeconomic indices. They tend to have "youthful vigor," growing rapidly while many churches with a more scattered membership are declining in size.[33]

American Journal of Sociology, 38 (Nov. 1932), 432-36. Cf. David M. Graybeal, "Churches in a Changing Culture," *Review of Religious Research,* 2 (Winter 1961), 121-28.

[31] C. J. Nuesse, "Membership Trends in a Rural Catholic Parish," *Rural Sociology,* 22 (June 1957), 123-30.

[32] Ross W. Sanderson, *The Strategy of City Church Planning* (New York: Harper and Brothers, 1932).

[33] F. Stuart Chapin, *Contemporary American Institutions* (New York: Harper and Brothers, 1935), pp. 196-204. ("Youthful vigor" was defined as a large Sunday school enrollment in proportion to church membership.)

Any significant change in the pattern of community life produces changes in the church. In a rural North Carolina school district which became part of an expanding metropolitan area, pressures on facilities compelled churches to launch building programs. Standards of religious performance changed to insist upon a full-time pastor, brick instead of clapboard edifice, and dining and recreational facilities in church. New financing techniques were needed to provide the new facilities and personnel, so harvest festivals, suppers, bazaars, auctions, and bake sales were added to church programs, and churches became social centers. Tensions between sacred and secular views of church activities and responsibilities were apparent within and between churches. Churches that refused to modify their beliefs about social activities continued to be strictly religious centers weakened by inadequate finances. Expansion of activities also necessitated more lay participation and leadership, with the latent consequence of helping persons move upward in the social class structure, thus facilitating expansion of the middle class. With change in long-established folkways and mores, the church adapted and yet provided a stable social matrix for its members.[34] The centuries long evolution of the church, from the portable Jewish tabernacle in the wilderness to the Jerusalem temple to the Christian church in many forms, continues as it adapts to social changes.[35]

Growth of Denominations and Large-Scale Religious Organizations. The rapid growth of the Southern Baptist Convention, which gained 4,000 churches in one decade and 4,000,000 members in less than one generation, is the result of many interacting factors. Biological growth is one; the South has the nation's highest birth rates. Southern Baptist migrants to the West and North have established new churches, making their denomination national instead of regional. Working class and wealthy people alike feel at home in the middle-class-dominated urban and village Southern Baptist churches, for the denomination's origin was among people considered underprivileged a generation ago, and it continues to serve many needs of persons with such backgrounds. Hence rural and recently-rural people predominate among new members recruited in cities. Local church independence allows great variability to meet the demands of local conditions. Many of the churches are centers of social life, offering members contacts where their personalities and interests are recognized and considered important. An aggressive lay leadership often organizes and controls new churches. Sunday school and adult Bible classes, enthusiastic singing, an aggressive press, and increasing social consciousness pertinent to the black, temperance, and politics are

---

[34] Albert Schaffer, "The Rural Church in a Metropolitan Area," *Rural Sociology,* 24 (Sept. 1959), 236-45.

[35] R. R. Martin, "The Church and Changing Ecological Dominance," *Sociology and Social Research,* 25 (Jan.-Feb. 1941), 246-57.

sources of vitality. But a biblical emphasis is perhaps the major cause of rapid growth. The Bible is the basis of most sermons. Doctrine is relatively simple and biblically based, allowing for a breadth in theological viewpoints. Aggressive leadership works for growth. A combination of theological, sociological, and psychological factors is thus involved in their expansion.[36] The Convention became the largest Protestant denomination in 1962.

The rapid growth of Child Evangelism, Youth For Christ, and the Inter-Varsity Christian Fellowship during the past generation has been attributed to certain social psychological features of their work. The social climate, created by the rise of totalitarianism, the Great Depression, World War II, and related events, was ripe for their remedy for spiritual hunger. Their use of color, drama, striking personalities, and mass groups was effective. They provided a challenge that was definite and yet simple. A strong sense of urgency, often associated with belief in the "soon return" of Christ, made them feel they were operating under divine imperatives. They satisfied for many a search for unity and fellowship that broke sectarian barriers. Their growth was closely related to that of many small evangelical denominations.[37]

Problems of Evaluation

Although growth is the standard most frequently used to evaluate church effectiveness, a church's basic purposes must be borne clearly in mind in any effort to determine its true worth. Only if a church accomplishes its objectives efficiently without compromise of ends or means can it be regarded as organizationally effective. Materialistic standards may cause loss of non-material values, which are the basic *raison d'être* of the church, if these ends are not consciously protected from default. Three criteria are essential for any organization's success. It must satisfactorily perform its objective functions as measured by institutional standards. Internal conflict must be minimized or regulated to prevent schism. Satisfactions for individuals must be maximized in order to assure continued membership. Reducing inconsistency of these criteria to a minimum is necessary for the success of any church.[38]

A study of 35 rural Baptist churches found four indicators of vitality.

---

[36] Charles G. Hamilton, "What Makes Southern Baptists Tick?" *Christian Century,* 68 (Oct. 3, 1951), 1125-26, and Harold E. Fey, "Why They Behave Like Southern Baptists," *Christian Century,* 64 (May 21, 1947), 648-49.

[37] Frank M. McKibben, "Sources of Vitality in the Religious Community. III. New Evangelistic Movements and Religious Education," *Religious Education,* 41 (July-Aug. 1946), 213-20, and Nevin C. Harner, "Crucial Challenges to Present Day Religious Education," *Religious Education,* 45 (May-June 1950), 159-64.

[38] Theodore Caplow, "The Criteria of Organizational Success," *Social Forces,* 32 (Oct 1953), 1-9.

These were youthful vigor (the percentage of members under age 45), benevolent and missionary giving, accessions to membership and baptisms, and consistent growth. The larger churches outstripped smaller ones on all four measures. The minimum vital church had about 100 members, at least 70 of whom were resident, and a budget enabling support of a full-time pastor.[39] Experience in California indicates that optimum size of urban Baptist churches is not more than 400 to 500 members.[40] Rural Kentucky churches of less than 300 members usually are unable to support an effective program.[41] Small churches are a liability rather than an asset in most denominations, but optimum size no doubt varies by denomination, community, and qualifications for membership. Numerical increases in size result in increased heterogeneity of membership, changes in interrelationships between members, a decline in harmony and integration, modifications of leadership roles and effectiveness, and diminished ego involvement by members whose present social participation tends to be in larger groups than formerly and to be based upon task involvement instead of personal recognition.[42]

Size of church membership, frequency of worship services, and educational activities were the three most significant indicators of church action in a thorough Missouri study. The index based upon them was a valid and reliable indicator of the effectiveness of church activity. Population growth or decline by townships in which churches were located accounted statistically for only about 16 per cent of the variations in the functioning of churches. The population per church and membership-to-population ratio were only slightly more related to church effectiveness.[43]

Since *ultimate* church goals are in the realm of values and are as much theological as sociological, scientists cannot discover them without special methodological adaptations. Most of a church's objectives may be subsumed under the headings of faith ("to cause people to accept a system of related values and beliefs—an ideology, or creed, or faith"), attitudes ("to cause people to adopt certain attitudes toward the divine, however defined, and toward their fellow men—attitudes derived from the ideology or faith"), and action ("to cause people to engage in certain behavior consonant with those attitudes"). Empirical analysis of church effectiveness is therefore possible, although most such work to date has not been very thorough.[44]

[39] LeRoy J. Day, *What Makes a Church Vital?* (New York: American Baptist Home Mission Society, 1944).

[40] Cecil G. Osborne, "Our Church Is Big Enough! " *Missions*, 157, no. 3 (Mar. 1959), 24-25.

[41] Harold F. Kaufman, *Rural Churches in Kentucky, 1947* (Lexington, Ky.: A.E.S. Bul. 530, Apr. 1949), p. 44.

[42] Wade F. Hook, "The Lutheran Church in the Carolinas Sociologically Interpreted," *Lutheran Quarterly*, 11 (Feb. 1959), 60-67.

[43] Holik and Hepple, *The Church in Rural Missouri*, pp. 247-76.

[44] Stanley K. Bigman, "Evaluating the Effectiveness of Religious Programs," *Review of Religious Research*, 2 (Winter 1961), 97-121 (quotations from p. 100).

Foreign Missions

Christian proselyting began in America during colonial days when missionaries were sent to the Indians. In 1812 the first American Protestant missionaries went to foreign lands. Catholicism also has devoted much money and many personnel to foreign missions, especially after 1914 when immigration began to dwindle.[45] Catholic missionary orders include the White Fathers, Society of the Divine Word, Congregation of the Immaculate Heart of Mary, Catholic Foreign Mission Society of America (Maryknoll Missioners), and Maryknoll Sisters of St. Dominic.

Christian missionaries are found on all populated continents and most major islands. In 1973 57,212 American missionaries were sent to other nations in addition to unknown thousands of independent persons and groups who were not in organized missions and agencies, aliens serving abroad under American sponsorship, seasonal and temporary assistants serving less than six months, missionaries on furlough in the U.S. (usually about 25 per cent of the total on the field), and home staffs of missionary societies and boards. No other nation sent more, but many had higher numbers in relationship to total population. Ireland headed the list with 3,229 per million population. Malta was next with 2,288, followed by Samoa with 1,149, Belgium with 969, Spain with 826, Netherlands with 797, and at least twelve more countries that exceeded the 279 rate of the U.S.A. Of the missionaries, 11,990 were Roman Catholic, 44,629 Protestant, 220 Orthodox, and 173 Anglican.[46] Missionary activity greatly exceeds that of the first decade of the century, when the missionary era supposedly was in full flower, for most groups other than the mainline denominations. Small fundamentalist and evangelical bodies make the greatest efforts in proportion to size.

The United States is also the greatest receiver of Christian missionaries. Its 16,746 aliens from abroad was followed in 1973 by Brazil with 15,472, France with 13,772, Italy with 9,388, Zaire with 8,985, and Argentina with 8,824. In every instance, the majority of these were Catholics.[47] From 1900 to 1980 the Christian population of Africa increased from 9.2 to 44.2 per cent of the population, largely as a consequence of the missionary movement. Similar changes occurred during the nineteenth century in Oceania. Although global Christianity grew from 558,056,332 in 1900 to 1,432,686,519 in 1980, Christians declined from 34.4 to 32.8 per cent of the world because total population increase was even greater.[48] Antagonism and resistance in Communist and Muslim nations have hampered its

---

[45] Kenneth Scott Latourette, "The Present Status of Foreign Missions," *Annals of the American Academy of Political and Social Science,* 256 (Mar. 1948), 63-71.

[46] David B. Barrett, ed., *World Christian Encyclopedia* (Nairobi: Oxford University Press, 1982), pp. 92–93, 799–805.

[47] *Ibid.,* pp. 804–5.

[48] *Ibid.,* pp. 4, 796.

growth in major parts of the world, and slow growth was evident in others, as in pre-Communist China where there were perhaps no more than five million Christians by 1950 after a century of intense missionary activities.[49] Numerous social forces help explain missionary successes and failures.

Social Influences Affecting Christian Missions

1. Religious values. A foremost influence on missionary work has been orthodox Christian doctrine. Belief in the universal validity of Christianity and in the doctrine that men can be reconciled to God only through Christ imposes a moral obligation to disseminate the gospel.

2. Revivalism. Nineteenth-century revivals stimulated evangelistic zeal; many dedicated their lives to missionary service and stimulated others to provide their financial support. Coming at a time when nationalism and humanitarianism were at a peak, the Moody revivals were one of the deepest sources of missionary enthusiasm.[50]

3. Church problems. Some missionary work represents a diversionary escape mechanism. Problems of local churches, denominations, or their leaders and the failure of churches to cope effectively with pressing needs of urban, industrial, secularizing America is covered up by enthusiastic missionary promotion.[51]

4. Education. The missionary movement was stimulated by the spread of knowledge about the misery of "savage, primitive, and heathen" peoples. Humanitarian interests in their physical, social, and economic well-being were intimately interrelated with spiritual concern. Many considered the mission field a place to prove the practical worth of Christianity.[52] The attitude that all problems of backward peoples are taken care of when they accept Christ is still common among the zealous. Few appeals are as effective in fund-raising for missions as those which emphasize physical misery, especially among orphaned children.

5. Ethnocentrism. All missionary work reflects ethnocentrism. Belief in the superiority of one's own religion is a dominant motive; typically accompanying it is a belief that other social customs are distinctly inferior to those of western industrialized nations. The traditional missionary enterprise may be viewed as "cultural imperialism" aimed at replacing native mores with those of the missionaries' home culture. The dogmatism associated with this outmoded belief in the overwhelming superiority of

---

[49] Ch'ien Tuan-sheng, *The Government and Politics of China* (Cambridge: Harvard University Press, 1950), pp. 15-16.

[50] Paul A. Varg, "Motives in Protestant Missions, 1890-1917," *Church History*, 23 (Mar. 1954), 68-82.

[51] John R. Everett, *Religion in Human Experience* (London: George Allen and Unwin, Ltd., 1952), pp. 482-84.

[52] *Ibid.*

the missionary-sending culture has sown seeds of antagonism against Christianity that will sprout and bear fruit for many decades.[53]

6. Race relations. The pre-Civil War controversy in churches over slavery had a deadening effect upon many missionary enterprises among American Indians.[54] Problems of race relations in the United States continue to hinder missionary work among dark-skinned peoples. Sending missionaries to foreign lands sometimes reflects prejudice in one's own: To salve consciences for mistreating a minority at home, people go to its homeland with the gospel. Sending missionaries may reflect feelings of cultural superiority as well as of religious concern: we send missionaries to convert the heathen to our way of life as well as to our religion. Paternalistic missionary work may thus serve to deepen prejudices about the inferiority of people with different racial or national origins.[55]

7. War. World War II greatly disrupted missionary activities through dislocating personnel and destroying housing, schools, and hospitals, especially in the Orient. Accentuated nationalism after the war has closed many doors of missionary opportunity. The destruction wrought in Europe shifted much of the burden of support for other nations' missions to the U.S. At the same time, as a result of inflation, increased donations have not kept up with increasing costs.

8. Social backgrounds of missionaries. The subculture from which missionaries come differs in many ways from that of public administrators and businessmen who are abroad. They generally adhere more rigidly to the formal sex code, profess and observe greater technical honesty, propound a theology not taken seriously by very many others in their homeland, and have taboos pertinent to tobacco, alcohol, and obscene language not typical of the population as a whole. Their social class backgrounds sometimes profoundly affect contacts with the people to whom they minister. The problems of a Baptist missionary wife in Africa trying to teach women how to wash clothes in a tribe in which this was a man's task would not have arisen among British missionaries of the Universities Mission to Central Africa who come generally from the upper middle class. Significant differences may also be observed between the work of Protestant and Catholic missionaries and of those from other distinguishable subcultures. Christian missions in most respects are widely diverse and highly differentiated.[56]

---

[53] L. A. Boettiger, "Missions and the Mores," Journal of Religion, 7 (Mar. 1927), 164-85.

[54] William M. Hiemstra, "The Disruptive Effects of the Negro Slavery Controversy Upon the Presbyterian Missions Among the Choctaw and Chickasaw Indians," Westminster Theological Journal, 11 (May 1949), 123-32.

[55] Buell G. Gallagher, Color and Conscience (New York: Harper and Brothers, 1946), pp. 56-61.

[56] G. Gordon Brown, "Missions and Cultural Diffusion," American Journal of Sociology, 50 (Nov. 1944), 214-19.

9. Social roles of missionaries. The missionary is a *"salesman of immaterial values."* [57] The intangible instruments of living he endeavors to sell usually have much less appeal than traders' material commodities. In his ethnocentric espousal of new religious values and rituals, he finds it very difficult to see the shortcomings of his religion, to refrain from judging all that he observes by his own cultural standards, and, in spite of lip service to the idea, to allow a truly indigenous church to arise out of the basic doctrines he preaches.[58] As a *sojourner* who conceives of his work as a job to be finished in the shortest possible time, the missionary is a stranger comparable to the marginal man. A non-permanent resident, he brings insulating mechanisms in his cultural baggage which may produce an aloofness between him and those he tries to reach. These devices protect him from having to associate with people who are educationally, socially, or culturally incompatible; they also are psychological barriers hindering the spread of his message.[59] Without adequate knowledge of indigenous religions, thought forms, and motives of action, the missionary cannot easily establish the points of contact which are essential for winning converts. His education is hence of prime importance to the effectiveness of his work.

The typical missionary is *an organizational man.* He must be a good member of the team, not an extremist. He must be able to adjust within the institutional machinery of both his over-all board and specific station. Personality appraisal has hence become very important in screening appointments. Conservatism and mediocrity is one price of a growing stress upon the organization. Growth and development of the missionary is often hindered by this trend. Specialization is prevented by the necessity that most be "general practitioners" engaged in a wide range of activities, and desires for status and security create problems. Many missionaries therefore lose sight of the organization as a means and make it instead an end in itself.[60]

Seven-tenths (71.2 per cent) of the world's 66,684 Protestant missionaries were from North America. An earlier analysis of those who were classified indicates that 61 per cent (but only 41 per cent of the North

---

[57] A. Irving Hallowell, "Sociopsychological Aspects of Acculturation," in *The Science of Man in the World Crisis,* Ralph Linton, ed. (New York: Columbia University Press, 1945), pp. 188-92.

[58] J. T. Hardyman, "Anthropology: Of Missionaries and for Missionaries," *Frontier,* 2 (Jan. 1959), 51-55; William A. Smalley, "The Cultures of Man and the Communication of the Gospel," *Journal of the American Scientific Affiliation,* 10, no. 2 (June 1958), 8-13.

[59] Paul C. P. Siu, "The Sojourner," *American Journal of Sociology,* 58 (July 1952), 34-44, and William A. Smalley, "Proximity or Neighborliness?" *Practical Anthropology,* 4 (May-June 1957), 101-4.

[60] Paul D. Clasper, "The Denominational Missionary and the Organization Man," *Foundations,* 2 (Jan. 1959), 57-71. This elaborates ideas intimated in William H. Whyte, Jr., *The Organization Man* (Garden City, N.Y.: Doubleday and Co., 1957).

Americans) were engaged in evangelism and church work, 19 per cent in education, 12 per cent in a health ministry, and 4 per cent in administrative, secretarial, financial, and other service positions. Under 4 per cent were agricultural and other specialists, social workers, YMCA leaders, and in other categories.[61] Even the missionary engaged to do evangelistic and church work, however, spends much time on mundane affairs. *Part-time missionaries* go to foreign lands under the guise of such activities as secretarial and business work, teaching school, or serving as foreign aid specialists. Off-duty hours are used to assist missionaries or to engage in their own programs of winning converts.[62] Protestant and Catholic organizations also are increasing their *lay missionaries* who assist in agricultural, industrial, administrative, medical, educational, social work, and related activities as an adjunct of the missionary program and who relieve religious personnel of secular duties.[63] Although role expectations and fulfillment undoubtedly are significant influences in every missionary program, social scientists have not systematically analyzed them.

10. Competition. Competition between the large number of philanthropic and religious organizations has made it increasingly difficult for many agencies to adhere to their traditional philosophies. Interdenominational "faith missions" provide an outstanding example of how social norms are changed by demands of practical expediency. The movement is named from its belief that faith in God alone without any appeal to men or to churches will provide the necessary material means. "Faith missionaries" were to depend solely upon God for their support and not to be limited by denominational organizations nor dependent upon any designated churches or individuals. Gradually their interpretation of "faith" changed. Some now teach that "faith" means telling men about needs and asking God for funds. Asking God includes public prayers and pleas for promises to pray that funds will be provided. Such requests are but thinly-disguised forms of asking men for finances. Other "faith missions" leaders state that the "faith" in their work refers to faith in Christ, not faith for finances; they imply thus that denominational programs have little or no such faith. A third adaptation stresses the idea that financial crises confront missionary boards only because the churches are failing. This, too, is a departure from the original "faith mission" position which uplifted "the unfailing faithfulness of God" even if all men, organizations, and institutions fail. "Faith missions" boards today typically refuse to send out missionaries whose financial support is not guaranteed. Faith

---

[61] M. Searle Bates, "What Are Missionaries Really Doing?" *Union Seminary Quarterly Review,* 15 (May 1960), 319-25.

[62] Richard O. Comfort, "Missionaries in Disguise," *Christian Century,* 74 (Nov. 20, 1957), 1381-82, and Arthur F. Glasser, "Vocational Witness," *His,* 18, no. 2 (Nov. 1957), 8-12, 18.

[63] Frederick Guest, "A New Kind of Missioner," *Catholic Digest,* 23, no. 7 (May 1959), 12-16.

once centered in God now appears to be centered in the faithfulness of Christian persons and churches.[64]

Jurisdictional disputes of major Protestant bodies have been solved by comity arrangements through the International Missionary Council, but Protestant-Catholic tensions and disputes growing out of foreign proselyting by many sects affect the work of all missionaries. When missionaries are seen by the nationals as transplanters of denominational competition or as parasites draining away economic resources, proselyting sects find ripe harvest fields awaiting their message of dissent.[65]

11. Conflict. Work on many fields has been profoundly affected by dissension among the missionaries. While personality conflicts are now minimized through careful screening of candidates, clashes between individualistic, strong-minded missionaries have carried over into unresolved tensions between the foreign staff and hired native workers. When the "self-support" idea associated with the concept of the indigenous church was first applied in Latin America, many native pastors previously paid by mission boards were reduced to extremely low salaries and suffered other injustices which produced tensions. Missionary boards also have competed with one another for national preachers; those which provide the most pay and other benefits have deprived others of native leadership.[66]

12. Politics. Many government treaties include reciprocal agreements to permit missionaries to work freely in each country. Government pressures have sometimes defended foreign missionaries exposed to persecution. Because of their interest in freedom of speech, assembly, the press, and especially religion, missionary organizations have engaged in pressure politics and on occasion have even embroiled the nation's foreign relations.[67]

13. Nationalism. Nationalism has been a root as well as a fruit of missions. Growing nationalism, the decline of colonialism, the revival of indigenous cultures, and the establishment of new nations in missionary areas have forced an emphasis upon the indigenous church administrated

[64] Norman P. Grubb, "The Decline of Faith in Faith Missions," *World Conquest,* 13, no. 3 (May-June 1954), 1-2. (Grubb is a leader in the World Evangelization Crusade founded by C. T. Studd in 1914 which, together with the China Inland Mission founded by J. Hudson Taylor in 1865, has served as a model for many "faith missions" organizations.)

[65] For example, Jehovah's Witnesses made great progress in rural Cuba in areas where the priest's annual visit was for the purpose of baptizing infants at $3.00 each. Lowry Nelson, *Rural Cuba* (Minneapolis: University of Minnesota Press, 1950), pp. 174-75, note 1.

[66] Juan M. Isais, "How Nationals Feel about Missions," *Christianity Today,* 2, no. 12 (Mar. 17, 1958), 14-15, and James F. McNiff, M. M., "Why Latin Americans Resent Us," *The Catholic World,* 188 (Dec. 1958), 219-22.

[67] Thomas A. Bailey, *The Man in the Street: The Impact of American Public Opinion on Foreign Policy* (New York: The Macmillan Co., 1948), pp. 199-211.

and financially supported by natives of the area in which it works. Allegations against missionaries for their supposed purchase of converts with material gifts, intervention in national politics, spying for foreign nations, and stirring up political revolts have led governments to compel withdrawal of missionaries from many areas. To protect Christian enterprises, control and leadership have been shifted to nationals. As a result, Christian churches of many missionary lands have renewed vigor, and "foreign missions" is becoming in some respects a thing of the past. The old pattern of philanthropic evangelism is being replaced gradually by an increasingly mature native church. Property and personnel have been turned over to the nationals of India, Japan, the Camerouns, Lebanon, and many other areas by American denominations. Most missionaries realize that nationalism may make them a liability rather than an asset to native Christians; they remain in the background, working through native leaders and helping missionary churches to help themselves. Yet much of what is labeled "indigenous" is indigenous in name only. Mere shifts of leadership and property to a national church do not carry out the principle. Elaborate organizational patterns imposed by missionaries are often perpetuated as if they were an essential element of Christianity.[68]

14. Culture patterns. The cultural milieu exercises a strong influence over the religious appeals, social organization, rites, ceremonies, and ethics of the young churches. Remarkable differences may be observed between Christian churches in the tropics and those in America and Europe. Animistic ideas and practices often remain in the former; in the latter ceremonialism tends to be less important and social welfare rather than personal salvation becomes more so.[69]

"Spiritual imperialism" which fails to appreciate cultural values and to deal with the natives as equals has seriously set back many mission programs. When this occurs, Communism, competing religions, or nationalism are typical scapegoats used by missionaries who unwittingly were largely to blame for their own failure.[70] The rapid spreading of Islam in Africa is a result of its adaptation to indigenous cultures, lack of racial discrimination, natural dissemination by laymen with non-missionary occupations, and indigenous support of schools and mosques from their very

---

[68] E. J. Bingle, "The Changing Pattern of Foreign Missions," *World Dominion and the World To-day,* 28 (Mar.-Apr. 1950), 100-5, and Harry Belshaw, "Africanization and the Church," *World Dominion and the World To-day,* 28 (Sept.-Oct. 1950), 288-91. The latter includes an excellent analysis of barriers to self-government of the African church.

[69] Ellsworth Huntington, *Mainsprings of Civilization* (New York: John Wiley and Sons, 1945), pp. 300-2.

[70] For a forthright account of a typical anti-white-missionary case, see Peter J. Brashler, "Perverseness in the Aru Adversity," *The Gospel Message* (Gospel Missionary Union), 64, no. 3 (Aug.-Sept. 1955), 1-4.

beginning. It is a demonstration of cultural adaptation as a key to successful proselyting.[71]

15. Indigenous religions. When missionaries bring a religion similar to
those already present among a people, their work is likely to grow more
rapidly than otherwise. Pentecostalism in Chile has outstripped other
Protestant groups because it is chiefly an indigenous movement with
spiritual fervor, a deep feeling of fellowship, and a sense of urgency to
proclaim the gospel as the expression of a simple, impressionable people
who have entered a new life in Christ.[72]

It is usually easiest to gain acceptance of the portions of the new religion that are closest to old beliefs and practices. When the missionary's
religious forms are adopted, they may be filled with a meaning or content that identifies them more with the "primitive religion" they supposedly replace than with the new type.[73] Objective and subjective meanings of religious practices may deviate so greatly that acceptance of a
new religion amounts to little more than putting old wine into new bottles.
The large number of "converts" among certain orientals when first confronted with American evangelism is a case in point. Accepting the invitation to "receive Christ as Savior" often amounted to no more than
either showing politeness or adding another god to an innumerable list.
Analogies between the indigenous and the new religion, often not sensed
by missionaries, have bridged the gap between their beliefs and practices,
contributing to syncretisms blending elements from both into new, unique
religious systems. Refusal to permit such adaptations, has contributed
to the failure of scores of missionary enterprises.

16. Sociopsychological needs. Desires of natives to gain emotional
security, personal prestige, and other rewards influence opportunists and
social outcasts to adopt Christianity before others.[74] Much of the Protestant success in winning converts from the educated classes reflects desires to gain prestige and information through contacts with Americans.
In Brazil the Roman Catholic Church has been a most effective channel
of upward social mobility. Many of its bishops and high dignitaries are of
lower middle class extraction.[75] Social bonds are also important. Once converts are won, their children, other family members, and friends are likely
to follow their footsteps into the new faith. A dominant motive in 56 per
cent of 4,000 new members of the Christian church in India was family

[71] Diedrich Westermann, "Islam in Africa," in *When Peoples Meet,* Alain Locke
and Bernard J. Stern, eds. (New York: Hinds, Hayden and Eldredge, rev. ed.,
1946), pp. 70-74.
[72] David C. Brackenridge, "Pentecostal Progress in Chile," *World Dominion and
the World To-day,* 29 (Sept.-Oct. 1951), 295-98.
[73] Albert G. Keller, *Societal Evolution* (New Haven: Yale University Press, rev.
ed., 1931), pp. 209, 314.
[74] Hallowell, "Sociopsychological Aspects of Acculturation," p. 196.
[75] Emilio Willems, "Letter to the Editor," *American Journal of Sociology,* 59
(July 1953), 59-60.

influence (34 per cent had Christian parents, and 22 per cent other Christian family members).[76]

Social Effects of Missions

Christian missions have the primary goals of making and strengthening converts, yet they have many additional social effects. Some are obvious, inevitable accompaniments of implanting a new religion in a cultural area; others are unintentionally produced latent consequences. Some effects are functional and others dysfunctional, but we will not label them because the same consequence seems from one frame of reference to contribute to the adjustment of society or its members, while from another it may seem destructive and injurious. For example, the eradication of polygynous marriage from a society may increase the respect and freedom accorded women, but it may also contribute to the collapse of traditional methods of social control and increase prostitution. The overlapping, interrelated effects of missionary work may be classified as religious, cultural, political, and social.

Religious Effects of Missions. Churches not only gain more adherents by evangelism in foreign lands, but they also gain strength in the homeland. The sense of fellowship of members is intensified by programs to extend their beliefs to "the regions beyond." Increased fellowship leads to increased loyalty and strengthens the entire organization.

The problems of missionary enterprises have increased cooperation within and across denominational lines. Missionary programs of the major branches of Christianity are part of a world-wide enterprise. American Catholic missions are integrated into the total program of the Roman Catholic Church; Protestant missions are coordinated both through denominational organizations like the Lutheran World Federation and interdenominational bodies, outstanding among which is the International Missionary Council. The need to avoid duplication of effort, as well as the meaninglessness of many denominational distinctions in foreign lands, has been a major source of cooperation in ecumenical organizations.[77] In spite of coordination and comity agreements by many missionary boards, there is a confusing multiplication of Christian groups in many regions. In the Union of South Africa alone there are over 1,100 separatist African denominations.[78]

---

[76] J. Waskom Pickett, as reported in J. H. Bavinck, *The Impact of Christianity on the Non-Christian World* (Grand Rapids, Mich.: Wm. B. Eerdmans Publishing Co., 1948), p. 77.

[77] John Dillenberger and Claude Welch, *Protestant Christianity* (New York: Charles Scribner's Sons, 1954), p. 178.

[78] Emory Ross, "Impact of Christianity in Africa," *Annals of the American Academy of Political and Social Science,* 298 (Mar. 1955), 161-69. For a discussion of the splintering and divisions of Christians in India see P. Oomman Philip, "Three Centuries of Christian Scandal," *Christian Century,* 60 (Nov. 17, 1943), 1332-34.

Both Christian and indigenous religions are influenced by their close association. Missionary Christianity sometimes acquires characteristics unknown to it in other cultures; it is increasingly under pressure to adapt to native customs and cultures. By 1930 it was apparent to skilled observers that it was "almost certain that only a Sinicized Christianity can permanently triumph in China." [79] Syncretism of Catholicism with native religions has been deliberately planned to substitute new meanings in old practices. This is much less disruptive in the culture and more effective in producing conversions than methods aimed at extirpating culture traits without providing substitutes.[80] In India, Christians in some areas have been identified as a separate caste; Hindu and Christian elements are strangely interwoven in work and worship in such communities. Caste distinctions have been retained by many Christians as a means of perpetuating a familiar type of group life.[81] The Christianity of American Indians and Eskimos is typically a new religion fusing native and Christain elements and reinterpreting tribal customs in the light of the new theology.[82] European-American Christianity similarly incorporates many pagan elements. Religions cannot be transplanted from one culture to another without being changed in at least minor respects.[83]

Christian religious concepts, ethical standards, and techniques also have penetrated Hindu society in India. In Indonesia Christianity has had little effect as a formal religion, but it stimulated Moslem reform to bring Islam into harmony with modern society and rational thought. Islam became a personal religion based on respect for the worth of the individual and recognition of his duty to his fellowmen.[84] Buddhists in the United States have adapted to American society so much that it is difficult to distinguish them from semi-Christian cults.[85] Successes of Christian missionaries in Japan have modified Japanese Buddhism. Western methods of propagating the faith and teaching the young were borrowed from

---

[79] Kenneth Scott Latourette, "Christianity in China," *Annals of the American Academy of Political and Social Science,* 152 (Nov. 1930), 63-71 (quotation from p. 71).

[80] M. D. W. Jeffreys, "Some Rules of Directed Culture Change Under Roman Catholicism," *American Anthropologist,* 58 (Aug. 1956), 721-31.

[81] Bede Griffiths, O.S.B., "Christ and India," *Commonweal,* 69 (Dec. 26, 1958), 331-33, and Hilda Raj, *Persistence of Caste in South India: An Analytical Study of the Hindu and Christian Nadars,* Washington, D.C., The American University, Ph.D. thesis, 1958.

[82] Ruth Shonle, "The Christianizing Process Among Preliterate Peoples," *Journal of Religion,* 4 (May 1924), 261-80, and Melville J. Herskovits, *Acculturation* (New York: J. J. Augustin Publisher, 1938), pp. 76-82.

[83] Theodor H. Gaster, ed. and reviser, *The New Golden Bough* by Sir James George Frazer (New York: Criterion Books, 1959), pp. 610-47.

[84] George W. Davis, "Some Hidden Effects of Christianity Upon Hinduism and Hindus," *Journal of Religion,* 26 (Apr. 1946), 111-24, and "The Religious Life of Indonesia," *Asian Review,* 55 (Oct. 1959), 309-13.

[85] R. F. Spencer, "Social Structure of a Contemporary Japanese-American Buddhist Church," *Social Forces,* 26 (Mar. 1948), 281-87.

Christianity. Mottoes, tracts, modern translations of ancient beliefs, and Buddhist scriptures were printed for mass circulation. Street corner services, Sunday schools, social service agencies, adapted Christian hymns, and even substitutes for Christian holidays were copied by the Buddhists. Few of the 126 new religions established in Japan since World War II are Christian, but almost all show the influence of Christianity.[86]

Reaction against missionaries among disinherited and lower class natives often crystallizes in the form of new religious sects. The cult of Eshu in Brazil has, in many sections, been transformed as a result of changes in the social structure, race relations, Catholicism, urbanization, and industrialization. Eshu, the malicious, has been changed into an evil being, often identified with Satan.[87] The John Frum movement, which promises a golden age after the abandonment of Christianity, and other Melanesian cults are organized around prophecies of an era of eternal happiness in which God or the ancestors will bring material goods ("cargo") after the social order has been overturned. Such cults are largely a reaction against the white man and his religion among people stimulated by socioeconomic deprivations. Embryonic nationalism is represented in such movements.[88]

Africa has thousands of separatist indigenous churches, sects, and cults. Some are separatist Christian groups resentful of attempted missionary control over the relationship of Christianity to tribal rites. Others display pentecostal features and heretical tendencies, combine tribal religion with distorted views of the Old Testament, revive tribalism, or are politico-religious cults like the Mau Mau movement. All reflect Christian failure to meet the challenges of indigenous tribalism. American divisions in Christendom, the desire for independence from foreign control, formalism and foreignism of life and worship in mission churches, the missionaries' ban on native techniques and implements of worship (dancing, drums, calabashes, etc.), the imposition of unintelligible hymns, failure of mission churches to appeal to the emotions, preoccupation of missionaries with education rather than evangelism, and promulgation of an unguided Biblicism which lacks any guarantee of doctrinal truth, have all helped magnify the fissiparous tendencies of Protestantism in Africa.[89]

---

[86] Everett, *Religion in Human Experience,* pp. 506-8, and Harry Thomsen, "Japan's New Religions," *International Review of Missions,* 48 (July 1959), 283-93.

[87] Roger Bastide, "Immigration et Métamorphose d'un Dieu," *Cahiers Internationaux de Sociologie,* 20 (Jan.-June 1956), 45-60.

[88] Jean Guiart, "Culture Contact and the 'John Frum' Movement on Tanna, New Hebrides," *Southwestern Journal of Anthropology,* 12 (Spring 1956), 105-16; Peter M. Worsley, *The Trumpet Shall Sound: A Study of "Cargo" Cults in Melanesia* (London: MacGibbon and Kee, 1957), and P. M. Worsley, "Cargo Cults," *Scientific American,* 200, no. 5 (May 1959), 117-28.

[89] Leonard J. Beecher, "African Separatist Churches in Kenya," *World Dominion and the World To-day,* 31 (Jan.-Feb. 1953), 5-12, and Geoffrey Parrinder, "Separatist Sects in West Africa," *ibid.,* 30 (Nov.-Dec. 1952), 343-46.

Sometimes the introduction of Christian missions contributes to increased secularism in society and eventually to a decline of both native and Christian religions. Traditional religious beliefs are undermined. The literacy introduced to enable reading of the Bible and religious literature makes possible reading from other sources, some of which are antagonistic toward Christianity. Translation of numerous non-religious works in the humanities and sciences has been a significant contribution by missions to education and diffusion of western culture in the Orient.[90]

Cultural Effects of Missions. Some elements in a culture influenced by missionaries are *incompatible* with Christianity. These include practices like idol worship, placation of evil spirits, head hunting, child marriage, and degradation of widows. Others are *adaptable* to the Christian message, easily retained by converts, although perhaps under a new rationale (vegetarianism, modes of worship, rituals, prayer posture, style of dress, etc.). Still others are *irrelevant,* although Christian ethics may have implications for their use. The proclamation of Christianity cannot consist merely of blanket categorizing of culture traits as approved or rejected. Methods must be adapted and purposes made clear in missionary work.[91]

Christian missions may promote societal integration or disintegration, depending upon effectiveness in relating the new religion to existing social patterns, the socio-religious environment to which the gospel comes, and the homegeneity of the Christian witness. The rate of social disintegration has been increased by Christians in areas affected by Catholic-Protestant, sect-church, and fundamentalist-modernist controversies.[92]

If the missionary's religion "takes hold," it usually changes the system of cultural organization radically. Among culture patterns broken under the influence of Christian missions in various lands are husband-wife relationships, economic behavior, sex standards, the initiatory system, the system or pattern of lineage, patterns of discriminatory segregation, and even traditional names. Respect for traditional institutions has been broken down without the provision of effective substitutes. Imposing a new religion without relating it to established ethical ideals and practices may eliminate instead of reinforce ethics.[93] The basic pattern

---

[90] Robert E. Park, "Missions and the Modern World," *American Journal of Sociology,* 50 (Nov. 1944), 177-83, and Tsuen-Hsuin Tsien, "Western Impact on China Through Translation," *Far Eastern Quarterly,* 13 (May 1954), 305-27.

[91] Bavinck, *The Impact of Christianity,* pp. 65-77.

[92] Justus M. van der Kroef, "Patterns of Western Influence in Indonesia," *American Sociological Review,* 17 (Aug. 1952), 421-30, and Hobart B. Amstutz, "In Malaya Today," *World Dominion and the World To-day,* 29 (Nov.-Dec. 1951), 330-33.

[93] Laura Thompson and Alice Joseph, "White Pressures on Indian Personality and Culture," *American Journal of Sociology,* 53 (July 1947), 17-22; Emilio Willems, "Protestantism as a Factor of Culture Change in Brazil," *Economic Development and Cultural Change,* 3 (July 1955), 321-33; Robert T. Parsons, "Missionary-African Relations," *Civilisations,* 3 (no. 4, 1953), 505-18; William Bascom, "African Culture and the Missionary," *ibid.,* 491-504; Ako Adjei, "Imperialism and Spiritual

of morality may lose so much of its underlying sanctions that the spread of Christianity means also the spread of immorality. In polygynous societies in which missionaries insist that male converts retain only one of their wives, many women released from marriage have no source of livelihood except prostitution. Christian converts in such societies sometimes resort to concubinage, which introduces new distinctions between women. Even when converts become convinced monogamists, relationships between husband and wife are considerably different from those of America and the subjective meanings involved in monogamy are not the same. Attitudes toward property are similarly related to the ethical system; introduction of new codes of honesty may change radically the entire pattern of socioeconomic organization. Lawlessness tends to increase rapidly during transition periods. Hence efforts of a mission board in Latin America to free serfs and Christianize Indians resulted initially in an increase of crimes against property.[94]

In the diffusion of culture traits, missionaries may oppose colonial administrators and commercial interests, but more often they work with them. The western trader and missionary may both introduce clothing to near-nudist peoples or increase the amount worn. Different motives are involved, but cooperation makes success more certain. Traders may try to extend the market for the white man's alcohol, while administrators and missionaries work together to oppose or control it. Missionaries, partly dependent upon colonial administrators for their well-being, have often worked with them to meet health and education needs and to bring about the acculturation, usually conceived in westernized terms, of isolated and preliterate peoples.[95]

Cultural arrogance is usually involved in efforts to replace native culture patterns with those of Western civilization. Holding that cultural diffusion should be entirely a one-way process, missionaries are prone to accept the ethnocentric view that everything indigenous is contrary to God's will, while everything distinctive of their home culture is good. Their converts have rejected native arts and crafts, music, games, and other cultural elements as if they were indelibly stained with a heathenism incompatible with Christian values. Christian converts could no longer be at home with their own people.[96] Mission stations are often "outposts of

---

Freedom: An African View," *American Journal of Sociology,* 50 (Nov. 1944), 189-98, and Gladys A. Reichard, "The Navaho and Christianity," *American Anthropologist,* 51 (Feb. 1949), 66-71.

[94] Edmund deS. Brunner, Irwin T. Sanders, and Douglas Ensminger, *Farmers of the World* (New York: Columbia University Press, 1945), p. 120.

[95] Brown, "Missions and Cultural Diffusion," pp. 216-17, and Wm. C. Smith, "Missionary Activities and the Acculturation of Backward Peoples," *Journal of Applied Sociology,* 8 (1922-23), 175-86.

[96] Adjei, "Imperialism and Spiritual Freedom"; A. Capell, "Native Cultures and the Christian Church," *World Dominion and the World To-day,* 28 (Nov.-Dec.

European civilization" at which white people may be seen at their best.[97] They may also be viewed as tools of Western cultural and political aggression.

Political Effects of Missions. Entrance to undeveloped territories by the great world powers has typically come by gradual penetration in which the first "civilizing" influence was that of missions. The flag has often followed the missionary, with the trader close behind. As a result, international political struggles, such as that between France and Germany to protect Roman Catholic missionaries in the Orient, have been directed toward much more than the ostensible protection of Western nationals. Colonial imperialism and Western capitalism have been intimately connected with modern Christian missions.[98]

The political partitioning of Africa by powers considered to be Christian, economic exploitation, and moral behavior of white people that indicated the Christian God must not care about what men do in their daily lives, contributed to a lack or loss of respect for Christianity by Africans. This outlook was also promoted by the Italian invasion of Ethiopia and accompanying failure of the "Christian" League of Nations to defend the member nation that was attacked. Racial prejudice in America and the Union of South Africa, divisions of Christians who professed to worship the same God, and the ethnocentrism of missionaries who refused to believe anything was worthy of respect in African religion and morals also lowered the reputation of Christianity. On the other hand, missionaries in South Africa were once the major champions of colored people who desired protection against injustice. Only through missionaries could news of cruelty against a native reach the ears of the government.[99] In India missionaries have been attacked by exploiters because, in their concern for tribal welfare, they offered aboriginals protection. Selfish exploitation of people in undeveloped areas has been limited by missionaries, as in 1898 when they joined with American merchants to exert pressure upon the U.S. State Department to halt the rapacity of European imperialists, especially Russians, in China.[100]

1950), 361-64, and Ronald and Catherine Brandt, *From Black to White in South Australia* (Chicago: University of Chicago Press, 1952).

[97] Park, "Missions and the Modern World," p. 183, and David M. Paton, *Christian Missions and the Judgment of God* (London: Student Christian Movement Press, 1953).

[98] Paul S. Reinsch, *World Politics at the End of the Nineteenth Century as Influenced by the Oriental Situation* (New York: The Macmillan Co., 1900), pp. 32-34; Thorsten V. Kalijarvi and associates, *Modern World Politics* (New York: Thomas Y. Crowell Co., second ed., 1946), pp. 36-37; John Lee (pseud.), "The Chinese Struggle for Democracy," *Annals of the American Academy of Political and Social Science,* 258 (July 1948), 31-52, and Parker Thomas Moon, *Imperialism and World Politics* (New York: The Macmillan Co., 1926), *passim.*

[99] James Bryce, *Impressions of South Africa* (New York: The Century Co., third ed., 1900), pp. 388-91.

[100] E. DeMuelder, S. J., "The Missionary Approach to Aboriginal Welfare,"

Missionaries have stimulated the development of democratic ideology. From the beginning of the move for independence in Korea, the leaders were Christians who had come under the influence of missionaries. Protestant missionaries in India introduced democratic ideals and methods through their educational system and through leadership training on how to conduct local, regional, and national church business. Demands of depressed classes and of the hill tribes for increased privileges have arisen largely from impulses implanted by missions.[101] When people in underdeveloped areas take the teachings of Christianity seriously, the associated democratic ideals may be called subversive or even communistic. Nationalistic revolutions in Africa have been authored largely by Christianity.[102] The Taiping Rebellion in China (1850-1864) was an indigenous movement aimed at establishing a Christian society.[103] Had it occurred a century later, missionaries might have supported it unequivocably even in opposition to government orders.

Missionaries in some respects have increased misunderstanding between peoples, but they have also built bridges of understanding. American missionaries have been more free of selfish political actions than those from Europe. They have served as "ambassadors of good will" helping to disseminate knowledge, even though it often was lopsided, about other peoples and cultures. Their great number, in comparison to businessmen and statesmen who have traveled or lived in other nations, and numerous speaking engagements while regularly home on furlough, have greatly multiplied their influence.[104] Their impact upon public opinion helped to cement other interests of the U.S. in its protective policy toward China and its later opposition toward Japanese domination.[105]

Through reducing languages to writing, breaking down intellectual and cultural isolation, and relieving certain tensions, Christian missions have begun to create a moral solidarity that can provide a basis for an integrated world society.[106] Even during war, ecumenical Protestant, Catho-

---

Indian Journal of Social Work, 14 (Mar. 1954), 366-75, and Thomas A. Bailey, *America Faces Russia* (Ithaca, N.Y.: Cornell University Press, 1950), p. 176.

[101] Latourette, "The Present Status . . . ," p. 66.

[102] Darrell Randall, "Is the Gospel Too Subversive for Africa?" *Saturday Review,* 36, no. 18 (May 2, 1953), 15-16, 49-50; Cecil Northcott, "Christian Democracy in Africa," *Christian Century,* 68 (Dec. 12, 1951), 1435-36, and a series of four articles on Africa by James H. Robinson, *Christian Century,* 73 (Jan. 11 to Feb. 1, 1956), 41-43, 77-80, 111-13, 137-39.

[103] E. R. Hughes, *The Invasion of China by the Western World* (New York: The Macmillan Co., 1938), pp. 66-68.

[104] Leland S. Albright, "The Missionary as Cultural Bridge Builder Abroad and at Home," in *Approaches to Group Understanding,* Lyman Bryson, Louis Finkelstein, and R. M. MacIver, eds. (New York: Conference on Science, Philosophy and Religion, 1947), pp. 706-15.

[105] Lawrence H. Chamberlain and Richard C. Snyder, *American Foreign Policy* (New York: Rinehart and Co., 1948), pp. 656-57.

[106] Park, "Missions and the Modern World."

lic, and Jewish organizations maintained relationships across barriers imposed by battle lines. If Christianity would overcome its internal dissension, if materialistic concomitants of traditional missions were sloughed off, and if general disrespect for non-Western culture traits were replaced by wholesome evaluation, missions conceivably could provide an ideological basis for international social solidarity.[107]

Other Social Effects of Missions. The contributions missions have made to raising the level of education, improving health, eradicating harmful superstitions, creating respect for women and underprivileged people, improving working conditions and agriculture, and meeting social needs resulting from war, famine, poverty, and disasters are too well known to need discussion here. "Secular" programs of aid to underdeveloped nations, such as the Point Four program, have received their major impetus and example from pioneering missionary work in education, agriculture, welfare, and health. In spite of the condescending attitude of superiority that has sometimes accompanied these activities, their disruptive effects upon established culture patterns, and other faults of Christian missions, tremendous good has been accomplished by them. Critics who condemn them for ruining native cultures usually fail to recognize that, in a world of advanced transportation and communication, such disruption is inevitable. Missionaries have speeded up the process, but they have also presented cultural alternatives that might have been lacking had the changes been introduced without their religious-cultural system. Even when mission programs appear to have brought no basic institutional changes, they have imparted ideals of the dignity of the individual which have contributed to the spread of democratic ideology.[108]

Through its missionary program, the church has informed Americans about other peoples and religions, established schools where nationals can learn to read and write, translated the Bible into native tongues, and reduced many languages to writing for the first time. The outstanding leader in the "literacy campaign" has been Frank Laubach, famous for the "Each One Teach One" method of education.[109]

". . . every advance into new territory made by printing has had as its motive an expanding religion. In the whole long history of the advance of printing from its beginning in China down to the twentieth century, there is scarcely a language or a country where the first printing done has not been either from the sacred scriptures or from the sacred art of one of the world's three great missionary religions." [110] Printing in

[107] Hugh Stuntz, "Christian Missions and Social Cohesion," *American Journal of Sociology,* 50 (Nov. 1944), 184-88.

[108] Marion J. Levy, Jr., *The Family Revolution in Modern China* (Cambridge: Harvard University Press, 1949), pp. 286, 304.

[109] Frank C. Laubach, *Thirty Years with the Silent Billion* (Westwood, N.J.· Fleming H. Revell Co., 1960).

[110] Thomas Francis Carter and L. Carrington Goodrich, *The Invention of Printing*

turn made popular education possible and contributed to the advent of political democracy. Modern nationalistic movements, which so often hinder further missionary advances, are in many instances a result of past missionary success. They reflect a reaction against pressures of social control which are inherent in the educational work of missionaries.[111] In the program to reduce languages into writing, the Summer Institute of Linguistics (Wycliffe Bible Translators) is prominent. Founded in 1942, its linguists were translating 680 languages in 38 countries in 1980; numerous other workers and countries were indirectly influenced through alumni of its summer school programs.[112]

Conclusion

We have seen that the missionary work of the church overlaps with all its other activities, so it may justly be termed a "missionary institution." Evangelism and religious education cannot be sharply distinguished, for they use many of the same techniques and have similar goals. Growth of churches, an indicator of successful missionary outreach, is related to characteristics of both churches and their environments. The church is directly dependent upon its community, although complete social determinism is lacking because many factors besides the environment are involved in church growth. The evaluation of church success is a complex task on which social science has only begun to work. In a society with much ideological, residential, and social class mobility, churches face the problem of winning the same people again and again as they shift their positions in the societal structure.

American foreign missionary enterprises are now more extensive than ever before. Numerous social influences affect foreign missions, and the effects are similarly diverse, creeping into every realm of religious, cultural, political, and social life. These effects are both functional and dysfunctional to individuals and society. It is therefore possible to select evidence on the basis of personal biases and build a case for either support or condemnation of American missionary work. So many interrelated factors and such great variation are involved that it is impossible to measure completely the over-all influence of Christian missions. The

---

in China—and Its Spread Westward (New York: Ronald Press Co., second ed., 1955), p. 26. Copyright 1955 The Ronald Press Company. Reprinted by permission.

[111] William Albig, *Modern Public Opinion* (New York: McGraw-Hill Book Co., 1956), p. 42, and Edgar T. Thompson, "Comparative Education in Colonial Areas, with Special Reference to Plantation and Mission Frontiers," *American Journal of Sociology*, 48 (May 1943), 710-21.

[112] Clarence W. Hall, *Two Thousand Tongues to Go* (New York: Harper and Brothers, 1958), and Kenneth L. Pike, "Our Own Tongue Wherein We Were Born," *The Bible Translator*, 10 (Apr. 1959), 70-82.

functional consequences to individuals seem to have outweighed the dysfunctional; if such is indeed the case, mankind as a whole is much the better, even from a strictly humanitarian perspective, than it would be had there been no missionary movement.

The revival of American Judaism has brought many of the problems and characteristics of Christian recruitment and missions into the synagogue. Other world religions, especially Buddhism and Islam, are also extending their missionary programs and, as a result, increasing their influence in America.

Cooperation within a group is an essential prerequisite for effective evangelistic efforts at home and abroad. Such efforts also represent instances of competition and contribute to other forms of antagonism. It is hence appropriate to look next at these basic social processes.

Selected References

Bachmann, E. Theodore, comp., "Doctoral Dissertations on Mission," *International Bulletin of Missionary Research*, 7, no. 3 (July 1983), 97–134. A bibliography with a subject index to 934 dissertations on mission-related subjects at 23 seminaries and 122 universities in the U.S. and Canada from 1945 to 1981.

Barkman, Paul F., Edward R. Dayton, and Edward L. Gruman, *Christian Collegians and Foreign Missions*. Monrovia, Calif.: Missions Advanced Research and Communications Center, 1969. Findings of a mailed questionnaire from over 4,900 delegates to the Ninth Missionary Conference of Inter-Varsity Christian Fellowship at Urbana, Dec. 1967.

Barrett, David B., *Schism and Renewal in Africa: An Analysis of Six Thousand Contemporary Religious Movements*. Nairobi, Kenya: Oxford University Press, 1968. A cross-cultural study of the phenomenon of independency among the churches of 34 nations in Africa as a response and reaction to Christian missions.

Barrett, David B., ed., *World Christian Encyclopedia*. Nairobi, Kenya: Oxford University Press, 1982. A massive compilation of data on twentieth-century churches and religions in 223 countries with projections to A.D. 2000.

Goddard, Burton L., ed., *The Encyclopedia of Modern Christian Missions: The Agencies*. Camden, N.J.: Thomas Nelson and Sons, 1967. Descriptions and addresses of 1,437 Christian (mostly Protestant) missionary sending and supporting agencies.

Heise, David R., "Prefatory Findings in the Sociology of Missions," *Journal for the Scientific Study of Religion*, 6, no. 1 (Spring 1967), 49–58 (commentaries by Alford Carleton and Elihu Katz, pp. 59–63). A review of sociological aspects of missionary activities: two major categories of strategies, two of tactics, and facilitating conditions and structural factors affecting the response.

Hessel, Dieter T., *Reconciliation and Conflict: Church Controversy over Social Involvement*. Philadelphia: Westminster, 1969. Tensions related to divergent concepts of the social mission of the church and alternative modes of social action.

Horner, Norman A., ed., *Protestant Crosscurrents in Mission: The Ecumenical-Conservative Encounter*. Nashville: Abingdon, 1968. Divergent philosophies and values of evangelicals and ecumenists pertinent to the Christian mandate, objectives, and strategy of world mission by three authors from each camp.

Jeffreys, M. D. W., "Some Rules of Directed Culture Change under Roman Catholicism," *American Anthropologist*, 58 (Aug. 1956), 721–31. On the deliberate use of syncretisms in Catholic missions.

Kraft, Charles H., *Christianity in Culture*. Maryknoll, N.Y.: Orbis Books, 1979. An intensive study of dynamic biblical theologizing in cross-cultural perspective which emphasizes the importance of dynamic equivalence.

Mehl, Roger, "Sociology of Missions," chapter 8 in *The Sociology of Protestantism*. Philadelphia: Westminster, 1970, pp. 163–189. Mission as a sociological phenomenon, sociological problems posed by it, and those problems born from mission contact with indigenous religions.

Nida, Eugene A., *Customs and Cultures*, 2nd ed. Pasadena, Calif.: William Carey Library, 1975. Anthropological and linguistic principles applied to Christian missions.

Philip, P. Oomman, "Three Centuries of Christian Scandal," *Christian Century*, 60 (Nov. 17, 1943), 1332–34. A discussion of splintering and divisions among Christians in India which reflect missionary influences.

Stipe, Claude E., "Anthropologists versus Missionaries: The Influence of Presuppositions," *Current Anthropology*, 21, no. 2 (April 1980), 165–168, with comments and replies pp. 168–179; 22:89, 181, 297–98; 23:338–40; 24:114–15. A discussion of the generally negative attitude of anthropologists toward missionaries, its sources, and the resulting bias in field work, followed by responses from numerous other anthropologists.

Varg, Paul A., *Missionaries, Chinese, and Diplomats*. New York: Octagon Books, 1977 (Princeton University Press, 1958). A study of the decline and failure of the American Protestant missionary movement in China, 1890–1952, including experiences of missionaries with diplomats.

Wax, Murray L., and Rosalie H. Wax, "Religion Among American Indians," *Annals of the American Academy of Political and Social Science*, 436 (March 1978), 27–39. An interpretation of tribal responses to Christian missionizing.

Winter, Ralph D., and Steven C. Hawthorne, eds., *Perspectives on the World Christian Movement: A Reader*. Pasadena, Calif.: William Carey Library, 1981. Eighty-seven essays, surveys, case studies, and reports on biblical, historical, cultural, and strategic perspectives on world evangelization.

Part Five: *Social Processes and the Church*

🏛 Chapter 10

Cooperation

All church activities involve cooperation, defined most simply as working together or activity for mutual benefit. No united action of any kind, hence no institutional behavior, is possible without cooperation. Early in history it became apparent that people could accomplish much more by working together than by acting independently. Out of mutual aid, common defense, and struggles with enemies for scarce goods and values grew the sense of togetherness or solidarity which is at the core of institutional unity. Common labor in which all shared the same task developed into group habits that distributed specialized duties. This division of labor led to the emergence of institutions like business, schools, and the church as well as to institutional roles and statuses.

In order to meet its functional requirements and survive, any organization must effectively safeguard its existence, relate itself to other organizations and the larger social system, pursue its goals, and establish working relationships between its members' roles. All these tasks demand cooperation, either by the entire group, or by a variety of subgroups related to each other as satellites around a central organizing administration or interest. The degree of consensus reached by members and subgroups often determines the degree to which the organization can accomplish its purposes effectively. Cooperative attitudes and behavior become so entwined with each other and so habitual for members that they operate unconsciously as if they were external forces and not personal acts.

Reciprocity is such that, though each gives, each also receives in the interaction process. Cooperation of members is evident as they engage in the church's rites and ceremonies, promote its interests through various activities, and play their institutional roles. Their informal social relationships are sometimes more significant than their formal, specialized tasks when it comes to promoting cooperation, a spirit of unity, and hence institutional success.

Basically, then, every aspect of church life involves or reflects cooperation. In this chapter we shall survey local, denominational, interdenominational, and interfaith church cooperation in America. We shall see that conflict (opposition, controversy, strife, discord, or antagonistic behavior) is paradoxically, yet inseparably, linked with cooperation.

Conflict as a Basis for Cooperation

Cooperative interaction within a church arises largely out of conflict. The need to work together in opposition to real or imaginary enemies is a basic source of the church. The enemies may be "spiritual wickedness in high places" (Eph. 6:12), personality traits deemed sinful, societal conditions, or other tangible or intangible, objective or subjective, foes. As members work together to oppose their enemies, worship, prayer, music, rites, and ceremonies bind them closer to one another and help to increase their cooperation and efficiency. The struggle for power in society often leads to cooperation for limited purposes by organizations otherwise in conflict with each other. European Catholic support of atheistic Mussolini and anti-Christian Hitler illustrates the tendency of churches to support the political causes believed most to further the saving of souls even if compromise on other grounds is necessary.[1] Protestant fundamentalists, who had strong anti-moving picture attitudes, cooperated with theaters to establish national prohibition. Political conflict makes strange bedfellows!

When contradictory values are present in society, the group-making role of conflict contributes to cooperation in a double sense: each set of beliefs attracts into an organization persons who are in accord with it; simultaneously each pushes toward the opposite group persons repulsed by it. Divergent perspectives on evangelism, e.g., divide Christians, hampering complete unity and reinforcing their division into major camps.[2]

Cooperative endeavors also grow out of the associated definitions of

---

[1] Thomas F. Hoult, *The Sociology of Religion* (New York: Dryden Press, 1958), p. 217.

[2] Franklin H. Giddings, "Are Contradictions of Ideas and Beliefs Likely to Play an Important Group-making Rôle in the Future?" *American Journal of Sociology*, 13 (May 1908), 784-91, and David O. Moberg, "A Sociologist's View of Contemporary Christian Evangelism," *Mid-Stream*, 8, no. 4 (1970), 17–31 (plus Discussion, pp. 31–39).

the situations that are involved in the conflicting and cooperative endeavors. Ideological concepts and communication play an important part in the formation and behavior of groups. Contrasting concepts like the elect and damned, spiritual and carnal, saved and unsaved, saints and sinners, have played a significant role in the history of religion. The solidarity of many groups is based partly upon concepts in their language; the outsider is readily identified by his failure to use the "correct" language. The religious group is a "speech community" held together by linguistic signs and psychological meanings. Convictions of the individual are reinforced through sharing religious singing, reading a creed, and participating in such rites as Holy Communion. The linguistic symbols are stabilized in the process of institutionalization. They confirm and strengthen the beliefs of members, identify them as being among the faithful, and indicate which persons and groups are alien to the faith.[3] Yet the linguistic symbols do not necessarily convey the same inner meaning to each worshiper. "Kneeling before the same altar . . . , saying the same creeds and singing the same hymns, one man worships the God who acts literally, another worships the God who acts metaphorically, a third worships the God who acts symbolically, and yet another worships the God who doesn't act at all."[4] "Passwords" thus are significant to church unity. They may be even more important than its basic doctrines.

Perceived differences in the nature and meaning of rituals lead both to cooperation and ideological conflict. Thus the Lord's Supper is a vexatious problem for those who seek organic unity in Christendom because there are so many variations of symbolic meaning and ritualistic conduct in celebrating it. Paradoxically, it is also a great potential uniter of Protestantism, for as communion it communicates a mystical union of the spiritual and natural realms of reality—union with God, with past and future history, and with the community of man.[5] Communion has united and divided both across and within denominational lines. Thus among Lutherans it has led to the organization of churches by believers who desired ordained clergymen to preach the Word and administer the sacraments.[6]

Perhaps the highest degree of cooperative endeavor with a religious base is found in monastic orders and in sectarian communal societies like

---

[3] Sven Wermlund, "Religious Speech Community and Reinforcement of Belief," *Acta Sociologica,* 3, no. 2-3 (1958), 132-46.

[4] William W. Bartley, III, "I Call Myself a Protestant," *Harper's,* 218, no. 1308 (May 1959), 50.

[5] William E. Hulme, "The Lord's Table—Great Uniter," *The Pulpit,* 29 (Apr. 1958), 102-4; and Report of Section IV, Oberlin Conference on Faith and Order, "The Table of the Lord," *Christian Century,* 74 (Oct. 9, 1957), 1195-96.

[6] Wade F. Hook, "The Lutheran Church in the Carolinas Sociologically Interpreted," *Lutheran Quarterly,* 11 (Feb. 1959), 60-67.

those of the Hutterites. Persecution is often a major force solidifying such groups. The sacrificial spirit essential to success apparently can persist for long periods of time only when motivated by powerful religious drives. Yet such groups have many "germs of internal conflict" which may lead to cleavages and even complete destruction of the communalistic way of life.[7] The Amana Society, Oneida Community, and the Shakers became disorganized as a result of such factors.

Cooperation of Local Churches

Local churches engage in cooperative activities both within and across denominational lines. Some of these are on a long-term basis; others involve only isolated incidents a few hours of the year. Some grow out of interchurch conflict which requires each group to make concessions to the other. Many have arisen to meet community needs which cannot be satisfied by churches in isolation.

Cooperation by churches with community agencies like Boy Scouts, Community Chest, and civic clubs is common. Many churches unitedly sponsor social welfare programs. Outstanding among these are union city missions which minister to spiritual, physical, and psychological needs of people in urban skidrow areas. Seeing the need for recreational services, religious education, and social welfare in blighted areas, many have enlarged their staffs with counselors, club directors, sports supervisors, and social workers until they have become social agencies with broadly diversified programs ministering to needs of people of all ages and not merely to alcoholics, homeless men, and "fugitives from family frustrations." Their programs sometimes are criticized as being an excuse used by churches for their failure to practice a religion that encourages skidrow people to attend worship services and other regular activities on an equal basis with others. Churches respond with the factual statement that these people "would not feel at home" in their programs and without missions would be completely neglected.

The most frequent type of cooperation of rural Kentucky churches has been the holding of special-day programs, most commonly at Thanksgiving, Christmas, World Day of Prayer, Memorial Day, and Holy Week or Good Friday. Churches cooperated less frequently in evangelistic campaigns, song services ("singspirations"), religious drama, and school baccalaureate services. Joint preaching services, especially Sunday evenings in the summer, were fairly common. Small churches without full-time pastors, were thus provided frequent worship services. Youth

---

[7] Lee Emerson Deets, "The Origins of Conflict in the Hutterische Communities," *Publications of the American Sociological Society,* 25 (May 1931), 125-35.

organization activities, Sunday schools, vacation Bible schools, other children's programs, and leadership training classes were common joint activities among churches too weak to sponsor effective programs alone. The coordinating organization was sometimes a denomination which sponsored regional or district programs, but more often it was a ministerial association, council of churches, Sunday school association, or committee established for a specific purpose.[8]

It may appear from the above that small churches are more likely than large ones to sponsor joint action programs. Such is not the case, although their need to cooperate may be greater. Two-thirds of the Kentucky churches with 400 or more members reported some type of cooperation; fewer than half as many churches with less than 400 members did. Churches in larger towns were more likely to cooperate with others. Only 14 per cent of open country and hamlet churches reported local cooperation, compared to 53 per cent in villages of 250 to 999, and 73 per cent in those of 1,000 or more. In Missouri rural churches 45.3 per cent of the large (100 or more members), 27.7 per cent of the medium (50 to 99 members), and 23.6 per cent of the small (under 50) church-type groups, and considerably fewer of each sect-type group, engaged in interdenominational cooperative activities.[9] This variation may be due to greater opportunity and recognition of the value of cooperation in larger villages. It may also reflect the more intense competition between churches in small centers where half a dozen churches may compete for a total population too small to give adequate support even to one. The larger communities also are more likely to have full-time ministers who are three times as likely as part-time pastors to be in cooperative churches.[10]

Protestant churches which cooperate tend to do so within a framework of values which leads to a variety of problems. In Springdale, N.Y., each church guarded its jurisdictional rights over members and lay leaders so they would not be drawn too strongly into cooperative ventures taking time and energy away from the church. While publicly promoting interchurch activities, churches privately disparaged each other. Ecumenical practice was ritualized by sharing responsibilities over a period of time, by non-sectarian sermons stressing areas of prior agreement, and by seating the members of each church separately in interdenominational services. This prevented any church from gaining unequal psychological or social access to members of another. Tacit anti-proselyting

[8] Harold F. Kaufman, *Rural Churches in Kentucky, 1947* (Lexington, Ky.: A.E.S. Bul. 530, April 1949), pp. 38-42.

[9] *Ibid.*, pp. 41-43, and Milton Coughenour and Lawrence M. Hepple, *The Church in Rural Missouri, Part II, Religious Groups in Rural Missouri* (Columbia, Mo.: A.E.S. Research Bulletin 633B, Sept. 1957), pp. 102-3.

[10] Kaufman, *Rural Churches in Kentucky*, pp. 42-43. The respective figures are 69 and 23 per cent.

agreements were accompanied by open competition through "non-sectarian" programs to attract outsiders.[11]

The Conciliar Movement

Many congregations and denominations band together in local or state councils of churches. By 1958 there were in the U.S. about 950 local and state councils, over 2,000 alliances of ministers, and some 2,200 interdenominational associations of lay men and women in local communities.[12] These organizations meet needs which cannot be met satisfactorily by churches in isolation from one another. They sponsor community-wide religious programs, conduct classes for lay workers, organize released-time religious education, influence local and state legislation, sponsor youth clubs and recreation centers, sustain religious radio programs, coordinate community religious activities, and plan home missions extension and community evangelism. Most churches cooperating in councils are members of denominations in the National Council of Churches (NCC). In some cases, like the Council of Evangelical Churches of St. Paul, Minn., churches which are more sympathetic to the National Association of Evangelicals have their own council parallel to or competing with the council cooperative with NCC goals and projects.

Some believe the conciliar movement represents the third major organizational period of American Protestantism. Initially churches were brought to the colonies from Europe. During a second period the denominational system predominated for a century and a half. In the emergent stage denominationalism may continue to stand side by side with the conciliar system, or local, state, and national councils of churches may gradually replace it.[13] Cooperative goal-oriented inter-, non-, and trans-denominational projects and associations for evangelism and social concern gained prominence among evangelicals in the 1970's and 80's.

Types of Local Church Unions

Social conditions have led many churches to unite in a more integrative and inclusive way. At least five types of such unions may be differentiated.

1. The circuit plan. This is a longstanding pattern in America in which one minister serves two or more churches. Sometimes it is referred to as a joint pastorate, the sharing of parishes by a clergyman, or, because

---

[11] Arthur J. Vidich and Joseph Bensman, *Small Town in Mass Society* (Princeton, N.J.: Princeton University Press, 1958), pp. 241-51.

[12] Truman B. Douglass, "Our Cooperative Witness to Our Oneness in Christ," *Christian Century*, 75 (Jan. 8, 1958), 41-44.

[13] W. B. Blakemore, "Councils Challenge Denominations," *Christian Century*, 74 (Dec. 4, 1957), 1442-43. (See Chapter 19.)

it involves dividing time, interests, and energy among constituents and services of more than one church, the division of the clergy. In many cases the only direct connection between the cooperating churches is the minister. In others modern transportation has made joint services and activities possible, often as missionary work of a sponsoring group which hopes that the outpost will grow into a self-sustaining church.

2. The multiple-church parish. Closely related are situations in which two or more churches secure and support on a continuous basis a professional religious educator, youth director, or other staff members to carry out programs that they separately would be unable to promote effectively. Often called *the larger parish plan,* it has been very effective in many communities, especially those with relatively low population density.[14] Various degrees of integration and denominational ties are found. The larger parish is above all a philosophy of service to the area surrounding the church and only secondarily an organization.[15] Sometimes, however, it becomes a masquerade for a denominationally-centered program that is blind to community needs.[16]

3. The federated church. Congregations of two or more denominations sometimes merge into a single functional organization for worship and other activities, each part continuing affiliation with its own denomination and thus formally restricting the nature of the cooperation. Improved relationships with other community institutions often result from the united front presented by formerly independent groups. Compromise of differences on mode of baptism, division of benevolences, church literature, and so on, must be made, but most participants believe they gain more than they lose by federation.[17]

4. The denominational community church. This type often results from comity arrangements when churching new or expanding communities. One denomination is given an exclusive privilege to establish a community church affiliated with that denomination. Concessions are made in membership qualifications to facilitate admission of members from other denominations. The church is protected from much denominational competition, has no question of the denomination from which to draw pastors, and may fall back upon the denomination for financial help.[18]

---

[14] Edmund deS. Brunner, *The Larger Parish* (New York: Institute of Social and Religious Research, 1934); and Mark Rich, *The Larger Parish and Effective Organization for Rural Churches* (Ithaca, N.Y.: Agricultural College Extension Bulletin 408, 1939).

[15] Marvin T. Judy, *The Larger Parish and Group Ministry* (New York: Abingdon Press, 1959).

[16] Mark Rich, "Is Denominationalism Resurgent?" *Town and Country Church,* 103 (Jan. 1955), 9.

[17] Ralph A. Felton, *Cooperative Churches* (Madison, N.J.: Drew Theological Seminary, 1947), pp. 28-35.

[18] H. Paul Douglass and Edmund deS. Brunner, *The Protestant Church as a Social Institution* (New York: Institute of Social and Religious Research, 1935), pp. 280-83.

5. The undenominational community church. United churches of this type sever all direct denominational connections. Anti-denominationalists regard this as the ideal; denominationalists condemn it. At least 2,000 such churches have been established. As of 1982 many of them were loosely related through the 15 state and 219 local groups of the National Council of Community Churches.

Sources of Local Church Unions

A major source of church unions is change in society and its values. The desire for a broader and more specialized church program brings pressures to unite. The dispersion of population from the typical rural community decreases the number of actual and potential church members. Increased mobility and the ease of modern transportation make it possible for fewer churches to provide a more excellent religious program than the many did in horse and buggy days. Certain types of situations are especially likely to result in united church programs. Nine are listed here.[19]

1. Rural communities with low population density. These often have local parishes organized denominationally on the circuit plan. Population decline has led also to unions of other types.

2. Fluctuating communities. The meager permanent population of a resort area, for instance, may find it impossible to maintain more than one church, and its vacationers are of many denominations. A community church often results.

3. Communities controlled by exceptional unifying forces. A mining or mill town dominated by a single industry may have a single church subsidized by the industry. Similarly prisons, the armed forces, hospitals, and welfare institutions typically provide chaplains representing only the major faiths. Denominational walls are ignored in such intramural programs.

4. Planned communities. Real estate promoters, public housing authorities, or others who plan "ideal communities" may insist upon church union under joint denominational auspices. New communities built around atomic energy plants, major dams, and housing corporations often have united churches.

5. Minority status in foreign communities. Where a few Americans are in foreign capitals or commercial centers, they sometimes organize union churches or conduct united religious services which become oases of Americanism in the foreign culture. Similar situations of small numbers

---

19 These are based chiefly upon Douglass and Brunner, *The Protestant Church,* pp. 276-80. Cf. Elizabeth Hooker, *United Churches* (New York: George H. Dora? Co., 1926).

and minority status may draw the Protestants or the Jews in an American community together into a united church.

6. Temporary pre-denominationalism. A "time-honored" pattern of building denominational churches has been to start as a "non-sectarian" Sunday school or "community" project. The leaders hope that during the non-denominational period "everybody" will become so involved that, when it is converted into a denominational church, they will become members of this church which they might otherwise never have considered joining.[20]

7. Stranded non-denominationalism. In the process of developing a new church, anticipated growth may fail to come. Real estate ventures that were too highly speculative, lack of anticipated change in the distribution of industry, or conflicts in the church fellowship about denominationalism or which denomination to join may cause a union church that was intended to be only temporarily pre-denominational to become a permanent community church.

8. Denominational mergers. Some local churches merge in anticipation of or following denominational mergers.

9. Denominational policies. Denominational leaders sometimes help produce union churches. Withholding home missions funds, when there is pronounced overlapping of parishes or weakness in many or all churches in a community, may stimulate the merger of several weak bodies. Two denominations sometimes exchange churches by merging the weaker congregation of one into the stronger of the other, and reversing the trade in another community.[21]

The Success of Union Churches

Many problems are found among union churches. With a great variety of denominational backgrounds, their membership may be divided on matters of doctrine, church finances, and polity. Major denominations may cooperate through comity arrangements to limit the number of churches in a community, but sects may begin competitive programs. Unless a church constitution or other agreed-upon guide to action is clear, serious questions arise whenever it is time to find a new pastor. The missionary program and other non-local activities may be hampered by internal dissension.

---

[20] Ethical implications of this technique are seldom considered. A sufficient justification for any program often is merely that "it works." The social scientist who evaluates it by the group's own norms can readily point out inconsistencies between ideals and action patterns when it operates on the utilitarian principle that the end justifies the means.

[21] W. F. Kumlien, *The Social Problem of the Church in South Dakota* (Brookings, S.D.: A.E.S. Bulletin 294, May 1935), pp. 38-39.

There were in Pennsylvania in 1954 over 200 "union churches" in which a Lutheran and an Evangelical and Reformed Church congregation shared the same church building. Some of the unions were over 200 years old. Only 24 of 190 studied had separate denominational Sunday schools. Fewer than half had church school boards or religious education committees. Union women's organizations were found in 43 per cent, one-fourth of which also had a denominational women's group. Union men's organizations were found in 14 churches and separate denominational ones in 36 more. Two-thirds of the churches had some youth work, one-third meeting weekly and over one-half monthly.[22]

An intensive study of about one-sixth of 603 known federated churches found they had a type of "hybrid vigor." Prolonged population decline usually preceded federation; subsequent population growth was correlated with success and decline with failure. Many were handicapped initially by an excess of property, most of which was in poor repair. Success followed a gradual development of Christian fellowship that was achieved through democratic processes aided by sympathetic guidance from outside officials. A major reason for success was the ability to secure adequately paid, well-trained, mature pastors. As a result, pastors had longer tenures than those either in denominational churches or in the weaker federations.[23] The 128 out of 4,529 churches inventoried in Indiana which were classified as non-denominational, community, union, or federated were generally smaller than denominational congregations. The 5 that were federated, however, were all formally recognized by the cooperating denominations and exceeded all except the Catholic Churches in average membership.[24]

Six of 47 West Virginia churches classified themselves as non-denominational community churches. One originated in a split in a denominational church, and five in active sponsorship by coal mining corporations which sought to make their communities more attractive, stable, and hence profitable. Two of the six were above and four below the average of the 47 in membership and financial strength. The success of the two was attributed to the personal influence of mining company officials who conferred special advantages of material support and prestige. Community churches in general neither realized their ideals nor achieved institutional superiority over denominational churches.[25]

Although the community church is in theory an inclusive body which is *the* religious organ of the entire community cutting across denominational

---

[22] "Union Churches," *Town and Country Church*, 98 (May 1954), 11.

[23] Ralph L. Williamson, *Federated Churches: A Study of Success and Failure* (Ithaca, N.Y.: Rural Church Institute, 1953).

[24] J. E. Losey, *The Rural Church Situation in Indiana* (Lafayette: Purdue University A.E.S. EC-153, Sept. 1957), p. 5.

[25] Mark Rich, *Some Churches in Coal Mining Communities of West Virginia* (Charleston: West Virginia Council of Churches, n. d.). The survey was made in 1949.

lines to include all Protestants, it seldom is truly such. Its membership is as selective as that of most other churches. Prejudices and traditions of the people prevent inclusiveness and shape each into a body with its own peculiar characteristics in terms of theological values accentuated, social classes represented, or beliefs pertinent to denominationalism.[26] Many community churches have succeeded, however, in drawing together people of many different denominational backgrounds and welding them into a unit that has a strong impact upon the community. In theory they have the opportunity to reunite Christians on the highest common denominator, but they are more likely than other churches to become theologically weak.[27]

Sources of Denominational Cooperation

Most American churches are members of one or another of the hundreds of bodies commonly called denominations.[28] Even "independent" churches are seldom completely independent; they usually are in organizations like the Independent Fundamental Churches of America, and some are integrally related to associational groups which for social or theological reasons avoid the label "denomination." Denominations provide for sharing of fellowship and of problems, education and exchange of pastors, publishing of educational materials, training lay leaders, promoting welfare activities, and supporting missionary enterprises. To discuss in detail the cooperation involved in the work of denominational administrators, boards, and committees is beyond our scope here. We shall examine, rather, some important sources of cooperation within and between denominations.

Conflict as a Source of Denominational Cooperation

Opposition to common "enemies" sometimes draws religious bodies together for specific purposes when they otherwise would not think of united endeavor. Thus in Oswego, New York, the strength of Catholicism has forced the individualistic non-Catholic churches to work together in a council that recognizes even the Jewish Synagogue as an informal member.[29]

---

[26] Douglass and Brunner, *The Protestant Church,* p. 283.

[27] Martin E. Marty, "The Remnant: Retreat and Renewal," *Christian Century,* 75 (Nov. 26, 1958), 1361-65.

[28] In Kaufman's study (*Rural Churches in Kentucky,* p. 38) fewer than three per cent of the churches were not affiliated with some established religious body, and only 10 of 505 churches in Missouri were non-denominational or federated (Coughenour and Hepple, *The Church in Rural Missouri,* pp. 55-57).

[29] W. Seward Salisbury, "The Structure of Religious Action in a Small City," paper read to the American Sociological Society, Atlantic City (Sept. 4, 1952), pp. 3-4 (mimeographed).

Controversy between religious bodies, as each tended to assert itself as the only true agent of God, grew out of religious liberty. Doctrinal storms and struggles continued into the twentieth century, but denominational contacts fostered by competition gradually produced a degree of understanding between rival groups. Sectional and racial provincialisms that contributed to divisions are gradually being overcome by political and social developments. Increasing secularism and growing power of Roman Catholicism drew the attention of many competitive Protestants to common enemies and challenging competitors. Gradually they became more willing to work together for self-defense as well as to present a stronger front against common foes. Competition and differentiation between denominations is thus being replaced by accommodating and synthesizing trends.[30]

Competition between denominations constitutes the historical background of comity arrangements. Overchurching and overlapping efforts of denominations in many communities led to situations detrimental to all churches involved. To prevent recurrence of such circumstances, many denominations work together in allocating fields of responsibility. In practice comity means that the denominations agree neither to duplicate one another's work nor to place a church in a mission field without regard for religious work already present there. Comity in foreign missions has resulted in several church unions, including the Church of Christ in Japan and the Church of South India, which united Congregational, Dutch Reformed, Presbyterian, Methodist, and Anglican Christians. Comity agreements imply the substantial equality of bodies which cooperate. Extremists and sect members who believe their group alone possesses the truth feel that any cooperation with such groups involves disloyalty to their faith. They therefore compete with the comity programs, showing no respect for their parceling of territory.

In the history of American comity, a standard of not more than one church for every 1,000 people "potentially homogeneous and reasonably accessible to the church building location" has evolved for the rural community. The earlier standard of 1,500 "available population" per urban or suburban church has been modified to "2,000 to 4,000 available population of Protestant preference." The latter has been challenged for its lack of an objective basis, vague definitions, and failure to recognize variations between communities. The urban comity standard was tested in 66 cities and towns in which population growth had exceeded 1,000 during the preceding decade. The average church membership in selected communities with populations of 10,000 or more was 482, and that for smaller communities was 270. The 429 Protestant churches had an average available population of 1,549, compared to an estimated state total of 1,191.

---

[30] H. Richard Niebuhr, *The Social Sources of Denominationalism* (Hamden Conn.: The Shoe String Press, 1954; c. 1929 by Henry Holt and Co.), pp. 234-35.

(The figure was obtained by subtracting official Jewish and Roman Catholic membership claims from a projection of the 1950 population.) The average ratio of membership to available population was thus one to four (24.4 per cent were members), a statistic based on membership only, without regard for additional Sunday school pupils and other constituents. It was suggested on the basis of these findings that (1) 10,000 population in a community should be the dividing line between rural and urban comity standards, (2) comity applications should be based upon the average active achievement of established churches in comparable communities rather than upon an excessive idealistic standard, (3) the average church can expect to realize as members one-fourth of its available population, and (4) variations within and among denominations by region should be carefully considered in attempts to apply comity standards. "A national numerical comity standard applying to all categories of urban and suburban population and to all the diverse regions of America and to the varieties of denominational patterns in each is not merely unscientific. It is a manifest absurdity." [31]

Mobility Between Churches

The movement of church members and clergymen between denominations has stimulated interdenominational cooperation by diminishing feelings of antipathy and intensifying the viewpoint that differences between Protestant denominations are trivial. The typical Protestant church grows much more by transfer of members than by evangelism (transforming people into church members for the first time). A large proportion of the transfer members come from other denominations. In eight large downtown churches studied a generation ago, from one-fourth to three-fourths of all members received transferred from other denominations. The pastors of 584 city churches of many denominations reported that 25 per cent of their transfers came from other denominations. Eight per cent of the pastors said more than three-fourths of their transferring new members came from other denominations, and 28 per cent said more than half.[32]

Denominational barriers are especially weak among suburban people. Mobility weakens denominational loyalties; even denominational churches have the atmosphere of united community congregations because of the wide range of religious backgrounds among members. The minister, Sunday school, and location are more important factors in choosing a suburban church than the denomination.[33] As Protestants move to suburban areas,

[31] Glen W. Trimble, "Population Requirements for Protestant Churching," paper presented to the Religious Research Fellowship, April 9, 1954 (mimeographed).

[32] Douglass and Brunner, *The Protestant Church*, pp. 54, 257. For more recent data see Christopher Kirk Hadaway, "Denominational Switching and Membership Growth: In Search of a Relationship," *Sociological Analysis*, 39, no. 4 (Winter 1978), 321–37.

[33] William H. Whyte, Jr., *The Organization Man* (Garden City, N.Y.: Doubleday and Co., n. d.; c. Simon and Schuster, 1956), pp. 407-11, 419.

they must adapt to numerous cross-pressures. Mixed marriages within Protestantism reflect the weakness of denominational distinctions and contribute to further weakening of them. The successful church adapts to this situation and attracts a constituency from heterogeneous backgrounds. By including diverse elements and appeals in its program, it becomes in essence a church of "mixed denominations," even while continuing a denominational program. [34] One suburban Baptist church with strict denominational membership qualifications and fewer than 300 members had members with backgrounds in at least eleven Protestant denominational families and about twice that many specific denominations.

Denominational lines are also weakening in urban churches, especially in the inner city and downtown areas. In Omaha and Council Bluffs, other denominations accounted for 45 per cent of the transfers into Episcopal churches, compared to 27 per cent into Congregational, 23 per cent into Presbyterian, 15 per cent into Christian, 14 per cent into Baptist, and 12 per cent into Methodist churches.[35] In 1953 the Virginia Methodist Conference reported that 33 per cent of its new members, exclusive of infant baptisms, came from other denominations, and 23 per cent of its transferring members changed to other denominations.[36] In addition, some persons actively participate in more than one church, satisfying some needs in each, and a similarly indeterminate number are carried as members on the rolls of more than one denomination.

Many clergy also cross denominational lines. In 1929 the Congregational Church ordained 96 men to the ministry but received 92 more from other denominations. In 1926 the General Council of the Presbyterian Church in the U.S.A. reported that 38.5 per cent of all accessions to its ministry during the preceding five years had been imported from other denominations. A large proportion came from denominations outside the Reformed family of churches to which Presbyterians belong. In a smaller, strongly urban denomination, considerably less than half had been trained under the church's own auspices.[37] Ministers withdrawing from the United Lutheran Church before World War II moved mainly toward Congregational churches, perhaps in a desire for more creedal and doctrinal freedom. Since the war they have moved chiefly toward episcopal and presbyterian types, apparently desiring the support of episcopal authority and a liturgical emphasis. Laymen moved in a diametrically opposite direction.[38]

---

[34] David Riesman, "Some Informal Notes on American Churches and Sects," *Confluence,* 4 (July 1955), 127-59.

[35] T. Earl Sullenger, "The Church in an Urban Society," *Sociology and Social Research,* 41 (May-June 1959), 361-66.

[36] W. E. Garnett, *The Virginia Rural Church and Related Influences, 1900-1950* (Blacksburg, Va.: A.E.S. Bulletin 479, May 1957), p. 54.

[37] Douglass and Brunner, *The Protestant Church,* p. 258.

[38] Theodore G. Tappert, "Directions in Lutheran Losses to Other Communions,' *Lutheran Quarterly,* 8 (Nov. 1956), 362-64.

Even in the small, relatively homogeneous Baptist General Conference, as of about 1950 one-third to two-fifths of the pastors had received no training in its school; by 1958 rapid denominational growth had raised this proportion to one-half. Of those who had some training in it, many had attended only the college, and many had not graduated. In a suburban eastern town with eight Protestant churches of various denominations, seven of the ministers had received some or all of their professional training in Baptist schools. The pastors of the Evangelical and Reformed, Episcopal, and Methodist churches were graduates of Baptist seminaries.[39]

Much movement between denominations reflects social aspirations and achievements. As a person climbs the ladder of socioeconomic success, he is likely to revise his activities within the church or even change his church membership. High prestige congregations are especially likely to receive social climbers of different denominational backgrounds.[40]

Common Beliefs, Traditions, and Goals

Cooperation also results from recognition of common beliefs, traditions, and objectives. Most Protestants are in the largest bodies, bodies that have been growing closer to one another in many ways. Their underlying unity of purpose was evident in frontier camp meetings, the prohibition movement, and interdenominational organizations like the American Bible Society and American Sunday School Union. Theological education is strongly interdenominational from the perspective of textbooks, course content, and student bodies. Interdenominational religious literature is widely distributed through books and such periodicals as the *Christian Century, Christian Herald, Christian Life,* and *Christianity Today.* Conflicts and tensions between denominations and their common heritage are increasingly understood. In 11 official hymnals used by 12 denominations of over 1,000,000 members, 23 selections appeared in all, and 241 were in a majority. Common elements far outnumbered diversities. Modern hymns reflect a more practical, ethical, and social viewpoint; earlier ones were more likely to be doctrinal or controversial.[41] Often one cannot determine a church's denomination from its ritual and ceremonies. Similarities between churches help increase cooperation.

Many denominations cooperate through such international organizations as the Lutheran World Federation, Mennonite World Conference, World Methodist Council, Baptist World Alliance, World Presbyterian

[39] Charles W. Griffin, "Are Baptists Awake to the Big Give Away?" *Baptist Leader,* 18, no. 4 (July 1956), 21.

[40] Leila Calhoun Deasy, "An Index of Social Mobility," *Rural Sociology,* 20 (June 1955), 149-51.

[41] John Wesley Buono, *Common Elements in the Hymnals of the Major Protestant Denominations in America,* Ph.D. thesis, University of Pittsburgh, 1952. But 62 per cent of the 3,008 selections appeared in only one hymnal.

Alliance, and Eastern Orthodox Episcopate. Ecumenical in the sense of having members in all parts of the world, they typically engage in relief operations, assist theological education, combat religious persecution, and cooperate in missionary programs.

Merger of Denominations

Cooperation can occur in spite of different ideologies. Theologically liberal and conservative groups sometimes work together on practical tasks related to social needs. The same activity may give them different satisfactions or grow out of different subjective intentions, but working together may develop group solidarity in spite of theological differences. Cooperation on specific issues may increase the recognition of similar interests and objectives which provide a basis for further cooperation and perhaps ultimate union. Groups of widely divergent doctrinal orientation hence are included in ecumenical bodies.

Cooperation of denominations reaches its highest level when two or more merge into a single body. American groups resulting from the merger of two or more denominations include the Evangelical Free Church of America (1950), United Church of Christ (1957), American Lutheran Church (1960), Evangelical Methodist Church (1960), Unitarian Universalist Association (1961), Lutheran Church in America (1962), Friends United Meeting (1965), Reformed Presbyterian Church, Evangelical Synod (1965), United Methodist Church (1968), The Missionary Church (1969), Primitive Methodist Church, U.S.A. (1975), International Pentecostal Church of Christ (1976), Presbyterian Church in America (1982), and Presbyterian Church USA (1983). Most of them united bodies that were closely related doctrinally and organizationally, but those in the United Church of Christ were widely divergent in both respects.

Merger does not always reduce the number of denominations; dissenters in each merging group, interpreting the compromises necessary for merger as deviation from "true" faith or polity, may withdraw to form new splinter groups. The Southern Methodist Church was thus organized in 1945 by congregations refusing to participate in the merger that created the Methodist Church, and organization of the United Church of Christ in 1957 led to creation of the National Association of Congregational-Christian Churches. Mergers have occurred largely under middle and upper-middle class influences. As sects that originate among the lower classes develop into middle class denominations, they grow more alike and find increasing opportunities to cooperate. New lower class sects originate among the underprivileged and are denounced by "respectable denominations," although many consider them wholesome in the sense that "trouble makers" are drained off from their own churches. In the history of modern religion the "trouble makers" for the respectable churches have included, simultaneously or consecutively, the Episcopalians, Congregationalists, Presbyterians, Quakers, Methodists, Baptists, and Disciples of Christ. "Trouble makers" are in some respects "the cranks" which turn the world! [42] Mobility on the church-sect continuum is an important source of mergers.

At least three types of norms sanction or call for church unity. One is the *dogmatic* argument that divine authority has revealed an unchanging pattern; all churches ought to accept and enter this sole authentic version of unity. Roman Catholics, many Anglo-Catholics, and the Eastern Orthodox hold this view, each claiming to be the only valid center for reunion of Christendom. The second is *pragmatic,* emphasizing the practical need for churches to unite and exert stronger influence. The rank-and-file of Protestantism tends toward this view. There are many *idealistic* interpretations. Some, like the Protestant Episcopal Church, find a strong sanction for union in the ideal of continuity. Others are convinced that division, which is the alternative to union, involves weakness, waste, and more seriously, an inherently divisive spirit and unkind deeds. The greatest opposition to unity comes from the groups that represent extreme variation theologically (such as fundamentalists), ecclesiastically (High-Church Episcopalians), or practically (many federated church groups). [43]

Opposition to Denominational Cooperation

Leaders recognizing the advantages of uniting two or more church groups are often frustrated in their efforts. A study of reactions to a proposed Presbyterian union concluded that religious convictions are far less significant hindrances to union than selfishness, pride, inertia, and fear. Vested interests of some Gospel Presbyterian clergymen, church officers, and professors were apparent in their opposition. Sources of the desire to continue as a separate body also included opposition to the National Council of Churches, love of the King James Version of the Bible, liking for the family-like features of a small denomination, pride in Scotch antecedents ("No one is good enough for us to join"), attachment to separate missionary ventures, and the desire to maintain racial segregation. Village and country churches generally opposed union, while city churches

---

[42] William Warren Sweet, *Revivalism in America* (New York: Charles Scribner's Sons, 1944), pp. 176-77.

[43] Douglass and Brunner, *The Protestant Church,* pp. 331-32. On relevant Roman Catholic dogmatism, see Jerome Hamer, "The Mission of Catholic Ecumenicism," *Cross Currents,* 6 (Spring 1956), 131-40.

favored it. Growing churches and presbyteries voted in its favor, but dying or inert ones were strong enough to prevent it. No denominational problems were solved by their victory.[44]

Three major Presbyterian denominations with common historical, ecclesiastical, and theological backgrounds have discussed the possibility of merger on various occasions since 1937. Content analysis of 40 documents on the subject revealed 66 themes used by Southern Presbyterians to oppose merger. Most frequently mentioned were those related to beliefs or doctrine. Church polity and practices were the other two major categories. Seven themes pertinent to racial inequality were mentioned in only 5 per cent of the paragraphs, and only 4 per cent referred to the conservative political and economic ideology of antiunion forces. Yet interview data and ecological analysis of the presbyteries' votes showed that the segregation issue was the major source of failure to merge. Ideological opposition apparently was a rationalization. The cultural and social basis for opposition distorted the perceptual world of antiunion members.[45]

Denominational periodicals are major factors in hardening denominational lines and resisting ecumenism. Editors and other leaders believe cooperation will lead to compromise of principles. Denominational departments which advertise in space rented for "news," the lack of funds to finance religious news agency services, the time element necessitating preparation weeks or even months in advance of publication, meager journalistic experience on the part of editors, poor planning, and lack of knowledge of how to gauge reader opinion and interest are also responsible.[46]

The obstacles to denominational mergers are of three main types. *Convictional* differences involve theological questions about God, the world, man, Christ, and the future. *Cultural* differences spring from divergent historical traditions, as among the various Lutheran synods, or contrasting social outlooks and loyalties, as in the case of Episcopalians and Methodists. *Temperamental* differences fall between and cut across the other two, and are evident especially in contrasts between traditionalists and modernists. Convictional distinctions are less divisive than the others, which are found in almost every convictional grouping. Protestants find it easier to cross convictional lines, in order to be with others of their own nationality and social class, than to remain within their theological communion if its worship involves unfamiliar speech and cultural orientation. Theological beliefs are less serious obstacles to unity than such questions of church order as the church's authority and polity, the nature of the ministry, and

[44] Renwick C. Kennedy, "Why Churches Do Not Unite," *Christian Century,* 69 (July 16, 1952), 825-27.
[45] Sanford M. Dornbusch and Roger D. Irle, "The Failure of Presbyterian Union," *American Journal of Sociology,* 64 (Jan. 1959), 352-55.
[46] R. E. Wolseley, "The Church Press: Bulwark of Denominational Sovereignty," *Christendom,* 11 (Autumn 1946), 490-500.

the nature and forms of worship.[47] It is likely that opposition to the ecumenical movement itself is based to a much greater extent upon cultural and temperamental differences than upon diverse theological convictions.

The Ecumenical Movement

Most definitions of ecumenicalism can be reduced to the idea of cooperation by churches on a universal or world-wide level. Organic merger of denominations, interdenominational cooperation of less than world-wide scope, and broad interfaith activities may also be considered aspects of the movement. The highest conceivable degree of universal cooperation is complete merger of all churches into one body. Degrees of ecumenism theoretically can be arranged upon a continuum from anarchical individualism, to noncooperating local churches, cooperation within denominations, loosely organized interdenominational cooperation, denominational mergers, interdenominational councils, international ecumenical organizations, and finally the universal "super-church."

Many recent conditions have stimulated the ecumenical movement. These include student Christian movements, attempts to relate religion to ethical and social problems, experiences in modern missionary enterprises, growing recognition of the social nature of divisions of Protestantism, the spread of theologies which do not follow denominational lines, the growth among Christians of a sense of world-wide community, and, above all, the Scriptural emphasis upon the church as the "body of Christ" transcending the ethnic, national, class, and racial barriers that divide men.[48] World War I gave the American churches an unprecedented stimulus to cooperate; spiritual efforts related to the armed forces and emergency services during and after the war reinforced, created, and sustained sentiments favoring church unity. A United Churches of Christ in America was proposed but not consummated; it reflected growing sentiment in favor of church union.[49] Current efforts by the Consultation on Church Union (COCU) eventually may be successful.

Considerations of sheer economy contributed to cooperative action. Many religious periodicals have merged as a result of decreasing circulation. Some ecumenical tendencies may hence be designated "ecumenicalism by default." [50] Cooperation for self-preservation occurred during the 1930's when churches appeared to be losing members and influence,

---

[47] Henry P. van Dusen, "Church Union: Recent Progress and Present Obstacles," *Christendom*, 8 (Winter 1943), 87-96.

[48] John Dillenberger and Claude Welch, *Protestant Christianity* (New York: Charles Scribner's Sons, 1954), pp. 290-95.

[49] Lefferts A. Loetscher, *The Broadening Church* (Philadelphia: University of Pennsylvania Press, 1954), pp. 100-1.

[50] Paul A. Carter, *The Decline and Revival of the Social Gospel* (Ithaca, N.Y.: Cornell University Press, 1954), pp. 184-85.

Communistic and Nazi ideologies threatened Christianity abroad, and liberal secularism, scientific rationalism, and logical positivism were attacking the very foundations of Christendom. A common front was presented against institutionalized evils as churches struggled for power in society through "social gospel" and "life and work" efforts. The "faith and order" belief that the church is the body of Christ and therefore tearing it asunder by denominational divisions is sinful, also contributed to increased cooperation. Theological endeavors and application of Christian principles to critical issues of modern society brought denominations ideologically closer. A return from divisive theologies to "pure religion," the desire to combine the peculiar insights of each group so that all might share them, and Biblical exhortations to unity in the faith were among the motives for church union.[51]

Meanwhile basic social conditions favored increased cooperation. Religious radio broadcasts were prohibited from slandering other groups, and those with nationwide audiences were almost of necessity ecumenically sponsored. As people had convenient access to preaching in denominations other than their own, they learned that the churches held much in common and that most differences were relatively insignificant. The advent of the automobile threatened rural churches and led many to consolidate. Movements of church members across denominational lines encouraged unity. Above all, mergers and unions of other organizations stimulated similar mergers for the sake of increased efficiency and effectiveness by churches. As the world "shrinks" through improved transportation and communication, religious organizations are brought closer to one another and cooperation is thrust upon them. The ecumenical movement can be explained partly as an outgrowth of the same forces that brought the United Nations into being. Similarly, the American melting pot encouraged unity in diversity. Much resistance to supra-denominational cooperation is removed when churches are assured that they will not lose their separate identities through federation. Neither complete creedal agreement nor a fixed form of local church polity is necessary to bring about functional unity. An ecumenical spirit may hence coexist with recognition and appreciation of the differences between denominational bodies. A commonly used slogan for contemporary ecumenism, organized around the principle of cultural pluralism,[52] is "In all things necessary unity, in all things doubtful liberty, in all things charity."

[51] *Ibid.*, pp. 185-87; J. L. Neve, *Churches and Sects of Christendom*, rev. ed. (Blair, Neb.: Lutheran Publishing House, 1952), pp. 479-82; and J. Milton Yinger, *Religion, Society and the Individual* (New York: The Macmillan Co., 1957), p. 293.
[52] Not all ecumenists work for confederation and cultural pluralism. Dr. E. Stanley Jones has been leading the Association for a United Church in a drive for a federal union of all Christian churches in which denominations would lose their identity and become one organic body, the Church of Jesus Christ in America.

Interdenominational cooperation faces much opposition. Theological differences are stressed by non-cooperators who promote denominational particularisms, regard religion as purely individualistic, or fear centralized control. But various sociological factors appear to be more significant hindrances to ecumenism. These include institutionalism and resistance to change because of loyalties to outmoded traditions; real or imagined threats to institutional independence; ethnocentric belief that one's own church alone has truly Christian doctrine or polity, hence cooperation compromises the truth; denominational bureaucracies which are blind to the need for cooperation, are committed psychologically to old traditions, or have a vested interest in maintaining the status quo; and the desires of churches on missionary fields to assert complete independence.[53]

Both sects and churches oppose ecumenism. Sects oppose it because of opposition to hierarchical authority and fear of losing the "true spirit of Christianity." Fearing compromise of its "faith and order," the sect can cooperate with other groups only on the level of "life and work." The church, at the other end of the continuum, may oppose ecumenism because it believes that it alone is the bearer of God's revelation. Denominational bodies, which fall between sect and church, are more likely to engage in cooperative enterprises and join ecumenical organizations.[54]

Ecumenical Organizations

Contemporary ecumenism emerged from several relatively independent movements including the World Student Christian Federation (1895), International Missionary Council (1921), and World Conferences on Life and Work (since 1925) and on Faith and Order (since 1910). The Life and Work and Faith and Order movements were the most significant influences producing the World Council of Churches (WCC), and the former was primarily responsible for the rise of the Federal Council of the Churches of Christ in America (FCC) founded in 1908 "to manifest the essential oneness of the Christian Churches of America in Jesus Christ as their divine Lord and Savior" and to carry out many practical activities.[55]

Cf. E. Stanley Jones, "Federal Union of Churches," *Christian Century*, 76 (Aug. 12, 1959), 925-26.

[53] Walter G. Muelder, "Institutional Factors Affecting Unity and Disunity," *The Ecumenical Review*, 8 (Jan. 1956), 113-26; and Roswell P. Barnes, "The Ecumenical Movement," *Annals of the American Academy of Political and Social Science*, 332 (Nov. 1960), 135-45.

[54] See Reinhold Niebuhr, "The Ecumenical Issue in the United States," *Theology Today*, 2 (Jan. 1946), 525-36.

[55] Leonard Hodgson, *The Ecumenical Movement* (Sewanee, Tenn.: The University of the South Press, 1951), and John A. Hutchison, *We Are Not Divided: A Critical and Historical Study of the F.C.C.C.A.* (New York: Round Table Press, 1941).

The FCC merged with 15 other national agencies in 1950 to form the National Council of the Churches of Christ in the U.S.A. (NCC). Agencies entering the NCC submerged their identity, but the 25 Protestant and 4 Orthodox denominations did not. The NCC is not a merger; it has no authority or control over member churches; neither can it prescribe a common creed, form of church government, or form of worship. In 1982 it consisted of 22 Protestant and 10 Eastern denominations which had 40,689,299 inclusive members, 138,495 churches, and 109,733 pastors serving parishes. Other communions participate in its many program units. It is unquestionably the largest ecumenical body in the U.S.

The National Association of Evangelicals (NAE) was established in 1942 "to provide a vehicle through which all believers in the Lord Jesus Christ may become united and articulate in relation to matters of common interest and concern." Although it includes 40 denominations and hundreds of congregations from 34 other groups, most are so small that their combined membership is not much over 3,500,000. Its role as a competitor of the NCC is apparent from the manner in which it establishes subsidiary organizations parallel to many in the NCC and at times openly opposes its action, though usually on a moderate and ethical level. Indirectly under its aegis, the National Sunday School Association (NSSA) was organized in 1946 to restore an evangelistic emphasis, make the Bible central in the curriculum, and emphasize spiritual power as an essential dynamic in Christian growth. By 1959 the NSSA was serving 28,000 churches representing 100 denominations with a constituency of about 10,000,000.[56] It merged into NAE's Commission on Education in 1979.

The chief interdenominational organization in militant fundamentalism is the American Council of Christian Churches (ACC) founded in 1941. Organized by Dr. Carl McIntire, a fundamentalist Presbyterian minister, it claimed 49 state groups with 1,508,771 members in 1982. Its purpose is "to expose and oppose liberalism, socialism, and near-communism threatening the very life of our nation; to unify those Protestants who believe in an inerrant Bible;...to obtain advantages for the propagation of the historic Christian faith in America and all lands." In its opposition to the NCC, WCC, and other groups, it has been accused of engaging in a "ministry of schism" in the U.S. and abroad, the latter initially through the International Council of Christian Churches (ICC) founded in 1948 which in 1982 claimed 334 denominations and associations of "Bible-believing churches" throughout the world. The ICC is closed to groups in or represented by the WCC or standing outside the stream of historic Christianity.[57]

---

56 Editorial, "Why Should Ecumenists Disown a Sunday School Convention?" *Christianity Today,* 4 (Dec. 7, 1959), 190-91.

57 Ralph Lord Roy, *Apostles of Discord* (Boston: Beacon Press, 1953), pp. 185-

Many additional organizations bear at least the semblance of ecumen-
icity. They include the Independent Fundamental Churches of America,
which in effect now functions like another denomination. The International Missionary Council, which had national missionary organizations
and councils in 35 nations, helped bring the WCC into existence. It has
been succeeded by the WCC Commission on World Mission and Evangelism, which had 57 councils of churches as members in 1982.[58]

The WCC was organized in 1948 after a series of conferences that
began in 1910. Official representatives of 147 Christian bodies met in
Amsterdam and established an official free fellowship of churches from all
parts of the world which accepts Jesus Christ as God and Savior. Working
closely with the NCC it cuts across theological, liturgical, and organizational lines to include representative Christian denominations from all but
Roman Catholicism and the most humanistic and fundamentalistic extremes of Protestantism. The official message adopted at its Second Assembly affirms "faith in Jesus Christ as the hope of the world" and can be
interpreted literally to include the basic doctrinal tenets of fundamentalism at the same time as it can be interpreted symbolically by theological
liberals.[59] Incorporated into the WCC program is a "new social gospel"
which sees a direct challenge to the church in social-ethical issues. Instead
of trying to reform the world simply by telling secular reformers what to
do, churches are challenged to correct their own faults and to transcend
barriers of race, nationality, and social class differences within their fellowship. "Let the Church be the Church!" has become a motto for the
ecumenical movement in its attempt to transcend particular and relative
interests like those of nations and denominations which were attempting
to subordinate it to their own service. As it becomes stronger, the WCC
will no doubt have more influence in the world, but it will also be in
danger of identifying itself with the Kingdom of God and hence of failing
to recognize that—like all other social institutions—it is not absolute, but
is subject to the limitations of human finiteness and the possibility of be-

---

202. On the organization and purposes of the ICC see also W. R. McEwen, "International Council of Christian Churches," *World Dominion and the World To-day,*
27 (July-Aug. 1949), 231-33. The ICC has published *The Reformation Review* since
1952; nearly every article includes negativistic references to churches not in the
ICC. The 1982 data are from Denise S. Akey, ed., *1983 Encyclopedia of Associations,* 17th
ed. (Detroit: Gale Research Co., 1982), pp. 1202, 1214.

[58]Akey, *1983 Encyclopedia of Associations,* p. 1237.

[59]"The Message of the Second Assembly, World Council of Churches, Adopted
at Evanston, Illinois, August 31, 1954," *Christian Century,* 71 (Sept. 22, 1954),
1123-24. Examples of statements which could be interpreted as fundamentalistic
are "Christ died for us" (the vicarious atonement), "He will come again as Judge
and King" (the second coming), and "Jesus Christ . . . , true God and true Man"
(the deity of Christ). The revised doctrinal statement adopted at New Delhi, India,
in 1961 is even more conservative.

coming the victim of the prejudices and illusions of its age. Now that it is "an institutional reality and not a transcendent hope," the WCC has become a relative, human, social institution.[60] In 1982 the WCC had 301 member agencies (Protestant, Anglican, Old Catholic, and Orthodox) from 100 countries and territories; 28 members are in the U.S. Conference for the WCC.

Contrasting values are often a source of tension within ecumenical bodies. Two sides to a disagreement may use the same language and appeal to the same values to arrive at opposite conclusions. Belief in "the Lordship of the living Christ" and in "the Bible as the Word of God" is shared by Christians who are theologically as far apart as ultra-fundamentalists and neo-orthodox liberals; the subjectively-intended meanings underlying these and other concepts are vastly different from one group to another. The degree to which social, cultural, and temperamental differences are basic to theological and organizational distinctions is a topic in need of sympathetic research.

Ecumenism in Catholicism and Judaism

Roman Catholicism may be considered an ecumenical religion, for it is found throughout the earth, and it consists of a large number of special orders and organizations. It has, however, remained aloof from other Christian groups because recognition of them through cooperation would imply the equality or validity of non-Catholic bodies. Pope John XXIII's ecumenical council (Second Vatican Council) has led to modified views of other Christians. Catholics hope their display of unity and strength will encourage other Christians to return to the "true Church." The Monks of St. Benedict have been working since 1924 to reunite the Byzantine (Orthodox) and western (Roman) rites.[61]

Within Judaism there are tendencies toward ecumenism as the traditional walls between Orthodox, Conservative, and Reform Jews are weakened by the necessity of unitedly opposing anti-Semitism, preventing persecution of Jews, and assisting in the establishment of Israel. Efforts to unite all rabbis into the Synagogue Council of America have met with little success, but the rabbis have cooperated with Jewish laymen to meet common needs through such organizations as the American Jewish Congress, American Jewish Committee, and Anti-Defamation League.

Interfaith Cooperation

Catholics, Protestants, and Jews do not openly cooperate on very many occasions. Leaders of all three are represented on many committees and

---

[60] Carter, *The Decline and Revival of the Social Gospel*, pp. 107, 189-91, 194, 225.
[61] Donald Attwater, "Monks of Unity," *Commonweal*, 71 (Jan. 15, 1960), 441-42.

boards designed to shape religious policies in a community, in the armed forces, and elsewhere. They cooperated to formulate and promote the UN Declaration of the Rights of Man; some also participated in unfruitful efforts of liberals to create a theology common to all three religions.[62]

All three religions have worked to diminish interracial tensions. Confronted with persecution of the Jews, they have cooperated to help gentiles understand Jewish culture and religion and to diminish anti-Semitic attitudes (Chapter 17). The National Conference of Christians and Jews is a leading interfaith organization designed to promote good relationships between members of the divergent religious groups. It sponsors an annual Brotherhood Week and promotes a policy of toleration, urging each group to "live and let live." Increasing attention to public policy by many religious groups creates strange coalitions around contrasting positions on issues like national defense, nuclear weapons, abortion, and religion in education.

Perhaps partly as a result of such efforts, American religion has developed an essential unity considerably different from patterns of interfaith relations found elsewhere. All three major faiths are so "Americanized" that some consider them to be little more than minor variations of a general American religion (Chapter 3).

Cooperation with Other Institutions

The church cooperates with all other major social institutions. Indirectly it works with the school, the family, social welfare agencies, government, and the economic order. It also cooperates directly with them through lending or renting facilities to community organizations, sponsoring agencies like scout troops and recreational clubs, announcing or giving other special recognition to community projects, providing leadership for programs considered worthy of church aid, and cooperating directly with civic, health, welfare, agricultural extension, and related organizations.

The church's work is interwoven with that of every other institution of society through complex reciprocal ties of cooperation and opposition. The paradoxically intermingled cooperative and antagonistic relationships between them are dealt with primarily in Chapters 13-14 and secondarily in other passages in this book. Let us now examine some types of conflict which are relevant to our analysis of the church as a social institution.

Selected References

Douglass, H. Paul, *Church Comity*. Garden City, N.Y.: Doubleday, Doran and Co., 1929. An old but excellent study of cooperative church extension in American cities.

Felton, Ralph A., *Cooperative Churches*. Madison, N.J.: Drew Theological

---

[62] Herbert W. Schneider, *Religion in Twentieth Century America* (Cambridge: Harvard University Press, 1952), pp. 68, 136-37.

Seminary, 1947. A survey of numerous types of church cooperation with primary data from both town and country churches.

Lee, Robert, *The Social Sources of Church Unity*. New York: Abingdon, 1960. Socio-cultural factors in the rise of the church unity movement.

Muelder, Walter G., "Institutional Factors Affecting Unity and Disunity," *The Ecumenical Review*, 8 (Jan. 1956), 113–26. An excellent sociological analysis with numerous implications for further research.

Niebuhr, H. Richard, *The Social Sources of Denominationalism*. Magnolia, Mass.: Peter Smith, and other reprint editions (New York: Henry Holt, 1929). The classic interpretation of social factors which gave rise to the American system of denominationalism.

Rouse, Ruth, and Stephen Charles Neill, eds., *A History of the Ecumenical Movement, 1517–1948*. Philadelphia: Westminster, 1954. An excellent survey of the development of the ecumenical movement.

Shelley, Bruce, *Evangelicalism in America: Its Rise and Development*. Grand Rapids: Eerdmans, 1967. A description of American evangelicalism, including the history of the National Association of Evangelicals (published at its twenty-fifth anniversary).

Chapter 11

Internal Church Conflict

All social processes may be reduced to the two main types of opposition and cooperation, i.e., striving against and striving with other persons and groups. The term "conflict" as used here includes all forms of opposition, avoidance, and dissociation between rival and competing individuals and groups.

Society consists of a congeries of groups which are held together in a shifting, dynamic equilibrium of opposing interests and efforts. As long as each group is channeled into separate territories of endeavor which are clearly demarcated, there is no serious conflict between them; when their interests and purposes overlap, encroach on each other, and become competitive, struggle occurs. The end result sought by each group is to improve, maintain, or defend its social position and values. This necessitates cooperation among members, but it also makes conflict a principal social process which is not only inevitable but essential to the maintenance of society itself.

Like other groups, local churches and their subgroups are created when people have common interests and needs that can be furthered best through collective action. Conflict between groups intensifies loyalties of members to their respective groups. The more of his own efforts and means one has devoted to a group for its ends, the more loyal and group-minded he is apt to be. Seldom is a local church so homogeneous in membership that there are not at least a few opposing cliques within it. On denominational levels this becomes all the more obvious; each hierarchical rank, each increment of size, and each new element of heterogeneity increases the potentialities for internal strife. In-groups and out-groups develop. Persons and factions with authority or prestige struggle to maintain their influence and privileges, while out-groups which lack these but believe themselves powerful enough either to achieve them or to secure compromises favorable to their position, actively challenge the status quo.[1]

In a broad sense, then, all church activities involve or grow out of conflict. Opposition against sin, secularism, undesired social conditions, and other forces, situations, and tendencies considered to be evil, is usually seen as a major, if not the only, task of the church. Sometimes opposition takes the form of intense conflict, but more often it is less acute. These three chapters on conflict are confined to a brief survey of some major types of religious conflict involving American churches. These include internal strife, the fundamentalist-modernist controversies, Catholic-Protestant tensions, interfaith struggles, and competition with other institutions. In lumping together such diverse forms of opposition, it is assumed that the reader realizes that there are great variations in the degree or intensity of conflict. No comparison of specific instances of conflict would be complete without allowing for such variation.

Only brief, indirect reference will be made to the forms of accommodation which end or suspend hostilities between groups. One of the most common in religious conflict is toleration—a "live and let live" solution in which each group insists its position is correct, but, since complete victory cannot be won, nothing more can be done about the situation than to let the opponent go his way. Compromise, arbitration, mediation, conciliation, and victory also terminate conflicts. Occasionally accommodation leads to amalgamation of two groups or assimilation of one by the other. Little systematic research interpreting religious conflict from the viewpoint of a consistent theoretical framework has been done.

Conflict Within the Local Church

Within a religious community the efforts of all members may be directed toward the same goal. Yet when that goal is defined in spiritual terms, attainment by one does not exclude others from reaching the same goal, as in most other types of competition. This "passive competition" involving parallel efforts is close to a type of cooperation; the members give one another mutual aid in concomitant striving to meet the standards

---

[1] George Vold, *Theoretical Criminology* (New York: Oxford University Press, 1958), esp. pp. 203-19, is one of the clearest succinct presentations of the "conflict school" of sociology.

of religious faith. Each person is judged by transcendental norms, not by comparison of a competitor's works with his own.[2]

Groups with overlapping memberships compete with one another for the time, attendance, and monetary contributions of mutual members, for the services of leaders, and for program time and facilities. To the stranger considering church affiliation the competition between such groups is often bewildering. Sometimes it is on an unethical level contradictory to the church's ideals; as a result the church is given uncomplimentary labels by nonmembers. Conflict may be linked with endemic competition between groups struggling for power. Difficulties of scheduling church facilities may cause tensions. One group may so dominate policy-making that others feel discriminated against. For instance, a youth organization may believe it is mistreated by a men's club dominated by leaders of the church's administration who are the final authorities in assigning dates and uses of facilities. If tension is prolonged, it is likely to result in bickering, quarreling, loss of members, and even division by a church split.

At times "some clique in the church assumes to be the bearer of the particular revelation once delivered to the saints and proceeds to control its own plans and purse with small regard to the church's central interest or its administrative unity."[3] When a clique centers around a strong leader who wishes to go his own way, frustration of his desires may prove disastrous for the church. Such problems have led to church constitution provisions to limit the term of office and the number of times officers may be re-elected. Pastors face many difficulties in coordinating activities and maintaining unity. When they are not prepared for their administrative tasks, they may become the focus of church strife.

Organic divisions (church splits) sometimes result from long periods of friction. Conflicting loyalties and an accompanying lack of consensus within the church are frequent causes. Personality clashes of leaders are often a source of discord although participants are led to believe that vital issues of doctrine or polity are basic.[4] Conflict may center upon contrasting loyalties focused around a tradition, a church-related or opposed activity, denominational or interdenominational connections, a doctrine which some believe is minimized or violated by others in the church,

---

[2] Georg Simmel, *Conflict*, trans. by Kurt H. Wolff (Glencoe, Ill.: The Free Press, 1955), pp. 69-71.

[3] H. Paul Douglass and E. deS. Brunner, *The Protestant Church as a Social Institution* (New York: Institute of Social and Religious Research, 1935), p. 94.

[4] Congregational disputes, often arising out of personality clashes, were the cause of closing in 13 per cent of closed churches in one study. Disagreement often began in the choir or centered on places of honor attained by some persons and denied to others. Theodore C. Scheifele and William G. Mather, *Closed Rural Pennsylvania Churches* (State College, Pa.: A.E.S. Bulletin 512, May 1949), pp. 7-8.

church facilities which some believe outmoded and others think ideal, questions of church location, "feuding" families, or the pastor's personal habits, abilities, or activities. Ministers who are "spiritually adolescent leaders with a thirst for power" often are at the root of church splits; chronically maladjusted neurotic leaders also are frequent causes.[5] Publicized issues often are only the immediate causal circumstance ("the straw that broke the camel's back") providing a rationalization for organic separation. Fear of deviating from established practices is common where lurking antagonisms wait to find expression in church quarrels. "Divisions in the church then result, not from real issues of belief and practice but from unrecognized antagonistic social attitudes." [6]

American church history includes countless examples of church divisions. Democratic government, the freedom of religion, assembly, the press, and speech, congregational church polity, conditions associated with the frontier, and an expanding population have made America an especially fertile seed-bed for new splinter groups. Issues that have split churches range all the way from deep theological and metaphysical problems to trivial questions of conduct. For example, Baptists at Long Run, Kentucky split in 1804 on the basis of a hypothetical problem: If Indians have killed four of a man's five children and the fifth is hidden nearby, would he be justified in telling a lie if the Indians ask if he has another child? When "Lying Baptists" were outvoted in formal church action, they withdrew from the "Truthful Baptists" to form their own congregation. The majority had upheld a type of conduct that none would conceivably have followed.[7]

Urban churches have split about the course of action to pursue when the surrounding population changes to include nonwhites or lower class persons. Other issues that have led to division include questions of removing the picket fence Grandfather Jones built, young people's parties in church, musical instruments, a new ritual or order of worship, the pastor's salary, and countless other details. To the outsider they often appear trivial or ridiculous; to participants they are interpreted as matters of life or death. Usually many issues combine and intensify the conflict.

The social processes underlying conflict need much additional study. Some evidence indicates that petty jealousies, bickering, back-biting, spites, and personal or factional quarrels are the most prevalent in small congregations which stress intensely emotional types of religious experi-

---

[5] Wayne E. Oates, *The Christian Pastor* (Philadelphia: The Westminster Press, 1951), pp. 46, 114.

[6] Anton T. Boisen, "Divided Protestantism in a Midwest County: A Study in the Natural History of Organized Religion," *Journal of Religion,* 20 (Oct. 1940), 359-81 (quotation from p. 372).

[7] Ernest Sutherland Bates, *American Faith* (New York: W. W. Norton and Co., 1940), p. 331.

ence.[8] Variations in regional and community settings, church polity, forms of worship, activity patterns, and theology perhaps are related to the nature and intensity of internal church conflict. Whether it results in organic division or not, it may contribute to personal maladjustments of members. Problems of religious loyalties are more likely to become a festering point for mental illness when they involve local church tensions than when they involve denominational loyalties. Children rebelling against parental authority pertinent to church affiliation sometimes become victims of mental illness. Religious tensions also are involved in the mental illness that arises out of crises in interfaith marriages.[9]

Protestant Denominational Conflict

Internal conflicts also occur in denominations. Sometimes churches of the same denomination are located so near each other that each infringes in evangelistic efforts upon territory and people considered by the other to be its "mission field." The wealthier farm families are the most likely to depart from an open country church to join a village church of the same or a similar denomination. This has brought churches within a denomination into acute competition with one another.[10]

"Family quarrels" within religious bodies also occur because of fund-raising for denominational projects. Quotas are sometimes arbitrarily assigned to churches on the basis of total membership without consideration of differences in the age, sex, occupational, and income distribution of members. Tensions arise between boards competing for funds, time on convention programs, space in denominational papers, and opportunities for promotion. These tensions are aggravated by personality clashes that sometimes emerge when strong leaders are brought into positions which demand semi-independent but coordinated action.[11]

Splinter Sects

Numerous religious denominations originated in conflict. Protestantism itself emerged chiefly out of the sixteenth century revolts against Roman Catholicism which were accompanied by much bloodshed and persecution. New splinter bodies continue to be formed; every denominational family has experienced some division as a result of doctrinal or other con-

---

[8] Bryan R. Wilson, "The Pentecostalist Minister: Role Conflicts and Status Contradictions," *American Journal of Sociology*, 64 (Mar. 1959), 494-504.

[9] Wayne Oates, *Religious Factors in Mental Illness* (New York: Association Press, 1955), pp. 77-78.

[10] Douglass and Brunner, *The Protestant Church*, p. 66.

[11] For descriptions of specific problems in major Protestant denominations see the series on "What is Disturbing the [Baptists, etc.]," *Christian Century*, 61 (March-Aug. 1944).

troversy. New groups usually do not begin with the intention of separating from parental bodies. They try to revitalize the church through internal reform, often assuming they are restoring doctrines or disciplines which belong to their group by virtue of its history and tradition. Intimate fellowship, study, worship, prayer, and service combine with criticism of the larger body to give the emergent body an identity of its own. Gradually it is set apart as a distinct sect with the ultimate result of complete independence.

Even sects that originate with the intent of increasing spontaneity, inward freedom, and personal piety crystallize into distinct groups. Institutionalization produces emphasis upon discipline or conformity to "the letter of the law" which destroys spontaneity and thus contributes to the rise of a new splinter group.[12] This process perhaps reached its height in nineteenth-century America when a type of religious laissez-faire believing that enlightened self-interest was God's instrument of guidance prevailed. "Each sect was prone to urge its claims as the sole avenue to salvation. And within each denomination the parties of accommodation and of self-assertion fought endless battles." [13]

The "faith missions" movement accentuated dissension in many denominations. Competition of faith missions with the denominational missionary program is closely related to the rise and spread of "nondenominational" fundamentalist churches. Many became new denominations in efforts to get away from what they considered to be the evils of denominationalism. Thus the Christian and Missionary Alliance began as an interdenominational movement of members *within* other churches; it rapidly developed into a new denomination which drew members *out of* other churches.

Ideological differences sometimes lie dormant like live coals awaiting winds of dissension to stir them into flame. When differences of theological opinion on such topics as Christ's return, the atonement, or tithing prevail within a denomination, the advent of another difference may be decisive. In U.S. Baptist history controversies over Bible societies, Millerism, Landmarkism, missions, slavery, anti-Masonry, and other topics have played a major role in the creation of splinter groups.[14] Similar issues have been the focus of conflict in many other groups.

The protest of new sects against "defects" in older churches may be either veiled or open. Thus Christian Science emerged out of Christianity-at-

---

[12] James Luther Adams, "The Sociology of Discipline and Spontaneity in Religious Groups," abstract of an address given to the Committee for the Scientific Study of Religion, Harvard University, Nov. 21, 1953 (mimeographed).

[13] H. Richard Niebuhr, *The Social Sources of Denominationalism* (Hamden, Conn.: The Shoe String Press, 1954), p. 234. This is the "dilemma of religious leaders" that Yinger gives as a major source of religious divisions. [J. Milton Yinger, *Religion, Society and the Individual* (New York: The Macmillan Co., 1957), pp. 140-42.]

[14] Robert G. Torbet, *A History of the Baptists* (Philadelphia: The Judson Press, 1950), pp. 283-313, 401-39.

large to emphasize relationships between the emotions and health when very few took them seriously. Since the emergence of psychosomatic medicine, Christian Science teachings about the power of mind over matter seem less queer. Moral Re-Armament arose partly as a protest against Christians' failure to make the Holy Spirit a living experience. Many churches no longer called for an all-out commitment; the sense of evangelistic and missionary urgency had evaporated; needs for the "cure of souls" were unmet as churches failed to relate Christian faith to modern psychological insights. When people are aware of social problems but are not led by their churches into clear thinking about them on the basis of religious insight, their concern may lead them into such sects as Moral Re-Armament.[15]

In their formative stages many sects emphasize one or a few doctrines at the expense of others. Stressing teachings that conventional churches neglect, they often severely magnify or distort the doctrine or practice. The sharp protest in the sect's infancy is generally led by aggressive leaders who define the uncared-for needs of followers. In time, the group restores better balance to its teachings; by the third or fourth generation of members it becomes a "respectable" group relatively inclusive and tolerant of the teachings of others (Chapter 5). In its early stages the sect may not want to be known as a church, for "church" is associated with hypocrisy, "empty" tradition, and tyranny. Some hence claim that they are neither church nor denomination but merely a "fellowship" or a "missionary alliance." Others emphasize their belief that they alone are "the true church" because they are returning to a New Testament or apostolic pattern of faith or polity.

Within a developing sect, conflict centered around the admixture of sect- and church-type elements may give rise to new schisms. In the Orthodox Presbyterian Church, itself a splinter group, strife arising over issues of eschatological freedom, Christian liberty regarding the use of alcohol, and independence of the foreign missions board led to the resignation of 29 ministers when the majority chose to retain unchanged standards. To relax its position would have meant a gain in membership and power in society, but it would also have meant a loss of some purity of the original ethic. Increasing structural complexity, accommodation to outgroups, and resort to rational argument more than charismatic leadership characterized the group as it moved away from the sect-end of the church-sect continuum. Throughout its development, sect and church characteristics intermingled and struggled with one another for dominance and power.[16]

---

[15] The Social and Industrial Council of the Church Assembly, *Moral Re-Armament* (Westminster, South Wales: Church Information Board of the Church Assembly, 1955), pp. 29-32, 45.

[16] Frank E. Houser, "The Structure and Institutionalization of a Protest Group," *Illinois Academy of Science Transactions*, 42 (1949), 130-39.

When a sect's protest position is attacked by outsiders, it tends to become even more firm in its deviant stand. The antiabolitionist position of Southern churches prior to the Civil War was largely a defense "on Scriptural grounds" which emerged out of the extremism of Northerners' protests against slavery.[17]

Sects based chiefly on ethnic distinctions tend gradually to be assimilated into the larger society as members become acculturated. But if prejudice is directed against them, the group may persist long after it otherwise would have collapsed. The Doukhobors in British Columbia are beginning to think, feel, and act increasingly like Canadians, but the assimilation process is retarded because certain individuals, especially in the occupations of farming, logging, and general labor in which Doukhobors keenly compete, hold intense prejudices against them. The rapidity of assimilation also contributed to formation of the fanatical Sons of Freedom movement within Doukhobor communities.[18] The old proverb, "the blood of the martyrs is the seed of the church," applies to most sectarian groups.

Sectarian secessions are unnecessary if minority groups can be accommodated within the larger church through monasticism, which provides opportunity to practice a rigorous ethic in a segregated community, or through ecclesiola, which are voluntary societies within the larger body one may have entered by birth. The secession of sects from churches typically entails alteration of hierarchical polity, the sacramental system, liturgy, or ethics only at the point which occasioned the breach, yet sects generally have a freer and simpler form of religious life than their parental body.[19]

Of 27 new denominations established from 1916 to 1944, two refused to enter into a union agreed on by a majority; four resulted from schisms in larger denominations; six represented sectarian divisions within small holiness or extremely fundamentalist sects; ten were new emotional sects whose adherents were generally "come-outers" but which arose without direct breach of a church organization; one was based on a doctrinal position and achieved without formal schism, and four were autonomous sects which claimed legitimacy through ordination by some Eastern Orthodox authority. They arose chiefly in rural areas among people who were in the stay-at-home segments of the population. Cultural lag due to isolation, repudiation of cultural advances, and reversion to American primitivism were evident in their stress on revivalism, preoccupation with individual sin, neglect of social injustices and problems, and

---

17 Anton T. Boisen, *Religion in Crisis and Custom* (New York: Harper and Brothers, 1955), pp. 126-28.

18 John P. Zubek, "The Doukhobors: A Genetic Study on Attitudes," *Journal of Social Psychology*, 36 (Nov. 1952), 223-39.

19 Roland H. Bainton, "The Sectarian Theory of the Church," *Christendom*, 11 (Summer 1946), 382-87.

repudiation of a professional ministry.[20] "For heresy as a rule is not the cause of a schism but an excuse for it. Behind every heresy lies some kind of social conflict, and it is only by the resolution of this conflict that unity can be restored." [21]

The non-theological foundations of religious conflict are evident also in the history of tensions between Lutheran synods. Geographical factors and poor travel accommodations led to administrative subdivisions. Linguistic distinctions and language preferences caused some to secede. Disagreements between confessional and interconfessional factions caused another split. Independent synods in border areas were often direct rivals. Tensions about affiliations, revivalistic methods, support of certain periodicals, and loyalties to competing theological seminaries were also prevalent. Any of these topics could produce heated debate; combinations of them evoked irreconcilable antagonisms which resulted in schisms.[22]

Such organizational conflict is not entirely destructive. Some denominational divisions helped to increase the number of ministers, provide for needs of previously neglected people, increase the energy, zeal, and faithfulness of laymen and clergymen, and generally enlarge the size and strength of the church as a social institution.[23] Other schismatic divisions, however, have had a blighting, stultifying effect upon organized religion as a whole as well as upon the groups directly involved. In Turbeville, S.C., a strong faction's intense opposition to unification of the Methodist Church in 1939 resulted in sharp cleavages between families and individuals, rampant malicious gossip, ridicule of each group by the other, weakening of family and connubial ties, hindering of progress in the school system, physical and mental breakdowns, and decelerated social progress in community cooperative activities.[24]

Church divisions resulting from internal dissension are often considered a symptom or source of disastrous defeat. They also are a source of vitality, for if a church permits its activities to lapse into "dead ritual," it soon loses members to a seceding sect. "Multiplication by division" may also be beneficial if resources for the support of more groups are adequate. Marcus Bach has compared Protestantism to the process of separation, subdivision, and growth called heterotype mitosis. "Eventually cells

---

[20] Harlan P. Douglass, "Cultural Differences and Recent Religious Divisions," *Christendom,* 10 (Winter 1945), 89-105.

[21] Christopher Dawson, "What About Heretics?: An Analysis of the Causes of Schism," *Commonweal,* 36 (Sept. 18, 1942), 514.

[22] Willard D. Allbeck, "Lutheran Separation—the Ohio Story," *Lutheran Quarterly,* 11 (Feb. 1959), 28-41. As the environmental factors decline, denominational mergers occur. See David L. Scheidt, "Recent Linguistic Transition in Lutheranism," *Lutheran Quarterly,* 13 (Feb. 1961), 34-46.

[23] Wade F. Hook, "The Lutheran Church in the Carolinas Sociologically Interpreted," *Lutheran Quarterly,* 11 (Feb. 1959), 60-67.

[24] Gus Turbeville, "Religious Schism in the Methodist Church: A Sociological Analysis of the Pine Grove Case," *Rural Sociology,* 14 (March 1949), 29-39.

are created that are different from the parent cell. . . . Mitosis is life. . . . Try to stop it. You can't do that any more than you can stop nature." [25]

Inter-Denominational Conflict

The underlying competitive spirit between denominations sometimes becomes apparent in efforts to establish the first church in a new suburb. Even when comity arrangements are made (Chapter 10), denominational leaders may adjust plans for selfish advantage to their own group. Open condemnation of other groups is common among fundamentalists; denominations commonly considered fundamental as well as "modernists" are denounced. Liberal extremists similarly criticize middle-of-the-road Christians. Minor sects often are victims of prejudice, particularly if socioeconomic or political differences accompany their religious distinctions. The Hutterites are a prominent current example of American persecution of socio-religious minorities. [26]

Few conflicts are as severe as those growing out of attempts to justify cleavages between groups that are similar doctrinally, historically, and organizationally. Hence churches and leaders in the Conservative Baptist Association and the General Association of Regular Baptists have been more vocal in their opposition to policies of the American Baptist Convention than other denominational families. As a result of denominational competition, minor differences have been accentuated. The virtues of one's own group are magnified, while errors, weaknesses, and inconsistencies widely attributed to religion are foisted upon others as if to say they alone bear guilt. The consciousness of common traditions and beliefs has been submerged. Stubborn perpetuation of the peculiarities of a sect has sometimes appeared to be its chief *raison d'être* long after real understanding of the peculiarities eliminated all true belief in them. Because of competition, Christians of one denomination have been delighted when some other Christian group has suffered defeats that actually were severely injurious to the whole of Christianity. Sectarian walls which divide denominations on the basis of theological differences are often a product of the vested interests of entrenched bureaucracies. [27]

Denominational competition is often based on nontheological grounds, reflecting socioeconomic status, nationality and racial differences, rural versus urban traditions, etc. A social system with free churches based on

---

[25] Marcus Bach, *Report to Protestants* (Indianapolis: The Bobbs-Merrill Co., 1948), p. 76.

[26] John D. Unruh, "What About the Hutterites?" *Christian Century,* 76 (July 8, 1959), 801-3.

[27] Charles C. Morrison, "The Nature of Protestant Disunity," *Christian Century,* 77 (Mar. 9, 1960), 281-84.

the principle of separation of church and state contributes to this competition, for each is permitted to extend itself at the expense of others. Southern Baptist churches accompany the invasion of their people into areas traditionally assigned to American (Northern) Baptists, and northern Baptist groups similarly establish churches in Florida. Roman Catholics are building churches in traditionally Protestant rural areas, while Protestants establish missions in congested urban areas occupied chiefly by Catholics.

The denominational pattern, with its lack of a united religious voice, weakens the church in its struggle for power. Thus one force contributing to the chaotic laws pertinent to divorce has been the disunity of American religion, especially Protestantism. Each state has its own laws; some absolutely prohibit divorce while others sanction remarriages even of people divorced many times. Such inconsistency weakens marriage and the family. Uniform national divorce legislation cannot be attained until more unity is achieved among its churches.[28] Denominational competition also has contributed to the founding of more churches than can be supported and operated adequately. "Overchurching" in many rural areas is associated with and presumably one cause of weak, struggling, poorly equipped, poorly supported, economically wasteful, marginal or submarginal churches with part-time or poorly qualified pastors and programs which generally fail to meet the needs of the people and the community.[29] Protestantism is weakened by "overchurching" in its competition with Catholicism and with other institutions for power. When numerous small churches depend upon a limited population base for their members, they are not likely to have much effect upon community life either individually or collectively.[30] Personal loyalty to and enthusiasm for one's church may be strong, however, when it is in a highly competitive situation.

Conflict in Judaism

It is often assumed that internal conflict in American religion occurs only in Protestantism. While its forms are different and often more publicly manifested, conflict is present in Judaism and Catholicism as well. Some of the numerous forms of world Judaism, each proclaiming itself to be the authentic form, "differ more widely from one another than from certain other religions. . . . The growth of new forms has

---

[28] Morris Ploscowe, *The Truth About Divorce* (New York: Hawthorn Books, Inc., 1955), p. 254.

[29] W. E. Garnett, *The Virginia Rural Church and Related Influences, 1900-1950* (Blacksburg, Va.: A.E.S. Bulletin 479, May 1957), pp. 53-54.

[30] C. C. Morrison, "The Wasted Power of Protestantism," *Christian Century,* 63 (May 12, 1946), 747-49.

usually been accompanied by conflicts and controversies between those who supported and those who opposed them." [31]

American Jewish conflict goes back at least to 1802 when Ashkenazic Jews founded a synagogue in Philadelphia, which already had a Sephardic synagogue. The two groups had different rituals. In Europe the Sephardim felt that they constituted a Jewish aristocracy, but in America the two elements mingled with little self-consciousness until the Ashkenazim began to increase relatively rapidly.[32] American Judaism is now neither Sephardic, Ashkenazic, nor East European but a product of all three interacting to produce a Jewry distinct from that of other cultures. Sephardic Jews have tended to remain Orthodox; the Ashkenazim were the chief supporters of Reform Judaism. East European Jews for cultural, social, and economic reasons fit in with neither group.[33]

The rise of Reform and especially Conservative Judaism out of the Orthodox Hebrew religion is similar to some Protestant splinters. The feeling that Orthodoxy was inadequate to meet American environmental demands, especially with regard to preserving ethnic solidarity, contributed to their emergence. Conservatism prevented complete alienation and religious disorganization of the East European Jew; it linked past Jewish culture with the opportunities of American society.[34] Other Jewish cleavages reflect national origins or, in the case of Hasidim ("Pious Ones") opposition to the Misnagdim, the enthusiastic mystical tendency of the former opposed by the latter. The Hasidic Jews were uprooted by Hitler from an isolated Carpathian Mts. area where westernization was at a minimum. After the war a remnant migrated to America, many to Brooklyn where they established kindergartens and all-day schools, acquired large buildings to use as Orthodox synagogues and residences for leaders, and won converts from other Jews through their singing, dancing, personable leaders, and devoted followers.[35]

Conventions and publications of Conservative rabbis are rife with heated discussions. Leftists in the Reconstructionist movement and rightists centered about the Jewish Theological Seminary of America debate the issue of the amount of liberty to be taken in officially sanctioning change of tradition. This problem is related to larger theological considerations, but there are no indications of an internal schism in Conservatism, for its foundation is the local congregations, which are not

---

[31] Maurice Simon, *Jewish Religious Conflicts* (London: Hutchinson's University Library, 1950), p. 7.

[32] Nathan Glazer, *American Judaism* (Chicago: University of Chicago Press, 1957), pp. 15-16, 21-23.

[33] Oscar I. Janowsky, "Historical Background," in *The American Jew: A Composite Portrait*, O. I. Janowsky, ed. (New York: Harper and Brothers, 1942), pp. 1-27; and Marshall Sklare, *Conservative Judaism: An American Religious Movement* (Glencoe, Ill.: The Free Press, 1955), pp. 21-24.

[34] M. Sklare, pp. 40, 249-52.

[35] Glazer, *American Judaism*, pp. 84, 144-46.

divided along parallel lines.[36] Attitudes toward cultural pluralism and assimilationism also divide Jews. Some wish to retain their ethnic distinctions; others believe Jews should be absorbed gradually into the American melting pot.

Conflict in Catholicism

The hierarchical polity of Roman Catholicism, its broad internal variation that satisfies a vast range of different interests and needs, and its power to suppress dissension through clerical appointments, the confessional, and excommunication minimize dissension and keep most internal conflicts out of public sight. History reflects many past tensions; occasionally a Father Coughlin or a Father Feeney is suddenly transferred or silenced. Jesuits have had many Catholic adversaries who disapproved of their intolerance or intellectual bias in militant Catholicism, especially against Protestantism.

Old Catholic Churches have broken away from the Roman hierarchy. Most of their leaders were connected with the Old Catholic Churches in Europe that organized in protest against the dogma of papal infallibility (1870), but they are no longer connected with or recognized by the European groups. They reject clerical celibacy and the authority of the pope but are otherwise similar to Roman Catholics. They have been torn by schisms, personal rivalries, depositions, and other internal conflict.[37]

"The ideological conflicts within the Catholic Church are far deeper than those which disturb Protestantism. For the universal Catholic Church must find formulas for community life which will be . . . both American and universal." [38] Cultural differences in church-state relationships, education, political ideology, and ecclesiastical dominance in the numerous nations where Catholicism is represented necessitate principles that can fit all types of circumstances. Papal sanction can be found for almost any conceivable position on church-state relationships, just as it can be used to oppose almost any position.[39] Hence, as Protestants can "prove" anything by quoting Scripture passages, Catholics can "prove" diverse positions by quoting popes.

Members of the Catholic hierarchy represent many conflicting political and social views. Some believe in an authoritarian form of government; others strongly support democracy. Some uphold and others oppose

---

[36] Sklare, *Conservative Judaism,* pp. 238-41.

[37] Elmer T. Clark, *The Small Sects in America,* rev. ed. (New York: Abingdon Press, 1949), pp. 170-76.

[38] Jessie Bernard, *American Community Behavior* (New York: The Dryden Press, 1949), p. 367.

[39] *Ibid.,* pp. 368-69.

labor unions. Some favor extension of tax support to parochial schools; others strongly insist upon private financing. Social and political ideas are often passed on by the lower clergy to parish members, many of whom obediently follow the suggestions as if they were official Church teaching and a matter of faith or morals under its proper jurisdiction. As a result, priests have much power in local politics where Catholics are numerous. Educated laymen in the Church are perhaps even more divided than the clergy. Many have been anti-clerical, openly opposing official Catholic positions on political and religious tolerance, contraception, censorship, parochial schools, or other issues, and rebelling even on issues within the realm of faith and morals.[40]

Catholic internal conflict is thus present in competing ideologies and interpretations of proper political, social, and ecclesiastical action. It is present between members of the hierarchy, between the laity and the hierarchy, and between ethnic groups (Chapter 17). A major trend in American Catholicism is the gradual re-alignment of internal power. The laity are increasingly native-born, well-educated, and members of the middle class. Power is shifting gradually away from the clergy in all but strictly religious matters as the laity realize that no political principle, even when enunciated by the pope, is obligatory to them, that Catholic leadership need not be accepted in matters which are not clearly in the realm of faith and morals, and that there is great diversity and sharp conflict between members of the hierarchy on numerous issues. American Catholics are Americans first and Catholics second on most matters of politics and social action. Roman Catholic flexibility results from nearly two millenniums of adjusting to its followers, reinterpreting its doctrine in order to prevent the loss of allegiance, and thus withstanding both internal attacks and external criticisms. Condemnation of the heresy of Americanism (defined as an attitude of mind which is open to the modification of Catholic teachings in order to win converts) by Pope Leo XIII in 1899 may have slowed the process of internal change, but it did not prevent it.[41] Catholicism in the U.S. clearly bears the imprint of American culture (Chapter 3).

The Fundamentalist-Modernist Controversies

Since human interest tends to center upon extremes, less popular attention is given to conventional Christianity than to deviations like fundamentalism and modernism. The fundamentalist-modernist controversy in Protestantism reached its peak in the 1920's when it centered upon issues of theological liberalism and biological evolution. Many be-

---

[40] *Ibid.*, pp. 365-75.
[41] *Ibid.*, pp. 366, 373-74.

lieve this controversy to be dead, but there are numerous indications of its continued survival. Analyses of the conflict generally focus upon fundamentalists as its initiator. "It always takes two to make a fight"; actually, modernists can be charged with initiating the strife, for they introduced changes that precipitated it. Yet they reflected a changing world. Modifications in the material culture and in accompanying ideologies led to religious changes which brought on "the fundamentalist controversy."

The terms "fundamentalist" and "modernist" are not defined by many who use them. Each often carries a derogatory or derisive connotation. Because of the variety of denotations and connotations loosely connected with each concept, most Christians prefer not to be labeled as either. We therefore must define these terms. We shall then examine representative issues in the Protestant controversy, its social sources and results, present trends, and finally analogous Catholic and Jewish controversies.

The Nature of Modernism and Fundamentalism

Modernists angered fundamentalists by efforts to make theology conform with the conclusions of scholarship and science and to apply Christian principles to society in an attempt to establish the Kingdom of God on earth. The other-worldly element of Christian ethics was minimized if not eliminated. The uniqueness of Christianity was denied; contributions of other religions to man's well-being were recognized. The "higher criticism" of the Bible, which emphasized scientific and historical techniques of checking its dependability, seemed to fundamentalists to remove all authority from the Book of Books. Human reason replaced Biblical revelation as the criterion for religious faith. The modernists' belief that God created the universe through an evolutionary process (theistic evolution) was to fundamentalists a crowning sin; it conflicted with literal interpretations of the Genesis account of God's fiat creation of the universe and life in six 24-hour days. Questions about Jesus' deity seemed to leave no room for belief in a supernatural Christ who came to earth to redeem man from his sins. Reinterpretations of biblical miracles added to fundamentalists' "proof" that the modernist was an enemy of God.

Modernism was "thinly disguised secular philosophy . . . only verbally Christian; . . . given a biblical veneer, its substance was evidently taken from the philosophy of science." [42] Its "chief aim was to rise above all theologies, creeds, and cults to a universal faith grounded in universal

---

[42] Herbert W. Schneider, *Religion in Twentieth Century America* (Cambridge· Harvard University Press, 1952), pp. 117, 119, 121. See also pp. 101-4.

evolution." [43] In place of the Bible as the central authority in Christianity, it substituted the historical or living Christ; a long series of reinterpretations of the New Testament emerged in its search for the Christ. "A God without wrath brought men without sin into a kingdom without judgment through the ministrations of a Christ without a cross." [44] While its essence was a method and not a creed, modernism's involvements with science, individualism, democracy, and humanism had a profound effect upon traditional Christian teachings and led to revision of many Christian doctrines.

"Fundamentalism was the organized determination of conservative churchmen to continue the imperialistic culture of historic Protestantism within an inhospitable civilization dominated by secular interests and a progressive Christian idealism." [45] The fundamentalist attitude was an essential aspect of the Protestant Reformation which substituted the Bible as an absolute authority in place of the Church of Rome. Those who insist that the Bible is infallible reaffirm a teaching of Luther and Calvin.[46] Broadly defined to include absolutist positions of any kind, fundamentalism is a "faith of stagnancy," whatever the object of faith may be. "Essentially, the fundamentalist mentality is that of a closed and authoritarian mind. . . . The danger and temptation of fundamentalism of any variety . . . is idolatry. Toynbee would call it the idolization of an ephemeral mode, or institution, or technique." [47]

Protestant fundamentalism rallies around five basic doctrines: the infallibility and inerrancy of the Bible, the deity and Virgin Birth of Jesus Christ, His vicarious atonement for the sins of mankind, His bodily resurrection from the dead, and His second coming—a bodily, visible return. Many also insist that the second coming will occur at the beginning of a literal 1,000-year reign on earth by Christ (the premillennial view), and that post- and a-millennialists are outside the fold of true Christianity. Fundamentalists also believe that heaven and hell are literal places; modernists consider such belief to be a cultural survival from an outmoded past.

[43] *Ibid.*, p. 120. Schneider distinguishes between the "complacent modernism" of 1900 to 1915 and "common sense liberalism" of 1915-1930. No attempt is made in our brief sketch to distinguish between the various types of modernism and liberalism, some of which are close to certain kinds of "liberal fundamentalism," but all of which are considered heretical by hyper-fundamentalists. As ideal types, the two opposing camps of modernism and fundamentalism are described here as logical opposites.

[44] H. Richard Niebuhr, *The Kingdom of God in America* (New York: Harper and Brothers, Torchbook ed., 1959), p. 193.

[45] Stewart G. Cole, *The History of Fundamentalism* (New York: Richard R. Smith, 1931), p. 53.

[46] Emile Cailliet, "The Mind's Gravitation Back to the Familiar," *Theology Today,* 15 (Apr. 1958), 1-8.

[47] Charles Harvey Arnold, "Biblical Authority in Contemporary Protestantism," *Religion in Life,* 23 (Summer 1954), 363-74. Quotations from pp. 365, 370-71.

The fundamentalist's sole basis of faith and conduct is the Bible.[48] Revelation, not verified experience, is the source of truth. The Bible is believed to *be* the Word of God, not simply to *contain* it, as liberals contend. The educational materials used in fundamentalist Sunday schools hence profess to cover the whole Bible; in fact they omit many significant portions. Emphasizing the letter more than the spirit of the Word, they are basically content- rather than pupil-centered.[49] Believing that "evil men and seducers shall wax worse and worse" (II Tim. 3:13) so all of man's efforts only increase misery, fundamentalists did not attempt to reform society through a social gospel as modernists did. They assumed, rather, that personal conversions will bring the Kingdom of God closer and closer to its earthly fruition when Christ will return and establish the utopian millennium. This individualistic emphasis upon "the soul as an insulated package in a vacuum" was seldom carried to its logical extreme; it was impossible to view the individual as being completely outside of his matrix of social relationships.[50]

The derisive term, "fighting fundamentalist," is a direct outgrowth of the controversial, negativistic spirit in fundamentalism. It has been called a "stubborn religion" which is "a twentieth-century movement of protest and unrest; it is apocalyptic, prophetic, critical of modern life and apprehensive of the future."[51] By its very nature fundamentalism resists changes in doctrine and "contends for the faith." Authoritarian dogmatism gives evangelism a clear objective: to lead people to accept Jesus Christ as Savior. Appealing to the emotions and conscience with the assurance of strong faith, fundamentalists often make more progress in evangelism than liberals that lack the zeal and fervor of a dogmatic message related to a theory of history in which people can find comfort and security in times of anxiety and confusion.[52] Many fundamentalist conversions come from the ranks of liberal church members. Proselyting efforts increase the tensions with modernists.

Even critics of fundamentalism admit that it has some sources of **strength lacking among liberals. If fundamentalists'** basic assumptions are granted, their position is clear and logical. They *know* exactly what they believe and are not merely seeking truth. This is in sharp contrast to the modernists' "muddled thinking and mingling of contradictory ideas"

---

[48] In fact, however, it is not only the Bible but a particular set of interpretations as well. For an analysis of two assumptions undergirding the fundamentalist view of the inerrancy of the Bible, see Marcius E. Taber, "Fundamentalist Logic," *Christian Century*, 74 (July 3, 1957), 817-18.

[49] Donald L. Leonard, *Fundamentalistic Christian Education: A Study of the Gospel Light Lesson Materials* (New Haven: Yale University Ph.D. thesis, 1953).

[50] Arthur W. Calhoun, *The Cultural Concept of Christianity* (Grand Rapids, Mich.: William B. Eerdmans Publishing Co., 1950), pp. 99-100.

[51] Schneider, *Religion in Twentieth-Century America*, p. 14.

[52] Bryan Green, *The Practice of Evangelism* (New York: Charles Scribner's Sons, 1951), pp. 202-4.

and the "more or less unconscious hypocrisy of liberalism." As a result, the "more radical minds that have broken with traditional religion completely are apt to respect the orthodox believer more highly than the muddled modernist. . . . Nothing is more difficult for the outsider to sympathize with, than the attempt to combine two loyalties; nothing harder to understand than the man who remains within the church without believing, who recites the creed with mental denial." [53] "A creed which is true to the facts of life, but false to their intellectual formulation, is preferable to a creed that is false to the facts but scientific in their presentation." [54]

Human reason and materialism are not a monopoly of modernism. A form of rationalism is involved in the assumption that only an inerrant Bible can be a worthy vehicle of Divine Revelation. Fundamentalists feel it is better to claim too much rather than too little for the Bible, for then people will read it. This leads to the all-or-nothing fallacy and to a counter-attack by rationalism itself: if there is even *one* error, the Bible cannot be the Word of God. Many persons reared with this attitude have been alienated from Christianity, becoming agnostics as a result of discovering "errors." A materialistic notion of truth in fundamentalism emphasizes mechanistic means of inspiration; the Bible becomes a "paper pope" to the believer. Jots and tittles of the written Scriptures are incorporated into the "foundation of faith;" historic Protestantism insists that this foundational position is rightly held by the "Living Word," Jesus Christ, alone.

The Nature and Events of the Conflict

Theologically it is possible to classify on a continuum at least five distinguishable parties to the controversies: fundamentalist, conservative, moderate, liberal, and modernist. Our concern is chiefly with the terminal groups, but often there are no clear-cut distinctions. Even highly orthodox leaders and groups have been labeled by hyper-fundamentalists as modernistic because they cooperate with liberals in community projects. Just as Ohio is "west" to New Englanders but "east" to Iowa farmers, so the fundamentalist and modernist labels are often applied from different vantage points in inconsistent ways.[55] The controversy cuts across de-

[53] John Herman Randall, *Religion and the Modern World* (New York: Henry Holt and Co., 1929), p. 145. Reprinted by permission of Holt, Rinehart and Winston, Inc.
[54] D. R. Davies, *On to Orthodoxy* (New York: The Macmillan Co., 1949), p. 32.
[55] Variations in usage are so great that certain modernists are sometimes labeled fundamentalists. Arnold ("Biblical Authority in Contemporary Protantism," pp. 365-71) seems to have done this in his fourth type of fundamentalism. His four types are (1) fundamentalism of the Word, which equates God's Word with the words of the Bible; (2) fundamentalism of the Spirit, which makes the "inner light" or the Holy Spirit the source of authority; (3) fundamentalism of the Cultus, in which a fixed liturgy or some organizational structure, office, or polity is deemed the essence

nominational lines. There often is closer fellowship between churches of different denominations united on the basis of common fundamentalist or liberal faith than between divergent churches in the same denomination. Fundamentalists are united by common support of interdenominational faith missions, Bible institutes, periodicals, evangelists, and welfare agencies.

Moderate fundamentalists and liberals often remain together in the same church. Concessions are made by each group, while hyper-fundamentalists, failing to gain control, often depart to establish new churches or to join those they know to be "true to the Word of God." On the basis of questionnaire responses the members of 50 Methodist Episcopal churches were classified theologically as fundamentalists, conservatives, average, liberal, or most liberal. All five categories were found in most churches, but each had a somewhat different distribution. Fundamentalists and conservatives ranged from 19.5 to 100 per cent of the membership. In the most liberal church, considerably over half were liberal or most liberal. Such variability in a church, especially when neither viewpoint can claim a majority, creates many problems for leaders. It bears the seeds of internal dissension and strife if it is not wisely managed.[56]

The Scopes trial in 1925, "heresy trials" of clergymen and seminary professors, polemic articles, books, and tracts, and fundamentalist attacks on higher education were major events in the conflict during the first three decades of the century. A major target of fundamentalist attack has consistently been the Federal Council of Churches, its successor, the National Council of Churches (NCC), and the World Council of Churches. Fundamentalists have continually levelled inconsistent charges against these groups. The charges range from their being anti-American, communistic, pro-Catholic, pacifistic, war-mongers, to free-love-supporting, anti-Christian organizations preparing the way for the extreme apostasy that they expect just before Christ's return. They conclude that "Every Christian in the United States should repudiate the NCC, separate from it, and separate from the denominations that are in it." [57] The NCC Broadcasting and Film Commission's "Advisory Policy Statement on Religious Broadcasting" in 1956 called for allocation of free radio and television time to broadcast religious programs as a public service and advised against the sale of such time. Its recommendation that allotment of time be made with "due consideration to the strength and representative

---

of the church and becomes a fetish, and (4) fundamentalism of a limited method, in which the scientific method in theology is crystallized as the only valid source of truth.

[56] Joseph Van Vleck, Jr., *Our Changing Churches* (New York: Association Press, 1937), pp. 159-61, 167-68.

[57] Carl McIntire, *Metropolitan Nicolai: Agent in Soviet Secret Police; How the Communists are Using the N.C.C.C.* (Collingswood, N.J.: 20th Century Reformation Hour, April 30, 1959), p. 3.

character of the councils of churches, local and national," was resented by churches and program sponsors outside the councils. Fundamentalists feared they would be removed from the air, as many claimed programs already had been, under NCC pressures.[58]

Splinters of Baptist and Presbyterian denominations, dissension within Methodist, Congregational, and Protestant Episcopal bodies, and hundreds of independent faith mission boards are tangible results of the controversies. Through missionaries the struggle was transplanted to foreign lands. The strength of fundamentalism in the 1920's resulted partly from an unofficial, informal alliance with exploiters of anti-Semitic and anti-Catholic feelings. Fundamentalism was indirectly involved in political discussions over the KKK and over Catholic nominee Alfred E. Smith in the 1924 and 1928 Democratic National Conventions. It was not a purely theological movement.[59]

The most impressive mid-century events in the controversy relate to the Revised Standard Version of the Bible (RSV) completed in 1952. "The New Bible" was burned in many churches. Protest meetings were held to attack it. Fundamentalist periodicals devoted hundreds of pages to its "errors." Sponsorship by a NCC agency, use of theologically and socially liberal scholars, and especially the translation of Isaiah 7:14 in which "young woman" replaced the King James Version (KJV) word "virgin" were criticized.[60] Dr. Carl McIntire led 1,127 clergymen, mostly members of the American Council of Christian Churches, to sign a declaration that the RSV is "unworthy of the name 'Holy Bible.' It is the Bible of modernism and higher criticism." The statement warned Christians against using the RSV and called upon churches to prohibit its use in worship services.[61] Attacks upon the RSV prompted articles, sermons, and declarations in its defense. The controversy helped make it a best seller; 1,600,000 copies were sold in the first eight weeks after publication.

Resistance against the RSV can be explained on sociological grounds. Many people are ignorant of both the problems of translation and the difficulties of transmitting documentary material down through the cen-

---

[58] Broadcasting and Film Commission, "Advisory Policy Statement on Religious Broadcasting" (New York: National Council of Churches, 1956); George Burnham, "Evangelical Broadcasting Outlook," *Christianity Today*, 2, no. 7 (Jan. 6, 1958), 28; and editorial, "The Scramble for Radio-TV," *Christianity Today*, 1, no. 10 (Feb. 18, 1957), pp. 20-23.

[59] Henry Steele Commager, *The American Mind* (New Haven: Yale University Press, 1950), pp. 178-83.

[60] Examples of literature produced against the RSV may be seen in any fundamentalist periodical of 1952 to 1954. Among the more prominent of these are *Moody Monthly, King's Business, Sunday School Times, Christian Beacon*, and *Sword of the Lord*.

[61] "Twenty-three in Area Join Attack on New Bible," Minneapolis *Star*, Jan. 12, 1953, p. 7.

turies. Study Bibles, commentaries, and concordances were nearly all built around the KJV. Customs of public use demand uniformity and perpetuate the traditional version. Certain KJV expressions are passwords of orthodoxy in some circles; modernizing them to fit current language patterns seemed to remove spiritual content, replacing the Word of God with the words of men. Sponsorship by a liberal organization made many fear its purchase would enrich an "enemy of the true gospel." Doctrines such as "soul sleep" had been built by certain sects around peculiarities of the KJV. Above all, minority groups need conflict in order to maintain their separate identity and a *raison d'être*. This necessity also helps account for the fact that the religiously based opposition to John F. Kennedy in the presidential election of 1960 was spearheaded by fundamentalists.

Social Sources of the Conflict

To the fundamentalist there is only one explanation of the fundamentalist-modernist controversies: the modernist has departed from the Word of God; he has capitulated to subversive doctrines of secular or even atheistic philosophers, scientific theorists, historians, and other scholars. Modernism indeed has adjusted to modern scholarship, but to explain the controversy around it on such terms alone is an extreme over-simplification. Some basic contributing factors are suggested and briefly discussed below. Their roots are deep in the history of American religion.

1. *The accumulation of scientific knowledge.* The growth of science and the piling up of historical facts, especially about religious literature, led to modifications of theology. The orthodox energetically reacted when they discovered that doctrines cherished as eternal, unchangeable truth were no longer held by many pastors. Evolution and theological modernism were basic issues. Psychological and sociological analyses of religion also made believers uncomfortable. Many felt that to explain is to explain away; that when one understands his religion, it has somehow disappeared. Hence the behavioral and social sciences were resented, distrusted, and opposed by those who felt their faith or their children's was being undermined by the new knowledge. Modernists endeavored to harmonize their religion with the findings and interpretations of science, and fundamentalists resisted such efforts.

2. *Rural-urban conflict.* The controversy was closely related to other phases of the conflict between rural and urban subcultures. Churches with the strongest rural influences tended to be the most conservative. People who were well adjusted to urban life tended to forsake fundamentalist doctrines and join liberal churches.[62] The constant influx of rural mi-

---

[62] Van Vleck, *Our Changing Churches,* p. 163.

grants into city churches prevented strictly geographic division, yet the strongholds of fundamentalism have generally been in rural areas and cities with strong rural influences. Anti-evolution agitation was strongest in the rural South; fundamentalists still emphasize evils of the city and defend agrarian life.[63] Yet it is perhaps not agrarianism per se that is involved but merely the correlates of relative educational backwardness and ignorance. Fundamentalist leaders and spokesmen were not limited to people of rural backgrounds. The desire for personal recognition, love, and fellowship is often not met satisfactorily in urban areas. Fundamentalism may have resulted partly from nostalgic longings for a more "rural" type of church life.[64]

3. *Traditionalism.* Modernism threatened traditional religion. Traditional values relative to family life, the economic order, recreation, education, etc. also were gradually succumbing to the encroachments of industrialization and associated trends. In a period of rapid social change the traditional religious values and social order were upheld by fundamentalism. It was oriented to the past; it was a "system-in-being," "orthodoxy challenged." [65] As an "intellectual rearguard action," it tried to fix Christianity in the rigid mold of a specific doctrinal complex and world view, to preserve certainty in a world of change, to hold on to simple, familiar, and therefore "safe" patterns in the face of new, bewildering problems.[66]

4. *Generational conflict.* Tension between an older and a younger generation was a basic element. Youth tends to be liberal, for it has few vested interests in the status quo. Especially during efforts to become emancipated from parents, it tends to react against all that is associated with them. Young people have somewhat more liberal theological beliefs than older people. Theological students generally have been more liberal than ministers already established in churches.[67]

5. *The search for security.* In a life of repeated adjustments to rapid social change, many seek a source of stability in the universe. The "old time religion" provided an assurance of salvation and a faith in the orderliness of a universe created and sustained by God.[68]

6. *Education.* As new knowledge was disseminated through education,

---

[63] J. Paul Williams, *What Americans Believe and How They Worship* (New York: Harper and Brothers, 1952), p. 99; Douglass and Brunner, *The Protestant Church,* pp. 292-93; and H. Richard Niebuhr, "Fundamentalism," *Encyclopaedia of the Social Sciences* (New York: The Macmillan Co., 1931), VI, 526-27.

[64] Paul A. Carter, *The Decline and Revival of the Social Gospel* (Ithaca, N.Y.: Cornell University Press, 1954), pp. 56-57.

[65] *Ibid.,* p. 47.

[66] John Dillenberger and Claude Welch, *Protestant Christianity* (New York: Charles Scribner's Sons, 1954), pp. 230-31; and William E. Mann, *Sect, Cult, and Church in Alberta* (Toronto: University of Toronto Press, 1955), pp. 155-57.

[67] George H. Betts, *The Beliefs of 700 Ministers and Their Meaning for Religious Education* (New York: Abingdon Press, 1929); and Van Vleck, *Our Changing Churches,* pp. 19-21. Presumably this remains true today.

[68] Commager, *The American Mind,* p. 179.

the controversy often became one of the educated and worldly-wise versus the uneducated and unsophisticated. Educated people were more likely to be theologically liberal than those with little or no education. Conviction and zeal rather than education characterized most fundamentalist leaders; Bible passages like I Corinthians 1:17-31 which decries the wisdom of the world were favorite sermon texts, and anti-intellectualism was evident in much of fundamentalism.[69] Leaders like Wm. Jennings Bryan attempted to defend the faith with logical, erudite arguments, but often they selected the most convincing assertions of fellow fundamentalists and the weakest statements of opponents. Fundamentalists believed it was far better to be a completely uneducated man of faith than to be a learned skeptic.[70] Extreme orthodoxy was often a reaction to increasing doubt about eternal verities.[71] When faith began to waver, the fundamentalist was told to contend fervently for it. Convincing others convinced himself.

7. *Socio-psychological compensation.* For many, especially in backward rural areas and in the lower classes, life on earth is one of hardship. An other-worldly religion offers them a glorious future when "the first shall be last and the last first." Using self-classifications of four categories (fundamentalist, conservative, liberal, radical), Sanderson's study of about a thousand urban churches revealed that 50 per cent more fundamentalist and 25 per cent fewer liberal churches than the average were located in socially and economically poor areas. Some less privileged people apparently find an escape in other-worldliness.[72] Immigrants, blacks, and people from "rural slums" are unlikely to worship in churches which have a liberal theology. Many problems of urban adjustment and assimilation are softened by fundamentalist sects. Believers are enabled by their faith to endure crises and strains; simple explanations of suffering prepare the way for spiritual and moral reorganization of sinners.[73]

8. *The Social Gospel.* The social theology of modernists emphasized many radical revisions of society. To fundamentalists this social gospel (described in Chapter 6) was no gospel at all; the gospel in the Bible seemed to be one for saving persons, not the social order. They distinguished between the temporal and the eternal world and separated affairs of the body from salvation of the soul. This theological dualism was threatened by modernistic efforts to apply scriptural principles to temporal

---

[69] Anti-intellectualism creates many problems in fundamentalist institutions of higher education. See John R. Brobeck, "A Christian View of Higher Education," *His*, 18, no. 6 (Apr. 1958), 5-7, 28.

[70] Norman F. Furniss, *The Fundamentalist Controversy, 1918-1931* (New Haven: Yale University Press, 1954), pp. 38-41.

[71] Carter, *The Decline and Revival of the Social Gospel*, pp. 55-56.

[72] Douglass and Brunner, *The Protestant Church*, p. 291.

[73] Mann, *Sect, Cult, and Church in Alberta*, pp. 154-56; and Van Vleck, *Our Changing Churches*, pp. 162-63.

affairs. Many fundamentalists interpreted the Sermon on the Mount as the constitution of a future Kingdom of Heaven; this directly contradicted liberal efforts to apply it to life on earth. (Such antinomian dualism was labeled "social modernism" by Pope Pius XI, for it implied that the benefit of clergy was not necessary to the management of secular affairs.) Other-worldliness thus constituted a mechanism of escape from both a social order and a social gospel that were felt to be highly undesirable and full of error.[74] Fundamentalists therefore gave many biblical passages a symbolic interpretation that made them apply to the salvation of the soul, Christ's second coming, or other "spiritual" doctrines. The same passages were taken literally by liberals as commands for use in present-day living, applicable directly to the current social order.

Religious individualism was closely related to a social individualism that opposed government interference with business. Fundamentalists gained the support of many industrialists as they attacked the social gospel, for these men were the targets of much reforming effort by liberals who examined and publicly exposed evils of the capitalistic system, employers, and other vested interests of the wealthy in the economic order. It was in this sense that "the main foundations of Fundamentalism were . . . a complicated mask behind which careful scrutiny reveals economic features in large part hidden from the mass of the population." [75]

9. *The struggle for power by religious leaders.* Modernists ignored fundamentalists during much of the controversy, believing the issues involved had been settled during the nineteenth century. When conservative leaders' desires for power in denominational affairs were thwarted and their voices ignored, "they not only intensified attachment to their beliefs, but they submitted themselves to undue emotional tension and change. Conservatives *became* fundamentalists. They suffered a sense of personal defeat when their views were being superseded." [76] Their desire for theological security, like-minded fellowship, and administrative leadership of their denominations made them assume the role of authoritarian agents of God preserving the "faith once for all delivered to the saints" (Jude 3).[77]

Fundamentalism lives by controversy. The specific issues shift from decade to decade, but essentially it is a protest movement centering upon defending the faith against intrusions it considers inconsistent with orthodoxy. Attacks upon evolution, the ecumenical movement, liberalism, secu-

---

[74] Schneider, *Religion in Twentieth-Century America,* pp. 14-15; and Commager, *The American Mind,* pp. 179-80.

[75] Harold J. Laski, *The American Democracy* (New York: The Viking Press, 1948), p. 278. See Furniss, *The Fundamentalist Controversy,* pp. 17-28; and Carter, *The Decline and Revival of the Social Gospel,* pp. 49, 55.

[76] Cole, *The History of Fundamentalism,* p. 334.

[77] *Ibid.,* pp. 328-37.

lar education, sinfulness in the media of mass communications, and various other subjects have engrossed its attention. Some of these are recurring topics; others involve battles fought and often lost with little subsequent effort to renew the struggle.

Some preachers are suspected of having used the crusade against modernism, evolution, ecumenicalism, and other isms to bolster waning church attendance, to increase periodical subscriptions, and in other ways to enhance their wealth or prestige.[78] The imputation of motives is always dangerous. Most fundamentalist leaders were sincere and honest in their efforts to proclaim and especially to defend the gospel as they understood it. After all, the Bible exhorts Christians to fight a good fight and to war against "spiritual wickedness in high places" (Eph. 6:12).

Consequences of the Conflict and Recent Developments

The controversy served as a corrective of extremisms in Christianity. Together with wars and depressions that undermined superficial optimism, it helped bring neo-orthodoxy, an intermediary form of liberalism linked with existentialism, to a dominant position in Protestant theology. It met many personality needs of people under stress in a changing world. It contributed to continuing study of the social and religious implications of evolutionary theory and led thinking persons to re-examine their theological position. It provided many with a rationalization for changing their church membership to a congregation more congenial in terms of social class composition. It increased the cooperation of many groups and was disastrously divisive for others. It led major denominations to re-examine their creeds and polity and was a wholesome antidote against non-critical adoption of new doctrines and practices.

On the other hand, the conflict deepened the gulf between educated clergy and uneducated parishioners. It undercut the intellectual prestige of religion in general and deflected attention from such important questions as changing responsibilities of the church in a society of increasing knowledge, advancing urbanism, and growing technology.[79] As a result, the total impact of Protestantism in American culture undoubtedly was weakened.

Within fundamentalism, moderate "evangelicals" near the center of the fundamentalist-modernist continuum, are often criticized by hyper-fundamentalists. Thus Billy Graham, world-famous evangelist who adheres to the basic tenets of fundamentalist doctrine, has been condemned for his willingness to cooperate with liberals in united evangelistic campaigns. Attacks upon the National Association of Evangelicals (NAE) by the

---

[78] Furniss, *The Fundamentalist Controversy*, pp. 29-33.

[79] Carter, *The Decline and Revival of the Social Gospel*, pp. 54-55; and Garnett, *The Virginia Rural Church*, p. 37.

American Council of Christian Churches (ACC) illustrate the same divisions. The ACC was organized to fight modernism; it believes the NAE has compromised its orthodoxy by refusing to take an outright stand against the NCC.

Conservative Protestants are engaged in much self-criticism; from it is emerging a new scholarship that is orthodox in Christian faith, yet neither anti-scientific nor anti-intellectual. Billy Graham has criticized many failures of the "orthodox," including their antinomianism, tendency to worship a creed instead of a Person, self-righteous "holier-than-thou" attitude, and internal controversies which result in name-calling, gossip, pride, and other sins.[80] Carl F. H. Henry similarly has criticized modernism as a perversion of scriptural theology and fundamentalism as a perversion of the biblical spirit; he believes evangelical Christianity must correct errors of doctrine and practice in both camps.[81] Because fundamentalism often has been identified with peripheral emphases in theological doctrine and methodology, has "proved itself impotent to change the theological and ecclesiastical scene," has lost every major theological struggle with modernism, and has failed to meet the demands of social situations confronting the church, a "new evangelicalism" is emerging. "The new evangelicalism embraces the full orthodoxy of fundamentalism in doctrine but manifests a social consciousness and responsibility which was strangely absent from fundamentalism. The new evangelicalism concerns itself not only with personal salvation, doctrinal truth and an eternal point of reference but also . . . believes that orthodox Christians cannot abdicate their responsibility in the social scene." [82]

Yet efforts to perpetuate the old type of fundamentalism are evident in the work of certain Bible schools, traveling evangelists, faith missions, religious periodicals, and even a college which boasts that its science classes use daily the very desk at which Scopes taught evolution in the early 1920's.[83]

Fundamentalists who live by mores and symbols of their own devising with no effort to associate with the universal Christian church have a "cultic orthodoxy." It attracts separatists who lack the security that comes from such association; they fear friendly conversation will lead to theological compromise and are highly critical, making others appear worse than they really are, because censure implies superiority. "Classical or-

[80] Billy Graham, "Evangelicals and Revival," *United Evangelical Action,* 12, no. 7 (June 1, 1953), 3-6, 8.

[81] Carl F. H. Henry, "Dare We Revive the Modernist-Fundamentalist Conflict?" *Christianity Today,* 1 (June 10 to July 22, 1957), 4 articles.

[82] Harold John Ockenga, "Theological Education," *Bulletin of Fuller Theological Seminary,* 4, no. 4 (Oct.-Dec. 1954), 4-5, 7-8. Quotation on p. 4. Reprinted by permission. Cf. Edward J. Carnell, "Post-Fundamentalist Faith," *Christian Century,* 76 (Aug. 26, 1959), 971.

[83] S. Hugh Paine, Sr., *The Duel: The Debate Between Bryan and Darrow Concerning the Authenticity and Genuineness of Holy Writ* (Dayton, Tenn.: William Jennings Bryan University, 1948), p. 14.

thodoxy," on the contrary, longs for authentic dialogue to explore historic themes with other Christians. The doctrine of the church is thus a central issue; it divides the theologically orthodox into two major camps.[84]

Because of changes within fundamentalism, with an increasing proportion deserting the folds of hyper-critical extremism to enter the more peaceful ranks of the "new evangelicalism," the conflict with modernism is much less prominent than a generation ago. Changes among liberals, as an increasing number have departed from extreme modernism to embrace neo-orthodoxy, have also contributed to its decline. However, the conflict has not disappeared. Most of the fundamentalist creed is incorporated into the "new evangelicalism" (although its acrimonious vituperation is lacking), which became "mainline evangelicalism" during the 1970's.

The passing of outstanding leaders contributed to the decline of the controversy. During the 1930's fundamentalists' energies were dissipated as they split into many small groups which, if consolidated, might have remained nationally effective. Their propaganda changed from a note of power and egoistic assurance of victory to one of petulance and even martyrdom. Ignored by modernists, they often said that they were God's "remnant" in a world of sinners who had a form of religion but denied the power thereof.[85] The great depression of the 1930's also contributed to diminished strife. Financial difficulties drew churches' concern away from theological discussions to practical problems of how to finance their operations. Human misery was so abundant and obvious that many conservatives turned their attention to the task of relieving it.

Most significant of all influences that ended the most virulent forms of the controversy, however, was the continued growth and diffusion of knowledge. Not only was the level of education rising, but radio was bringing to the people modernistic leaders who had been labeled as heretics. Hearing them firsthand, they discovered that their teachings were less anti-Christian than they had been led to believe; even the doctrines of Harry Emerson Fosdick "were not, after all, the instruments of Satan." [86] As it became impossible for any respectable scholar to refute certain tangible findings of the sciences, fundamentalists who went into higher education modified their views and in turn had an impact upon the churches from which they came. They demonstrated that evangelical faith was not destroyed by modern knowledge. Thus the fundamentalists lost the battle. And yet the modernists, in their failure to change basic doctrines of orthodox faith, also lost.

The controversy continues, but generally in milder form.[87] The post-

---

[84] Edward John Carnell, "Orthodoxy: Cultic vs. Classical," *Christian Century*, 77 (Mar. 30, 1960), 377-79.

[85] Furniss, *The Fundamentalist Controversy*, pp. 179-81.

[86] *Ibid.*, p. 180.

[87] See Arnold W. Hearn, "Fundamentalist Renascence," *Christian Century*, 75 (Apr. 30, 1958), 528-30; and editorial, "Change of Format, No Change of Heart," *Christianity Today*, 2, no. 13 (Mar. 31, 1958), 23-25.

World War II "revival of religion" brings together the intellectual and emotional aspects of Protestantism in creative interchange. The instruments and insights of modern scholarship and science increase understanding of the Christian message, yet this is done in the context that "faith is the gift of the Eternal God and stands above us and the best of our human devices. Therefore it [the theological renaissance] cuts across the theological divisions of American Protestant history." [88] Extreme fundamentalists and extreme modernists alike deplore this trend, but the bulk of American Protestants—liberal, evangelical, conservative—are enabled to discuss their views creatively and constructively. Dichotomous divisions of the past are transcended by such debate; wide gulfs separating Protestants in the past appear to be narrowing for the mutual benefit of all. By 1980 moderate fundamentalists preferred to be labeled as "evangelicals," and the term "modernism" was largely displaced by "liberalism."

The Controversy in Catholicism

Although most Protestant fundamentalists were strongly anti-Catholic, Catholicism meets all theological requirements of the fundamentalists' minimum five-point definition. The chief difference is that the ultimate authority is not an infallible Bible but an infallible Church. Revelation as interpreted by the Church hierarchy and tradition rather than empiric rationalism is to the Catholic the basic source of truth.[89]

A creative, but sometimes destructive, tension between the Catholic and modernist position has prevailed throughout church history. Its earliest major manifestation perhaps occurred in the controversies related to Gnosticism (c. 200 A.D.).[90] Contemporary modernism in Catholicism sprang up at the same time as it did in Protestantism and for basically the same reasons. The centralized organization of the Church, however, made it simple to compel modernists either to conform to its teachings or to leave the Church. The Encyclical *Pascendi Gregis* in 1907 by Pope Pius X brought an end to modernism's development in the official Catholic press and pulpits. By 1910 its leaders had been excommunicated, professors and priests were required to take an oath of fealty to essential doctrines, and the Church was formally purged of modernism. The American atmosphere of optimism, belief in progress, and belief in universal brotherhood was a fertile breeding ground for modernistic theology, however. Many Catholics adopted its tenets, and philosophers like George Santayana published essays to justify and defend it. Neo-Thomism as a de-

[88] Robert T. Handy, "Fundamentalism and Modernism in Perspective," *Religion in Life*, 24 (Summer 1955), 381-94. Quotations from p. 394.

[89] Laski, *The American Democracy*, pp. 286-87.

[90] Wilford O. Cross, "Catholic and Modernist," *Anglican Theological Review*, 41 (Apr. 1959), 95-104.

fender of Catholic faith developed to serve the Church; it uses the Tho-
mistic appeal to reason instead of the ecclesiastical appeal to authority.
Thus some of the modernistic methods officially condemned by the
Church are gradually being accepted by it.[91]

Modernists in Catholicism have been less likely to leave their Church
than those in Protestantism. The emotional effects of mystic ecstasy, "the
religious thrill," come to the Catholic modernist in the religious ritual
which centers on the Mass because of the effects of long years of conditioning, even if he no longer believes in the truth of the articles of faith.
The liberal Protestant is likely to withdraw from his original denomination
or from all church connections, for he lacks a firm ritualistic foundation
and has only a reasoning approach to his faith. Ritual is thus, for the
Catholic, a conservative force that so firmly binds him to a system that
the appeal of reason is of no avail in efforts to break his church bonds.[92]

Roman Catholicism is changing today, as in the past. It therefore can
be expected to survive the impact of the vast social, technological, and
political changes of the twentieth century. The great diversity which is
possible and permissible within it is, paradoxically, a source both of weakness and strength, of division and unity.

The Controversy in Judaism

Judaism is similarly divided, although less along doctrinal than historical lines which separate those who emphasize Zionism as a symbol of the
continuous historical existence and living culture of the Jews from those
whose religion is little more than a modern philosophy. The extreme modernists among the Jews are the Reconstructionists who regard Judaism as
a civilization.[93] Along the continuum toward "Jewish fundamentalism"
follow the Reform, Conservative, and finally Orthodox Jews. For the
liberal Jew the homeland of Israel has become the focus of piety. In both
liberal Christianity and liberal Judaism a new loyalty has replaced a fundamentalist emphasis upon the authority of the Bible.[94]

Revelation dominates in *Orthodox Judaism*. The inspiration of the
Old Testament and Talmud is accepted; the Torah is considered to be
the work of God rather than of Moses. Orthodox Jews attempt to live up

---

[91] Schneider, *Religion in Twentieth-Century America*, pp. 121-22, 132-33, 183;
and Horace M. Kallen, "Modernism," *Encyclopaedia of the Social Sciences* (New
York: The Macmillan Co., 1933), X, 564-68.

[92] Luther Sheeleigh Cressman, "Ritual the Conserver," *American Journal of
Sociology*, 35 (Jan. 1930), 564-72.

[93] Sklare, *Conservative Judaism*, pp. 241-45; Mordecai M. Kaplan, *Judaism as a
Civilization* (New York: The Macmillan Co., 1934); and M. M. Kaplan, *The Future
of the American Jew* (New York: The Macmillan Co., 1948). Reconstructionist views,
however, are increasingly incorporated into Reform and Conservative Judaism. It has
never been a truly distinct organic group but is chiefly a movement for internal reconstruction of Judaism.

[94] Schneider, *Religion in Twentieth-Century America*, pp. 86, 102-3, 130-31.

296 SOCIAL PROCESSES AND THE CHURCH

to the Torah's precepts as far as modern conditions permit, while Reform and Reconstructionist Jews completely adjust their religion to modern life and culture. Yet American Orthodoxy might better be called orthopraxy, for its concern is more with correct practice of religious regulations and customs than with doctrinal details. Great diversity is present in its customs as well as in its beliefs, and it has been modified so greatly by the American culture that it is unlike Orthodox Judaism elsewhere. The high costs of keeping the dietary laws and the Sabbath, maintaining separate Orthodox social welfare institutions, and supporting an intensive program of weekday religious education have contributed to the financial weakness of its synagogues and defection from its ranks.[95]

Reform Judaism was transplanted to America from Europe, especially Germany. Emerging mainly during the second half of the nineteenth century, it taught that the Messianic aim of Judaism is not to restore the old Jewish state but to unite all God's children in confessing His unity. The world-wide dispersion of the Jews was for the high-priestly mission of leading all nations to a true knowledge and worship of God. The doctrine of immortality was applied only to the soul; belief in a bodily resurrection was rejected. The Hebrew language was replaced in prayer with "an intelligible language." Laws regulating diet, priestly purity, and dress were rejected as not conducive to holiness and obstructive to modern spiritual elevation. Only the moral laws of the Mosaic code and ceremonies adapted to modern civilization were accepted as binding. Reform Judaism emerged partly as the religion of economically comfortable Jews who wanted to be accepted by the non-Jewish world. Its ritual is close to that of middle-class Protestantism. Nineteenth century rationalism was a major influence on its modification of ancient prayers, rituals, and doctrines. The retention of circumcision and the traditional ban on intermarriage were results of a continuing identification with Judaism as a national movement; they occurred in spite of the rational ideology of the leaders.[96]

Conservative Judaism arose largely out of protests against the liberalism of Reform Judaism. It can be traced to the adoption of liberal principles by the Reform group in 1885 and to a strong, emotional protest against the serving of shrimp, a forbidden food for the Orthodox, at the first graduation dinner of Hebrew Union College (1883). Orthodoxy was too severe for them and Reform too un-Jewish. The movement grew with efforts to center Judaism upon common Jewish elements in religion, culture, intellectual pursuits, and philanthropy. It was stimulated by Zionism.[97]

---

[95] David de Sola Pool, "Judaism and the Synagogue," in *The American Jew*, Janowsky, ed., pp. 28-55.

[96] Glazer, *American Judaism*, pp. 45-56.

[97] *Ibid.*, pp. 56-59. 91-94.

The *Zionist movement* was the focus of many internal differences. The Orthodox were able only gradually to reconcile Zionism with their age-old hope of messianic redemption. Reform Jews generally opposed the idea of establishing a new national state, but East European immigrants were strongly inclined toward socialism, anarchism, and Zionism. American Zionism was primarily a "movement of secular salvation" which tended to disintegrate traditional Orthodoxy. Great variation was found among the Zionists; some were religious and others solely in search of revived Jewish national culture. The movement did not prosper until Hitler began persecuting Jews in 1933, causing thousands of them to emigrate from Germany to Palestine. In 1935 the Central Conference of American (Reform) Rabbis adopted a neutral position on Zionism, abandoning the official hostility adopted in 1897, and in 1937 they went on record regarding Palestine, affirming "the obligation of all Jewry to aid in its upbuilding as a Jewish homeland by endeavoring to make it not only a refuge for the oppressed but also a center of Jewish culture and spiritual life." [98] Little opposition to the Zionist movement remained after the Nazi pogroms. American Jews provided large sums of money for the relief of European Jews and the establishment of Israel.

Judaism as a distinct religion has survived in America largely because of its internal variations. The Reform movement provided a cushion for the disintegrative effects of emancipation from traditional Orthodoxy, which no longer was acceptable to the German Ashkenazim Jews. It prevented complete assimilation and loss of identity. Conservatism similarly offered a mode of living for the alienated and a cushion for the effects of dissolving Judaism as a highly traditional, integrated, sacred system. It prevented the complete religious disorganization and alienation of Jews of East European origins.[99] Variations and adaptations within Judaism, each severely criticized by groups refusing to accept them, are thus one of the foundations which make possible the continued existence and strength of Judaism in America.

Conclusion

We have seen that a number of social forces contribute to internal conflict in religious organizations. Variations in ethnic background, traditions, social class, linguistic patterns, education, and mobility of members lead to differences in theological doctrines, norms pertinent to cultural pluralism and assimilationism, ideological views of innovation and adaptation, and attitudes toward church ritual and other action patterns. Vested interests are perpetuated by entrenched groups, including denominational

---

[98] From the statement as quoted in Glazer, p. 104.
[99] Sklare, *Conservative Judaism,* pp. 246-52.

bureaucracies, while those who are not in positions of power struggle for recognition and dominance. Personal jealousies and rivalries increase the possibilities for conflict. Out of these and related factors come internal controversies that often are considered "purely religious" but upon analysis prove to reflect a host of interwoven social, psychological, historical, theological, philosophical, and economic factors.

The internal sources of church conflict in turn reflect basic social forces in the modern world. Urban residence, migration, the insecurities which accompany free enterprise and democratic individualism, a heterogeneous population, the cultural lag of social institutions failing to keep up with technological change, and the rapid expansion of scientific and other knowledge directly or indirectly stoke the fires of religious controversy. Yet, paradoxically, these very same forces, both inside and outside of churches, make cooperation ever more essential for the survival of the church. Cooperation and conflict are coexistent. As the modern division of labor becomes ever more complex, both play an increasingly important role in man's institutions.

The social composition of opposing groups in any controversy is a primary key to understanding it and the alignment of persons and groups into opposing camps. Lower class persons and other "have-nots" who are victims of social discrimination nearly always form their own religious bodies. People who are socially or geographically isolated cling to old beliefs and habits, while those in the mainstream of new scientific, scholarly, or commercial developments are likely to adopt "modern" forms of behavior, clothing old doctrines with new semantic meanings or liturgical garb. Those who become identified with peculiar customs which identify the group as quaint are likely to lend a hallowed air to those customs and to brand deviation from them as heresy.

Dysfunctional effects of internal religious conflict are readily apparent. It results in wasted resources of time, energy, and material goods. Personalities of participants may be damaged. "Overchurching," with all of its associated problems, grows very largely out of competition. Conflict between factions reduces the church's impact on persons and on society by preventing unified action to promote goals believed desirable by all the churches. These and other immediate effects often differ, of course, from the long-range consequences.

Church conflict also has numerous constructive or functional effects. It promotes internal unity in the groups involved, binding their members closer to one another. It helps relieve personal tensions through the cathartic release which often results. It clarifies the goals and values of the group as it is forced to indicate its position on controversial issues and keeps groups alert lest they fail to maintain their position in the competitive social system. It perpetuates the larger religion of which any specific church group is a part, for it provides more subgroups and variations within that religion, thus making possible the satisfaction of a greater variety of personal and social needs. It also is a source of innovation to fit emerging needs and interests of people in a changing world, leading to new activity patterns, interest groups, ethical teachings, and doctrinal formulations to fit the changing times. Much of the vitality of the church as a social institution is a direct result of conflict.

These same forces and similar results are characteristic of conflict between the major church bodies and between the church and other social institutions. These are examined in the next two chapters.

Selected References

Buzzard, Lynn, interview, "War and Peace in the Local Church," *Leadership*, 4, no. 3 (Summer 1983), 20–30. Characteristics of and principles about church conflicts based on mediation-arbitration experiences of the Christian Conciliation Service in the Christian Legal Society. (See also Harvard Business School Case Services, "Anatomy of a Church Fight," *ibid.*, pp. 96–103.)

Dodd, C. H., G. R. Cragg, and Jacques Ellul, *More Than Doctrine Divides the Churches*. New York: World Council of Churches, 1952. Social and cultural factors which hinder church unity and promote misunderstandings among Christians.

Fray, Harold R., Jr., *Conflict and Change in the Church*. Philadelphia: Pilgrim Press, 1969. A clinical study of the use of conflict in Eliot Church, Newton, Mass., as a discipline for renewal; published to stimulate thinking and reflection by others.

Hoge, Dean R., *Division in the Protestant House: The Basic Reasons Behind Intra-Church Conflicts*. Philadelphia: Westminster, 1976. Research on divisions in the United Presbyterian Church leads to core questions of religious truth, authentic life, and the suggestion that neo-evangelicalism could be creative and redemptive.

Leas, Speed, and Paul Kittlaus, *Church Fights: Managing Conflict in the Local Church*. Philadelphia: Westminster, 1973. Strategies for dealing with conflict.

Lewis, G. Douglass, *Resolving Church Conflicts: A Case Study Approach for Local Congregations*. San Francisco: Harper and Row, 1981. A theory of conflict and its management with applications to ministry in the church and in the world.

Metz, Donald L., *New Congregations: Security and Mission in Conflict*. Philadelphia: Westminster, 1967. A sociological analysis of goal conflicts and other tensions in six young Presbyterian congregations.

Mickey, Paul A., and Robert L. Wilson, *Conflict and Resolution: A Case-Study Approach to Handling Parish Situations*. Nashville: Abingdon, 1973. The nature of local church conflict and how to handle it constructively.

Moberg, David O., *The Great Reversal: Evangelism and Social Concern*, rev. ed. Philadelphia: Lippincott, 1977. An analysis of divisions between advocates of individual soul-winning and of structural change in twentieth-century Protestantism.

Rausch, David, "Jews Against 'Messianic Jews,'" in *New Religions and Mental Health: Understanding the Issues*, ed. Herbert Richardson (New York: Edwin Mellen Press, 1980), pp. 39–47. Jewish Defense League demonstrations against Melech Yisrael, a Messianic (Christian) congregation.

Wood, James R., *Leadership in Voluntary Organizations: The Controversy over Social Action in Protestant Churches*. New Brunswick, N.J.: Rutgers University Press, 1981. A theory of leadership legitimacy to explain how Protestant ministers successfully advocated social action on racial equality issues even when a majority of their congregations opposed it.

᧤   Chapter 12

Interfaith Conflict

Religious conflict is evident in interfaith relations as well as within churches and denominations. In America it has been observed between Christianity and nativistic Indian religions, oriental religions, and Islam, as well as between the dominant Protestant, Catholic, and Jewish religions which are the focus of attention here. Our survey of Protestant-Catholic tensions and causes of conflict is followed by a summary of relationships between Christians and Jews which includes the problem, sources, theories, and effects of anti-Semitism and the accommodative adjustments of Hebrew Christians. The chapter concludes with suggested sources of increased tolerance and good will between the major faiths in pluralistic America.

Protestant-Catholic Tensions

Most analyses of Protestant-Catholic relationships are distinctly partisan because the subject is emotion-laden for so many people. Nearly all sources of information are colored by obvious or covert biases that distort the facts. Bigotry, especially by anti-Catholics, has been so common that any criticism of Catholicism is likely to be labeled by intellectuals as well as by pro-Catholics as intolerant and unfair, and any objectively-based compliment paid the Catholic Church is criticized by its opponents as bowing at the Pope's feet.[1]

Historical accounts of American anti-Catholicism rarely recognize sufficiently the contemporary stimuli that contributed to its periodic outbreaks. Even non-Catholic scholars tend to view these events oversimply as based upon bigotry or irrational ignorance. Current interfaith quarrels indeed are partly a continuation of irrational past struggles, but the tensions have a continuing social, psychological, and ideological basis which must not be overlooked in analyzing the subject.[2]

Protestant dominance in America has made its side chiefly one of attack and the Catholic position chiefly one of defense. Yet the struggle is not entirely one-sided. Protestant propaganda has emphasized its defensive position in the face of Catholic growth in numbers and power as Roman Catholicism has advanced from a position of weakness in colonial America to the largest religious body. (The largest Protestant category, as we saw in Chapter 2, is Baptist, which about two-thirds as many prefer, but it has over 30 bodies.) Description of Catholicism as the dominant American religion is not wholly amiss, for only rarely is Protestantism sufficiently united to warrant reference to it as a unit.

Issues in the Conflict

In 183 letters to the author and publishers of a non-fictional best-seller treatment of the Catholic Church in America, 695 tension items expressing adverse feelings against Catholics or the Church were distinguished. Catholics were charged with persecuting Protestants, tolerating illiteracy and vice, being totalitarian, producing bad effects on national and international politics, infiltrating the free press, attempting to control Congress, insidiously controlling socioeconomic affairs, having adverse family mores, endangering American education, etc. The tension items were of three major types: value-charged terms and epithets, fears of Catholic intentions and influence, and personal experiences and "known facts" concerning Catholics.[3] Content analysis also indicates the presence of Protestant-Catholic tensions in periodical literature.[4] How widespread these accusa-

---

[1] Paul Blanshard claims that fear of being associated with "anti-Catholic fanatics" has prevented many American liberals from honestly analyzing the implications of Catholic dominance and has become a tool in the hands of the Catholic hierarchy. Cf. *American Freedom and Catholic Power* (Boston: Beacon Press, 1949), p. 266.

[2] Charles L. Sewrey, "Historians and Anti-Catholicism," *Christian Century,* 73 (Mar. 14, 1956), 333-35.

[3] Gordon C. Zahn, "The Content of Protestant Tensions: Personal Experiences and 'Known Facts'," *American Catholic Sociological Review,* 16 (Mar. 1955), 12-22; and Gordon C. Zahn, "The Content of Protestant Tensions: Fears of Catholic Aims and Methods," *ibid.,* 18 (Oct. 1957), 205-12.

[4] John J. Kane, "Protestant-Catholic Tensions," *American Sociological Review,* 16 (Oct. 1951), 663-72; and Orlo Strunk, Jr., "Protestant-Catholic Tensions: A Repetition

tions and attitudes are in the general population is unknown. They do, however, play a prominent part in the interaction of Catholics and non-Catholics in many local communities, and they occasionally appear in discussions of national and international issues.

The issues involved in the tensions between Catholics and Protestants[5] may be classified under seven major categories: politics, education, freedom, family welfare, divergent mores, economics, and religion. They are frequent subjects of articles in *Christian Century* and *Christianity Today,* prominent Protestant periodicals, in the Catholic *America,* and in other religious publications.[6]

1. *Political issues.* All of the conflict may be considered political, for it is out of immediate issues of political legislation, administration, and legal interpretation that most open clashes between Catholics and Protestants emerge. The most directly political sources of tension follow.

Alleged Catholic influence upon elections. It is charged that "the Catholic vote" is influenced unduly by the Catholic hierarchy and that democratic institutions are thereby undermined. Catholics deny this and state that they are divided politically just as Protestants and Jews, hence there is no such thing as *"the* Catholic vote." Local studies sometimes reveal a strong influence by the priest upon politics,[7] but they also reveal wide variation in the voting of Catholic citizens and legislators (Chapter 14).

The holding of political and juridical offices by Catholics. Anti-Catholics charge that such officers cannot be trusted to uphold national welfare, for whenever it is in any way believed contradictory to the welfare of Catholicism, the Church will receive preferment. Primary loyalty is to a foreign ruler, the pope, and to an authoritarian Church-dominated form of government. This belief has been a source of discrimination against Catholics wherever they have been a clear minority. The best known twentieth-century national events reflecting this issue are the 1928 and 1960 presidential election campaigns. In 1928 the Democratic candidate, Alfred E. Smith, was defeated partly because of anti-Catholicism.[8] The

---

and Extension Study in Simple Frequency-Type Content Analysis," *Boston University Graduate Journal,* 5 (1957), 156-57.

[5] The term "Protestant" is used in this section to refer to non-Catholics, most of whom are Protestants or have Protestant religious preferences. Many individual Catholics and Protestants take a position different from that indicated here. The "Catholic" position here is that of the Church hierarchy in most cases, or that of most Catholic people, and the "Protestant" position is that characteristic of leaders in major Protestant denominations, as far as these respective positions can be discerned.

[6] John J. Kane, *Catholic-Protestant Conflicts in America* (Chicago: Henry Regnery Co., 1955), pp. 5-9, includes a content analysis of items of tension in *Christian Century* and *America;* other portions of Kane's book are a basis for many statements in this chapter.

[7] Dewey Anderson and Percy E. Davidson, *Ballots and the Democratic Class Struggle* (Stanford University, Calif.: Stanford University Press, 1943), p. 74.

[8] Cf. Edmund A. Moore, *A Catholic Runs for President* (New York: Ronald Press

Catholic response to such charges emphasizes the "loyalty and service to every fundamental ideal and principle upon which the Republic was founded and has endured." [9] It is only in matters of faith and morals that the Catholic official must follow the dictates of his Church. Protestants charge that "faith and morals" can be defined so broadly that a Catholic president would not be a free man because of his dual allegiance.[10] Careful analysis of Catholic U.S. Supreme Court justices has found, however, that as a group their ideas cannot be distinguished from ideas of colleagues.[11]

Ego-involvements of Catholics, as in every minority, lead them to claim prejudicial discrimination whenever a Catholic's advance in career is blocked, even if obvious inferiority or incompetency is involved. Catholics are sometimes wanted for civic boards and committees regardless of abilities simply so they will be represented. Religious bias is also expressed in an anti-Protestant direction. In local elections Catholics are favored in certain communities. In the 1896 presidential election when William Jennings Bryan was the Democratic candidate, large numbers of Catholic Democrats deserted their party because of his radicalism and close identification with Protestantism in spite of his general support from the Catholic press.[12]

Separation of church and state. The First Amendment to the Constitution of the United States declares that "Congress shall make no law respecting an establishment of religion." This has been interpreted historically and legally to mean that there shall be no established church, that neither states nor the federal government may aid or prefer one religion above another, that neither may force a person to engage in religious activities, that no taxes may be levied to support religious institutions, and that a "wall of separation between church and state" must be maintained. Catholics have sought a reinterpretation to permit use of public funds to support certain church-sponsored educational and welfare institutions without favoritism toward or discrimination against particular religions. The controversy focuses on public aid to church-sponsored hospitals and

---

Co., 1956). Moore concluded that "there is no evidence that religious controversy has disappeared as a potentially divisive force in the political life of the United States" (p. 200). This opinion is justified by events in 1960. However, even the strongest Protestant candidate of the Democratic Party most likely would have lost the 1928 election. Richard Hofstadter, "Could a Protestant Have Beaten Hoover in 1928?", *The Reporter,* 22, no. 6 (Mar. 17, 1960), 31-33.

[9] John Tracy Ellis, *American Catholicism* (Chicago: University of Chicago Press, 1956), p. 159. Ellis states that discrimination to keep Catholics out of posts of leadership is commonly recognized by educated Catholics although it operates more subtly than it did during the 1928 election campaign (p. 149).

[10] James Curry, "Politics, the Pope, and the Presidency," *Eternity,* 10, no. 2 (Feb. 1959), 13-15, 47.

[11] Harold W. Chase, Margaret Jane Green, and Robert Mollan, "Catholics on the Court," *The New Republic,* 143, no. 14 (Sept. 26, 1960), 13-15.

[12] Robert D. Cross, *The Emergence of Liberal Catholicism in America* (Cambridge: Harvard University Press, 1958), pp. 105, 257.

schools; Catholics claim aid is constitutional; their opponents claim it is not. Many anti-Catholics are convinced that long-range plans of the Catholic Church include repeal of the First Amendment and a pattern of church-state relationships which will severely restrict non-Catholics. Foremost among the organizations working to uphold church-state separation is Americans United for the Separation of Church and State, which was organized as POAU in 1948.[13]

Diplomatic representatives to the Vatican. Catholics claim the Vatican is a political state; Protestants say it is primarily a religious center and hence oppose the appointment of diplomatic representatives. President Roosevelt's "personal representative," Myron C. Taylor, appointed in 1939, was tolerated only because of special World War II conditions. Opposition led to the withdrawal of such a representative during Truman's presidency.[14] Subsequent reappointments have been sporadic.

International politics. Anti-Catholics claim that the Catholic Church has maneuvered behind the scenes to help cause many wars, revolutions, and other political disturbances and that it now is engaged in anti-Communistic endeavors leading to World War III. Governments are wittingly or unwittingly used by the Church in its endeavors to defeat Communism.[15] Catholic response typically empasizes the evils of atheism, the persecution of Catholics in Soviet satellites, and the attack upon *all* religion by Soviet Communism. One phase of the competitive struggle to influence international affairs is the programs in Washington, D.C., to train foreign diplomats. In 1919 the Jesuit School of Foreign Service was established in Georgetown University and in 1958 the Protestant School of International Service in the American University. The latter was partly a reaction to the effectiveness of the former.

Anti-democracy. Catholicism is charged with being autocratic and fascist-supporting. Political conditions in Italy, Spain, and Latin America are cited as evidence of what would occur with Catholic control of America. The Catholic reply emphasizes the strength of individualism and appointment of Protestants to high government positions in European nations dominated by Catholicism. They charge that similar appointments of Catholics are not made in "Protestant America" and that this proves Protestants are really the more anti-democratic.[16]

Taxation of church property. Large property holdings by the Catholic

---

13 For Catholic criticisms of POAU see Lawrence P. Creedon and William D. Falcon, *United for Separation* (Milwaukee: Bruce Publishing Co., 1960).

14 William F. O'Brien, "General Clark's Nomination as Ambassador to the Vatican: American Reaction," *The Catholic Historical Review*, 44 (Jan. 1959), 421-39.

15 Paul Blanshard, *Communism, Democracy and Catholic Power* (Boston: Beacon Press, 1951); and Avro Manhattan, *The Catholic Church Against the Twentieth Century*, rev. ed. (London: Watts and Co., 1950).

16 Erik von Kuehnelt-Leddihn, "The Catholic Temper," *Confluence*, 2, no. 4 (Dec. 1953), 92-105; and Michael P. Fogarty and H. Stuart Hughes, "Catholicism and Democracy: An Exchange," *Commentary*, 26 (Aug. 1958), 119-26.

Church give it a substantial interest in taxation policies. Protestant churches have a similar vested interest in the conventional practice of not taxing church property but they claim that this privilege is abused by the Catholic Church when it holds non-taxable but income-producing property and thus gains an "unfair" advantage over competing businesses. In addition, the tax burden of other property holders is greater when church property is untaxed; the Catholic Church is the chief target of criticism.[17]

In nearly all political issues, it has been demonstrated that Protestants use religious influence in politics in the very manner and on the same subjects they condemn in Catholicism. Efforts to check the political dominance of one religious group tend to establish the dominance of another.[18] The political aspects of Protestant-Catholic tensions are so prominent that nearly every major periodical has carried articles related to the subject. A Seminar on Religion in a Free Society in May, 1958, discussed these questions. Supporting religious pluralism, it concluded that "The point of the Catholic Church, the point of the Jewish faith and the Protestant Church, is personal holiness. . . . whatever our differences in organization, structure, and method, there is this one same end in view." [19]

2. *Educational issues.*

Public education. Catholics protest against state laws requiring Bible reading, prayers, or hymn singing in schools, for these reflect Protestant dominance. Some Protestants oppose religious education in public schools through released time classes, and most of them oppose the use of garbed nuns, brothers, and priests as public school teachers. Local conflicts have arisen when Catholics with children in parochial schools have become members of the public school board, when Catholic facilities with crucifixes and other symbols of Catholicism have been rented for public school use, or when Catholic voters have refused to support programs to improve public school facilities.

Parochial schools. Non-Catholics sometimes attack the curriculum and quality of teaching in parochial schools, but more often they are concerned with problems of church-state separation referred to above and in Chapters 8 and 14. Catholics feel that they suffer "double taxation" when they pay taxes for public schools while supporting parochial schools by tuition and contributions. Many Catholics think government ought to help pay tuition, furnish health services, subsidize transportation, pay for textbooks and supplies, and provide services like school lunches for parochial

[17] In a California city studied by Anderson and Davidson over one-third of all taxable real estate was owned by the Roman Catholic Church; the entire tax burden was borne by only two-thirds of the real property (*Ballots and the Democratic Class Struggle*, pp. 75-76).

[18] Kane, *Catholic-Protestant Conflicts*, pp. 126-46.

[19] Donald McDonald, reporter, *Religion and Freedom* (New York: The Fund for the Republic, 1958), p. 48.

school pupils. Anti-Catholics believe such public contributions would be only an entering wedge undermining the public school system. Catholics counter-charge that Protestant emphasis upon principles is a smoke-screen for monetary interests and reflects fear that free competition of public and private education would result in a private school victory.

Partisanship has blinded discussants to certain important facts. Each tends to compare the opponent's actual situation with his own ideal. Proponents of public schools charge that parochial schools are "undemo-cratic," for they foster class consciousness, spread undemocratic attitudes, impede cultural integration, and slow down social mobility. No effort is made to discover how many scholars from parochial schools strengthen democratic values. Leaders in independent schools often condemn public schools for lack of discipline. However, the private school can slough off offenders; the public school is required to accept their discards and all others who come. Selection policies in terms of social class and other traits also must be evaluated in order to get a fair comparison of the two types of schools. The public school is criticized for its "progressive educa-tion." That this is a straw man is apparent when specifics desired in private schools are listed; they comprise progressive education in its best sense.[20]

3. *Freedom.* Pointing to the history of other nations in which Cathol-icism is or has been dominant, many Protestants feel that freedom of religion, speech, the press, and assembly are threatened by Catholicism.

Freedom of speech and the mass media of communications. The strength of Catholic censorship of the movies, radio, and television, high-lighted by events associated with such controversial Catholic-opposed films as *Martin Luther,* has provided a factual basis for much discussion.[21] Censorship grows out of centuries of Catholic tradition. It is criticized by non-Catholics as unjustifiable when extended to public libraries, book stores, and non-Catholic publications. Catholics believe that what is in-jurious to them also injures others, hence they uphold the welfare of all people of good will by these activities.

Freedom of assembly and religion. Pointing to the persecution of Prot-estant missionaries in nations like Spain, French Canada, and Colombia, Protestants insist that the Catholic Church unfairly uses state power to pre-vent religious teachings other than its own and demonstrates its true colors of intolerance and suppression of non-Catholic teachings.[22] They ob-

---

[20] Leighton H. Johnson, "Unemphasized Aspects of the Independent-School Ques-tion," *School and Society,* 87 (May 23, 1959), 239-40.

[21] For examples, see editorial, "The 'Martin Luther' Controversy," *Commonweal,* 65 (Mar. 15, 1957), 603-5; editorial, "Censorship in Chicago," *Christian Century,* 74 (Jan. 23, 1957), 102-3; and Bosley Crother, "The Strange Case of 'The Miracle'," *Atlantic Monthly,* 187, no. 4 (Apr. 1951), 35-39.

[22] The Confederation of Evangelical Churches in Colombia reported in July, 1956, that since 1948, 47 churches and chapels had been destroyed by dynamite or fire and many others damaged, that over 200 Protestant schools had been closed, that in the last six months over 40 Protestant churches had been closed and their members forced

ject to treaties of friendship, commerce, and navigation which exclude traditional provisions concerning mutual freedom of worship and liberty of conscience in both nations. For example, the 1955 treaty with Haiti omitted the religious liberty clause because officials in Haiti feared Catholic criticism on the grounds of a Concordat between Haiti and the Vatican; much discussion of the danger to religious liberty appeared in the Protestant press.[23] Catholic responses refer to their persecution by Protestants in various lands, comparative silence of Protestants when Catholicism suffers infringements of religious liberty, and differences between a land of "religious unity" and the United States with numerous religious groups, none of which claims a population majority. Within Catholicism is an ever-increasing movement favoring freedom of religion as inevitably linked with the Christian spirit.[24]

4. *Family welfare.* Catholicism has stimulated and supported legislative activities which strengthen traditional divorce laws, forbid dissemination of birth control information, forbid therapeutic abortion and euthanasia, prevent the adoption of babies by parents of any religion other than that of the natural parents, prohibit sex education in public schools, and provide public funds for sectarian welfare. Conflict over pro- and anti-Catholic policies in hospitals and welfare has occurred in many communities. Protestants condemn the application of Catholic canonical law to non-Catholic patients in Catholic hospitals partially supported by public funds. Friction arises out of mixed marriages involving Catholics, for the procedures required for the Catholic to remain in good standing in his Church involve a one-sided commitment by the non-Catholic to respect the other's religion and rear the children in Catholicism.

On such topics of faith and morals Church influence on Catholic legislators and administrators often is evident. Catholics believe their values are based upon "natural law" and should be applied to all mankind. They resent critics who try to impose prohibition and anti-gambling laws on all people. Their Church is suspicious of any proposals to regulate child welfare; it has a strong vested interest both economically in its welfare institutions and theologically in its belief that religion is more important to the proper rearing of children than secular and temporal welfare. Gradual change is occurring in Catholicism as a result of pressures

to meet clandestinely for worship, and that 75 Protestants had been martyred. By January, 1958, the number of Protestant martyrs had increased to 80. Cf. W. Stanley Rycroft, "Facts for Fr. Kelly," *Christian Century,* 75 (Jan. 22, 1958), 108-9. The solution to such problems cannot come by legislation alone. Cf. Marshall K. Powers, "The Legal Status of Non-Roman Catholic Mission Activities in Latin America," *International Review of Missions,* 49 (Apr. 1960), 201-9.

[23] E.g., Clyde W. Taylor, "How Treaties May Affect Christian Missions," *United Evangelical Action,* 14 (Sept. 15, 1955), 387-88, 402.

[24] A. F. Carrillo de Albornoz, *Roman Catholicism and Religious Liberty* (Geneva· World Council of Churches, 1959), and John Tracy Ellis, "American Catholicism in 1960: An Historical Perspective," (Reprint from *The American Benedictine Review,* March-June 1960), Collegeville, Minn.: St. John's Abbey, 1960.

from its laity. Acceptance of the rhythm method of birth control, reinterpretation of old rules to provide a way to save the mother's life in case
of a tubular pregnancy, and legitimization of non-use of extraordinary
means to prolong the lives of the ill who are beyond medical hope are
adaptations of traditional Catholic dogma.[25]

5. *Divergent mores.* Other moral teachings create conflict.

Sterilization of mental defectives. Catholics oppose sterilization, saying it interferes with divine law and violates the supreme intrinsic worth
of the person. Many non-Catholics believe that preventing such sterilization by legislation is an unwarranted extension of Catholic power.

Gambling. Most Protestants define all gambling as sinful. Catholics
sponsor games of chance to raise Church funds, interpreting gambling as a
purely personal matter. Clashes often occur between those who favor
regulated gambling and those who oppose all gambling. In many of these
a secondary issue is Catholicism's struggle for power and the associated
anti-Catholic reaction. Gambling is legalized in some states for non-profit
and religious institutions only; Protestants insist that such gambling breaks
down public morals.

Use of alcoholic beverages. Protestants have led in the prohibition
movement, while Catholics have held that the use of alcohol is as personal a matter as eating when it does not result in drunkenness.

6. *Economics.* Many Protestants oppose Catholic policies for economic
reconstruction and labor relations.[26] The cooperation of European
Catholicism with certain socialistic governments is condemned. The differences partly reflect the generally higher position of Protestants than of
Catholics on the socioeconomic scale. As Catholics rise into the middle
classes, the importance of this source of tensions presumably will diminish.

7. *Religion.* The entire controversy may be subsumed under "religion,"
but certain phases of it are particularly religious in nature.

Dogma of Catholicism. Outstanding among religious issues is Roman
Catholic insistence that it is the ONE true religion. It refuses to cooperate
on an equal basis with other churches; to do so might imply recognition
of them as "true" religions. Refusal to work with ecumenical organizations also is related to other doctrines.[27] It aggravates anti-Catholicism.

Veneration of saints and the Virgin Mary. Many Protestants interpret
the reverence Catholics give to saints and the Virgin as a form of idolatry.
Misunderstanding Catholic theology and claiming that lay Catholics also
misinterpret it, Protestants criticize "lucky" medals and amulets, prayers

[25] Jessie Bernard, *American Community Behavior* (New York: Dryden Press,
1949), note 25, p. 374; and Kathryn Boardman, "Life Saving 'Limit' Cited," St.
Paul *Dispatch,* April 1, 1959, p. 33.

[26] Kermit Eby, "The Catholic Plan for American Labor," *Christianity Today,* 1, no.
15 (Apr. 29, 1957), 12-15.

[27] For a concise comparison of some major Protestant and Catholic doctrines see
Kenneth Underwood, *Protestant and Catholic* (Boston: Beacon Press, 1957), pp.
386-89.

offered to saints, and preservation of relics as pagan superstitions. Protestant opposition has prevented such acts as the erection of a statue of St. Maurice, the patron saint of foot soldiers, at Fort Benning, Georgia.

The Ten Commandments. America's three major religions agree that there are ten commandments but do not agree upon how they should be listed. Derived from Exodus 20 and Deuteronomy 5, commandment I in the Catholic version is divided by most Protestants into I and II, while Protestant X is Catholic IX and X. Lutherans and Jews have still different numbering. When used in public schools and community activities, each group protests if another's version is used.

Church membership definitions. The contrast between the voluntary manner of joining most Protestant churches and the Catholic interpretation of membership creates misunderstanding. Under Catholic law any person validly baptized as Catholic, even without knowledge or consent of non-Catholic parents, is and remains a Catholic until death or excommunication. Protestants often criticize Catholic membership statistics as vastly over-stated. Friction arises when legal interpretation of church membership is needed to apply child welfare or other laws.

Foreign missionary work. Protestant missionaries to areas where Catholicism is dominant have alarmed Catholics by winning more converts than Catholics have won from Protestants (chiefly because of the disparate size of the potential proselyte populations). Legal and extralegal reprisals have had repercussions in America.

Proselyting. The most severe of all directly religious clashes relate to efforts of both religions to win converts. Catholics began by the 1930's to engage in evangelistic activities similar to those of Protestants. The charges that they appeal to fear and ignorance, magnify dogma and authority, and repeat a half-dozen or so verses over and over as the scriptural basis for the entire Catholic position[28] may also be brought against much Protestant evangelism. A common goal of the Catholic press is the winning of converts. Pressures also are used on secular newspapers to publish materials favorable to Catholicism.[29] Certain Protestant organizations and periodicals like *Christian Heritage* (*The Converted Catholic*) have been established primarily to convert Catholics.[30] Knights of Columbus advertisements in popular periodicals and Catholic sub-groups like the Paulists have convert-making as a major goal.

In 1954 questionnaires from 2,219 Protestant clergymen in 23 cities indicated that they had received 51,361 members from Catholicism dur-

---

[28] These characteristics of Catholic advertisements to win converts are outlined in Charles M. Crowe, "So This Is Good Will!" *Christian Century,* 62 (Apr. 4, 1945), 427-29.

[29] Heinz H. F. Eulau, "Proselytizing in the Catholic Press," *Public Opinion Quarterly,* 11 (Summer 1947), 189-97.

[30] For brief descriptions of a few of them see Ralph Lord Roy, *Apostles of Discord* (Boston: Beacon Press, 1953), pp. 156-77. By 1976 *Christian Heritage* was defunct.

ing the past decade. This led to the estimate that 4,144,366 Catholics had been converted to Protestantism in contrast to the 1,071,897 converts Roman Catholics claimed, "presumably from Protestantism," during the same period.[31] The different nature of membership definitions, sampling considerations (incomplete response, urban bias, assuming members and clergymen are equally distributed, and unqualified mathematical projection to the national level), reliance upon clergymen's memories to cover a decade, and the propagandistic purposes of the survey are some of the study's methodological weaknesses.[32] In 1958 the *Christian Herald* asked similar questions of 10,000 Protestant pastors in 14 cities chosen because of their Catholic strength. Only 917 replies were received from active ministers, three-fifths of whom used the same methods for taking Catholics into the membership as for others. They reported receiving 7,011 Catholics during the preceding three years and losing 1,227 members to the Catholic Church. Most transfers of religion were due to intermarriage, but educational and recreational programs also were important sources of conversions.[33] To generalize from sample returns of only nine per cent is very hazardous. Perhaps non-respondents were embarrassed because of an excess of conversions away from Protestantism. It is more likely, however, that most did not reply because of a lack of converts, time, interest, or the necessary information.

A nation-wide survey by an independent research firm concluded that 1,434,000 Roman Catholics in the U.S. had become Protestants and 2,370,000 Protestants had turned to Catholicism.[34] Here, too, problems of definition and sampling interfere with confident conclusions. Since more Americans nominally identify themselves with Protestantism, Catholics have a much larger potential missionary field than Protestants, and this latter report may be closer to the truth than the *Christian Herald* surveys. Perhaps the greatest problem in evaluation lies in the question of whether to count dormant or fallen-away persons as converts when won to the other faith. If a convert's grandparents were Catholic, is he a convert from Catholicism?

Types of Anti-Catholicism

As a result of varying combinations of emphasis upon and disagreements about the preceding issues, there are at least six main types of opposition to Catholicism. (1) The "if-they're-for-it-I'm-against-it" person

[31] Will Oursler, "Who Said Conversion Is a One-Way Street!" *Christian Herald,* 77, no. 4 (Apr. 1954), 20-22, 34, 73. The 1959 *Official Catholic Directory* claimed 140,411 converts during 1958. This was the 13th successive year in which over 100,000 converts were recorded.

[32] Glen W. Trimble, "What Has Dr. Poling Proved?" News Release from the Massachusetts Council of Churches, April 16, 1954.

[33] "Conversion Is Still a Two-Way Street," *Christian Herald,* 81, no. 3 (Mar. 1959), 26-28, 73.

[34] "Catholics Dispute 'Loss' to Protestant Faiths," (A.P.), Minneapolis *Star,* April 2, 1954, p. 13. The survey was made for the *Catholic Digest.*

has an entirely negative creed, lacks positive convictions of his own faith, and opposes pope, saints, priests, purgatory, parochial schools, and Catholics who run for public office. (2) The Protestant "bigot" cultivates all the "facts," with special reference to the "dirt" about Catholics. He knows the worst and will not listen to the best about them, calling fellow Protestants who have a good word for Catholics naïve or misinformed. (3) The "when-they-get-to-be-the-majority-they'll-destroy-our-freedom" group collect data on persecutions of Protestants in Italy, Spain, Colombia, and Argentina. They know little about those American Catholics whom they consider a negligible minority, who are concerned for civil liberties and who publicly disavow Catholics who advocate seizure of secular power. (4) Those who fear the "vast-monolithic-structure" of the Catholic Church believe it to have members of one mind, one vote, and one fear of democracy. (5) The "Catholicism-is-clericalism" type reasons that all Catholics are anti-American gamblers and drunkards who believe Protestants are going to Hell, for he sees the local priest promote bingo, use wine in the Mass, teach Roman Catholicism as the only true religion, and raise funds for the parochial school. (6) The final type sees his own religion as a positive heritage and takes issue with Catholics on the basis of Christian convictions in an effort to be faithful to the gospel.[35]

It is often assumed that problems of interfaith relations are one-sided, the minority group being "sinned against" by the majority. In fact, however, white American Protestants, the nation's majority group, also are an object of prejudice and discrimination. Future sociologists may devote as much attention to anti-Protestantism as to anti-Catholicism and anti-Semitism.[36] All sides in the struggle need understanding, love, and faith in the honesty and motives of the others if their continuing dialogue is to prove fruitful. Knowledge of the basic causes of the conflict can help promote wholesome relations between them.

Causes of Protestant-Catholic Conflict

Many interacting factors make Catholic-Protestant tensions a continuing American problem. All have their roots in past history, but our primary interest here is not the historical development of the problem, for most of its events are symptoms of deep underlying causes. The controversy is two-sided in its origins, both Catholics and Protestants being

---

[35] Robert McAfee Brown, "Types of Anti-Catholicism," *Commonweal,* 63 (Nov. 25, 1955), 193-96.

[36] For a first step toward such analysis see John W. Dykstra, "Anti-Protestant Bias," *Christian Century,* 75 (Sept. 17, 1958), 1048-50. Illustrations of such prejudice may be found in Thomas Sugrue, *A Catholic Speaks His Mind on America's Religious Conflict* (New York: Harper and Brothers, 1952), pp. 47-48. WASPs (White Anglo-Saxon Protestants, often equated with "all white Protestants") are a common target of derision among intellectuals.

responsible for it.[37] All of the causes are so interrelated that no incident
in the conflict may be understood adequately without reference to its
total cultural setting.

1. *Psychological roots of the conflict.* Ethnocentrism, authoritarian
personality, and social interaction concepts of the causes of religious conflict are incomplete but partial explanations. Catholicism has a different
psychological appeal than most of Protestantism. Part of the lack of
understanding between the two groups may flow from differential socio-
psychological conditioning within the respective religions. Projection perhaps has played a part both in making Catholicism a scapegoat for
socio-economic problems and in unconscious projecting of undesirable
characteristics in one's religion to the other group. The impatience of
Protestants with the prominent display of Catholic personages and events
in the press and with the strength of Catholic influence in community and
national affairs may reflect "an unconscious unwillingness to accept
the consequences of our boasted individualism and our opposition to
regimentation." [38]

2. *Cultural differences.* Catholicism has been linked with an Old World
culture proud of its conservatism, adherence to fixed dogma, and emphasis on hierarchical privileges; Protestantism is culturally tied to a liberal,
pragmatic, and democratic society. Cultural differences contribute to misunderstanding and conflict.[39] Contrasts between the cultural backgrounds
of the dominant Protestant religions (northwestern Europe with a strong
pietistic and puritanistic tinge) and those of most Catholics (southern
and eastern Europe) have increased dissension. Cultural conflicts are
reflected in contrasting positions on such matters as gambling and the
use of alcohol. The Irish Catholics brought with them to America anti-
English sentiments which transferred readily into anti-"Anglo-Saxon"
Protestant ideas. Many prejudices of both Catholics and Protestants were
thus imported from the Old World.[40]

3. *Economic and social inequality.* Catholics in the U.S. have had
more lower class members than Protestants. Misunderstanding between
the social classes complicates problems of interfaith relations. When the

---

[37] This is the basic theme of Kane's "symptom-cause thesis" (*Catholic-Protestant Conflicts*).

[38] F. Ernest Johnson, "Sources of Vitality in the Religious Community," *Religious Education*, 41 (July-Aug. 1946), 193-202. Quotation from p. 196.

[39] Ellsworth Faris, "Sociology of Religious Strife," *Journal of Religion*, 15 (Apr. 1935), 207-19.

[40] Elizabeth K. Nottingham, *Religion and Society* (Garden City, N.Y.: Doubleday and Co., 1954), p. 80. The English also brought antipapal attitudes to America as Ray Allen Billington has indicated in *The Protestant Crusade, 1800-1860* (New York: Rinehart and Co., 1952). The Protestant Irish from Ulster were among the most fervent anti-Catholics a century ago. See Rowland Tappan Berthoff, *British Immigrants in Industrial America, 1790-1950* (Cambridge: Harvard University Press, 1953), pp. 187-202.

Irish first immigrated in large numbers in the 1830's and 1840's, anti-cheap labor, anti-alien, and anti-republican feelings were expressed against them and often intensified the problems associated with their minority religion. Catholicism's marginal position in many communities makes it the subject of "hysterical legislation" or of powerful lobbying that cultivates Catholic favor for political or commercial reasons. Thus Catholics often are in an ambiguous position because the American social order has been primarily Protestant.[41] Protestant domination of public schools and other institutions led early to Catholic attempts to withdraw into separate parallel institutions. Catholic separatism continues as secularism is attacked by the Church. Insecurity in regard to economic and social provisions for the future may also cause a psychological transfer of feelings which aggravates interfaith tensions.

4. *Rural-urban conflict.* Catholics are primarily urban in the U.S., whereas traditional Protestantism represents rural virtues and frontier values. Protestant-Catholic tensions relative to repeal of the Prohibition Amendment to the Constitution reflected the conflict between rural and urban views. Paradoxically, Catholicism often attempts to maintain in an urban society values which are characteristic of rural people. This is most obvious in its teachings pertinent to contraceptives.

5. *Ignorance.* Each side has failed to appreciate the other's merits and contributions. Many charges made by both are based upon misunderstanding.

6. *The struggle for power.* As a minority religion, Catholicism has been struggling for recognition. As both Protestant ecumenicalism and Roman Catholicism grow, the increasing strength of each becomes a challenge to the other.[42] Both are stronger as a result, for the faithful member feels to some extent a compulsion to demonstrate the superiority of his religion. Political interests of Catholicism in international affairs linked with its struggle against Communism, the desire of both Protestants and Catholics to wield greater political influence, and efforts of each to extend its principles to all of society, contribute to tensions. Parochial schools and Catholic welfare initially were results of anti-Catholic prejudice, but they also have increased prejudice.[43]

7. *Bureaucratic and church-like qualities of Catholicism.* Certain characteristics of the Roman Catholic Church contribute to tensions with non-

---

[41] D. W. Brogan, "The Catholic Church in America," *Harper's Magazine,* 200, no. 1200 (May 1950), 40-50.

[42] Charles Y. Glock, "Issues That Divide: A Postscript," *Journal of Social Issues,* 12, no. 3 (1956), 40-43; and Herbert Wallace Schneider, *Religion in Twentieth-Century America* (Cambridge: Harvard University Press, 1952), pp. 53-54.

[43] John O'Grady, *Catholic Charities in the U.S.* (Washington: National Conference of Catholic Charities, 1931); and Peter and Alice Rossi, "Background and Consequences of Parochial School Education," *Harvard Educational Review,* 27 (Summer 1957), 168-99.

Catholics. Outstanding among these is its bureaucratic hierarchical structure which is highly resistant to change. The history of the conflict of science and religion illustrates the adjustment problems faced by such a large organization. In addition, Catholicism is a "church" in the Troeltschian sense of the term, attempting to associate itself with every aspect of the social order. Such a relationship is very difficult to maintain in modern industrial-secular societies. Continuing belief in it inevitably causes friction with other religious bodies which wish to maintain an equal position of privilege. The current domination of all parish and subsidiary organizational affairs by the Catholic clergy is as much due to default of the laity as to episcopal authoritarianism.[44] If the "absolute despotism" of Catholicism were replaced by a parliamentarian organization, the Church would undergo such tremendous change that it would no longer be greatly distinct from Protestantism.[45]

8. *Problems of social control.* Many problems grow out of the weakness of each religion's control over members in a society which provides opportunity to deviate from the paths of righteousness as defined by their church. If a church could exercise sufficient control over its members, it would not need to turn to the state for legislation to support its teachings. Much of the conflict comes out of efforts to gain governmental help and to enforce church dogma upon the entire population. The increasing insistence in many dioceses that Catholic children not attend public schools, and accompanying dogmatics on birth control and ecumenical affairs may be viewed as dikes erected in an attempt to prevent the defection from faith that so often results from rising socioeconomic status.[46]

9. *Different value systems.* Basic to the conflict are profound differences in values. Divergent definitions of the Christian church prevent cooperation and union. The Catholic teaching that political authority comes from God and not from the people is in marked contrast to implications of the Protestant doctrine of the priesthood of the believer. It often plays a major part in the ideological struggle pertinent to political organization. Such leading Catholic publications as the *Catholic World, Ave Maria,* and the *American Ecclesiastical Review* have carried articles explaining that it is impossible for good Catholics to believe in religious freedom as generally understood in America, that Catholics could accept the American concept of church-state separation only as a temporary expedient and not as an ideal, and that they must obey instructions from pastors on voting and other citizenship duties when religious or moral questions were, in the judgment of the Church, involved.[47] These issues are controversial within Catholicism; many Catholics reject positions held by leaders in

---

[44] Kane, *Catholic-Protestant Conflicts,* pp. 49-69.

[45] David W. Soper, "As Catholics See Us," *Christian Century,* 65 (Nov. 3, 1948), 1169-71.

[46] David Riesman, "Some Informal Notes on American Churches and Sects," *Confluence,* 4 (July 1955), 127-59.

[47] Sewrey, "Historians and Anti-Catholicism."

their Church on various political questions. Nonetheless, these issues do point up certain genuine conflicts of values involved in the political aspects of Protestant-Catholic tensions. When current Catholic publications take a position different from that of the past on political or other issues, they are suspected of political expediency by critics who know about past statements and have been told by Catholics that their Church is everywhere and at all times the same.

Differences in social policies result from divergent ethical ideas which ultimately reflect contrasting theological conceptions.[48] The Catholic physician who refuses to take a child's life to save its mother in childbirth complications sincerely believes in the Catholic interpretation of the commandment not to kill, even if it means letting the mother die. The Protestant ethic, by contrast, insists that a partly lived life must have precedence over one that has not fully begun. Non-Catholics frequently assert that behind this policy of Catholic medicine lies the ulterior motive of making more Catholics, while Catholics are tempted to believe that Protestants deliberately choose to kill infants.[49]

When relationships between the central ethical-religious system and practical problems of life are overlooked, the possibilities for misunderstanding and conflict are vastly increased. Differences sometimes grow out of divergent interpretations of the same Scriptures and nearly always may be traced partly to basic contrasts in theological values. In Catholicism salvation is provided through objective, institutional means supplied by the Church; in Protestantism it is subjective, based upon the relationship of the individual's conscience to God. Thus controversy regarding the problem of religious liberty may be related to the Catholic doctrine "that objective religious truth is one, that the Church is the divinely appointed guardian of that truth on earth, and that all other denominations and sects are to some degree in error." [50] Catholics and Protestants agree that people must be allowed to choose and follow the truth, but divergent concepts of truth and different values pertinent to the freedom of propagating error create pronounced practical contrasts between them. The relatively peaceful coexistence of many religions in America occurs in spite of different values. If a revival of emphasis upon theological distinctions occurs, we can expect interfaith tensions to increase as a result of conflicting value systems.[51]

---

[48] Edward Duff, S.J., *The Social Thought of the World Council of Churches* (New York: Longmans, Green and Co., 1956), pp. 309-20; W. H. Van de Pol, *The Christian Dilemma: Catholic Church-Reformation,* trans. G. Van Hall (New York: Philosophical Library, 1952); Gustave Weigel, S.J., "Catholic and Protestant Theologies in Outline," *The American Scholar,* 25 (Summer 1956), 307-16.

[49] Margaret Mead, "The Ethics of Insight-Giving," Appendix II in *Male and Female* (New York: William Morrow and Co., 1949), pp. 446-47.

[50] Joseph H. Fichter, *Social Relations in the Urban Parish* (Chicago: University of Chicago Press, 1954), p. 204.

[51] *Ibid.,* p. 207. Cf. Arnold and Caroline Rose, *America Divided: Minority Group Relations in the United States* (New York: Alfred A. Knopf, 1948), pp. 54-60; and

10. *Confusion of ends and means.* In the struggle for power and influence, religious groups are prone to lose sight of their basic religious values and objectives in efforts to win the struggle. "It is not the religious activities of a denomination . . . which cause other denominations . . . to regard it with suspicion; these, under our law of religious freedom, are respected and admired. It is the secular activities . . . which set other denominations . . . to eying it askance." [52] When the system of man's inner world of faith is extended to the outer world and imposed upon all mankind, disastrous effects inevitably occur. When Protestants see Catholicism as an energetic pressure group aiming at dominating the nation's social and political life, they become alarmed and attack the institution which seems more like a political machine seeking to perpetuate and strengthen itself than an ecclesiastical organization promoting men's spiritual welfare. They feel that the religious values of Catholicism have been subverted and what once were considered means toward ends have become ends of the organization. [53]

Thinking Catholics, on the other hand, tend to see Protestants as having a highly subjective religion. Catholics view their Church on earth as Christ, while Protestants consider Christ in the believer as comprising the universal church. Since Protestant authority is the Bible, Catholics consider them to be intellectually anarchical; they cannot find convincing answers in the Bible about certain topics. The Catholic believes he has an objective authority in his Church in contrast to the Protestant's religion of his own invention. The Catholic does not see Protestant denominations as separate branches on the same tree of Christian faith as Catholicism, but as a wholly different kind of growth. Many of them believe Protestants have idolized the nationalistic state or, even worse, individual opinion. [54] Although they comprise the largest American religious body, Catholics consider theirs a minority religion. When criticisms are directed against political involvements of their Church, the typical reaction in most Catholics is that they are unjust victims of bigotry. Both groups have a tendency in the struggle for power to focus attention more upon organizational means than upon their basic goals of spiritual welfare for persons.

No one of these ten causes serves as an explanation of all the issues in the controversy, but each throws some light upon them. Review of the issues and their causes will make their interrelationships clear to anyone at least nominally acquainted with American religion.

Karl Mannheim, *Ideology and Utopia* (New York: Harcourt, Brace and Co., 1949) p. 31.
[52] Sugrue, *A Catholic Speaks His Mind,* p. 20.
[53] *Ibid.,* pp. 23-24, 58-59, 63-64.
[54] Soper, "As Catholics See Us."

Jewish-Christian Tensions

Friction between Protestants and Catholics contributes to problems of
Jews, for it sharpens differences between the religious groups. American
Jews have often been targets of discrimination in employment, housing,
politics, business, higher education, resorts, clubs, and synagogue location.
A substantial proportion of Americans, especially in rural communities
where there are few Jews, have hostile attitudes toward Jews. Sociometric
analysis of roommate choices by preparatory school boys found ethnocentrism along broad religious lines. Protestants tended to choose Protestants, Catholics chose Catholics, and Jews chose Jews. Catholic and
Protestant exclusion of Jews was greater than their exclusion by Jews.
Each group had good insight into the social responses received from the
others.[55] Sociometric studies of other students have had similar findings.
At least in latent form, awaiting economic, social, psychological, or
political circumstances that might arouse it, anti-Semitism is "a most
peculiar disease" in America.[56]

There are relatively few important differences between liberal Judaism
and liberal Protestantism. Traditional patterns of Jewish religious organization have been accommodated to denominational pluralism and the
secular state, for Judaism has no central hierarchy; it is centered in
the local congregationally-governed synagogue or temple. Anti-Semitism
therefore is based chiefly upon economic and cultural factors. Religious
factors are important, nevertheless. By religion the Jew is a unique type
of out-group member in a dominantly Christian society. His religion is
both "strikingly different from Christianity and . . . the indispensable
foundation of Christianity."[57] Long after a secularized Jew's religious
fervor is gone, he is identified as a Jew. Even if he becomes a Christian,
he is likely to be designated a "converted Jew." This indicates that religion
is not the sole basis for Jewish identity and illustrates its intricate interrela-
tions with other cultural factors in the problem.

American anti-Semitism often has had a religious tinge. It has been led
by preachers like Gerald Winrod, William D. Herrstrom, and Gerald
L. K. Smith, who held anti-Semitic rallies in churches and published pam-
phlets, books, and periodicals like *The Defender Magazine* and *The Cross
and the Flag* "in the name of Christ." By calling itself "Christian" and
appealing to people's fears and frustrations, the anti-Semitic movement

---

[55] R. E. Goodnow and R. Tagiuri, "Religious Ethnocentrism and Its Recognition
Among Adolescent Boys," *Journal of Abnormal and Social Psychology,* 47 (Apr.
1952), 316-20.
[56] "The Fortune Survey," *Fortune,* 36, no. 4 (Oct. 1947), 5-6; and Carey McWilliams, *A Mask for Privilege* (Boston: Little, Brown, and Co., 1948), pp. 110-12.
[57] Henry Enoch Kagan, *Changing the Attitude of Christian Toward Jew* (New
York: Columbia University Press, 1952), p. 4.

gained followers among sincere Protestants and Catholics.[58] Groups like the Ku Klux Klan and Posse Comitatus use similar appeals.

A major difficulty anti-Semites face is the use of the Old Testament by both Christians and Jews. Most Jewish heroes are also Christian heroes, and Jesus was a Jew. Several techniques are used to overcome this difficulty. Some deny that Jesus was a Jew at all, saying "secondary meanings" have been given the term "Jew" in the past two centuries "by Yiddish propagandists." Others deny that any such thing as anti-Semitism really exists, reinterpreting the term until it loses all meaning. More common is the "device of the dishonest disclaimer," the denial that the writer is anti-Semitic. Some throw the burden for anti-Semitism back upon the Jews who are said to be themselves responsible for it. Substitutes like "Zionist" and "Khazar" are used so the term "Jew" will not appear with embarrassing frequency in their writings. Fear is aroused by linking Jews with Communism, bureaucracy, or whatever group, activity, or ideology may be the most unpopular or feared at the time. Names are twisted to sound Jewish ("Ike the Kike," Harry Solomon Truman," etc.), and parenthetical "real names" accompany references to "Jewish enemies disguised under Anglo-Saxon names" ("Sidney Hillman, or more correctly Schmuel Gilman"). Highly emotionalized language is used. Other anti-Semites, Jewish sources, and bogus "authorities" like the *Protocols of the Learned Elders of Zion* or the *Benjamin Franklin Prophecy* are often referred to. Innumerable other techniques and tricks are used in their clever hatemongering.[59]

Christian Sources of Anti-Semitism

Anti-Semitism is not fostered only by the "lunatic fringe"; it grows out of certain basic Christian teachings. The Jew has been persecuted because he rejected and crucified Jesus. Christians appropriated the Hebrew Scriptures, reinterpreting all blessings promised and bestowed upon Israel to apply to the Christian Church ("the true Israel"), while all curses, rebukes, and threats of punishment by God toward Israel were retained for the Jews.[60]

Roman Catholicism has opposed anti-Semitism in no uncertain terms. Yet its teachings that it is the only true Church, that all outside it need conversion, and that the only definite solution for the Jewish question is conversion to Christianity, make its position seem somewhat paradoxical.

---

[58] Roy, *Apostles of Discord*, pp. 26-117; and Wallace Stegner, "The Radio Priest and His Flock," in *The Aspirin Age, 1919-1941*, Isabel Leighton, ed. (New York: Simon and Schuster, 1949), pp. 232-57.

[59] Margaret L. Hartley, "The Subliterature of Hate in America," *Southwest Review*, 37 (Summer 1952), 177-90.

[60] Isacque Graeber, "The Truth About Anti-Semitism," *Social Action*, 12, no. 1 (Jan. 15, 1946), 2-11.

Some statements of neo-orthodox theologians like Karl Barth may be taken out of context to support anti-Semitism. Their condemnation of Jews as being under God's judgment is parallel to condemnation of all others, including Christians. Since this theology "is opposed to the kind of Christianity which involves acceptance of the 'only right religious tenets,' . . . and is instead concerned solely with man's acceptance or non-acceptance of Jesus as the Christ," any anti-Semitic tendencies in neo-orthodoxy flow out of the Jews' rejection of "the Christ of faith," not out of anti-Judaism as such.[61] Liberal Christianity places itself on a higher plane than Judaism, but it allows no room for the view that the Jews crucified Jesus. Rather, "he is crucified by any and all men who deny the principle of love of God and neighbor." [62]

References to ancient Judaism continually crop up in Christian sermons, Sunday school lessons, and publications. Anti-Semitism is unconsciously fostered when biased hearsay accounts are passed on with little attempt to discover such things as what the Torah (Law) really means to Jews. They forget the New Testament teaching that Jesus laid down his life and insist that Jews killed him. They identify sinful, despicable Bible characters as Jews and gloss over the Jewish identity of those who are honored and respected.[63]

Certain issues both produce and reflect tensions between Judaism and Christianity. In the early Christian era they competed with each other in efforts to win converts. Christian spokesmen "proved" their religion's superiority by God's rejection of the Jews as the chosen people. Some of their efforts involved extreme misinterpretations of Judaism and of Bible doctrines. Jesus' criticisms of fellow-Jews were exaggerated; the Jewish people as a whole were charged with the entire guilt for his crucifixion, and Jews were even described as atheists. The early competition for converts has been replaced by one-sided evangelism. Contemporary Judaism is not a proselyting religion, but both Protestantism and Catholicism try to win Jewish converts. Some premillennial fundamentalists disseminate propaganda to Jews on a world-wide basis, believing that they will not win many, if any, converts immediately, but that after the "rapture" of Christians "to meet the Lord in the air" many Jews (some specify exactly 144,000 because of Rev. 7:4) will be converted during a great tribulation immediately preceding Christ's utopian millennial kingdom on earth. Some Jews are flattered to receive recognition as God's chosen people, even if in a strange theological framework; others are offended at being made special targets of evangelism by Jews for Jesus or Christian "missions to the Jews."

[61] A. Roy Eckardt, *Christianity and the Children of Israel* (New York: King's Crown Press, 1948), pp. 66-73, 83-89. Quotation from pp. 86-87. Eckardt prefers the term "neo-Reformation" to refer to "neo-orthodox" theology.
[62] *Ibid.*, p. 117.
[63] See James A. Pike, "The Roots of Bias," *Look*, 25, no. 6 (Mar. 14, 1961), 49-52.

Ultimately, not Christianity but "Christians" are responsible for injustices against Jews which are presumed by their perpetrators to be in the name of Christ. Acceptance of the principle of generic vengeance—that Jews are cursed and persecuted because they killed Christ—is diametrically opposed to the Christian principle of individual dignity and accountability as well as to the Gospel of Love emphasized throughout the New Testament.

Theories of Anti-Semitism

Anti-Semitism in many ways resembles the problems associated with racial tensions (Chapter 17). Its causes have been traced to ethnocentrism, the authoritarian personality, projection of guilt feelings, frustration-aggression complexes, and subconscious rebellion against Christian moral restraints or Christ's claims upon the individual. Many social-psychological theories of anti-Semitism emphasize religion. One of the most common is that Jew-hatred is at root a concealed hatred of Christianity, for it attacks universal love and attempts to replace it with the principle of force in human relations. Perhaps this is why anti-Semitism thrives among fundamentalists; it is most common among those who consciously or subconsciously feel Christianity as a repression. The Chosen People concept is easily twisted into the belief that Jews try to destroy Gentiles. The over-aggressiveness of many Jews, a result of minority status, is easily interpreted as a threat to the majority. Intentional propaganda against Jews may be interpreted as a result of their symbolizing Christ, democracy, and progressivism.[64]

Anti-Semitism is based upon a vicious circle. Jews experience prejudice and discrimination because of their separateness from other population segments; separateness in turn results largely from prejudice and discrimination. The Jew symbolizes the fact that Christianity is still a live root of western civilization. He is used as a theological testimony to the truth of Christian tradition.[65] Religion is hence related to anti-Semitism in far more significant ways than the mere identity of its target in terms of religious affiliation.

A major reason for the distinctiveness of anti-Semitism in contrast to other forms of ethnocentric prejudice is the fact that Jews have lived as a distinct group among other self-centered groups and not on a territory

---

[64] Excellent surveys of the causes of anti-Semitism which provide much of the basis for this discussion are Arnold and Caroline Rose, *America Divided*, pp. 277-306; George E. Simpson and J. Milton Yinger, *Racial and Cultural Minorities*, rev. ed. (New York: Harper and Brothers, 1958), pp. 288-345; and James Parkes, *An Enemy of the People* (Baltimore: Penguin Books, 1946), pp. 82-110. Many additional theories and sources directly linked with religion are presented in these references.

[65] Salo W. Baron, *Modern Nationalism and Religion* (New York: Harper and Brothers, 1947), p. 269.

of their own. Conscious Jewish nationalism is evident in Zionism, but unconscious Jewish nationalism has resulted from the dilemma of not having a country of their own until modern Israel was founded. Internationalism among Jews is motivated by their peculiar group identification and an ecological distribution that points to internationalism as a solution to their problem. If no one had his own country, the Jewish situation would not be peculiar. Unaware of the unconscious nationalistic motivations underlying their internationalism, Jews fail to understand the peculiar nationalistic nature of anti-Semitic counter-nationalisms.[66] The Zionist movement has not eliminated the suspicion that Jewish brotherhood encourages cheating gentiles, for it has added the belief that Jews have divided loyalties and would not hesitate to betray our nation in any showdown between the two. Zionism, largely a result of anti-Semitism, has thus become another source of rationalizations supporting anti-Semitism.[67] Unhappiness with Israel's policies intensifies tensions.

Disapproval of Jewish-Christian marriages by both religions helps divide Jew from gentile. Yet efforts to prevent intermarriage are not a serious source of misunderstanding when they are mutually believed desirable and do not imply degradation of each other. They have repercussions, however, in resentment against Jews for "clannishness," opposition to social equality in college organizations, and related problems. Tensions also appear in discussion and action pertinent to religion in public education. Jews generally object to segregation of children by released time classes; they believe it promotes sectarianism and anti-Semitism. They protest against Christmas celebrations and use of Christmas carols in public schools. "There are few issues on which Jewish organizations in the United States are more united than on opposition to religion in the public schools." [68] This often makes them oppose the practices of dominant Protestant or Catholic groups.

Contemporary Judaism: Results of Prejudice

Many characteristics of American Judaism may be traced partly or entirely to opposition it has faced as a minority religion. It is largely an ethnic religion, preserving social solidarity and identity in a society which once threatened to submerge Jews into a general assimilated population.[69] As a denomination parallel to others, it is taking the form

---

[66] Gustav Ichheiser, "The Jews and Anti-Semitism," *Sociometry,* 9 (Feb. 1946), 92-108.

[67] T. Valentine Parker, *American Protestantism: An Appraisal* (New York: Philosophical Library, 1956), pp. 45-46.

[68] Leo Pfeffer, "Issues That Divide," *Journal of Social Issues,* 12, no. 3 (1956), 21-39. Quotation on p. 31.

[69] Marshall Sklare, *Conservative Judaism* (Glencoe, Ill.: The Free Press, 1955), pp. 32-40. Cf. Kurt H. Wolff, "An Elementary Syllabus in the Sociology of the Jews,"

of "symbolic Judaism," whose chief function is to serve as a symbol for the expression of Jewishness. The post-war revival of Judaism was less a religious revival than a reflection of the fact that in the new suburban environment Jews attend the synagogue primarily to feel and express their Jewishness, rather than to practice the traditional religion. Emerging symbolic Judaism grows out of the middle class acculturation of Jews who are relatively devoid of religious traditions.[70]

Contemporary Judaism strongly resists total assimilation. Jewish college students are less inclined than Catholics and Protestants to favor inter-marriage. Many attach high importance to religion in the sense of over-all Jewish identification, but their religious beliefs are often highly secularized.[71] Pluralism, which attempts to maintain social integration and cultural identity without an ecological base, is favored over assimila-tionism. Completion of the natural history cycle of ethnic relations, which includes the stages of isolation, competition, conflict, accommoda-tion, and finally complete assimilation, appears unlikely in the near future of American Judaism.[72] Its survival as an ethnic group is largely a result of centuries of persecution and deep roots of religious tradition. It is primarily family ritual that has transmitted the distinctive re-ligious beliefs and practices of Judaism from generation to generation.[73]

Personality damage in the victim of anti-Semitism is difficult to evalu-ate. The Jewish child called a "Christ-killer" by gentile playmates who have heard that Jews crucified Jesus may never forget the incident. He may never understand how the crucifixion, which has caused him per-sonal humiliation, can be considered by Christians an occasion in which love and grace were poured out upon a sinful world. The suffering that results from discrimination in housing, employment, and education may be far less injurious than the poisoned minds of both victims and ag-gressors. Callousness to suffering and insensitivity to injustice among the majority cause among the victim minority a sense of insecurity, super-

---

Social Forces, 24 (May 1946), 451-61; M. Zborowski, "The Children of the Cove-nant," *Social Forces,* 29 (May 1951), 351-64; and Lawrence H. Fuchs, *The Political Behavior of American Jews* (Glencoe, Ill.: Free Press, 1956), for additional sugges-tions of the consequences of anti-Semitism.

[70] Herbert J. Gans, "American Jewry: Present and Future," *Commentary,* 21 (May 1956), 422-30; and Herbert J. Gans, "The Future of American Jewry," *Commentary,* 21 (June 1956), 555-63.

[71] Alvin Scodel, "Some Correlates of Different Degrees of Jewish Identification in Jewish College Students," *Journal of Social Psychology,* 49 (Feb. 1959), 87-94; and Joseph Maier and William Spinrad, "Comparison of Religious Beliefs and Practices of Jewish, Catholic, and Protestant Students," *Phylon,* 18, no. 4 (1957), 355-60.

[72] Amitai Etzioni, "The Ghetto—A Re-Evaluation," *Social Forces,* 37 (Mar. 1959), 255-62; and Aaron Antonovsky, "Aspects of New Haven Jewry: A Sociological Study," *YIVO Annual of Jewish Social Science,* 10 (1956), 128-64.

[73] David R. Mace, *Hebrew Marriage: A Sociological Study* (New York: Philosoph-ical Library, 1953), pp. 264-65.

sensitive imagining of slights when none were intended, and even a desire to run away from self and the noblest traditions of one's people.[74] Prejudice and discrimination thus multiply themselves in a vicious circle harmful to all who are involved.

Until recently there have been very few sociologists of the Jews, although Jewish sociologists have been numerous. This, too, reflects anti-Jewish prejudice. Many entered the social sciences to escape their Jewish identity and promote the equality of all people. To study Jews would have exposed them to the possibility of being identified as "Jewish Jews." Third generation Jews, however, feel a need for identification with a group smaller than the total society; in America this need is met by church membership and pride in ancestors. Younger Jewish scholars therefore are less reluctant to make sociological studies of the Jews.[75]

Some Jews react to discrimination and prejudice with self-hatred (Jewish anti-Semitism). Seeking to escape from their Jewishness, some move into non-Jewish neighborhoods and avoid all customs that might identify them as Jews. Some merely sever ties with traditional Judaism; others try to forget their Jewishness entirely and become part of the non-Jewish environment.[76]

Jewish Christian Converts

Thousands of Jews through the centuries have become Christians. Almost invariably the convert was cut off from his Jewish people as if dead. In some cases conversion was preceded by an inner breach with the synagogue; joining a Christian church merely completed assimilation into the gentile population. In 1866 the Hebrew Christian Alliance was founded in England; extended to North America in 1915, it developed into the International Hebrew Christian Alliance in 1925. It has stood consistently for the principle that it is wrong to expect Jewish converts to identify themselves with and lose themselves in the nation in which they live, for Christianity is not bound to any nationality. Jewish Christian Synagogues and Hebrew Christian churches have been established in many communities as a result of anti-Semitism among Christians, the wish to preserve national identity, the desire to be Christian witnesses to Jewry, and the dislike of much theology and practice in gentile churches. Jewish converts have been suspected of seeking material gain by transfering religious allegiance; others have been put on a pedestal

---

[74] Louis Finkelstein, "The Jewish Minority," in *Group Relations and Group Antagonisms*, R. M. MacIver, ed. (New York: Peter Smith, 1951), pp. 85-95.

[75] Seymour Lipset, "Jewish Sociologists and Sociologists of the Jews," *Jewish Social Studies*, 17 (July 1955), 177-78.

[76] Abraham I. Golomb, "Jewish Self-Hatred," *YIVO Annual of Jewish Social Science*, 1 (1946), 250-59.

and regarded as a sort of "circus curiosity." Slights against Jews and other wounds have pushed many of them away from other churches to those of the Hebrew Christians.

Contrary to popular opinion, modern Christian missions to Jews have been at least as successful as the average Christian mission program.[77] Yet only a minute proportion of those subjected to Christian propaganda have become Christians. Informal but effective isolation from old social contacts has resulted from conversion. Many converts could not adjust to gentile churches and social surroundings, slipped away from their church membership, or even lost faith in Christ. Name-changing, intermarriage with gentiles, and removal from Jewish neighborhoods are common among Hebrew Christians.[78]

Hebrew Christians claim to combine the best elements of Christianity and Judaism, ideologically identifying with both. They see their conversion as a fulfillment of the Jewish religion, accepting Jesus as Christ, the Jewish Messiah. The Hebrew Christian Church enables a more natural and gradual move away from Judaism than is possible in a gentile church. The social features associated with Christianity cannot take hold in the short period of time that is sometimes involved in the religious aspects of conversion. Marginality between two religions creates confusion for the persons involved and restricts their social relations. The Hebrew Christian movement is primarily a protest against the position that the Jewish convert is typically forced to occupy. It uses history and theology to justify its attempt to transform the social world into one in which the Jewish convert will have recognized status. Second generation Jewish Christians tend to become almost exclusively Christian, so Hebrew Christians can be considered an intermediate step in the conversion of Jews to Christianity.[79]

Reduction of Interfaith Tensions

Anti-Semitism has been condemned by the major Christian denominations; all try to promote human brotherhood and reduce anti-Jewish prejudice.[80] To what extent their efforts are fruitful is not fully known. They appear to have been crowned with partial success, but it remains to be seen what would happen if serious economic depression or other

---

[77] H. L. Ellison, "The Church and the Hebrew Christian," in *The Church and the Jewish People,* Göte Hedenquist, ed. (London: Edinburgh House Press, 1954), pp. 143-67.

[78] Ira O. Glick, "The Hebrew Christians: A Marginal Religious Group," in *The Jews,* Marshall Sklare, ed. (Glencoe, Ill.: The Free Press, 1958), pp. 415-31.

[79] *Ibid.*

[80] Kagan, *Changing the Attitude of Christian Toward Jew,* pp. 10-11; Yves M.-J. Congar, O.P., *The Catholic Church and the Race Question* (Paris: UNESCO, 1953), pp. 50-55; W. A. Visser 't Hooft, *The Ecumenical Movement and the Racial Problem* (Paris: UNESCO, 1954), pp. 35-41.

adverse conditions were to produce the kind of environment that is a breeding place for intergroup strife.

It is commonly assumed that, with increasing efforts of all major religious groups to produce a society in which members apply religious principles to daily life, religious bigotry and tensions will naturally decline. This may not be the case at all. However, some sources of increased tolerance and reconciliation may be exploited by those who wish to spread good will. We shall briefly mention a few which stress improvements in Catholic, Protestant, and Jewish religious education as a means toward reduced interfaith friction.

1. *Recognition of elements shared.* Barnes has stated that "upon at least 95 per cent of all matters of strictly religious import, Catholics and Protestants were in agreement." [81]   This percentage may be too high, but all three religions overlap. Knowledge of common doctrines, hymns, attitudes, limitations, goals, and problems can increase appreciative understanding of each group by the others and thus diminish feelings of antagonism that exist.

2. *Recognition of the contributions of others.* In the heat of conflict each protagonist tends to magnify the others' supposed flaws, inconsistencies, and sins. Such acts obscure common enemies like Communistic atheism and "godless materialism" and prevent recognition of needs by each for the others. The contributions of Catholicism, particularly, to American life and culture have been overlooked. They include a faithful habit of worship, an accompanying emphasis upon symbolism that promotes a spirit of trust in the supernatural, numerous welfare activities, and influence on vast numbers of Catholic immigrants. Had it not been for the Catholic Church's control over these foreign-speaking lower-class immigrants in American cities, crime might have been much more widespread than it actually was.[82] Catholic, Protestant, and Jewish churches help maintain order and perform other valuable functions in society.

3. *Self-recognition and correction of faults and shortcomings.* Each group has inconsistencies relevant to the very issues of the controversy. Protestants insist upon church-state separation while they benefit from tax exemption and uphold clergymen's right to act as representatives of the state in performing weddings. Catholics insist divorce is sinful, yet do not consider the divorce of a convert married before conversion a violation of this principle. Each group assumes ulterior motives are behind the others' programs. Thus, Catholic efforts to integrate the races are considered by many Protestants to be a shrewd piece of propaganda

---

[81] Harry Elmer Barnes, *Social Institutions* (New York: Prentice-Hall, Inc., 1942), p. 684.

[82] William Sweet, *The American Churches* (New York: Abingdon-Cokesbury Press, 1947), pp. 93-109.

when cultural conditions make this policy a source of Negro conversions. Similarly, Catholic welfare is criticized as simply providing opportunity for proselyting. When Protestants engage in the same types of agricultural, medical, educational, or social work activities in foreign missions for the purpose of winning converts, the motives they condemn as "opportunistic" in Catholicism are applauded as prudent in their own behavior. Catholic desires to win a majority of the population to their religion are designated by Protestants as evidence of a "Catholic plot." Yet the devout Protestant desires few things more than to have his nation become predominantly Christian in his sense of that term.

4. *Recognition of social change.* The need to change many methods in order to meet new conditions effectively can promote interfaith relations. It can lead to internal adjustments which adopt and adapt contributions from the others.

5. *Removal of faulty images.* Each needs to recognize the inadequacy and often gross inaccuracy of estimates made of each other's religious position. As ignorance breaks down, mutual respect and understanding are promoted. Constructive dialogue between groups is a basic element in improved intergroup relations. The typical American receives much of his information about religions other than his own from sources in his own denomination rather than from representatives of the other religion. The opportunity for bias under such circumstances is great; a warped perspective is inevitable.

Churches are improving their religious education in this respect. Sharp distinctions between Christians and Jews are beginning to erode; rabbis are admitted into some ministerial associations and exchange pulpits with Christian ministers. Christians increasingly recognize their Hebrew heritage. Yet "the general influence of religious education . . . and of religious worship is to predispose those who share in it to view their Jewish neighbors with an unfriendly eye; and their Christian convictions form a well-watered seed-bed for the instillation of antisemitic prejudice from other sources." [83]   The type of religious education experienced by Christians in learning about Jewish customs reflected in the Bible is related to their attitudes toward Jews. An experiment tested the efficiency of various educational approaches aimed at reducing Christians' prejudice against Jews. The *indirect group method,* in which the rabbi instructor transmitted information under favorable circumstances without specific mention of anti-Jewish prejudices and without encouraging students to speak of their own experiences with or personal attitudes toward Jews, neither reduced nor increased anti-Jewish prejudice. A *direct group method,* which included dynamic participation of students as a group with their Jewish instructor in discussions of anti-Jewish attitudes, per-

---

[83] James W. Parkes, *Judaism and Christianity* (Chicago: University of Chicago Press, 1948), p. 176.

mitting correction of misinformation about Jews by the instructor and a type of group catharsis for hostility as students evaluated their own experiences and attitudes, was much more effective. Attitude scale scores became more favorable toward Jews; values about them were reoriented. When the indirect method was combined with a *focused private interview* of the student with the rabbi instructor on contemporary Christian-Jewish relations, the results were less favorable than those of the direct method.[84]

Many efforts by Jewish agencies like the Anti-Defamation League to reduce anti-Semitism may have latent consequences which have the opposite effect. Refuting accusations, clinics to deny specific anti-Jewish rumors, and disproof literature to counteract anti-Semitic propaganda sometimes furnish enemies of the Jews with ammunition. Straightforward information to create a favorable stereotype of Jews and to expose anti-Semitic motives, goals, associations, and sources of funds appears more effective.[85]

The prospects for improved mutual understanding of Protestants, Catholics, and Jews are bright. On most great social issues their basic convictions are the same.[86] Events have clearly indicated, however, that education alone is insufficient to solve the intense problems of interfaith relations. It helps crush prejudices in some persons but strengthens those of others. It also makes differences more clear and prominent. Religious education therefore needs to be supplemented by "education in action" which involves "learning by doing" in cooperative enterprises.

6. *Cooperation.* If Catholics, Protestants, and Jews could work together more often in the role of church member as equals to promote community welfare and attain spiritual goals, they would be more likely to recognize wholesome qualities in their co-religionists and to speak of their work in terms of *we, our,* and *us.* When this occurs, common bonds of in-group feeling are developed which go beyond the denominational lines that divide the groups.[87] Such cooperation is possible in efforts to curb the advance of secularization, promote a mutual spirit of brotherhood and respect for all men, defend the religiously-minded minority against the repercussions from attacks on other minorities, and oppose evil in society or a specific community. Distrust increases with strangeness, tolerance with familiarity. Cultural pluralism provides a framework

---

[84] Kagan, *Changing the Attitude of Christian Toward Jew.*

[85] Solomon A. Fineberg, "Strategy of Error," *Contemporary Jewish Record,* 8 (Feb. 1945), 25-30.

[86] Benson Y. Landis, "Protestants and Catholics," *Commonweal,* 42 (July 27, 1945), 356-58; Robert McAfee Brown, "A Step Forward in Catholic-Protestant Understanding," *Christianity and Crisis,* 17 (Apr. 1, 1957), 35-38; and Robert D. Cross, "Changing Image of Catholicism in America," *Yale Review,* 48 (June 1959), 562-75.

[87] Faris, "Sociology of Religious Strife."

for such cooperation. Democracy itself is, in a sense, a "universal faith" with a creative "spiritual" basis.[88]

The chief agency attempting to combine the approaches of education and cooperation between the major faiths is the National Conference of Christians and Jews (NCCJ) founded in 1928. In February 1983 it had 77 regional offices serving as human relations centers. Its purposes are expressed in its by-laws as the promotion of "justice, amity, understanding and cooperation among Protestants, Catholics, and Jews," and the analysis, moderation, and finally elimination of intergroup prejudices in a social order dominated by "the religious ideals of brotherhood and justice." Research, education, conferences, workshops, and coordination of community efforts to reduce prejudice are at the heart of its program. It created the international Religious News Service in 1934.

Conclusion

Our discussion has shown that conflict between Protestantism, Catholicism, and Judaism is very extensive, highly complex, and greatly variegated. Interfaith conflict arises largely from traditional attitudes of each faith toward the others—attitudes formed in historical situations considerably different from current circumstances. Today the conflicts are complicated by many new factors, such as differences in members' relative socioeconomic positions, rural and urban backgrounds, length of residence in America, and minority or majority social status. Pressures of a changing society have influenced interfaith relations—pressures associated with such trends and conditions as industrialization, urbanization, the rising level of living, changes in the status of the respective ethnic groups, physical mobility, struggles between institutions, conflicting norms in American life, and the increasing sophistication of American people. Conflict between the faiths cannot be ascribed merely to differences in religious doctrines, although such differences are important.

American interfaith conflict is a hodgepodge of many contradictory tendencies. None of the major faiths is neatly organized in a set position with regard to the others. Inside each are pronounced differences in outlook toward other groups—differences ranging from bitter hostility to avid cooperation. Movements toward increased tolerance and cooperation are found alongside of movements representing severe discord. The picture is complicated and lines along which relations are being established are frequently confused.

It is impossible to foretell how interfaith conflict will move in the future, since it will be compounded out of multitudes of adjustments

[88] Frederick Mayer, "The Meaning of Religion and Education," *The Personalist,* 40 (Jan. 1959), 41-53.

along numerous lines of unpredictable events. We may surmise that it will continue to adjust to the emerging pattern of integrated American life. The principles of democracy, the crystallizing of national values, the increasingly interdependent economic and social adjustments of all people, and the growing acceptance of cultural pluralism will set the framework of action for the religious faiths. Internal changes in all churches will result; their relationships to each other will be modified accordingly.

Selected References

Billington, Ray Allen, *The Protestant Crusade, 1800–1860: A Study of the Origins of American Nativism.* Chicago: Quadrangle Books, 1974 (Macmillan, 1938). Anti-Catholicism which emerged from Protestant fears that democratic institutions would crumble as a result of Roman Catholic values and Catholic immigration.

Glock, Charles Y., and Rodney Stark, *Christian Beliefs and Anti-Semitism.* New York: Harper and Row, 1966. A major study based on survey research (note strengths and weaknesses identified in book reviews in religious and social science journals).

Hager, Don J., Charles Y. Glock, and Isidor Chein, eds., "Religious Conflict in the United States," *Journal of Social Issues*, 12, no. 3 (1956), 1–67. Six articles analyzing religious conflict, especially Protestant-Catholic tensions.

Kane, John J., *Catholic-Protestant Conflicts in America.* Chicago: Henry Regnery Co., 1955. An excellent survey and analysis by a Catholic sociologist which can serve as a basis for further research.

Menendez, Albert J., ed., *The Best of Church & State 1948–1975.* Silver Spring, Md.: Americans United for Separation of Church and State, 1975. Articles, editorials, news stories, and reviews selected from *Church & State* magazine.

Moore, Edmund A., *A Catholic Runs for President.* New York: Ronald Press Co., 1956. An analysis of the 1928 campaign in which Al Smith, a Catholic, was the Democratic candidate.

Olson, Bernhard E., *Faith and Prejudice: Intergroup Problems in Protestant Curricula.* New Haven: Yale University Press, 1963. Analysis of how church-school materials treat other racial, ethnic, and religious groups.

Raab, Earl, ed., *Religious Conflict in America: Studies in the Problems Beyond Bigotry.* Garden City, N.Y.: Anchor Books, 1964. Analyses of modern interreligious conflicts.

Richardson, Herbert, ed., *New Religions and Mental Health: Understanding the Issues.* New York: Edwin Mellen Press, 1980. Papers on mental health, proposed legislation against cults, special-interest groups, conversion, judicial decisions, and governmental studies related to legislative regulation of religious practices.

Tussman, Joseph, *The Supreme Court on Church and State.* New York: Oxford University Press, 1962. A historical summary of decisions and supporting arguments pertinent to the First Amendment.

Underwood, Kenneth, *Protestant and Catholic.* Boston: Beacon Press, 1957. A thorough socio-historical study of Catholic-Protestant relations in Holyoke, Mass., which has shifted from a Protestant to a Catholic population majority.

△ Chapter 13

Inter-Institutional Conflict

The conflict of the church with other institutions is referred to directly or indirectly in nearly every chapter of this book. It is a natural result of the fact that the church is located in the world, its members are members also of other institutions, and its values are not always those dominant in society. (The enmity of God and His people against "the world" and the "heathenism" surrounding them is a major theme of the Bible.)

A prominent area of historical conflict between the church and other institutions is that of religion and science. Much of this chapter is devoted to an analysis and interpretation of the relationships between these two general (diffused-symbolic) institutions. A briefer survey of some aspects of conflict between the church and other institutions follows. The chapter concludes with some general sources and results of conflict within the church as well as between it and other institutions.

The Conflict Between Science and Religion

The voluminous amount of literature pertaining to the relationship of science and religion is best classified as philosophical, theological, or literary. Our purpose is to indicate the reality of the conflict, its nature and causes, some reciprocal interrelationships, and trends. This obviously supplements the sections on scientific method and the sociology of religion in Chapter 1. The church's dependence upon the results of scientific research and technology will be omitted from this survey.[1]

The Presence of Conflict

The history of science is replete with illustrations of church opposition to new discoveries and interpretations (theories) of the universe. Recent events in the controversy have centered upon such topics as Biblical miracles, the deluge, the age of the earth, free will versus determinism, cultural relativity, the inherent sinfulness or goodness of man, the antiquity of man, demonism, birth control, and educational philosophy. Christian controversy with science has not involved Catholics alone, as anti-Catholics sometimes imply. Disputation relevant to Darwinism, evolution in public schools, and other issues for over a century have been prominently centered in Protestantism. The most spectacular incident was the trial in 1925 of John T. Scopes who violated Tennessee law in a public school by teaching the Darwinian theory of evolution there. Recent conflicts over teaching creationism and evolution pick up the battle but are also a reaction against the dogmatism of evolutionism. Generally, the greater the degree of theological orthodoxy, the greater the opposition to science; the greater the degree of theological liberalism, the greater the acceptance of science.[2] The conflict between fundamentalists and modernists, as we saw in Chapter 11, is partly a struggle between modern science and orthodox religion.

Some who have studied the relationships between science and religion insist that the conflict is only between theology and science. It is indeed on the level of intellectual, hence theological, concepts that the clashes have most often occurred. Organized conflict, however, involves social groups, and theology is always a direct or indirect outgrowth of religious institutions; it represents an effort to systematize and make intelligible the beliefs and norms which are at the core of the institution. Thus, whether the conflict with science is conceived of as involving religion, theology, or ecclesiastical bodies, the church as a social institution is directly involved.

The Nature of the Conflict

Whether or not a *necessary* conflict exists, churches' efforts to defend their faith have led many to believe that science and religion are es-

---

[1] E.g., a concordance to the Revised Standard Version of the Bible was rapidly compiled by use of electronic equipment (Clair M. Cook, "Automation Comes to the Bible," *Christian Century*, 74 [July 24, 1957], 892-94), and social research methodology is applied increasingly to problems of churches. The role of scientific planning in church work and personnel needs for it are dealt with in *Search* (New York: National Council of Churches, 1960).

[2] Harry Elmer Barnes' discussions of science and religion are organized around this

sentially antagonistic and irreconcilable. Some scholars have attempted to identify religion with ignorance. As a result, the acceptable sphere of religion in modern life continually shrinks as walls of ignorance are pushed back; many believe that nothing will remain mysterious. God and the supernatural are relegated to the sphere of religion in this dualistic division of the universe. They gradually diminish in size and significance as scientific knowledge expands. Religion "becomes the sign and symbol of an intellectual naïveté quite uncongenial to the scientific temper,— an atavistic emotional response to life's more serious difficulties." [3] Religious laymen, sensing this, become anti-intellectual and anti-scientific.[4] They do not recognize the tendency of scientific endeavor to enlarge the scope of man's recognized ignorance by raising more problems than are solved.

Dogmatic religion, whether based on revelations of a papal or a paper authority, invariably opposes advances in knowledge which contradict conventional interpretations and dogma. Allegiance to tradition predominates over allegiance to truth in such groups.[5] The same type of dogmatism is found among "scientific fundamentalists" who have made a cult of scientism by believing that no convictions arrived at through nonempirical scientific methods can be accepted as truth.[6] They have made science an ultimate value instead of a means toward ends. Conflict between them and those who recognize the validity of knowledge from nonempirical sources is inevitable.

The postulates undergirding religious investigation are based ultimately upon some form of revelation and usually are easy to identify, but those which are basic to science are seldom listed explicitly and are difficult to discover. Scientists usually postulate the existence of a universe with a more-or-less deterministic type of order that can be observed verifiably. Most American religionists assume the free will of persons who act independently; paradoxically, they also assume the sovereignty of an omnipotent, omniscient, and omnipresent God. Social scientists generally as-

---

type of continuum. See *The Twilight of Christianity* (New York: The Vanguard Press, 1929), pp. 301-72; and *Social Institutions in an Era of World Upheaval* (New York: Prentice-Hall, Inc., 1942), pp. 693-99.

[3] Arthur L. Swift, Jr., *New Frontiers of Religion* (New York: The Macmillan Co., 1938), p. 63.

[4] Merle Curti, "Intellectuals and Other People," *American Historical Review,* 60 (Jan. 1955), 259-82.

[5] Charles A. Ellwood, *The World's Need of Christ* (New York: Abingdon-Cokesbury Press, 1940), p. 81.

[6] H. Richard Rasmusson, "The Preacher Talks to the Man of Science," *Scientific Monthly,* 79 (Dec. 1954), 392-94. Even the "objectivity" of sociologists of religion is sometimes basically a "thinly disguised antipathy to organized religion and to nonmaterialist philosophies" which is a product of "advocates of the modern cult . . . [of] dogmatic secularism," according to Thomas Ford Hoult in a book review, *American Sociological Review,* 24 (Oct. 1959), 735.

sume man's personality and behavior to be in some sense determined by heredity and environment, while Christianity assumes a human mind which is both independent and capable of physical-social conditioning.[7] Private worlds of experience are admissible as theological evidence, but generally they are excluded from science because they are nonempirical.

The progress of science undermines the literal authority of the scriptures of any religious faith, for science recognizes the authority only of experience (including empirical observation) and the accompanying reason which interprets experience. In addition, all scriptures reflect the "science" of the place and time in which they were written. Dogmatic religion tends to adhere to these reflections of an out-moded science as well as to the basic message of faith imparted by them. Conflict with science is an inevitable result.[8] Belief in the universality of the Genesis flood and in God's creation of distinct, immutable species has been a source of much antagonism between churches and schools.

The scientist's devotion to the scientific method has latent consequences which sometimes intrude upon his non-scientific statuses and roles and cause him to reject religion. In his role of scientist, he is concerned with limited, accessible segments of nature, relies upon a relatively small range of techniques for discovering truth, strives for an objectivity that prevents his personal interest from intruding, accepts only verifiable generalizations, and operates within an ethical framework that is not obviously religious. Hence he is likely to reject non-scientific techniques for the discovery of truth even in his non-scientific roles, to fail to see the larger problems of life that deal with ultimate reality, to reject personal involvement in religion, to refuse empirically non-verifiable generalizations, and to believe that religion is not necessary for an ethical system that can help produce a better life for man in society. The habits and sentiments of the scientist thus tend to limit his perspective, making him fail to appreciate the benefits of personal religion.[9]

Science and religion have been considered competitors in showing men how to get what they want. This conflict is often won by science; tangible results of research and invention are readily discernible, while the results of appeals to Deity usually must be explained in other-worldly terms that often fail to satisfy those whose desires are not granted. As man's knowledge expands, church leaders are compelled to make their teachings about the material universe, physical and mental health, and other subjects conform to or harmonize with modern science.

[7] George Y. Rusk, "The Spiritual Nature of Man: A Study in Catholic Psychology," *Journal of Social Psychology*, 27 (May 1948), 151-58. See the references to Father Coogan presented in Chapter 17.

[8] Edgar S. Brightman, *A Philosophy of Religion* (New York: Prentice-Hall, Inc., 1940), p. 483.

[9] Gordon W. Allport, *The Individual and His Religion* (New York: The Macmillan Co., 1951), pp. 111-13.

The conflict of religion with science is thus partly a conflict between idealized and practical methods of meeting man's needs.

A major source of conflict has been the resistance of organized religion to change. Vested interests, such as the priesthood, try to maintain their power when it is encroached upon by scientific developments. Resistance to change is ingrained in institutions. When supernatural sanctions are added to ordinary resistance to innovation, conservatism or obscurantism inevitably results. While one effect is to control the rapidity of change and thus to increase the stability of society, another is to hinder many beneficial changes resulting from scientific endeavor. Perhaps the only condition under which science inevitably conflicts with religion is that in which religion is under the tutelage of magic and superstition, absolutely unwilling to change any details of creed and conduct.[10]

At the root of the controversy are two different normative systems which have two different theories of knowledge, two different approaches to reality, two different methods of extending knowledge, and two different attitudes of mind.[11] Only as doctrinal differences are reconciled can there be true peace between science and religion.

Differences Between Science and Religion

Contrasting characteristics of empirical science and conventional religion accentuate the conflict, but they also provide a basis for understanding it and reconciling the two modes of dealing with the universe. The ten listed may be considered as a composite description of constructed or ideal types which are never found in reality in pure form but which describe tendencies drawn out to their logical extremes. The Judeo-Christian religion is the focus of discussion; conclusions do not apply to all religions. The definition of science presented in Chapter 1 is implicit. The specific items overlap, yet at the core of each is a distinct thought.[12]

1. The method of science is basically inductive, while that of religion, with its emphasis upon revelation, is typically deductive.

2. Science stresses objectivity with impartial observation and de-

---

10 L. L. Bernard, "The Sociological Interpretation of Religion," *Journal of Religion*, 18 (Jan. 1938), 1-18.

11 Dennis A. Routh, "The Churches and Science," *Hibbert Journal*, 52 (Oct. 1953), 56-64. Cf. William L. Kolb, "Values, Positivism, and the Functional Theory of Religion: The Growth of a Moral Dilemma," *Social Forces*, 31 (May 1953), 305-11.

12 This discussion is partly based upon Clifford Kirkpatrick, *Religion in Human Affairs* (New York: John Wiley and Sons, 1929), pp. 469-72. Kirkpatrick views the contrasts between science and religion as demonstrating their incompatibility; here they are presented as helping to establish and clarify their compatibility.

scription. Religion assumes a definite value position that precludes complete objectivity by encouraging identification of and cooperation with that which is believed to be "good" and opposition to all that is "evil."

3. Science is basically agnostic, doubting new or isolated findings and emphasizing the need for empirical observation and verification before new ideas are accepted. Religion is based upon faith in God; "without faith it is impossible to please him" (Heb. 11:6; cf. Hab. 2:4). In religion faith is a virtue and doubt a vice.

4. Science seeks naturalistic explanations of phenomena; it denies mystery except as it denotes ignorance which science may ultimately dispel. Religion stresses supernatural explanations. Mystery is prominent in it because revelation of some things is lacking, there are problems of interpreting what has been revealed, and supernatural beings or forces are believed to intervene in many events.

5. Science stresses continuous variation, seeing degrees of "black and white" in most subjects. Religion leans toward discrete variables, like dichotomies of saints and sinners, good and evil, God and mammon, and light and darkness, which imply an either-or classification.

6. The chief emphasis of science is upon description of empirically observable facts; that of religion is upon subjective and normative evaluations.

7. Science is dynamic, ever-changing, and hence never final or absolute in its conclusions. The heart of revealed religion is relatively static and dogmatic, for its basic concepts and principles are revealed on a "once for all" basis. The growth of science hence involves accumulation of new "facts" and theories; that of religion involves accumulation of new interpretations and adaptation of old revelations.

8. Science is deterministic, tending to believe that all events are mechanistic results of antecedent conditions. Religion is voluntaristic, emphasizing man's free will to choose among alternatives of action.

9. The values of science come from non-scientific sources; ultimate values cannot originate in science. Religion is a basic source of the major values of society. Science also views values as relative in time and place, while religious groups consider their basic values to be absolute, unchangeable, and universal.

10. In conclusion, science is basically a method of study and investigation, while religion is basically a system of faith and worship. This summarizes the other contrasting features. When science is defined as a body of systematized knowledge, the bounds of that knowledge are delimited by reference to the scientific method in order to distinguish scientific from philosophical, theological, or other types of knowledge. Similarly, if science is defined in terms of its areas or fields of knowledge (chemistry, economics, zoology, etc.), these, too, are determined by reference to the scientific method.

Since science and religion have different functions in society, they can be allies for the common good whenever neither dogmatically commits itself to an antiquated, exclusive, and unadjustable tradition or to a belief that it has the sole key to man's successful adjustment to the universe. A survey of semi-religious ethical values in science, its limitations, and interrelationships between science and religion will make this more clear.

Moral Aspects of Science

Many have been led by the conflict to think science is opposed to all religion and hence *ipso facto* immoral. Actually, science is neither moral nor immoral. It is amoral because it is but a method which involves searching for truth whatever the truth may be. Yet the scientific approach to phenomena shares many ethical characteristics with the Judeo-Christian religion.[13]

An outstanding characteristic of science is its demand for *intellectual honesty*. Making findings conform to a preconceived conclusion by "doctoring" data is a form of cheating, lying, or dishonesty that is not tolerated in science. When prejudices cause one to stack up all available evidence on one side of a controversial subject and consciously or subconsciously to ignore or slight evidence on the other side, he has lost his scientific competence.[14]   Similarly, when consciousness of personal bias is so strong that one "leans over backwards" to overcome or correct it, he is in danger of presenting an inaccurate picture and hence being dishonest. It is especially important in the sociology of religion to be aware of this demand, for most men have definite convictions with respect to religion. These may be so strong that they intrude at the most inopportune moments if there is no conscious attempt to control them. Discussions and studies of religion which are uncontrolled by the ethics of science tend to generate more heat than light. Rigid adherence to scientific methodology and careful use of scientific instruments and techniques help control distorting prejudices.

Love of truth is a basic characteristic of science. Surely the Founder of the Christian Church who said, "I am the truth" (John 14:6; cf. John 1:14, 17; 8:32; 18:37), would not object to attempts to learn the truth!

The scientific method involves *self-discipline*. To look objectively at certain subjects requires so much effort that scientists constantly emphasize the need to verify their findings. Verification by replication of one's own experiments is desirable; it is even better to have others with

---

[13] Earl E. Speicher, "Religious Aspects of Scientific Method," *Crozer Quarterly*, 9 (Apr. 1932), 189-202.

[14] Yet this technique is frequently used by many propagators of Christianity. Can science actually be more ethical than they?

different value systems repeat one's observations. In the ultimate sense, there is no such thing as "complete objectivity," yet it is a goal toward which scientists strive in their observations and conclusions.

The scientific method implies *humility*. Scientific facts are constantly accumulating; theories and laws of science change with new evidence. Human knowledge is so vast that one can never know more than a portion of all that there is to be known even in his own discipline. The scientist therefore is willing for his findings to be replaced by new scientific facts and interpretations and to let his work be superseded by more recent data. He avoids sweeping generalizations and carefully qualifies conclusions in a humility that all too often is lacking in religious leaders who claim to follow the teachings of a Bible that emphasizes humility as one of the greatest virtues (Proverbs 11:2; 29:23; Micah 6:8; Luke 14:11; James 4:6-10; etc.).

In addition to the "method-mores" that relate to the scientist's status and role as scientist are "welfare-mores" which relate to the basic goals of his work.[15] He aims to promote the welfare of mankind. Shared ethical-moral principles help science and religion to complement each other.

Limitations of Science

Science has other limitations besides those imposed by the ethics of scientific procedure. It is based upon certain assumptions or postulates which are themselves unproved and usually unprovable. Scientists are limited to the tools and techniques that are available. In few major areas is this more significant than in the sociology of religion. Measuring instruments and tools for analysis of religious phenomena are neither numerous nor highly developed. Minute distinctions, which often are crucial in testing hypotheses, cannot be measured accurately with crude instruments.

Science cannot explain behavior in the ultimate sense of accounting for its first causes. When they scientifically state causes, scientists deal with sequences of events and basically describe successive stages of a routine of experience. Since each phenomenon or stage has a host of antecedents stretching back into the unobservable past, scientists can never arrive at the final, ultimate, original cause of any event. From their incomplete evidence they can theorize about such matters as the origin of the universe, but they cannot certainly determine the exact time or precise manner in which it took place. Circumstantial evidence is not proof. Yet some concept of causation underlies all man's conscious activity. The goal of causal knowledge is never fully attained, but efforts can bring one from many converging angles ever nearer to it.

---

[15] Read Bain, "The Scientist and His Values," *Social Forces,* 31 (Dec. 1952), 106-9.

When it is empirical, the concept of causality helps avoid pitfalls of irrational thinking by ordering thoughts about complex problems into a logical system which is susceptible to test by facts.[16]   A major goal of science is to improve the tools and techniques that make it possible to discover such cause-and-effect relationships so events can be predicted more accurately and controlled more completely.

Because of these and other limitations, scientific facts, principles, and laws of one generation are errors in the next. For as knowledge accumulates and becomes more precise, testing of relationships is possible and new facts are discovered which modify the old theories and laws. That which is verified today may be modified tomorrow, and that which is unverified today may be confirmed tomorrow. Scientific knowledge is not absolute; in common with all human knowledge, it is relative to time and place. Scientific generalizations are neither certainly true nor certainly false; they are only more reliable or less reliable, depending upon the evidence that supports them.

Science also is limited by the time it takes to arrive at scientific conclusions. When man is faced with the necessity for an immediate or early choice of action, it usually is impossible to set up experiments to test the consequences of alternatives before him. Experiments in the social sciences and hence in the church may take a generation or more to complete. Because of the high value placed on human life and freedom it often is impossible to experiment at all. Hence there is a need to deliberate, experiment, and reflect upon problems *before* such pressures come. Long-range basic research (pure science) and the analysis of practical problems (applied science) when correlated with one another, often through theories of the middle range, offer great promise for the future of man and the church.

Numerous religious concepts and beliefs are outside the realm of contemporary science. This does not invalidate these concepts and beliefs, for science "does not bring a total revelation or outlook upon the universe." [17] To be sure, the goal of science is nothing less than complete interpretation of the universe, but that goal is an ideal marking out a path scientists take, not a destination they shall reach. The more a scientist knows, the more he knows he does not know. There is a measure of truth to the aphorism that a specialized scholar has learned "more and more about less and less until he knows everything about nothing."

Science cannot determine the values toward which man ought to strive. If it is given goals, it can assist in testing their validity and consistency and in choosing effective means for working toward them. Thus, if

---

[16] R. M. MacIver, *Social Causation* (Boston: Ginn and Co., 1942), pp. 5, 384-85, 392-93.

[17] Benjamin Ginzburg, "Science," *Encyclopaedia of the Social Sciences* (New York: The Macmillan Co., 1937), 13, p. 602.

it is desired to prolong human life, scientists can indicate effects of overeating, tobacco, alcohol, or pessimism upon longevity and thus provide a basis for religious ethics. Although science may contribute to ethical systems, it is not concerned primarily with the morality of either the end or the means; it simply tells which means will be effective to a given end. Science tells what is, not what ought to be, except as it interprets values already provided for it. The ultimate source of moral values is not in science but, from the Hebrew-Christian perspective, in God.

Interrelations of Science and Religion

Both science and religion search for truth. The search of each usually benefits both functionally. "Religion, like science, demands objectivity, reality. If it does not represent objective reality, it cannot endure any more than science." [18] " . . . all untrammelled scientific investigation, no matter how dangerous to religion some of its stages may have seemed for the time to be, has invariably resulted in the highest good both of religion and of science." [19] To insist revelation can come only through one source or by one method, whether that of sensory experience, intuition, logical analysis, or the sifting of tradition, would seriously impoverish mankind. Interactive use of these methods of science and religion to discover truth contributes much to man's welfare.[20] Science and religion share such basic values as honesty, humility, self-discipline, faith (though in different objects), the use of logical powers of the intellect, belief in the worth of man, and faith in the significance of his enterprises. Science is rooted in a moral order which religion helps create and sustain.

As science developed, it exposed many superstitions and errors of traditional religion. Natural explanations of phenomena gradually have replaced many supernatural ones. The very substance of modernistic religion is taken from the philosophy of science.[21] Christ has been attributed with having a "scientific spirit" because "He verified his fundamental assumption that this is a spiritual world by inductive methods. Thus he passes the test of scientific consistency by living and demonstrating his theory." [22] Hence, it may appear that science has completely triumphed over religion until all that remains is its old institutional

[18] Ellwood, *The World's Need of Christ*, p. 220.
[19] Andrew D. White, *A History of the Warfare of Science with Theology in Christendom* (New York: George Braziller, 1955), p. viii.
[20] Hornell Hart, "The Alienation of Science and Religion," *Christian Century*, 60 (June 30, 1943), 764-65.
[21] Herbert W. Schneider, *Religion in Twentieth-Century America* (Cambridge: Harvard University Press, 1952), pp. 119-20.
[22] A. J. Todd, *The Scientific Spirit and Social Work* (New York: The Macmillan Co., 1919), p. 75.

structure with entirely new normative content. Such, however, is not the case. Those who adhere to traditional norms basic in America's dominant religions recognize that not the basic beliefs but only interpretations of them have changed. This helps account for the strength of contemporary religion. While some desire that science become the basis for religion,[23] others see science as a servant of religion,[24] and still others consider them allies.[25] The last of these viewpoints increasingly dominates twentieth-century American thought.

Neither science nor religion has been mortally wounded. Both have arisen out of the conflict with an ability to work together which might not have developed without it. Many associations help to correlate science and religion. They include the American Scientific Affiliation, a large association of committed Christians who are scientists; Conference on Science, Philosophy, and Religion; Institute on Religion in an Age of Science; Unity-in-Diversity Council (International Cooperation); and the Creation Research Society, which emphasizes scientific investigations and interpretations that support the literal six-day creation account of the Bible.[26]

The highly visible conflict between religion and science has often obscured the more significant and less visible indirect cooperative relationships between them.[27] Yet there is never complete agreement by all scientists on the interpretations of scientific findings, and there is far from complete agreement of theologians on interpretations of the faith "once and for all delivered to the saints." Hence we cannot expect complete agreement between scientists and religionists in the many areas of overlapping interest; their conflict is perpetual.

The horizons of scientific analysis will be extended as scientists devote increased time and attention to religious phenomena and institutions; simultaneously, churches will benefit from the knowledge science can give about such topics as the extent to which religious ideals are reached, the best methods for achieving them, and the ways in which social processes operates in and with relationship to religious institutions.[28]

---

[23] "Religion can at best only hope to generalize upon the basis of the facts which have already been discovered by science." Barnes, *The Twilight of Christianity*, p. 364.

[24] "Far from destroying the humanities or religion, science may, in fact, actually strengthen religious aspirations and make them capable of realization." Herbert A. Bloch, *Disorganization: Personal and Social* (New York: Alfred A. Knopf, 1952), p. 601.

[25] Warren Weaver, "Science and Faith," *Christian Century* 72 (Jan. 5, 1955), 10-13; and Rasmusson, "The Preacher Talks to the Man of Science."

[26] The purpose and addresses of most are in Denise S. Akey, ed., *1983 Encyclopedia of Associations* (Detroit: Gale Research Co., 1982).

[27] Robert K. Merton, *Social Theory and Social Structure*, rev. ed. (Glencoe, Ill.: The Free Press, 1957), p. 606.

[28] See E. P. Pfatteicher, *Christian Social Science* (New York: Falcon Press, 1933), p. 4: "Every new development in the social science of today has forced me back upon the consciousness of the splendid heritage that is mine in the Word of God and

"The intelligent Christian . . . will not fear the intrusion of science into the sanctuary." [29]

If religious revelations indeed are from an omniscient God, there can be no true conflict of revealed truth with facts discovered by science. But there can be, as in the past, a great deal of disagreement growing out of the interpretations both of science and revealed religion. In the future when facts of science, as contrasted to hypotheses and theories, conflict with teachings of the church, it is likely that endeavors to adjust interpretations of the churches' teachings to the facts will be increased. A flexible religion which adapts to meet changing conditions of man in a changing society is likely to dominate the religious scene.[30]

> "Science will give us knowledge of the facts, but there it must stop. Religion, depending on science in the realm of fact, dares us and encourages us to press on into the realm of value. It is only superstition, ignorant both of the facts of religion and of its values, that will think to sever this union of the disciplined mind and the courageous heart." [31]

Conflict of the Church with Other Institutions

The church competes with other institutions for the time of mutual members. School programs are often a focus of tension between religious and educational leaders, for a great deal of time is demanded for class-related and extra-curricular activities, and church calendars include numerous youth activities afternoons and evenings during the week as well as on weekends. Leaders of sect-type congregations sometimes have a "chip on the shoulder" and feel that school authorities deliberately undermine their program. In rural communities where there is relatively little organized leisure aside from church and school programs, agreements sometimes are made between community leaders to have a calendar of events that leaves one or two evenings each week exclusively for the churches. Competing churches in a small community may thus be compelled to cooperate with one another in opposition to what they conceive to be a common danger.

When institutions compete with one another for people's time, it is easy to forget the welfare of individuals because of concern for the in-

---

in the application of that Word by men of heroic mould as social scientists with a starting point, a center and a goal."

[29] Joseph H. Fichter, S.J., *Social Relations in the Urban Parish* (Chicago: University of Chicago Press, 1954), p. 5.

[30] J. Milton Yinger, "Some Consequences of the Scientific Study of Religion," *Religious Education,* 52 (Sept.-Oct. 1957), 350-54.

[31] George Hedley, *The Superstitions of the Irreligious* (New York: The Macmillan Co., 1951), pp. 41-42. Reprinted by permission.

stitution as such. Struggles between institutional factions injure persons who become unfortunate victims caught between conflicting group identifications. The church may compete with family life, especially if families are divided religiously among two or more congregations. Family plans for joint leisure-time projects sometimes are thwarted by the church's demand that one or more members participate in certain activities, spend time alone for devotional purposes, or engage in certain religious rites and ceremonies. Protestant churches often demand much time from the faithful member; in many families there are few evenings when no member is engaged either in attending a church-related activity or serving the church through a committee or other sub-group.[32]

The church, especially if it is near the sect-end of the church-sect continuum, opposes conditions in other institutions which it considers evil. The centuries-long struggle between political and ecclesiastical institutions is well known. States have contested and decreased the churches' power by limiting the number and functions of the clergy, secularizing the law and courts, disbanding ecclesiastical orders, dispossessing the church of land, and laicizing marriage and other relationships. American churches have engaged in numerous political activities in their struggle for power (Chapter 14). In their current relationships with government, they try either to influence government, to ignore it, or else to withdraw from the society which they believe to be secular and evil.

In most religious bodies, compromise with the social order predominates. It is neither attacked nor evaded but is accepted with little serious ethical evaluation. Identification of the church with its culture is made obvious by its foreign missionary programs (Chapter 9). It has often been assumed by American missionaries that all moral and cultural values at variance with those predominant in America are non-Christian. Christianity at home has conformed itself to the social order; abroad it has become an element at war with the culture.

Churches in conflict with certain culture traits often adopt inconsistent systems of values. Baptists in the South condemn mixed bathing; their northern brethren sponsor "splash parties" for church youth. Just the opposite applies to tobacco: Most northern Baptist groups condemn its use as sinful, while many southern Baptists not only condone it but directly depend upon it for their livelihood. Within sect-type bodies there have been pronounced differences in attitudes toward the use of cosmetics and jewelry, attendance at movies, and recreational activities like "joy-riding" on Sundays. Increasing urbanization, economic prosperity, and associated trends have markedly diminished the condemnation of such practices even by Holiness and Pentecostal sects. Such contrasting reactions

---

[32] To what extent this divides or unites the family and strengthens or weakens the church we can only speculate upon until systematic research has probed the problem carefully. Lenski's Detroit area studies indicate that white Protestant churches weaken kinship ties while Catholicism uses or strengthens them. Gerhard Lenski, *The Religious Factor* (Garden City, N.Y.: Doubleday and Co., 1961), pp. 219-27.

toward the social order and established culture traits not only reflect conflict between the church and society but also provide a basis for internal strife in many groups.

By attacking evils, church groups attempt to make their ethical and moral systems clear to the world. They seldom are sufficiently united to make themselves widely heard. Furthermore, they generally criticize only minor culture traits and rarely aim their criticism at basic culture patterns.[33] The church generally takes for granted the economic and political systems that dominate its culture. Christianity has "failed to keep Christ at its head and to demand the imitation of Christ in every department of life, whether of individuals or of communities." [34]

By some of its programs the church unwittingly tends to undermine social institutions of which it approves. An outstanding illustration is the parochial and Christian day school movement. If strong in the community, these private schools contribute to a progressive deterioration of the public school system. Churches may state that they believe in maintaining the public school system, but a latent effect of supporting schools for constituents is the weakening of public schools. By duplicating personnel, facilities, and equipment, the church weakens the entire educational system.[35] (Protagonists, however, point to monetary savings for public schools, the virtues of educational competition, and the issue of "distributive justice," claiming private schools should share the benefits of tax funds.)

The church is often contrasted to other institutions as the carrier of religion, the counterpart or even equivalent of life itself, aloof from secular interests and yet running through all the activities of individuals in every phase of life. However, organized religion sometimes takes sides among the various parties of secular strife and, in the struggle for power, becomes equivalent to an equal, involved in a multitude of changing "secular" relationships while theoretically rejecting such involvement.[36] The church may hence be either an ally or an opponent of other institutions and institutionalized practices. Ideally it is above direct partisanship because of its emphasis upon a sacred ethic that undergirds all of life, criticizes evil, and praises good wherever it is found.

Conclusions about Religious Conflict

In these three chapters we have seen that churches must share people, space, wealth, and other elements with each other and with other institu-

---

[33] The Social Gospel movement is in some respects an outstanding exception, but its emphases have not pervaded a majority of local churches and church members even within a single denomination (Chapter 6).

[34] Ellwood, *The World's Need of Christ*, p. 100.

[35] For a case in point see editorial, "Churches Undermine Public Schools," *Christian Century*, 66 (June 29, 1949), 782.

[36] Georg Simmel, *The Web of Group-Affiliations*, trans. Reinhard Bendix (Glencoe, Ill.: The Free Press, 1955), p. 158.

tions. Since these resources often are limited, conflict is a frequent result. "Appeasement or isolation. Gradualism, ameliorism, Fabianism, reform; or revolution. Conciliation or aggression. These are words which recur throughout all studies of conflict. Religious institutions are no more immune to the problems of strategy which they represent than are economic or political institutions."[37] Let us summarize some conclusions about sources and functions of church conflict.

Sources of Conflict

The cultural setting plays a significant role both in producing a conflict and shaping the direction it takes. American emphasis upon freedom of speech, the press, assembly, and religion creates a fertile breeding ground for religious dissension. It has caused an almost constant emergence of relatively minor tensions and thus has prevented the extreme revolutionary upheavals that disrupt all social life. As religious groups show varying degrees of resistance to America's rapid social change, cultural lag becomes a basis for tensions within and sometimes between them. Vested interests stubbornly resist change; progressive members, chiefly from the younger generation, stimulate it. Generational conflict thus accentuates religious strife. Cultural conflicts are involved in many struggles. Rural interests are arrayed versus urban, old world versus new, middle class versus lower or upper class, and ethnic group versus ethnic group. Such tensions are so important that it is often impossible to determine how much church strife is basically religious.

Conditions like war, prosperity, and depression in society influence the churches' conflict and cooperation. In Middletown the great depression increased the competition between churches and decreased their cooperativeness even within the same denomination.[38] A non-cooperative, competitive spirit in churches is perhaps greatest in communities with insufficient population and wealth to provide them with adequate support.

Group identifications lead persons to take sides in conflicts and help determine their intensity. When numerous cross pressures are involved because of the many roles people in complex societies play, group conflicts are likely to be weakened by competing loyalties. When there is no internal conflict because a person's meaningful social classifications coincide, his ego-investments in the religious group are likely to produce intense involvement in the conflict and the strife is apt to be severe.

---

[37] Jessie Bernard, "The Sociological Study of Conflict," in The International Sociological Association, *The Nature of Conflict* (Paris: UNESCO, 1957), pp. 33-117. Quotation from p. 94.
[38] Robert S. Lynd and Helen Merrell Lynd, *Middletown in Transition* (New York: Harcourt, Brace and Co., 1937), pp. 303-4.

Informal groupings within a church's formal structure significantly influence the behavior of members and of the institution. When social distance between conflicting groups is small, the intensity of conflict tends to be great; the most severe conflicts generally occur between cliques within a church.[39] A struggle for status and power by individual leaders is often involved in religious conflict. Personal ambitions and jealousies intrude and are easily confounded with the struggle of rival principles or organizations.

Values that go deeper than mere group identification are supremely involved in religious conflict. Religious bodies are founded upon fundamental premises which may be "impregnably ensconced in an enveloping blanket of silence." [40] Religious values are a source of consensus, solidarity, and integration but also of misunderstanding, cleavage, and disintegration in society. Radical variations are found in the value-orientations of churches. When people are strongly committed to their religious groups and values, conflict on religious grounds may be intense; when religious allegiance is trivial with only a low intensity of conviction, conflict seldom is severe. Divergent values within or between churches about beliefs and functions of the group are a significant source of tension.[41] Inability to communicate effectively also reflects group values and contributes to conflict. Key words and phrases reflect basic theological orientations and are used to identify the orthodoxy or lack of orthodoxy of leaders; in effect these become catchwords, slogans, and labels used in conflict. Quaker emphasis upon "concern," fundamentalist use of "born again," and neo-orthodox employment of "transcendence" help members in each group to recognize friend and foe. All cultural conflicts are conflicts of meanings.[42] This is even more true in religious struggles than in most other types.

Much religious conflict has been based upon oversimplified dichotomizations. Christians have engaged in many controversies involving antitheses which, when viewed objectively, appear to be false. The controversies are concerned with justification by works or by faith; belief in church leaders or in the Bible as the ultimate authority; belief in the priesthood of clergymen only or in the priesthood of believers; belief in

[39] Robert H. Jordan, "Social Functions of the Churches in Oakville," *Sociology and Social Research,* 40 (Nov.-Dec. 1955), 107-11; James S. Coleman, "Social Cleavage and Religious Conflict," *Journal of Social Issues,* 12, no. 3 (1956), 44-56; and Walter Firey, "Informal Organization and the Theory of Schism," *American Sociological Review,* 13 (Feb. 1948), 15-24.

[40] William Albig, *Modern Public Opinion* (New York: McGraw-Hill Book Co., 1956), p. 247.

[41] Robin M. Williams, Jr., "Religion, Value-Orientations, and Intergroup Conflict," *Journal of Social Issues,* 12, no. 3 (1956), 12-20.

[42] Thorsten Sellin, *Culture Conflict and Crime* (New York: Social Science Research Council, Bulletin 41, 1938), pp. 59-60.

transubstantiation or in mere symbolism in Communion; and belief in the gospel or in the church as the means of salvation.[43] Reconciliation of normative conflicts like these can come through improved insights into the validity of both alternatives, clarifying the fact that mediating positions are possible.

Religious conflict presents special problems that are usually absent in conflict of other types. The private nature of personal religious experience threatens established groups by making possible the creation of new creeds or new interpretations of doctrine. Family transmission of religious beliefs from one generation to the next builds religious differences into children at an early age and tends to create different types of personalities as well as to perpetuate conflicting sets of values. Association in religious groups and dissociation from others make it easy for sociopsychological mechanisms of projection, rationalization, and compensation to create suspicions, fears, mistrust, and hostility within each group against others from which it is isolated.[44]

Functional Effects of Conflict

Religious conflict cannot be understood without appreciation of its functions. An outstanding result is cooperation for mutual offensive and defensive action. The social identification that grows out of mystical experiences shared by members of a religious fellowship not only draws them together but makes them feel sorry for and sometimes hostile toward others in society who are not in the inner circle.[45] Conflict is often necessary to maintain group unity; sometimes in the church's struggle against "the world, the flesh, and the devil," it is convenient to have tangibly perceptible opponents. Aggressive behavior against heresy has strengthened the consciousness of unity in Roman Catholicism, and Protestantism's protests have frequently held groups together that otherwise were on the verge of splintering.[46]

Conflict forces contending groups to make their claims clear. Consequently these claims will often be modified by them. Sometimes tensions are relieved and minority opinions recognized through the social interaction which occurs in conflict.

A comparison of three types of organizations—those which were in conflict with others, those in competition, and those faced with neither conflict nor competition—found several effects of conflict upon organi-

---

[43] Humphrey Whistler, *False Alternatives at the Reformation* (London: S.P.C.K., 1957).

[44] Coleman, "Social Cleavage and Religious Conflict."

[45] Anton T. Boisen, "Divided Protestantism in a Midwest County: A Study in the Natural History of Organized Religion," *Journal of Religion*, 20 (Oct. 1940), 359-81.

[46] Georg Simmel, *Conflict*, trans. Kurt H. Wolff (Glencoe. Ill.: The Free Press, 1955), pp. 97-98.

zations. Conflicting groups more actively pursued their goals than those faced only with competition; the latter were more active than those without competition. Groups faced with opposition were more likely to develop a complex organizational structure, to have frequent meetings, especially for executive or planning purposes, to have flexible activities and techniques, and to have a strong cohesive relationship among members.[47] Similar effects of conflict seem to occur in local churches. If they are unaware of any competitors or foes, socially or spiritually conceived, they may have a gradually declining program and influence. American denominations generally are stronger than corresponding bodies in Europe. This characteristic undoubtedly reflects differences in economic and physical resources and the heterogeneous population of America, but it is also due to the strength of competing religious bodies. "If all the people in the world were to be converted to Christianity, the organized Christian church would also wither."[48] Opposition often strengthens the church.

Selected References

Barr, David L., and Nicholas Piediscalzi, eds., *The Bible in American Education.* Philadelphia: Fortress Press, 1982. Essays on the dialectical relationship between the Bible and various educational and cultural forces during American history.

Burtt, E. A., "The Value Presuppositions of Science," *Bulletin of the Atomic Scientists,* 13 (Mar. 1957), 99–106. Postulates of science.

Casserley, J. V. Langmead, *Morals and Man in the Social Sciences.* New York: Longmans, Green and Co., 1951. Relationships between Christian theology and social science, with analyses of relativism, freedom and determinism, rationality, and other basic concepts of social science theory.

DeSanto, Charles P., Calvin Redekop, and William L. Smith-Hinds, eds., *A Reader in Sociology: Christian Perspectives.* Scottdale, Pa.: Herald Press, 1980. Several of the 40 chapters deal with tensions related to Christian values in the profession and discipline of sociology.

Journal of the American Scientific Affiliation. A scholarly quarterly devoted to the interface of all the sciences with Christianity (P.O. Box J, Ipswich, MA 01938).

Lehman, Edward C., Jr., "The Scholarly Perspective and Religious Commitment," *Sociological Analysis,* 33, no. 4 (Winter 1972), 199–213. Research on the relationships between scholarly orientation and religiosity among urban midwestern college faculty members.

Lyon, David, *Karl Marx: A Christian Assessment of His Life and Thought.* Downers Grove, Ill.: Inter-Varsity Press, 1981. An appreciative biographical analysis and commentary which relates Marx's background and thought to Christianity.

MacKay, Donald M., *The Clockwork Image: A Christian Perspective on Science.*

[47] Arnold M. Rose, "Voluntary Associations under Conditions of Competition and Conflict," *Social Forces,* 34 (Dec. 1955), 159-63. The study was of 91 voluntary organizations "of all types" in Minneapolis and St. Paul.

[48] Arnold W. Green, *Sociology: An Analysis of Life in Modern Society* (New York: McGraw-Hill Book Co., 1952), p. 45.

Downers Grove, Ill.: Inter-Varsity Press, 1974. A brain physiologist's critique which includes a strong indictment of the "nothing buttery" fallacy (ontological reductionism) often found in the sciences.

Maduro, Otto, *Religion and Social Conflicts*, trans. Richard R. Barr. Maryknoll, N.Y.: Orbis Books, 1982. A sociological analysis of the diverse involvements of religion, especially Latin American Catholicism, in liberation struggles using Marxist theoretical models.

Moberg, David O., "The Encounter of Scientific and Religious Values Pertinent to Man's Spiritual Nature," *Sociological Analysis*, 28, no. 1 (Spring 1967), 22–33. Neglect of the spiritual nature of humanity in the social sciences, evidences for its ontological reality, and suggestions for scientific research that recognizes it.

Phenix, Philip H., "The Scientific Faith of American Scientists," *Christian Scholar*, 38 (June 1955), 99–113. The presuppositions and credo of scientists and their implications for religious faith.

Simmel, Georg, *Conflict and the Web of Group Affiliations*, trans. Kurt H. Wolff. New York: Free Press, 1955. A theoretical analysis of social characteristics, causes, and effects of conflict.

Part Six: *Inter-Institutional Relations*

🏛 Chapter 14

The Church and Other Institutions

In the previous chapter, as well as in other earlier passages we have dealt with relationships between the church and such institutions as social work, business, schools, and science; later we shall note some connections between the church and various institutions and professions devoted to health and the treatment of social problems. Here we shall briefly survey relationships of the church to the family and government. Although the social dynamics of institutional interaction are complex and their effects very difficult to evaluate, no complete picture of the church as a social institution is possible without examining them. We shall see that religious norms and action have a profound influence upon other institutions and that this influence is reciprocal.

The Church and the Family

An intimate connection prevails between the dominant American religions and family values. The Catholic conception of marriage as a sacrament which confers God's grace, the Protestant view that it is a holy ordinance, and the Jewish belief that it is *kodosh*, a sacred consecration, all endow marriage with a sacred element. They imply that, ideally, husband and wife serve God; they thus promote the stability of marriage. Widely diffused biblical teachings and church interpretations about marriage, sexual intercourse, children's and parents' responsibilities, as well as concepts of God as the Heavenly Father, the church as the bride of Christ, mankind as a brotherhood, and all believers as spiritual brethren, have clear implications for the family. Although traditional religious teachings about the position of women in the home and in the church have encouraged patriarchalism and kept women subordinate to men, American society is moving gradually toward increased equality between the sexes. Even Mormons, whose religion upholds patriarchal authority as a divine endowment necessary in this life and in eternity, are moving toward more lenient child discipline and democratic interaction in most family matters.[1]

By promoting self-examination through prayer and forgiveness in the humble recognition that all men are imperfect, the Judeo-Christian religion "helps overcome those egocentric blocks to happiness in marriage that are well-nigh universal." [2] Its educational influence, ideals, and constructive fellowship promote wholesome motivations, neighborliness, and loving service that shifts attention from self to others. Solutions to family problems are discovered in church discussion groups and therapeutic counseling. Yet, with all these potential contributions, it is very difficult to assess the consequences of religion for family life and vice versa. Research has been piecemeal, directed chiefly toward subjects that are the most susceptible to statistical analysis. It is therefore dangerous to make conclusive statements about the importance of religion to family life. Many of the data included in this section are based upon inference and hence should be taken as suggestive and tentative, not as definitive findings on the relationships between religion and various aspects of family life.

Religious Life-Cycle Rituals

Church membership is more significant to many Americans for its rites of passage than for any other specific function. These ceremonies symbolize changed roles and statuses as people pass into each new stage of life.[3] Varying with the ethnic group, life-cycle rituals help to cushion shock, carry people over crises and symbolize passage from one stage of life to the next. They recognize changes of status and associated problems connected with the realities of the life-cycle, and they do so with "no pretence that the rhythms of mood, of guilt, of unhappiness and

---

[1] Victor A. Christopherson, "An Investigation of Patriarchal Authority in the Mormon Family," *Marriage and Family Living,* 18 (Nov. 1956), 328-33.

[2] James A. Peterson, *Education for Marriage* (New York: Charles Scribner's Sons, 1956), p. 332.

[3] Arnold van Gennep, *The Rites of Passage* (Chicago: University of Chicago Press, 1960).

grief do not occur." [4] They remind men that what happened in the past will happen again and again in the future. The church calendar with its sacred days and special religious festivities embodies the "social memory." All life-cycle ceremonials involve commitment, either by one who undergoes the rite or by him on whose behalf it is experienced. This commitment may be to a social group like the church, or to God who is worshiped by it.[5]

In Roman Catholicism and certain Protestant churches, life-cycle rituals have been elevated to the position of *sacraments*—ceremonies which confer or symbolize a special measure of divine favor or grace upon worthy recipients. Violation or omission of the rituals is avoided for fear of incurring God's wrath or not securing clear and safe passage from one stage of life to the next. In other groups these rituals are *ordinances* with only symbolic value. In still others they are simple ceremonies with little or no direct spiritual significance. Formal ritualism is almost completely absent among groups like the Quakers which consider biblical ceremonies to have only spiritual meanings that need not or cannot be conveyed by tangible rituals.

Orthodox Jews perhaps have the most complete set of life-cycle rituals in America. Special rites are associated with circumcision, naming of babies, redemption of the first-born, beginning religious education, the *bar mitzvah* ceremony for boys entering adolescence, betrothal, the groom's reading of the Torah in the synogogue on the Sabbath before his wedding, marriage, confession and proclamation of faith at the time of death, the funeral, interment, and mourning.[6]

Infant baptism symbolizes the sacredness of life, the need for cleansing from sin, the belief that children are a gift from God, and parental responsibility for children's spiritual life. Acts of purification, anointing, and circumcision have similar subsidiary significance. They publicly declare the child's parenthood, dedicate him to the faith of his parents, add his name to the church register, and emphasize the importance of the church to the family and individual. Some Christian groups condemn infant baptism because they believe baptism symbolizes entrance into a new life of union with Christ which can take place only by conscious choice of a responsible person. Criticizing belief in the magical efficacy of baptism as a detrimental superstition, many substitute a religious ceremony of christening or infant dedication.

Confirmation, first communion, and "believer's baptism" symbolically liberate the child from parental responsibility for salvation and establish

---

[4] Everett C. Hughes, *Cycles and Turning Points* (New York: National Council of the Episcopal Church, n.d.), p. 6.

[5] *Ibid.*, pp. 8-14.

[6] Sister Frances Jerome Woods, C.D.P., *Cultural Values of American Ethnic Groups* (New York: Harper and Brothers, 1956), pp. 52-55.

personal responsibility for religious faith and practice. Departmental promotions in the church school are associated with the child's life stages; his religious instruction is adapted to meet changes in interests and capacities. These promotions usually are automatic and bear little symbolic meaning, but they are analogous to the puberty ceremonies associated with changing roles and statuses in preliterate societies.

Through the wedding ceremony the church tries to impress the husband and wife with the sacredness, religious responsibilities, and permanence of marriage. Social pressures, tradition, and esthetic values cause most Americans to value church weddings highly even if they have no formal church connections. Of 54,748 couples married in 1949 only 9.5 per cent had been married in civil ceremonies. Most civil weddings occurred among the divorced, partners of different religious faiths who were prohibited a church wedding, older persons with no great emotional needs for a church wedding, persons with no formal religious affiliation, and hasty marriages.[7]

Nearly all Americans wish to have their funeral service conducted by a church representative.[8] The funeral is the opposite of initiation ceremonies. The deceased is considered a member of the group until conventional rituals formally recognize through public farewell and disposal that he has departed. Survivors often consider the funeral as a symbol of initiation into the heavenly community. Ceremonials connected with bereavement distract attention from sorrow, releasing or relaxing tensions and helping to carry them back into the mainstream of life.[9] The exact significance of the funeral varies greatly between and even within denominations. To some it symbolizes the end of life; to others, the beginning of eternal life. Some comfort the bereaved by reminding them of the deceased's religious faith and devotion, future in heaven, and end of earthly trials. Others comfort by drawing sorrowing minds away from the deceased to God. Some try to cover up and minimize demonstrations of grief; others institutionalize mourning and decree that the widowed wear black garments for a specified period of time. Ceremonial is often "the cloak that warms the freezing heart, . . . the firm stick upon which the trembling limbs may lean; . . . a house in which one may decently hide himself until he has the strength and courage to face the world again." [10]

---

[7] J. V. DePorte, "Civil Marriage in New York State, Apart from New York City," *American Sociological Review,* 17 (Apr. 1952), 232-34.

[8] Even admitted agnostics desire a churchly atmosphere or a minister to say a few words on behalf of the deceased. James H. S. Bossard and Eleanor S. Boll, *Ritual in Family Living* (Philadelphia: University of Pennsylvania Press, 1950), p. 123.

[9] Thomas D. Eliot, "Bereavement: Inevitable but Not Insurmountable," in *Family, Marriage and Parenthood,* Howard Becker and Reuben Hill, eds. (Boston: D. C. Heath and Co., 2d ed., 1955), pp. 657-58.

[10] Hughes, *Cycles and Turning Points,* p. 8. Cf. LeRoy Bowman, *The American Funeral* (Washington, D.C.: Public Affairs Press, 1959).

Sustenance Rituals in the Family

Grace at meals, family prayers, and even family worship, as well as religious feasts, fasts, and festivals, may be interpreted as sustenance rituals related to economic interests and material maintenance. These have been more common in rural than urban families and perhaps have declined in their incidence, although evidence is contradictory and inconclusive.[11]

An increasingly substantial body of evidence, however, indicates that ideals taught by churches are not attained by a majority of their families. A nationwide survey of Methodists found only one family in five had daily family worship, and one-tenth never said grace at meals.[12] Although over half of 387 midwestern Congregational-Christian families had some kind of family group worship, this was so broadly interpreted that it included bedtime prayers for children, prayer at mealtime, and "silent periods." [13] Over 300 of 417 families in one Protestant church were passive or irregular church participants, and only 30 were among the very active members. Church participation was directly correlated with overt religious practices in the home. Once religious rites were established, families clung to them long after church participation declined. Bereavement in a family was more likely to cause decreased participation than divorce, and participation was especially low if the husband-father had no church membership. Families with children generally were more active in church than the childless, although small children had a limiting effect upon participation.[14]

One-third or fewer of 16,000 children entering Catholic parochial schools in 33 states showed the expected amount of home training pertinent to five prayers and five basic dogmas, although over half knew the Sign of the Cross. Children from the most rural areas were the best trained religiously, and those who came from areas with a high rate of mixed marriages had the poorest record.[15] Religious observances by 8,363 white

[11] William F. Ogburn, with the assistance of Clark Tibbitts, "The Family and Its Functions," in President's Research Committee on Social Trends, *Recent Social Trends in the United States* (New York: McGraw-Hill Book Co., 1933), p. 674; "The Quarter's Polls," *Public Opinion Quarterly,* 11 (Summer 1947), 303-4; David O. Moberg, "Die Säkularisierung und das Wachstum der Kirchen in den Vereinigten Staaten," *Kölner Zeitschrift für Soziologie und Sozialpsychologie,* 10, no. 3 (1958), 430-38.

[12] Murray H. Leiffer, "What Are Our Sources of Spiritual Strength?", *Christian Advocate,* 131 (Jan. 19, 1956), 75, 85, 87, 91. Cf. findings for an evangelical denomination in Ohio reported by Elmer G. Homrighausen, "Do Church Members Practice Spiritual Disciplines?," *Theology Today,* 10 (July 1953), 252-54.

[13] Erston M. Butterfield, "A Study of Family Worship," *Religious Education,* 43 (Jan.-Feb. 1948), 26-30.

[14] Sarah Frances Anders, "Religious Behavior of Church Families," *Marriage and Family Living,* 17 (Feb. 1955), 54-57.

[15] John L. Thomas, S.J., "Religious Training in the Roman Catholic Family," *American Journal of Sociology,* 57 (Sept. 1951), 178-83.

urban Catholics in the South fluctuated with the individual's life-cycle. Over three-fourths performed their Easter duties (78.9 per cent) and attended Mass every Sunday (78.6 per cent), but only about two-fifths (43.3 per cent) received Communion monthly or more. The best record for all three was held by the 10 to 19 age group, presumably because of supervision by mothers and teachers. Religious fidelity was lowest among those aged 30 to 39; it was hindered by social distractions, marriage, absorption in family responsibilities, preoccupation with economic striving, and possibly practices like birth control which prohibit reception of the sacraments. Marked improvement was noted in later age decades, except for the Communion criterion among the oldest persons.[16]

Family ritual ("prescribed procedure, arising out of family interaction, involving a pattern of defined behavior, which is directed toward some specific end or purpose, and acquires rigidity and a sense of rightness as a result of its continuing history") seemed in studies of Bossard and Boll increasingly concerned with secular rather than religious matters. Middle class families were the most religious and participated the most often in church activities. Among lower class families religious practices died out as the family grew. Few upper class families had grace at meals, family prayers, or family Bible reading, but nearly half attended church regularly on Sunday mornings. Social compulsions made them attend together at Christmas, Thanksgiving, Easter, and during Lent. Although more dogmatic about the importance of a church christening, confirmation, wedding, and funeral than others, the upper classes felt that religion is highly personal and intimate, so open involvement in family religious ritual would be embarrassing. Among Orthodox Jews the Passover was the most cherished family rite; it was closely identified with family unity.[17]

Religious Intermarriage

All major American churches encourage certain types of mate selection; all oppose interfaith marriages and hedge them in with restrictions not emphasized for intrafaith weddings. For a marriage of a Catholic and non-Catholic to be considered valid by the Roman Catholic Church, the Catholic party must declare his or her intention of continuing to practice the Catholic faith and promise to do all in his or her power to share that faith with the children born of the marriage and to have them baptized and raised as Catholics. The non-Catholic must be informed of that dec-

---

16 Joseph H. Fichter, S.J., "The Profile of Catholic Religious Life," *American Journal of Sociology*, 58 (Sept. 1952), 145-49. Women were more faithful at all ages than men, but past disproportions of the sexes may have been greater than today's.

17 Bossard and Boll, *Ritual in Family Living*, pp. 29, 75-81, 120-23. Christmas also is an American family festival. Cf. Mark Benney, Robert S. Weiss, Rolf Meyersohn, and David Riesman, "Christmas in an Apartment Hotel," *American Journal of Sociology*, 65 (Nov. 1959), 233-40.

laration and promise and must receive instruction in the essentials of the Catholic faith. Orthodox and Conservative Jewish rabbis stubbornly oppose intermarriage, considering it treason against Judaism. Reform rabbis generally consider every mixed marriage "a nail in the coffin of Judaism" but perform such weddings in the fear that a Christian clergyman would otherwise influence the couple.[18] Protestants usually view mate selection as a personal matter and have no formal system of control over interfaith marriages, but most denominations discourage them through education and propaganda. Clergymen, realizing they serve as civil as well as ecclesiastical agents when they officiate, hope religious sanctions will help partners realize marriage is more than a purely civil contract.

Church efforts to prevent intermarriage are not fully successful. Attitudes of youth toward mixed marriages appear increasingly tolerant.[19] Churches find it difficult to maintain in-group loyalties. Spouses in 6.4 per cent of the nation's marriages as of March 1957 belonged to different faiths. Of all marriages in which one spouse was Protestant, 8.4 per cent involved a Roman Catholic and 0.2 per cent a Jewish partner. Among marriages in which one mate was Catholic, 21.2 per cent involved marriage to a Protestant, and 0.4 per cent to a Jew. Among Jews, 4.2 per cent of the marriages were to a Protestant, and 3.0 per cent to a Catholic. If marriages occurred at random in respect to religion, 44 instead of 6 out of every 100 couples would have involved an interfaith marriage.[20] Local studies also have revealed a tendency to marry within one's own religion even after nationality barriers are dissolved, although mixed marriage rates are surprisingly high in many areas.[21] In the 1970's 10 per cent of Jews, 11 per cent of Protestants, and 23 per cent of Catholics had mixed marriages, but for marriages performed by their religion when they were age 16, equivalent figures were 15, 16, and 39. Membership changes hide much intermarriage.[22]

Mixed marriage rates appear highest when the proportion of people in a population is small so there is a scarcity of prospective mates within the group. Closely-knit ethnic subgroups in a religious community deter intermarriage; fidelity to the ethnic group, minority social status, language, and prejudices reinforce the religious factor in reducing mixed marriage.

---

[18] Milton L. Barron, *People Who Intermarry* (Syracuse, N.Y.: Syracuse University Press, 1946), pp. 29-33.

[19] W. E. Garnett, *The Virginia Rural Church and Related Influences, 1900-1950* (Blacksburg, Va.: A.E.S. Bulletin 479, May 1957), p. 59.

[20] "Religion Reported by the Civilian Population of the United States," *Current Population Reports,* Series P-20, no. 79, Feb. 2, 1958. Interdenominational marriages were not reported.

[21] Ruby Jo Reeves Kennedy, "Single or Triple Melting-Pot? Intermarriage in New Haven, 1870-1950," *American Journal of Sociology,* 58 (July 1952), 56-59; Loren E. Chancellor and Thomas P. Monahan, "Religious Preference and Interreligious Mixtures in Marriages and Divorces in Iowa," *ibid.,* 61 (Nov. 1955), 233-39.

[22] Andrew M. Greeley, *Crisis in the Church* (Chicago: Thomas More Press, 1979), p. 123. Cf. Norval D. Glenn, "Interreligious Marriage in the United States: Patterns and Recent Trends," *Journal of Marriage and the Family,* 44, no. 3 (Aug. 1982), 555-66.

Interfaith marriages are often a means of upward social mobility for women, so the incidence among minority groups is generally highest among members with high socioeconomic status. Mixed marriage is most frequent among those with only loose ties to their church, so many mates are converted to the religion of their partner. Special problems for Jews are created by programs to reduce prejudice and anti-Semitism, for a latent effect of such programs is increased opportunity and temptation to intermarry.[23]

Even if both partners claim religious indifference, conflicts centering on religion arise in interfaith marriages. The proportion of them that are successful is smaller than among those which have not crossed religious boundaries. Common results include the changing of religion by one partner, divided religious loyalties in the family, deviation from church standards of birth control, diet, and other behavior, difficulties with relatives and friends, problems of child rearing, children who are more likely than others to enter mixed marriages, marital discord, divorce, and separation. The incidence of these problems appears to be somewhat greater than in intrafaith marriages.[24] Several of these consequences are directly related to maintenance of institutional religion, so churches see interfaith marriages as a threat to their stability. Their opposition to such weddings may be based less upon concern for the persons involved than for the perpetuation of ecclesiastical rites and organizations.[25]

Mixed marriages across denominational lines within the major faiths may result in tensions as severe as in many interfaith weddings. Of every

[23] *Ibid.;* Alfred C. Clarke, "An Examination of the Operation of Residential Propinquity as a Factor in Mate Selection," *American Sociological Review,* 17 (Feb. 1952), 17-22; Peter A. Munch, "Social Adjustment Among Wisconsin Norwegians," *ibid.,* 14 (Dec. 1949), 780-87; Jerold S. Heiss, "Premarital Characteristics of the Religiously Intermarried in an Urban Area," *ibid.,* 25 (Feb. 1960), 47-55; Gerald J. Schnepp and Louis A. Roberts, "Residential Propinquity and Mate Selection on a Parish Basis," *American Journal of Sociology,* 58 (July 1952), 45-50; Clark E. Vincent, "Interfaith Marriages: Problem or Symptom?" in *Religion and the Face of America,* Jane C. Zahn, ed. (Berkeley: University Extension, University of California, 1959), pp. 67-87; Harvey J. Locke, Georges Sabagh, and Mary M. Thomes, "Interfaith Marriages," *Social Problems,* 4 (Apr. 1957), 329-33; James H. S. Bossard and Harold C. Letts, "Mixed Marriages Involving Lutherans—A Research Report," *Marriage and Family Living,* 18 (Nov. 1956), 308-10; and Hershel Shanks, "Jewish-Gentile Intermarriages: Facts and Trends," *Commentary,* 16 (Oct. 1953), 370-75.

[24] Ray Baber, "A Study of 325 Mixed Marriages," *American Sociological Review,* 2 (Oct. 1937) 705-16; Judson T. Landis, "Marriages of Mixed and Non-Mixed Religious Faith," *ibid.,* 14 (June 1949), 401-7; J. S. Slotkin, "Jewish-Gentile Intermarriage in Chicago," *ibid.,* 7 (Feb. 1942), 34-39; James H. S. Bossard and Eleanor S. Boll, *One Marriage, Two Faiths* (New York: Ronald Press Co., 1957); Murray H. Leiffer, "Mixed Marriages and Church Loyalties," *Christian Century,* 66 (Jan. 19, 1949), 78-80; Murray H. Leiffer, "Mixed Marriages and the Children," *ibid.,* 66 (Jan. 26, 1949), 106-8; Ray E. Baber, *Marriage and the Family* (New York: McGraw-Hill Book Co., 2d ed., 1953), pp. 103-7; and John J. Kane, *Marriage and the Family: A Catholic Approach* (New York: Dryden Press, 1952), pp. 153-54.

[25] Vincent, "Interfaith Marriages: Problem or Symptom?" Cf. Howard M. Bahr, "Religious Intermarriage and Divorce in Utah and the Mountain States," *Journal for the Scientific Study of Religion,* 20, no. 3 (Sept. 1981), 251-61.

100 mixed marriages entered in 1951 and 1952 by United Lutherans, 57 were with other Protestants, 20 with Roman Catholics, one with a Jew, 3 with other non-Protestants, and 19 with non-church members. In about 35 per cent of these marriages performed by Lutheran pastors, both partners remained active in their respective churches. The non-Lutheran became Lutheran in 40 per cent, and in 10 per cent the Lutheran joined his spouse's church. The other 15 per cent dropped completely out of church or out of contact with the officiating pastor.[26] Since a wide range of faith and practice may be found within a denomination and even within a single large congregation, spouses from the same church may differ in the nature or intensity of religious beliefs, desired types of family religious practices, or ethical principles about drinking, dancing, smoking, contraception, or other matters.[27]

Religion and Marital Adjustment

Most studies have found that church attendance and membership, mutual enjoyment of church activity, conservative sex morals and religious attitudes, church sanction of the marriage ceremony, and similar indicators of religiosity are related to good marital adjustment.[28] Fellowship provided in the church in the midst of lonely urban society and solutions to common problems found through discussion groups and educational activities of the church may be part of the explanation, but it may also simply reflect a tendency of social conformists to be better adjusted than those who deviate from the norms of their society.[29] The deviant, whether an extreme saint or sinner, may be a poor matrimonial risk.

Yet the presence of marital problems among church-attending as well as non-attending people is well known.[30] The rather consistent correlation between better adjustment and religiosity cannot establish causation; it may simply reflect factors other than religion which are present in the

[26] Bossard and Letts, "Mixed Marriages Involving Lutherans."

[27] James A. Pike, *If You Marry Outside Your Faith* (New York: Harper and Brothers, 1954), pp. 150-53. These problems related to religious variations between mates are ignored by most family researchers.

[28] For examples see Lewis M. Terman, *Psychological Factors in Marital Happiness* (New York: McGraw-Hill Book Co., 1938), pp. 109, 163-64, and Gerald J. Schnepp and Mary M. Johnson, "Do Religious Background Factors Have Predictive Value?" *Marriage and Family Living*, 14 (Nov. 1952), 301-4. Somewhat contradictory but inconclusive findings are reported in Peterson, *Education for Marriage*, pp. 319-31, and Clifford Kirkpatrick, "Factors in Marital Adjustment," *American Journal of Sociology*, 43 (Sept. 1937), 270-83.

[29] Harvey J. Locke, *Predicting Adjustment in Marriage* (New York: Henry Holt and Co., 1951), p. 243, and Harvey J. Locke and Georg Karlsson, "Marital Adjustment and Prediction in Sweden and the United States," *American Sociological Review*, 17 (Feb. 1952), 10-17.

[30] F. Bernadette Turner, "Common Characteristics Among Persons Seeking Professional Marriage Counseling," *Marriage and Family Living*, 16 (May 1954), 143-44.

cultural backgrounds, personalities, or social experiences of the marital partners.

Religious Influences on Sex and Fertility

Jewish and Christian teachings have held consistently that sexual intercourse should be limited to marriage and that sex must always be considered in the larger framework of love, marriage, procreation, and the family.[31] Although sex education in the church sometimes indirectly imparts knowledge about masturbation and other forms of sexual misconduct,[32] research demonstrates that there are differences between the religious and non-religious. The Kinsey studies found that the incidence of both pre- and extra-marital coitus was lowest among the religiously devout in all three major religions, next lowest among the moderately religious, and highest among the religiously inactive. Studies of sexual behavior of college students, premarital relationships of engaged and married couples, and premarital pregnancies all point to the conclusion that religious beliefs and activities are associated with low rates of premarital coitus.[33] A gradual breakdown of religious controls over behavior may be one reason for the apparent increase in pre-marital sexual intercourse.[34]

Lack of sexual gratification in marriage results in less intense negative sentiments over the marital relationship for religiously-oriented than for non-religious marriage partners.[35]

Most Protestants and Jews accept birth control as a means of family planning. Their ideal of parenthood as a stewardship includes both child-spacing and limitation of the total number to assure good health for mother and child and to encourage child rearing under the best possible circumstances. Certain Judeo-Christian groups, however, teach on the basis of Genesis 1:28 and 9:1-7 supplemented by interpretations of Onan's

[31] Roland H. Bainton, "Christianity and Sex," in *Sex and Religion Today,* Simon Doniger, ed. (New York: Association Press, 1953), pp. 17-96.

[32] Alfred C. Kinsey *et al., Sexual Behavior in the Human Female* (Philadelphia: W. B. Saunders Co., 1953), p. 139.

[33] *Ibid.,* pp. 55-56, 304-7, 318-19, 331, 342-45, 424, 437, 443; Alfred C. Kinsey, Wardell B. Pomeroy, and Clyde E. Martin, *Sexual Behavior in the Human Male* (Philadelphia: W. B. Saunders Co., 1948), pp. 465-95; Ernest W. Burgess and Paul Wallin, *Engagement and Marriage* (Chicago: J. B. Lippincott Co., 1953), pp. 337-42; Eugene J. Kanin and David H. Howard, "Postmarital Consequences of Premarital Sex Adjustments," *American Sociological Review,* 23 (Oct. 1958), 556-62; and Harold T. Christensen, "Studies in Child Spacing: I—Premarital Pregnancy as Measured by the Spacing of the First Birth from Marriage," *ibid.,* 18 (Feb. 1953), 53-59.

[34] William F. Ogburn and Meyer F. Nimkoff, *Technology and the Changing Family* (Boston: Houghton Mifflin Co., 1955), pp. 5, 50-57, 138-39, 261-62. This may also account for the contrary findings reported by Lee G. Burchinal and Elmer W. Bock, "Religious Behavior, Premarital Pregnancy, and Early Marriage," *Alpha Kappa Deltan,* 29, no. 2 (Spring 1959), 39-44.

[35] Paul Wallin, "Religiosity, Sexual Gratification, and Marital Satisfaction," *American Sociological Review,* 22 (June 1957), 300-5.

sin (Genesis 38:8-10) that limitation of family size is sinful. Orthodox Jews oppose the use of contraceptives except when the wife's life will be endangered by conception, for the Talmud teaches that nothing may be done to prevent natural conception and birth. They believe the Lord will provide sustenance for all who are born and hold that Catholic teachings about birth control descended from Jewish tradition.[36]

The Roman Catholic Church teaches that the primary purpose of marriage is the procreation and rearing of children. Birth control other than "virtuous continence" is condemned as "frustrating the marriage act," "criminal abuse," "perversion of the right order," and "intrinsically evil." Any use of matrimony which deliberately frustrates the sex act in "its natural power to generate life is an offense against the law of God and of nature, and those who indulge in such are branded with the guilt of a grave sin." [37] Sterilization, abortion, and even artificial insemination with the husband as donor are similarly condemned. The only permissible forms of birth control are abstinence from sexual intercourse and the rhythm method. Legislative and administrative action to enforce these standards in birth control clinics, hospital codes for doctors, social welfare policies, and foreign aid programs has resulted in conflict within numerous states and communities with groups which have different values. As a result of the world's "population explosion," however, they and other religious bodies are trying to develop demographic policies that are "realistic, yet doctrinally sound." [38]

Differences in fertility between religious groups are partly a result of these variations in ethical teachings. Jews, who (except for the Orthodox minority) have the most favorable attitudes toward birth control, have the fewest children; Catholics, with a theology opposed to contraception, have the most, and Protestants fall in between.[39] Desired size of family and the extent to which birth control techniques are used are similarly related to religion. In a nationwide study in 1955, 88 per cent of Protestant couples and 70 per cent of the Catholics reported that they were using birth control measures.[40] Catholics who use contraception

---

[36] Rabbi S. I. Levin, Minneapolis, Aug 4, 1959.

[37] Pope Pius XI, *Casti Connubii, Encyclical Letter on Christian Marriage* (Dec. 31, 1930), The Missionary Society of St. Paul the Apostle in the State of New York, 1941, par. 56, p. 17. Other quotations are from sec. 13 and pars. 53-62, pp. 5, 16-19.

[38] Flann Campbell, "Birth Control and the Christian Churches," *Population Studies,* 14 (Nov. 1960), 131-47; George A. Kelly, *Overpopulation: A Catholic View* (New York: Paulist Press, 1960); Richard M. Fagley, *The Population Explosion and Christian Responsibility* (New York: Oxford University Press, 1960); and James O'Gara, "Catholics and Population," *Commonweal,* 71 (Dec. 18, 1959), 339-42.

[39] Frank Lorimer, *Culture and Human Fertility* (Paris: UNESCO, 1954), pp. 183-98; and Charles F. Westoff, "Religion and Fertility in Metropolitan America," in *Thirty Years of Research in Human Fertility* (New York: Milbank Memorial Fund, 1959), pp. 117-34. Most Catholic-Protestant disparity disappeared in the 1970's.

[40] Ronald F. Freedman, Pascal K. Whelpton, and Arthur A. Campbell, "Family Planning in the U.S.," *Scientific American,* 200, no. 4 (Apr. 1959), 50-55. Many Cath-

techniques contrary to Church doctrine justify their non-conformity by defense mechanisms of rationalization and compartmentalization of religion. Over half of 244 Catholic physicians were found to violate their Church's position by giving device-contraception advice.[41]

Socioeconomic factors other than religion are significantly related to fertility patterns. Catholics follow the same general social class trends as Protestants; the higher their social class, the smaller the average family.[42] Yet completed Catholic families tend to be slightly larger than others within each class category except at the very lowest levels. Catholics with secular education are more like Protestants in their fertility behavior than those with parochial education.[43] Other findings support the conclusions that religion is a more important determinant of fertility than nationality, that Jewish fertility is less influenced by social and psychological variables than that of Christians, that education and economic pressures appear more significant influences on attitudes and behavior of young Mormons than religious tradition, that the general influence of American society has significantly reduced the fertility rates of Catholics, and that groups like the Hutterites with religious teachings which oppose birth control and have a social system and attitudes favorable to large families can double every sixteen years even if they delay marriage to the age of at least 19 or 20, have no immigration, and strongly taboo sexual relations before marriage.[44]

We may conclude that social and economic conditions are more significant influences on reproductive behavior than religious doctrines per se. As new techniques of birth control are developed, it is likely that ethical formulations of Roman Catholicism will continue their evolu-

---

olics were not necessarily violating Church precepts, for they used only the rhythm method for "serious motives."

[41] Eugene J. Kanin, "Value Conflicts in Catholic Device-Contraceptive Usage," *Social Forces*, 35 (Mar. 1957), 238-43; and Sydney S. Spivack and Jerald T. Hage, "Religious Influences and Contraceptive Advice Given by Physicians," *Abstracts of Papers Delivered at the 54th Annual Meeting of the American Sociological Society* (Sept. 3-5, 1959), p. 34. (Device-contraception was approved by 98 per cent of non-Catholic physicians.)

[42] Frank W. Notestein, "Class Differences in Fertility," *Annals of the American Academy of Political and Social Science*, 188 (Nov. 1936), 22-36.

[43] P. K. Whelpton and Clyde V. Kiser, "Social and Psychological Factors Affecting Fertility . . . ," *Milbank Memorial Fund Quarterly*, 21 (July 1943), 221-380, and 22 (Jan. 1944), 72-105; and Westoff, "Religion and Fertility . . ."

[44] Douglas G. Marshall, "The Decline in Farm Family Fertility and Its Relationship to Nationality and Religious Background," *Rural Sociology*, 15 (Mar. 1950), 42-49; Erwin S. Solomon, "Social Characteristics and Fertility: A Study of Two Religious Groups in Metropolitan New York," *Eugenics Quarterly*, 3 (June 1956), 100-3; Lowry Nelson, "Education and Changing Size of Mormon Families," *Rural Sociology*, 17 (Dec. 1952), 335-42; Samuel A. Stouffer, "Trends in the Fertility of Catholics and Non-Catholics," *American Journal of Sociology*, 41 (Sept. 1935), 143-66; Albert J. Mayer and Sue Marx, "Social Change, Religion, and Birth Rates," *ibid.*, 62 (Jan. 1957) 383-90; and Joseph W. Eaton and Albert J. Mayer, *Man's Capacity to Reproduce* (Glencoe, Ill.: The Free Press, 1954), pp. 48-57.

tionary modification toward the liberal attitudes and practices already held by a substantial proportion of its members. "Secular pressures" on marital behavior are accepted less rapidly by them than by Protestants, but their influence is clearly evident.[45] Although Detroit Area Study evidence indicates that the earlier trend toward convergence of family size of Catholics and others was reversed during the 1950's when Catholic families increased more rapidly,[46] there is at present no solid support for the belief that Catholics will soon become a majority of the population. The celibacy of their clergy and religious orders helps to counterbalance the large families of laymen. The March 1957 Census survey revealed that the cumulative fertility rate (number of children ever born per 1,000 ever-married women) of Baptists was higher than that of Roman Catholics. The latter were only slightly above all Protestants.[47]

Church Influences on Child Rearing

The high value placed upon children in American culture may partly result from long-term influences of the Judeo-Christian religion. In addition, the various churches affect their people in other ways. Protestants, in keeping with their theology, usually teach self-control and personal accountability, thus relying upon internalized social controls; Catholics stress external controls to guide the child.[48]

Parents are the child's first and usually most significant teachers of religion. Answers to questions about the nature of the universe, the origin of life, and innumerable other topics convey and clarify religious ideas. Religious beliefs, affiliations, and activities of children are directly related to their early training. Thus in Bell's study of 9,614 youths, only 4.2 per cent of the Catholics, 2 per cent of the Protestants, and none of the Jews had adopted a faith different from that of either parent, and 81.1 per cent had the same affiliation as that of both. In homes with divided church loyalties, they were more than twice as likely to accept the mother's faith as the father's.[49] Almost three-fourths of the children enrolled in

---

[45] J. Anthony Samenfink, "A Study of Some Aspects of Marital Behavior as Related to Religious Control," *Marriage and Family Living*, 20 (May 1958), 163-69.

[46] Gerhard Lenski, *The Religious Factor* (Garden City, N.Y.: Doubleday and Co., 1961), pp. 212-19.

[47] Paul C. Glick, "Intermarriage and Fertility Patterns Among Persons in Major Religious Groups," *Eugenics Quarterly,* 7 (Mar. 1960), 31-38. The respective figures for women aged 15 to 44 are Baptist, 2,359; Roman Catholic, 2,282; all Protestants, 2,220; Jews, 1,749. A large number of Negroes and the rural South background of a majority of Baptists probably account for their high fertility. The rate among Methodists was 2,155; Lutherans, 2,013; Presbyterians, 2,001, and "Other Protestants," 2,237.

[48] Daniel R. Miller and Guy E. Swanson, *The Changing American Parent* (New York: John Wiley and Sons, 1958), pp. 158-74; and Lenski, *The Religious Factor,* pp. 208-10.

[49] Howard Bell, *Youth Tell Their Story* (Washington, D.C.: American Council on

the church schools of 325 churches in 18 Protestant denominations had parents who were active participants in the church's program.[50] More adolescents drop out of Sunday school because of parental indifference than for any other reason.[51] According to Ralph N. McEntire's study, over 90 per cent of the youth who remained in the church and progressed through its various departments came from homes in which parents were church members actively supporting the program.[52]

Ethical values of children are closely related to family experiences and often are taken directly from the overt behavior of parents. When concepts of right and wrong of 1,100 children in grades 5 through 9 were correlated with ideas of right and wrong of others who presumably influenced them, the following correlation coefficients were obtained: Child and his parents, .545; child and his friends, .343; child and his club leaders, .137; child and his school teachers, .028; child and his Sunday school teacher, .002. The child's moral concepts were closer to those of his mother than his father, perhaps because of the more intimate relationships typically enjoyed with the mother. The choice of friends and of clubs and their leaders may be primarily a product of family influences, so to some extent these correlations may be indirect results of the causal influence of parental guidance.[53] Juvenile delinquency is inversely related to adolescents' and parents' church participation, to the knowledge of religion imputed to parents, and to religious rapport and discussion of religion with them.[54] When parents are "significant others" to adolescents, parental expectations are so interiorized that they influence religious attitudes and self-expectations as well as other aspects of behavior.[55]

The personal adjustment of youth is related to religion. Those with above average personalities and other indicators of good mental, personal, and social adjustment are much more likely to be faithful participants in church groups. Marriage adjustment studies have shown a similar relationship between background religious experience and good adjust-

---

Education, 1938), p. 196. Cf. Murray H. Leiffer, "Why Do We Choose the Churches We Attend?," *Christian Advocate,* 131 (Feb. 2, 1956), 137, 157-60, and Snell Putney and Russell Middleton, "Rebellion, Conformity, and Parental Religious Ideologies," *Sociometry,* 24 (June 1961), 125-35.

[50] Helen F. Spaulding and David W. Will, *A Study of the Church Relationships of Parents of Children in the Elementary Division of the Church School* (New York: The Committee on Children's Work, National Council of Churches, 1958), pp. 4-13.

[51] Leonard Carroll, "Why We Lose Adolescents," *Bethel Seminary Quarterly,* 1, no. 3 (May 1954), 54-66.

[52] Lloyd A. Peterson, "The Place of the Church in Youth Guidance," *Report of Governor's State Conference on Youth* (St. Paul: State of Minnesota, 1948), pp. 32-33.

[53] Hugh Hartshorne, Mark A. May, David E. Sonquist, and Chester A. Kerr, "Testing the Knowledge of Right and Wrong," *Religious Education,* 21 (Oct. 1926), 539-54.

[54] F. Ivan Nye, *Family Relationships and Delinquent Behavior* (New York: John Wiley and Sons, 1958), pp. 35-36, 147-49.

[55] Bernard C. Rosen, "The Reference Group Approach to the Parental Factor in Attitude and Behavior Formation," *Social Forces,* 34 (Dec. 1955), 137-44.

ment.[56] When a home is basically unhappy and traumatic through deprivation of love and support or through rigid relationships with absolutist supernatural creedal concepts and inelastic externalized values, "the seed for future agnosticism may have been sown"; some agnostics therefore come from fundamentalist Protestant backgrounds.[57]

The family and church are not the child's only sources of religious education. The total community provides the matrix for personal development and makes its impact upon him.[58] Churches which cooperate closely with parents undoubtedly play a significant part in the development of personality. They cultivate faith in God, promote a sense of belonging, develop responsible participation in social activities, provide a "Benevolent Other" in whom to confide, and support high aspirations. Yet **if we were able to factor out their respective influences, the church** undoubtedly would be found far less significant than the family in personality development and character formation.

Religion and Family Problems

Numerous studies support the conclusion that marital maladjustment often is linked with lack of religious influences on the marriage. Thus divorced couples were much less likely than a comparable group of happily-married to belong to a church or to begin an affiliation with one at the time of marriage. Never attending church was associated with marital maladjustment and attending four times or more a month with happiness. Mutual interests in church are associated with adjustment, but when church attendance becomes an individualistic activity, it appears to have a disruptive effect upon a marriage.[59]

The lowest divorce rates generally are found among Jews and Catholics, followed in order by Protestants, interfaith marriages, and, highest of all, marriages in which neither partner has religious affiliation.[60] Catholic dogma strongly opposes divorce, yet numerous divorces occur among Catholics, and, perhaps partly because of their generally lower social class position, they account for more than their share of desertions, an-

---

[56] Lester Beals, "A Study of Certain Home Factors and Their Relationship to the Personal Adjustment of Children," *School and Society,* 72 (July 22, 1950), 55-57; Anton T. Boisen, *Religion in Crisis and Custom* (New York: Harper and Brothers, 1955), pp. 21-40; Terman, *Psychological Factors in Marital Happiness,* pp. 230-31, 234-36, 395-96, 412.

[57] Richard V. McCann, "Developmental Factors in the Growth of a Mature Faith," *Religious Education,* 50 (May-June 1955), 147-55.

[58] Cf. William L. Troyer, "Christian Nurture and Recent Social Science Investigation," *Religious Education,* 42 (Nov.-Dec. 1947), 351-56.

[59] Locke, *Predicting Adjustment in Marriage,* pp. 239-42, 257-58.

[60] H. Ashley Weeks, "Differential Divorce Rates by Occupation," *Social Forces,* 21 (Mar. 1943), 334-37; Landis, "Marriages of Mixed and Non-Mixed Religious Faith"; Stephen Somogyi, "Differential Divorce Rates by Religious Groups," *American Journal of Sociology,* 46 (Mar. 1941), 665-85.

nulments, and legal separations. Divorce trauma is somewhat more likely to disturb divorced Catholics than Protestants. Differences are also observable in religious and other post-divorce behavior of Catholics and Protestants. The latter are more likely to enter a second marriage.[61]

People sometimes turn to the church for help when they get into trouble, but this is not universally true. The religious devotion of 100 Chicago families struck by the great depression was not significantly changed as a result, although a few discontinued church participation because of their lack of suitable clothing or of money for contributions.[62] Help or advice was sought in 57 of 109 cases of trouble among 62 New York City families. Relatives, druggists, and bartenders were consulted more often than clergymen. It seemed as if ministers were removed from the vicissitudes of life, for even in depression times clergymen lived fairly well. Many families felt that their failure to know and understand their problems through experience vitiated their usefulness as spiritual advisers.[63]

Many latent effects of church work are overlooked or even totally unsuspected before competent research reveals startling findings. Although Roman Catholics have a strong family tradition, a national survey representative of living college graduates found that 48 per cent of all Catholic women graduates were unmarried, as compared to 23 per cent of the Jewish and 21 per cent of Protestant ex-coeds.[64] The high value churches place upon legitimacy makes illegitimacy a disgrace which many innocent children have been unable to overcome. Stress upon sexual continence before marriage sometimes leads to an unhealthy preoccupation with sex. Religious concepts of sin may be psychologically harmful if behavior or drives which are an inevitable part of normal life are alleged to be sinful. Marriage counselors have found that religion is often "one of the most positive assets in the formation of permanent adjustments," but it may also become a major source of difficulty if the counselor is unfamiliar with the doctrines and policies of his clients' religious groups.[65] Maladjusted ministers may perpetuate pathology or accentuate problems

[61] Thomas P. Monahan and Loren E. Chancellor, "Statistical Aspects of Marriage and Divorce by Religious Denomination in Iowa," *Eugenics Quarterly*, 2 (Sept. 1955), 162-73; Thomas P. Monahan and William M. Kephart, "Divorce and Desertion by Religious and Mixed-Religious Groups," *American Journal of Sociology*, 59 (Mar. 1954), 454-65; William J. Goode, *After Divorce* (Glencoe, Ill.: The Free Press, 1956), pp. 34-38, 100, 105, 145-46, 157, 190.

[62] Ruth Shonle Cavan and Katherine H. Ranck, *The Family and the Depression* (Chicago: University of Chicago Press, 1938), pp. 107-8.

[63] Earl L. Koos, *Families in Trouble* (New York: King's Crown Press, 1946), pp. 86-89.

[64] Ernest Havemann and Patricia Salter West, *They Went to College* (New York: Harcourt, Brace and Co., 1952), p. 55. For divergent findings see John L. Thomas, "Catholic College Spinsters?," *Social Order*, 2 (1952), 357-62.

[65] John F. Cuber, *Marriage Counseling Practice* (New York: Appleton-Century-Crofts, 1948), pp. 114, 132.

in the families to which they minister. Moralizing without contributing to practical solutions may increase people's difficulties. Many clergymen fallaciously focus attention upon immediate, specific problems in their marriage and family counseling rather than on the underlying sources of trouble.[66]

Although the church often binds up men's wounds, at times it helps create them. Disagreements and maladjustments centered on religion are apparent among couples of the same religion as well as in interfaith marriages. Variations in theological orientation, fervor of faith, and social class composition within a denomination introduce many potential areas of conflict. Disagreements may relate to questions of local church affiliation, religious practices in the family, or certain aspects of religious creeds or dogma. If these differences accentuate other disagreements, they are especially difficult to overcome. When there is no common universe of discourse because of widely divergent philosophies of life, the family may be on its way to complete disruption.[67] Religion sometimes causes guilt feelings for certain types of sexual relationships in marriage; highly detrimental conflicts may result from repression of such feelings. Absorption in religion may become a substitute for divorce among the neurotic, enabling a family to continue functioning together when it otherwise could not do so, but such absorption by one partner may make the mate feel neglected and increase resentment and tensions. Religious formalities may be substituted for personal deficiencies. Cruel fathers may cloak their brutality with pious prayers and penitential phrases. Selfish or indolent mothers may hide behind a verbal religious barrier. Formal religious activities may be used as a shelter to hide dishonesty and social inadequacies.[68] Many of these "hypocrites in the church" are sincere in their faith, but personal and social inadequacies are not solved automatically by superficial religious activities.

Common prayer may significantly reinforce family unity if all members are in basic accord on religion. But if one marital partner is accustomed to formal, ritualistic prayers and the other to emotionally expressive, spontaneous utterances or to the quiet devotion of silence before God, family prayers may become a major source of tension. Similarly, if a child is forced against his will to participate in family devotions that are meaningless to him, he may become alienated from the religion of his parents. It is hence just as unwise to approve all family

[66] H. Walter Yoder, "Spiritual Processes and Marriage Failure," *Journal of Pastoral Care*, 10 (Spring 1956), 34-39.

[67] For an illustrative case see Rockwell C. Smith, "Religion in Family Life," in Becker and Hill, *Family, Marriage and Parenthood*, pp. 601-4.

[68] Jessie Bernard, *Remarriage: A Study of Marriage* (New York: Dryden Press, 1956), pp. 94-95; Robert L. Dickinson and Lura Beam, *A Thousand Marriages* (Baltimore: Williams and Wilkins Co., 1931), pp. 373-74; M. C. Elmer, *The Sociology of the Family* (Boston: Ginn and Co., 1945), p. 121.

religious rituals indiscriminately as it is to condemn them unreservedly. Time, place, personnel, and other pertinent circumstances must be considered in any attempt to evaluate fairly the merits and demerits of family religion.

When problems arise in family life, most contemporary churches emphasize helping people overcome their difficulties rather than condemning them for their sinfulness, as often tended to be the case in the past. Many activities in the church's history of welfare activities, help to prisoners, treatment of the mentally ill, and assistance to persons with other needs may be criticized for their failure to meet modern standards of social work, but they have generally approximated the standards contemporary to such work. Today formal marriage and family life education supplements the influence of sermons, disciplinary action toward the wayward, and other traditional activities of the church to cope with or prevent family problems. The Cana Conferences among Catholics, youth programs, educational literature, church school education, and pre- and post-marital counseling are among church efforts to promote wholesome marriage and family life. Although churches, like other institutions, tend to think more highly of themselves than they ought to think, they contribute much to successful continuance of the family. "The large and generally favorable effect of religious teachings upon marriage and the home is now commonly recognized." [69]

Conclusion

Every family in America, religious or not, is affected to some degree by the church. The family is even more significant for the well-being of the church. When a child develops attitudes of contempt or hatred for his father, it is difficult to teach him in church to love his Heavenly Father. When he is exposed to marital maladjustment at home, he is not likely to look forward to being "united with Christ" as a part of the Christian church married to the Bridegroom. The family thus provides the background of experience and attitudes upon which religious institutions depend in building their interpretations of the ultimate purpose of life and the universe. The attitudes and habits encouraged by churches are successfully established in children's lives only when there is cooperation and help from the families in which they spend so much more time.

The first sin of a child is typically against a parent; the voice of developing conscience tends to be parental voices projected as if they were the voice of God. God is a father image from the psychiatric perspective, an object of ambivalent feelings of love and fear. Some

---

[69] John Sirjamaki, *The American Family in the Twentieth Century* (Cambridge: Harvard University Press, 1953). p. 36.

long for refuge in the "arms of a Mother Church," and certain types of religious experience may be seen as forms of regression flowing out of mother fixation. Many of the deepest concepts of religion may thus be traced to family relationships.[70] The church and the family are inter-related in a never-ceasing process of reciprocal interaction. Neither can be fully understood apart from the other.

There seems to have been a long-range trend toward a secularization of family life—a decline in supernaturalism and in religious beliefs and practices. This decline may be attributed to the increasing specialization of social institutions, the withdrawal of religion from public schools, delegation of religious education to Sunday schools and other church agencies, discontinued recognition of the father as the priest of the family, increased explanation of the mysteries of the universe by science instead of by religion, and the ease of mobility, diversity of moral standards, and multiplicity of personal contacts which result from urbanization and inventions like the automobile and radio.

Although substantial changes unquestionably have occurred in family religious practices, this does not necessarily mean that the "spirit of religion" has changed along with changes in its form. Churches have indeed modified activities relevant to family life to meet current needs, but it is possible that the new "bureaucratic" urban conditions have created a social milieu more likely to encourage religious faith than the older "individuated-entrepreneurial urbanism." [71] A study of 428 students and 380 of their parents found that formal aspects of religion were declining but informal practices like bed-time prayers and a regular religious story-telling hour were increasing.[72] Interviews with another cross-section of families also failed to find significant differences between religious practices of contemporary families and the childhood families of the parents.[73] Among Mennonites the new emergent type of family was found to rate higher on a marital success index, to have less conflict between family members, and to experience less anti-social behavior in children than the traditional, more authoritarian type of family. No significant differences were observed in the degree of acceptance of Mennonite values.[74] It is dangerous to equate changes in outward form with change in the inner meanings of religion. Religious practices as such may decrease in number or frequency while religious motivations may increasingly pervade every area of life or vice versa.

[70] Clifford Kirkpatrick, *Religion in Human Affairs* (New York: John Wiley and Sons, 1929), pp. 87-90.

[71] Guy E. Swanson and Jean Isaacson, "Religion and Bureaucracy," Appendix 4 in Miller and Swanson, *The Changing American Parent*, pp. 276-95.

[72] Floyd M. Martinson, "Trends in Family Religion," *Abstracts of Papers*, Society for the Scientific Study of Religion (Apr. 12, 1958), p. 5.

[73] Moberg, "Die Säkularisierung."

[74] J. Howard Kauffman, *A Comparative Study of Traditional and Emergent Family Types Among Midwest Mennonites*, Ph.D. thesis, University of Chicago, 1960.

Perhaps it is true that "If anything at all is to be done about the family, it will have to come about finally by bringing a change in the hearts of the people." [75] But that which is "in the hearts" of men is largely a result of community and family pressures. To change hearts therefore involves changing families and other groups as well as changing persons. As social institutions, families and churches tend to be self-perpetuating agencies only slightly modified from one generation to the next. Linked with all the rest of society, they cannot be changed radically without a complete social revolution. Nevertheless, change does occur by gradual evolutionary modifications hardly discernible from one generation to the next, but it is obvious when seen in broader historical perspective. Such change does not necessarily involve either the moral degeneration often assumed by traditionalists nor the secularization postulated by many social scientists. Old institutional forms of religion vanish from the family as they evolve into new behavior patterns adapted to the changed social environment, but religious attitudes, motivations, and behavior continue to be an effective influence on family life.

The Church and Government

Politics as the art or science of governing enters into all church activities, for like all institutions the church is "political" in the sense that it is an administrative organization operating through a polity that includes organized roles and statuses and accompanying duties and privileges. The church also has direct relevance for the political institutions of society, for it serves as an organ of social control, helps harmonize conflicting interests, mobilizes citizens for defense, reinforces the laws and ethics of society, crusades for improvement of the social order, and helps socialize citizens who in America are the source of political authority and power. Types of church government or polity are summarized in Chapter 4. Here we shall survey church-state relationships and the reciprocal influences of the church and government on each other. Related aspects of church-state relations are presented in Chapters 6, 8, 12, and elsewhere.

Church-State Relations

There are five possible relationships between church and state, all of which have been observed in American history. (1) Active hostility which results in the churches' going underground has occurred only to small minority religions that have been persecuted as subversive. (2) Each may intimately support the other, so that membership in one

[75] Carle C. Zimmerman, *Outline of Future of the Family* (Cambridge, Mass. Phillips Book Store, 1947), p. 100.

means membership in the other. (3) One church may be established by the state with others tolerated. (4) The church may exist within a state because of the support it receives from another stronger state, as in the case of foreign missions. Or, as is the predominant pattern in United States history, (5) church and state may be legally separate, existing side by side with distinct spheres of concern. Because these spheres are not always well-defined, there often is uncertainty and conflict, especially in overlapping and residual areas not clearly relegated to one or the other of the two institutions.[76]

The general pattern of American church-state relations is based upon the First Amendment to the Constitution (strengthened by the Fifth and Fourteenth Amendments). It provides for freedom of each citizen to enjoy peaceably and without interference his religious worship in the way he deems most suitable. Article 6 of the Constitution specifies that no religious test shall be required as a qualification for any office or public trust under the United States.

Religious liberty as a constitutional right, an American innovation, is a growing concept in the world. By 1960 even the United Nations was actively working to extend the freedom of religion. Religious liberty provides individual freedom in the choice of creed, autonomy for religious organizations, and equality of differing religious groups before the law. It has been maintained in the United States by separatism rather than jurisdictionalism. All religions have been relegated to the sphere of private interests to be invaded only when public safety appears to be involved.[77]

American religious freedom and toleration are the products of numerous historical factors. Among these factors are the large number and wide variety of competitive sects in the colonies with no established church common to all, the relative indifference to religious interests in the late 18th century because of the distractions of the tremendous opportunities of the expanding economic and social system, Locke's theory that religion is a purely personal matter, the dominance of Protestantism with its tradition of toleration based upon its emphasis on direct access of the believer to Divine truth through the Bible, the identification of religious freedom with the larger struggle for liberty, the need for settlers which encouraged acceptance of immigrants with various faiths, the looseness of contacts with parental churches in Europe, and even the very small number of Catholics and Jews in America at the time of the Revolution. Frontier revivals emphasized inner spiritual experience and the equality of all in the sight of God, thus accelerating acceptance of "left wing" Protestantism, which stressed religion as a way of life rather than

---

[76] John H. Otwell, "Christian Conceptions of Church and State," *Religious Education*, 45 (Jan.-Feb. 1950), 35-40.

[77] Guido de Ruggiero, "Religious Freedom," *Encyclopaedia of the Social Sciences* (New York: The Macmillan Co., 1934), 13, pp. 239-45.

a creed and upheld individualistic political doctrines that supported church-state separation.[78] Out of such influences has come the "great tradition of the American churches," the voluntary principle of church support which is a corollary of constitutional separation of church and state.[79]

American church-state separation is softened by shifting interpretations and practical modifications. It is sometimes by-passed entirely on the local level where direct and indirect subsidies are allocated by government to churches and religious agencies for various purposes. Deeply conflicting viewpoints within and between the religions make church-state relations a significant area of persistent tension (Chapter 12). A long heritage of conflict has produced prejudices and preconceptions that impede logical discussion, and there is a deficiency of basic assumptions from which argument can proceed. New issues are created by rapid expansion of governmental functions. Since churches often lean heavily upon the courts to settle specific disputes, strife is not confined to semi-private discussions. Court decisions, based largely upon tradition, are in many respects inadequate to solve the problems, but they serve the cause of progress by showing clearly that tradition is inadequate in a world of rapidly evolving institutions and practices.[80]

Traditional Catholic doctrine teaches the supremacy of the spiritual over the temporal, meaning supremacy of the Church over the state whenever there are clashes of interest. It supports union of the Church with government as an ideal to be subverted only when no alternative is possible and then only temporarily. When other religions are present within the state, the Roman Catholic Church should have a privileged position; others are to be tolerated only for practical political reasons.[81] Many Catholics reject these traditional teachings, however. Although such contributions by liberal Catholics to the separation of church and state have been the result more of practical considerations than of principles, the Church today has "no idea of preparing on earth . . . for the transformation of her spiritual sovereignty into an absolute and universal supremacy. Entirely devoted to her work of spiritualizing and sanctifying mankind, she unreservedly admits the full sovereignty in its own field, of her temporal partner, the State." [82]

---

[78] Robin M. Williams, Jr., *American Society* (New York: Alfred A. Knopf, 1951), pp. 319-21; Jessie Bernard, *American Community Behavior* (New York: Dryden Press, 1949), pp. 362-63; Ernst Troeltsch, *Protestantism and Progress,* trans. W. Montgomery (Boston: Beacon Press, 1958), esp. pp. 117-26, 174-77, 204-7.

[79] Winthrop S. Hudson, *The Great Tradition of the American Churches* (New York: Harper and Brothers, 1953).

[80] Walter B. Rutland, "Church-State Relations in America: Status and Trends," *Social Forces,* 28 (Oct. 1949), 83-86.

[81] Antonio Márquez, "Catholic Controversy on Church and State," *Theology Today,* 15 (Jan. 1959), 531-41.

[82] Joseph LeCler, S.J., *The Two Sovereignties,* trans. Hugh Montgomery (London: Burns Oates and Washbourne, 1952), p. 185; cf. pp. 171-78.

American Catholics are divided on the very issues about which Protestants often assume there is a monolithic, official Catholic position. Not all Catholics agree that federal aid to parochial schools is desirable, that an ambassador to the Vatican should be appointed, that the media of mass communications should be censored, or that an official (Catholic) religion should be established in America. "Strictly speaking, there is no such thing as Catholic politics . . . The immediate and primary objective of government is the good of man in his temporal achievement. This objective is different from the objective of religion: the good of man in his eternal achievement." [83]

The Roman Catholic doctrine of politics is based upon a mystical theory of *natural law,* the belief that a God-given law governs the universe. Man never knows it completely, but revelation and reason have revealed it in part; it is man's responsibility to carry out its precepts. There is nowhere a systematic, complete, and definitive formulation of the principles of social justice believed to be the necessary guides to institutions and the social order. From papal encyclicals and other Catholic writings, Shields concluded that these essential laws of social justice fall under three concepts: (1) *Common Good.* Man's end on earth is to achieve the highest good; this can be done only in association with others, so the purpose of society is to promote the end common for its members. (2) *Functional Association.* To promote the common good, people must cooperate as members of functional groups. (3) *Subsidiarity.* Functional associations have authority to regulate only those affairs of members which bear on the purpose of the group. Hence they may be ranked hierarchically on the basis of function, with the higher organizations coordinating, supervising, and aiding activities of the lesser ones but not performing their functions. These principles are in the area of faith and morals; "in the Catholic view the prime task and mission of the Church is to restore Christian beliefs to their rightful place in human affairs." [84] Even if Catholics devoutly follow the teachings of their Church, there is room for much variation on specific issues within the framework of these principles.

Most Protestants believe in the separation of church and state, but precise implications of its relevant, subjectively intended meanings as well as political applications vary widely. Historical evidence supports the contention that their denominations will support it at least as long as they cannot capture political power.

The logical meaning of church-state separation was operationally defined by a special North Carolina Baptist Convention committee. It

---

[83] Senator Eugene J. McCarthy, "Religion and Politics," *Catholic Digest,* 23, no. 10 (Aug. 1959), 6-13 (condensed from *America,* April 11, 1959), italics deleted.

[84] Currin V. Shields, *Democracy and Catholicism in America* (New York: McGraw-Hill Book Co., 1958), pp. 90-94 (quotation from p. 93). See Gregory Baum, "Protestants and Natural Law," *Commonweal,* 73 (Jan. 20, 1961), 427-30.

recognized that there is no such thing as absolute separation but that at least six principles are involved: distinct reasons for being, so church and state have different basic functions; separate publics, the government including all persons born in its territory and the church including only those who are part of the fellowship of faith; different methods, the state using police power, military action, and taxation to achieve its objectives and the church using instruction, worship, prayer, and love rather than compulsion; separate administrations, with neither using the other to achieve its own ends; separate sources of support, so churches depend on stewardship and not on tax funds for revenue, and separate educational programs, so neither will monopolize channels of knowledge.[85]

There is no clear line between the spheres of governmental and religious action in America. The "wall of separation" is no longer, if indeed it ever was, a distinct partition separating the two.[86] They are so interrelated in their impact upon the lives of citizens that they can be considered separate only in principle. The principle provides a guide to action, however, as long as both institutions accept it as valid. Current pressures to secure governmental support for ecclesiastical agencies and activities could lead ultimately to a form of vertical pluralism or multiple establishment similar to that of certain other nations.[87] More likely a new form of church-state relations as unique as the principle of religious liberty was when it became part of the Constitution of the United States in 1789 may emerge out of the dynamic processes of legislation, administration, and jurisprudence.

Government Influences the Church

People's attributes and names for their gods change in accordance with the form of their government. Church polity, as well as linguistic symbolism, reflects organizational patterns of the state in which the church develops. Catholicism and feudal monarchy hence have closely parallel structures, while many denominations that originated in America reflect democratic government in their insistence that Christ is the unseen head of the church, that it therefore cannot have authoritarian leaders, and that all members should have an equal voice in the conduct of church

---

[85] C. Emanuel Carlson, "Steps Taken but Answer not Found for Religious Liberty in Welfare State," *Report from the Capital* (Baptist Joint Committee on Public Affairs), Jan. 1959, pp. 1-2.

[86] P. F. Drucker, "Organized Religion and the American Creed," *Review of Politics*, 18 (July 1956), 296-304. For summary discussions of issues related to government and religious freedom see Lynn R. Buzzard and Samuel Ericsson, *The Battle for Religious Liberty* (Elgin, Ill.: David C. Cook Publishing Co., 1982).

[87] David O. Moberg, "Religion and Society in the Netherlands and in America," *American Quarterly*, 13 (Summer 1961), 172-78. Cf. Lenski's discussion of the "drift toward compartmentalization" in *The Religious Factor,* pp. 326-30.

affairs. In the future we may even see reference to God Himself as if He were a committee chairman or the president of a democratic group!

Governmental forms profoundly influence relationships of the church to the rest of society. Numerous variations among churches of the same denomination located in different areas reflect restrictions and limitations imposed by state regulations pertinent to incorporation, property ownership, safety, zoning, and similar controls. Even the parish of the Catholic Church, which theoretically admits no right by the state to make laws governing its operation, is usually a legal corporation and is subject to civil law.[88]

Religious liberty is not interpreted as permitting acts under the guise of religious beliefs that tend to injure the health, safety, or morals of the public. Such minority religious practices as polygamy, snake-handling, and flagellation have been prohibited by government in its task of protecting the general welfare and preventing wholesale license which would permit every citizen to become a law unto himself. In 1958 the Kansas State Board of Health applied a 1912 regulation prohibiting common drinking cups to prevent the use of the common Communion chalice in churches as "a potential source for the transmission of communicable disease." [89]

The American government has supported religion by sanctioning nonsectarian religion in public schools, assisting foreign missionaries, supporting chaplains in Congress, the Armed Forces, and correctional institutions, exempting religious contributions from taxable income, reducing postal rates for religious publications, making church property tax exempt, and giving numerous indirect economic benefits.

Church Influences on Government

The church has exerted a profound influence upon American political life in two ways. First, by direct efforts to affect political affairs and second, indirectly through the consequences of its spiritual and social ministry. Western democracy has been consistently allied with and molded by Protestantism,[90] and all major religions of America support its democratic form of government. Judaism has engaged in an almost continuous struggle against various forms of tyranny since the days of the ancient pharaohs, so there can be no question about its stand. Even the Roman Catholic Church has made concessions to democracy, although unqualified approval of democratic processes cannot come from an authoritarian re-

---

[88] Joseph H. Fichter, S.J., *Social Relations in the Urban Parish* (Chicago: University of Chicago Press, 1954), pp. 182-84.

[89] "Storm in a Cup," *Time,* 71, no. 20 (May 19, 1958), 62.

[90] James Hastings Nichols, *Democracy and the Churches* (Philadelphia: Westminster Press, 1951), and Troeltsch, *Protestantism and Progress.*

ligion. Catholic philosopher Jacques Maritain sincerely believes that democracy has its philosophical roots in the basic teachings of Christianity. All the major churches try to prove that the roots of democracy either lie in their own tradition or have similarities to their highest social ethic.[91]

The church has provided sanctions to support the civil rights movement by its emphasis upon the universal fatherhood of the Creator, the brotherhood of man, the golden rule, and similar teachings.[92] To be sure, certain fundamentalist and authoritarian minority sects have been accused of violating the civil rights of those with whom they disagree, but churches as a whole have upheld civil liberties in practice as well as in theory. Similarly, by providing sanctions for the ethical and legal system of folkways, mores, and laws of society, the church indirectly performs a political function.

When the church effectively influences government, it may become a revolutionary force in society. Biblical teachings about social, political, and economic relationships have many radical social implications. They have contributed to gradual or sudden modifications of many social institutions and community conditions.[93]

The impact of religion on government is not always functional, however. When a church is identified with national institutions and values, overweening confidence in the rightness of political goals can lead it to perpetuate tyranny and support other evils in the name of "Christian civilization," the American Way of Life, or moral absolutes.[94] When religious diversity is great, religion may disrupt national unity as rival religious groups in their struggle for power seek to use government to accomplish their aims. Such civil wars have been avoided in the United States because of the "unity in diversity" ideal and the fact that every church is a minority religion.

Churches have profoundly influenced certain aspects of American foreign policy. The principle of religious liberty was used to stimulate immigration from Europe. Christian missionaries have been "powerful advance representatives" of their home country and have been protected by their government in times of rebellion or nationalist uprisings, often to the embarrassment of the nation's diplomats. Jewish interest in Zionism and Israel has had a significant impact upon foreign affairs with

---

[91] Jacques Maritain, *Christianity and Democracy* (New York: Charles Scribner's Sons, 1944); and Walter G. Muelder, "National Unity and National Ethics," *Annals of the American Academy of Political and Social Science,* 244 (Mar. 1946), 10-18.

[92] Dorothy I. Height and J. Oscar Lee, *The Christian Citizen and Civil Rights* (New York: Federal Council of the Churches of Christ in America, 1949).

[93] Maurice Fraigneux, *Christianity Is Revolutionary,* trans. Emma Craufurd (London: Cassell and Co., Ltd., 1954); William Dale Morris, *The Christian Origins of Social Revolt* (London: George Allen and Unwin, Ltd., 1949); Robert Gordis, *Politics and Ethics* (Santa Barbara, Calif.: Center for the Study of Democratic Institutions, 1961).

[94] James Luther Adams, "Religion and the Ideologies," *Confluence,* 4 (Apr. 1955), 72-84.

Arabian states. Diplomatic relations with such nations as Argentina, Colombia, Italy, and Spain have been enhanced by the strength of American Catholicism and endangered by the persecution of Protestant missionaries. Opposition to the president's representative to the Vatican in the 1940's came largely from churches, and it is conceivable that Catholic opposition to Communism has had a much greater influence on the "cold war" than most people realize.

To promote their specific values pertinent to legislation on liquor control, gambling, education, war, political corruption, racial discrimination, marriage, child labor, social welfare, atomic warfare, and a host of other social and economic issues, churches have been political pressure groups throughout American history, playing a major part in nearly every major politico-economic change. They were arrayed on both sides of the slavery question. They had more to do with passage of the Prohibition (18th) Amendment to the Constitution than even the Anti-Saloon League, and they have engaged in many anti-vice crusades. In some cases they have thus sought to advance partisan economic or ecclesiastical interests, but more often they have been concerned with basic ethical principles and human needs in their attempts to register judgments of the religious conscience. As a result, the major religious bodies have been surprisingly united on social creeds on the national and international level, even though in the local community and on specific details there often has been an equally high degree of disunity and sectarian rivalry among them.[95]

Concern of the church with morality has led it into an ever-broadening concern with political affairs, for moral issues are involved in almost every activity of man and hence in most if not all corporate decisions made through government. The social gospel movement (Chapter 6) has left its mark on many aspects of national and international policy, and current lobbying on local, state, and national levels is becoming an increasingly formalized program that goes far beyond simple opposition to "liquor, war, and sin." Anti-liquor crusading is no longer considered *the* way to solve all social problems, although it does continue in modified form in many denominations. Some church lobbying is basically humanitarian, promoting the general welfare, but some is protective in character striving to defend vested interests of the specific church. Church lobbies in Washington, D.C., have two chief functions: (1) informing, advising, and persuading legislators and administrators, and (2) channeling information about legislation and other governmental action to the church public.[96]

---

[95] Harry F. Ward, "Organized Religion, the State and the Economic Order," *Annals of the American Academy of Political and Social Science,* 256 (Mar. 1948), 72-83; and Muelder, "National Unity and National Ethics."

[96] Luke E. Ebersole, *Church Lobbying in the Nation's Capital* (New York: The Macmillan Co., 1951).

Churches also affect government through their influence on members. Education in church programs to make "good citizens" undoubtedly affects political affairs, although it is impossible to isolate these effects from those of all other factors which influence behavior. Support of the nation in time of war, assistance to immigrants adjusting to the new American culture, the message of security and peace in times of disaster, and perhaps even the provision of a "safety valve for the discharge of discontents against something other than the property system" [97] through revivalism have had clear political implications. Support of politics as a vocation in which religious principles can be demonstrated helps to break the dichotomy of "sacred and secular" and upholds the sacredness of all legitimate, moral, and beneficial activities of mankind.[98] Although churches do not ally themselves with specific political parties, as tends to be the case in Europe, they play a definite part in public elections. Religious views and affiliations of a candidate are more important than political and economic ones in some communities. To be elected to office in Utah, he must generally be a Mormon; in the South he must be a Protestant and in some local areas more specifically a Baptist or a Methodist; in certain northern cities, especially in New England, he will not succeed unless he is a Catholic.

When the members of a church hold the same basic political and economic views, it is perhaps more often as a result of common nonreligious traits which helped bring them together in the church than of their common religion. When churches take a political stand that identifies them with a specific party or economic philosophy, they generally do so because most of the members already identify themselves with that party or philosophy. A majority of Catholics support the Democratic Party, but most of them belong to the lower social and economic classes which are predominantly Democratic. Most Southern Baptists are Democrats, but so are southerners in general. American religious affiliation is associated with political and economic opinion mainly because certain denominations are made up of members from rather distinct income and status groups.[99] Usually the socioeconomic position of a church's members, more than religious doctrine, determines what political viewpoint (if any) it will adopt. This is evident, with some qualifications, from voting patterns observed in many elections. Since the mid-1920's Jews have voted chiefly for Democratic candidates. Northern Protestants vote mainly for Republicans, but Protestant voting patterns generally are

---

[97] Harold D. Lasswell, *Politics: Who Gets What, When, How* (New York: Peter Smith, 1950), p. 107.

[98] See Jerry Voorhis, *The Christian in Politics* (New York: Association Press, 1951).

[99] Wesley and Beverly Allinsmith, "Religious Affiliation and Politico-Economic Attitude: A Study of Eight Major U.S. Religious Groups," *Public Opinion Quarterly,* 12 (Fall 1948), 377-89.

more influenced than those of Catholics by differences in occupation and degree of commitment to the church as a significant reference group.[100] Although there is some evidence from comparative analyses of voting behavior in 1948, 1952, and 1956 that youth, especially among Catholics, may be deviating from traditional voting patterns of their group, Detroit Area Study data suggest that among young adults the religious factor is increasingly prominent as an influence on party preference.[101]

Religion and politics meet in the mind of the politician. If he is devout, religious judgment is brought to bear upon political issues. Yet among congressmen regional and party loyalties are far more significant influences on voting than religious ideology. Urban northern Democrats vote with other urban northern Democrats regardless of religion, and the one Republican Catholic senator voted more like other Republicans than like other Catholics.[102] The ideas of the nation's Catholic Supreme Court justices similarly are not distinguishable as a group from those of non-Catholics. In fact, their action on cases has often been contrary to that which would have been expected on the basis of Catholic doctrine.[103]

Churches at times have recommended specific patterns of voting or other political behavior to their members. The 1960 election campaign involved pronounced political efforts by certain Protestant groups as well as by the Roman Catholic bishops in Puerto Rico. Such work does not always accomplish its intended purpose and indeed may have manifest or latent effects highly detrimental to the church as appears to have been true in the latter instance.[104] In local politics religion is more likely to be involved in school board elections than in any other single issue. When both Protestants and Catholics are relatively powerful in a local community, tensions may reach a high level. When board members have a vested interest both in a parochial school system and in keeping taxes low, the public school system is likely to suffer.[105]

[100] David Gold, "On Description of Differential Association," *American Sociological Review,* 22 (Aug. 1957), 448-50; Oscar Glantz, "Protestant and Catholic Voting Behavior in a Metropolitan Area," *Public Opinion Quarterly,* 23 (Spring 1959), 73-82; L. H. Fuchs, "American Jews and the Presidential Vote," *American Political Science Review,* 49 (June 1955), 385-401; Werner Cohn, "The Politics of American Jews," in *The Jews,* Marshall Sklare, ed. (Glencoe, Ill.: The Free Press, 1958), pp. 614-26.
[101] Moses Rischin, *Our Own Kind: Voting by Race, Creed, or National Origin* (Santa Barbara, Calif.: Center for the Study of Democratic Institutions, 1960); Luke Ebersole, "Religion and Politics," *Annals of the American Academy of Political and Social Science,* 332 (Nov. 1960), 101-11; Lenski, *The Religious Factor,* pp. 124-35.
[102] William Bates, "Catholic Congressional Voting: Is It Truly Liberal?" *Social Order,* 6 (Mar. 1956), 104-6.
[103] Harold W. Chase, Margaret Jane Green, and Robert Mollan, "Catholics on the Court," *The New Republic,* 143, no. 14 (Sept. 26, 1960), 13-15.
[104] Norman Cousins, "Sin and Political Behavior," *Saturday Review,* 43, no. 49 (Dec. 3, 1960), 34, 64; and Thomas J. Liggett, "End of a Clerical Venture," *Christian Century,* 78 (Aug. 9, 1961), 952-54.
[105] For a prominent illustration see Gainer Bryan, Jr., "Public School, Roman Style?" *Christian Century,* 74 (Oct. 16, 1957), 1234-35.

Although Protestants, Catholics, and Jews agree that the church is morally and ethically superior to the state, their views of what is moral and ethical vary considerably. Protestants generally oppose legalized gambling while many Catholics sponsor games of chance to raise money for religious purposes. Catholics and Orthodox Jews oppose contraceptives as taking into man's hands prerogatives that belong to God alone, while most Protestants and other Jews support birth control within broad limitations. Fluoridation of water to help reduce tooth decay is supported by most churches, but Christian Scientists oppose it as compulsion to take medicine. Moderate use of tobacco and alcohol is upheld as personal privilege by some religious groups while others condemn one or both as injurious to health or morals. Vaccination, dissection of human cadavers, sterilization, blood transfusions, and euthanasia are other controversial topics in religious circles which sometimes become political issues.

Within the same religious body may be found many political and economic viewpoints, especially if its membership cuts across occupational and class lines. Controversies over these matters have contributed to major cleavages, like those of Baptists, Methodists, and Presbyterians over the issue of slavery before the Civil War. Internal dissension has created serious problems for denominational leaders and has made many adopt a stand-off policy of not acting on any controversial issue.

Social action committees and resolutions in Protestant bodies have solidified the *libertarians* who support and persistently recommend "the religious philosophy of limited government inherent in the Declaration of Independence." [106] Libertarians believe that man's inalienable rights and responsibilities must not be usurped by the state and that the church must help protect them. They consider taxation for social welfare to be sinful because it involves "taking by force" from the person taxed to help others; such help is moral only when offered voluntarily out of love, they believe. Libertarians cut across denominational, theological, and social lines to include members of all major denominations, fundamentalists and liberals, business and clergy persons, employers and employees. Their publications include *The Freeman*, published by the Foundation for Economic Education, *The Intercollegiate Review* of the Intercollegiate Studies Institute, and *Modern Age*, also published by ISI. (*Faith and Freedom* and *Christian Economics* are now defunct.) These cooperate closely with each other and with other conservative periodicals like *Human Events* and *National Review*. Sincerely believing that "that government is best which governs least," libertarians are accused of providing respectable channels for irresponsible charges of "Old Deal" groups that are presumed to have ulterior motives for their right-wing political inter-

---

[106] From the descriptive statement in *Faith and Freedom*, 6, no. 10 (June 1955), 2.

ests.[107] Their views are in sharp contrast to those of such Christian periodicals as *Sojourners, Radix, The Other Side, Christianity and Crisis,* and *The Christian Century.*

Conclusion

The political influence of the church is seldom that of a single voice unitedly promoting exactly the same goals. Libertarians oppose political liberals within denominational bodies, and the denominations often take divergent stands on major issues of national and international affairs. Except on generalities, a united front by churches seems to be the exception rather than the rule. This partly reflects the dominance of Protestantism with its emphasis upon the right of private judgment and the authority of the conscience of the individual citizen.

The reciprocal influences of church and state on each other, the great variability of the relationships between churches and political institutions, and the manner in which religious values reflect the general culture are clearly illustrated by the history of the churches' attitudes and action pertinent to war. Religious sanctions have supported the nation's wars, yet during peacetime churches have passed through pronounced waves of pacifism and have worked strenuously to perpetuate peace. Wars have had a profound impact upon churches and the religious faith of members. American wars indicate clearly that Judeo-Christian teachings have not been universally applied and that the church, in its concern with the problems of war and peace, reflects its society even more than it influences it. War is a symptom of an egoism that is contrary to Jewish and Christian teachings. Continuation of the war-oriented spirit of power politics in international relations reflects the failure of churches to indoctrinate the majority of the population with values antithetical to war.

Churches often face a dilemma in politics similar to that faced in wartime. If they rigidly support religious ethics of loving the enemy and doing good to all men, they lose members and influence. If they depart from their ethics to support war's brutality, they abdicate their opportunity to mold society after the ideal religious pattern and reduce their influence until all they can do is soften the harshness of certain subsidiary problems induced by war. If the religious leaders openly indicate the spiritually devastating effects of warfare upon combatants, they are in danger of losing their jobs; if they declare the war is a holy cause or bolster morale by assuring the salvation of all who die in battle, they may deny basic truths of their church. Hence church-type religious bodies tend to accept and support war, while sects that are outside of society's basic value-structure contradict the prevalent pattern of social behavior without modifying their religious position. Sects have nothing to lose by op-

---

[107] George Younger, "Protestant Piety and the Right Wing," *Social Action,* 17, no. 5 (May 15, 1951), 5-35.

posing a war that society is engaged in, but churches, linked with political, economic, professional, and other groups that have an emotional, psychological, and economic stake in society, can lose much.[108] The position of churches on war is one of the most tangible evidences of the fact that the church as a social institution is a part of society, not apart from it. The same tends to be true of other changes and proposed reforms in society; churches uphold the status quo; sects oppose it.

Church constituents for whom religion in the family is a prominent concern are more unwilling to have the church play an active role in politics than those for whom saliency of religion in the family is absent.[109] Does this indicate that the more religious people are, the less concerned they are about the impact of religion on their political institutions? Does it suggest that religious families recognize the dangers of identifying the church with some political party or movement to such an extent that it will be corrupted by undesirable aspects of the political program? Or does it reflect a feeling by the relatively non-religious families that the church ought to be gaining new tasks and functions to replace what they believe to be outmoded ones?

Selected References

Baron, Salo W., "Impact of Wars on Religion," *Political Science Quarterly*, 67 (Dec. 1952), 534–72. An excellent socio-historical survey.

Besanceney, Paul H., S.J., *Interfaith Marriages: Who and Why.* New Haven, Conn.: College and University Press, 1970. A review of the research and insights of social scientists.

Bossard, James H. S., and Eleanor S. Boll, *One Marriage, Two Faiths.* New York: Ronald Press Co., 1957. A collection and interpretation of case studies of interfaith marriages which deserves replication.

Ebersole, Luke Eugene, *Church Lobbying in the Nation's Capital.* New York: Macmillan, 1951. A study of lobbyists and lobbying for churches and religious organizations.

Fowler, Robert Booth, *A New Engagement: Evangelical Political Thought, 1966–1976.* Grand Rapids: Eerdmans, 1982. An analysis of the diverse involvements of evangelical Christianity in political and social issues.

Gordon, Albert Isaac, *Intermarriage: Interfaith, Interracial, Interethnic.* Westport, Conn.: Greenwood Press, 1980 (Beacon Press, 1964). An interpretation of the various types of intermarriage based in large part upon in-depth interviews about personal and family histories.

Gray, Robert M., and David O. Moberg, *The Church and the Older Person*, rev. ed. Grand Rapids: Eerdmans, 1977. A survey of research on religion and aging together with implications for action.

Hoge, Dean R., and Kathleen M. Ferry, *Empirical Research on Interfaith Mar-*

---

[108] J. Milton Yinger, *Religion in the Struggle for Power* (Durham, N.C.: Duke University Press, 1946), pp. 176-218. Cf. Ray H. Abrams, *Preachers Present Arms* (Philadelphia: Round Table Press, 1933).

[109] Benjamin B. Ringer and Charles Y. Glock, "The Political Role of the Church as Defined by Its Parishioners," *Public Opinion Quarterly*, 18 (Winter 1954-55), 337-47.

riage in America. Washington, D.C.: U.S. Catholic Conference, 1981. A review and summary of available research on interfaith marriage with special attention to Catholics.

Hughes, Everett C., *Cycles and Turning Points.* New York: National Council of the Episcopal Church, n.d. A sociological analysis of the significance of initiatory and other life-cycle religious rituals and their relevance to Christianity.

Journal of Church and State. A scholarly journal with significant articles, book reviews, lists of doctoral dissertations, and notes on worldwide news events related to church-state relationships (Baylor University, Waco, TX 76798).

Kaslow, Florence, and Marvin B. Sussman, eds., *Cults and the Family.* New York: Haworth Press, 1982 (*Marriage and Family Review*, vol. 4, no. 3/4). Original papers on family responses to conversion of members to new religious movements, the utopian quest for perfect families, therapy for former cult members, etc.

Kauffman, J. Howard, "Marriage and Family Alternatives," in *A Reader in Sociology: Christian Perspectives*, ed. Charles P. DeSanto, Calvin Redekop, and William L. Smith-Hinds (Scottdale, Pa.: Herald Press, 1980), pp. 505–31. A summary of alternative arrangements and proposals with an evaluation based on both biblical perspectives and empirical evidence. (See also Robert W. Herron, "What Makes a Family Christian?" pp. 533–44; James H. Phillips, "The Future of Monogamous Marriage from a Christian Perspective," pp. 545–68, and Charles P. DeSanto, "Premarital Sex: A Christian Perspective," pp. 569–81.)

Kelley, Dean M., ed., "The Uneasy Boundary: Church and State," *Annals of the American Academy of Political and Social Science*, vol. 446, Nov. 1979. A preface and 12 articles on various aspects of church-state relationships.

Liebman, Robert C., and Robert Wuthnow, eds., *The New Christian Right: Mobilization and Legitimation.* Hawthorne, N.Y.: Aldine, 1983. Original articles on the emergence and changing forms of the "New Christian Right," religion and politics, political involvements of fundamentalists and evangelicals, the Moral Majority, and similar subjects.

Schlesinger, Benjamin, ed., *The Jewish Family: A Survey and Annotated Bibliography.* Toronto: University of Toronto Press, 1971. Surveys on Jewish families and intermarriage, a 429-item annotated bibliography, an appendix of 172 books of fiction on Jewish life, and statistical data.

Stokes, Anson Phelps, and Leo Pfeffer, *Church and State in the United States*, rev. ed. Westport, Conn.: Greenwood, 1975. A monumental work on American church-state relations.

Young, Kimball, *Isn't One Wife Enough?* Westport, Conn.: Greenwood, 1970 (Henry Holt and Co., 1954). A comprehensive account of plural marriage among the Mormons.

Zwier, Robert, *Born-Again Politics: The New Christian Right in America.* Downers Grove, Ill.: Inter-Varsity Press, 1982. An analysis and appraisal of Christianity and politics with special emphasis on the period from 1977 to 1981.

Part Seven: *The Social Psychology of Religion*

🏛 Chapter 15

The Church Member

The importance of church members is obvious, for without them there could be no churches. Furthermore, democratic society considers institutions to be instruments rather than ends in and of themselves, and any functional effects of the church on society must come through persons acting either individually or in groups.

We shall survey various characteristics of church members, including indications of the degree to which their beliefs and activities are consistent with the ideal patterns churches recommend. The extent to which their religious participation "makes a difference" in life is a crucial indicator of the degree to which membership is more than a mere formality. Long after formal membership is discontinued, the church's influence presumably continues if it has helped to stabilize personality, build character, and establish wholesome social relationships, or, conversely, if it has contributed to personal or social maladjustments. Many church leaders suspect that principles and practice do not coincide in members' lives, but often, fearing what they might find, they resist research which will disclose the facts. They would be comforted if they knew a majority of their members were practicing the disciplines encouraged by the church.

Attitudes of Church Members

Living in a small New York town and participating in its life for an extended period, Schanck and his wife joined the Baptist and Methodist churches and conducted informal interviews with all members of both churches about church rites and behavior which the church tabooed. Significant discrepancies were evident between attitudes members were willing to give out for publication and their private attitudes. In 85 per cent of the cases, private attitudes were less conservative. In 77 per cent of the comparisons of nonmembers' public attitudes with members' private ones, nonmembers were more liberal. (See Table 8.)

Table 8
Attitudes of Church Members and Nonmembers in a New York Town

	51 Methodists		38 Nonmembers
Type of Attitude	Public (Per cent)	Private (Per cent)	Public (Per cent)
Attitude Toward Baptism:			
Baptism is real	58.8	41.2	21.0
Baptism is symbolic	37.3	39.2	47.4
Baptism is superstitious	3.9	19.6	31.6
Attitude Toward Card Playing:			
Use of face cards is wrong	90.2	19.6	23.7
Only gambling is wrong	3.9	72.6	73.7
Any card games may be played	5.9	7.8	2.6

Source: Richard L. Schanck, "A Study of a Community and Its Groups and Institutions Conceived of as Behaviors of Individuals," *Psychological Monographs,* 43, no. 195 (1932), 44, 46.

These relationships prevailed in 85 attitudes toward the nature and form of baptism, the Lord's Supper, ownership of church property, theater attendance, card playing, and other topics. Public attitudes of Baptists and Methodists toward religious symbols (the form and nature of baptism and the Lord's Supper) were more conservative than their public attitudes toward their religious code (card playing, theater attendance, and the minister's freedom of expression). Their public attitudes toward compensation for the choir and janitor were the most conservative of all. This study is tangible evidence that a church's norms are not always accepted by its members, even though they presumably agree with its creed. Yet members are closer to agreement with each other than to agreement with persons who choose not to join the church.[1]

---

[1] Richard L. Schanck, "A Study of a Community and Its Groups and Institutions Conceived of as Behaviors of Individuals," *Psychological Monographs,* 43, no. 195 (1932).

Attitudes toward death are conditioned by religious faith. A student questionnaire revealed two chief frames of reference, temporal and spiritual. Roman Catholics and fundamentalist Protestants were more consistently spiritual, thinking of death as a transition to an after-life more than in terms of what happens to the body. Regardless of religion, all who reported frequent church attendance had more consistent attitudes and more spiritually oriented responses. Religious dogma presents ready-made answers to questions about topics like death. Although the religious view is generally expected to alleviate anxiety about dying, emotional responses suggesting fear of death or of the dead were more common among spiritually than temporally oriented individuals. Upper and lower class persons gave more consistently spiritual responses than the middle income group. This supports Veblen's suggestion that the middle class life orientation is temporal, secular, and means-oriented, while the upper and lower classes are more likely to be trans-temporal and fate- or luck-oriented.[2]

The conditions under which members live most nearly in accord with the precepts of their church have received little systematic study. Comparison of an isolated Mormon village with villages in Utah suggests that isolation of a religious group from the main body of its religion contributes to the maintenance of distinctive institutions and beliefs. Individual members scattered about in a large, strange society, however, may rapidly lose their religious distinctives.[3]

When a church body makes an official pronouncement on a social, economic, or political issue, the climate of opinion prevalent in its membership is often assumed to coincide with the official policy. A comparison of Episcopal pronouncements with attitudes of a national sample of Episcopal laymen indicates that on nine issues the church was more liberal in its policy and more receptive to social change than were the parishioners. The greatest danger of offending members' collective sentiments came on issues directly related to power distribution in society. On topics like war, labor, government control, and the church's political role, members not only had definite convictions but also had a clearly identifiable self-interest. However, on ideological or moral issues like human rights, conscientious objectors, and intermarriage with Catholics, no collective will had become solidified, and the church had greater opportunity to exert its leadership through strong and clear-cut pronouncements.[4] Parishioners with most of

[2] William A. Faunce and Robert L. Fulton, "The Sociology of Death: A Neglected Area of Research," *Social Forces,* 36 (Mar. 1958), 205-9.

[3] Thomas F. O'Dea, "The Effects of Geographical Position on Belief and Behavior in a Rural Mormon Villiage," *Rural Sociology,* 19 (Dec. 1954), 358-64. Wilford E. Smith also found rural families to be more orthodox than urban ("The Urban Threat to Mormon Norms," *Rural Sociology,* 24 [Dec. 1959], 355-61). Much "leakage" of church members may result from living in an urban, impersonal society among people of heterogeneous religious and cultural characteristics.

[4] Charles Y. Glock and Benjamin B. Ringer, "Church Policy and the Attitudes of

their group affiliations in church-related organizations participated most actively in church rituals, felt most strongly that the church was important in their personal lives, and most believed that the church influenced their opinions. Yet those most committed to the church were the least likely to endorse an active political role for it. Males, younger members, and the college educated were more willing than others to have the church participate actively in public affairs. Even when the variables of sex, age, and education were controlled, the inverse relationship between church commitment and permissiveness toward an active church role in politics remained. The most committed members were the most inclined toward the traditional view that the church must not "meddle" in politics.[5]

Both clergymen and fellow constituents exert a significant influence on members for whom the church is a reference group, i.e., a vital and meaningful organization which is part of one's frame of reference in developing self-concepts, making decisions, or appraising social situations. In a semi-rural Utah community male Mormons with high conformity to ritualistic behavior norms of their church were more likely than other males to hold the attitudinal values most emphasized by the church. Church participation was a stronger influence on attitudes than religious beliefs.[6] Members tend to shift attitudes on various aspects of religious faith, practice, and social implications in the direction of the majority and of clergymen, the experts in the religious field.[7]

Church Participation Studies

Religious interests are by no means negligible among contemporary Americans. Over 90 per cent of 271 persons aged 18 to 30 in four Minnesota communities were church members and over 70 per cent were active in the church. The highest ranked of 43 discussion topics or activities in all 18 sub-categories by sex, age, marital status, and place of residence was "having a wholesome religious life." Three-fourths of all adults in 1981 felt following God's will was very important to them.[8]

The more mobile a Protestant population is, the lower the proportion

Ministers and Parishioners on Social Issues," *American Sociological Review*, 21 (Apr. 1956), 148-56.

[5] Benjamin B. Ringer and Charles Y. Glock, "The Political Role of the Church as Defined by Its Parishioners," *Public Opinion Quarterly*, 18 (Winter 1954-55), 337-47.

[6] John Democritos Photiadis, *Behavioral Conformity to Church Teaching as a Function of the Sentiments of the Individual and Membership Group Identification*, Ph.D. thesis, Cornell University, 1958.

[7] H. E. Burtt and D. R. Falkenburg, Jr., "The Influence of Majority and Expert Opinion on Religious Attitudes," *Journal of Social Psychology*, 14 (Nov. 1941), 269-78.

[8] Marvin J. Taves and Robert R. Pinches, "The Community Relations of Older Rural Youth," *Minnesota Farm and Home Science*, 16, no. 1 (Oct. 1958), 19-20, and R. R. Pinches and M. J. Taves, "Fitting Young Adults into the Community," *ibid.* 16, no. 3 (May 1959), 3, 6, and Princeton Religion Research Center, *Religion in America 1982* (Princeton, N.J.: The Gallup Poll, 1982), p. 148.

who are church members. Low levels of home ownership and other in-dices of low socioeconomic status are correlated with low church mem-bership rates. Catholic studies demonstrate that urban families which change place of residence have a slightly but consistently better record of Mass attendance, Easter duties, Holy Communion, valid marriages, and children in Catholic schools than families that are more stable.[9]

Age and education are related to variations in Catholic participation. The better educated generally are more active. The highest percentage of religious observance occurs in youth, with declines to the 30-39 decade and an upswing in succeeding years. Males in the thirties and early forties have the lowest record of all. Adult supervision is perhaps the main rea-son for the higher observance of adolescents and pre-adolescents. Institu-tional controls become more lax in the twenties; numerous social distrac-tions accompany emancipation from school and home ties. During the succeeding decade family responsibilities deter attendance, the persistent practice of birth control bars many from penance and the Eucharist, and the husband is preoccupied with occupational and economic striving. Fol-lowing the thirties, social and economic aspects of life are more settled. The sense of belonging in the parish and an accompanying security of so-cial relations probably fortify group religious practices. Slightly lower par-ticipation in extreme old age can be attributed primarily to physical disabilities. The aged also spent their formative years in an era when Catholics were not widely encouraged to receive Communion weekly.[10]

Ritualistic behavior even in church does not always conform to ex-pected norms. Persons entering the Catholic Cathedral in Syracuse, New York, were observed to see how many sacramentally dipped a finger in the font of holy water and made the sign of the cross. Both rites were kept by 975 persons (62.7 per cent) and neither by 414 (26.6 per cent); 28 (1.8 per cent) dipped the finger but made no sign of the cross, and 140 (8.9 per cent) made the sign without dipping the finger. A J-curve may describe the pattern of conformity in most groups; the majority engage in the expected behavior, with declining numbers in each category further removed from it. Observations of genuflection in two Catholic churches, time of arrival at church on Sunday, and Catholic student beliefs regarding the Deity support the hypothesis. The pattern is less clearly substantiated in regard to Episcopalian participation in congregational singing and silent prayer upon taking places in the pew.[11]

---

[9] Joseph H. Fichter, S.J., *Social Relations in the Urban Parish* (Chicago: University of Chicago Press, 1954), pp. 94-106. The Protestant differences might disappear if more atten-tion were given to Pentecostal-Holiness and other sectarian groups.

[10] *Ibid.*, pp. 83-91, 107-20. For generally comparable findings in an urban north-ern parish see Joseph B. Schuyler, "Religious Observance Differentials by Age and Sex in 'Northern Parish',"· *American Catholic Sociological Review,* 20 (Summer 1959), 124-31.

[11] Floyd H. Allport, "The J-Curve Hypothesis of Conforming Behavior," *Journal of Social Psychology,* 5 (May 1934), 141-83.

Many variations in religious participation may be attributed to differences in values. Conflicts between values espoused by the various institutions pull participants in different directions. When religious teachings are recognized to have implications contrary to such social patterns as "second-class citizenship" for Negroes, conspicuous consumption to "keep up with the Joneses," or measuring people's worth by their material possessions, people may grow cool toward the church that emphasizes such teachings and either find another that is more congenial to their values or drop out of church entirely.

The degree of faith or normative commitment is related to one's regular practice of religion. Persons with sectarian religious beliefs in the Columbus, Ohio, metropolitan area were more frequent church attenders than those with church-type attitudes. Sectarians belonged to more church subgroups, derived more satisfaction from religion than "secular" groups did, and drew more of their close friends from within the religious group.[12] In an Idaho Latter Day Saints church extremely orthodox members whose religion seemed to permeate the entire life differed from the extremely unorthodox in several respects. Males tended toward the extremes of orthodoxy and unorthodoxy more than females, perhaps because of the dominant role of males in Mormonism. A cyclical pattern by age similar to Fichter's findings for Catholics was observed. Orthodoxy reached its highest levels at ages 18-19 and 60 and its lowest levels at about age 30 and in old age. Income was more consistently related to orthodoxy than occupation; highest orthodoxy occurred among members with annual incomes less than $2,000 and at about $8,000, with lowest orthodoxy at $5,000 and in the highest income categories. Few differences in orthodoxy were observed between the single and married, but divorced persons were at the two extremes. Converts and those who had served as missionaries were more orthodox than other members.[13]

When a religious group is a minority in society, its influence over members is sometimes so dissipated that it loses many distinctive features and gradually is assimilated into the general population. Roman Catholics attend Mass less regularly when they are a minority participating in social institutions dominated by Protestants.[14] But when they suffer a degree of persecution, they are driven to form closely-knit communities and their minority position strengthens their observance of religious practices. In

[12] Russell R. Dynes, "The Consequences of Sectarianism for Social Participation," *Social Forces*, 35 (May 1957), 331-34. Cf. Phillip E. Hammond, "Contemporary Protestant Ideology: A Typology of Church Images," *Review of Religious Research*, 2 (Spring 1961), 161-69; and Nicholas J. Demerath, III, "Social Stratification and Church Involvement . . . ," *ibid.*, 146-54.

[13] Glenn M. Vernon, "Background Factors Related to Church Orthodoxy," *Social Forces*, 34 (Mar. 1956), 252-54.

[14] Meyer F. Nimkoff and A. L. Wood, "Effect of Majority Patterns on the Religious Behavior of a Minority Group," *Sociology and Social Research*, 30 (Mar.-Apr 1946), 282-89.

American small towns Catholics attend Mass much more regularly than in cities, especially if the cities have few Catholics; the social control of the group is stronger over its members, and personal contacts between the clergy and the faithful are facilitated by the small number of Catholics in the parish. Thus in Bloomington, Indiana, with only 1,200 Catholics in a city of 28,000, Sunday Mass attendance is estimated at 75 per cent, compared to only 15 to 20 per cent in the San Antonio Mexican population, nearly all of whom are at least nominally Catholic, and only 46 per cent attendance of all Catholic parishioners in New Orleans.[15]

Catholic students at the University of Minnesota who often attended Mass and received communion, and who attended Mass the first Friday of each month, were more likely than other Catholics to have only Catholics as friends. Attitudes toward birth control were also related to homogeneity of friendships. These findings indicate that other Catholics constitute a reference group for those who most faithfully practice their religion.[16] The degree of members' self-identification with the church undoubtedly varies. It is likely that one's sense of group identification is greater in groups which are ethnic or religious minorities than in the denominations of the majority.

A test was made of the hypothesis that "attitudinal response is a function of the relative strengths of momentary forces toward or away from membership in groups with conflicting norms." Catholics in experimental groups of introductory psychology students were questioned on personal attitudes toward general religious, Catholic, and other opinion items. Their responses were closer to the orthodox Catholic position than Catholic control students in a large heterogeneous class. There were no significant differences between responses of the experimental group, who were first briefed by discussion on basic assumptions which underlie the opinions of all Catholics, and a control group of Catholics questioned in a small room but not experimentally aroused to the fact of their common Catholic affiliation. These findings suggest that the relevance of Catholic membership to selected attitudes is increased by reminders of common group membership. However, among "evangelical Protestants" (mostly Lutherans) and Jews, no significant differences were found between those isolated for discussion of Protestant or Jewish assumptions before answering the items and those in the large control group. Religion may be a more salient and powerful influence upon Catholics than upon others.[17]

---

[15] François Houtart, "A Sociological Study of the Evolution of the American Catholics," *Sociaal Kompas,* 2 (Jan.-Apr. 1955), 189-216.

[16] Gertrude Neuwirth, "The Implication of Reference Group Behavior for Religious Participation," Summary of Papers Presented at the March 6, 1958, meeting of the Minn. Chapter of the Society for the Scientific Study of Religion (dittoed), pp. 2-3.

[17] W. W. Charters, Jr., and Theodore M. Newcomb, "Some Attitudinal Effects of Experimentally Increased Salience of a Membership Group," in *Readings in Social Psychology,* Eleanor E. Maccoby, Theodore M. Newcomb, and Eugene L. Hartley,

Does Religion Permeate Daily Living?

"Official morality" in the church often deviates from private beliefs and behavior. Many members publicly proclaim certain doctrines and ignore their practical implications. Such deviation is encouraged when people observe others violating prohibitions.[18]

Findings on the effects of religious education in the late 1920's shocked many church leaders. Scores on Bible knowledge tests were related to scores on tests to measure cheating, lying, class loyalty, and altruism (unselfishness) and to teachers' ratings on various conduct traits. The sample of 485 pupils in grades 7 through 12 was selected from public schools and schools for delinquents to be representative by intelligence, occupation, other socioeconomic characteristics, types of communities, character levels, and sex. No significant relationship was observed between Biblical information and various phases of conduct. Mere Biblical knowledge did not insure proper growth in character, so traditional methods of Bible instruction needed revision in order to accomplish desirable results in children's character.[19]

Investigation of deceit among children in public and private schools revealed that 28 per cent of the Catholics, 26 per cent of the Jews, and 43 per cent of the Protestants were honest on achievement tests designed to detect cheating. The respective figures for dishonesty were 47, 47, and 40 per cent, while 25, 26, and 17 per cent were "confessors" (dishonest, but later confessing their cheating). It is likely that these variations resulted less from different religious influences than from such associated social factors as place of birth, ancestry, and socioeconomic background. Protestants enrolled in Sunday school were not significantly different in cheating behavior from those not enrolled; the same was true of Jews receiving and not receiving religious instruction.[20] Among Protestant denominations analyzed separately, more cheating than average, when intelligence was controlled, was found among Baptist, Episcopal, and United Brethren children. Less than average cheating occurred among Christian, Christian Scientist, Lutheran, Presbyterian, and Reformed children. Methodist groups were divided. It was impossible to account for all denomina-

eds. (New York: Holt, Rinehart and Winston, Inc., 3d ed., 1958), pp. 276-81. It may be argued, however, that this experiment was highly exploratory and not definitive.

[18] Charles K. Warriner, "The Nature and Functions of Official Morality," *American Journal of Sociology*, 64 (Sept. 1958), 165-68; and Don L. Kimbrell and Robert R. Blake, "Motivational Factors in the Violation of a Prohibition," *Journal of Abnormal and Social Psychology*, 56 (1958), 132-33.

[19] Pleasant R. Hightower, *Biblical Information in Relation to Character and Conduct* (Iowa City: University of Iowa Studies in Character, III, no. 2, 1930).

[20] Hugh Hartshorne and Mark A. May, *Studies in the Nature of Character*, I, *Studies in Deceit* (New York: The Macmillan Co., 1928), pp. 295-300, 356-62, *passim*.

tional differences on the basis of socioeconomic factors alone. Different ethical standards may prevail between churches, especially when nationality and religious groupings are identical and reinforce each other.[21]

A survey of members in an evangelical denomination in Ohio found that 20 per cent never prayed, 25 per cent never read the Bible, 30 per cent never attended church, 40 per cent never gave to the church, 50 per cent never attended the church or Sunday school, 90 per cent never had family worship, 95 per cent never invited another person to Christ, and 95 per cent never tithed. All of these activities were recommended by their churches. In the Methodist Church there were 625,000 inactive members in 1941 and 1,735,000 a decade later. Even active members often fail to practice holy habits advocated by their church. As a result, missions to church members are often conducted by local churches and denominations.[22]

A nationwide Methodist opinion survey found that subscribers to *Christian Advocate* were closer to traditional Methodist positions about games of chance, profanity, dancing, tobacco, drinking, driving faster than the speed limit, and similar topics than a general cross-section of members. Younger members were more broad-minded than older ones, and the less regular church attenders had more deviant attitudes than those who attended often. Dancing, formerly considered sinful by most Methodists, was objected to by only 24 per cent of the *Advocate* subscribers and 15 per cent of the others; use of tobacco was condemned by about twice as many, and drinking of alcohol by a significant majority in even the most liberal sub-categories. Sixty-nine per cent of the general sample believed the church should advocate and teach total abstinence; less than half believed it wrong for Methodists to buy a chance on a charity raffle, and only 40 per cent objected to playing bingo. Fewer than one-third criticized speculative buying of stocks, but two-thirds said "a good Methodist" would not drive faster than the speed limit.[23] About half stated that their family had no period of worship other than grace at meals; one-fifth had daily family worship. The younger the respondent, the less likely he was to share in daily family worship. Half of the women and two-fifths of the men did some "inspirational reading." Only one in ten reported that grace is never said in their homes. Of six types of worship experiences, Sunday church service was first in the proportion (60 per cent) who considered it the most helpful and significant religious experience; it was followed by daily devotions (13 per cent), church school including youth services (7.5 per cent), grace at meals (3.5 per

---

[21] *Ibid.*, pp. 254-56. (Related findings are included in Chapter 17.)

[22] Elmer G. Homrighausen, "The Church in the World: Do Church Members Practice Spiritual Disciplines?" *Theology Today*, 10 (July 1953), 252-54.

[23] Murray H. Leiffer, "Methodists Don't Do That. Or Do They?" *Christian Advocate*, 131 (Jan. 5, 1956), 10-11, 29-31; and Murray H. Leiffer, "Finding Out What Methodists Think," *ibid.*, 130 (Dec. 29, 1955), 1594-95, 1615.

cent), religious radio and television programs (1.5 per cent), and inspirational reading (1.4 per cent).[24]

Orthodox Jews similarly deviate from behavior traditionally considered ideal in their religion. As Jewish religious observance becomes secularized, assimilation is so accelerated that some question the survival of Judaism in America.[25]

Inconsistencies between church members' behavior and religious ideals sometimes result from failure to see practical implications of the ideals. Economic factors often have more influence than religious values. Thus, industrialists have engaged in sensational acts of philanthropy attracting much public attention while persistently exploiting their laborers, selfishly grasping power, and greedily piling up wealth. Often they have been leading members of churches, but their "religion appears to have been partly a mask for economic advantage . . . whether or not it was consciously so used." [26] Attitudes and actions of church members tend to follow those predominant in their communities and social classes (see pertinent sections of Chapters 3, 14, and 17). While professing loyalty to democracy, their daily behavior often is inconsistent with democratic ideology.[27] This fact reflects a basic dilemma of churches with voluntary membership. To continue operation, a church must win sufficient new members to replace those lost by death, migration, and other departures. This necessitates appealing to approved life styles and cherished values of people in the community who otherwise would brand the program, message, or worship patterns as eccentric, un-American, or otherwise objectionable. Accommodation to community values reduces the influence of the church over members; failure to accommodate maintains a "pure" message or mission but typically eventuates in institutional decline.[28]

While the U.S. can be considered a "Christian nation" on the basis of the affiliations of a majority of its people, it may be far from that in terms of their daily conduct. Faith is not always accompanied by "works"! There is, rather, a continuum of orthodoxy along which church members may be ranked. Few are in the extreme position in which religion permeates all of their beliefs and actions, and few are at the other extreme in which

---

[24] Murray H. Leiffer, "What Are Our Sources of Spiritual Strength? " *Christian Advocate,* 131 (Jan. 19, 1956), 75, 85, 87, 91.

[25] Howard W. Polsky, "A Study of Orthodoxy in Milwaukee: Social Characteristics, Beliefs, and Observances," in *The Jews,* Marshall Sklare, ed. (Glencoe, Ill.: The Free Press, 1958), pp. 325-35.

[26] Liston Pope, *Millhands and Preachers* (New Haven: Yale University Press, 1942), p. 20.

[27] For this reason Gabriel Vahanian believes we are now in a post-Christian era. "This Post-Christian Era," *Nation,* 189 (Dec. 12, 1959), 438-41.

[28] Albert T. Rasmussen, "Contemporary Religious Appeals and Who Responds," in Jane C. Zahn, *Religion and the Face of America* (Berkeley: University Extension, University of California, 1959), pp. 1-16.

religion has no impact upon behavior. Most fall between the two poles. Part of the reason for this characteristic may be ignorance of church teachings. Three hundred adult church attenders had median scores of only about 30 per cent on an easy ten-item test of general Bible knowledge. Ignorance of biblical history or only sketchy acquaintance with it was evident in 83 per cent.[29] But life is influenced when people see tangible things to do.

Laymen donate substantial amounts of labor that would otherwise require payment from the church treasury. A study of 341 rural churches belonging to 23 denominations in 44 states found that 25,612 church members and 5,329 nonmembers had contributed labor valued at $280,-578 in the year 1948. The 72 types of donated labor were rated for their monetary value, harmful effects and social values of promoting fellowship, creating church loyalty, enlisting church workers, and helping low-income people to give. Church suppers had high social values but low economic and stewardship values. Sales projects brought in little money, were poor publicity, and interfered with stewardship values. Among the most beneficial projects were various forms of constructing and beautifying church property, transporting people to church, providing musical services, and sponsoring dramas. Group projects generally were more interesting, provided more fellowship, and developed more church loyalty than individual work. Most labor gifts were contributed by men and increased their interest and pride in the church.[30] Regular contributions of time and energy are given for Sunday school teaching and administration, singing in the choir, handling church finances, church visitation programs, committee work, etc. The hours per member per year spent in such activities range from zero to perhaps several hundred. This could be made a major part of any index to identify nuclear or core members.

Church Membership and Community Participation

Church members are more likely than non-members to join other community organizations. When farm ownership and land classes were held constant in a New York study, participation in organizations other than the church was greater among Protestants than Catholics. Among the Protestants, Congregationalists, Presbyterians, and Friends were slightly more active than Baptists and Methodists.[31] Surveys of urban populations

---

[29] Thomas Roy Pendell, "Biblical Literacy Test," *Christian Century,* 72 (Oct. 21, 1959), 1212-13.

[30] Ralph A. Felton, *Men Working: A Study of Voluntary Labor Gifts* (Madison, N.J.: Drew Theological Seminary, 1949).

[31] W. A. Anderson, "Social Participation and Religious Affiliation in Rural Areas," *Rural Sociology,* 9 (Sept. 1944), 242-50.

have produced similar findings. In Bennington, Vermont, Protestants averaged 2.54 memberships in voluntary associations, Catholics 1.12, and persons with no church affiliation 0.79. Only in the upper social class did persons with no professed affiliation have significantly more memberships than Catholics.[32] Forty-five per cent of the Jews interviewed in a 1955 national NORC sample belonged to no organizations, compared to 63 per cent of the Protestants and 69 per cent of the Catholics. Corresponding figures for memberships in one organization are 25, 20, and 17 per cent and for memberships in two or more 30, 17, and 14 per cent, respectively.[33] Even when urban neighborhoods are controlled by economic status and family characteristics, Protestants exceed Catholics in formal memberships and attendance. Catholics, however, report more informal group participation,[34] and differences are diminishing.

The greater activity of church members in voluntary social organizations may explain such phenomena as the tendency of members to adopt new farm practices more rapidly than nonmembers. Significant interaction between farmers occurs in church settings and contributes to the diffusion of new techniques.[35]

Differences in educational aspirations and attainment of Protestants and Catholics have been noted. Thus 58 per cent of Protestant but only 47 per cent of Catholic high school students in a San Francisco-Oakland Bay area study wanted to go to college. Social class variations appeared responsible for the differences.[36] The relatively small number of Catholics in science and scholarship has become a major source of concern to the Roman Catholic Church.[37] Catholic students in a predominantly Protestant university were more likely to enroll in B.S. and less likely to

---

[32] John C. Scott, Jr., "Membership and Participation in Voluntary Associations," *American Sociological Review,* 22 (June 1957), 315-26.

[33] Charles R. Wright and Herbert H. Hyman, "Voluntary Association Memberships of American Adults: Evidence from National Sample Surveys," *American Sociological Review,* 23 (June 1958), 284-94. Yet Catholic families were more likely than Protestant to include persons with organizational memberships; this may be due to larger family size. (1981 Gallup Poll results are similar.)

[34] Wendell Bell and Maryanne T. Force, "Religious Preference, Familism, and the Class Structure," *Midwest Sociologist,* 19 (May 1957), 79-86.

[35] James H. Copp, *Personal and Social Factors Associated with the Adoption of Recommended Farm Practices Among Cattlemen* (Manhattan, Kansas: A.E.S. Technical Bulletin 83, Sept. 1956); and Herbert F. Lionberger and C. Milton Coughenour, *Social Structure and Diffusion of Farm Information* (Columbia, Missouri: A.E.S. Research Bulletin 631, Apr. 1957), pp. 19, 92.

[36] Alan B. Wilson, "Residential Segregation of Social Classes and Aspirations of High School Boys," *American Sociological Review,* 24 (Dec. 1959), 836-45.

[37] S. J. Weigel, "American Catholic Intellectualism: A Theologian's Reflection," *Review of Politics,* 19 (July 1957), 275-307; and Thomas F. O'Dea, *American Catholic Dilemma: An Inquiry into the Intellectual Life* (New York: Sheed and Ward, 1958). Gerhard Lenski suggests that both conscious and subconscious levels of thought and action inhibit the development of scientific careers among Catholics. See *The Religious Factor* (Garden City, N.Y.: Doubleday and Co., 1961), pp. 202-3, 248, 253-55.

take a liberal arts program than Protestants. This contradicts typical conclusions about the "Protestant ethic"; apparently it was adhered to more by Catholic than Protestant students! [38] Perhaps this reflects the continuing rise of Catholics in the general social and occupational structure. Third generation Catholics do not differ significantly by occupation from white Protestants of comparable backgrounds.[39] Yet a high level of religious commitment is very strongly related to the American work ethic.[40]

Church Attendance Patterns

Sample surveys reveal clear differences in church attendance by gender, age, religion, and other variables. During an average week of 1981 41 per cent of adults (35 per cent of males and 46 per cent of females) attended church or synagogue; only 28 per cent had not attended (other than for weddings, funerals, and special holidays) within the preceding six months. Rates increased with age from 32 per cent for those under 30 to 49 per cent for those who were 65 or more. Among Catholics the weekly rate was 53 per cent and for Protestants 40 per cent compared to 74 and 44 per cent, respectively, in the peak year of 1958. Rates were highest (44 per cent) in rural areas and cities under 50,000 and lowest (38 per cent) in cities of 50,000 to 999,999. They were higher in the Midwest (47) and South (44) than in the East (39) and West (32 per cent). Church members (55), evangelicals (66), those of very high spiritual commitment (72), and those who watched religious television (52) or heard religious radio (57 per cent) within the past week had higher weekly records than their counterparts.[41]

In a New York City parish with 14,000 Catholics, 3,000 attended other churches and 2,000 were too young, old, sick, or otherwise unable to attend. Sunday Mass attendance was about 6,500—80 per cent of those who might be expected but under half of all parishoners. Artificial parish boundary lines, which help account for this, can destroy the community life of the parish.[42]

Church attendance patterns vary with social conditions. In the suburban

[38] Helmut R. Wagner, Kathryn Doyle, and Victor Fisher, "Religious Background and Higher Education," *American Sociological Review*, 24 (Dec. 1959), 852-56.

[39] Seymour M. Lipset and Reinhard Bendix, *Social Mobility in Industrial Society* (Berkeley: University of California Press, 1959); John Kosa and John Nash, "The Social Ascending of Catholics," *Social Order*, 8 (Mar. 1958), 98-103; and Neil J. Weller, "A Comparative Study of Vertical Mobility Among Catholics and Protestants," paper presented at the annual meeting of the American Sociological Society, Sept. 5, 1959. But see Lenski's contrary conclusions in *The Religious Factor*, pp. 76-95.

[40] Research and Forecasts, Inc., *The Connecticut Mutual Life Report on American Values in the '80s: The Impact of Belief* (Hartford: Connecticut Mutual Life Insurance Co., 1981), pp. 159-82.

[41] Princeton Center, *Religion in America 1982*, pp. 42-45, 101.

[42] Joseph B. Schuyler, "Potential Elements of Organization and Disorganization in the Parish—As Seen in Northern Parish," *American Catholic Sociological Review*, 18 (June 1957), 98-112.

fringe of Flint, Michigan, attendance was lower for both Catholics and Protestants than in the central city even after age, education, occupation. and size of household were controlled. As elsewhere, older, white collar, and highly educated persons attended more frequently than others. Proximity to church was closely related to Catholic attendance rates.[43] A Los Angeles study of four large churches similarly found that participation varied directly with the distance of members' residences from the church; the church's pulling power in drawing new members rarely exceeded ten miles.[44]

The very poor chapel attendance record of Protestants in the Army results from previously acquired attitudes. The importance of public worship is not impressed upon Protestant youth. Church life is typically regarded more as a social affair than an opportunity for confronting God, for Protestants tend to emphasize theologically horizontal (man-man) rather than vertical (man-God) relationships. Primary loyalty is generally given to a local church or its minister rather than to Christ. As a result, many Christian persons must be won for the church all over again when they join the armed forces or move to a new community.[45]

Sex Ratios of Churches

The sex ratio (number of males per 100 females) in the U.S. in 1930 was 102.5 and in 1940 it was 100.7, but the sex ratio of church memberships reported in the 1936 Census of Religious Bodies was 78.5. Religious bodies with the most children enrolled as members tended to have the most equitable sex distributions. The highest sex ratio (99.1) was reported by the Church of Jesus Christ of the Latter-day Saints (Mormons). It was followed by Norwegian Lutherans (95.8), Missouri Synod Lutherans (93.2), and the Roman Catholic Church (91.7). The Church of **Christ, Scientist, had the lowest sex ratio (31.3), followed by four black** Baptist and Methodist bodies which ranged from 56.7 to 61.1. Southern denominations had higher sex ratios than their northern counterparts.[46]

Sex ratio differences between denominations can be explained by many factors. Where family solidarity is greatest, the whole family is most likely

[43] Basil G. Zimmer and Amos H. Hawley, "Suburbanization and Church Participation," *Social Forces,* 37 (May 1959), 348-54.

[44] Merle E. Fish, Jr., *Adjustment of Large Downtown and Boulevard Churches in Los Angeles to Socio-Cultural Factors in the Community,* Ph.D. thesis, University of Southern California, 1959; *Dissertation Abstracts,* 20 (July 1959), 401.

[45] Chaplain Tracy Early, "Why Army Church-going Lags," *Christianity Today,* 3, no. 21 (July 20, 1959), 12-13. Many soldiers also attend civilian churches. Three-fourths of the new members joining urban Baptist churches analyzed in 150 studies came by transfer of church letter; 38 per cent of the losses were by erasure. The study by Rev. James Scott is reported in "Urban Evangelism," *The City Church,* 9, no. 5 (Nov.-Dec. 1958), 16.

[46] T. Lynn Smith, *Population Analysis* (New York: McGraw-Hill Book Co., 1948), pp. 186-88.

to be members together in the same church. Denominations that are "old-world" in tradition and emphasize the patriarchal family are the most likely to emphasize family church memberships which include children. These are "churches" as contrasted to "sects" in Troeltsch's typology (Chapter 4). Variations in membership policies contribute to differences in the degree to which a church approximates the sex ratio of its community. The more children included in a church, the higher its sex ratio tends to be, for at birth boys slightly outnumber girls, and children have little opportunity or inclination until adolescence to renounce the membership conferred upon them by parents. Churches retaining inactive members on their rolls are more likely to have an equitable sex ratio than those which regularly eliminate such persons. Immigration also has affected the sex composition. Ethnic groups with excesses of males among the long-distance migrants have had higher sex ratios in their churches than other denominations.

Leadership opportunities of the sexes, both in and outside the church, have no doubt drawn disparate proportions of women into churches. Groups founded and dominated by women tend to have extremely low sex ratios, while those like the Mormons which most emphasize male dominance have relatively high sex ratios. Social class differences may also contribute to variations. Middle class people may be more likely to become members and participate in church activities as a family unit than the lower classes. Different types of doctrinal emphasis may appeal differently to the sexes and contribute to some extent to unequal sex ratios. The age of a denomination may be partly responsible for variations; evidence suggests that the older, more traditionally oriented ones have higher sex ratios. Psychological and social sex differences also may enter into variations in identification with and participation in church. If women indeed are more highly expressive emotionally, this may be a major reason for low sex ratios in Pentecostal and Holiness groups. The roles of women may also be more compatible with religious activity than those of men in American society.

The sex ratio of rural farm communities is far higher than that of urban areas. In 1940 the urban sex ratio was 95.5, but that of urban churches in 1936 was 78.6. The rural population had a sex ratio of 107.8, but the sex ratio of rural churches was only 78.4. This indicates that men are more underrepresented in rural than in urban churches, although one might expect the opposite on the basis of the traditional character of much religion, the nature of social life in the rural community, and the larger proportion of men in rural areas. In order to have the same sex ratio in rural as in city churches, the rural church ratio would have to be 12.4 per cent higher.[47]

---

[47] *Ibid.* Females comprised 49 per cent of the rural Mo. population, but 55 per cent of the participating members in rural churches. Cf. Milton Coughenour and Lawrence M. Hepple, *The Church in Rural Missouri, Part II, Religious Groups in*

Among church members, women also are generally more faithful participants than men. At every age group among 8,363 white urban Catholics, women were more faithful than men in their religious observances.[48] Steel mill workers interviewed in Ellwood City, Pennsylvania, frequently indicated that, although they were church members, they left the practice of religion to their wives.[49] All research on Protestants and Catholics reaches similar conclusions about the higher religiosity of females.

Explanations of Low Sex Ratios in Churches

Only speculation prevails as to why Christian church membership and participation includes disproportionately high numbers of women. Some explanations offered are *psychological*. Women may face more crises in life because of their role in child-bearing and hence may be more inclined toward religion. Other theories assume that males and females are innately different mentally and psychologically, women as a result having a "natural" inclination toward religion. Thus it has been said that woman is "a creature of intuition, of mystical emotion, rather than of intellect and rational inhibition." [50] She was a slave of man for ages, had no will of her own, and lacked experience and environment to develop the "later mental products of the evolutionary process" which presumably advanced more rapidly in her master.[51] Females with feminine personalities differ significantly from masculine males in all six values measured by the Allport-Vernon-Lindzey scale. Females rank higher on esthetic and religious values; value systems are closely related to the basic elements of personality.[52]

Social psychological attempts to explain the excess of women over men in the church emphasize differences in the socialization process and in social experiences of males and females. Girls are given more rigid training in moral and ethical behavior, which either is directly related to or strengthened by religious indoctrination stricter than boys generally get. Men are trained to be more self-sufficient emotionally, psychologically, and economically. Church is sometimes considered to be only for "sissies" and women, especially among lower class men who consider the church's role in providing solace in time of suffering, sorrow, and personal or social inadequacy to be its primary function. Thus subjectively intended meanings of church participation may not be the same in the two sexes.

Rural Missouri (Columbia, Missouri: A.E.S. Research Bulletin 633B, Sept. 1957), p. 63.

[48] Fichter, *Social Relations in the Urban Parish*, pp. 116-19.

[49] Charles R. Walker, *Steeltown* (New York: Harper and Brothers, 1950), p. 44.

[50] Frederick M. Davenport, *Primitive Traits in Religious Revivals* (New York: The Macmillan Co., 1905), p. 293.

[51] *Ibid.,* pp. 292-94.

[52] S. V. Didato and T. M. Kennedy, "Masculinity-femininity and Personal Values," *Psychological Reports,* 2 (1956), 231-50.

Other explanations of the low sex ratio in church are primarily *sociological*. The church's traditional "extra" activities as well as worship services may be more appropriate for females than for males. The roles of women are chiefly family-centered, with a tendency to depend largely upon personal influences. Religion, dealing largely with personality, is perhaps more easily appreciated by them than by men.[53] Men perhaps engage in more activities that provide opportunities for social interaction in primary groups than the typical housewife. Contacts made during work, coffee breaks, commuting between work and home, and in clubs or the neighborhood tavern may satisfy most of men's needs for mingling with other people. Women have fewer such outlets outside the church. Cultural standards demand that women be more pious, so institutional norms are different for women than for men. The family and "culture-bearer" roles of women appear more consistent with the values and functions of religion than the secular roles typical of the male.[54]

The church has long provided outlets for creative energies of women when other institutions were more exclusively male-dominated and male-operated. Sunday school work in many churches is an almost exclusively female activity. Missionary groups, auxiliaries, and prayer circles also tend to be dominantly feminine. This results partly from the greater amount of time available among women for such activities, but it also is a partial cause of women's greater interest in church. Some of the gossiping, displaying of new clothing, and emotional appeals that attract women to church activities may drive men away. Similarly, women can gain social status in church when they lack such opportunities elsewhere. The reputation of being the best women's guild executive, Sunday school teacher, cook for church dinners, or even purveyor of "news" about people, gives prestige to many women who, especially in the past, have been kept in a subordinate position elsewhere in society.

The differential longevity of the sexes also helps explain the greater number of women than men in the church. Male death rates are higher in every decade of life, so more women survive into adulthood and especially into old age.

Among Jews, men have been relatively more active than women in the church. The male-oriented nature of traditional Judaism is responsible for this difference from Christianity. In over half of the Conservative synagogues studied, however, the predominance of women in the Friday

---

[53] L. Wyatt Lang, *A Study of Conversion* (London: George Allen and Unwin, Ltd., 1931), pp. 44-45.

[54] Fichter, *Social Relations in the Urban Parish*, pp. 91-93. This type of explanation is much more satisfactory than outmoded ones that speak, e.g., of religion as having a narcotic element which provides a refuge from the bitter facts of life; since women use fewer other narcotics than men, they are more likely to get their narcotics through religion! See Ernest R. Groves, "An Unsocial Element in Religion," *American Journal of Sociology*, 22 (Mar. 1917), 657-62.

night congregations indicates that patterns of activity are changing. Revision of women's status has helped maintain Jewish institutions, compensating for destruction of the unity of the Jewish sacred system. Although women still have limited status, mixed seating of the sexes is symbolic of radical change.[55]

Evidence that the sex differences in religious participation are due primarily to cultural rather than biological elements also comes from other sources. Sex differentials in Catholic religious observance in European and Latin American countries vary between three to two and two to one with females always in the lead. In America the leadership of women is generally much less. New York male Puerto Ricans have markedly higher rates of religious practice than males on the Island. The cultural milieu is apparently the chief factor influencing sex differentials of religious practice.[56]

Effects of Unequal Sex Ratios in the Church

Regardless of its causes, differential church participation of the sexes has numerous significant effects upon church life and work. When women are church members without their husbands, they often are unable to contribute as much financially as they would otherwise. Widows with small incomes, adolescent and working girls, and "church widows" (a colloquial term for wives whose husbands have no interest in church) often constitute more of an economic liability than asset for the religious body. They clearly are assets in other respects, of course.

The disproportionate number of women among foreign missionaries reflects the excess of young women in the church, the great prestige of this vocation, the greater religious devotion of women, and perhaps the frustrations of women indoctrinated against mixed marriage. Since there usually are more unmarried women than men in the church, some must choose either to remain unmarried or to marry outside of their church. Faced with the dilemma of whether to endure pangs of conscience for violating the church's standards of marriage or to endure the frustrations of celibacy, many find compensating sublimations in religious and humanitarian activities; others renounce their faith, and some suffer depression or more severe forms of mental illness.

[55] Marshall Sklare, *Conservative Judaism* (Glencoe, Ill.: The Free Press, 1955), pp. 29, 53-54, 86-90.

[56] Joseph B. Schuyler, S.J., "Age and Sex Differentials in Religious Observance," *Proceedings of Fall Meeting,* Society for the Scientific Study of Religion (Oct. 31-Nov. 1, 1958), pp. 10-11 (abstract). Schuyler claims that in U.S. Catholicism the women's lead over men is at most 10 per cent. This is not consistent with the findings of Fichter reported at the beginning of this section. For pertinent data on Christians and Jews drawn from national surveys in 1957 and 1958 see Bernard Lazerwitz, "Some Factors Associated with Variations in Church Attendance," *Social Forces,* 39 (May 1961), 301-9.

Many churches face problems of lay leadership because of the large proportion of women in their membership. In small congregations, it is difficult to find enough qualified male members to fill church offices which traditionally are the exclusive domain of men. Youth organizations may be dominated by female leadership. This encourages a still greater sexual lop-sidedness of participation as adolescent boys are given the impression that church activities are not for men. Thus cause and effect are inseparably intertwined in regard to the church's sex composition. Although women are more numerous in churches, the status of women workers in the church is generally lower than their status in other occupational fields.

Why Do People Join Churches?

Active members of three rural Kansas churches expressed four chief types of reasons for their support of the church. Their consensus was that church is good for the children, that it promotes wholesome social relationships for youth, that it provides an orderly method for expression of religious impulses, and that it develops and helps bring into expression a "sense of community" when it is the only church in the area. Most members had given little previous conscious thought to the question of why they were loyal to the church.[57]

Family loyalty was found in a Methodist survey to be the most important reason for joining a specific local church (34.0 per cent placed it first); this was closely followed by denominational loyalty (31.2 per cent). Other influences listed were nearness to home (11.4), the appeal of the total church program (11.1), the minister's preaching (6.8), and attendance by friends (5.5). Proximity to church, effective preaching, and a good church program were considered supporting rather than determining reasons for membership in a particular church by the researchers.[58]

First-time joiners of Protestant churches in the Pittsburgh area were most likely to have been contacted by the following agencies, in order of statistical importance: Sunday school (42.6 per cent), friendliness of individual members, pastoral work of the minister or an employed staff member, subsidiary organizations and educational systems of the church, worship and preaching services, evangelistic visitation, and church publicity. When members entering the church by transfer from other churches and by reclamation are added to those making their first public declaration of church vows, the influences credited by new members for their act of joining were as follows:

[57] F. D. Farrell, *Kansas Rural Institutions: V. Three Effective Rural Churches* (Manhattan, Kansas: A.E.S. Circular 256, June 1949), pp. 31-32.

[58] Murray H. Leiffer, "Why Do We Choose the Churches We Attend?" *Christian Advocate*, 131 (Feb. 2, 1956), 137, 157-60.

Pastoral cultivation by ministers	61.4 per cent
Sunday school	24.0
Friendliness of church members	14.3
Pastoral cultivation by lay officers or members	9.5
Special evangelistic services	7.8
Inner religious experiences	5.3
External pressures, sickness, death, etc.	1.7

Aside from the Sunday school, "the member winning pattern more often effective than any other single pattern, begins with a friendly lay member, continues in a pastoral contact, and is then divided between the preaching worship service and the subsidiary organizations of the church." [59]

The reasons people express for joining churches may not be the "real" reasons, but they can disclose socially acceptable reasons and rationalizations. Analysis of other influences in operation at the time of joining also can help us understand current increases in church membership. Few stress the need for a personal, "voluntary" decision to join the church more than Baptists. A study of 104 out of 107 persons who had joined five congregations in four Baptist denominations during the preceding twelve months revealed a large number of influences upon their decisions. These influences were classified individually by a panel of judges as to whether or not each was more likely to be "sacred" or "secular" for a person joining a Baptist church. The outstanding reasons given for joining were family, friendliness in the church, "spiritual reasons," and nearness of the church to home. Fifty joined the church in spite of knowledge that some other Baptist church was nearer to their homes; in only two cases were the reasons given for going to the more distant church unequivocably judged to be "sacred." "Sacred" influences predominated over "secular" in responses to questions about certain specific factors that affected their decisions to join. Nevertheless, reasons classified by the judges as "secular" also were very numerous and played an important part, according to respondents' own evaluations.[60] The analysis of motivations for even a single act is very difficult. It can never result in absolute empirical certainty because subjective and objective data and intuitive and empirical evidence are so interrelated. Available knowledge supports the tentative conclusion that the recent rapid growth of American church membership may actually be a result of increasing secularization of society rather than of a contrary trend. The reasons for joining the church, satisfactions achieved by church participation, and evidence of increasing secularization in church programs and members' lives support that hypothesis.[61]

Over 75 per cent of the members received into a large Protestant

[59] John H. Shope, *The Agencies and Techniques Used for Winning New Members for the Protestant Churches in Allegheny County, Pennsylvania, in 1947*, Ph.D. thesis, University of Pittsburgh, 1949, p. 94.

[60] David O. Moberg, "Die Säkularisierung und das Wachstum der Kirchen in den Vereinigten Staaten," *Kölner Zeitschrift für Sociologie und Sozialpsychologie*, 10, no. 3 (1958), 430-38.

[61] *Ibid.*

church over a three year period were first assimilated into some phase of the church's organized social life. Nearly half of those in youth groups were non-church members; over half of the persons first associated with the church through youth organizations eventually entered full church membership.[62]

Joiners of new sects appear to have psychological traits that are compatible with the sect's ideology. Psychologist Hedda Bolgar has demonstrated that theosophists tend to be married couples in which the wife is dominant and the husband's mother very strong-willed. Much personal resentment and aggression may be bound up with religious doctrines, like those of Unity, that stress peace, unity, and the lack of dogmatic rancor. As the sect ages and acquires second-generation members, the distinct associations of sect ideology and the psychology of the true believer may diminish.[63]

Jehovah's Witnesses lead a rather encapsulated existence. Their ideology, rooted in preindustrial traditions embodied in the Bible, appeals strongly to people who are alienated in the complexity and ambiguities of modern civilization.[64] By simple acts of propagating the faith, members gain the distinction of being "ministers." Analysis of the Seattle audience of Krishna Venta, who was claimed to be Christ, revealed two chief types of attenders, seekers and observers. Observers came primarily to satisfy curiosity and were not likely to return. Seekers had strong religious interests that were not satisfied through normal institutional channels. They learned of Krishna predominantly through newspaper advertising, while observers learned of him chiefly by word-of-mouth. Both skepticism of observers and favorable impressions of seekers increased with exposure. Cult-prone persons appear to be institutionally alienated but religiously intense.[65]

The highly individualistic nature of Protestantism, which emphasizes personal salvation and looks upon conversion as largely a psychological experience, is a source of what is often labeled secularism. Competition among churches leads to persuasion methods used in business rivalry. Slack ties with the supernatural, instrumentalistic functionalism, and democratic lay domination rather than ecclesiastical control hence tend to prevail. Economic institutions tend to predominate over others, including the church, in our "business-minded culture." [66]

In the Park Forest suburb of Chicago, Whyte found that the most im-

---

[62] Charles Lee Wilson, "A Social Picture of a Congregation," *American Sociological Review*, 10 (June 1945), 418-22.

[63] David Riesman, "Some Informal Notes on American Churches and Sects," *Confluence*, 4 (July 1955), 127-59.

[64] Joseph Bram, "Jehovah's Witnesses and the Values of American Culture," *Transactions of the New York Academy of Science*, 19 (1956), 47-54.

[65] William R. Catton, Jr., "What Kind of People Does a Religious Cult Attract? " *American Sociological Review*, 22 (Oct. 1957), 561-66.

[66] John Sirjamaki, "A Footnote to the Anthropological Approach to the Study of American Culture," *Social Forces*, 25 (Mar. 1947), 253-63.

portant considerations in choosing a church were, in order, the minister's personality, abilities, and qualifications; the Sunday school; convenient location; the denomination, and the music. Friendship, stability, and kinship with others are also demonstrated and symbolized by the church.[67]

Jewish congregations have experienced impressive growth since World War II. Membership is open to all Jews without test of applicants' beliefs, but occasionally with screening for abhorrent moral conduct, financial irresponsibility, or nonconformity to religious observances. Dominant motivations for joining are the desires to give children a Jewish education, to attend religious services on the High Holidays (*Rosh Hashanah* and *Yom Kippur*), and to have children confirmed.[68]

Church joining often reflects a quest for social status and respectability. Persons "engaged in the promotion and management of consistently profitable illegal enterprises . . . frequently maintain membership in such conventional institutions of their local communities as churches." [69] People are attracted to a group when their self-images coincide with its norms. They are drawn most strongly toward it when they are not forced to choose between it and alternative behavior which has stronger social sanctions. When they join because they are truly interested in the group's aims, they generally find a place in it.[70]

American churches generally are closely linked with community patterns of social stratification. Each tends to cater to the religious needs of a segment of the population. While some persons cling to a church because of tradition, others shift allegiance as they or the churches change their class characteristics. Theology is relatively unimportant to most people in the selection of a church. "They go where they find their own kind of people. During their lifetimes they may belong to several different churches as a result of mobility up or down or because of moving to a new community where the levels of the churches are different." [71] Problems of relationships between the American (Northern) and Southern Baptist Conventions may be traced partly to cultural differences in members' backgrounds. These differences lead to variations in theology, pat-

---

[67] William H. Whyte, Jr., *The Organization Man* (Garden City, N.Y.: Doubleday and Co., 1956), pp. 407, 417, 419-21.

[68] Marshall Sklare, "Church and the Laity Among Jews," *Annals of the American Academy of Political and Social Science,* 232 (Nov. 1960), 60-69.

[69] Solomon Kobrin, "The Conflict of Values in Delinquency Areas," *American Sociological Review,* 16 (Oct. 1951), 653-61. Quotation from p. 657.

[70] Joseph H. Fichter, "Die Soziale Struktur der Gruppe in einer Pfarre," *Kölner Zeitschrift für Soziologie und Sozialpsychologie,* 7, no. 1 (1955), 43-54; and Harrison M. Trice, "Sociological Factors in Association with A.A.," *Journal of Criminal Law, Criminology, and Police Science,* 48 (Nov.-Dec. 1957), 378-86.

[71] W. Lloyd Warner *et al., Democracy in Jonesville* (New York: Harper and Brothers, 1949), pp. 166-67. This may be why Hans Toch and Robert Anderson found that denominational affiliation gives little clue to beliefs about God, Jesus Christ, the Bible, Church, Epistemology, or Metaphysics. Cf. "Religious Belief and Denominational Affiliation," *Religious Education,* 55 (May-June 1960), 193-200.

terns of worship, and relationships with other denominations that make southerners who feel out of place in northern churches form their own congregations in the North.[72] Belonging to a church is a popular demonstration of anti-Communism and loyal Americanism. It is possible that many who would not otherwise have done so have joined churches because of hatred for and fear of atheistic Communism.[73]

Types of Church Members

There are great differences in the meaning of church membership from the viewpoint both of subjective interpretations and objective behavior. Members may be ranked on a series of continua according to the nature and frequency of participation in religious behavior, the degree to which they believe in official church tenets of faith and action, the extent to which religious considerations permeate other areas of life, or willingness to serve as propagandists for their religion, to mention only a few possible variables. Thus, on the basis of willingness to give witness to their faith, Evangelist Bryan Green classified Christian laymen into four overlapping categories. "Saints" are marked by such high qualities that their lives are like a speech recommending their religion to others. "Ecclesiastical Christians" serve as office-holders, witnessing primarily to persons already within the sphere of the church. "Speaking Christians" are able to express their faith in speech either to groups or to individuals in private. "Christians who are also experts or leaders in public or industrial life" are doctors, teachers, managers, politicians, and other influential persons in society who help break down the "crust of materialism" and gain recognition for spiritual values, thus making it easier for others to accept the Christian faith and to see practical outlets for Christian values.[74] Clergymen sometimes refer to the "busybees" who do all the work, the "special agents" who will serve only on assignments of their own choice, and the "I.W.W.'s" who answer "I won't work!" Such observations by nonscientists indicate the possibility of empirically classifying church members.

Every religious institution has two types of members. *Denominationalists* have a primary interest in the welfare of their institution. Transgressions against others may be committed on its behalf that men would never seriously consider committing for themselves. A passion for the institution may develop which is greater even than one's love for himself; this may

[72] Robert G. Torbet, "Historical Background of the Southern Baptist 'Invasion'," *Crusader,* 14, no. 8 (Sept. 1959), 6-7.

[73] P. E. Kraemer, "Kanttekeningen bij een Jaar Amerika," *Sociologisch Bulletin,* 8, no. 4 (1954), 98-121.

[74] Bryan Green, *The Practice of Evangelism* (New York: Charles Scribner's Sons, 1951), pp. 248-56.

lead to physical or symbolic martyrdom. *Religionists* have a primary interest in the service of God and the improvement of human character, regarding institutions as a means toward that goal. Unless institutions are maintained, the greater objectives may not be realized, so church members face the dilemma posed by the need for both the institution and the basic objectives it serves.[75]

The most thorough and systematic classification of church members to date was developed in Father Fichter's studies of 8,363 white Catholics aged 10 and over in southern urban parishes. Three institutional criteria (baptism, place of residence, and ethnic origin) stemming from a regulatory pattern established by the Catholic Church and three personal criteria (self-intention or meaning of membership, religious observance, and social participation) were used to classify parishioners. Four types are emphasized—the nuclear, modal, marginal, and dormant—but saints and "dead" members are also recognized.[76] Each type may be considered a segment of a continuum that ranks members from the most to the least faithful.

1. The *saint* is the member whose life completely conforms to his church's ideology. Since this involves an intangible, humanly immeasurable inner perfection that can be known to God alone, the social scientist cannot clearly separate saints from nuclear members.[77] Only after death is sainthood declared in Catholicism on the basis of extraordinary holiness of life and heroic virtues. The medieval saint specialized in the social functions of conserving values and contributing to social reform as a symbol and interpreter of the spiritual solidarity of society. As the "center of gravity for moral and spiritual values" was transferred from the church to the community, the saint became departmentalized, traditionalized, and conventionalized, losing his role of leadership in moral and spiritual affairs. When sectarianism triumphed as a logical result of Protestant individualism, the social significance of the saint tended to be destroyed by the heterogeneity of expectations for saintly character. Modern heroes replacing the saints are seldom identified with the church.[78]

Among his studies of altruistic love, Sorokin included an analysis of 3,090 Christian-Catholic saints. His discoveries led to the following conclusions. Their longevity exceeded that of contemporaries. The proportion

[75] Louis Finkelstein, "Institutionalism and the Faith," in *Conflict of Loyalties,* R. M. MacIver, ed. (New York: Institute for Religious and Social Studies, 1952), pp. 89-98.

[76] Fichter, *Social Relations in the Urban Parish,* pp. 7-79.

[77] *Ibid.,* p. 23. This definition of "saint" differs from the Protestant theological definition which considers all true believers in Christ to be saints, even if they are imperfect.

[78] John M. Mecklin, "The Passing of the Saint," *American Journal of Sociology,* 60, no. 6, part II (May 1955), 34-53; reprinted from 24 (Jan. 1919), 353-72. Francis Heiermann, S.J., strongly criticized Mecklin's thesis. See *ibid.,* 25 (July 1919), 24-40.

of saints originating in the upper classes has diminished, and the lower and poorer classes have increased their proportion since the beginning of Christianity. Thirty-five per cent became saints in spite of parental opposition or indifference. Women have inferior opportunities to be officially sanctified in Catholicism. The proportion of saints who live in the "secular world" is increasing, perhaps because of the relative decrease in hermits, monks, and others living in secluded milieus. They are replaced more and more by secular "good neighbors." Even in terms of sensate utilitarian and hedonistic values, the unselfish, loving, and saintly are paid dividends of vitality, long life, peace of mind, and happiness.[79]

Another study of Roman Catholic saints and *beati* (persons officially beatified) found that 78 per cent from the first to the mid-twentieth century had been born into the upper class (landed nobility), 17 per cent into the middle class (merchants, industrialists, professionals, and free farmers), and only 5 per cent into the lower class (manual laborers). Only in the first and the last three centuries were there striking departures from the dominant pattern. The proportions of the general population in the various classes over the centuries were opposite to that of saints; perhaps 5 per cent were upper, 10 to 15 per cent middle, and 80 to 85 per cent lower class members.[80] The predominance of aristocratic backgrounds among Catholic saints may reflect a desire of early Church leaders to reach the upper classes, the intimate linkage of medieval Church dignitaries with the leaders of society, and the criterion of voluntary acceptance of poverty sometimes used in determining sainthood. Gradual gain in the proportion of middle class saints since the thirteenth century has paralleled the growth of the middle classes. Hagiographers later in time report higher social status for the saints than those closer to the time in which they lived; "the status of a saint was never reduced in the later telling of his tale, except of course under the impact of modern scholarly and critical investigation." [81] Saints, representing the highest human realization of the religious profession, reflect the transient social hierarchies of earth.

2. *Nuclear* church members are the most active participants and the most faithful believers. In practice they include the saints, for saints cannot be unequivocally identified by empirical techniques. The personal moral code of the nuclear member is based upon religious beliefs that conform to the teachings of his church; it extends to, integrates, and controls his roles in all other institutions and associations. Nuclear members meet all institutional and personal criteria for membership. In Fichter's

---

[79] Pitirim A. Sorokin, *Altruistic Love* (Boston: Beacon Press, 1950).

[80] Katherine and Charles H. George, "Roman Catholic Sainthood and Social Status: A Statistical and Analytical Study," *Journal of Religion*, 35 (Spring 1955), 85-98.

[81] *Ibid.*, p. 97.

analysis they received Holy Communion weekly or oftener and belonged to a parish organization. In his study of 8,363 white parishioners aged 10 years and over, only 5.7 per cent met the qualifications. Their social background usually involved membership in a "good" family closely attached to the parish church, more education and more years in Catholic schools than modal parishioners, birth into Catholicism rather than conversion, and membership in the lower middle socioeconomic class as salaried and wage workers. American, rather than European, and rural, rather than urban, ways of life seemed most conducive to the development of nuclear members.[82]

Most lay leaders come from among nuclear members. These "core participants" appear to be attached to their church primarily through application of some form of faith, whether it centers upon ritual, divine revelation, charismatic leadership, or some combination of these.[83] Most of the "militant laity" who are anxious to share their faith with others also come from their ranks.[84] They comprise the nucleus of families and persons who work closely with professional church leaders as an inner circle guiding its activities and those of subsidiary organizations. Sometimes they are labeled by critics as the "clique that's in control," "the inner circle," or "pastor's pets." And such indeed they are; they are considered the "ideal" members. They are the "church pillars" who become recognized as dependable leaders and render such outstanding service that they are retained as officers year after year even in churches that insist upon rotating specific positions. The tendency to be pillars appears to be socially inherited, the same families providing church officers for several successive generations in the same church in rural communities.[85] In Protestant denominational politics, certain families play a dominant long-term role in leadership, especially in smaller bodies. From among the ranks of nuclear members occasionally emerge a "remnant" who, as a creative minority, deviate from majority patterns of mediocre religion to instill new vigor and introduce new insights that make the church a prophetic influence in society.[86] Some nuclear members, however, may be "religious hangers-on" who are deficient in other social relationships and find personality outlets in church organizations and activities.[87]

[82] Fichter, *Social Relations in the Urban Parish*, pp. 21-30.

[83] W. Seward Salisbury, "The Structure of Religious Action in a Small City," abstract of paper presented to the Committee for the Scientific Study of Religion, Nov. 3, 1951. (Fichter also uses the term "core Christian" to describe the nuclear parishioner.)

[84] Paul H. Furfey, "The Missionary Role of the Parish," in *The Sociology of the Parish*, C. J. Nuesse and Thomas J. Harte, eds. (Milwaukee: Bruce Publishing Co., 1951), pp. 303-22.

[85] Farrell, *Kansas Rural Institutions*, pp. 20-21.

[86] Martin E. Marty, "The Remnant: Retreat and Renewal," *Christian Century*, 75 (Nov. 26, 1958), 1361-65.

[87] H. Paul Douglass and Edmund deS. Brunner, *The Protestant Church as a Social Institution* (New York: Institute of Social and Religious Research, 1935), p. 49.

3. The *modal* church member is the "ordinary member" who helps make up the mass of the membership. While not a model of what his church believes members ought to be, he is indeed a living model demonstrating to outsiders what a "typical" Catholic, Methodist, or other member is. "Average" both from the statistical viewpoint of frequency and the tendency to "live up to his religion in a 'middling sort of way'," the modal membership includes about 70 per cent of urban Catholic parishioners.[88]

The ideal pattern of social solidarity based upon Christian love is not met by modal members. Occupational, political, and socioeconomic status considerations are more significant in promoting cooperation and group unity among them than religious factors. Even in church organizations, personal friendships, similar education and age, personal interest in a concrete, specific activity, and recognition from other persons are more significant to social solidarity than such "higher" motives as love for God, church membership, and loyalty to the parish.[89]

4. The *marginal* member is the "marginal man" of the church. Internal psychological value conflicts, imperfectly institutionalized roles, and socioreligious distance (i.e., a remoteness from the goals and values considered ideal by the church) characterize the marginal or fringe member. Approximately 20 per cent of the Catholics studied by Fichter were marginal in terms of failure to meet the Church's minimum standards of Mass attendance, annual reception of Communion and penance, and Catholic education of children. The same people tended to be negligent in all three religious obligations.[90]

The values of the major social institutions, which affect everyone in some manner, tend to be inconsistent with one another, so compartmentalization is likely in the complex behavior of the individual playing his multiple roles in situations involving numerous social statuses, unless he has a central integrative system of values. Marginal Catholics try to reconcile contradictory values and patterns of conduct. Though they believe that democracy and brotherhood are worthy ideals, they assume **black Catholics are not fit to attend the same schools and churches as** whites. They profess honesty while giving in to deceptions demanded by their occupational roles. Modal parishioners may also engage in incon-

---

[88] Fichter, *Social Relations in the Urban Parish*, pp. 40-41. Mistaken generalizations about all religion or an entire church often result from casual observations of these members.

[89] *Ibid.*, pp. 42-55; and Joseph H. Fichter, S.J., "Religious Values and the Social Personality," *American Catholic Sociological Review*, 17 (June 1956), 109-16. Even the majority of lay leaders in a suburban Catholic parish were modal members; their activity in parish organizations was used to support other social roles, especially those pertinent to child rearing. (Frank Cizon, "Some Characteristics of Leaders in a Catholic Suburban Parish," paper presented at the Annual Meeting of the Religious Research Assn., Indianapolis, June 16, 1961.)

[90] Fichter, *Social Relations in the Urban Parish*, pp. 56-62.

sistent behavior, but they are neither aware of the inconsistency nor psychologically frustrated by it as are marginal members. Relativity of moral values pertinent to such problems as those involved in sex and marriage is common among marginal Catholics. They also tend to be anti-authoritarian, opposed to the hierarchical structure or "dictatorial" policies of the Church. As the church has lost some functions to other institutions, the marginal member seems to have substituted non-religious institutional "escape mechanisms" and activities for those centered in the church. He may thus be viewed as a "product of institutional inconsistency." [91]

5. *Dormant* members are even further removed from the ideal. Sometimes included in membership statistics, they more accurately consist of persons who are not members but have a church preference. Variously labeled as "inactive," "strayed sheep," "leakage," or "fallen away" members, they may once have met minimum institutional requirements for membership, may occasionally attend a church service, and do not join any other church. Their church contacts are only intermittent and sporadic. Approximately one-third of the baptized Catholics studied by Fichter were dormant. Most had unobtrusively departed from parish life with no publicity of their withdrawal and without any public dismissal or excommunication. Their departure improved internal social relationships of the church, for many dormant members are unassimilable, cantankerous, shirking, or indifferent persons who are a discredit to their church.[92]

In addition to social forces contributing to marginality, dormant Catholics were found to come from families that neglected the child's religious nurture. Over three-fourths lacked religious training. They were most numerous on the lowest socioeconomic level and likely to come from disorganized families. Forty per cent of the dormant Catholics referred to attitudes or behavior of priests as factors that led to dormancy. Many mentioned traumatic experiences, such as disappointment with the clergy and lay leaders or sudden realization that the Church's teachings on subjects such as birth control or racial segregation were contrary to personal ideals. Many were "drifters" who could present no reasons for having left the Church; these included some very aged, whose physical and mental apathy made them incapable of meeting institutional demands, and "social strainers" who had subordinated their religious values in efforts to gain higher social status.[93]

Backsliding in Protestantism may be greatest in groups that demand of members the least in personal sacrifice or discipline. A cheaply-bought membership is apt to wear away rapidly. The individual may come to believe that a system of salvation which requires little of him must be of

---

[91] *Ibid.*, pp. 58-67.
[92] *Ibid.*, pp. 15, 68-73.
[93] *Ibid.*, pp. 73-79.

little value. Members of conservative churches are more loyal than those of liberal ones, perhaps because their churches are smaller and make more demands upon members.[94]

6. The *dead* church member has formally joined another denomination. He hence is "dead" to his old religion and "alive" as one of the other five types of members in his new church.[95] Such members may be carried simultaneously on the formal records of two or more religious bodies because of deficiencies in bookkeeping or failure to notify the former church of their action. (This category also includes persons who are physically dead but not yet removed from church membership lists.)

While this typology refers particularly to Catholic parishioners, it could be applied also to Protestants and Jews after developing appropriate modifications for classifying constituents of the other faiths. The findings from such an application might prove remarkably similar in spite of obvious differences in church values and organization. Variations in subjectively-intended meanings of membership and its social significance that are indicated by this typology and related studies need to be recognized in any serious analysis of church members.

Types of Jews

The most common classification of Jews divides them into Orthodox, Conservative, Reform, and secularized categories. Many other typologies are possible. On the basis of various combinations of self-images of Jews living in predominantly gentile communities, nine types of Jews were distinguished. The first four represent the "more comfortable" forms of psychological adjustment and the latter five the "less comfortable" forms. (1) The *comfortable in-group Jew* has a strong attachment to Jewish traditions and is sustained by the life of the Jewish community. He is likely to be Orthodox. It is unimportant to him whether or not he is accepted by gentiles. (2) The *comfortable participant* desires status in both Jewish and gentile groups and feels he has won respect from both. He protects himself from direct encounters with anti-Semitism by selective socializing with gentiles in the life of the larger community. (3) The *comfortable assimilationist* has dissociated himself from the Jewish community. He does not deny his Jewish origin, but participates selectively in the gentile group and has found among them a role in which he is accepted. He considers Jewish opinion about himself unimportant. (4) The self-esteem of the *self-sustainer* is based typically upon a career or the pursuit of

---

[94] J. Milton Yinger, *Religion, Society and the Individual* (New York: The Macmillan Co., 1957), p. 98; and Frederick A. Bushee, "The Church in a Small City,' *American Journal of Sociology*, 49 (Nov. 1943), 223-32.

[95] Fichter, *Social Relations in the Urban Parish*, p. 69n.

ideological causes which place him in a group where he is not confronted with decisions on "Jewishness." What Jewish or gentile groups think of him is not the basis of his self-respect. (5) The *uneasy assimilationist* wants acceptance by both gentiles and Jews but feels rejected by the Jewish community. He may be married to a gentile and feel guilty about having deserted the Jewish community. When psychological stress is great, he may attempt to free himself from his sense of guilt by passing as a gentile. (6) The *self-conscious participant* wishes acceptance by both groups and has gained respect among Jews. Occasional rebuffs in the larger community make him feel that gentiles scorn him because he is a Jew. To prove that he is acceptable by gentile standards, he may emulate upper middle class gentiles. (7) The *disowned Jew* cares for status only in the Jewish community but is rejected by it. Jews are embarrassed by or ashamed of him, often because of his exaggerated or ill-becoming expression of Jewishness. (8) The *frustrated assimilationist* wants acceptance only by gentiles but feels that they look down upon him because he is Jewish. If his feelings of rejection are sufficiently strong, he will pass for gentile in order to gain acceptance. (9) The *rejected Jew* wants acceptance from both Jews and gentiles but feels rejected by both. He is deeply ambivalent and has conflicts for having left the fold without gaining acceptance in the gentile group; he is the most marginal of all types. In his search for acceptance, psychological stress may force modification of either values or participation patterns that brings him closer to one of the other eight types.[96]

One survey found that Jewish religious identification is related to the degree of Americanization. Second generation Jews (parents in this study) and their children were predominantly Conservative or Reform rather than Orthodox, as the following summary indicates:

	Parents	Grandparents
Orthodox	16	81
Conservative	43	11
Reform	30	5
Religious, but unclassified	4	—

Depending upon interpretation, these Jews may be considered as either very near assimilation or highly ethnocentric.[97] "Church membership" among Jews may refer even more to identification with a total sub-culture than to a set of specifically religious beliefs and practices; religion to them

---

[96] John P. Dean, "Patterns of Socialization and Association Between Jews and Non-Jews," *Jewish Social Studies,* 17 (July 1955), 247-68. Critical comments on this paper are given by Julian L. Greifer, Leo Srole, and Joshua Trachtenberg, *ibid.,* pp. 269-81. The degree and type of involvement in Jewish ethno-religious groups is related to their orientation to gentile opinions and hence to political attitudes. See Edgar Litt, "Jewish Ethno-Religious Involvement and Political Liberalism," *Social Forces,* 39 (May 1961), 328-32.

[97] Marshall Sklare, Marc Vosk, and Mark Zborowski, "Forms and Expressions of Jewish Identification," *Jewish Social Studies,* 17 (July 1955), 205-18. Cf. discussions by Isidor Chein, Werner J. Cahnman, Leibush Lehrer, and others, *ibid.,* pp. 219-37.

epitomizes a complex configuration of faith, rituals, and self-identification. Yet in many communities where they are few in number no unique Jewish way of life can be discerned.[98]

Non-Church Members

Analysis of church membership is incomplete without reference to the significance of nonmembership. When nonmembership is a product of deliberate disagreement with or opposition to the values advocated by a church, the church has clearly affected the nonmember's behavior. If he is eligible for membership, his behavior is more a threat to the church than if he could not join it except under the most unusual circumstances. It is perhaps the greatest threat of all if he is an ex-member or apostate who is a living symbol of the inferiority he now imputes to the church's values. Some nonmembers who are ineligible aspirants for membership may attempt to "enter the fold" of salvation through some opening other than the institutional gate. The only nonmembers who are not oriented in some way to a religious body are persons entirely indifferent to the prospect of membership, especially if they are completely ignorant of the group.[99]

The behavior of even strongly irreligious and highly skeptical persons is influenced by the church when their actions pertain in any manner to religion. They must continually recognize that religious belief is present in other persons, even if not in themselves; hence the church they ignore or despise influences their conduct.

In small communities, nonmembers are likely to become known as either intransigents who have repeatedly resisted evangelistic approaches or those who are immoral, unreliable, irresponsible, and "without self-respect." The latter are totally neglected in church recruiting and evangelism.[100]

Many nonmembers have had at least nominal connections and identify with a religion. Only 2.7 per cent of Americans aged 14 and over in 1957 claimed they had no religion; by 1981 that figure had increased to 7 per cent of adults, 68 per cent of whom claimed to be church members. Most of the unchurched—nonmembers and inactive members—have a Christian background and beliefs, but other interests, work schedules, or illness compete with churchgoing and many have had problems with the church. They are more likely to be mobile, single or divorced, young, and male than active members. One-fifth want deeper spiritual meaning than they

---

[98] See, e.g., Morris Freedman, "The Jews of Albuquerque," *Commentary*, 28 (July 1959), 55-62. Compare the "natural Jewishness" of a Massachusetts suburb described in Evelyn N. Rossman, "Decade in Northrup," *ibid.*, 28 (Sept. 1959), 214-22.

[99] Cf. Robert K. Merton, *Social Theory and Social Structure*, rev. ed. (Glencoe: The Free Press, 1957), pp. 289-92, 296.

[100] Arthur J. Vidich and Joseph Bensman, *Small Town in Mass Society* (Princeton, N.J.: Princeton University Press, 1958), pp. 251-52.

found in the church, and 60 per cent believe most churches and synagogues "have lost the real spiritual part of religion." Seventeen per cent
of nonmember adults had attended church within the previous month in
1981.[101] Cuber's study in the Detroit area found that from 18 to 37 per
cent of the people attending 18 regular worship services of four churches
were nonmembers, and 32 per cent of 1,000 members attended less than
once a year. Hence no clear line can be drawn between "church people"
and "nonchurch people." A church's social control extends far beyond
the limits of membership and attendance, so not even approximate measures of "real participation in church culture" can be secured because of
the great variations among both members and nonmembers.[102] In many
respects church membership can be considered as a continuous rather
than a discrete variable.

Lay Leadership in the Church

Studies of lay leadership in churches generally focus upon persons appointed or elected to church offices. Such studies neither eliminate from
the ranks of "leadership" those who are mere office holders nor include
those non-officers who are influential leaders of church programs, activities, and values.

The opportunities for lay leadership in the typical American church
are great; there are many offices, committees, and boards in the church
and its subsidiary organizations. This is true in Catholicism as well as
Judaism and Protestantism. Societies in the Catholic parish may be classified as liturgical (groups that assist in the religious services), sociospiritual
(groups with sanctification as the primary objective), educational, amelio-
rative (engaged in "works of mercy"), and recreational. A type of self-
selection operates; members in each of these groups have more in common
than the church membership has as a whole. Perhaps not more than one-
third of Catholic parish members are participants in parochial organizations, although an average of 13.2 societies was found in 23 urban southern parishes. The work of each is typically done by fewer than ten persons.[103]

In small rural Protestant churches the distinction between lay leader
and minister is often vague. Part-time preachers, lack of insistence upon
an ordained clergy, and variations in definitions of the ministry make it
difficult to determine if certain persons should be classified as ministers or

[101] "Religion Reported by the Civilian Population of the United States: March 1957,"
Current Population Reports, Series P-20, No. 79, Feb. 2, 1958; Princeton Center, *Religion
in American 1982*, pp. 23, 41, 101; Princeton Religion Research Center, *The Unchurched
American* (Princeton, N.J.: The Gallup Organization, 1978).

[102] John F. Cuber, "Marginal Church Participants," *Sociology and Social Research,*
25 (Sept.-Oct. 1940), 57-62.

[103] Fichter, *Social Relations in the Urban Parish,* pp. 52-54, 155-62, 189.

as lay workers. Churches in the larger Kentucky towns that have full-time ministers and large memberships are more likely to have leadership training courses than are the churches without full-time pastors which are most in need of special training for laymen.[104]

Control of church affairs reflects the socioeconomic structure of the community. Membership of church boards of 387 Protestant churches from nine denominations consisted overwhelmingly of the favored economic classes. Proprietors, managers, and professional men accounted for more than half of the board chairmen. Bankers were most favored for the chairmanship in relationship to their total number on the boards, with manufacturers in second place and farmers and lawyers almost equally tied for third. In the absence of contrary evidence, it may be assumed that this leadership has immediate effects upon sermon references to the profit motive, organized labor, and other class-related topics.[105] Even in Protestant churches which have a substantial proportion of wage laborers, leadership tends to come predominantly from white-collar, proprietary, or professional members. In New Haven churches located in wage-earner neighborhoods, leadership was in the hands of white-collar workers who previously had lived in the area and had moved away but continued commuting to church.[106] In the 19 churches of Oakville, Oregon, most officers were men of higher socioeconomic status than other members, were younger than members in general, and were nearer in social distance to each other than members generally were.[107] The financial and technical control of another large Protestant church was found to reside disproportionately in its upper class members. The leadership of subsidiary organizations, however, cut across all classes represented.[108] Persons of prominence in a community sometimes accept leadership positions in a church which are of only symbolic significance, exchanging their prestige for the status symbol.[109] Nevertheless, Protestant churches are largely middle-class institutions. The boards that control them may reflect their membership much more nearly than cursory analysis suggests.

Church members in a large Kentucky study were better educated than nonmembers. They had higher incomes, were more active in community organizations, were older, and included more women. Officers were even better educated than the general membership, had higher incomes, were

[104] Harold F. Kaufman, *Rural Churches in Kentucky, 1947* (Lexington, Ky.: A.E.S. Bulletin 530, Apr. 1949), pp. 26-29.

[105] Jerome Davis, "A Study of Protestant Church Boards of Control," *American Journal of Sociology*, 38 (Nov. 1932), 418-31. No comparisons of members and officers are provided in this excellent study.

[106] John W. McConnell, *Evolution of Social Classes* (Washington, D.C.: American Council on Public Affairs, 1942), pp. 167-75.

[107] Robert H. Jordan, "Social Functions of the Churches in Oakville," *Sociology and Social Research*, 40 (Nov.-Dec. 1955), 107-11.

[108] Wilson, "A Social Picture of a Congregation."

[109] Vidich and Bensman, *Small Town in Mass Society*, p. 233.

more active in community organizations, were slightly older, and were as likely to be men as women despite the higher proportion of women in the membership.[110]

In open country churches men are much more likely to be leaders in the church and its auxiliary organizations than women, while in urban centers an opposite tendency prevails. Attitudes and traditions against female leadership may be stronger in rural areas. Urban churches also have more auxiliary organizations in which women are culturally expected to assume positions of leadership. Of persons studied in Kentucky who were officers in organizations other than the church and its subsidiaries, 88 per cent were church members. If religious teachings have a real impact upon members' lives and an import for community affairs, churches may wield tremendous influence. If, on the other hand, religion is compartmentalized so that religious observances are designated only for certain times and places instead of qualifying all behavior, the churches' influence upon the community may be very slight.[111] The overlapping of church leadership positions with those of other institutions contributes to community integration. Activities are coordinated without bureaucratic clearinghouses simply because a few persons hold a wide variety of leadership roles. Sectarian groups without such connections therefore tend to be at conflict with the rest of the community.[112]

A generation ago, one-eighth of all rural church members served at any given time as teachers or officers of Sunday schools.[113] Typical qualifications sought in the selection of such workers are religious piety, personal consecration, loyalty ("faithfulness") to the church, and willingness to serve. The teaching has often been inferior and has helped drive some thinking persons away from the church. Volunteers for teaching assignments and other youth leadership positions often include those least capable to take such responsibilities. Many inner needs of such persons are met by religious service, among them release from guilt, relief from boredom, and escape from family tensions. Volunteers are sometimes selfishly grasping for solutions to their own problems, subconsciously subordinating the church's welfare to their own personal needs.[114] A result of such long-standing problems is the insistence in many churches that all Sunday school teachers complete certain training courses and meet other qualifications before serving in any official capacity.

In the small Protestant church a large proportion of members must be

[110] Harold F. Kaufman, *Religious Organization in Kentucky* (Lexington, Ky.: A.E.S. Bulletin 524, Aug. 1948), pp. 30-34.

[111] *Ibid.* Fichter similarly found Catholic parochial lay leaders to have an average of 2.2 memberships in nonreligious social organizations in addition to 2.95 memberships in religious groups. See *Social Relations in the Urban Parish*, p. 33.

[112] Vidich and Bensman, *Small Town in Mass Society*, pp. 258-84.

[113] Douglass and Brunner, *The Protestant Church*, p. 159.

[114] Wayne E. Oates, *The Christian Pastor* (Philadelphia: Westminster Press, 1951), p. 63.

nuclear if the church is to survive. In the large church there has been an increasing professionalization of leadership as paid workers have been hired for religious education, counseling, recreational leadership, social work, music, and church visiting. These special staffs often "get people out to church more successfully than they get the church out to people." [115] They diminish the role of the lay worker in the church. Laymen who serve tend to have their contributions channeled chiefly into activities aimed at self-perpetuation of the bureaucratic organization.[116] As a church grows larger, it takes on an increasing number of secondary group characteristics. The spontaneity, informality, and intimacy of primary group interaction tend to disappear; laymen are used proportionately less. The member accepts less and less personal responsibility for the work of his church, shifting it to paid workers. He tends to give proportionately less money to the church, so the paid staff must depend increasingly upon the smaller gifts of a larger number of persons. Thus "the usefulness of the individual church member has decreased in direct proportion to the increase in the size of the congregation." [117] The degree of participation by members varies inversely with the size of the church. These tendencies can be counteracted by providing for more subcommittees and small, natural groupings within the church.

Lay leadership in Catholicism differs from that in most of Protestantism. Authority flows from the top, and the parish priest is the primary leader of all parochial groups. The success of the lay leader depends upon a combination of elements which includes his relationships with the priest; relationships with the members, functions, and goals of the group; interests of the priest, members, and leader, and peculiar characteristics of parochial groupings, in addition to his own leadership qualities.[118] The impact of the American democratic culture upon Catholicism is clearly evident from Fichter's study of 245 white lay leaders. Three-fourths (76.7 per cent) of them believed that in order to obtain cooperation from the members of a parochial organization, all important issues should be submitted to the membership. Furthermore, 71.5 per cent believed that the best position of the priest in parochial organizations on questions that are not a matter of faith and morals is not in having complete control or power of final decision, but in giving only advice and direction instead. An additional 6.1 per cent believed that the priest should have an equal vote with the parishioners.[119] In Catholicism new organizations among the lay elite arise to meet new crises. In the fourth century these were pre-

---

[115] Douglass and Brunner, *The Protestant Church*, p. 93.

[116] Paul M. Harrison, "Churches and the Laity Among Protestants," *Annals of the American Academy of Political and Social Science*, 332 (Nov. 1960), 37-49.

[117] Oates, *The Christian Pastor*, p. 73.

[118] Fichter, *Social Relations in the Urban Parish*, pp. 30-39; and John J. Kane, "Church and the Laity Among Catholics," *Annals of the American Academy of Political and Social Science*, 332 (Nov. 1960), 50-59.

[119] *Ibid.*, pp. 36-37. Since Vatican II the laity have played a more active role.

dominantly monasteries; in the twentieth they are largely associations organized for special purposes within the Catholic value system.[120]

Entrepreneurship may be more apparent in American churches than in commercial enterprises. Adult Bible classes and other activities dominated by laymen provide the esthetic pleasures afforded by efficient organization, self-management, and making each individual "count" (if only by being counted). "A 'good cause' justifies a zeal that would often appear self-serving and egregious in a salesman, [and often is associated with] a quasi-religious enthusiasm for efficiency and good management for their own sakes . . ." [121] Leadership in the church also provides training and business experience that would otherwise take years to get. The church thus helps suburbanites and others to rise in their administrative and business positions. Lay as well as professional church leadership often involves striving for personal status and prestige in the "social game" of a local community.[122]

The larger and more nearly universal the membership of a church, the more it may be expected to accommodate its doctrines and practices to those of the general community. Yet this does not necessarily result in the choice of church officers who are compromisers. Selection of the more pious or devout among the many persons eligible for holding church offices is common in Protestantism. In Lutheran churches of Württemberg, Germany, sectarian groups within the church, which emphasize a pietistic, religiously conservative religion and comprise ecclesiola in ecclesia, provide much of the church's leadership.[123] The same presumably is true in the typical American church.

Conclusion

We have noted great variations in people's religious behavior and attitudes. By 1962 Glock summarized these under five dimensions of religiosity. The *ritualistic* dimension pertains to what people do, all of their private and public religious practices. The *ideological* pertains to their religious beliefs, the *intellectual* to knowledge of their religion, and the *experiential* to their emotions, feelings, sensations, and perceptions related to God and ultimate reality. The *consequential* dimension differs, for it pertains to all the relationships and behavior in everyday life that

---

[120] Andrew R. Breines, *The Catholic Layman in Time of Crisis,* Ph.D. thesis, University of Wisconsin, 1958; and Leo R. Ward, C.S.C., *Catholic Life, U.S.A.* (St. Louis: B. Herder Book Co., 1959).

[121] Riesman, "Some Informal Notes on American Churches and Sects."

[122] Norton E. Long, "The Local Community as an Ecology of Games," *American Journal of Sociology,* 64 (Nov. 1958), 251-61; and Whyte, *The Organization Man,* pp. 326-27.

[123] Peter L. Berger, "Sectarianism and Religious Sociation," *American Journal of Sociology,* 64 (July 1958), 41-44.

are a result of the other four dimensions which can be interpreted as more directly connected with one's relationship with God. It is in the theological domain of "works" in contrast to faith. The indicators of each dimension vary in both kind and degree.[124] (See Chapter 19.)

Fukuyama modified these dimensions in his analysis of 4,095 members in 12 Congregational-Christian churches. Four distinctive styles of religion emerged from study of various aspects of religious beliefs and practices, attitudes on ethical and moral issues, and cultural pursuits. (1) The intellectually oriented (cognitive) members (22 per cent) were well informed about the Bible and religion in general. They viewed sermons as something to think about and were most numerous among men aged 20 to 29, college graduates, and persons of high socioeconomic status. (2) The organizationally oriented (cultic) member was the most common type (44 per cent). These are the "active" members who are "church pillars." Faithful in attendance, contributing generously to church budgets, and donating much time to the church or its organizations, they were most likely to be middle-aged and married with children. (3) The belief oriented (creedal) members (28 per cent) emphasized the importance of assent to traditional creeds and saw beliefs as important in defining their religious position. They included a large proportion of females, older people, persons with high school or less education, and others with low socioeconomic status. (4) Devotionally oriented (devotional) members (23 per cent) emphasized feeling and emotion rather than knowledge and intellect. Daily Bible reading for devotional purposes and a view of the Christian as one who had experienced conversion were stressed. They were most numerous among females, older persons, those with only grade school education, and those of low socioeconomic status. About one-third of all members studied could be described by one of the above styles, one-third by two or more, and two per cent by all four. One-third, however, were not definable by any of the four types; they are "nominal church members." Church membership for most Protestants and Catholics is primarily a cultic or organizational matter.[125] It is along such lines that further fruitful research may be expected. Church membership and participation is not a unitary phenomenon; it is important to distinguish between the wide variety of members and memberships when relating religion to the various topics which are the subject of social science research.

Since the church's encounter with the daily affairs of social life occurs primarily through its members, the church's impact on the world depends

---

[124] Charles Y. Glock, "On the Study of Religious Commitment," *Religious Education*, 57, Research Supplement (July-Aug. 1962), pp. S-98 to S-110; Charles Y. Glock and Rodney Stark, *Religion and Society in Tension* (Chicago: Rand McNally, 1965), Chapter 2. Cf. Snell Putney and Russell Middleton, "Dimensions and Correlates of Religious Ideologies," *Social Forces*, 39 (May 1961), 285-90.

[125] Yoshio Fukuyama, "The Major Dimensions of Church Membership," *Review of Religious Research*, 2 (Spring 1961), 154-61.

significantly upon the extent to which its values are incorporated into their minds and expressed in their behavior. The vitality of a religion is not indicated by mere statistics of membership, church attendance, or religious preference. Its influence upon people, and through them upon society, is the true test of its social significance.

Selected References

Borhek, James T., and Richard F. Curtis, *A Sociology of Belief*. Melbourne, Fla.: Krieger, 1981 (Wiley, 1975). Characteristics of belief systems and their implications for social organization.

Campbell, Thomas C., and Yoshio Fukuyama, *The Fragmented Layman: An Empirical Study of Lay Attitudes*. Philadelphia: Pilgrim Press, 1970. A sociological survey of a representative sample of members in the United Church of Christ focusing on types of church participation in relationship to social issues.

Caplovitz, David, and Fred Sherrow, *The Religious Drop-Outs: Apostasy Among College Graduates*. Beverly Hills, Calif.: Sage Publications, 1977. Apostasy—the relinquishing of religious beliefs and identity—among graduating college seniors during the 1960s is related to such variables as intellectualism, radicalism, adjustment, and "higher values."

Glock, Charles Y., and Robert Bellah, eds., *The New Religious Consciousness*. Berkeley: University of California Press, 1976. Studies of religious behavior and groups in the San Francisco Bay Area.

Glock, Charles Y., Benjamin Ringer, and Earl Babbie, *To Comfort and to Challenge: A Dilemma of the Contemporary Church*. Berkeley: University of California Press, 1967. Report and analysis of survey research in the Episcopal Church which reveals tensions between the goals of the clergy and the laity.

Greeley, Andrew M., *The American Catholic: A Social Portrait*. New York: Basic Books, 1977. A descriptive and analytical summary of research on the latter stages of the acculturation of Catholic ethnic immigrant groups into American society.

Greeley, Andrew M., *Crisis in the Church: A Study of Religion in America*. Chicago: Thomas More Press, 1979. Survey research to identify the characteristics of alienated, unchurched, dissatisfied, communal, and disidentified Catholics.

Johnson, Roger A., ed., *Views from the Pews: Christian Beliefs and Attitudes*. Philadelphia: Fortress Press, 1983. Chapters by sociologists and theologians focused around empirical data from a survey of lay and clergy members of the Lutheran Church in America.

Kotre, John N., *The View from the Border*. Chicago: Aldine-Atherton, 1971. Comparisons of the beliefs and values of 50 Catholic graduate students who consider themselves in the Catholic Church with 50 who consider themselves out.

Paloutzian, Raymond F., *Invitation to the Psychology of Religion*. Glenview, Ill.: Scott, Foresman and Co., 1983. An introductory survey of the psychology of religion with research findings centered on the question, "How does religion work in people's lives?"

Stark, Rodney, and Charles Y. Glock, *American Piety: The Nature of Religious Commitment*. Berkeley: University of California Press, 1970. Survey research with many measures revealing significant differences between church members of different denominations.

Wuthnow, Robert, *The Consciousness Reformation*. Berkeley: University of California Press, 1976. Survey research findings on non-traditional religious participation in a California community.

Chapter 16

Religious Conversion and Revivalism

Sociologically *conversion* refers to any relatively sudden emergence of a new role, outlook, belief, group identification, character, or personality; it includes personal "mutations" and changes in political, economic, or social outlook as well as religious reorganization of one's life. Conversion or a functional equivalent is essential to the preservation of churches insofar as they are voluntary organizations. Although religious conversion is largely social in its definition, background influences, effects, and propagation, sociologists have given it relatively little attention. Perhaps it is regarded by them as by psychologists "as a kind of psychological slum to be avoided by any really respectable scholar." [1]

In theory at least, nearly all Christian groups work for and expect conversions. With their minimization of emotion, church-type groups tend to give conversion a broad, loose, or indefinite meaning. Sect-types generally demand a regenerate church membership and preserve the revival technique to produce it. While they usually deny the social aspects of conversion, claiming it to be purely supernatural, their efforts to make converts and their expected results of conversion indicate that their working definition is social as well as theological.

Christian history has seen many meanings and methods of conversion.

---

[1] Walter Houston Clark, *The Psychology of Religion* (New York: The Macmillan Co., 1958), p. 188.

Where state and church are united so all citizens are considered church members, there is no need to recruit members by conversion. At least six specific types of meaning are given to the term conversion: (1) In the New Testament it means a turning about or a change of attitude toward God. (2) It refers to renunciation of one religion and adherence to another or to change from one branch of a religion to another. This is a prominent usage in Catholicism; anyone who comes into the Church from non-Catholic sources is a convert. (3) Fundamentalists emphasize the "acceptance of God's plan of salvation," typically defined to include repentance of sin, faith in Jesus Christ, asking forgiveness, and regeneration, which in some groups must be accompanied or proved by assurance, spiritual gifts, or other manifestations. (4) Another concept involves consciously or voluntarily becoming religious, as distinguished from merely conforming to the religious ways of one's family or other group. (5) The term sometimes connotes adopting a Christian as contrasted to a non-Christian quality of life, or (6) any abrupt transfer from one type of living or philosophy of life to another, especially if this change is toward what is considered socially a higher form of life. These usages overlap and are to some degree interchangeable.

In Protestantism three major conversion patterns are found.[2] In liturgical churches, such as the Lutheran and Episcopal, confirmation is the rite most directly associated with what is called conversion in other bodies. It refers to accepting Christ as Savior and Lord and becoming a church member after a period of educational preparation which emphasizes Christian doctrine and the duties of members. No stress is placed upon an emotionally intense experience; it is difficult if not impossible for most persons in this pattern to indicate any given time at which a change from "lost" to "saved" took place.

A second pattern is characteristic of such denominations as the Methodists, Baptists, Congregationalists, and Presbyterians. Historically they emphasized the old-fashioned revival as a source of conversions, but today this is rare. Preparatory classes for prospective members, especially youth, are held, and there is a distinct trend toward the confirmation pattern. Many adults are received into membership by letters of transfer from other churches or by the "reaffirmation of faith" of persons whose former church membership status has lapsed. Their conversion is assumed to have occurred at some past date.

Most younger sect-type bodies emphasize traditional revivalistic conversion patterns. Commitment to Jesus Christ as Savior and Lord tends to be accompanied by an emotional upheaval, a sudden break with the past, and sharp awareness of a radical reversal of status before God from being lost to being saved. Other-worldliness receives major emphasis.

All three groups share essential goals as the focus of educational and

2 Harry C. Munro, *Fellowship Evangelism Through Church Groups* (St. Louis: Bethany Press [for the Cooperative Publishing Association], 1951), pp. 128-31.

evangelistic efforts. These include personal commitment to Christ, dedication to a Christian way of life, and vital membership in a local church. There are variations in interpretations of what these goals mean, in the emotional intensity and expression of religious experiences, and in the behavior patterns expected of the faithful, but all Christian groups regard becoming a Christian as surrendering to God, obeying His will, and identifying oneself with the church. Some refer to the experience as conversion; others speak of regeneration, confirmation, salvation, deciding for Christ, coming to Jesus, joining the church, being born again, and the like.

An increasing number of Catholics and liberal Protestants view conversion as a process repeated again and again whenever a person engages in any behavioral change or attitudinal repentance. Nevertheless, our discussion will emphasize the traditional (revivalistic) view of conversion since it is the most distinct, though not necessarily most effective, expression of religious commitment.

The Social Nature of Conversion

Psychologists have given much attention to psychological processes in the conversion experience, but they have tended to neglect the manner in which these processes are influenced by group experiences. Religious conversion has much in common with intellectual synthesis, creative imagination, emphatic resolution of the will, and even "falling in love." Indeed, so many of its characteristics are similar to love, and the speech of love is used so often by those involved in mystical religious experiences, that some psychologists have treated religious devotion as erotic in its origin or motivation.[3] Such similarities do not, however, prove that the energies displayed are simply or purely sexual.

Conversion sometimes reflects the release of repressed social feelings. Early socialization may have taught one that certain types of behavior are sinful or that only persons with distinctive religious beliefs can be saved. These ideas may be repressed until there is a carefree, amoral, or even immoral type of behavior which seems to deny ever having been exposed to such teachings. Then suddenly, upon conversion, repressions are released, a strong sense of guilt emerges, and beliefs appear to have been fashioned anew in a very abrupt manner. What has really occurred, however, is that past social experiences have suddenly emerged from the unconscious into the conscious mind. Past influences have begun a process of unconscious preparation that has steadily developed until it suddenly overcomes all resistance, bursts forth into consciousness, and becomes for a time the dominant factor therein, according to this interpretation.[4]

---

[3] Radoslav A. Tsanoff, *Religious Crossroads* (New York: E. P. Dutton and Co., 1942), pp. 211-12.

[4] J. C. Flugel, *Man, Morals and Society: A Psycho-Analytical Study* (New York: International Universities Press, 1945), pp. 204-5; Alfred C. Underwood, *Conversion: Christian and Non-Christian* (New York: The Macmillan Co., 1925), pp. 247-49, 252-57.

Conversion, like mental illness, arises out of an internal conflict between the ideal and actual self, often is accompanied by guilt and a sense of estrangement from other people, involves acute awareness of unattained possibilities, often involves pathological behavior, and reveals natural self-healing tendencies of the personality. The emotional disturbances involved may be constructive and purposive, serving to break up malignant attitudes and habits and making possible a new synthesis of the personality. [5]

Sociologically, conversion may be considered as the development of a new conception of self in which the entire personality or, as the theologian would say, soul is reoriented around new values. In the adolescent it may accompany the process of developing adult viewpoints; in the adult it may involve turning away from one system of values to another. It is the equivalent of what some psychologists call convergence, in which wholeness of being is built, unification of character is achieved, and a new integrated self replaces the divided self that was torn between conflicting groups, values, or desires. As such, it involves the whole person, not merely one or a few segments of life. The universe is viewed from a new perspective. All things become new (II Cor. 5:17). Mere drifting and impulsive actions tend to be checked by this new orientation of life. New loyalties produce a new way of life. New meanings of God, the world, life, and society become internalized and result in responses different from those of the past. Whether the conversion takes place abruptly or gradually, it involves a new conception both of self and of relationships to others. Self-realization involves social realization.

Conversion may also be seen as a phase in the socialization of the individual. Socialization includes the entire process by which the person learns to adjust to life in society, conform to group standards, get along with other people, and function as an effective part of the group. It reflects all of his formal and informal educational experiences from the time of birth. The person who has been reared in a relatively Christian environment usually grows gradually into a mature Christian person. His "conversion" may be only the final step in a lengthy process of preparation without any radical transformation of conduct, ideals, or character. Such conversion so often occurs in adolescence that it is traditionally expected in non-liturgical churches that members' children will join the church in early adolescence or late pre-adolescence, and in liturgical churches it has been institutionalized into confirmation rites. Conversion involves "the final casting off of childish things, the initiation into complete manhood," [6] rather than a form of regression into childish behavior.

---

[5] Anton T. Boisen, *The Exploration of the Inner World* (New York: Harper and Brothers, 1936), pp. 59-60, 121-22, 204, 209, 281; and A. T. Boisen, *Problems in Religion and Life* (New York: Abingdon-Cokesbury Press, 1946), pp. 112-13.
[6] Havelock Ellis, *The Dance of Life* (Boston: Houghton Mifflin Co., 1923), p. 222.

Conversion includes growing out of a selfishly motivated life into one that includes social motives and impulses. "Conversion is the climax of the 'unselfing' process." [7] When it has advanced to a high degree, the convert is willing and able in his mind to take the point of view of others, seeing his role in life and especially in religious circles as part of a pattern of group activity. The "generalized other" becomes an internalized reference point by which behavior is evaluated.[8] Conversion involves changes in group identification with accompanying changes in attitudes and actions. When the convert leaves behind his life of sin and enters the life of grace, he departs from one social group and joins another. His group loyalties change; old customs and beliefs are denied, and a new set of norms is accepted. The permanence of the conversion usually is correlated positively with the extent to which the old associations have been broken and new ones substituted. Profound alterations of the personality, resocialization, and development of a new conception of self, accompany the shifts in group identification.

With changes in patterns of association come changes in other actions and in attitudes that are often far-reaching in both their immediate and long-range implications. If the outward shifting of group membership takes place suddenly, it may involve a radical change of character "from sinfulness to righteousness or from indifference to spiritual awakening." [9] The later in life a conversion comes, the more intense and revolutionary it is likely to be, for the changes are more difficult and drastic as habitual associations and patterns of behavior have been more strongly established through repetitive experiences.[10]

Repentance and faith, turning from sin and to God, are not merely philosophical or theological concepts. They involve group identifications to such an extent that "loving the brethren" is given in the New Testament as a necessary indication of possessing eternal life (I John 3:14; 4:7-12). Scripturally and sociologically, conversion cannot involve mere inward mystical experiences that do not influence one's group associations. To some extent conversion is an internal psychic readjustment of the human organism or soul as it becomes one with itself and hence "has no primary reference to any external object." Institutionalized conventions and traditions sometimes may be fatal to true internalized religious experience, but in order to experience complete conversion and have the "new inward harmony proceeding from a psychic centre that is at one alike with itself

---

[7] Frederick Morgan Davenport, *Primitive Traits in Religious Revivals* (New York: The Macmillan Co., 1905), p. 316.

[8] Cf. George Herbert Mead, *Mind, Self, and Society* (Chicago: University of Chicago Press, 1934), pp. 151-54.

[9] Boisen, *The Exploration of the Inner World,* p. 307.

[10] Paul E. Johnson, *Psychology of Religion,* rev. ed. (New York: Abingdon Press, 1959), pp. 128-29.

and with the Not-Self," it is necessary to be accepted as part of a group fellowship and to have wholesome relationships with its members.[11]

The sociological interpretation of conversion as the development of a new conception of self, a phase in socialization, and a shifting of group identifications is neither a complete nor exclusive explanation. That which is conversion sociologically may not be considered conversion at all from the perspective of the religious leader, and some experiences the latter calls conversion may seem to the sociologist to involve no sociological changes. Nevertheless, the sociological perspective can assist the religious worker and make him more effective in efforts to attain his goals. Theological interpretations similarly can help the sociologist of religion understand the process.

Types of Conversion

In most cases of conversion no new teachings have been imparted and no new loyalties and standards acquired. The individual has been under tension because of some inner conflict and has resolved this conflict through a commitment or re-commitment to loyalties, doctrines, or standards already his. A person with a maladjusted personality may shift from one religion or denomination to another in the search for inner security, peace, or happiness. Conversions on mission fields which involve proselyting from other religions are often of this kind, as are some of mystics who emerge from their experiences with new insights that may result in the establishment of a new cult or in emotional reinforcement of traditional beliefs.[12] Either through reinforcing the teachings of the group in which one has been socialized or through reacting against it, conversion reflects the social life and conditioning of the persons involved.

Changes in group identification may take place through *reflexive conversion* in which there is a change of feelings toward persons of a particular group followed by changes in association patterns and finally a change in ideology. It may also occur through *ideological conversion* in which there is first a change in ideology followed by changes in association preferences and lastly a change in the feelings aroused by contact with persons of a particular religious identity.[13]

Many have classified conversions as gradual or sudden. Sudden conversions almost invariably grow out of past experiences, whether recollected and recognized or not. They often are the climax of a gradual

---

[11] Quoted passages are from Ellis, *The Dance of Life,* pp. 218 and 225; see also pp. 219, 227-28.

[12] Boisen, *The Exploration of the Inner World,* pp. 207-8.

[13] Daniel Glaser, "Dynamics of Ethnic Interaction," *American Sociological Review,* 23 (Feb. 1958), 31-40. Glaser presents these as a hypothesis of the sequence in which changes in ethnic identification occur. It is here hypothesized that they apply also to changes in religious identification.

process which has acted consciously or subconsciously over a period of time. These eruptive, dramatic experiences are most likely to occur when problems have accumulated pertinent to desires or tendencies that must be repressed for social reasons. Such conversion involves sudden release from feelings of fear and estrangement and a sense of fellowship with God resulting in a new conception of self and of one's role in life. The sudden event appears to be the conversion; actually it is either a point of departure or arrival in a process. It differs so little in fact from gradual conversions that depth analysis of specific cases leads to almost complete banishment of the distinction.[14] The conversion crisis hence is not a sudden, disruptive event. Seen in broadest perspective, conversion is a process that lasts throughout life.[15]

An early study analyzed data of many groups selected to give "a true picture of conversion in modern Christian communities." Conversion was found to be a distinctively adolescent phenomenon with most cases between ages 12 and 19 and nearly all between 10 and 25. Feeling seemed to play a larger part in the religious lives of females; males were influenced more by the intellect and volition. Conversion involved a process of "unselfing" in which the individual was called out from self-centeredness into active sympathy with the world outside himself. New powers or abilities emerged; life was lived on a higher plane as he realized the possibilities of development. Youth brought up in Christian circles went through similar phases of growth into enlarged spiritual life during the same age period as converts. Their emotional and psychological symptoms of stress were much the same, and the result was similar.[16]

Three types of religious awakening were compared by Clark. The *definite-crisis type* involved an emotional crisis in which a definite change of attitude seemed to have been effected. The *emotional-stimulus awakening* had no emotional upheaval or one of greatly reduced intensity, yet the subject looked back to some event that was a stimulus awakening the religious consciousness. Typically it involved going forward in a public meeting, joining a church, being confirmed, or standing in a Sunday school decision day service. Although life and attitudes remained unchanged, the emotional stimulus stood out in memory as a starting point of the religious life. In the third type, *gradual awakening,* no obstructions to the enlarging and growing religious life were observed, hence no change of attitude was necessary. If deep stirrings of the emotional life were ex-

---

[14] Sante de Sanctis, *Religious Conversion,* trans. Helen Augur (New York: Harcourt, Brace, & Co., 1927), pp. 65-86; Boisen, *Problems in Religion and Life,* pp. 116-17; Tsanoff, *Religious Crossroads,* pp. 218-21; and Leon Salzman, "The Psychology of Religious and Ideological Conversion," *Psychiatry,* 16 (1953), 177-87.

[15] This is a major theme of L. Wyatt Lang, *A Study of Conversion* (London: George Allen and Unwin, Ltd., 1931).

[16] Edwin D. Starbuck, *The Psychology of Religion: An Empirical Study of the Growth of Religious Consciousness* (New York: Charles Scribner's Sons, 1899).

perienced, they found their place in the process of development and were not regarded as determining in their influence. Of 2,174 cases, 6.7 per cent experienced a definite-crisis awakening, 27.2 per cent an emotional-stimulus experience, and 66.1 per cent no definite awakening whatever. Although the data were not directly comparable to those of earlier studies, there was some evidence that the proportion passing through the definite-crisis awakening conventionally called conversion was diminishing with increasing emphasis upon religious training.[17]

Earlier studies found the mean and the modal year for conversions to be the sixteenth, and the median the seventeenth. Clark's definite-crisis and emotional-stimulus subjects experienced conversion earlier, the modal year being the twelfth, but typically with a lapse of about five years if impediments then hindered the normal process. The variability of the age of religious awakening, with a shift of three and a half years in one generation, indicates that it is not simply a biologically determined pubertal experience;[18] it is sociocultural.

Males were more likely than females to have a definite-crisis conversion. Persons who were exposed to a stern theology which emphasized total depravity, hell fire, damnation, and eternal punishment of the unsaved were more likely to experience a crisis awakening and much less likely to experience the gradual type than those whose theological exposure had been to a moderate theology dominated by the love of God, forgiveness, the ideals of Christ, and service. Individuals from groups that emphasize confirmation were much less likely than others to experience a definite-crisis or emotional-stimulus conversion. Those who had poor home training in religion or irregular Sunday school attendance during childhood, those who were reared in rural areas, and persons who were in a full-time religious vocation or planned to enter one were more likely than others to have a definite-crisis experience.[19]

Clark's findings demonstrate that social influences are significantly related to variations in religious experiences. His types of awakening may be interpreted from the perspective of social roles. The definite crisis type involves a *sudden change of role*. The individual comes out from sin and the world through an abrupt crisis, changing his habits to conform with his social role in a new religious group. The emotional-stimulus awakening involves a *sudden role identification* with abruptly increased involvement in a group of which one already is a member. This is common among persons reared under consistent religious influences; their lives are not radically changed by conversion because they have already been developing in the direction involved. The gradual awakening may be termed *role assimilation*, for it involves a learning process without any

17 Elmer T. Clark, *The Psychology of Religious Awakening* (New York: The Macmillan Co., 1929).
18 *Ibid.*, pp. 54, 63-68.
19 *Ibid.*, pp. 73-74, 84-88, 100-3, 109-19.

crisis experience. Gradual change of role begins with learning in childhood or some later date.[20]

A study of 399 members in the Mission Covenant Youth, an organization of an evangelical, revivalistic denomination in Sweden, indicated 16.0 per cent to have experienced a sudden change of role, 55.8 per cent sudden role identification, and 28.2 per cent role assimilation. The sudden change of role was much more likely than sudden role identification to have occurred at revival meetings. The order was reversed for camps, other formal meetings, and informal situations. Sudden change of role probably dominates in the first generation of a revivalist movement, but when children of the first generation develop, imitation of their parents' experience of conversion takes the form of a sudden role identification; they do not change roles but reinforce previously learned ones.[21]

Sudden role identification took place almost exclusively during puberty, the modal age being 14 to 15 years, with a mean of 16.6 for the boys and 15.6 for the girls. Sudden change of role occurred at a somewhat later age, and was more frequent among those who lived in rural districts, those with limited education, and men. Educational differences were due to the breaking down of fundamentalist beliefs by higher education, extracurricular school activities which had to be given up to meet Covenant standards, strengthening of the student's emotional and intellectual life by the Swedish system of education so that he would not be swayed easily by opinions or ideologies, and greater opportunities in higher education to contact attitudes incompatible with Covenant role expectations. Sex differences may have been due to the greater similarity of the female than the male role to Covenant norms pertinent to smoking, use of alcohol, card playing, and sometimes sex. Men also had more opportunities to be in touch with secular attitudes. As a result, many more women than men were members; the change from the habit system of the average man to the Covenant position was greater and more violent than that of the average woman.[22] It is likely that American conversion patterns reflect similar influences, for conversion is clearly affected by cultural norms and conditions.

The Incidence of Conversion

Over one-third of American adults say they have been born again or experienced a turning point in their lives when they committed themselves to Jesus Christ.[23] Certain religious groups still emphasize the need for a fairly distinct conversion experience in order to become a member, but

[20] Hans L. Zetterberg, "The Religious Conversion as a Change of Social Roles," *Sociology and Social Research*, 26 (Jan.-Feb. 1952), 159-66.
[21] *Ibid.*
[22] *Ibid.*
[23] Princeton Religion Research Center, *Religion in America 1982* (Princeton, N.J.: The Gallup Poll, 1982), p. 31.

most church members probably have had only the gradual type of awakening, if any. A panel of 200 research subjects, selected to secure variety and range of religious background and experience as well as of education, sex, age, marital status, and occupation, did not include any persons who experienced conversion as usually defined, although at least one had what might be called a deconversion or loss of faith. They reflected developmental growth in their religious concepts. Reactions against rigid, absolutist conceptions of God as the individual moved toward maturity had led many to change their concepts of the Deity as a pictorial, personal, anthropomorphic God or to react entirely against them in favor of deconcretized, spiritualized concepts of the Deity.[24]

Pratt estimated that at least nine out of ten religious conversion cases reported in psychological studies would not have had any violent or depressing experience to report if they had not been reared in a church or community which taught them to look for it or even to cultivate it. Without such social experiences, the gradual and almost imperceptible nature of the process of religious maturation makes it impossible to single out an emotional experience of conversion.[25]

Christian groups that have aimed at maintaining a converted membership have not been able to uphold that standard for a very long period of time. With the coming of the second generation, religious development of the converts' children hinders their having distinct conversion experiences. Conversion tends to be "watered down" with the passage of time until its operational definition fits the actual experiences produced in the group. It may involve raising a hand at a Sunday school decision day, going forward at a meeting, shaking hands with an evangelist, signing a decision card, answering "Yes" to the question, "Do you believe in Jesus?," or almost any overt act that seems to reflect a religious decision or emotion.[26] Four generations seem involved in the American pattern. The first had its religious roots in the evangelistic enthusiasm of the Moody and Sankey revivals. Religion was basic to their very existence; it was a source of energy for missionary and philanthropic endeavors as well as for personal living. The second generation inherited their religion. It was a secure personal possession and a source of strength for Christian living, but most lacked the overflowing vitality which had made their fathers' personal evangelism so effective. The third generation, brought up under the new religious education, generally failed to have personal religious experience rooted in their spiritual life; religion became something passed down to them which they felt obligated to sustain. Their church work represented their parents' interests and not their own. Their religious ob-

24 Richard V. McCann, "Developmental Factors in the Growth of a Mature Faith," *Religious Education,* 50 (May-June 1955), 147-55.

25 James Bissett Pratt, *The Religious Consciousness* (New York: The Macmillan Co., 1920), pp. 152-54.

26 George A. Coe, *The Psychology of Religion* (Chicago: University of Chicago Press, 1916), pp. 155-56.

servances were a tribute to the memory of the past rather than symbolic of a living, creative, present reality. The fourth generation is undergoing religious education in church schools, but it is not at all deeply affected by what it is exposed to. Religion is largely irrelevant to daily life and interests. Like economic wealth according to a proverbial saying, family fortunes in religion are accumulated by the first generation, enjoyed by the second, dissipated by the third, and lost to the fourth.[27]

The Half Way Covenant adopted in 1662 in the New England Congregational churches admitted to baptism, and upon adulthood to the civil rights of membership, the children of baptized members, even if not of communicant status. It illustrates the tendency for the religion of one generation to be "watered down" by the next. Moral and religious requirements for church membership became progressively lower until a majority of members in many churches no longer claimed to have had any definitely religious experience. Membership in the church and citizenship in the community became synonymous; the influence of the church waned until it became largely a secular institution. Disciplinary control over members was greatly weakened as accident of birth rather than religious conviction became the source of church membership.[28]

Social Influences on Conversion

The language used in conveying the religious message of the need for conversion is a social product and a social instrument used in a social setting. The results expected when efforts are made to win converts are largely social, involving, as we have seen, modifications in socialization, group identifications, roles, and statuses. Conversion is influenced by social factors in many additional ways. Some sect leaders strangely insist that social influences are not at all involved in religious conversion but at the same time exert strong social pressures upon persons they wish to convert.[29]

1. Norms of the religious group affect the forms conversions take and teach prospective converts how to be saved and what to expect as an

---

[27] Henry P. Van Dusen, *The Plain Man Seeks for God* (New York: Charles Scribner's Sons, 1933), pp. 20-24; as cited in Douglas Clyde Macintosh, *Personal Religion* (New York: Charles Scribner's Sons, 1942), pp. 311-12.

[28] Winthrop S. Hudson, *The Great Tradition of the American Churches* (New York: Harper and Brothers, 1953), pp. 65-67; and Macintosh, *Personal Religion,* pp. 279-80.

[29] Numerous Biblical references indicate the importance of a person's background to his religious faith and works. The wisdom literature includes the admonition to train a child in the way he should go, for then even when he is old he will not depart from it (Proverbs 22:6). The Apostle Paul indicated that Christian faith is impossible without preachers to bring the message of salvation (Romans 10:14-15). Many examples are given of persons whose childhood experiences affected their entire lives. Among these is Timothy, who was influenced by the faith of his mother and grandmother (II Timothy 1:5).

accompaniment of the experience. The nature of repentance and self-surrender is socially defined. Some groups emphasize outward manifestations, such as discontinuing the use of tobacco or lipstick or wearing certain types of clothing; others stress social participation in group activities or general personality traits.

The doctrinal system of a church controls converts' experiences. A theology of crisis produces crisis experiences; a theology that emphasizes development produces a church membership that gradually grows in faith and works. Even the age at which religious problems become acute and conversion typically occurs is that which social usage declares suitable. Society tends to "define the age and range and sex to which religious experience is presented as a problem to be solved." [30] The language forms and vocabulary used to express religious experiences grow out of participation in a particular group. When required to tell of personal experiences, converts use clichés and follow instructions. Doctrinal beliefs are influenced by the language used; self-interpretations of motivations grow out of social influences operating before, during, and after conversion.

The Covenant youth studied by Zetterberg had been influenced by many church activities to learn the roles expected of them in the group. Over four-fifths had attended Sunday school, Bible classes, and religious clubs; eight-tenths had been brought up in a family in which at least one parent was a member of the Covenant church. [31]

A group's conception of salvation varies with the socioeconomic segment of society that is dominant in its membership and with the world image emphasized in the segment of society it represents. Concepts of "from what" and "for what" one wishes to be redeemed, and according to the particular church can be redeemed, vary widely. [32] The forms of salvation expected may become so institutionalized that they are highly artificial and mean little to many in whom they are induced.

2. The general cultural milieu influences the forms and results of conversion. Christian converts in India experience a distinctly Indian form of Christian conversion. Mass conversions in America often are devoid of significance for many persons involved, but the isolated Christian convert in India is much less likely to persist in his new faith than the one who comes as part of a mass movement of an entire village, hamlet, or other group that has social solidarity. Psychological introspection is impossible on a uniform basis among Christians in India because the group

---

[30] Margaret Mead, "Adolescence in Primitive and in Modern Society," in *Readings in Social Psychology,* 3d ed., Eleanor E. Maccoby, Theodore M. Newcomb, and Eugene L. Hartley, eds. (New York: Holt, Rinehart and Winston, Inc., 1958), pp. 341-49. Quotation from p. 347.

[31] Zetterberg, "The Religious Conversion."

[32] Hans H. Gerth and C. Wright Mills, *From Max Weber: Essays in Sociology* (New York: Oxford University Press, 1946), pp. 280-81.

consciousness of one caste is significantly different from that of another.[33] Proselytes have been won by terrorism. Thus Spanish Jews, tortured during the Inquisition and shocked by the massacre of 1391, professed Christianity to escape persecution.[34]

When a religion is brought to a new culture, it must determine which of its elements are irrelevant cultural traits and which are essential to the faith. When alien cults enter a world of religiously indifferent traditions, only slight changes, if any at all, occur in culture traits of the converts. The "paganisms" of Christian syncretisms partly result from this tendency.

In a society which highly emphasizes the value of entertainers, "conversions" sometimes result from opportunities to gain personal publicity or fame. The total cultural setting in which evangelistic efforts take place must be considered by those who wish to win true converts. In America the most effective techniques seem to involve elements of the democratic process in which thoughtful discussion in an atmosphere of mutual respect is present. When there is dogmatic argument, attack upon sincerity, or criticism of the present religion, the evangelist often arouses defense reactions that prevent conversion.[35]

3. Changes in social status may contribute to conversion. Certain persons depart from churches of relatively low social status to join those of higher status as they rise on the socioeconomic ladder. Most of the converts in 135 Mennonite churches had previous church affiliations. They came from low-income, low-education, and farm-occupation groups. Eighty per cent of the churches' membership were offspring of Mennonites; new joiners came because they intimately knew one or more members. The higher the formal education of members, the more apt they were to leave the church. Members who left tended to join more liberal denominations.[36] Socioeconomic influences are intricately interwoven with patterns of conversion and religious mobility.

4. Predisposing social background experiences contribute to conversion, as already intimated. Publicity of sudden, dramatic conversions conveys the impression that they resulted from the immediate revival or other situation in which the conversion occurred. Upon investigation most are found to grow out of a prolonged background of conditioning influences. The Apostle Paul was exposed before conversion to Stephen's martyrdom and the testimonies of Christians he persecuted (Acts 8:1; 9:1-30). Jerry McCauley, the famous mission convert and organizer, stated that he did not know any man to be permanently reclaimed by

33 Angus Stewart Woodburne, "The Psychological Study of Conversion in India," *Journal of Religion*, 1 (Nov. 1921), 641-45.

34 Cecil Roth, *A History of the Marranos* (New York: Meridian Paperbacks, 1959).

35 Harrison Sacket Elliott, *The Process of Group Thinking* (New York: Association Press, 1938), pp. 160-61.

36 John A. Hostetler, "Religious Mobility in a Sect Group: The Mennonite Church," *Rural Sociology*, 19 (Sept. 1954), 244-55.

Christianity who did not have a good mother.[37] Of 100 Protestant converts from Catholicism, 83 were influenced by other people and 92 mentioned dissatisfaction with the Catholic Church.[38] Many external influences were evident on Starbuck's subjects who had experienced developmental growth rather than a distinct religious conversion. Foremost among influential forces was the home which affected 39 per cent of the females and 52 per cent of the males. This was followed by friends and the example of other people, which together influenced 34 per cent of the females and 42 per cent of the males. The church or its pastor, publications, and crisis experiences like death and illness also stimulated conversion.

General religious development without distinct transitions were most likely to emerge when there were religious surroundings in childhood, when children were kept reasonably free from dogmas they were incapable of assimilating, when their needs were met carefully at every point in development, and when there was a continual mixture of faith and doubt, permitting freedom to question all things and yet enough trust and insight to remain firmly rooted in religion.[39]

Evangelistic efforts to produce conversions face problems similar to those of political propaganda. What appears to be conversion often is activation of previously held ideas and experiences, many of which have been forgotten and repressed into subconsciousness. Very few persons are converted by campaign propaganda to vote for a candidate for whom they would not have voted otherwise. Half of those studied in the 1940 and 1944 presidential campaigns had decided for which party to vote at least six months before the election. One fourth made and held their decision after they knew who the nominees were. Seventy per cent of the decisions corresponded to voting tendencies in groups with social characteristics similar to their own. Predispositions were deeply rooted; they could not be easily changed by campaigning. The strongly partisan devoted the most attention to campaign propaganda and were exposed to much more of their own than opposition influences. Thus the "bottleneck of conversion" lies in the fact that those who most read and listen to propaganda read and hear chiefly that which supports the position they have already taken; those who are eligible for conversion read and listen the least.[40] It is likely that a similar bottleneck is present in propaganda aimed at securing religious conversions. Many a pastor has been dismayed at the small number or complete lack of the non-converted at "evangelistic services," and the majority of those who attend even the most widely advertised revival crusades are church members already converted

---

[37] Davenport, *Primitive Traits in Religious Revivals,* pp. 309-10; see also pp. 317-18.

[38] Russell O. Berg, "Why Catholics Become Protestants," *Christian Herald,* 83, no. 8 (Aug. 1960), 22-24, 46, 76-80.

[39] Starbuck, *The Psychology of Religion,* pp. 294-310.

[40] Paul F. Lazarsfeld, Bernard Berelson, and Hazel Gaudet, *The People's Choice,* 2d ed. (New York: Columbia University Press, 1948), pp. xxi, 94-95.

to the evangelist's basic position. Those who "need" the religious message the most are the least likely to receive it through conventional channels.

Social Effects of Conversion

The definition of conversion makes it necessary for changes to occur in order to apply the term correctly. It is in the light of modern needs that modern patterns of repentance and acceptance of redemption occur, hence modern religious experiences have their own distinctive emphasis and expression.[41] What is defined as conversion today might not have been considered such had it occurred a generation ago, and vice versa. As social conditions change, the overt nature of conversion changes. Most contemporary "conversions" occur in the institutionalized framework of regular church activities and are primarily a means of joining the church.

Despite the theological doctrine that the converted and the natural man are radically different, "converted men as a class are indistinguishable from natural men; some natural men even excel some converted men in their fruits; and no one ignorant of doctrinal theology could guess by mere every-day inspection of the 'accidents' of the two groups of persons before him, that their substance differed as much as divine differs from human substance." [42] Yet the lives of many converts might have been much further from ideal had they never received whatever measure of grace has touched their lives. Whether as a result of gradual growth or sudden conversion, sanctification changes the lives of many people; their personalities are changed and they indeed are born anew.[43]

Conversion often involves a shifting of the center of organization of a personality. Major systems of value are reoriented in the saltatory, complex, organizational process of becoming; basic character trends may be changed and one may be freed from the bonds of inadequate adjustment.[44] Victory over "evil habits" is a common concomitant. Deep-seated habits sometimes are destroyed by the act of complete commitment. "When a new self-ideal is sincerely accepted, old habits seen to be inconsistent with this new standard are inhibited." [45] Since habits seldom are formed suddenly, many groups give great attention to helping converts develop new external habits to accompany a new internal reorientation of values. "Wherever converts 'stick' it will be found that habit-formation, particularly through a new social fellowship, follows the conversion crisis." [46] Reorganization of the personality thus involves both positive as-

---

[41] Gene E. Bartlett, "Will Modern Conversion Convert?" *Christian Century,* 64 (May 14, 1947), 619-21.

[42] William James, *The Varieties of Religious Experience* (New York: Random House, Modern Library ed., n.d.), p. 233.

[43] *Ibid.,* pp. 234-36.

[44] Gordon W. Allport, *Becoming* (New Haven: Yale University Press, 1955), pp. 87-90; and Percival M. Symonds, *Dynamics of Psychotherapy,* I, *Principles* (New York: Grune and Stratton, 1956), p. 161.

[45] Lang, *A Study of Conversion,* p. 141.

[46] Coe, *The Psychology of Religion,* p. 168.

pects of rebuilding a life and a negative aspect of sloughing off undesirable habits and associations. Concrete expression of the conversion is necessary if the experience is to have permanence. In many groups leaders insist upon a public declaration of the convert's determination to lead a new life. This act helps to settle the matter decisively, for if it were purely subjective and secret it might be disregarded in times of temptation. It brings moral support and encouragement from the religious community and holds before the convert the fear of censure should he fail in his struggle to live a new life. Public identification with the group helps the newcomer; it also strengthens the group, giving it greater social solidarity as members recognize their common backgrounds and share their struggles to live the new life.

Attitudes of the convert are closely related to group experiences during and after conversion. If he is not given a role and status that make him feel he belongs to the group, he is likely to become a backslider. The internalization of a new-found faith is greatly intensified and accelerated by strong social commitments (public testimonies, personal witnessing, or baptism) which involve the entire personality and make the new birth become more than an empty phrase. Similar influences, processes, and effects are associated with conversion into cults and other new religious movements.[47]

Many (though not all) converts have broken the bonds of undesirable habits, developed altruistic behavior, experienced a radical change in moral values, carried out difficult restitution, received an intense missionary zeal, subdued egoistic impulses, and received increased physical and mental vitality from their conversion.[48] The specific fruits of conversion vary, however, with the environment within which the convert's development has taken place. Thus the Hindu convert to Christianity often far excels the American Christian in the virtues of humility and resignation to the will of God, for in the East passive virtues are exalted, while active and aggressive ones are stressed in the West. The feeling of assurance emphasized as a result of conversion in many Protestant groups is in harmony with the theological doctrine of justification by faith. The Catholic result of conversion is more typically a state of compunction than of assurance; if immediate, unmediated deliverance were offered, repetition of sacrifices in the Mass and a mediating priesthood to offer them would be unnecessary.[49]

47 L. L. Bernard, "Attitudes and the Redirection of Behavior," in Social Attitudes, Kimball Young, ed. (New York: Henry Holt and Co., 1931), pp. 59-60; and J. G. McKenzie, Psychology, Psychotherapy and Evangelicalism (New York: The Macmillan Co., 1940), pp. 109-14. Cf. James T. Richardson, ed., Conversion Careers: In and Out of the New Religions (Beverly Hills, Calif.: Sage, 1978).

48 Many examples of conversions that had no apparent wholesome effects can be found. To state dogmatically that either extreme type of result is inevitably the case seems unwarranted in the light of present knowledge.

49 Underwood, Conversion, pp. 248-57.

Post-Conversion Experiences

A study of 100 autobiographies of persons who had experienced religious conversion indicated that 5 per cent of the women and 7 per cent of the men had experienced complete relapses. Nearly all (93 per cent) of the women and most (77 per cent) of the men had gone through post-conversion struggles with old habits, periods of inactivity and indifference, efforts to attain an ideal, storm and stress, or doubts. Problems experienced after conversion are the same in kind, although different in degree, as those experienced by adolescents in the absence of conversion.[50]

A pastor furnished Starbuck with the results of two types of evangelistic effort in the same community. In revival meetings conducted by a professional evangelist there were 92 converts; 62 were dropped before six weeks, and 30 were received into full membership. Of the 30, only 12 remained members in good standing at the time of the report. Of 68 converts who were the result of regular church work in homes, Sunday school, revival meetings of the pastor, and similar activities, 16 were dropped before six weeks, 52 were received into full membership, and 40 were in good standing at the time of the report.[51] Of 73 Boston converts "brought to Jesus" by two popular evangelical preachers, only one changed his overt behavior in an altruistic direction after conversion. Thirty-seven changed their speech patterns so they repeated the words, "Our Lord Jesus Christ," and similar religious expressions more often than before conversion. The remaining 35 changed neither overt behavior nor speech patterns. In terms of altruistic transformations, Sorokin concluded that nearly all momentary religious conversions are superficial and that this helps explain why the alleged "religious revival" had so little effect upon the deeper currents of social life and moral conditions.[52]

Follow-up studies of conversions are difficult, for groups that emphasize conversion seldom keep records of converts who do not join churches as a result of their experience. The memories of those who emphasize the need for a distinct conversion are deceptive; all who change and become faithful church workers are remembered, while those who drift away are forgotten. One exploratory study followed up conversions in a Child Evangelism class, a Baptist daily vacation Bible school, evangelistic programs of a local church, and another church's program in which the pastor emphasized a process of conversion that involved accepting Christ as Savior and continuing a life of commitment. The evidence indicated that inter-

[50] Starbuck, *The Psychology of Religion,* pp. 353-66.
[51] *Ibid.,* p. 170.
[52] Pitirim A. Sorokin, "Studies of the Harvard Research Center in Creative Altruism," Winchester, Mass., Harvard University Research Center in Creative Altruism, n.d.

weaving evangelistic efforts with the entire program of the church was more effective in producing church growth and spiritual development of members than a program of isolated periodic evangelistic programs and revivals.[53]

Dropping out of church or Sunday school does not invariably mean that the person is permanently lost to the church. In a Baptist General Conference survey, over one-third of 145 Sunday school superintendents and 27 per cent of 222 pastors had at one time or another dropped out of Sunday school. The primary reason for their later return was a conversion experience. Other factors effective for a few were changed work, new location of residence, the influence of some person, family influences, consecration of one's life, or opportunities for service. The modal age of dropping out was 14, but many quit between ages 17 and 24. In another study of over 600 youths who had quit Sunday school, only three cases were found in which one or both parents also attended.[54] No matter how it is measured, backsliding appears more closely related to family environment than any other factor. "Deconversion" of persons so reared that they "always" have been believers usually occurs without overt signs of moral degeneracy in general cultural terms. However, from the perspective of the group they leave, such persons may be very degenerate because of concomitant rejection of distinctive marks of membership in the church they have forsaken.

The new convert is not always eagerly received in church. He may face difficult problems of assimilation in his efforts to identify with the new group. The convert to Catholicism often experiences feelings of loneliness in the dilemma that, while he is a Catholic, he does not know how to act like one. Parish activities that seem natural and correct for others are complex and difficult for him. Even more difficult is the maze of distinctions involved in relationships between lay members, the priest, and the hierarchy. Many converts never fully internalize and live the institutionalized roles expected of Catholics.[55]

The convert is sometimes overly enthusiastic about his new faith. He may conform to a higher degree than others to the group's ethical norms, and he may zealously try to win additional converts. This may result partly from a feeling that he is on trial and must ensure acceptance by the group; it also comes from ignorance of the nuances of patterned and permissible departures from the group's norms. The long-established members have acquired this knowledge unwittingly in the course of their

53 David O. Moberg and Norris A. Magnuson, "A Follow-up Study of Converts," *Bethel Seminary Quarterly*, 3, no. 2 (Feb. 1955), 50-58.
54 Leonard Carroll, "Why We Lose Adolescents," *Bethel Seminary Quarterly*, 1, no. 3 (May 1953), 54-66.
55 John D. Donovan, "The Social Structure of the Parish," in *The Sociology of the Parish*, C. J. Nuesse and Thomas J. Harte, C.Ss.R., eds. (Milwaukee: The Bruce Publishing Co., 1952), pp. 83-85.

socialization; the convert, lacking acceptable alternatives, may become a rigid conformist in efforts to live up to the strict letter of the normative code.[56]

In Catholic parishes with a large proportion of converts, as in many black communities, much of the religious life must be organized on an individual rather than family basis because converts generally enter the Church as individuals. Problems of unfamiliarity with Catholic traditions, customs, and doctrines are then more common than when families reinforce Church teachings. In such parishes, interfaith marriages also tend to be common, and numerous associated problems arise from the Church's conflict with prevailing community standards.[57] It is not surprising that Fichter found no converts among nuclear parishioners. Some, however, were very active in "the broader apostolate," devoting much time to Catholic organizations and activities on the supraparochial level.[58]

Like most Protestants, Catholic laymen generally expend little effort toward the making of converts. They passively accept the status quo, fear the possibility of arousing antagonism, believe Protestantism is crumbling so ex-Protestants will enter the Church automatically, lack knowledge of proper methods, and get discouraged at the lack of immediate results in their few feeble proselyting efforts. Self-satisfaction from parish activities leads them to neglect efforts to draw others into the fellowship.[59]

Conclusion

The sociological interpretation of conversion treats it as a human rather than a supernatural phenomenon. Ultimate causation and supernatural significance are outside the realm of social science. To understand the social processes in conversion is not to demonstrate that no supernatural elements are involved. Those who believe in an omnipotent God must believe that He can work through influences and processes that may appear purely natural to the detached human observer.

Although religious conversion is largely and primarily an individual matter involving new personality commitments, it has profound social implications. To Christianize the social order without Christianizing individuals is even more difficult than the impossible attempt to Christianize individuals without influencing the social order. The community cannot build its life upon religious values unless persons who comprise it are so

---

[56] Robert K. Merton, *Social Theory and Social Structure*, rev. ed. (Glencoe, Ill.: The Free Press, 1957), p. 352.

[57] Thomas J. Harte, C.Ss.R., "Racial and National Parishes in the United States," in *The Sociology of the Parish*, Nuesse and Harte, p. 174.

[58] Joseph H. Fichter, S.J., *Social Relations in the Urban Parish* (Chicago: University of Chicago Press, 1954), p. 28.

[59] Paul Hanly Furfey, "The Missionary Role of the Parish," in *The Sociology of the Parish*, Nuesse and Harte, pp. 305-7.

building their lives. Higher motivations than mere selfish grasping cannot characterize a society unless they characterize a large proportion of its members.[60] Both religious education and revivalistic conversion have changed some people's values and produced the social commitment necessary for improved personal adjustment and social relationships. When broadly defined, conversion is still a common phenomenon.[61]

Religious Revivals

All major Protestant denominations in America have engaged in revivalistic endeavors. Variations between their revivals do not involve differences in kind but only in degree. The revivals shared many elements, and all can be traced back to the Great Awakening in the eighteenth century; it fixed the pattern of frontier religion.

Revivals cannot break out at any place or time; the cultural milieu must provide an atmosphere which makes them possible. The techniques of professional revivalists aim at producing the necessary conditions. When unsatisfied longing for vital religious experience is absent and when people's minds are preoccupied with other interests, revival efforts fail. Revivals may therefore occur without spreading to adjacent areas. They are localized because conditions that help produce them are local conditions.[62] Conditions which have commonly contributed to past revivals include social maladjustments and rapid intellectual advance. When people are frustrated, they seek an outlet for their feelings or turn to what they hope will be a solution. Revivals are hence more common among isolated rural people and lower class city dwellers than others. They were common on the frontier and often occurred in immigrant groups. Lower class persons with poor education are more than ever looked down upon in periods of rapid intellectual development. They can relieve tensions and gain recognition through conversion. Anti-intellectualism hence is associated with many revivals.

The revival is likely to be a movement of social reorganization or integration. Many revivals seem to have operated like safety valves discharging discontent without serious injury to established institutions. They thus may have served as a harmless and disguised protest of the working class against businessmen and other vested interests in the social order. Their cathartic emotional outlet may have done more to prevent drastic attacks on established institutions than many realize.

---

60 Charles A. Ellwood, *The World's Need of Christ* (New York: Abingdon-Cokesbury Press, 1940), pp. 25-33.

61 W. H. Clark, *The Psychology of Religion*, pp. 211-18; and Paul E. Johnson "Conversion," *Pastoral Psychology*, 10, no. 95 (June 1959), 51-56. For a more recent survey of major perspectives and research on conversion which views it as the establishment of personal identity and wholeness, see V. Bailey Gillespie, *Religious Conversion and Personal Identity* (Birmingham, Ala.: Religious Education Press, 1979).

62 Underwood, *Conversion*, pp. 198-202.

The immediate social environment receives great attention from the effective revivalist. He uses publicity, united prayer, and cooperative labor to focus attention on one common purpose, hope, and expectation, that of soul-winning. Conversions and pseudo-conversions result from the heightened suggestibility of the crowd situation. When publicity stunts and psychological trickery are the main source of "conversions," backsliding is common. "It is interesting that many who believe that conversions are effected by God unaided should arrange that potential converts shall be exposed to the utmost social pressure, persuasion and emotional arousal." [63]

Revivals have contributed to the rise and growth of new sects by originating new groups and splitting old bodies. Revivalism has softened denominational distinctions by stressing the need for conversion without reference to denominational affiliation. It has contributed to an overemphasis upon the emotional, ecstatic, mystical, and personal in religion. Many churches became so concerned with saving souls that they failed to see the relationships of these souls to society as a whole and the need to influence civic and economic affairs in order to help individuals. The social gospel was born in reaction against revivalism. The emphasis upon lay leadership, the push for interdenominational fellowship, the quest for personal morality or holiness, the attack upon segregation, and other activistic characteristics of American religion can be traced partly to preparation in theory and practice by revivalism. Many social reforms have been stimulated by revivals. Abolition of slavery, the establishment of benevolent and missionary organizations, the founding of many colleges, the unification of American culture on a level that transcends narrow provincialisms, and even the growth of religious liberty [64] were encouraged by revivals. The basic economic order remained unchanged, however, and may even have been hindered from wholesome change by them. Numerous other shortcomings of the nation were spared adverse criticism; revivalistic movements kept attention from them.

Appraisals, Cycles, and Trends of Revivals

Church membership records indicate that large numbers entered the churches during revival years in the eighteenth and nineteenth centuries. A large decline in usual rates of membership additions followed the revivals. The longer and more intense the revival had been, the longer was the duration of the depression in additions that followed. The interval between revivals increased, and regular religious education gradually re-

[63] Michael Argyle, *Religious Behaviour* (London: Routledge and Kegan Paul, 1958), p. 2.

[64] Charles Hartshorn Maxson, *The Great Awakening in the Middle Colonies* (Gloucester, Mass.: Peter Smith, 1958), pp. 149-51.

placed revivalistic methods of gathering in members. Early revivals began in the church with a re-vival of members, but since about 1875 they have emphasized the conversion and recruitment of new members.[65]

Numerous follow-up studies have been made of decisions in recent Billy Graham crusades. These have generally been biased either for or against the evangelist and have found what they sought. Many new church members have been gained by the campaigns, but numerous referrals have been members of churches. Many decisions do not represent conversion but only consecration or re-dedication. Criticism of revivalism has stressed its theological shallowness, psychological trickery, economic costs, divisive influence, emotional emphasis, and other weaknesses. This criticism has had a profound influence upon many contemporary evangelists, making them especially cautious not to abuse their privileges.

A fairly regular cycle of revival campaigns in New York City has been observed. Finney's campaign in 1832 was followed in 1876 by Moody, in 1917 by Billy Sunday, and in 1957 by Billy Graham. McLoughlin predicted in 1957 that the next great revival campaign in that city will come in about 1997 and that Graham's effective campaigns would soon end, for past periods of revivalistic fervor of such broad scope have lasted on the average about ten years.[66] The rise and fall of revivalistic enthusiasm and conversions may be related to the life cycle of churches and the growth pattern of religious sects (Chapter 5).

With the decline of emotional revivalism by the early twentieth century, new evangelistic techniques emerged. Visitation evangelism, fellowship evangelism, adult Sunday school classes with an evangelistic emphasis, telephone evangelism, evangelistic appeals in regular worship services, use of mass communications, and other developments succeeded the old time revival (Chapter 9). "Evangelism in depth" became an emphasis in many churches.[67] Interviews with 46 religious leaders in twelve Protestant denominations indicated that all Christian groups, liberal, fundamentalist, neo-orthodox, and neo-evangelical alike, are earnestly concerned about evangelism. All use what they consider to be scriptural appeals in efforts to win others for Christ. The main channel of their work is the local church. Even when united mass campaigns are held, the local churches' role in both preparation and follow-up work is stressed. Christianity is emphasized more as an entire life than as a sudden decision or entrance into church membership alone. A spirit of generosity toward other groups

---

65 Samuel W. Dike, "A Study of New England Revivals," *American Journal of Sociology*, 15 (Nov. 1909), 361-78.

66 William G. McLoughlin, Jr., "Billy Graham: In Business With the Lord," *Nation*, 184 (May 11, 1957), 403-10. But Graham was still very active in 1983 and annually continued to be one of America's ten most admired living men. See John Pollock, *Billy Graham: Evangelist to the World* (New York: Harper and Row, 1979).

67 Cecil Northcott, "Needed: Evangelism in Depth," *Christian Century*, 74 (June 26, 1957), 782-83.

which recognizes common objectives seems characteristic of a large proportion of church leaders.[68]

Emotionalistic revivalism has declined for many reasons. Among them are the passing of the isolated frontier, the spread of churches into all communities, increasing heterogeneity of the population, urbanization, and increased education. Stress upon religious education accompanied the decline of revivalistic conversions. Emotions were drained off through radio, motion pictures, and other forms of escapism, and emotionalism was condemned in "respectable" churches. As revivalistic methods became conventionalized and ritualized, often along bureaucratic lines, "revivals" tended to lose their spontaneity and freshness of spirit and, for the most part, were replaced by new institutional forms of evangelism. Yet basic ideas of evangelical religion persist, ready to be stirred up by religious leaders when tensions arise from disturbing social climates and rapid social change.[69]

As noted in Chapter 2, the bulk of the mid-twentieth century "revival" lies outside of traditional revivalism. It draws its strength from close identity of religion with national values. God is presented as useful in achieving individual and group goals. He is "packaged" safely as "the Lord of individual lives." Free enterprise, democratic ideals, and the American Way of Life are sanctified. Modern techniques of mass manipulation are used. Catholicism and non-Christian religions are Protestantized as dominant groups become culture religions by a process of secularization through syncretistic fusion. The revival of interest in religion does not seem to involve a reawakening to Christian faith nor a rebirth of humble surrender to God.[70]

Selected References

Begbie, Harold, *More Twice-Born Men*. New York: G. P. Putnam's Sons, 1923. Interesting descriptions of cases of religious conversion which are suitable for comparative analyses.

Busséll, Harold L., *Unholy Devotion: Why Cults Lure Christians*. Grand Rapids: Zondervan, 1983. An examination of the moral and religious values, interests, and goals which are shared by evangelical Christians and current cults.

Dike, Samuel W., "A Study of New England Revivals," *American Journal of Sociology*, 15 (Nov. 1909), 361–78. A socio-historical analysis and appraisal of early American revivals and their effects on church membership trends.

---

[68] David O. Moberg and Norris A. Magnuson, "Current Trends in Evangelism," *Journal of Pastoral Care*, 10, no. 1 (Spring 1956), 16-26.

[69] Timothy L. Smith, "Historic Waves of Religious Interest in America," *Annals of the American Academy of Political and Social Science*, 332 (Nov. 1960), 9-19.

[70] Martin E. Marty, "A Revival of Interest," *Christian Century*, 75 (Nov. 12, 1958), 1296-99; Will Herberg, "There Is a Religious Revival!" *Review of Religious Research*, 1 (Fall 1959), 45-50; and A. Roy Eckardt, "The Rise and Fall of Popular Religion," *Religion in Life*, 28 (Autumn 1959), 587-94.

Firebaugh, Glenn, "How Effective Are City-Wide Crusades?" *Christianity Today*, 25, no. 6 (March 27, 1981), 412–17. An empirical follow-up in 1979 of inquirers, ministers, and lay leaders in churches in Billy Graham's 1976 Seattle Crusade.

Hoge, Dean R., with Kenneth McGuire, C.S.P., and Bernard F. Stratman, S.M., *Converts, Dropouts, Returnees*. Washington, D.C.: U.S. Catholic Conference, and New York: Pilgrim Press, 1981. Analysis of sociological factors in dropping out from, returning to, and being converted to the Catholic Church based on interviews with 200 persons in each of the three categories.

Hostetler, John A., *The Sociology of Mennonite Evangelism*. Scottdale, Pa.: Herald Press, 1954. An empirical study of membership gains and losses.

James, William, *The Varieties of Religious Experiences: A Study in Human Nature*. New York: Penguin Books, 1982 (New York: Longmans, Green and Co., 1902). A classic study in the social psychology of religion.

Lang, Kurt, and Gladys Engel Lang, "Decisions for Christ: Billy Graham in New York City," in *Identity and Anxiety*, ed. Maurice R. Stein, Arthur J. Vidich, and David Manning White. New York: Free Press, 1960, pp. 415–27. A study which includes empirical data.

Lofland, John, *Doomsday Cult: A Study of Conversion, Proselytization, and Maintenance of Faith*, enl. ed. New York: Irvington Publishers, 1977. Excellent research on the "Divine Precepts" cult.

Richardson, James T., ed., *Conversion Careers: In and Out of the New Religions*. Beverly Hills, Calif.: Sage Publications, 1978 (*American Behavior Scientist*, 20, no. 6, July-Aug. 1977). Nine studies of new religions (including the Jesus Movement and Catholic charismatics) dealing with topics like conversion processes, consequences, theories, and deprogramming.

Smith, Timothy L., *Revivalism and Social Reform: American Protestantism on the Eve of the Civil War*. Baltimore: Johns Hopkins University Press, 1980. The significant role of revivalistic Protestantism in American social life.

Sweet, William Warren, *Revivalism in America*. Magnolia, Mass.: Peter Smith, 1965 (New York: Scribner's, 1945). A historical survey of the origin, growth, and decline of revivalism.

Weisberger, Bernard A., *They Gathered at the River*. New York: Octagon Books, 1979 (Boston: Little, Brown and Co., 1958). The story of the "great revivalists" and their impact on religion in America.

Zablocki, Benjamin David, *Alienation and Charisma: A Study of Contemporary American Communes*. New York: Free Press, 1980. Research on 60 urban and 60 rural communes, many of which are religious; supports the claim that those who joined from 1965 to 1975 did so largely because they were overwhelmed with the many choices offered by society.

Chapter 17

The Church and Social Problems

From time immemorial, organized religion has been concerned with behavior that deviates from social norms. Sins against the deity and sins against society have generally been synonymous, and religious nonconformity has been a crime among many peoples. The definition of crime has grown out of the Code of Hammurabi, the Mosaic law, and other legal codes based at least partly on religious doctrine. Modern philosophies for treating criminals and other deviants are linked with religion, and the church has been a significant source of numerous reforms aimed at social problems. Today most Americans consider one of the church's tasks to be the prevention, alleviation, and treatment of social and personal problems. Jewish and Christian social ethics are alike concerned with them. Much of the practical training of clergymen is oriented toward them. Even evangelistic efforts are slanted in part toward solving them or reclaiming sinners from them.

Numerous other portions of this book deal with social problems—problems that are highly significant for persons engulfed in them as well as for the total society and institutional groups which they impinge upon. We already have examined certain aspects of the church's relationship to such problems as population pressures, social welfare needs, nationalism, social conflict, anti-Semitism, and family disorganization. Here we shall survey in somewhat greater detail the church's relationship to certain additional problems, most of which have been given much attention by church leaders. Racial prejudice and segregation, social class distinctions, mental illness, and crime will receive the bulk of our attention. Since minority group religions have their distinct features largely because of **segregation and discrimination, certain aspects of black, American Indian**, and other ethnic religions are described. Our treatment of the topics covered is brief and suggestive rather than exhaustive.

Religious leaders commonly assume that among the effects of their work are both character education, which prevents people from becoming social deviants, and personal development which supports mental health. They believe that as churches meet the spiritual needs of men, they increase well-being and promote societal health. Many scholars deny their claims, however, because evidences of the negative influence of religion on certain areas of life are almost as easy to find as those which are positive.[1] We shall stress empirical data rather than statements of opinion. As we shall see, religion in the generic sense has both functional and dysfunctional effects. Since there are such great variations in church doctrines and programs, all conclusions reached must be qualified in terms of the specific time, place, and groups upon which they are based.

Religion and Prejudice

Relationships between religion and ethnic prejudice are so complex that scholars arrive at contradictory conclusions. Some studies have shown that the anti-religious and indifferent tend to be the most tolerant toward **blacks, followed by Jews, Protestants, and Catholics. Others have found** certain Protestants to be more liberal than Jews and others less liberal than Catholics, with the religious more tolerant than those who are not church members or regular attendants.[2] This divergent evidence, together with observed correlations between religiosity and certain types of outgroup prejudices, rigid and conventional moral codes, and nationalistic attitudes, has led to the hypothesis that "only certain types of religious training are effective in lessening intergroup hostility."[3]

---

[1] For an excellent debate on the role of religion in the field of morals and crime see John Edward Coogan, S.J., "The Myth Mind in an Engineer's World," *Federal Probation*, 16, no. 1 (Mar. 1952), 26-30; replies by Ruth S. Cavan, Donald R. Taft, Karl A. Menninger, Lowell J. Carr, Harry Elmer Barnes, and Negley K. Teeters, *ibid.*, 16, no. 2 (June 1952), 24-31, and no. 3 (Sept. 1952), 36-42; and Coogan's conclusion, "Secularism Alien to Our Covenant Nation," *ibid.*, 16, no. 3 (Sept. 1952), 42-47.

[2] For examples see Abraham L. Rosenblum, "Ethnic Prejudice as Related to Social Class and Religiosity," *Sociology and Social Research*, 43 (Mar.-Apr. 1959), 272-75; Jack R. Frymier, "Relationship Between Church Attendance and Authoritarianism," *Religious Education*, 54 (July-Aug. 1959), 369-71, and Bruno Bettelheim and Morris Janowitz, *Dynamics of Prejudice* (New York: Harper and Brothers, 1950), pp. 50-52, 96-97.

[3] Robin M. Williams, Jr., *The Reduction of Intergroup Tensions* (New York· Social Science Research Council, Bul. 57, 1947), p. 68.

Ethnocentrism is present to some degree in every group and has been linked with religious identifications throughout history. When a group's roots are chiefly in a specific church or religion, the more exclusive and sectarian the group, the stronger its prejudices against non-members are likely to be. Dogmatic religious organizations which stress their own merits are blind to their demerits. In trying to limit contacts with outsiders they may nourish an authoritarianism that feeds prejudice. Certain conventional teachings of Christians unintentionally contribute to anti-Jewish sentiments (Chapter 12); churches may also accentuate and reinforce attitudes of antipathy toward other groups. This often occurs in Protestant-Catholic relationships, partly from stressing distinctive religious doctrines and partly from opposition to inter-faith marriages. Anti-black attitudes are indirectly fostered by identifying righteousness with the color white and sin with black, as in the "Wordless Book" used in fundamentalist child evangelism. This is easily transferred in the mind to anti-colored, pro-white racial prejudices.[4]

Church members tend to reflect attitudes of prejudice and acts of discrimination which are institutionalized in their community, for they are members of an entire social system. Pietistic religion hence may be accompanied by a concept of morality that sees no evil in involuntary segregation of blacks and that fails to see the larger latent implications of community customs. Even the proffering of religion to condemned black criminals is one aspect of a ritual by which complete subordination to the caste system and to the total society was upheld.[5] (But see Chapter 19.)

Old-fashioned religious revivalism techniques are commonly used by agitators against Jews and blacks. Rigid stereotypes which make all on their side the "saved" and all opposed to them the "damned" are exploited. Many agitators are themselves revivalists who weave a doctrine of hate into their religious message. Appealing to fundamentalists in the major denominations as well as in splinter groups and independent congregations, they attempt to identify basic religious tenets with anti-Semitic, anti-black, anti-Catholic, anti-internationalist, and other negative doctrines, trying to make religious people accept the rest of their message. Colorful emotional appeals have been used in their "ministries of hate" to spread views which are antithetical to basic Christian truth. Some of the best known "apostles of discord" were ex-Communist Kenneth Goff who preached against the "Jew-controlled Communist party," blacks,

---

[4] A popular fundamentalist chorus is worded, "My heart was black with sin, Until the Savior came in. His precious blood, I know, Has made it white as snow." Only by a process of extreme circumvolution in biblical interpretation can black be used as a scriptural symbol of sin, although white is often associated with purity. Sin is referred to as scarlet and "red like crimson" in Isa. 1:18.

[5] Allison Davis, Burleigh B. Gardner, and Mary R. Gardner, *Deep South* (Chicago: University of Chicago Press, 1941), pp. 529-34.

and Catholics; Gerald L. K. Smith, who headed the Christian National Crusade attacks upon the "Jew-nited Nations" (UN) "For a White Christian America"; Gerald Winrod of *Defender Magazine* notoriety; and cowboy evangelist Harvey H. Springer who published the anti-Catholic *Western Voice*, "America's Outstanding Prophetic Weekly."[6] Passionate self-interests are thus disguised in the noble garments of religious idealism.

But only a minority on the fringes of Christianity engage in actions designed to promote intergroup prejudice. The majority try to promote love and tolerance. This is evident from analysis of materials published for use in Sunday schools[7] as well as from the numerous church projects aimed at developing high principles of motivation. The National and World Councils of Churches and all major Christian bodies promote spiritual principles of justice, love, righteousness, liberty, and equality. The Jewish religion, dominated by the idea that there is but one God who created the universe and mankind, consistently repudiates racial exclusivism and injustice. Prejudice is increasingly seen in America as a moral issue. Much interest focuses on black-white relationships.

Black Religion in America

The distinctive features of black religion are largely a result of its historical background of slavery and racial discrimination. Slavery was once rationalized as good because it brought heathen souls into contact with Christianity and led to their salvation. It also was upheld by a philosophy that incorporated certain aspects of Biblical doctrine as a rationalization for the subordination of slaves. Yet in the late eighteenth century significant groups of Protestants took a stand favoring emancipation. Religious motivations became a significant force behind the abolitionist movement. As a result of internal disagreements, chiefly over emancipation, many denominations were split into northern and southern branches in the pre-Civil War era. When war broke out, churches and the clergy supported the cause; God's blessing was invoked on behalf of each side in the War Between the States.

Blacks initially were allowed to worship and even to become members in predominantly white congregations. However, preachers faced difficul-

---

[6] Ralph Lord Roy, *Apostles of Discord* (Boston: Beacon Press, 1953); Leo Lowenthal and Norbert Guterman, *Prophets of Deceit* (New York: Harper and Brothers, 1949); Arthur Derounian, "Hate-Mongers Among the Clergy," *American Mercury,* 62 (Mar. and June 1946), 278-85, 761-62; and Nathan Perlmutter, "Evangelist Demagogue, 1952 Model," *Commentary,* 14 (Oct. 1952), 334-38.

[7] Frank and Mildred Moody Eakin, "Can Sunday School Fight Prejudice?" *Christian Century,* 67 (Nov. 15, 1950), 1358-59; and F. and M. Eakin, *Sunday School Fights Prejudice* (New York: The Macmillan Co., 1953).

ties of adapting sermons to a diverse audience that included greatly different interests, backgrounds, needs, and vocabularies. Masters and slaves often were embarrassed in each other's presence. Segregation in society inevitably led to separate commemoration of the Lord's Supper, separate Sunday schools, and other forms of segregation in churches. Initially black congregations were organized and maintained within white churches and subordinate to them, but independent black churches became symbols of religious emancipation from white authority and control. Personal ambitions of black leaders, special needs for social intercourse and spiritual benefit, displeasure with white control, and discrimination contributed to secession from white churches. The first Negro Baptist church was established in 1773 and the first Protestant Episcopal Church for Negroes in 1787. The African Methodist Episcopal Church was founded in 1816 and the African Methodist Episcopal Zion Church in 1820.

The most rapid growth of black churches occurred during the Reconstruction era when much assistance came from the North. Resentment against white control over Negro Baptist associations and tensions pertinent to Sunday school literature led to formation of the National Baptist Convention in 1880. However, in 1917 it was split during a struggle for power among its leaders, a common source of many black denominations.[8]

Social Functions of Afro-American Churches

Many major functions of black religion originated in discrimination, first as slaves and later as "second class citizens" distinguished by skin color and various cultural features. *Social protest* has been a dominant trait. Ministers were expected to lead the slaves as spokesmen begging favors from the master. The black church emerged as a protest against exclusion and segregation and in the current decade played a leading part in such activities as sit-ins. The church is a *symbol of group identification* in efforts to improve conditions of the race. *Self-expression* in the cathartic release provided by emotional religious worship helps blacks forget personal trials and gives them the social recognition of fellow-worshipers. The lack of centralized control over the local church undoubtedly helped make Baptists the most popular denomination. *Emotional escapism* is provided through old-time black preaching. Linked with the closely related psychological mechanism of compensation, it provides a foundation for literalistic theological tendencies. Blacks easily identify themselves with

---

[8] For further details see general histories of blacks in America and such works as Willis D. Weatherford, *American Churches and the Negro* (Boston: Christopher Publishing House, 1957); Carter G. Woodson, *The History of the Negro Church,* 2d ed. (Washington, D.C.: Associated Publishers, 1945); and Dwight W. Culver, *Negro Segregation in the Methodist Church* (New Haven: Yale University Press, 1953).

the Israelites escaping from bondage in Egypt, the Savior born in a manger, prophetic judgments against the rich, the free gift of grace to every believer, and similar Bible references.[9] *Personal adjustment* is promoted as the believer finds escape from the hardships of life and is temporarily freed from the world's humiliations. Migrants from rural areas are aided in their adjustments to the strain of city life. The church buoys up hope, giving members a sense of community on earth and a faith that the last will be made first in the future life when those who are rich in things of the spirit receive their reward. Both lay and professional *leadership opportunities* are provided which would be absent if there were no separate black institutions. Nearly half the adults in 570 black churches in 17 rural South counties held some church position,[10] and blacks have a higher ratio of ministers than the general population, although they lack their proportionate share of all other professions. The *social control* of the church has been a stabilizing force in the black community. Generally supporting the status quo, diverting attention from current social issues to an other-worldly future, and protesting against vices common among lower class blacks, the church has been a conserving force in a milieu of social disorganization. *Socioeconomic service* is evident in the church's assistance to black business and professional men as well as in aid given the needy. The success of Father Divine's Peace Mission movement was partly a result of economic satisfactions provided through low cost meals, "extensions" or "heavens" which really were hotels, and other tangible services supplied to followers. *Recreational programs* are not highly advanced in the black church, but choirs, instrumental ensembles, and other musical attractions entertain those who attend. Popular preachers use humorous illustrations, flights of oratory, and even sexual innuendo when denouncing sin. The exciting experience of "getting the Spirit" and speaking in tongues, dancing in church aisles, or shouting praise to God in an emotional lower-class church undoubtedly has a recreational element for participants and observers. The church often serves as a *community center* which is subject to no outside control. Sewing circles, burial associations, missionary societies specializing in charitable tasks for the black community, 4-H clubs, and even a few cooperatives are promoted by churches for the entire black community. The church serves as an important center of social life for a large segment of the population. Although it plays a relatively less significant part in many of these functions than in the past, it remains a powerful force in black life.[11]

---

[9] E. T. Krueger, "Negro Religious Expression," *American Journal of Sociology,* 38 (July 1932), 22-31; William H. Pipes, *Say Amen, Brother!* (New York: The William-Frederick Press, 1951); Robert Lee and Ralph L. Roy, "The Negro Church," *Christian Century,* 74 (Oct. 30, 1957), 1285-87.

[10] Ralph A. Felton, *These My Brethren* (Madison, N.J.: Drew Theological Seminary, 1950), pp. 38-39.

[11] Cf. Kelly Miller Smith, "Religion as a Force in Black America," in *The State of Black America 1982*, James D. Williams, ed. (New York: National Urban League, 1982), pp. 197-237.

Black Cults

Islam, Muslim sects, and wide variety of cults have been relatively successful in urban areas. Blacks have been attracted by their antagonism to conventional Christianity, promises of material rewards, charismatic leaders attributing social evils to the sins of Caucasians, titles which imply sainthood or importance, and panaceas offered to appease hunger, heal disease, and even to bring death to enemies. Rejecting the possibility of attaining their goals within the general framework of American values and institutions, the cults are essentially authoritarian and win their greatest growth and influence during periods of acute distress and crisis in black life. Record has hypothesized that they depend upon a steady stream of rural migrants to replenish and maintain their strength and that traffic into and out of them reflects fluctuations in the social status of their joiners.[12]

Segregation and Integration in Churches

Few blacks and whites worship together in the same local church. Even when congregations do not formally exclude persons of other races, social pressures typically compel them to solicit members only from their own. Most people do not "feel at home" in a group with customs and interests alien to their own background. Doctrinal sanctions uphold segregation in some churches, while others become unwitting instruments of segregationists by sponsoring private schools when public schools are involved in integration controversies. The most segregated hour of the week may still be 11:00 A.M. Sunday, the customary Protestant worship hour, but most of it is by the minorities' choice. In accord with the homogeneous unit principle, they want autonomy and freedom to retain the worship styles of their own subculture.

Yet concepts of social justice basic in the struggle for black rights have come largely from religion; "the present movement to do away with segregation as an ultimate ideal has stemmed mainly from the churches."[13] By 1956 all major religious bodies in both the North and South had made pronouncements officially sanctioning the principle of desegregation. In spite of sporadic opposition and failure to follow denominational recommendations on the congregational level, more and more church members

---

[12] Wilson Record, "Extremist Movements Among American Negroes," *Phylon,* 17 (First Quarter, 1956), 17-23. See also Erdmann D. Beynon, "The Voodoo Cult Among Negro Migrants in Detroit," *American Journal of Sociology,* 43 (May 1938), 894-907; Charles S. Braden, "Islam in America," *International Review of Missions,* 48 (July 1959), 309-17; and C. Eric Lincoln, *The Black Muslims in America* (Boston: Beacon Press, 1961).

[13] Anson Phelps Stokes et al., *Negro Status and Race Relations in the United States, 1911-1946* (New York: The Phelps-Stokes Fund, 1948), p. 50.

challenge segregation on moral and spiritual grounds. Integration within church congregations, as well as in church-related colleges, theological seminaries, and hospitals, also has progressed significantly during the past decade.[14] Christians on the whole are somewhat more favorable toward abolition of the American "caste system" than secularists in the same community. Preachers in general have been more positive and articulate on the issue of race than laymen; many nevertheless uphold the status quo rather than work to reduce racial discrimination.

The interracial relations of Catholics do not differ greatly from those of Protestants. Four types of segregation have been discerned within Roman Catholicism. *Traditional* segregation is a relic from slavery conditions in which two races worship in the same church with separate seating for blacks. *Compulsory* segregation provides separate institutions for minority groups; without segregation they perhaps would be completely neglected. *Theoretical* or planned segregation results from rationalizations by whites about blacks' pride in having their own institutions and maintaining group identity. *Voluntary* segregation comes from true desires of minorities themselves to be separate from the majority.[15]

Catholic integrationist policies also tend to be of four types, although not directly parallel to the segregation patterns. (1) The minimal policy integrates blacks only into "essential" activities of worship; "nonessential" parish activities remain segregated. (2) All church institutions are opened to blacks in a definite but incomplete break with biracialism; a racial parish and compensatory segregation remain in the diocese. (3) Complete official integration prevails in most northern dioceses. No special parish or school is maintained for blacks; only voluntary segregation remains. (4) Complete actual integration includes blacks in all forms of Catholic life that are governed by free choice of the people. Steady progress is being made toward this highest form of integration, which means the death of prejudice.[16] Since 1937 the Church has had an educational program designed to reduce interracial prejudice. Catholic Interracial Councils have been established in many large cities; numerous parishes have been integrated.

Less than 7 per cent of the nation's civilian nonwhite population aged 14 and over in March 1957 were Roman Catholic by preference, compared to 61 per cent Baptist, 17 per cent Methodist, and 10 per cent other Protestant.[17] Since Catholicism is relatively weak in the South, a smaller proportion of its churches was implicated in the grosser forms of segrega-

14 Frank S. Loescher, "Racism in Northern City Churches," *Christian Century*, 73 (Feb. 8, 1956), 174-76; "Segregation Status," *Christianity Today*, 1, no. 11 (Mar. 4, 1957), 29; Social Welfare Dept., *How Racially Inclusive Are Cleveland Area Churches?* (Cleveland, Ohio, Church Federation, 1958).

15 John LaFarge, S.J., "Caste in the Church. II. The Roman Catholic Experience," *Survey Graphic*, 36 (Jan. 1947), 61-62, 104-6.

16 *Ibid.*

17 "Religion Reported by the Civilian Population of the United States: March 1957," *Current Population Reports: Population Characteristics*, Series P-20, No. 79, Feb. 2, 1958.

tion. Its hierarchical structure and power of excommunication can impose standards of integration on a parish; most other churches cannot do so until members themselves favor it. Fellowship between members is less emphasized than in Protestant churches, so integration is less difficult. Many blacks also are attracted to Catholicism because Catholic schools, welfare, and community agencies have served all people, regardless of nationality or color. Catholics recorded 75,000 black converts, 8 per cent of all conversions, in the decade ending in 1955.[18] They claimed 389,111 black members in 1950 and 615,964 in 1960 but 1,300,000 in 1982 when about 4 per cent of all blacks were Catholic. Although over 11 per cent of the U.S. population is black, this is remarkable growth when the initially low black membership is considered. Growth was greatest in large cities that received many black migrants.[19]

In race relations as in other respects, Protestant and Catholic churches as well as minority religions like Christian Science reflect the larger society. Integrationist policies exist more on the national or supraparochial level than in local parishes. Where pro-segregation attitudes are strong, the clergy fear taking a stand for immediate integration; if they do, they may preach to empty churches, lose members, and lose financial support. Radical minority groups like the Methodist Layman's Union organized in 1959 "to save the Methodist Church from integration and disunion" silence the voice of moderate reason.[20] Since the church is made up of the persons who comprise society itself, it seldom is a "spearhead of reform." [21] Yet denominational action supports local churches and pastors who wish to initiate change, contributes to an uneasiness in many members over social inequities, and thus indirectly encourages gradual revision of folkways and laws. The most effective sermons about race relations are preached by example, not by words. As long as churches remain segregated through subtle techniques, they give moral sanction to segregation in other areas of social life.

The Church and the American Indian

The religion of American Indians similarly reflects discrimination. Early white settlers had varying views of the indigenous natives. Some

---

[18] Francois Houtart, "A Sociological Study of the Evolution of the American Catholics," *Sociaal Kompas,* 2 (Jan.-Apr. 1955), 189-216.

[19] "Negro Catholic Converts Cited," St. Paul *Dispatch*, March 12, 1960, p. 4, and Felician A. Foy, O.F.M., and Rose M. Avato, eds., *1983 Catholic Almanac* (Huntington, Ind.: Our Sunday Visitor, 1983), p. 552.

[20] Thomas Reeves, "Methodist Layman's Union Victim," *Christian Century,* 76 (Sept. 2, 1959), 995; Stanley Rowland, Jr., "Jim Crow in Church," *Nation,* 182 (May 19, 1956), 426-28; C. J. Nuesse and Thomas J. Harte, C.Ss.R., eds., *The Sociology of the Parish* (Milwaukee: Bruce Publishing Co., 1951), pp. 166-74; and Joseph H. Fichter, S.J., *Social Relations in the Urban Parish* (Chicago: University of Chicago Press, 1954), pp. 48, 63, 117-18, 205.

[21] Gunnar Myrdal, *An American Dilemma* (New York: Harper and Brothers, 1944), p. 877. See William T. Liu, "The Community Reference System, Religiosity. and Race Attitudes," *Social Forces,* 39 (May 1961), 324-28.

were determined to convert them or to kill them. Pestilences among Indians were regarded as God's judgment falling for the benefit of His chosen (white) people, and even the pioneer clergy looked upon extreme violence and cruelty toward them without feelings of compunction. America became a new promised land to be conquered with God's approval by forcing back and exterminating the red Canaanites. Only the Baptist and Quaker dissenters in Rhode Island and Pennsylvania had attitudes which today would be considered enlightened.[22] Missionaries to the Indians brought "the Bible in one hand and a textbook in the other." They contributed much to Indian welfare but also made it easier for other white men to exploit and subjugate them. Missionary work has continued to the present day; with growing emphasis upon Indians as persons, some past mistakes are being corrected.[23]

Indian migrants to urban areas often face discrimination in Christian churches as well as elsewhere. As members of the lower social classes, they cannot dress as well for church as middle class people. Mission chapels established especially for them perpetuate segregation. In many respects, Indians represent a greater indictment of American democracy than Negroes. Injustices of the past and present explain their reluctance to accept the invitation to adopt the white man's religion.

Disillusionment, discrimination, and stress encourage the development of new religions and revitalization of the old. Nativistic cults hence emerged among the Indians. The Peyote cult, the Prophet Dance in the Northwest (including the Smohalla and Shaker cults), and various other fusions of Christian and pre-Christian elements revive and perpetuate traditions of the past. They also are reform movements which emphasize mystical experiences, immediate physical benefits, deferred spiritual blessings, a special revelation of the Creator's teachings, physical and moral regeneration of the individual and group, and the perpetuation of social and cultural group identity. They provide new statuses for persons striving for social recognition, and they combine anti-native and anti-white sentiments. Revival of native elements often reflects deprivation; it expresses in ritual symbolism basic attitudes of rejecting white culture, feelings of loss or damage, aggressive retaliation, and self punishment. Combining native and Euro-American systems of religion, these sects represent an effort either to thwart extinction or to re-establish native sociocultural systems and political autonomy.[24]

---

22 Buell G. Gallagher, *Color and Conscience* (New York: Harper and Brothers, 1946), pp. 54-56, and Carey McWilliams, *Brothers Under the Skin* (Boston: Little, Brown and Co., 1943), pp. 52-53.

23 G. E. E. Lindquist, *The Indian in American Life* (New York: Friendship Press, 1944), pp. 111-40, 164; B. Frank Belvin, *The Status of the American Indian Ministry* (Shawnee: Oklahoma Baptist University Press, 1949); Harold E. Fey, "Haunted by History," *Christian Century,* 73 (Mar. 21, 1956), 363-65.

24 Fred Voget, "Reformative Tendencies in North American Indian Nativistic

Some nativistic cults are *reversion religions* which stress abstention from all food and equipment which has its source in the white man and a return to old ways under leadership of a seer or prophet. Others, like Peyotism, are *amalgamation religions* aimed at peaceful living under the new conditions. Retaining old customs and eschewing Christian theology, most Peyote sects in the Native American Church teach that Christ came to save white people, but peyote (a cactus eaten in religious meetings to bring color visions and extreme lassitude) came to save Indians. Their religion thus constitutes a reaction against the subordinate position often given Indian converts in Christian organizations. It provides them with purpose and self esteem; hence it grows most rapidly in areas of extreme economic distress.[25]

Religion and the Immigrant

Immigration, with subsidiary problems of assimilation, was a major social problem of past generations. Religious motivations have been prominent among many groups of immigrants from the time religious dissenters helped found the English colonies till the Nazis' quasi-religious purges of the Jews.[26] The persecution of dissenters from bigoted New England religion led to the founding of Rhode Island. Religious discrimination in America also has been apparent in the treatment of Quakers, Jews, Unitarians, Catholics, Baptists, Mormons, Jehovah's Witnesses, Hutterites, Amish, and other groups at various times and places. When immigrants identified partly or solely by religious distinctives appear to threaten economic interests, antagonisms are accentuated, as in the case of Irish Catholics in the 1840's and 1850's and eastern Europeans early in this century. The "sheep" in Biblical accounts of God's final judgment are readily identifiable as one's own nationality as well as religion and the "goats" as all others.

While the faithful sing hymns and recite creeds about the universal brotherhood of all believers, they are likely to remain aloof from brothers of another nationality or skin color. When immigrants transplant their na-

Movements," abstract of paper presented to the Committee for the Scientific Study of Religion, Oct. 13, 1952; Melville J. Herskovits, *Acculturation* (New York: J. J. Augustin Publisher, 1938), pp. 76-90; Anthony F. C. Wallace, "Revitalization Movements," *American Anthropologist,* 58 (Apr. 1956), 264-79; David F. Aberle and Omer C. Stewart, *Navaho and Ute Peyotism* (Boulder: University of Colorado Press, 1957).

[25] Ruth Underhill, "Religion Among American Indians," *Annals of the American Academy of Political and Social Science,* 311 (May 1957), 127-36.

[26] ". . . religion as a cause of emigration from Sweden is a factor historians cannot ignore, however much they may differ as to its relative importance." George M. Stephenson, *The Religious Aspects of Swedish Immigration* (Minneapolis: University of Minnesota Press, 1932), p. 9.

tive church, it becomes a center of allegiance holding the group together, preserving old-world culture traits, perpetuating the native tongue, and thus helping to retard assimilation. Ethnic distinctions have multiplied the Protestant denominations and made a significant contribution to variations among Catholic and Orthodox parishes. Catholic groups like the Poles and Italians complain that the Church is dominated too much by the Irish; in local parishes conflict and prejudice also have been prominent between older settlers and recent immigrants. National parishes with jurisdiction over an ethnic group are a territorial solution to such problems. They rest basically upon language differences, hence none are English or Irish. In 1948 there were 1,535 national parishes in the U.S., 10 per cent of the total. Of these 466 were for Poles, 314 for Italians, 206 for Germans, 152 for Slovaks, and 114 for French (mostly French-Canadians). The dual system of national and territorial parish organization has led to many problems for the Church, although it increases social control over immigrants and has other advantages. In Chicago only 8 national parishes were altered in a century; anomalies like a French parish in a district with no Frenchmen and a German parish with an entirely black congregation have hence been observed.[27] Since the Second Vatican Council most national parishes have been absorbed into the territorial diocesan system by boundary changes, but some new ones for groups like Hispanics and Koreans have been formed for linguistic reasons.

Immigrants with a religion similar to American Protestantism tend to be assimilated more rapidly than those with Buddhist, Moslem, or even the Catholic religion. Among Roumanians, for example, Baptists moved more rapidly toward assimilation than the Orthodox, even though the former attended church more faithfully and were more fundamentalistic. Their religion was closer to the dominant American pattern; the Roumanian Orthodox Church and its members were the chief bearers of those fragments of Roumanian culture that survived.[28]

Although Old World religions have promoted ethnocentrism and hindered assimilation, they also have contributed to social well being, preventing much social disorganization, reducing problems related to immigration, and profoundly influencing the churches that received immigrants. American Catholicism, e.g., has gradually blended together "the intensely sentimental Catholicism of Spain; the fiercely Puritanical Catholicism of Ireland; the relaxed and affectionate Catholicism of Italy; the reasonable and sophisticated Catholicism of France; the deeply devotional Catholicism of Hungary and Poland."[29]

[27] Houtart, "A Sociological Study of the Evolution of the American Catholics," and Nuesse and Harte, *The Sociology of the Parish*, pp. 154-77.
[28] Peter G. Trutza, *The Religious Factor in Acculturation*, Ph.D. thesis, University of Chicago, 1956.
[29] Thomas Sugrue, *A Catholic Speaks His Mind on America's Religious Conflict* (New York: Harper and Brothers, 1951), p. 42.

Illustrative of groups which have faced greater social problems than others are the Mexicans and Japanese. Most Mexican immigrants are Roman Catholics. Catholic ritual in Mexico has been fused with indigenous rites, images, tributes, and sacrifices. Many priests of this syncretistic religion exploit the people, live hypocritically, and support restrictions of religious liberty. The religion of the Mexican immigrant to the U.S. tends gradually to slip away. He does not incur the enmity of the priest and reproach of the people that would come were he to drop religious duties in the homeland; he benefits economically by no longer paying tithes, first fruit taxes, and other contributions required in Mexico. Low economic resources and high tuition costs prevent him from sending children to parochial schools. Immigrant priests experiencing difficulty in their own adjustment to the new culture cannot cope with these problems. Protestant propaganda calls weaknesses of Catholicism to immigrants' attention. **Missing the vivid, colorful, pagan pageantry of Mexican Catholicism, they** may become non-fanatic American Catholics, Protestants, members of a **folk cult, religiously indifferent, or unbelievers. Many Protestants discrimi**nate against them as "just greasers who can never amount to anything" with high crime rates, the Catholic religion, and needs for costly community and health services. Even while sending missionaries to Mexico, they are aloof from, if not openly discriminatory toward, Mexicans in church and in personal relationships.[30]

Adoption of the Christian religion has helped many Japanese immigrants become acculturated. Christian churches aided their adjustment by helping find jobs, sponsoring kindergartens and nursery schools through which children were introduced to the public schools, and converting them to an American religion. The relocation of Nisei students during World War II brought many into non-segregated Christian churches for the first time and was an effective interracial educational process both for them and for white Americans. An increasing proportion of the Nisei-Christians worship with white people rather than in segregated Japanese-American churches. Buddhism lost out in the competitive struggle because it had fewer organized activities and, during the relocation period, lacked the outside contacts used so effectively by Christians in the resettlement process. Christian churches crushed Japanese solidarity by breaking down the orientation toward Japan and the Japanese conception of family-centered collective responsibility. The Nisei who have remained in Buddhist churches have forced them to adopt such Christian practices as Sun-

---

[30] Manuel Gamio, *Mexican Immigration to the United States* (Chicago: University of Chicago Press, 1930), pp. 108-27, 195-209; Ruth D. Tuck, *Not With the Fist: Mexican-Americans in a Southwest City* (New York: Harcourt, Brace and Co., 1946), pp. 152-57; and George E. Simpson and J. Milton Yinger, *Racial and Cultural Minorities,* rev. ed. (New York: Harper and Brothers, 1958), pp. 598-601; cf. Yvan D. Illich, "The Pastoral Care of Puerto Rican Migrants in New York," *Sociaal Kompas,* 5, no. 5-6 (1958), 256-60.

day school, regular Sunday services, youth organizations, evangelism, and hymn singing.[31]

Authoritarian, perfectionist, and exclusive tendencies of minority group religions hinder assimilation. Those outside "the true faith" are considered heretics, pagans, or unenlightened. Differences between groups are perpetuated, and social interaction, especially intermarriage, is hindered. Tensions between nationality groups within the same faith often become evident. If such religious incompatibility is accentuated, it could lead to a serious rift in American solidarity.[32] On the other hand, the mingling of a large number of religious groups in America which has accentuated religious differences has also increased mutual toleration, for each recognizes it is a minority dependent upon peaceful coexistence. Religious ideals associated with intergroup relations and with the ecumenical movement help to soften antagonisms between America's churches; the struggle for power between Protestants and Catholics and even between Christianity and other religions drives churches into closer cooperation; as a result respect for each other increases.

Social Class Divisions and Religion[33]

The dominant Protestant churches in America have developed into "a kind of middle-class ghetto." [34] Socioeconomic distinctions are a primary source of new sects (Chapter 5), for lower class groups tend to split off from the middle class majority and form their own denominations. As membership in these, in turn, moves upward in the class structure, lower class members again are drawn into new splinter groups.

On the basis of the dominant social class position of members as indicated in numerous scattered studies, the leading denominational families in America may be ranked from high to low in the following approximate order: Episcopal, Unitarian, Congregational, Presbyterian, Christian Scientist, Friends, Methodist, Disciples of Christ, Lutheran, Baptist, Mormon, Eastern Orthodox, Assemblies of God, Pentecostal, Holiness, and Jehovah's Witnesses. Jews fall in about the same position as Christian

---

31 S. Frank Miyamoto, as cited in Arnold and Caroline Rose, *America Divided* (New York: Alfred A. Knopf, 1948), pp. 223-24, 228; Robert W. O'Brien, *The College Nisei* (Palo Alto: Pacific Books, 1949), pp. 9-10, 115-16, 119-20; and R. F. Spencer, "Social Structure of a Contemporary Japanese-American Buddhist Church," *Social Forces,* 26 (Mar. 1948), 281-87.

32 An opinion of Henry P. Fairchild, *Race and Nationality as Factors in American Life* (New York: Ronald Press Co., 1947), pp. 110-11, 136; cf. Gerhard Lenski, *The Religious Factor* (Garden City, N.Y.: Doubleday and Co., 1961), pp. 324-30.

33 For resources on this subject see David O. Moberg, "Social Class and the Churches," *Information Service,* 37, no. 12 (June 14, 1958), 6-8, which lists 72 sources and summarizes major generalizations from them.

34 A. D. Mattson, *Christian Social Consciousness* (Rock Island, Ill.: Augustana Book Concern, 1953), p. 23. This is a major theme of Gibson Winter, *The Suburban Captivity of the Churches* (Garden City, N.Y.: Doubleday and Co., 1961).

Scientists (Orthodox Jews lower; Reform and Conservative Jews some-what higher), and Roman Catholics as a whole are just above the Baptists, who rank relatively low because they include such a large proportion of the black population. Great variations are evident from one community to another. Some Episcopal churches draw their members from a lower level of the class structure than certain Baptist or Methodist congregations in the same community. Nationality distinctions are often linked with the class differences between churches.

A larger proportion of business, professional, and white collar people than skilled and unskilled laborers belong to a church and are active in it, and more farm owners and managers than tenants and laborers are members. Relatively few local Protestant churches succeed in drawing members from all social classes in their community.

Sectarian attacks upon formalism in worship, symbolism in church architecture, and even "liberalism" in doctrine often reflect a protest by lower class persons against things they cannot afford to have because of economic limitations or against doctrinal implications they cannot fully understand because of limited educational backgrounds. Religious organizations protect the status of their members and leaders and reflect the established social order of the community, thus accentuating the gulf between various segments of the population at the same time as they duplicate it. The sect provides socially unattached segments that have lost a sense of belonging to a settled society with a new sense of identity and personal worth.

Lower class people who participate in the church tend to use church resources more in their leisure-time activities than upper middle and upper classes do. They also contribute a larger proportion of their incomes to religious purposes. Taken as a whole, however, persons with higher incomes, more prestigeful occupations, more years of schooling, and positions of active leadership in other community organizations tend to be the most active in the church.

Every aspect of the church—its beliefs, rituals, emotional expression in worship, leadership, membership, sub-organizations, teachings for practical living, etc.—is influenced by social class. That is why it has been referred to repeatedly throughout this book.[35] Class-related cultural values permeate the work of Protestant, Catholic, and Jewish churches. These values are often contradictory to doctrines which the church purports to uphold; the church is indeed at war with the world as it tries to introduce attitudes and behavior patterns contrary to the tendency of its age. Upward social mobility, for instance, is so strongly emphasized in American culture that it often takes precedence over religious goals and obligations.

---

[35] Index references will help locate relevant passages. William McKinney and Wade Clark Roof, "A Social Profile of American Religious Groups," in *Yearbook of American and Canadian Churches 1982*, Constant H. Jacquet, Jr., ed. (Nashville: Abingdon, 1982), pp. 267–73, note the persistence of the socioeconomic status hierarchy of a generation ago.

Cliques in church groups and members' attitudes toward politico-economic issues typically reflect socioeconomic considerations much more than religious values.

Many of the class-related phenomena in religion reflect American voluntarism which permits an individual to choose his church. The interests of the common laborer and the professional man are greatly different. Informal communication between them is difficult. Religious ritual, social activities of church organizations, applications of religion to everyday life, and even spiritual truths therefore must be adapted to the dominant group served by the church; others, sensing the church's irrelevance to their needs, will not "feel at home." As the population composition of the community served by a church changes, it must either adapt its program to the new population, attract members from a distance, move to the new location of the kind of people it serves, or gradually die. Valiant efforts are being made by a few exceptional churches to integrate members from diverse social classes; time and research will indicate the conditions under which such efforts are successful.

Once established, class identifications of churches are self-perpetuating and self-justifying. When most members are from one segment of society, they attract new members from the same segment. Socioeconomic distinctions tend to solidify class-related institutions which consciously or unconsciously impose effective barriers against people from societal positions different from the majority of members. This problem is not new. Some of the earliest Christian groups were tempted to deviate from the teachings of Christ by showing deference to certain people (James 2:1-13).

Class distinctions between churches are thus both functional and dysfunctional. While they hinder application of such concepts as universal brotherhood and prevent direct service by the typical church to all segments of its community's population, they also help increase its influence over the specific groups to which it ministers. What a church loses in breadth of control in the community, it may gain in depth. What it loses from identification with a given class and the tendency to overlook its sinfulness, it may gain by increased cohesiveness of members who remain in the congregation.

Mental Illness

Mental illness is a social concept from the perspective of its definition and its impact upon society. It is primarily in relationship to others that certain persons are described as mentally ill, neurotic, maladjusted, or unsocialized, while others are labeled well-adjusted, healthy, or socialized. The church contributes to both mental health and illness, so it is appropriate to survey various aspects of its relationship to mental hygiene.

Religious faith and practice do not prevent mental illness; psychoses occur among the religious as well as among "the unjust." If one could thoroughly fulfill the Law as summarized by Jesus' statement that man should love God and his neighbor (Matthew 22:36-40), "such a person would be psychologically incapable of neurosis. . . . Even those psychological manifestations of 'normal stress,' experienced daily by us all, would largely disappear if we fulfilled the injunction literally." But no mortal man can completely fulfill the Law; even at his best, man is imperfect. Hence there are religious neurotics just as there are "spiritually dead" persons who are healthy in the normal usage of the word.[36]

Although Jewish neurotics are much less likely than others to become drug addicts or alcoholics, the Jewish incidence of reported psychoneurosis is about two and one-half times that of the general population. Cultural and social class differences appear more significant than religious affiliation as explanations of variations in psychiatric disorder rates; the high Jewish rate reflects greater acceptance of psychiatry by Jews than others.[37] No statistically significant relationship between denomination and type of psychosis has been found among Protestants. Religious convictions are more likely than formal affiliation to be important factors in symptoms and treatment of mental disorders. Yet even when the moral issues linked with religion or conflict with institutional religion are precipitating factors, they may be symptoms more than causes of personality disintegration.[38]

No Hutterites (a communal, pacifistic Mennonite sect scattered in isolated midwestern and Canadian colonies) are confined to mental hospitals. Medical doctors serving them also report fewer psychosomatic and nervous symptoms than among others, so it was believed that there is very little mental illness among them. Strong social solidarity and clearcut social expectations protect members from the necessity of facing life's uncertainties in the spirit of normlessness often found among persons adrift in large cities. Intensive screening, however, found that one in every 43 living Hutterites had experienced symptoms researchers diagnosed as mental disorder, and 57 per cent of these were actively ill at the time

[36] Paul E. Meehl, "Religion and the Maintenance of Mental Health," in *Society's Stake in Mental Health,* in Robert L. Jones et al. (Minneapolis: Social Science Research Center of the Graduate School, University of Minnesota, 1957), pp. 52-61 (quotation from pp. 60-61).
[37] Bertram H. Roberts and Jerome K. Meyers, "Religion, National Origin, Immigration and Mental Illness," *American Journal of Psychiatry,* 110 (Apr. 1954), 759-64; Robert M. Eichler and Sidney Lirtzman, "Religious Background of Patients in a Mental Hygiene Setting," *Journal of Mental and Nervous Disease,* 124 (1956), 515-17; August B. Hollingshead and Fredrick C. Redlich, *Social Class and Mental Illness* (New York: John Wiley and Sons, 1958), pp. 203-5.
[38] Samuel Southard, "Religious Concern in the Psychoses," *Journal of Pastoral Care,* 10 (Winter 1956), 226-33; Wayne Oates, "The Role of Religion in the Psychoses," *Pastoral Psychology,* 1, no. 4 (May 1950), 35-42.

of study. The traumatic social consequences of mental illness were minimized by the economic, psychological, and social support, and love demonstrated for the patient.[39] Children of the Old Order Amish, less completely isolated from the outside world, nevertheless lack the complication
of adult roles that results from living in a complex society where numerous vocational choices are open. Expected to live an agrarian life, they
need not face frustrations of others in preparing for life. They are more
likely than less isolated Mennonites and others to show an interest in
adult objects rather than in toys, and to identify models of persons they
most desire to be like in terms of abstract moral and religious attributes, rather than to name specific persons. Amish pupils in the same
schools as other children are more introverted, withdrawn, submissive,
and slightly less emotionally balanced.[40]

Although much of the evidence is subjective, resting largely upon psychiatric and clinical sources and dealing with the relatively intangible subject of the inner man, there is reason to believe that personality maladjustment and mental illness are sometimes created and aggravated by religion. Religious fidelity itself may be analyzed as mental illness. If an
American were to adhere literally to such teachings of Christ's Sermon on
the Mount (Matthew 5:1-7:29) as walking the second mile or giving the
plaintiff in a law suit more than he asks for, he would be considered mentally ill because such acts are so inconsistent with American culture norms.
Diligent and exclusive pursuit of religious goals makes a person eccentric.

Any religion that merely ministers to unconscious cravings for self-
punishment, relief of guilt-feelings, or repudiation of unpleasant reality
is regarded by psychiatric theory as a neurotic or psychotic religious system.[41] When a religion itself can be considered neurotic, it is inevitable
that faithful members have neurotic symptoms. Yet the flagellant,
serpent-handler, glossolalist, or fasting sectarian is not pathological from
the perspective of his religious group. His strange behavior is a symbol of
conformity to group ideals, a sign of group identification, a reflection of
personal submersion into the sect. The faithful member keeps religious
doctrines in the larger context of related cult teachings and does not de-

---

[39] Joseph W. Eaton and Robert J. Weil, *Culture and Mental Disorders* (Glencoe,
Ill.: The Free Press, 1955); Bert Kaplan and Thomas F. A. Plaut, *Personality in a
Communal Society* (Lawrence: University of Kansas Publications, Social Science
Studies, 1956), pp. 102-5.

[40] Manford H. Kuhn, "Factors in Personality: Socio-Cultural Determinants as
Seen Through the Amish," in *Aspects of Culture and Personality*, Francis L. K. Hsu,
ed. (New York: Abelard-Schuman, 1954), pp. 43-65; and Elmer Lewis Smith, "Personality Differences Between Amish and Non-Amish Children," *Rural Sociology*, 23
(Dec. 1958), 371-76. But is it fair to use standard personality tests which incorporate
non-Amish standards? Are they maladjusted only when in the worldly, alien atmosphere of the school or only when judged by its standards?

[41] Karl A. Menninger, *The Human Mind* (New York: Alfred A. Knopf, 1949),
pp. 466-68.

tach himself from a social group to live in a world of his own making, as many of the truly mentally ill do.[42]

The mental and emotional problems of many persons reflect clashes in cultural norms related to religious differences. Conflicts between Jew and Gentile, Catholic and Protestant, and members of competing denominations sometimes have mobilized hatreds, prejudices, and intolerance of members. Tensions also grow out of conflicting regional patterns of social ethics pertinent to dancing, theater attendance, mixed bathing, cosmetics, jewelry, alcohol, tobacco, etc. Some migrants react against all religion as a result of the social and personal maladjustments emerging from such variations, while others seek out new sects with standards of public morality similar to those of their home community.

Escapism, "the neurotic function of religious belief," sometimes is dysfunctional for mental health. Ascetic monasticism, celibacy, or other forms of self-denial may be used to escape the burdens of family life and the rigors of society. Prayer may be used as an escape mechanism by the indolent or neglectful. Dependence upon God may be used as an excuse for evading responsibilities of medical care, soil conservation, insect control, or crime prevention. The religious cults which condone antisocial personal habits and periodic confession which replaces painful personality reorganization alike emphasize a type of pseudo-holiness that permits neglect of obvious social duties.[43]

Repressions based on anxiety for evil thoughts, marital maladjustment resulting from the belief that God is punishing through sending undesired children, and similar aspects of guilt feelings are sometimes linked with mental illness. Even Calvinism, perhaps the dominant theological tradition in America, may contribute to loneliness, anxiety, doubt, and feelings of unworthiness and guilt which cause personal and social deviations.[44] Intense propagandizing by authoritarian religions which have strongly intolerant attitudes toward other groups contributes to a bigotry which is often considered a mark of a warped personality. Devotional religious literature may be used to strengthen unwholesome egocentric personality tendencies.[45] Clergymen have unwittingly fostered mental illness through sermons which feed on fear, shame, remorse, guilt, or sadistic tendencies of hearers, through an unrealistic, purely moralistic attitude toward mental disorders, and through perpetuation of cultural mytholo-

---

[42] Wayne Oates, *Religious Factors in Mental Illness* (New York: Association Press, 1955), pp. 63-64, 68-69.

[43] Wayland F. Vaughan, *Personal and Social Adjustment* (New York: The Odyssey Press, 1952), pp. 61-63; Robert Ezra Park, *Race and Culture*, ed. Everett C. Hughes (Glencoe, Ill.: The Free Press, 1950), p. 366.

[44] See *Escape From Freedom* (New York: Rinehart and Co., 1941) and other writings of Erich Fromm.

[45] Joseph Havens, "The Egocentric Use of Devotional Literature," *Pastoral Psychology*, 4, no. 38 (Nov. 1953), 37-42.

gies and folk misconceptions pertinent to child welfare, sex hygiene, adolescent behavior, and personal deviations. Symptoms of the struggle associated with spiritual awakening in normal personality development are similar to those of certain nervous disorders, but they have vastly different results and need markedly different treatment.[46]

Intensive analysis of 68 mental patients who had a high degree of religious confusion or sensed a need for a minister's friendship indicated that religious ideas and experience played a significant role in the causation and precipitation of their illness. Conflicting loyalties to a holiness sect and an older group, religious influences associated with the family, religion used as a "last straw solution" to sexual and family problems, and use of religion as a rationalization to supply the ideational content or form of the illness were noted. In 9 of the 35 cases in which religious influences were absent, hospital chaplains stimulated a religious concern which aided recovery.[47]

The Preventive and Adjustive Influence of Religion

Many of religion's social functions help prevent mental illness by supporting wholesome personalities. The single-mindedness referred to in the Bible is the socio-psychological concept of integration, "the forging of approximate mental unity out of discordant impulses and aspirations."[48] Religion itself can be explained partly as a quest for unity in the disorder of life. Religious interests help to integrate the mind and personality, promoting inner security and encouraging a realistic estimate of one's own nature, including a balanced perspective of both strengths and weaknesses. The integration of members into groups of like-minded believers also contributes to their personal integration. In many cultural islands religion has been an omnipresent component of every activity, unifying and integrating the total life of the community. Thus in certain southwestern Spanish-American villages religious significance and ritual are at the core of all institutional activity. A simple, devout Catholicism pervades planting and harvest, birth and death, sickness and health, marriage and recreation, leadership and authority. It sanctions the villagers' daily affairs and provides solace for their misfortunes.[49]

Character education programs contribute to mental health; they guide

---

[46] Roberto Assagioli, "Spiritual Development and Nervous Disease," *Journal of Psychotherapy*, 3 (1956), 30-46.

[47] Wayne E. Oates, "The Role of Religion in the Psychoses," in *Religion and Human Behavior*, Simon Doniger, ed. (New York: Association Press, 1954), pp. 88-106.

[48] Gordon W. Allport, *The Individual and His Religion* (New York: The Macmillan Co., 1951), p. 92.

[49] Lyle Saunders, *Cultural Difference and Medical Care* (New York: Russell Sage Foundation, 1954), pp. 48-49.

the never-ending process of personality development centered around the internalization of standards of right and wrong and the development of wholesome habits. The conscience has a distinctly social base related to cultural norms and social experiences; the church plays a part in building maturity.[50] By promoting altruistic love, social fellowship, and a religious faith which aids many to face anxiety and defeat gracefully, the church stimulates the development of social maturity and helps members find their lives by losing them in service to others.[51] The provision of wholesome outlets for feelings of hostility through holy wars, proselyting efforts, and other channels has a similar effect. Thus the shunning of deviant members by the Amish gives a positive outlet for aggression; by identification with the person who is shunned, the individual can expel his own bad or unacceptable impulses.[52]

Religious escapism often is a similar source of mental health. Thus consolation for the dying and bereaved gives hope in time of sorrow and provides for readjustment without complete demoralization. The nonreligious are more likely to suppress memories and feelings regarding death than the religious, who tend to focus on the after-life in order to control anxieties concerning death.[53] Whenever escapism helps and does not hinder man's social relationships, it makes life richer and more satisfying. Christianity is not necessarily disgraced by theories that it originated as a "fantasy escape of the oppressed."[54]

Prayer can help conquer neurotic attitudes, heal conflicts, overcome loneliness, and renew the sense of belonging to a larger whole. It may result in a mental catharsis, which relieves one of pent-up emotions, or in self-suggestion, which helps solve problems. The thought alone that is in prayer thus changes the universe, to say nothing of the supernatural impact believers hold prayer to possess.[55] Combat soldiers in World War II who prayed when threatened by external danger were less apt to be overcome by psychoneurotic disturbances than those who did not pray. Prayer

---

[50] Gordon W. Allport, *Becoming* (New Haven: Yale University Press, 1955), esp. pp. 19, 73; and Richard V. McCann, "Developmental Factors in the Growth of a Mature Faith," *Religious Education,* 50 (May-June 1955), 147-55.

[51] Anton T. Boisen, "The Sense of Isolation in Mental Disorders: Its Religious Significance," *American Journal of Sociology,* 33 (Jan. 1928), 555-67; Pitirim A. Sorokin, *Altruistic Love* (Boston: Beacon Press, 1950).

[52] Charlotte G. Babcock in "Discussion" of Kuhn, "Factors in Personality," p. 61.

[53] Herman Feifel, "Older Persons Look at Death," *Geriatrics,* 11 (Mar. 1956), 127-30; and Irving E. Alexander, Randolph S. Colley, and Arthur M. Adlerstein, "Is Death a Matter of Indifference?" *Journal of Psychology,* 43 (1957), 277-83.

[54] See Abram Kardiner, *The Psychological Frontiers of Society* (New York: Columbia University Press, 1945), pp. 435, 437, 450.

[55] James Houston Shrader, "Prayer: Factual Data, Rationale, Verification," *Religious Inquiry: Exploratory Studies on Empiric Approaches to Religion,* no. 18 (Oct. 1957), 3-22; Donald L. Robertson, "Prayer Helps Maintain Health," *Christian Century,* 74 (Jan. 16, 1957), 73-75; and Paul E. Johnson, "A Psychological Understanding of Prayer," *Pastoral Psychology,* 4, no. 36 (Sept. 1953), 33-39.

was a highly approved activity in their emergency situations; an over-whelming majority believed it to be very helpful.[56]

Perhaps because of these influences of religion, many studies have found it related to various types of personal and social adjustment. "Be-lievers" among university students and church-attending youths have a personal-social adjustment that is superior to others.[57] Personal adjust-ment of the aged is superior among those who have religious beliefs and engage in religious activities, even though many of their church-related experiences have maladjustive implications.[58] Neurotic World War II soldiers attended church less often than soldiers in general.[59] Character ratings and reputations of people tend to be positively linked with their religious observance, perhaps because morality and ethical conduct are traditionally linked with religion.[60]

On the other hand, a study of students and Minneapolis people aged 15 to 70 found that most correlations between religiosity (favorableness toward religious beliefs) and humanitarianism (measured by attitudes toward Negroes, charity, conscientious objectors, German spies, treatment of criminals, unmarried mothers, etc.) were small and negative. Religios-ity tended to vary directly and humanitarianism inversely with the con-servatism of church denominations.[61] Dogmatic religious orientations are inversely related to the degree of concern with social matters in large communities, but in a small upper New York township a positive correla-tion of .64 between church attendance and honesty and of .41 between church attendance and kindness was discovered.[62]

Religious conservatives have lower I.Q.'s, consider more things wrong in themselves, worry about fewer things, are more susceptible to sugges-

56 Arnold M. Rose, "Conscious Reactions Associated with Neuropsychiatric Break-down to Combat," Psychiatry, 19 (Feb. 1956), 87-94; and Samuel A. Stouffer et al., The American Soldier: Combat and Its Aftermath (Princeton, N.J.: Princeton Uni-versity Press, 1947), pp. 108-9, 136, 172-91.

57 Daniel G. Brown and Warner L. Lower, "Religious Beliefs and Personality Characteristics of College Students," Journal of Social Psychology, 33 (Feb. 1951), 103-29; and Carol Larson Stone, Church Participation and Social Adjustment of High School and College Youth (Pullman, Wash.: A.E.S. Bul. 550, 1954).

58 Robert M. Gray and David O. Moberg, The Church and the Older Person, rev. ed. (Grand Rapids, Mich.: Wm. B. Eerdmans Publishing Co., 1977).

59 Samuel A. Stouffer et al., Measurement and Prediction (Princeton, N.J.: Prince-ton University Press, 1950), p. 526.

60 Allport, The Individual and His Religion, pp. 66-67, and Robert J. Havighurst and Hilda Taba, Adolescent Character and Personality (New York: John Wiley and Sons, 1949), pp. 62-69.

61 Clifford Kirkpatrick, "Religion and Humanitarianism: A Study of Institutional Implications," Psychological Monographs, 63, no. 9 (whole no. 304, 1949). This study does not measure religiosity in terms of actual religious activities; if church participation or some other measure of behavior had been used, the results might have been different.

62 Walter Houston Clark and Caroline M. Warner, "The Relation of Church Attendance to Honesty and Kindness in a Small Community," Religious Education, 50 (Sept.-Oct. 1955), 340-42; Warner L. Lowe, "Religious Beliefs and Religious De-lusions," American Journal of Psychotherapy, 9 (1955), 54-61.

tion, and are more likely to refer to their parents as reasonable or lenient than religious liberals. Anti-church persons tend to be more radical in all areas of politico-economic and social issues than pro-church persons,[63] but conservatism in one area of life is not necessarily correlated with conservatism in others. One study of five types of liberalism-conservatism (political, economic, religious, social, and esthetic) found all possible variations and combinations in a sample of 246 male students.[64]

The apparently contradictory findings about religion and certain personality traits may be largely due to people's individual differences, the great variations in and among religions, and the use of different criteria, indicators, measurement tools, and techniques. Almost anything churches do may aid one person while harming another.

Therapeutic Aspects of Religion

The alienation of psychiatry from religion which was so widespread two or three decades ago is gradually being replaced by cooperative arrangements in which the common roots, purposes, and techniques of both are recognized and the members of each profession are aware of their limitations and the other's contributions to "the cure of souls." The Institutes of Religion and Health which publishes the *Journal of Religion and Health* has a staff of 80 professionals providing out-patient psychiatric, clinical, and pastoral counseling services. Wholistic Health Centers, clinical psychologists sponsored by churches, and other formalized pastoral-care programs are scattered across the nation. There are differences between the philosophies, goals, and methods of the healing professions, but their therapy and theoretical orientations have much in common.[65] Clinical training of ministers is directly related to the church's acknowledged role in the mental health movement. Personal counseling, confession of sin, group therapy, and even the constructive use of anxiety are used therapeutically.

The popular "peace of mind" cultism of Norman Vincent Peale and others is both praised and condemned. The self-centered, hero-worship-

---

63 T. A. Symington, *Religious Liberals and Conservatives* (New York: Columbia University Teachers College, Contributions to Education No. 640, 1935); T. H. Howells, *A Comparative Study of Those Who Accept as Against Those Who Reject Religious Authority* (Iowa City: University of Iowa Studies in Character, 2, no. 3, 1930); Philip M. Kitay, *Radicalism and Conservatism Toward Conventional Religion* (New York: Columbia University Teachers College, Contributions to Education No. 919, 1947).

64 Willard A. Kerr, "Untangling the Liberalism-Conservatism Continuum," *Journal of Social Psychology,* 35 (Feb. 1952), 111-25. Cf. Robert A. Harper, "Is Conformity a General or a Specific Behavior Trait? " *American Sociological Review,* 12 (Feb. 1947), 82-86.

65 Samuel Z. Klausner, *Role Adaptation of Ministers and Psychiatrists in a Religio-Psychiatric Clinic* (New York: Bureau of Applied Social Research, Columbia University, 1957), pp. 59-64; Don C. Shaw, "The Christian Roots of Psychoanalysis," *The Chaplain,* 10, no. 5 (Oct. 1953), 14-26; R. Lofton Hudson, "When Religion and Psychotherapy Meet," *Review and Expositor,* 52 (July 1955), 325-35.

ing, "believe in yourself" program of "positive thinking" has been accused of turning the church into a service station and of making God subservient to personal ambition. The how-to-do-it formula for securing peace of mind helps many, but its superficiality has dubious mental health and theological implications. To imply, as some religious leaders have, that in it lies the whole cure for all mental and emotional problems is gross over-simplification.[66]

Christian Science stresses the belief that the only reality is God; all else is illusion. The power of Divine Mind is believed to cure ills, harmonize inter-personal relations, provide for material needs, and ameliorate one's lot in mortal existence in other ways. The ill call upon practitioners for healing; if the cure fails, the patient lacked faith or was the victim of collective errors in others' minds. The body's natural recuperative powers, which operate both with and without the intervention of human healers, eventually result in cures for most ailments treated. Analysis of testimonial letters suggests that problems of health are a major factor leading people into the Church of Christ, Scientist. Much attention is given to disorders that are very insignificant in daily living, and many ailments were self-diagnosed by writers. Dramatic "cures" may hence be due to mistaken diagnosis or to psychogenic factors. In 1951 about 8,500 practitioners, mostly women, were active in the U.S.[67]

Faith healing has been practiced in many religions as well as outside of religion entirely. Groups that base their appeal partly or largely upon it include New Thought, Unity School of Christianity, Divine Science, Christian Science, the Church of the Nazarene, the International Church of the Foursquare Gospel, Father Divine's cult, part of the Christian and Missionary Alliance, and various Pentecostal and Holiness groups. Quackery and deception associated with much "faith healing," as well as naturalistic explanations of the autosuggestion of prayer and the healer's power of suggestion over functional disorders, have placed faith healers on the defensive. Systematic follow-up surveys are resisted, perhaps because their results are similar to one study of 350 professed healings. Within six months 39 had died, 5 became insane, 301 showed no change

---

66 Norman Vincent Peale, *A Guide to Confident Living* (Englewood Cliffs, N.J.: Prentice-Hall, 1948), is the outstanding book of this type. Comparable approaches in Judaism and Catholicism are Rabbi Joshua L. Liebman, *Peace of Mind* (New York: Simon and Schuster, 1946), and Bishop Fulton J. Sheen, *Peace of Soul* (New York: Whittlesey House, 1949). Critical interpretations are given by William L. Miller, "The Gospel of Norman Vincent Peale," *Union Seminary Quarterly Review,* 10, no. 2 (Jan. 1955), 15-29; Warren Weaver, "Peace of Mind," *Saturday Review,* 37, no. 50 (Dec. 11, 1954), 11, 49-50; and Paul Hutchinson, "Have We a 'New' Religion?," *Life,* 38 (Apr. 11, 1955), p. 140.

67 R. W. England, "Some Aspects of Christian Science as Reflected in Letters of Testimony," *American Journal of Sociology,* 59 (Mar. 1954), 448-53; Orlo Strunk, Jr., "Motivational Factors and Psychotherapeutic Aspects of a Healing Cult," *Journal of Pastoral Care,* 9 (Winter 1955), 213-30. Christian Scientists testify to the healing of disorders which, according to their theology, are non-existent errors!

of condition, and 5 who had suffered from certain nervous diseases apparently had been cured.[68] A spontaneous cure may be only a shift from one form of neurotic expression to another.[69] While such transference is not true healing, it has a functional effect if it means the difference between adjustment and maladjustment in society. Often, however, the new symptom is more grievous and disabling than the first. The major Christian denominations have recently revived their interest in the faith healing process.[70]

Catholicism and other religions support numerous shrines to which the physically infirm and emotionally unbalanced make pilgrimages hoping to be healed. The most famous is Lourdes, France, which dates back to 1858. Only 54 of its cures have been confirmed by the Roman Catholic Church as truly miraculous (beyond the realm of what medical science considers natural law). Yet a social-psychological "miracle" occurs there regularly as invalids return "finding life worth living. They arrive as social rejects and return to fuller participation in society."[71] They have received a legitimized role, a place in society as performers of minor economic tasks or as "cross bearers." Reaffirmation of their faith increases Catholic solidarity and establishes a sense of brotherhood based upon what they share in common.

Suicide, Alcoholism, and Drug Addiction

Catholics have lower rates of suicide than Protestants. Jews, in spite of their urban residence, occupational distribution, and anti-Semitism, have the lowest rates of all. Durkheim theorized that these differences are due to variations in the degree of social cohesion of the groups. Catholicism has an authoritarian, traditional, and anti-individualistic element in its ethic, while Protestantism is individualistic and permits a high degree of free inquiry. Since Protestants have a less intensive collective life (less social cohesion), their suicide rates are higher than those of Catholics and especially of Jews. Much that is extra-religious has been incorporated into Catholic and Jewish religion. Definitions of almost every conceivable social situation have evolved; members are furnished a satisfying, definite, constraining set of collective representations (socially shared values,

[68] The study by Gaebelein is reported in Wade H. Boggs, Jr., *Faith Healing and the Christian Faith* (Richmond: John Knox Press, 1956), pp. 27-28.

[69] Percival M. Symonds, *Dynamics of Psychotherapy, I. Principles* (New York: Grune and Stratton, 1956), pp. 147-49.

[70] Cf. Charles S. Braden, "Study of Spiritual Healing in the Churches," *Pastoral Psychology*, 5, no. 44 (May 1954), 9-15; and Carl J. Scherzer, *The Church and Healing* (Philadelphia: Westminster Press, 1950), pp. 169-84.

[71] Samuel Z. Klausner, *Lourdes: Participation and Observation* (New York: Bureau of Applied Social Research, Columbia University, 1958), p. 31; see also pp. 23-26, 29-31.

ideas, and ritualistic symbols about the universe) which are sufficient for meeting most situations. The communicant who fails to find or refuses to accept the representations is provided socially therapeutic techniques, like the confessional, which prevent complete personal disorganization. Anomic suicide, which reflects a disruption of social norms or the lack of regulation of man's activities by them, and egoistic suicide, which springs from excessive individualism in which man no longer finds a basis for existence in life, are thus much more frequent among Protestants.[72]

Reliable estimates indicate that over 10,000,000 Americans are either addicted to alcohol or are problem drinkers who need special help. Many activities of rescue missions, Salvation Army Harbor Light units, religious counseling clinics, and other church-related agencies are oriented toward problems associated with alcohol. For many alcoholics medical treatment is inferior in the long run to spiritual treatment; without some form of the latter, the former usually fails. The effectiveness of Alcoholics Anonymous is partly due to its religious basis. Six of its famous twelve steps to recovery mention God; the last refers to recovery as a "spiritual awakening." The religious approach to the alcoholic provides him with a sense of superhuman help, a feeling of being accepted, a means of handling his ultimate anxiety, a foundation for personality in a meaningful philosophy of life, and a unifying commitment to group-transcending values. Much religious therapy substitutes religious satisfactions for those previously received through alcohol.[73]

The strong prohibitionist tendencies of evangelical Protestantism are less than two centuries old. Drinking was general in early America, common even at church gatherings. Since the time of Finney and other nineteenth century evangelists, however, Protestants have worked closely with temperance organizations to restrict the production, sale, and use of alcohol.[74] Current educational aims of churches range from temperate drinking to complete abstinence from all alcoholic beverages.

Variations in religious mores as well as in cultural influences help explain the different patterns of use of alcohol. Protestants who are faithful to their religion consume little or none; Catholics and Jews use more, and the non-churched use the most of all. Strong social mores among Orthodox Jews place a stigma upon drunkenness and alcoholism which makes it unlikely that a Jew will turn to alcohol as a solution for emotional problems,

[72] Emile Durkheim, *Suicide,* trans. John A. Spaulding and George Simpson (Glencoe, Ill.: The Free Press, 1951), pp. 152-70, 208-9, 258-61, 327-29, 373-76; Ruth Shonle Cavan, *Suicide* (Chicago: University of Chicago Press, 1928), pp. 40-41.

[73] Percy M. Sessions, "Ego Religion and Superego Religion in Alcoholics," *Quarterly Journal of Studies on Alcohol,* 18 (Mar. 1957), 121-25; Howard J. Clinebell, Jr., *Understanding and Counseling the Alcoholic Through Religion and Psychology* (New York: Abingdon Press, 1956), pp. 67-154; Isidor Thorner, "Ascetic Protestantism and Alcoholism," *Psychiatry,* 16 (May 1953), 167-76.

[74] Mark Mohler, "Conversion of the Churches from Wet to Dry," *Current History,* 25 (Oct. 1926), 6-13.

as the young, rebellious, fundamentalist Protestant or Mormon is likely to do. Low Jewish alcoholism rates are also due to integral identification with the family and a historical tradition internalized at an early age. Ceremonial use of alcohol, ingroup identification as a minority, constant references to the hedonism of outsiders, and other ethnocentric religious ideals and sentiments thus combine to account for much of the distinctive behavior of Jews relevant to the use of alcohol.[75]

There is incomplete and fragmentary evidence that drug addicts may include disproportionate numbers of Roman Catholics, the non-religious, and persons of non-Jewish and non-Christian religions.[76] Some have found that church attendance has been given up by addicts. This may result from real or imagined social ostracism after becoming addicted or from the anomie which is partly responsible for the addiction. If spiritual solace can satisfy some of the desire for euphoria, religion may be useful as a therapeutic device.[77]

Crime and Juvenile Delinquency

Popular opinions hold that religion is a major preventive and cure for delinquency and crime. Contrary views are less publicized in America where religion is so popular. Only a brief survey of this vast topic is possible here.

Numerous studies have found that Roman Catholics provide more than their proportionate share of offenders, while white Protestants and Jews furnish less than their share. When socioeconomic and other factors are controlled, however, differences between religious groups tend to disappear. The lower social class position of Catholics and black Protestants helps explain their higher crime rates. Lower class offenders and blacks are more likely to receive official discipline rather than referral to social agencies and other off-the-record treatment; hence they are overrepresented on police and court records. In addition, Catholic church affiliation more than that of some other groups may be merely nominal, the result of "accident of birth" rather than of true religious commitment. Problems of social disorganization among first and second generation immigrants affect more Catholics than others. Larger families among them increase the number of potential juvenile delinquents per population unit. When,

[75] Charles R. Snyder, *Alcohol and the Jews* (Glencoe, Ill.: The Free Press, 1958); Nathan Glazer, "Why Jews Stay Sober," *Commentary,* 13 (Feb. 1952), 181-86.
[76] See Alan S. Meyer, ed., *Social and Psychological Factors in Opiate Addiction* (New York: Bureau of Applied Social Research, Columbia University, 1952), pp. 36-37; and Bingham Dai, *Opium Addiction in Chicago* (Shanghai: The Commercial Press, 1937).
[77] Michael J. Pescor, "A Statistical Analysis of the Clinical Records of Hospitalized Drug Addicts," *Public Health Reports,* Supplement No. 143, 1943.

in addition, the occupational distribution, educational level, and age-sex ratios are taken into consideration, religion remains only a very minor part of the complex network of interacting causative forces in the pattern of group differences.

Most prisoners claim to be church members, and few are avowed atheists. In fact, in one study the percentage of prisoners who admitted that they were religiously indifferent was less than that of the general population.[78] In an anonymous sample of 50 Michigan prisoners, only 4 per cent stated they never had a church connection. Over half claimed church-going families, but one-third of this group stated that one parent, usually the father, did not attend church. Over three-fourths claimed to have studied the Bible in church schools for a median duration of four years.[79] Findings like these led Barnes and Teeters to conclude that "the population of any state penitentiary is far more religious—and orthodoxly so— than the law-abiding college professors, scientists and scholars of the country." [80] Additional evidence, however, casts doubt on this conclusion.

Prisoners often declare falsely that they are church members. On the chance that parole boards may hear about their religion and hence act favorably on their behalf, inmates have made false statements, attended chapel regularly, joined the prison choir, recited Bible passages to guards, and changed their stated religious preference.[81] When all available evidence is carefully evaluated, it appears that prisoners are somewhat less religious than the general population. Of 2,343 inmates 51 per cent declared they had no religious preference. When verification of preference was requested, clergymen named by them were the least responsive of nine types of informants, only 12 per cent replying to letters sent from the prison's mental health office. This implies that, in a substantial proportion of cases, the claimed affiliation was so loose and casual that the inmate's name was not recognized by the minister.[82] The average prisoner in America's largest prison (Southern Michigan in Jackson) was found to have had no connection with the church for 20 years. Few knew the name of a clergyman, and very few were members in good standing. Under 4 per cent of the "Catholic" inmates in an Illinois prison had come up to the average Catholic practice of receiving the sacraments several times

[78] Philip M. Smith, "Organized Religion and Criminal Behavior," *Sociology and Social Research,* 33 (May-June 1949), 362-67.

[79] Philip M. Smith, "Prisoners' Attitudes Toward Organized Religion," *Religious Education,* 51 (Nov.-Dec. 1956), 462-64.

[80] Harry Elmer Barnes and Negley K. Teeters, *New Horizons in Criminology,* rev. ed. (Englewood Cliffs, N.J.: Prentice-Hall, 1945), p. 735.

[81] Donald R. Taft, *Criminology,* 3d ed. (New York: The Macmillan Co., 1956), pp. 276-81, 357-58; Leo Kalmer and Eligius Weir, *Crime and Religion* (Chicago: Franciscan Herald Press, 1936), pp. 19-28; Hans von Hentig, *The Criminal and His Victim* (New Haven: Yale University Press, 1948), pp. 334-35.

[82] Donald Clemmer, *The Prison Community* (Boston: Christopher Publishing House, 1940), p. 51; cf. Kalmer and Weir, *Crime and Religion,* pp. 49-64.

yearly.[83] Only 59.5 per cent of 172 Wisconsin prisoners, compared to 88.1 per cent of their presumably law-abiding brothers, had married women of their own religion.[84] Insofar as religiously mixed marriage reflects less intense religious faith, this is further evidence that the prisoners were less concerned about religion. Mixed marriages may also have compounded the problems that contributed to their criminality.

Over 70 per cent of 1,700 juvenile delinquents in Judge Lyons' Minneapolis court were without a church program, and only 20 per cent of 5,900 Florida delinquents were church attenders. Two Oregon studies showed 83 and 90 per cent of the cases to be without church affiliation, and in Buffalo 80 per cent were without church programs.[85] Of 162 delinquent girls, only 2.1 per cent attended church regularly, and interviews showed that religion had never been integrated into their home life. Negative, indifferent, or actively hostile attitudes toward religion were found in 95 per cent, presumably as a projection of hostility because the subjects felt rejected, unwanted, and unloved by their families.[86] Two-fifths (43.6 per cent) of 2,137 boys picked up by Detroit police for offenses were regular church attenders, and only one-seventh never attended. Those who were recidivists in the following year were much less likely to be regular attenders than the non-repeaters. Church attendance lowered the general likelihood that a boy would get into trouble; it was part of a total cultural complex in which boys from more favorable home and community conditions were more likely to attend church.[87]

Church leaders eagerly publicize evidence like the above. Yet comparisons of delinquent with non-delinquent children indicate that exposure to religion does not prevent delinquency. Mursell found that inmates of a reform school had received as much religious training as the children outside and that religious education, knowledge, attitudes, and background as measured by psychological tests could not be regarded as causes either of delinquent or non-delinquent behavior.[88] Eighty-three delinquent girls had social attitudes more favorable to Sunday observance and the Bible than a control group of 100 non-delinquents.[89] Over half of 761 delin-

---

[83] Coogan, "The Myth Mind."

[84] John Lewis Gillin, *The Wisconsin Prisoner* (Madison: University of Wisconsin Press, 1946), pp. 24, 239, 256.

[85] Jay Edgerton, "The Judge Likes the Juveniles," Minneapolis *Star,* Apr. 2, 1954, p. 26.

[86] Sister M. Dominic, R.G.S., "Religion and the Juvenile Delinquent," *American Catholic Sociological Review,* 15 (Oct. 1954), 256-64.

[87] William M. Wattenberg, "Church Attendance and Juvenile Misconduct," *Sociology and Social Research,* 34 (Jan.-Feb. 1950), 195-202; cf. Sheldon and Eleanor Glueck, *Unraveling Juvenile Delinquency* (New York: The Commonwealth Fund, 1950), pp. 166-67, 249, 252.

[88] Reported in Negley K. Teeters and John Otto Reinemann, *The Challenge of Delinquency* (Englewood Cliffs, N.J.: Prentic Hall, 1950), p. 159.

[89] Studies by Warren C. Middleton, Paul J. Fay, and R. R. Wright cited by Milton

quents in Passaic, New Jersey, were attending church services weekly, were regular church school attenders, and fulfilled the religious obligations of their church. Only 6.8 per cent did not claim some church connection. The unusually low incidence of delinquency among Jews was attributed to Judaism's pervasiveness into everyday life, the social solidarity of Jews, and discrimination against them.[90]

Mere tabulation of religious preferences, backgrounds, and memberships as related to crime and delinquency throw little light on the subject. The meaning of religion to the individual, self-identification as religious or non-religious, and the degree to which religion has become a significant frame of reference have not been controlled in studies of religion and delinquency. Lacking such analysis, we can only hypothesize on the basis of incomplete evidence that most religion is a deterring factor in crime causation. Religious activity similarly seems associated with successful adjustment of past offenders, but studies to date are fragmentary and inconclusive, dealing only with crude indices of religious behavior.[91]

The Church Accentuates Crime Problems

Some aspects of crime and juvenile delinquency are undoubtedly increased and their prevention and treatment made more difficult by certain aspects of church work. Knowledge of these dysfunctional consequences is based chiefly upon "educated guesses" and should be considered only as hypotheses until systematic research has tested them. Among alleged dysfunctions of the church and religion are the doctrine of free will, which bolsters the classical theory of crime and penology; Protestant traditions which presumably contribute to disrespect for law through their stress upon personal liberty; the tendency of churches to support easy "solutions" and poorly planned programs of social reform; sanctification of the status quo, which upholds cultural causes of delinquent behavior; support of a "duality of morals" by sanctioning intergroup prejudices and groups like the KKK; sectarianism which hinders effective treatment of offenders; stimulation of anxieties and guilt reactions that lead to anti-social behavior; compartmentalization of religion and ethics which supports the attitude that "business is business"; religious fanaticism which contributes to personal demoralization through loss of self-control, and certain reli-

---

L. Barron, *The Juvenile in Delinquent Society* (New York: Alfred A. Knopf, 1954), p. 169.

90 William C. Kvaraceus, *The Community and the Delinquent* (New York: World Book Co., 1954), pp. 373, 405-8.

91 For examples see Sheldon and Eleanor Glueck, *Juvenile Delinquents Grown Up* (New York: The Commonwealth Fund, 1940), and Ralph W. England, "A Study of Postprobation Recidivism Among Five Hundred Federal Offenders," *Federal Probation,* 19, no. 3 (Sept. 1955), 15, note 18.

gious practices that are criminal.[92] Such practices include Jehovah's Witnesses' use of evangelization techniques which violate city ordinances, conscientious objectors' refusal to obey compulsory military service laws, and the illegal acts of whipping cults, snake-handlers, and other bizarre sects.

The church tends to reflect more than to counteract the values and customs of society, even when they have anti-social implications. Falling in line with the spirit of its age, the church supports most delinquent tendencies of society. When adults obviously violate religious ethical principles, the child is influenced toward thinking that "anything is all right if you can get by with it," "everybody has his racket," and "everybody else is doing it." Told not to lie, the child also is instructed to tell the hostess of a dull party that he had "a lovely time." When he has a stomach ache from eating green apples, he is expected to say that he "feels just fine." After his fifth birthday, parents may tell the bus driver he is under five. Observing "smart business deals" enshrouded in a spirit of "let the buyer beware," padded expense accounts, and listing of personal expenses in tax reports as if they were business expenditures, the child is influenced more by parental example than by verbal church teachings. All too often churches themselves "spread a velvet cloak to hide and nourish such admitted evils." [93] Failing to develop in members a conscience consistent with high moral principles, churches implicitly abet anti-social attitudes and conduct by stressing faith and minimizing its specific applications to daily life. Worse yet, they themselves are implicated at times in criminalistic behavior.

White collar crime and other offenses within churches is a neglected subject in criminology. It includes misappropriation of designated funds, sexual offenses by the clergy, violation of anti-gambling and public safety laws, evasion of taxation, and falsification in publicity. Semi-criminal techniques have been used by sect leaders as a guise for securing economic gain. So-called religious corporations have solicited funds by fraudulent claims that they will be used for summer camps, boys towns, and similar causes. Denominational leaders have flagrantly violated the rules of their constitutions in order to retain power. Clergymen have testified in court to the "good character" of confirmed moral delinquents. One pled so earnestly for parole of a juvenile delinquent into his supervisory custody that the judge complied with his wish on the assurance of pastoral

---

[92] These criticisms are gleaned from numerous criminology and juvenile delinquency texts.

[93] Robert M. Lindner, *Stone Walls and Men* (New York: Odyssey Press, 1946), p. 254. See also Barron, *The Juvenile in Delinquent Society,* pp. 169-70; George A. Vold, *Theoretical Criminology* (New York: Oxford University Press, 1958), pp. 257-59; Mabel A. Elliott, *Crime in Modern Society* (New York: Harper and Brothers, 1952), pp. 257-59.

guidance, observation, and report. Within six months the boy shot and killed a policeman who apprehended him in an act of serious crime. The pastor had neither seen nor heard of him since the date he assumed his trust.[94]

Many criticisms of the church are valid; each may apply to certain cases of anti-social behavior. Selective search for the church's faults is easily rewarded, as is the opposite bias. Scientific objectivity and moral integrity disclose evidence on both sides of the subject.

Church Control of Crime and Delinquency

Cooperation by church leaders with juvenile courts, probation officers, and institutions for treating offenders is increasing. Some churches hire social workers to do preventive and rehabilitative work. Many support leisure-time youth programs, camps, and social service agencies designed partly to cope with these problems. Religious education and theological training of church leaders often includes an orientation to the problem and treatment of crime and delinquency as well as to preventive programs aimed at improved family life, personality adjustment, and character education.[95]

Chaplains in correctional institutions help to rehabilitate inmates. Some are paid by the institution; others are church employees who are volunteers on the prison staff. Although some inmates testify that the chaplain's ministry provided comfort, helped them "see the right," and made them better persons, the majority react to the chaplain as "a fraud," an insincere figurehead, or a sky pilot who, like everyone else, has his racket. No facts are available to indicate how many are genuinely changed, but prison conversions that resulted in radically transformed lives attest to the fact that some are helped permanently. For many inmates religious services are merely a diversion from the ordinary routine; there is good reason to believe the majority of Catholic and Protestant prisoners are religiously insincere.[96] Although many serious-minded church workers and progressive chaplains are giving much thought to their work and its improvement, the 1945 statement of Barnes and Teeters may still be valid: "Serious attempts to evaluate the effectiveness of religious work among convicts have never been made." [97]

---

[94] J. Lindsay Almond, Jr., "The Church and Juvenile Delinquency," *Lutheran Quarterly,* 1 (May 1949), 205-13.

[95] For descriptions of the programs at Harvard Divinity School and Union Theological Seminary see Richard V. McCann, "Juvenile Delinquency and the Church's Opportunity," *Religious Education,* 50 (Mar.-Apr. 1955), 88-92; and Robert Lee, "The Church and the Problems of Delinquency," *ibid.,* 52 (Mar.-Apr. 1957), 125-29.

[96] Clemmer, *The Prison Community,* pp. 234-38; cf. Kenyon J. Scudder, *Prisoners Are People* (New York: Doubleday and Co., 1952), pp. 136-48.

[97] Barnes and Teeters, *New Horizons in Criminology,* p. 735.

Mandatory religious requirements in child care and legally enforced church attendance for the probationer equate religion with punishment and imply that salvation rather than rehabilitation is the goal sought by the court. Religion as the basis of placement in foster homes or institutions may not only undermine social work knowledge and skills but may also violate American principles of church-state separation and voluntary entrance to and exit from organized religion.[98]

Delinquency reflects the churches' failure either to reach large numbers of people or to train them effectively to live in accord with Judeo-Christian ethics. No studies indicate that there are fewer delinquents or less crime in highly churched areas than in areas with few churches or ministers. Indeed, the highest homicide and assault rates in the nation are found in southern states which comprise "the Bible Belt." The higher states rank in the average number of ministers, churches, and church members aged 13 and over per 100,000 population, the lower is their general social well-being as measured by indices of economic welfare, education, culture, housing, voting, medical facilities, and health.[99]

Numerous interrelated social limitations on the church and deficiencies of its programs and personnel help explain why the church fails to prevent crime and delinquency. Churches typically minister primarily to successful elements of society; they do not reach the lower classes which provide the bulk of those legally adjuged to be delinquent. Religion fails today as in the past "to penetrate in any real and vital way the experience of the gang boy."[100] Recreational and delinquency prevention programs are obstructed by members' fears that their children will be contaminated by delinquents or that church property will be abused. The belief that such "worldly" activities do not belong in church also hinders their support. Even when delinquents come under religious influence, they resist attitudes foreign to their backgrounds. In addition, parents of pre-delinquent children seldom call on a minister for help until the situation is so acute that preventive measures are ineffective.[101]

Some church personnel are inadequately qualified educationally, emotionally, or socially for their work and as a result are ineffective. Follow-

---

98 Charles H. Boswell, "If I Were a Judge," *Federal Probation,* 15, no. 1 (Mar. 1951), 29; Don. J. Hager, "Religion, Delinquency, and Society," *Social Work,* 2 (July 1957), 16-21; Don J. Hager, "Race, Nationality, and Religion," *National Probation and Parole Association Journal,* 3 (Apr. 1957), 129-41.

99 Austin L. Porterfield, *Youth in Trouble* (Fort Worth: The Leo Potishman Foundation, 1946), pp. 109-10. It must be recognized, however, that the largest number of churches per population unit is found in rural areas where churches generally have poorly developed programs.

100 Frederic M. Thrasher, *The Gang* (Chicago: University of Chicago Press, 1927), p. 492. Cf. Arthur L. Swift, Jr., "Gangs and the Churches," *Union Seminary Quarterly Review,* 11, no. 4 (May 1956), 43-50.

101 Charles V. Gerkin, "The Pastor and Parents of Delinquent Children," *Pastoral Psychology,* 6, no. 57 (Oct. 1955), 8-13.

up of tangible results of religious work with offenders in prisons and jails is usually inadequate, so the "converts" often become backsliders, failing to develop new friendships, group identifications, and personal habits that would enable them to escape the depressing influences of a society that encourages them to return to their sinful ways.[102] Other-worldly doctrines antagonistic to church promotion of social justice and community reform, ineffective educational techniques, the belief that abstract dogma alone is sufficient to change conduct, and competition with other societal influences also help explain shortcomings of church programs in character education and rehabilitation.

Conclusion

We have seen that certain aspects of religion accentuate personal-social problems while others implicitly and explicitly prevent, alleviate, and treat the same problems. The interconnections of the functional and dysfunctional concomitants and effects of religion are very complex. The "black" and "white" are not clearly distinguishable; they overlap and are omnipresent in the impact of the church upon people and society. Religious factors are so intertwined with the total culture that their influence is not easily isolated for analysis. The origins of many problems lie partly in culturally patterned defects that involve a "pathology of normalcy." [103] Everything that is good can be abused.

These generalizations indicate the need for caution in assessing the impact of the church. There are great differences between churches as well as between the teachings and examples of religious leaders within them. The tendencies toward self-assertion, self-perpetuation, and self-aggrandizement in religious institutions may foster intolerant attitudes and maladjusted personalities even though the religion itself is basically tolerant and adjustive.[104] Variations in the degree of religious self-identification may be significantly associated with the church's influence on a person. Church affiliations are often nominal, not necessarily representing acceptance of the faith and practice for which the church stands. Samples used in studies of deviant behavior may not represent a true cross section of groups analyzed. The impact of the same religious influences upon individuals varies. Thus remorse, repentance, and confession may have

---

102 John Lennart Cedarleaf, "The Chaplain's Role with Delinquent Boys in an Institution," *Federal Probation,* 18, no. 1 (Mar. 1954), 40-45; William C. Nau, "Let Them Know About It," *ibid.,* 15, no. 3 (Sept. 1951), 36-37.

103 Erich Fromm, "Individual and Social Origins of Neurosis," *American Sociological Review,* 9 (Aug. 1944), 380-84.

104 Cf. Commission on Human Rights, *The Main Types and Causes of Discrimination* (New York: United Nations, 1949), p. 22.

either functional or dysfunctional consequences.[105] The differential internal responses may be subject to environmental variations but they never are easy to measure and analyze. The degree to which religion is effective in the prevention and treatment of mental illness, delinquency, and other problems may be related to the priority, frequency, intensity, and duration of the religious influence, but these have not yet been subjected to objective measurement.[106]

As a variegated institution consisting of dozens of major branches and thousands of local congregations, the church's impact upon deviant behavior is highly complex and heterogeneous, whether seen from the perspective of its role in the prevention, causation, or treatment of such problems. Analysis of this impact is a major area for future research by social psychologists and other social scientists.

Selected References

Abramson, Harold J., *Ethnic Diversity in Catholic America*. New York: John Wiley and Sons, 1973. An analysis, based in large part upon survey research, of persistent differences between Catholics from ten different ethnic backgrounds.

Barnett, Homer G., *Indian Shakers*. Carbondale: Southern Illinois University Press, 1957. A description of the doctrine, ritual, and effects of this messianic cult of the Pacific Northwest.

Brotz, Howard, *The Black Jews of Harlem*. New York: Free Press, 1964. Description of Harlem's largest Black Jewish congregation plus analysis of Black nationalism and protest leadership.

Demerath, Nicholas J., III, *Social Class in American Protestantism*. Chicago: Rand McNally and Co., 1965. Research data on the complex relationships between social class and religion.

Donaldson, William J., Jr., ed., *Research in Mental Health and Religious Behavior*. Atlanta: Psychological Studies Institute (620 Peachtree St. N.E., 30308), 1976. Thirty-five theoretical, empirical, and analytical articles comprising "an introduction to research in the integration of Christianity and the behavioral sciences."

Eaton, Joseph W., and Robert J. Weil, *Culture and Mental Disorders*. Glencoe, Ill.: Free Press, 1955. Mental health of the communal Hutterites compared to that of other populations.

Fauset, A. H., *Black Gods of the Metropolis*, 2nd ed. Philadelphia: University of Pennsylvania Press, 1971. Negro religious cults of the urban North.

Fichter, Joseph H., *Religion and Pain: The Spiritual Dimensions of Health Care*. New York: Crossroad Publishing Co., 1981. Research on the responses of professional personnel in Catholic general hospitals to the suffering of patients.

Frazier, E. Franklin, *The Negro Church in America*, and C. Eric Lincoln, *The Black Church Since Frazier*. New York: Schocken Books, 1974. Reprint of Frazier's 1964 study with Lincoln's 1970 James Gray Lectures at Duke University.

---

[105] John D. Copp, "Remorse, Repentance, and Confession," *Pastoral Psychology*, 7, no. 63 (Apr. 1956), 42-45.

[106] See Sutherland's theory of differential association in the genesis of criminal behavior. Edwin H. Sutherland and Donald R. Cressey, reviser, *Principles of Criminology*, 5th ed. (Chicago: J. B. Lippincott Co., 1955), pp. 74-81.

Johnstone, Ronald L., "Negro Preachers Take Sides," *Review of Religious Research*, 11, no. 1 (Fall 1969), 81–89. Research on the divergent approaches of black clergy to political and social issues.

LaBarre, Weston, *The Peyote Cult*, 4th ed. Hamden, Conn.: Archon Books, 1975. An anthropologist's study of peyotism.

Lincoln, C. Eric, *The Black Muslims in America*. Boston: Beacon Press, 1961. A history, description, and analysis of the origins, rationale, and implications of the Black Muslim movement.

Marriott, Alice, and Carol K. Rachlin, *Peyote*. New York: Thomas Y. Cromwell Co., 1971 (Mentor Books, 1972). A very readable, largely first-hand account of the use of peyote and the Native American Church.

Marx, Gary, *Protest and Prejudice: A Study of Belief in the Black Community*, rev. ed. New York: Harper and Row, 1969. Survey research on militancy, civil rights, black nationalism, and anti-Semitism among American blacks.

Moberg, David O., *Inasmuch: Christian Social Responsibility in the Twentieth Century*. Grand Rapids: Eerdmans, 1965. A sociologist's interpretation of the application of biblical values to current human needs.

National Clearinghouse for Mental Health Information, *Bibliography on Religion and Mental Health 1960–1964*. Washington, D.C.: Government Printing Office, PHS Publication Nos. 1599, 1967. An extensive annotated bibliography arranged in 14 sections.

Nelsen, Hart M., and Anne Kusener Nelsen, *Black Church in the Sixties*. Lexington: University Press of Kentucky, 1975. Description and interpretation including data from survey research.

Nelsen, Hart M., Raytha L. Yokley, and Anne K. Nelsen, eds., *The Black Church in America*. New York: Basic Books, 1971. Historical and sociological analyses of black religion.

Oates, Wayne E., *Religious Factors in Mental Illness*. New York: Association Press, 1955. An analytic interpretation of religion and mental illness from the perspective of those who are ill.

Pettigrew, Thomas F., and Ernest Q. Campbell, *Christians in Racial Crisis*. Washington, D.C.: Public Affairs Press, 1959. A study of the dilemmas and varied responses of clergy in the Little Rock school desegregation crisis.

Reed. William Standish, *Healing the Whole Man—Mind, Body, Spirit*. Old Tappan, N.J.: Revell Power Books, 1980. A plea for wholistic medicine, by the founder and president of Christian Medical Foundation International, which has perceptive conclusions based on experience, study, and observation.

Simpson, George E., *Black Religions in the New World*. New York: Columbia University Press, 1978. History, belief systems, and rituals of black religious groups since the slave-trade era.

Part Eight: *Professional Leadership in the Church*

🏛 Chapter 18

The Clergy

In Catholic and Anglican traditions the clergyman is usually referred to as "priest"; in Judaism he is a "rabbi," in Reformed churches a "minister," and in Lutheran and other Protestant denominations a "pastor." Yet the terms overlap and often are used interchangeably. The church has always charged clergymen with responsibility for its ordinances, liturgy, sacraments, "pastoring the flock," preaching, teaching, and administration. Great variety and adaptability of the ministerial office is evident; the distinction between clergy and laity has been a source of both conflict and creative tension. Since all specific offices of the clergy are interrelated, sharp distinctions between them do violence to what the profession actually is.

In Protestantism in 1952 there were an estimated 184,900 workers in the local parish (ministers, directors of religious education, music directors, church social workers, sextons, etc.); 5,270 in denominational programs (executives, editors, secretaries, clerical workers, etc.) besides thousands of publishing house employees; 1,920 in inter-church national or area programs; 12,800 campus, institutional, and military workers (teachers of religion in colleges and prep schools, denominational chaplains, seminary professors, student movement secretaries, house parents, chaplains, and "Y" secretaries); 18,610 workers in missionary enterprises; tens of thousands of employees in church agencies for children, the aged, and the handicapped; and dedicated persons in many fields of work appointed to do specialized missionary jobs.[1] Although church leadership includes all of these types of workers, this chapter is limited to the professional ministry. The 218 American religious bodies in the 1983 *Yearbook* reported a total of 508,452 clergy of whom 291,722 were serving parishes.[2] We shall survey the backgrounds and recruitment of the clergy, their education, roles and role conflicts, division of labor, and social control over the ministry, their social status, standards for success, and problems.

Recruitment of the Ministry

Occupational choice of the ministry results from factors similar to those which influence entry into other professions. Specifically religious values appear to be more important among Catholics entering the clergy than among Protestants and Jews, who are more often motivated by humanistic values.[3] Most rabbis come from assemblies with a good program of Jewish training, such as the Leaders Training Fellowship, which gives special attention to the best qualified youth at ages 14 to 18 so that they will later become either lay or professional leaders in the congregation.[4]

Two generations ago Simmel, noting that European priests came from all social classes, said it was impossible for the priesthood to engender class hatred, for every family had some relative in it. Cutting across all other groups, an inter-regional uniformity of the clergy was both an effect and a cause of its purposive unity.[5] Protestant clergymen have come largely from rural communities and the middle or lower middle class. The majority have come from within their respective denominations, which often are strongest in rural areas. The proportion with rural backgrounds tends to reflect the ecological distribution of churches, so the role of rural areas as suppliers of the ministry may have been overstressed. Persons

---

[1] John Oliver Nelson, "A Listing of Church Vocations," *International Journal of Religious Education,* 28, no. 7 (Mar. 1952), 6-10. Nelson summarizes duties and training requirements for 48 church vocations. (Recent statistics are unavailable.)

[2] Constant H. Jacquet, Jr., ed., *Yearbook of American and Canadian Churches 1983* (Nashville: Abingdon, 1983), p. 232. Many who retire or leave the ministry continue to be listed in denominational reports, but this is balanced by thousands more in non-reporting denominations. For example, one analysis indicates that many rabbis, particularly in Orthodox Jewry, were not included in the *Yearbook* statistics. See "Report on American Rabbis," *Information Service,* 36, no. 33 (Nov. 30, 1957), p. 1.

[3] Eli Ginzberg, Sol W. Ginsburg, Sidney Axelrad, and John L. Herma, *Occupational Choice: An Approach to a General Theory* (New York: Columbia University Press, 1951), pp. 14-15.

[4] I am grateful to Rabbi Kassel Abelson of Minneapolis for many facts relevant to the rabbi.

[5] Georg Simmel, *The Web of Group-Affiliations,* trans. Reinhard Bendix (Glencoe, Ill.: The Free Press, 1955), pp. 143-44.

now in the ministry came from a society which had a higher proportion of rural people than at present. The rural population supplies many people for other occupations by heavy out-migration. When such variables are considered, disproportionate contributions of rural areas to the ministry tend to disappear. Felton's study of 1,709 ministerial students found that rural areas supplied *fewer* than their proportionate share of seminary students.[6]

Family influences significantly affect vocational choice of the ministry. Ministers' homes provide as much as 25 times their "natural quota" of clergymen. Home training was the most prominent of 16 situations and events that influenced choice of the ministry by 1,573 theological students. In 15 per cent the father's occupation was the ministry. This was exceeded only by farming with 25 and skilled labor with 19 per cent. They listed as the person most influential in their decision the pastor (34.0 per cent), mother (17.4 per cent), father (11.2 per cent), evangelist (6.4 per cent), college teacher (5.8 per cent), Sunday school teacher (5.0 per cent), followed by missionary, friends, and others. Over three-fourths included the minister in their three choices.[7] Almost three-fourths of 140 Yale divinity students came from homes with a strong religious interest; three-fifths had one or more relatives in religious or social work. Their specific type of religious work most often had been influenced by association with persons and programs of the type chosen.[8]

Pious, church-going parents, especially mothers, are a major influence on Catholics' choice of a religious profession. Members of the religious order they eventually enter also influence vocational recruitment. One-fourth of the seminarians studied by Fichter had a brother in the priesthood or a religious order.[9] The typical American Catholic bishop is one of several children, others of whom also may have entered religious vocations. Coming out of northern, native-born stock of Irish or German background, he is apt to have a capable, industrious father who gave his children a Catholic high school education.[10] Protestant and Jewish decisions to enter the ministry are often deferred until the late teens or early twenties, but Catholics encourage career selection of the priesthood, at least on a trial basis, by the end of grade school. In some families a tradition of having at least one clergyman each generation holds a heavy hand over youth. In others, family or personal tragedies are conceived to be a re-

---

[6] Ralph A. Felton, *New Ministers* (Madison, N.J.: Drew Theological Seminary, 1949), pp. 25-26.

[7] *Ibid.*, pp. 7-11.

[8] Robert O. Smith, "Personality and Cultural Factors Affecting the Religion of One Hundred and Forty Divinity Students," *Religious Education*, 43 (Mar.-Apr. 1948), 106-11.

[9] Joseph H. Fichter, S.J., "The Religious Professional," *Review of Religious Research*, 1 (Winter 1960), 89-101.

[10] John D. Donovan, "The American Catholic Hierarchy: A Social Profile," *American Catholic Sociological Review*, 19 (June 1958), 98-112.

sult of sin, and efforts are made to compensate by having a member enter the ministry. Church recruitment pressures have used psychological trickery to get decisions to enter the ministry by appeals implying that any able person who refuses publicly to acknowledge willingness to be called into the ministry is carnal, backsliding, or undedicated. Conscientious youth are then faced with the dilemma of publicly professing a "call" they do not expect to receive or of facing the displeasure of their elders.

Essays by 306 theological students, mostly Methodist, on motivations for entering the ministry showed four major factors were common to most cases: early religious training, participation in church youth activities, influence of a pastor, and higher than average marks in school. Books, parental pressure, and "instantaneous religious experience" were of little or no importance. "A call to the ministry seems to be conditioned more by coldly rational than by emotional factors." [11] Yet many of the more thoughtful Christian youth fail to enter seminaries because they are confused about the nature of a call, have not been directly encouraged to give it serious consideration, sense the low standards of many seminaries, see the ministry as an unexciting occupation, or feel sinful and timid.[12]

Many groups have insisted upon a divine "call," a subjective, emotional experience which semi-miraculously reveals God's will that one should become a clergyman. Some sects teach that it is the only important qualification. The call may result from "hearing the voice of God," heeding Biblical commands, or a combination of circumstances.[13]

The chief reason for entering the ministry by 38 per cent of 1,704 students from 57 Protestant seminaries was "a definite call of God." All agreed this was one reason, but there was wide disagreement as to the definition of a call and the manner in which it comes. For most it was a gradual process combining situational factors, personality, abilities, and attitudes of understanding or devotion.[14] In a Missouri rural church survey, 62 per cent of church-type and 85 per cent of sect-type clergymen included a call to preach among reasons for entering the ministry. Greater stress upon religious conversion was associated with greater emphasis upon a ministerial call.[15] Protestant denominations which emphasize a

---

[11] "Strange Role for Univac," *Newsweek*, 55, no. 15 (Apr. 11, 1960), 84. The study was by Marvin T. Judy at Southern Methodist University.

[12] Walter D. Wagoner, "The Ministry: Image and Reality," *Christian Century*, 77 (Apr. 20, 1960), 464-66.

[13] Edwin J. Omark, "Called to the Ministry," *Bethel Seminary Quarterly*, 2, no. 2 (Feb. 1954), 5-9.

[14] Felton, *New Ministers*, pp. 15-17. Other leading reasons were the "need of man and society for Christ" (31 per cent) and the desire "to serve mankind" (26 per cent).

[15] Lawrence M. Hepple, *The Church in Rural Missouri*, Part III, *Clergymen in Rural Missouri* (Columbia, Mo.: A.E.S. Research Bulletin 633C, Dec. 1958), pp. 182-84. Home influence and the desire to serve people were the other major reasons given by both groups.

divine call provide clergymen for others. "The Unitarian denomination furnishes practically no ministers, but must recruit its prophets from emancipated ones of more orthodox denominations." [16]

Personal ambition and striving for status are sometimes underlying motivations making men feel a call to the ministry. When the call is an emotional experience by persons unqualified for their self-chosen vocation, ruthless elimination or relegation to marginal positions commonly results. Personal bitterness may cause negativistic attitudes toward religion as ex-clergymen protect their self-images through psychological processes of rationalization and compensation. As problems associated with both naïve conceptions of the call and ignoring a divine imperative in recruitment are reckoned with, conceptions of what constitutes a call are increasingly similar. [17]

Verbally expressed life goals of ministers emphasize service to God and mankind more than the "security" and "getting ahead" that are dominant in other groups. [18] Unconscious motivations leading men into the ministry have included identification with a priest who became a substitute for an inadequate father, unconscious attempts to sublimate socially unacceptable wishes in order to master some childhood trauma, and confused sexual and aggressive drives. [19] Some try to solve inner conflicts through the ministry, counseling, or related vocations. Such a person "seeks to use the misfortunes of others for purposes of self-relief or . . . attempts to get rid of inferiority feeling by playing God to those who have need of help." [20] Because many inadequate personalities have been "led to accept the call" and have failed to overcome serious weaknesses during their preparation, theological seminaries systematically assist students to overcome defects and, when these efforts fail, prevent them from entering the ministry. Misfits are found in every profession; the ministry is not unique in this respect.

Many drop out of theological education. A comparison of 229 "per-

[16] Everett C. Hughes, *Men and Their Work* (Glencoe, Ill.: The Free Press, 1958), pp. 29-30.

[17] "God does not call a person to do something without reference to his own creative gifts to that person in the first place." Wayne E. Oates, *The Christian Pastor* (Philadelphia: The Westminster Press, 1951), p. 58. See Carroll A. Wise, "The Call to the Ministry," *Pastoral Psychology,* 9, no. 89 (Dec. 1958), 9-17; and Daniel D. Williams, "The New Spirit in Theological Education," *Union Seminary Quarterly Review,* 11, no. 1 (Nov. 1955), 33-38.

[18] John B. Holland and Charles P. Loomis, "Goals of Life of Rural Ministers," *Sociometry,* 11 (Aug. 1948), 217-29; and Orlo Strunk, Jr., "Theological Students: A Study in Perceived Motive," *Personnel and Guidance Journal,* 36 (Jan. 1958), 329-32.

[19] Margaretta K. Bowers, "Some Observations on the Unconscious Motivation Determining Religious Vocation," *Abstracts of Papers and Addresses* (11th meeting, Society for the Scientific Study of Religion, Apr. 21, 1956), pp. 2-3; and Gotthard Booth, M.D., "Unconscious Motivation in the Choice of the Ministry as Vocation," *Pastoral Psychology,* 9, no. 89 (Dec. 1958), 18-24.

[20] Ernest R. Groves, "Professional Training for Marriage and Family Counseling," *Social Forces,* 23 (May 1945), 447-51. Quotation from p. 450.

sistent" and 28 "nonpersistent" ministerial candidates in evangelical and fundamentalist schools found that more of the persistent believed they had a "call" to the ministry and were altruistically motivated. All whose initial consideration of the ministry had been made after entering college persisted in their plans. Those who made both the initial consideration and final decision within the same year and those who decided before age 13 or after 25 were more likely to persist in their training.[21]

A study of 111 ex-ministers concluded that the best-trained men withdraw while mediocre and emotional types remain in the ministry. Intellectual reconstruction involving shifts in beliefs was evident in 40 cases, and family considerations—especially the wife's health and welfare—in 20. Inefficient church administration was a factor in 43 cases; some of these felt seminary training had not prepared them adequately, and others left because of problems of placement, uncertainty of tenure, lack of a guaranteed salary, and other problems of finances and administration.[22] Many entered church-related college teaching or editing of religious publications; they did not withdraw from the ministry in its broadest sense.

Education of the Clergy

The level of education of the American clergy appears to have declined continuously from colonial times to about 1930; it then held its own and began a gradual rise. Nevertheless, in 1952 only one-third of the rural clergymen in Missouri church-type and 1.2 per cent of those in sect-type bodies had received any seminary education; 29 per cent of church-type and 82 per cent of sect-type ministers had less than a college education.[23]

Church doctrines pertinent to the clergy are related to the provision for and accessibility of theological education. As standards have risen, correspondence schools and "diploma mills," often stressing evangelical doctrines, have granted numerous fraudulent degrees to ministers who need the prestige degrees carry.[24] Great emphasis upon sacraments and liturgy, as in Catholicism and other church-type bodies, is accompanied by high standards for the clergy. Every Protestant body provides for exceptions from its educational standards. The average level of education, consequently, is lower than the ideal. The episcopal polity of Catholicism

[21] Harold W. Darling, *A Comparative Study of Persisting and Non-Persisting Ministerial Candidates in Evangelical Colleges*, Ph.D. thesis, Purdue University, 1958; *Dissertation Abstracts*, 20 (Aug. 1959), 586-87.

[22] H. G. Duncan, "Reactions of Ex-Ministers Toward the Ministry," *Journal of Religion*, 12 (Jan. 1932), 100-15.

[23] Hepple, *Clergymen in Rural Missouri*, pp. 160-61.

[24] William W. Sweet, "The Rise of Theological Schools in America," *Church History*, 6 (Sept. 1937), 260-73; and Enock C. Dyrness, "Fake Degrees in the Pulpit," *Christianity Today*, 3, no. 16 (May 11, 1959), 8-10.

enables it to adhere more closely to its usual minimum standard, eight years of preparation after high school, than many Protestants, for whom college plus three or four years of seminary and a year of internship are typical requirements. The rabbi of a modern Jewish congregation is expected to have completed college plus four to six years in a postgraduate rabbinical school which he can enter only after meeting certain qualifications of background and knowledge of Jewish lore. Preparation for the rabbinate hence parallels and exceeds the Protestant pattern.

Minority clergy are especially deficient educationally. Over 11 per cent of the U.S. population but only 4.9 per cent of its theological students in 1982 were black.[25] Two per cent of white but 54 per cent of black rural Virginia ministers had only a high school education or less. Relative poverty, shortage of scholarships, congregational polity, inadequate education at the time of relatively late decisions to enter the ministry, and discrimination by seminaries of white denominations have contributed to racial differences in ministerial education.[26]

Numerous evaluations of ministerial education have been made. Many clergymen feel inadequately trained in the social sciences and in the clinical work, counseling, and related activities increasingly thrust upon them. Curricular changes in seminary education, courses in specialized vocations within the ministry, and in-service training for those already in the ministry are designed to meet the demands of modern society.

Roles of the Clergy

The clergyman shares many loyalties to groups and institutions with others, but usually his loyalties to a church, to his denomination, to his profession, and often to larger ecumenical organizations go beyond the layman's. Regardless of denomination, relationships with constituents have similar patterns of leadership, control, status, and provision of material sustenance. Hence a solidarity between clergymen may override antagonisms between religious groups and usually distinguishes the minister from other believers in his church.[27]

[25] Jacquet, *Yearbook*, p. 262. The latter figure has climbed steadily from the 2.6 per cent reported in 1970. In the 1980 Census of Population 6.8 per cent of all clergy were black.

[26] W. E. Garnett, *The Virginia Rural Church and Related Influences, 1900-1950* (Blacksburg, Va.: A.E.S. Bulletin 479, May 1957), pp. 50-51; William Coolidge Hart, "The Negro in the Christian Ministry," *Christian Century*, 76 (Mar. 18, 1959), 319; and Harry W. Roberts, "The Rural Negro Minister: His Educational Status," *Journal of Negro Education*, 17, no. 4 (1948), 478-87.

[27] Simmel, *The Web of Group-Affiliations*, pp. 161-62. For discussions of the nature of the ministry as a profession see Lee Braude, "Professional Autonomy and the Role of the Layman," *Social Forces*, 39 (May 1961), 297-301; and Warren O. Hagstrom, "The Protestant Clergy as a Profession: Status and Prospects," *Berkeley Publications in Society and Institutions*, 3 (Spring 1957), 1-12.

The clergyman may be seen from many perspectives, for he has diverse and multiple tasks. He may seem considerably different when performing duties associated with one of his roles from what he is when engaged in another. The typical interrelated and overlapping roles include preacher, educator, institutional representative, administrator, group leader, counselor, and symbolic roles.[28]

1. *Preacher.* Preaching is a dominant duty of Protestant ministers. It overlaps with and supports all other work, even helping listeners resolve personality problems when it is of a therapeutic type.[29] In his public speaking the minister deals with ideals, goals, and other normative topics. In other roles he is apt to see the world and people as they actually are, far short of the ideals he proclaims. Sometimes this normative emphasis makes ministers overbearing, dogmatically giving "the only correct answers" to many problems beyond the scope of their qualifications.[30] The task of "interpreting the Permanent to a world of Change"[31] is difficult. Changes in theological conceptions from liberalism and fundamentalism toward neo-orthodoxy reflect problems of interpreting and proclaiming God's message to a world racked with serious social problems which seems to have change as its only constant. Yet a substantial proportion of the Protestant clergy hold conservative theological beliefs; in a 1978 self-classification 53 per cent of the clergy chose evangelical, 34 per cent traditional, 22 per cent fundamentalist, 15 per cent liberal, 10 per cent charismatic, 8 per cent neo-orthodox, 9 per cent other, and 2 per cent did not know.[32]

Sermon time in the typical Protestant church has been reduced from 90 minutes or more a century ago to 20 or 30 minutes.[33] Preaching nevertheless remains the most important part of the church service, the most attended church activity, the most important reason for attending, and the most important church source of guidance for living.[34] Yet good preaching is hindered by pressures of other duties. Hasty mechanical sermon preparation is typical. Sermons are assembled, not grown; parts

---

28 Classifications of clergical roles vary considerably. For an example that deviates from this see Hepple, *Clergymen in Rural Missouri*, pp. 206-18.

29 Oates, *The Christian Pastor*, pp. 66-68.

30 Roy A. Burkhart, "Is the Church Authoritarian?" *Pastoral Psychology*, 5, no. 43 (April 1954), 25-28.

31 Robert S. and Helen Merrell Lynd, *Middletown in Transition* (New York: Harcourt, Brace and Co., 1937), pp. 307-8.

32 *Evangelical Christianity in the United States: National Parallel Surveys of General Public and Clergy* (Princeton, N.J.: The Gallup Poll and Princeton Religion Research Center, 1979), p. 251. (Instructions were to "choose as many as you feel apply.")

33 Gerald B. Smith, "Preaching Goes Modern," St. Paul *Sunday Pioneer Press*, Sec. 3, pp. 2-3, Sept. 14, 1958.

34 William Israel Gorden, *The Speech Activities of First Community Church, Columbus, Ohio*, Ph.D. thesis, Purdue University, 1958; *Dissertation Abstracts*, 19 (Feb. 1959), 2186.

are fitted on a chassis outline instead of resulting from the maturation of ideas through meditative study.[35]

Preaching for conversions in the role of *evangelist* is emphasized in sect-type groups. In the major denominations such preaching is incorporated into pastoral sermons, is subordinated to evangelistic campaigns, or consists chiefly of appeals to join the church.

2. *Educator.* The minister teaches in his pulpit ministry as well as in visitation, counseling, and work connected with church schools, leadership-training, membership classes, and other educational activities. He also teaches by his example of religious devotion, personal conduct, and family life.[36]

3. *Institutional representative.* The minister is expected to speak *for* his church as well as *to* it. As its official representative in the community, he symbolizes his church and is a "public relations man" publicizing its work, defending its policies, and protecting its interests, leaders, and members. This task is very difficult if he is not committed with a clear conscience to its objectives, doctrines, operational strategy, and affiliations. When a church has reached a high degree of institutionalization, its pastor may be primarily an organization man working for a denominational hierarchy and almost deifying the institution he serves.[37]

The minister of a prominent church often is expected to be active in community affairs. In rural areas and among minority groups he may be a true community leader, representing a much broader constituency than his church membership. He is apt to have close contacts with such community leaders as the school superintendent, county agricultural agent, Community Chest director, and civic club presidents. Ministers in large cities usually are not considered top leaders, and church influence is not apt to be crucial in making community decisions. Church leaders may be highly significant, however, in the role of restating settled policies and interpreting new ones. Ministers are often desired as board members of civic and charitable agencies because they are effective channels of communication to the people. When they use such positions for selfish reasons, people react against them, reject them as community leaders, and replace them with persons not obviously seeking personal gain.[38] In community

---

[35] Willard L. Sperry, "What's Wrong with the Clergy?" *American Mercury,* 62 (Apr. 1946), 412-18.

[36] Jean M. James found that Catholic laymen expect their priests above all else to be living examples of complete dedication to God. Cf. "The Social Role of the Priest," *American Catholic Sociological Review,* 16 (1955), 94-103. Over half of the time of the average Episcopal priest is spent in educational activities. Cf. Charles E. Whipple, *The Teaching Ministry of the Priest in the Episcopal Church,* Ed.D. thesis, New York University, 1959; *Dissertation Abstracts,* 20 (Feb. 1960), 3412.

[37] William H. Kirkland, "The Organization Man and the Ministry," *Christian Century,* 75 (Apr. 23, 1958), 492-94; and William H. Whyte, Jr., *The Organization Man* (Garden City, N.Y.: Doubleday and Co., 1956).

[38] Floyd Hunter, *Community Power Structure: A Study of Decision Makers* (Chapel Hill: University of North Carolina Press, 1953), pp. 82-83, 117-18.

power struggles related to gambling, prostitution, and other vices, clergymen are expected to support reform crusades.

The clergyman serves as a representative of government as well as of
his church when he solemnizes marriage vows. He is not permitted to
wed persons without a license, and he must file pertinent forms in a
government office.

4. *Administrator*. Many churches are big business in terms of property
holdings as well as budget. Some employ business managers, but in most
the pastor has responsibilities of coordinating church groups, purchasing
equipment, selecting and overseeing lay workers, planning and supervising the church program, integrating activities with those of the denomination and of ecumenical and community agencies, adjusting denominational directives to fit the needs and resources of the local church, and
serving as chairman or ex officio member of church boards and committees. These executive activities require many hours weekly. The Catholic parish priest is charged with direct responsibility for all of these administrative and business duties even when he delegates them to others.

5. *Group leader*. The minister typically is expected to lead a complex
series of sub-organizations as well as the church itself. If those considered
important are not already established, he must take the primary responsibility for founding social, recreational, educational, or welfare agencies.
As either the chairman or the "power behind the throne," he guides many
activities of sub-organizations.

6. *Counselor*. Counseling is as old as the ministry. It cannot be separated from other ministerial work except for analytic purposes. Much of
it relates directly to family crises and the life cycle.

The minister's counseling differs from that of other professions, for his
frame of reference is unique. He often is a friend who has known his
counselees prior to their special need, and much of his counseling takes
place indirectly in family situations. His position prevents rigid screening
of clients and attracts people of greatly different types, for he is socially
and economically accessible. He often is received as a representative of a
universal God with a universal gospel who is concerned for the whole of
life, not only a compartmentalized subdivision. He tries to lead counselees
into conformity with a normative system. Since many problems of adjustment are alleviated by wholesome spiritual attitudes, the clergyman with
insight into the social and psychological foundations of personality can
be of inestimable value to the mental health of his people.

Since love and the development of healthy personalities are at the core
of pastoral work, a mental health orientation supported by insights from
the behavioral sciences can provide a frame of reference for all the
preaching, visiting, counseling, and administrative tasks of the pastor [39]
Yet clergymen's goals of counseling are less often those of mental hygiene
than are those of other professions. Clergymen tend to emphasize tradi-

---

[39] Russell R. Bletzer, "The Minister as Counselor," *Pastoral Psychology*, 8, no. 72
(Mar. 1957), 28-34.

tional values and methods, but an increasing proportion get beyond the superficial level of mere advice-giving to help people help themselves by gaining understanding of their problems, their personality deficiencies and strengths, and the resources available to help them resolve difficulties. Emotional re-education that produces the "more abundant life" often occurs through such counseling.[40]

The most formalized counseling arrangement is the Catholic confessional. Through it the parishioner discharges spiritual responsibilities, replaces his independence with dependence on God, and obtains relief from a sense of guilt. The clergyman in the confession booth is identified as a mediating representative of God and becomes a moral judge. Group counseling, which brings together persons with similar problems for the purpose of producing insight and restoring wholesome social relations, is also being used by some pastors.[41]

The minister's counseling overlaps with that of lawyers, medical doctors, teachers, marriage counselors, social workers, psychiatrists, and clinical psychologists. Each profession believes it knows what is best for the client, but cooperation is gradually replacing the mutual distrust and suspicion that once prevailed between these helping professions. The attitudes of clergymen toward other professional people who deal with problems of family life vary greatly. Interviews with a cross-section of clergy in 14 denominations without official local welfare agencies found the majority to be cooperative toward social work, but 35 per cent had clearly noncooperative attitudes. Ministers with college and seminary education were more favorably disposed toward social workers than those who had only Bible school training, but an even more pronounced relationship was found between favorable attitudes and course work in psychology and sociology.[42]

The effectiveness of pastoral counseling is weakened by inadequate preparation, gullible acceptance of anti-religious presuppositions simply because they are cloaked in religious terminology, and a search by some ministers for solutions to their personal problems through learning about problems of others. Studies of pastors' qualifications for counseling have invariably found shortcomings, many of which could have been overcome through increased education in the social and behavioral sciences.[43]

---

[40] Richard K. Kerckhoff, "The Profession of Marriage Counseling as Viewed by Members of Four Allied Professions: A Study in the Sociology of Occupations," *Marriage and Family Living,* 15 (Nov. 1953), 340-44; and Arthur M. Tingue, "The Minister's Role in Marriage Preparation and Premarital Counseling," *ibid.,* 20 (Feb. 1958), 11-17.

[41] H. Walter Yoder, "Spiritual Processes and Marriage Failure," *Journal of Pastoral Care,* 10 (Spring 1956), 34-39. Casual observation suggests the hypothesis that the theological orientation of a minister has a direct bearing upon the methods he uses to help people. Fundamentalists and other authoritarians seem to emphasize directive counseling, while the neo-orthodox and liberals lean toward non-directive techniques.

[42] David O. Moberg and Russell Voight, "The Protestant Minister and Social Work," *Midwest Sociologist,* 19, no. 1 (Dec. 1956), 38-44.

[43] Ernest R. Groves, "A Decade of Marriage Counseling," *Annals of the American*

PROFESSIONAL LEADERSHIP IN THE CHURCH

7. *Symbolic roles.* The ordained clergyman is a *pastor* serving as an "undershepherd of the Great Shepherd" to meet church members' needs for spiritual sustenance and health. Physical, mental, moral, and social healing; religious, educational, and vocational guidance; ministry to the dying and bereaved, and ministry through pastoral aids are among his duties.

The minister is a *prophet* when bringing the will of God to bear upon the personal or social lives of men. His position as a spokesman for God is sometimes symbolized in church architecture through elevating the pulpit from which God's Word is read and preached. In its purest form the prophetic role involves charismatic leadership.

When the minister concentrates on administering sacramental means of grace, he plays the liturgical role of a *priest* who is part of an institutional system, an intermediary between God and man, and a symbol both of God and the church. In theory non-sacramentarian bodies omit this function; in practice every clergyman who administers the ordinances of baptism and Communion, performs wedding ceremonies, conducts funerals, prays publicly *for* his people, and tries to bring God's grace to them is a priest. As priest, he defends existing regulations through supervising traditional rituals and ceremonies. Representing continuity, the priest is at conflict with the prophet, who seeks to purify society and the church. Traditional leadership dominates the priestly role, which mediates between the sacred and the secular in all of its specific functions.[44]

The clergy also symbolize and support societal integration by providing acceptable definitions of social situations. Reminding believers of the work of God and reminding nonmembers of the specific church and religion he represents, the minister is a tangible symbol of God and the church.[45]

Role Integration

The typical pastor specializes as much as possible in those roles which he believes he can perform well and in which he has the greatest interest.

Academy of Political and Social Science, 212 (Nov. 1940), 72-80; Andrew L. Wade and Joel V. Berreman, "Are Ministers Qualified for Marriage Counseling?," *Sociology and Social Research,* 35 (Nov.-Dec. 1950), 106-12; John A. Clippinger, "Attitudes Toward Pastoral Training of Sixty-One Outstanding Pastors," *Religious Education,* 48 (Mar.-Apr. 1953), 113-16; Robert L. Clingan, "Rural Pastors Advise on Professional Training," *Church Management,* 25, no. 7 (Apr. 1949), p. 68; and Ronald A. Ward, "The Relevance of Ministerial Training," *Religion in Life,* 25 (Winter 1955-56), 55-64.

[44] E. O. James, *The Nature and Function of Priesthood* (New York: Vanguard Press, 1955); and Alfred Bertholet, "Priesthood," *Encyclopaedia of the Social Sciences* (New York, The Macmillan Co., 1934), 12, 388-95. For problems pertinent to one aspect of the priestly role see Robert L. Fulton, "The Clergyman and the Funeral Director: A Study in Role Conflict," *Social Forces,* 39 (May 1961), 317-23.

[45] Oates, *The Christian Pastor,* pp. 26-42; and Talcott Parsons, *Essays in Sociological Theory, Pure and Applied* (Glencoe, Ill.: The Free Press, 1948), pp. 298-99.

As a result, clergymen are sometimes classified as pulpiteers, administrators, pastors, teachers, counselors, evangelists, or public relations men. Some minimum degree of competence is needed for each of the many roles, and they must be adapted to the particular parish.

All of the clergyman's roles are within a single framework. Unless he is in a specialized ministry, he is invariably considered the leader of a church. His total task is integrated around this position; his specific duties arise out of it. "Away from church, the pastor is apt to be viewed as the church." [46] A clarity of direction for all his overlapping tasks is provided when his chief role as minister or institutional leader is given proper perspective by a wholesome balance between vocational traditions and the needs of men in contemporary culture.[47] Whether he conceives of himself as a general practitioner, parish promoter, community problem solver, father-shepherd, interpersonal relations specialist, believer-saint, scholar, evangelist, liturgical leader, educator, representative of the church-at-large, or church politician, his master role is that of clergyman; all his other roles are subservient to it.[48]

Roles of the Rabbi

The rabbi is a leader by virtue of his advanced training. His roles are similar to those of the Protestant minister, but his public relations work has assumed much greater significance because of the problems associated with anti-Semitism. He possesses no special sacramental powers. In Reform Judaism the rabbi usually conceives of himself first as a teacher, then as a preacher, pastor, and public relations man for his congregation and for Judaism as a whole.[49]

The Orthodox rabbi has an ambiguous position. He served the first Jewish settlement without connection with any one congregation. He answered questions about Jewish tradition and served as a religious "ornament." In the area of second settlement he has often led an adult study group. Preaching is not an important duty. He receives only a nominal salary but collects fees for special services and compensation for super-

[46] A'Delbert Samson, *Church Pastors in Four Agricultural Settlements in Montana* (Bozeman, Mont.: A.E.S. Bulletin 539, April 1958), p. 3.

[47] Walter Harrelson, "The Christian Minister—Citizen of Two Worlds," *Baptist Leader,* 21, no. 6 (Sept. 1959), 14-15; Robert G. Middleton, "Let the Minister Be a Minister," *Foundations,* 2 (July 1959), 198-206; and Samuel W. Blizzard, "The Parish Minister's Self-Image of His Master Role," *Pastoral Psychology,* 9, no. 89 (Dec. 1958), 25-32.

[48] Samuel W. Blizzard, "The Protestant Minister's Integrating Roles," *Religious Education,* 53 (July-Aug. 1958), 374-80.

[49] Saul Mendlovitz, "The Role of the Rabbi," *Abstracts of Papers and Addresses* (11th meeting, Society for the Scientific Study of Religion, Apr. 21, 1956), pp. 3-4. See Jeshaia Schnitzer, "Rabbis and Counseling: Report on a Project," *Jewish Social Studies,* 20 (July 1958), 131-52.

vising the manufacture and handling of kosher foods and beverages. In the large synagogue, the sexton (*shammes*) is one of the most important permanent staff members. He arranges for the services, distributes honors, keeps equipment in order, collects money, and assists laymen with administrative duties. The cantor (*chazzen*) who sings and chants the important prayers is also prominent in Orthodoxy. Large sums are paid for those who are famous, especially for the High Holiday services at which the cantor is advertised as the featured attraction.[50]

The Conservative rabbi has crucial functions as preacher and priest in the worship program. He leads many educational and social activities of the congregation, spearheads promotional activities, coordinates and integrates the disparate interests and viewpoints represented in the congregation, explains Jewish ritual and law to inquirers, and counsels individuals, families, and groups. Jewish welfare and philanthropy has been transferred from the synagogue to independent agencies. The rabbi has had little preparation for this change and also lacks a clear ideological basis for Conservatism. Hence he faces problems of role-adjustment and self-conception, and a search for legitimation is prominent within the profession.[51]

Seven types of rabbis discovered in interviews all reflect aspiration to the traditional role of scholar-saint and a trend toward a new Americanized scholar-saint role as the characteristic type. They are ranked as if on a continuum. (1) The Traditional rabbi tries to adhere to Orthodox belief and practice. He has little influence, is pessimistic about the future, and has hope only in his faith that Messiah will come. Near him is (2) the Free-Lancer who earns his livelihood from rabbinic services and religious ceremonies but turns his back on the synagogue and communal responsibility. (3) The Modern Orthodox rabbi staunchly adheres to traditional Judaism but is an organizer and administrator, sacrificing scholarship to build up the synagogue as the center of the Jewish community. (4) The Conservative rabbi, changing traditional values and rabbinical functions for the sake of revitalizing the Jewish community, is a religious specialist with middle-of-the-road values, functions, and role aspirations. (5) The Social Reformer organizes and leads social action groups rebuilding the Jewish community and legitimizing liberal-democratic values and goals in terms of prophetic Judaism. (6) The Traditionalistic Reform rabbi also tries to rebuild Jewish civilization about the synagogue, reasserting traditional values and forms which older Reform Judaism repudiated. (7) The Intellectual Reform rabbi has rejected the traditional scholar-saint role and substituted modern Western values for the Jewish value system. His

---

[50] Marshall Sklare, *Conservative Judaism* (Glencoe, Ill.: The Free Press, 1955), pp. 50-52.

[51] *Ibid.*, pp. 159-98, 222-29, 238-41; Albert I. Gordon, *Jews in Transition* (Minneapolis: University of Minnesota Press, 1949), pp. 170-72; Norman Miller, "Changing Patterns of Leadership in the Jewish Community," *Jewish Social Studies*, 17 (July 1955), 179-82.

authority rests on philosophies of humanism, idealism, rationalism, and the scientific method. His major functions parallel those of the liberal Protestant minister whom he emulates.[52]

Roles of the Catholic Priest

The Catholic pastor's roles are similar to those of the Protestant clergyman. Officially charged with "the cure of souls," his duties include supervising parishioners' faith and morals, celebrating the Mass, administering sacraments, instructing the faithful in Christian doctrine, and other duties prescribed by canon law.[53] As *mediator* he is "the special pleader between God and the people, a kind of channel through whom supernatural life flows to the laity, a sort of distribution center for sanctifying grace."[54] As *father* he is an undershepherd charged with the care of souls, providing fatherly care, guidance, and sacramental confession. Two generic roles overlap with all others: The *communal* role views the parishioner as a social being in a matrix of social relationships, and the *administrative* role cuts across many other duties.[55] Roles of the specialized clergy vary according to their particular order, its functions, and its discipline. These orders have shifted historically from a familistic or *Gemeinschaft* type toward the *Gesellschaft* type.[56]

Priests possess a combination of types of authority that may be labeled the "charisma of office." When the pope speaks in the sphere of office (*ex cathedra*) his statements bear weight and must be obeyed. Similarly, the priest's personal life has no direct influence upon such roles as confessor and administrator of the Mass, for his office, not his person, gives him special powers. Charisma has thus been institutionalized in the Catholic bureaucracy.[57] (See Chapter 4.)

Role Conflicts of the Clergy

Many problems emerge in the ministry from tensions and conflicts related to competing demands of multiple roles and problems of establishing self-identification.[58] Six types will be briefly discussed.

---

52 Jerome E. Carlin and Saul H. Mendlovitz, "The American Rabbi: A Religious Specialist Responds to Loss of Authority," in *The Jews,* Marshall Sklare, ed. (Glencoe, Ill.: The Free Press, 1958), pp. 377-414.

53 C. J. Nuesse and Thomas J. Harte, eds., *The Sociology of the Parish* (Milwaukee: Bruce Publishing Co., 1951), p. 5.

54 Joseph H. Fichter, *Social Relations in the Urban Parish* (Chicago: University of Chicago Press, 1954), p. 125.

55 *Ibid.,* pp. 123-37.

56 E. K. Francis, "Toward a Typology of Religious Orders," *American Journal of Sociology,* 55 (Mar. 1950), 437-49.

57 Helen Constas, "Max Weber's Two Concepts of Bureaucracy," *American Journal of Sociology,* 63 (Jan. 1958), 400-9.

58 James M. Gustafson, "An Analysis of the Problem of the Role of the Minister," *Journal of Religion,* 34 (July 1954), 187-91.

1. *Prophet versus institutional leader.* Being a spokesman for God is not always compatible with caring for the church as an institution. Upholding church interests tends to silence God's judgment upon man's institutional behavior. Inroads of time and worrisome concern with administration encroach upon spiritual work. Material favors received for the church may carry hidden price tags of political or business obligation. This clashing of the prophetic preacher with the priestly statesman is evident in southern clergymen. A majority privately favor school desegregation on the basis of religious principles but are compelled to refrain from direct action to promote it. A few are avowedly integrationists or segregationists, but the majority are either *prudent integrationists* who indicate sympathy for integration through one or two public actions but generally avoid public commitment or *"the silent"* who are ambivalent in private view and refuse to take a public stand, "caring for their own people without getting entangled in politics." [59]

The need to uphold tradition hinders the intellectual freedom necessary to cultivate prophetic insights. Routine duties consume time and energy, and laymen withhold information about public and professional life; hence clergymen lack the clarity and conviction needed to preach about the actualities of current life.[60]

2. *Working with individuals versus with groups.* At times the minister is oriented toward personal counseling and help and at times toward working with groups. Shifting from one to the other trying to decide which is more important creates tensions. Spiritual and judgmental functions may be performed well when preaching to a group, but negativistic or critical personal counseling can ruin both the pastor's ministry and the life of his counselee.

3. *Time allocation.* If the minister arranges his schedule around traditional duties, progressive members criticize him as behind the times; if he extends himself in "new" areas of pastoral work, traditionalists say he is untrue to his calling. As ministerial roles become more specific and formal, ambiguity increases. Each clergyman must evaluate his roles and assign to each the time that will best meet the demands of his position. He often feels as if his time is insufficient for any of his functions.[61] Sometimes this is due to inability to tell when he is on or off duty. Feeling subject to call at all times, irritated by trifling interruptions, and perplexed by com-

---

[59] Ernest Q. Campbell and Thomas F. Pettigrew, "Men of God in Racial Crisis," *Christian Century,* 75 (June 4, 1958), 663-65; and "Vignettes from Little Rock," *Christianity and Crisis,* 18 (Sept. 29, 1958), 128-34, 136.

[60] Sperry, "What's Wrong with the Clergy? " and Kenneth W. Underwood, *Protestant and Catholic* (Boston: Beacon Press, 1957), pp. 374-75.

[61] Samuel W. Blizzard, "The Roles of the Rural Parish Minister, the Protestant Seminaries, and the Sciences of Social Behavior," *Religious Education,* 50 (Nov.-Dec. 1955), 383-92; and Samuel W. Blizzard, "The Minister's Dilemma," *Christian Century,* 73 (Apr. 25, 1956), 508-10.

peting duties, ministers have strongly individualistic vocational attitudes and claim longer working hours than their records justify.

Over the past generation the minister's work-time distribution apparently has involved increasing emphasis on administration. In the early 1930's the percentage distribution of weekly work duties of 687 ministers was homiletical, 28.7; pastoral, 24.9; ministerial, 20.7; administrative, 11.4; educational, 5.4; civic, 5.1, and mechanical, 4.0.[62] The average working day of 251 midcentury rural ministers in 22 Protestant denominations was 9 hours and 17 minutes. The role of administrator consumed 37 per cent of his time, followed by pastor (26), preacher and priest (18), organizer (11), and teacher (8 per cent).[63] Rural Missouri ministers in 1952 spent 10.7 hours weekly in visitation, 7.4 in sermon and speech preparation, 6.4 in Bible reading, 5.8 in general reading, 3.3 in the Sunday schedule, 1.9 in conferences, and 1.2 hours in weekday religious services.[64]

4. *Material versus spiritual objectives.* Inner conflicts result from the minister's need to justify his work in "spiritual" terms when so many necessary activities are "non-spiritual." His conscience may lead in directions he cannot go because of realities of social situations. His observable behavior may seem to indicate more concern for worldly success than for clearly spiritual values. The "call of God" is nearly always to a more prosperous church which offers improved material advantages. Self-defenses indicate that such fields have greater "challenge" or "opportunity for service," but inner struggles and problems of social relationships may reflect the intricate web of conflicting values. "All told, the minister is a bit too sensitive about himself as a holy man caught in very earthly situations. With large individual exceptions, the profession at large seems the victim of a mild vocational psychosis." [65] When there is lack of consensus as to his basic role, these problems are accentuated. For instance, Pentecostal bodies retain the ideal of a non-professional, charismatic ministry, yet require institutionalized leadership for their existence. This disparity combines with low social status to accentuate role conflicts and status contradictions.[66]

5. *Specialization versus "general practice."* A multitude of specialized roles and duties are tending to replace the general practitioner. High,

62 H. Paul Douglass and Edmund deS. Brunner, *The Protestant Church as a Social Institution* (New York: Institute of Social and Religious Research, 1935), p. 119.

63 Samuel W. Blizzard, B. B. Maurer, and G. A. Lee, "Rural Ministers—Work Long Day," *Science for the Farmer* (Pa. State University), 3, no. 4 (Spring 1956), 14.

64 Hepple, *Clergymen in Rural Missouri*, pp. 219-28. The data from the studies cited are not strictly comparable, so it is hazardous to speculate on the nature of trends.

65 Douglass and Brunner, *The Protestant Church*, p. 132.

66 Bryan R. Wilson, "The Pentecostalist Minister: Role Conflicts and Status Contradictions," *American Journal of Sociology*, 64 (Mar. 1959), 494-504. Wilson's conclusions are based upon British research but very likely apply to ministers in American groups similarly emerging out of sectarianism into denominationalism.

often unrealistic, expectations cause the conscientious minister to fear failure. He is plagued by guilt feelings and frustration for not having fully done the job. Mental breakdown may result.[67]

6. *Frustrated self-conceptions.* The typical minister thinks preaching is his most important role, followed in order by pastor, priest, teacher, organizer, and administrator. Yet he devotes the most time to administration, the role he likes least. His major criticisms of his profession are lack of sufficient time and conflicts between roles.[68] The rabbi sees scholarship as his dominant role, but this is the one least expected by his congregation. Both inner conflicts and conflict with them and his community result. He hence must compromise and sacrifice, becoming "something of a trapeze artist," in efforts to balance expectations and performance.[69]

Mental illness sometimes results from tensions related to personality or work, deviations from ideal expectations, competition within the profession, economic stringencies, role contradictions, the gulf between ministers and laymen, problems of serving many masters, emotional difficulties, and vocational maladjustments.[70] Like others, ministers who break down tend to come from families with much disharmony and parental rejection. Early fundamentalist faith commonly leads to problems of adjustment when exposed to liberalism. Religious beliefs are clearly a part of ministers' illness.[71] Many "vocational neuroses" are rooted in the nature of the profession. "Guilty knowledge" acquired through hearing confessions and becoming an "expert" on heresy, unholy knowledge, and ungodliness may add to the minister's personal problems.[72] Yet there may be no more mental breakdowns than in other occupations; the ministry is such a public profession that burnout and illness among its personnel are conspicuous.

[67] Wesley Shrader, "Why Ministers Are Breaking Down," *Life,* 41, no. 8 (Aug. 20, 1956), 95-104; and William H. Hudnut, Jr., "Are Ministers Cracking Up? " *Christian Century,* 73 (Nov. 7, 1956), 1288-89.
[68] Samuel W. Blizzard, "Self Image of the Minister as a Community Leader," *Abstracts of Papers and Addresses* (11th meeting, Society for the Scientific Study of Religion, April 21, 1956), pp. 4-5. Laymen also want ministers to concentrate on preaching and pastoral work. Cf. Charles Y. Glock and Philip Roos, "Parishioners' Views of How Ministers Spend Their Time," *Review of Religious Research,* 2 (Spring 1961), 170-75.
[69] Sidney I. Goldstein, "The Roles of an American Rabbi," *Sociology and Social Research,* 38 (Sept.-Oct. 1953), 32-37.
[70] Carl W. Christensen, "The Occurrence of Mental Illness in the Ministry: Introduction," *Journal of Pastoral Care,* 13 (Summer 1959), 79-87; John W. Whitcomb, "The Relationship of Personality Characteristics to the Problems of Ministers," *Religious Education,* 52 (Sept.-Oct. 1957), 371-74; and David Blain, "Fostering the Mental Health of Ministers," in *The Church and Mental Health,* Paul B. Maves, ed. (New York: Charles Scribners Sons, 1953), pp. 253-65.
[71] Carl W. Christensen, "The Occurrence of Mental Illness in the Ministry: Family Origins," *Journal of Pastoral Care,* 14 (Spring 1960), 13-20.
[72] Hughes, *Men and Their Work,* pp. 80-81; and Karl R. Stolz, *The Church and Psychotherapy* (New York: Abingdon-Cokesbury Press, 1943), pp. 230-56.

The Division of Labor in the Ministry

With increasing complexity of society, specialization has increased in the ministry as in other occupations. The typical pastor is expected to perform a multitude of specialized tasks in a more formal manner than a century ago. As the part-time frontier lay preacher was replaced by a full-time, educated, institutional-minded professional, some of the "earthiness" and spontaneity of religious services vanished. Preaching tended to become remote from people's daily lives and problems.[73] Even today religious groups that successfully reach the laboring classes tend to have lay preachers and a high degree of spontaneity and lay participation.

The professional minister was one of the few educated people in the early American community. He was called upon to be the minister, teacher, doctor, lawyer, and adviser on problems of all types. Today he must rely upon others for specialized tasks outside the central area of his ministry. Even the rural minister now needs some specialized training, for the organizations he participates in and the kinds of help available for solving problems are significantly different from those of the city pastor.[74]

The large church may employ a senior pastor, who is in charge of worship services and coordinates all pastoral duties, as well as a minister of music, religious education director, minister of counseling and pastoral care, minister to youth, and church administrator. This multiple ministry makes the pastor's load lighter, clarifies his specific duties, and permits specialized training for specialized tasks. Practical problems associated with such working arrangements arise because the specialties are so new that roles and statuses may not be clearly specified. In addition to specialization within the local church, many clergymen function in institutional settings. Seven types will be briefly discussed.

1. The *military chaplain* serves with officer rank in the armed forces to minister to their members. He conducts religious rites, ceremonies, and services and is a "repository of confidences" who spends much time counseling men in trouble. He is an important channel of communication. Role conflicts occur when chaplains are expected to sponsor social activities they believe to be inconsistent with their role as clergymen. They face problems when they return to civilian life because normal relationships with churches have been severed. The chaplain must minister to people

---

[73] David E. Lindstrom, *Rural Life and the Church* (Champaign, Ill.: The Garrard Press), 1946, pp. 45, 145-46; and David E. Lindstrom, *American Foundations of Religious Liberty* (Champaign, Ill.: The Garrard Press, 1950), p. 44.

[74] Richard O. Comfort, "The Training of the Rural Ministry," *Town and Country Church,* no. 84 (Dec. 1952), 1-2; Carl A. Clark, "Specialized Seminary Training for the Rural Minister," *Review and Expositor,* 52 (July 1955), 336-42; and Samuel W. Blizzard, "The Parish Minister's Self-Image and Variability in Community Culture," *Pastoral Psychology,* 10, no. 97 (Oct. 1959), 27-36.

from many denominations, overriding denominational distinctions and in a sense becoming unfaithful to his own denomination. Should he speak as a military officer or as a messenger of God? Does his position imply approval of war? These and other dilemmas are resolved by compartmentalization and rationalization in which the role of military officer usually takes precedence over the role of clergyman.[75]

2. *Prison chaplains* are employed by large correctional institutions to help rehabilitate inmates through counseling, religious services, and religious and moral education. Many pastors near institutions without full-time chaplains serve prisons, reformatories, or rehabilitation centers on a part-time basis.

3. The *hospital chaplaincy* has ancient historic roots but only recently emerged as a specialty. These clergymen help many patients recover by providing opportunities for worship, religious education, and counseling in which they listen, offer advice, help restore sound judgment, and tie the individual into larger contexts. Psychiatrists and other workers with mental patients sometimes have antipathetic attitudes toward clergymen because unwise types of religious teaching and counseling can do inestimable harm. As more ministers are trained in clinical work and have sufficient psychiatric orientation to recognize the psychiatrist's role without either slighting it or trying to usurp it, the hospital chaplain is increasingly accepted and desired on the clinical staff. By 1950 about one-third of the state hospitals had full-time chaplains, mostly Protestants. Part-time Jewish chaplains were used in about one-third, half of which held weekly Jewish services. Over 90 per cent had Protestant and almost as many had Catholic religious services.[76]

4. *Industrial chaplains* are employed by many large industrial firms to conduct religious services and counsel employees. These chaplains are sometimes criticized as being "captive" either to industrial management, which may employ them for ulterior motives, or to labor. "Christian ethical teachings" easily become rationalizations for privilege of one group or another.[77]

5. The *college chaplain or campus pastor* often has multiple, ambiguous roles which make it difficult to know if his primary task is counseling students, conducting religious services, teaching classes, publicizing the school, or finding outlets for students' "practical" religious assignments.

75 Waldo W. Burchard, "Role Conflicts of Military Chaplains," *American Sociological Review*, 19 (Oct. 1954), 528-35; L. Alexander Harper, "The Chaplain: A New Look," *Christian Century*, 74 (Feb. 13, 1957), 194-96. C. Stanley Lowell, "I Was a Chaplain," *ibid.*, 61 (June 28, 1944), 773-74.

76 *The Mental Health Programs of the Forty-Eight States* (Chicago: The Council of State Governments, 1950), p. 192.

77 C. H. Cleal, "The Work of Industrial Chaplains," *World Dominion*, 33 (Mar.-Apr. 1955), 110-14; and "Captive Chaplains," *Christianity Today*, 2, no. 7 (Jan. 6, 1958), 29.

He may serve a church-related college or sponsor a club-like center adjacent to a public institution's campus.

6. *School chaplains* are hired by private boarding schools to conduct religious services, provide personal counseling, and serve as instructors or dormitory supervisors When their aid results in rebellion against parental standards, they face special problems. Often they have no time during the school year that can justly be called their own.

7. The *village chaplain* employed in suburban Park Forest, Illinois, to work with the police and fire departments may be setting a new pattern for interfaith cooperation. He is a "roving pastor," calling on persons of any religion who may need his help.[78] Clergy similarly are on call to help people by request or referral at many major shopping centers, airports, and motels.

Social Control and Status of the Ministry

Theological seminaries exert control over the ministry through admission and dismissal policies which include personality as well as scholastic standards. During theological training the clergy are given a new formal language, new definitions of their wishes, new reference groups and ego ideals. They are impressed with their dependence upon the professional community for successful placement and advancement and are "punished" for inappropriate beliefs or behavior. The ministry thus tends to become a community without physical locus in the larger society. Stresses and strains between the profession and its clientele are undoubtedly related to variations in social control objectives and patterns of the diverse groups which have been involved in their respective backgrounds. Professional recognition through ordination ceremonies and advancement in the ministry are significantly influenced by seminary personnel.[79]

The profession has an embryonic code of ethics controlling its members. Competition and cooperation among the clergy and the accompanying striving for success also influence many activities. Short pastorates reflect efforts to climb in the profession by changing churches. Much more migration from church to church occurs in congregational denominations than in those with a highly bureaucratic structure. Clergymen's opinions of one another are significant in changes of pastorates, either through recommendations to church pulpit committees or through a presbytery or bishop. If, as in medicine, a tightly-knit "inner circle" of established leaders in an area controls appointments, excludes or penalizes intruders, enforces professional rules, or controls competition, its influence may be of

---

[78] Rev. Joseph L. Hughes as told to Bernard Asbell, "I'm the Whole Town's Chaplain," *Saturday Evening Post,* 232, no. 22 (Nov. 28, 1959), 22-23, 83, 86.

[79] William J. Goode, "Community Within a Community: The Professions," *American Sociological Review,* 22 (Apr. 1957), 194-200; and Hughes, *Men and Their Work,* pp. 31-32, 61.

PROFESSIONAL LEADERSHIP IN THE CHURCH

crucial importance to the careers of new recruits to the ministry. When ambitions to succeed professionally blind a minister to his need to succeed in terms of less tangible religious ideals, he may injure churches and human lives. Honorary degrees and other special preferments are among the instruments used in the competitive struggle.[80]

The most effective control over typical Protestant clergymen is the church congregation. Striving for status is reflected in many relationships with members. Ministers who wish to maintain influence over their congregations almost invariably are forced to compromise or silence convictions on issues tinged with social, political, or economic implications. Thus many "have surrendered all they have to preach about in order to keep the privilege of preaching."[81] Soon after entering the ministry, most clergymen who once thought of the church as an instrument of social reform become adjusted to their members' standards and focus attention upon personal sins and religious consolation for human problems. Those who do not adjust often are forced out of the church or even out of the ministry. The majority try to cure societal problems by converting individuals, but these efforts usually support the status quo and are ineffective in dealing with socioeconomic problems.[82] When the Protestant Episcopal Church takes a partisan position on a social issue, its ministers usually adopt this view in spite of opposition from members. When the denomination compromises on an issue, the minister tends to compromise with the views of his members.[83] Theoretically the influence of parishioners on pastors should be greater in congregational than in episcopal bodies, and the presbyterian type should fall between the two.

Church members' images of the clergy contribute to ministers' self-conceptions and to the structuring of their activities. Deliberate selection policies and subtle social controls after a pastor is installed in a church tend to make him emphasize the roles most expected from him.[84] Prox-

[80] Myles W. Rodehaver and Luke M. Smith, "Migration and Occupational Structure: The Clergy," *Social Forces,* 29 (May 1951), 416-21; Myles W. Rodehaver, "Ministers on the Move: A Study of Mobility in Church Leadership," *Rural Sociology,* 13 (Dec. 1948), 400-10; Luke M. Smith, "The Clergy: Authority, Structure, Ideology, Migration," *American Sociological Review,* 18 (June 1953), 242-48; Oswald Hall, "The Stages of a Medical Career," *American Journal of Sociology,* 53 (Mar. 1948), 327-36; Ray H. Abrams, "The Clergy and Their Honorary Degrees," *Crozer Quarterly,* 11 (Apr. 1934), 190-204.

[81] Arthur L. Swift, Jr., *New Frontiers of Religion* (New York: The Macmillan Co., 1938), p. 113.

[82] *Ibid.,* pp. 113-14; Liston Pope, *Millhands and Preachers* (New Haven: Yale University Press, 1942), pp. 143-61, 203; and Jerome Davis, "The Social Action Pattern of the Protestant Religious Leader," *American Sociological Review,* 1 (Feb. 1936), 105-114.

[83] Charles Y. Glock and Benjamin B. Ringer, "Church Policy and the Attitudes of Ministers and Parishioners on Social Issues," *American Sociological Review,* 21 (Apr. 1956), 148-56.

[84] Luke M. Smith, "Laymen's Images of Parish Clergymen," *Proceedings* (Society for the Scientific Study of Religion, Fall meeting, 1958), p. 11.

imity of his residence to the church probably is related to the degree of
control that the congregation exercises over him.[85] Popular fiction using
clergymen as leading characters minimizes their liturgical roles, organizational ability, pulpit oratory, and theological learning. "Sincerity, unselfish
concern for the poor and outcast, fearless denunciation of evil from the
pulpit, and wise, sympathetic counsel to the erring and perplexed" are
extolled and admired.[86] The writers reflect the values Americans generally desire in clergymen.

In colonial America the ministry was one of seven professional occupations, but by 1936 its duties and privileges were shared by over 290
others. By 1790 declining esteem for the ministry was evident; the mer-
chant and politician gradually replaced it in functional community leadership. The clergyman's social status is still colored by past high prestige.
Among disadvantaged minorities he still serves as the chief professional
aid of the sub-society with a role comparable to that of colonial times.[87]
Prestige scales rank clergymen high in contemporary society, with missionaries only slightly lower. Among 24 occupations the clergy was recently rated highest for honesty and ethical standards.[88]

Educational demands on the clergy and their status in society are directly related to the socioeconomic level of the denomination's membership. People in churches with high prestige seek clergymen who will
further enhance the church's standing and competitive membership recruitment. The demands and facilities for an educated ministry are thus
both cause and effect of the class level of a denomination's membership.[89] This undoubtedly is related to the failure of denominations with
the best educated ministry to meet the needs and interests of lower class
people.

Success in the Ministry

Although people grant clergymen high social status, they mercilessly
criticize their weaknesses and faults. Methodist laymen, who perhaps are
typical of Protestants, desire ministers who stress denominational loyalty,

---

[85] Stanley H. Chapman, "The Contemporary Pastorate," *American Sociological Review*, 9 (Dec. 1944), 597-602.

[86] Gilbert P. Voigt, "The Protestant Minister in American Fiction," *Lutheran Quarterly*, 11 (Feb. 1959), 1-13. Voigt analyzed 50 ministerial characters in fiction "that deserves to be called literary."

[87] Stanley H. Chapman, "The Minister: Professional Man of the Church," *Social Forces*, 23 (Dec. 1944), 202-6.

[88] Theodore Caplow, *The Sociology of Work* (Minneapolis: University of Minnesota Press, 1954), pp. 53-55, and Princeton Religion Research Center, *Religion in America 1982* (Princeton, N.J.: The Gallup Poll, 1982), p. 14.

[89] Pope, *Millhands and Preachers*, p. 116. Variations in the influence of Protestant and Catholic clergy upon beliefs, attitudes, and behavior patterns related to social class mobility are analyzed in Gerhard Lenski, *The Religious Factor* (Garden City, N.Y.: Doubleday and Co., 1961), pp. 256-87.

cooperate with other denominations in Thanksgiving and pre-Easter services, preach against liquor, and proclaim equal opportunities and responsibilities for all races and nationalities. They do not want ministers who are apologetic for being in the ministry, give an impression of pessimism or defeatism in preaching on church goals, hesitate to take the initiative on Christian issues, fail to spend adequate time in study, fail to start services punctually, lack dignity in ministerial functions, have annoying pulpit mannerisms, make grammatical mistakes, speak indistinctly, are hesitant and bashful in meeting people, do not furnish challenging leadership for men as well as women and children, permit an individual or group to control church policies, show intolerance toward those who disagree with them, are undemocratic in church affairs, are anti-Semitic, soft-pedal missionary giving to boost the local church budget, appear untidy, have bad breath or noticeable body odor, are lax in meeting financial obligations, lose control of their tempers, do not get along well with their wives, or are divorced. Remarkably high agreement was found between lay leaders, youth, women, and Methodist Youth Council members.[90]

Laymen emphasize clergymen's personal attributes more than those of most other professions. They are expected to meet professional qualifications of education and experience, but also to be personally likable, friendly, sincere, tactful, sympathetic, adaptable to all types of people in a wide variety of group situations, level-headed, and good conversationalists with a sense of humor. Emphasis on personal qualifications minimizes social factors significantly related to success in the ministry. Concepts of success in bureaucratic, sacramental churches emphasize fulfillment of formal ritual duties and conformity to tradition; charismatic, instrumentalist churches use the offices, structure, and ritual as means toward achieving a series of goals.[91] The highly controlled, authoritarian setting of the military or prison chaplaincy—in contrast to the permissive atmosphere of the democratic church—means its demands upon clergymen are significantly different. The primary group qualities of much rural life (in contrast to city anonymity), social class differences in moral standards and daily life habits, variations related to members' ethnic backgrounds, and differences in community traditions are related to the minister's success. If he understands the implications of divergent social characteristics, he can adjust to them and meet people's needs successfully; if not, he can fail miserably. Unfortunately, many ministers are woefully ignorant of the communities they serve.[92] Sometimes the minister is expected mirac-

---

[90] Murray H. Leiffer, *The Layman Looks at the Minister* (New York: Abingdon-Cokesbury Press, 1947). The items listed here represent those on which 90 per cent or more of the 1,500 respondents agreed.

[91] Smith, "The Clergy: Authority, Structure, Ideology, Migration."

[92] Facts about 117 cities were compared with ratings given these cities on a series of scales. The coefficient of correlation of opinions of clergymen with facts was only .36 compared to .59 for educators. See Edward Lee Thorndike, "Facts vs. Opinions: An

ulously to increase church membership in a community of diminishing population, to reduce delinquency in a society which creates and abets it, or to bring into the church persons who have few social characteristics in common with its members.

Success in the ministry as indicated by advancement, in contrast to such professions as law and medicine, usually depends upon frequent moving to new places of employment. Relatively few "successful" Protestant and Jewish clergymen spend most of their professional careers in a single community. Those who do are judged successful because they have built large congregations.[93] Climbing the ladder of professional success is evident in Catholicism as well as Protestantism and Judaism. The best example is seen in the success of an illiterate peasant's son who became the Supreme Pontiff—Pope John XXIII.

Personal background is related to Methodist ministers' success as measured by salaries. The most successful are more likely than others to come from small families, to have well-educated parents and professional or proprietor fathers, to live in a large community and attend large schools in childhood, to have a high degree of intercommunity residential mobility, to begin high school at an early age, to have more education, and to major in the social sciences or philosophy rather than religion in college. They were accepted by parents as equals at an earlier age, and their mothers viewed the ministry favorably. This background apparently is related to the social skills which enable maintaining a good reputation even when subjected to the tests of gossip which raise or lower prestige and influence church attendance and contributions, thereby affecting bishops' appointments.[94]

Social Problems of the Clergy

In addition to the difficulties associated with recruitment, education, role conflicts, long working hours, competition, increasing specialization, bureaucratization, social control, and social climbing already suggested, many ministers face other problems, nine of which follow.

1. *Low income.* From 1929 to 1949 the incomes of employees of religious organizations dropped from $200 above to $750 below the national

---

Empirical Study of 117 Cities," *Public Opinion Quarterly*, 2 (Jan. 1938), 85-90. The situation may have improved since that time.

[93] "Success in the ministry" as typically defined involves circular reasoning and evaluation on the basis of cultural norms. Normative "spiritual" criteria like those listed in the Bible (I Tim. 3:1-7; Titus 1:5-11, etc.) deviate sharply from some current cultural values.

[94] Philip J. Allen, "Childhood Backgrounds of Success in a Profession," *American Sociological Review*, 20 (Apr. 1955), 186-90. See also James Otis Smith and Gideon Sjoberg, "Origins and Career Patterns of Leading Protestant Clergymen," *Social Forces*, 39 (May 1961), 290-96.

average income. No other occupational group suffered such a great loss. A parallel situation prevailed in Canada.[95] Marked improvements have since occurred in most denominations. In 1981 the median weekly earnings of clergy in the Current Population Survey were $284, compared to $289 for all full-time workers; the $285 for male clergy was far below the $347 average for all males.[96] As of 1956, ministers in home missions enterprises receiving part or all of their income from a denominational agency had salaries considerably below those needed to maintain a modest but adequate level of living according to Bureau of Labor Statistics standards. Ministers' salaries were about on a par with accounting clerks who worked under supervision of trained bookkeepers. They were below those of carpenters, electricians, auto mechanics, painters, pipe-fitters, plumbers, truck drivers, and many other skilled laborers.[97]

Salaries vary by denomination, type of church served, educational preparation, and subsidiary benefits received. Inclusion of ministers under the Social Security Act in the 1950's helped raise salaries as many churches made their pastors qualify for the maximum benefits, available in 1960 only to persons with incomes of at least $4,800. The low incomes of ministers, many of whom have as much formal education as the minimum required for a Ph.D. or M.D. degree, may reflect the rural orientation of many churches. The clergy are expected to serve out of love for God rather than for material gain. Salaries seldom keep pace with inflation. Fringe benefits like discounts on purchases, reduced fares on transportation lines, free admission tickets, contributions of food, and other material gifts reduce the problem. Yet conspicuous consumption, forced upon many clergymen, leads them to live beyond their means with resulting difficulty in paying bills. Recruitment problems are no doubt related to low incomes.

2. *Old age and retirement.* Many ministers, especially outside denominations with pension plans, have faced severe economic difficulties in old age. Owning no home at retirement, the minister with limited financial resources is tempted to stay in active service longer than is advisable for either his personal welfare or that of his church. Churches fearing "life sentence" pastorates refuse to call ministers in the later decades of their careers for fear they might "settle down" and refuse to retire after abilities seriously decline. Stereotyped ideas about older men and desires to appeal to youth, to have outstanding pastors at low salaries, and to influence the pastor all incline churches toward youthful ministers. As a

---

[95] U.S. Dept. of Commerce statistics reported by Willmar Thorkelson, "This Week in Religion," Minneapolis *Star,* Oct. 13, 1951, p. 6; and editorial, "Pastors' Pay Under Street Sweepers'," *Christian Century,* 66 (Mar. 9, 1949), 292-93.

[96] Bureau of Labor Statistics, "1981 Weekly Earnings of Men and Women Compared in 100 Occupations," U.S. Dept. of Labor, March 7, 1982, Table 3.

[97] Anne O. Lively, *Incomes of Home Missions Ministers* (New York: Bureau of Research and Survey, National Council of Churches, 1956). Sampling bias in this study of ministers in 14 major Protestant denominations favored the younger, better-educated, and slightly better-paid ministers in the North Central region of the U.S.

result, many are "laid on the shelf" by their fifties. With educational standards rising and retirement age falling, the minister's professional career is being cut short at both ends.[98] A marginal economic position, dependence upon charity after a life of service, forced unemployment before retirement age, and loss of power and influence contribute to clergymen's problems of old age.[99]

3. *Family pressures.* The ministry continues to be a rural-type occupation involving the entire family. The parson's wife is expected to participate in church activities. Members don't want "solemn saints," "wifely pastor's assistants," or "protecting mother models" in the parsonage. Yet the need to provide special training for the minister's wife is not met by most theological seminaries.[100] Children of the clergy often are expected to be paragons of virtue; if they are like other children, the minister may be severely censured. Yet they are more likely to enter the ministry than other youths, and many more than their statistical share have become famous.

4. *Short tenure.* Protestant pastorates are shortest in marginal rural churches, typically averaging only two or three years, somewhat longer in successful rural churches, and longest in highly developed, successful city churches. Ministerial moves often involve relatively great distances. The frequency and distance of moving have led some to classify the ministry as a "nomadic occupation."[101] Because of short tenure, many pastors are frustrated. Hoping to lead a congregation, they often must subserviently follow its members, even sacrificing principles to do so. Difficulties are multiplied if preceding clergymen have left unpaid bills, personal enmities, or a reputation for indecency because of a belief that the end justifies the means in the battle against sin. Loyalties may have been built around a charismatic minister who won disciples to himself rather than to the church, or an overly competent pastor may have done nearly all the church's work without using lay leadership. The new minister may then find it impossible to meet the standards expected of him.[102]

---

[98] John Irving Daniel, "Premium on Youth," *Christian Century,* 65 (May 19, 1948), 478-80; and Aute L. Carr, "Are Ministers Obsolete at 50?" *ibid.,* 75 (Apr. 16, 1958), 463-64. Social security legislation covering ministers may counteract this trend.

[99] Donald L. Hibbard and John Park Lee, "Presbyterian Ministers and Their Widows in Retirement," *Journal of Gerontology,* 9 (Jan. 1954), 46-55; E. H. Moore and C. Hammer, "Ministers in Retirement," *Sociology and Social Research,* 32 (July-Aug. 1948), 920-27; Justin Wroe Nixon, "Parity for Pastors," *Christian Century,* 69 (Feb. 6, 1952), 154-56; and Ethel Shanas and Robert J. Havighurst, "Retirement in Four Professions," *Journal of Gerontology,* 8 (Apr. 1953), 212-21.

[100] Betsy Rupman Deekins, "Model Wives for the Clergy," *Church Management,* 33, no. 3 (Dec. 1956), 28; and Louise M. Porter, "Have Experience, Will Teach," *ibid.,* 35, no. 12 (Sept. 1959), 44-45.

[101] Vincent H. Whitney and Charles M. Grigg, "Patterns of Mobility Among a Group of Families of College Students," *American Sociological Review,* 23 (Dec. 1958), 643-52.

[102] Graham R. Hodges, "The Crime of the Omnicompetent Clergyman," *Church Management,* 30, no. 6 (Mar. 1954), and Anonymous, "A Much-Maligned Man Talks Back!" *ibid.,* 33, no. 3 (Dec. 1956), 20, 30-31.

5. *Social change.* Changes in the church and in society create problems. The minister is "caught between the times" as changing patterns of specialized duties are expected of him for meager financial rewards. He may have memorized a "catalog of sins" that became outmoded as time-linked cultural items went out of date. Memorized Bible passages from old versions seem strange to a generation reared on the Revised Standard Version. The liturgy of some denominations has changed as new books of worship have been adopted. "Yesterday the minister knew what was proper during divine worship. Tomorrow he will know again. Meanwhile, he is caught in an experimental, ambiguous phase between the times."[103] Change, including efforts to overcome sexism, proceeds slowly.

6. *Personal isolation.* Professional responsibilities impede close friendships in the community he serves. Efforts to prevent all semblance of favoritism may prohibit a sense of belonging or of feeling wanted when he has no friend in whom to confide at times of personal and professional problems.

7. *Crime in the ministry.* Occasionally a clergyman is apprehended for a criminal offense. Like the medical doctor, the minister is sometimes tempted by sexually frustrated women in his parish. When he commits an offense, it is likely to receive much more publicity than comparable deeds by other persons. It may be projection more than fact that makes ministers the subject of gossip alleging sexual irregularities. White-collar crime occurs in the ministry; misrepresentation of education through shortcut degrees sold by diploma vendors is a borderline case. As in other occupations, the full extent of these offenses is unknown.[104]

8. *Part-time pastorates.* The "yoking" of churches by which one minister serves two or more congregations is more common among major than minor denominations, perhaps because they have more churches close enough to permit such circuits. Economically poor communities, areas of low population density, and regions with a large number of competing denominations are apt to have "divided pastors" shared by more than one congregation. Part-time pastorates by students, semi-retired ministers, and lay preachers have similar causes and effects. Pastoral visitation, attendance at conferences, and services provided to the people all suffer in this kind of arrangement. The claims of two vocations may also tear the pastor inwardly. Yet only at such costs are many marginal churches able to remain in operation. These problems are especially acute among such groups as rural blacks.[105]

9. *Women Clergy.* The admission of women into the ministry results

---

[103] Clarence Seidenspinner, "Between the Times," *Christian Century,* 65 (Oct. 20, 1948), 1108-9.
[104] Crime in the ministry has not been systematically studied, but temptations of clergymen are common subjects of popular literature, movies, and television.
[105] Harry W. Roberts, "The Rural Negro Minister: His Work and Salary," *Rural Sociology,* 12 (Sept. 1947), 284-94.

partly from economic limitations of church resources. At least 77 bodies ordain or license women for the ministry; major denominations are gradually liberalizing provisions enabling them to enter the ministry. In the 1981 Current Population Survey only 5.0 per cent of all clergy (about 14,100) were women, but in 1982 they comprised a fourth (23.7 per cent) of the students in theological schools. They face special problems of prejudice, credibility, placement, rivalry, and ordination. Yet there is growing support for women in that career. Sect-type and liberal bodies are more open to employing them than denominations closest to the church-type. The Minnesota Poll in 1956 found 59 per cent of respondents open to having a woman as religious leader of a church and 35 per cent opposed. Men were both more willing and less opposed than women.[106]

Conclusion

Difficulties associated with the profession accentuate the problems of recruitment to the ministry. Following significant shortages of clergy during the 1950's and early 1960's in most mainline Protestant bodies, the membership declines and accompanying budgetary problems led to staff reductions even as priorities were shifted from church planting to social justice. Employment prospects are less bright for their seminarians than for those in the growing evangelical and fundamentalist churches. The steady increase of Catholics has not been matched by equivalent growth in the number of priests (from 55,581 in 1962 to 58,085 in 1982), so 843 parishes were without resident clergy in 1982, and lay deacons are now performing duties once limited to priests. The decline of brothers and sisters in Catholic religious orders (from 184,853 in 1962 to 129,250 in 1982) poses many additional problems.[107]

Such difficulties, however, may help to resolve other problems. When churches compete for ministerial candidates, they become more willing to pay appropriate salaries, and when the candidates compete for positions, they may adapt better to local needs. Increased professionalization of the ministry forces some marginal churches to unite, thus becoming more efficient. The shortage in the growing conservative groups, however, encourages ambitious persons who are incapable of meeting the strenuous demands of a college-plus-seminary education to secure short-cut training and find congregations willing to become victims of faulty theology, weak preaching, and misguided pastoral methods.

---

[106] Bureau of Labor Statistics, *Labor Force Statistics Derived from the Current Population Survey: A Databook*, Vol. I (Washington, D.C.: Government Printing Office, 1982), Bulletin 2096, p. 664; Barbara Brown Zikmund, "Women in Ministry Face the '80s," *Christian Century*, 99, no. 4, (Feb. 3–10, 1982), 113–15; "Public Approves Idea of Women in Clergy," Minnesota Poll Release, Minneapolis *Sunday Tribune*, July 22, 1956.

[107] Jacquet, *Yearbook*, p. 259; Bureau of Labor Statistics, *Occupational Outlook Handbook*, 1982–83 Edition (Washington, D.C.: Government Printing Office, 1982), pp. 124–28.

Frustrations in the ministry make many a clergyman "an isolated, lonely, tired individual who is cut off from the fulfillment of the . . . basic functions in society that offer him personal satisfaction in fulfilling his call to service."[108] Prevented by social pressures from living as they believe men ought to live, frustrated by an unfulfillable self-image of the minister as one ordained to a holy calling, filled with vocational guilt for spending major blocks of time on "pointless parish piddling," disillusioned by the politics of professional advancement, embittered by the bureaucracy that makes them office managers, committee maneuverers, and publicity directors instead of scholars and preachers of God's Word, sensing the double standard which expects the clergy and their families to live according to different ethical and moral standards from laymen, and sometimes sensing cleavages between doctrinal, social, political, or economic beliefs and what they are expected to preach, many ministers resolve their inner struggles by entering other vocations. The problems and frustrations of the clergy are not all unique. They reflect a culture with increasing specialization in all vocations which is filled with inconsistencies and paradoxes and dominated by secular values.

The ministry provides numerous satisfactions which are lacking in other vocations. The clergy get more attention than many other occupational groups because they touch the lives of a substantial proportion of the nation's people. The vast majority are well adjusted and happy in their service to God and man.[109]

Selected References

Carroll, Jackson W., Barbara J. Hargrove, and Adair T. Lummis, *Women of the Cloth: New Opportunity for the Churches.* San Francisco: Harper and Row, 1983. Sociological study of women as clergy.

Carroll, Jackson W., and Robert L. Wilson, *Too Many Pastors? The Clergy Job Market.* New York: Pilgrim Press, 1980. Research in 12 denominations on reasons for and consequences of the oversupply of clergy, plus suggestions for action.

Davies, Horton, *A Mirror of the Ministry in Modern Novels.* New York: Arno, 1970 (Oxford University Press, 1959). A survey of portraits of the clergy in novels by 15 authors since 1850.

Douglas, William, *Ministers' Wives.* New York: Harper and Row, 1965. Findings of involvement in ministry, motivations, meanings, fulfillments, frustrations, and other topics from questionnaires and in-depth interviews.

Ebaugh, Helen Rose Fuchs, *Out of the Cloister: A Study of Organizational Dilemmas.* Austin: University of Texas Press, 1977. A sociologist's study of Catholic religious orders for women, including struggles of change from 1960 to the early 1970's and nuns' reasons for staying and leaving.

Fichter, Joseph H., *Organization Man in the Church.* Cambridge, Mass. Schenk-

---

[108] Oates, *The Christian Pastor,* p. 62.

[109] Paul Arthur, "The Sacrifices I Make to Stay in the Ministry," *Church Management,* 35, no. 2 (Nov. 1958), 12; Raymond E. Gibson, "Don't Pity the Parson," *Christian Century,* 76 (July 1, 1959), 778-79; and Paul Waitman Hoon, "Building Up Breaking-Down Parsons," *ibid.,* 74 (Nov. 6, 1957), 1313-14.

man Publishing Co., 1974. Church personnel, ecclesiastical structures, and the social world of American Catholicism.

Fichter, Joseph H., *The Rehabilitation of Clergy Alcoholics: Ardent Spirits Subdued*. New York: Health Sciences Press, 1982. Research on the problems, treatment, recovery, and ministry of alcoholic clergy.

Hadden, Jeffrey K., *The Gathering Storm in the Churches*. Garden City, N.Y.: Doubleday and Co., 1969. Survey research showing significant contrasts between the clergy and laity in Protestantism which reflect underlying structural tensions and theological differences.

Hamilton, Charles, *The Black Preacher in America*. New York: William Morrow, 1972. The black minister as leader of the black community as well as of the church, its primary institution.

James, E. O., *The Nature and Function of Priesthood*. New York: Vanguard Press, 1955. An anthropological review and analysis of literature on the priesthood in the religions which fed into Christianity.

Menges, Robert J., and James E. Dittes, *Psychological Studies of Clergymen: Abstracts of Research*. New York: Thomas Nelson and Sons, 1965. Supplement I, *Ministry Studies,* 1, no. 3 (Oct. 1967), 1–79. An excellent tool for discovering resource materials on most aspects of the ministry.

Niebuhr, H. Richard, and Daniel D. Williams, eds., *The Ministry in Historical Perspective*. New York: Harper and Row, 1983 (1956). The historical development of the Protestant ministry since the Reformation.

Oates, Wayne E., *The Christian Pastor,* rev. ed. Philadelphia: Westminster, 1981. A pastoral psychologist's analysis of the role of the Christian pastor and his functions as a "man of crisis" with practical suggestions for "the average pastor in a specific church."

Pruyser, Paul W., *The Minister as Diagnostician*. Philadelphia: Westminster, 1976. An analysis of pastoral care which strongly argues that clergy should not try to be second-rate psychologists or psychiatrists but should have their own unique role.

Quinley, Harold E., *The Prophetic Clergy: Social Activism among Protestant Ministers*. New York: John Wiley and Sons, 1974. Report of a survey of 1,580 parish clergy in nine Protestant denominations in California.

Rudge, Peter F., *Ministry and Management*. London: Tavistock Publications, 1968. "The Study of Ecclesiastical Administration" from the viewpoint of organizational theory and other social science perspectives.

Samson, A'Delbert, *Church Pastors in Four Agricultural Settings in Montana*. Bozeman, Mont.: Agricultural Extension Service Bulletin 539, April 1958. A sociological analysis of the clergy in four areas of Montana.

Schuller, David S., Merton P. Strommen, and Milo L. Brekke, eds., *Ministry in America*. San Francisco: Harper and Row, 1980. A report and analysis of assessment criteria, models, and areas of ministry based on a massive in-depth survey of 47 U.S. and Canadian denominations.

Ziegler, Jesse H., ed., "Education for Ministry in Aging: Gerontology in Seminary Training," *Theological Education,* 16, no. 3 (special issue, Winter 1980), 267–414. Papers, project abstracts, guidelines, strategies, models, and references related to the project of the National Interfaith Coalition on Aging to stimulate ministries with, for, and by aging and elderly people.

Part Nine: *Conclusion*

🏛   Chapter **19**

Change with Continuity:
From the 1960's to the 1980's

Change is so continual in American religion, even as it is in modern society, that it can be argued that the only thing "permanent" is change.[1] Individuals change their beliefs, behavior, roles, affiliations, social identity, and sometimes their worldview as they pass through the life cycle. Religious institutions at all levels—congregations and parishes, denominations, parachurch associations, and ecumenical organizations— similarly change over time. The same applies to the scholarly disciplines that study religion. Yet when one seeks common themes and threads that run through the past, present, and evolving future, it is amazing how much remains basically the same.

Even in the systematic study of religion, the accumulation of scholarship is not far beyond the early classical studies. Recent scholars have a tendency to forget the basic questions raised by classical writers, to elevate them to a "sainthood" that hampers new work, to identify themselves with one or another of the masters, ignoring the others, and to separate theory from quantitative data.[2] In addition, each generation tends to focus its attention upon new sets of questions while humanity remains basically the same from age to age, with only peripheral details changing

---

[1] See David O. Moberg, "The Christian and Social Change," *Paraclete: Journal of the National Association of Christians in Social Work,* 4 (Summer 1977), 3-25.

[2] Charles Y. Glock and Phillip E. Hammond, eds., *Beyond the Classics: Essays in the Scientific Study of Religion* (New York: Harper and Row, 1973), pp. 409-11.

significantly. Although numerous, most changes represent only minor variations in the way in which relatively stable religious realities are expressed and handled.[3]

That may be why, during revision of the first edition of this book, it became apparent that its generalizations are still quite up-to-date. Even the implications for action needed little more than minor adaptations of factual details. Nevertheless, it is appropriate to sketch some pertinent recent developments, supplementing those indicated in the list of selected references at the end of each chapter.

Characteristics of American Religion

The dominant religion in America is still Protestantism, although the Catholic Church is slowly gaining in proportionate membership strength. The *1983 Yearbook of American and Canadian Churches* reports that 59.7 per cent of the population are members of a church, but this is a conservative figure because many religious groups are omitted, some have only old statistics, and in many bodies children who are active participants are ineligible for membership. For the 1983 *Yearbook* the Church of God in Christ headquartered in Memphis reported an increase of 3,300,000 over its previous 425,000 as of 1970; and the Church of Jesus Christ of Latter-day Saints (Mormons) included unbaptized youths for the first time: they account for 650,000 of its 3,500,000 members. Other large percentage increases occurred in the Church of God based in Cleveland, Tennessee (5.01 per cent), the Assemblies of God (3.23 per cent), and the Seventh-day Adventist Church (3.05 per cent).[4] Among the large omitted groups are the Church of Christ, Scientist, which may have 250,000 or more members, and the Native American Church of North America, a cult centering on the ceremonial use of peyote, which claims 400,000.[5] Thousands more are members of the other 1,000-plus groups Melton has identified.[6] Still more are in the independent congregations that have sprung up over the past generation; some of these carry names indicative of a denominational family (Baptist, etc.), while others are community churches, transdenominational fellowships, part of the charismatic movement, or "just Christian," usually emphasizing an evangelical orientation centered on faith in Jesus Christ and the authority of the Bible. A majority of their members have come from other Christian bodies, so the overall

---

[3] For example, Christians historically have centered these universals around human nature: people are created in God's image, but this includes autonomy, or "freewill"; all succumb to the temptation to sin, so changes in society alone, however important, cannot accomplish human perfection.

[4] "Churches Claim Gain in Members," *Milwaukee Journal,* July 2, 1983, p. 4.

[5] David B. Barrett, ed., *World Christian Encyclopedia* (Nairobi, Kenya: Oxford University Press, 1982), p. 718.

[6] J. Gordon Melton with James V. Geisendorfer, *A Directory of Religious Bodies in the United States* (New York: Garland Publishing, 1977), pp. 8-9.

picture may be like a "circulation of elites" shifting from one congregation to another.

Significant changes have occurred in Catholicism since the Second Vatican Council (1962-1965). Use of the vernacular instead of Latin in the Mass has made its worship services intelligible to persons reared outside that Church who see significant similarities to "high church" Episcopalianism and Lutheranism. This may be part of the reason for the increasing proportion of the population whose religious preference is Catholic— a rise from 20 per cent in 1947 to 28 per cent in 1981, while Protestant preference fell from 69 to 59 per cent.[7]

Catholics increasingly cooperate with non-Catholics in a wide variety of programs; regulations limiting interfaith activities have been relaxed for almost all non-sacramental functions. Increased cooperation has also been evident from the Protestant, Jewish, and Orthodox sides, so not all of this change is in the direction of a "protestantization" of Catholicism. Some Protestant groups have adopted liturgical components of worship which once would have been labeled "strictly Catholic," and there is a much freer two-way exchange of religious music than in the past.

Changes are occurring in Judaism as well. The Arab-Israeli Six Day War in 1967 and subsequent events in Israel stimulated interest in community life. In March 1983 the Central Conference of American Rabbis (Reform Jews) approved a resolution defying the traditional Jewish law which accords Jewish status only to those children whose mothers are Jewish. To the consternation of Orthodox Jews, that resolution declares that a child of a mixed marriage shall be presumed to be Jewish regardless of which parent is a Jew.[8] Since about 1971 Rabbi Francis Barry Silberg has conducted a Brit Chayyim ceremony of life for girls, parallel to the Brit Milah covenant of circumcision for male babies; this ceremony for girls has been included in at least one Reform Jewish prayer book.[9] Even though there has been increased solidarity within the Jewish community as a whole through its support of Israel since the Six Day War, events like these contribute to intra-Jewish tensions.

Overarching the developments within each religious family is increased attention to the thesis that America has a civil religion. Expressed in a set of beliefs, symbols, and rituals linked with the idea that political structures and events are part of a transcendental dimension by which God is at work, it gives the nation a divine destiny. The biblical symbols of chosen people, promised land, and New Jerusalem are invoked on behalf of the public domain. Yet this coexists with religious pluralism on the private level, so no one specific religion is singled out as "correct," and divergent

[7] Princeton Religion Research Center, *Religion in America 1982* (Princeton, N.J.: The Gallup Poll, 1982), p. 23.

[8] "Definition Splits Jews," *Milwaukee Journal,* June 25, 1983, p. 4.

[9] Gretchen Schuldt, "Girls Initiated into Jewish Faith," *Milwaukee Sentinel,* July 2, 1983, part 1, p. 7.

values sometimes are identified as its characteristics. Allegedly this admixture allows for satisfaction both of society's needs for cohesion and commitment by its members and of personal needs for identity and belonging by the same social processes, but the extent to which it actually accomplishes this is not fully established.[10] Whether there really is a national civil religion is still an open question; the answer depends partly upon how loosely "religion" can be defined.

Other recent developments include the growth of evangelicalism, the charismatic movement, the "electronic church," and the parachurch movement. "Evangelical" is the label now preferred by most of the theologically conservative Protestants who dislike being called "fundamentalists." By the early 1970's it was apparent that most mainline Protestant bodies were declining while evangelical groups continued to grow. When Jimmy Carter, openly declaring himself to be a born-again Christian, was elected President of the U.S. in 1976, the terms "evangelical" and "born-again" became so popular that they were used in a wide variety of both secular and religious ways. Many religious leaders and organizations that once labeled themselves as "liberal" or "neo-orthodox" identified themselves with the word "evangelical," although their definitions often deviated from that of such groups as the National Association of Evangelicals.

National surveys using a narrow definition (born-again Christians who have encouraged other people to believe in Jesus Christ and who believe in a literal interpretation of the Bible) concluded that from 17 to 19 per cent of adults were evangelicals.[11] Scattered among all the Christian denominations, but mostly Protestant, they were more likely than others to be personally involved in charitable activities, to have a right-wing political ideology, to rate themselves high in the quality of their Christian life, to attend church more than once a week, to watch religious programs on television, to read the Bible daily, to be members of Bible study or prayer and meditation groups, to be part of the charismatic renewal movement, to consider religious faith as the most important influence in their lives, to try hard to put their religious beliefs into practice, to hold orthodox Christian beliefs, to receive personal comfort and support from their religious beliefs, and to be very happy.[12]

The charismatic movement in Catholicism did not become a schismatic

---

[10] Robert N. Bellah, "Civil Religion in America," *Daedalus*, 96 (Winter 1967), 1-21; Robert N. Bellah, *The Broken Covenant: American Civil Religion in Time of Trial* (New York: Seabury, 1975); John A. Coleman, "Civil Religion," *Sociological Analysis*, 31, no. 2 (Summer 1970), 67-77; Phillip Hammond, "The Sociology of American Civil Religion: A Bibliographical Essay," *Sociological Analysis*, 37, no. 2 (Summer 1976), 169-82; Meredith B. McGuire, *Religion: The Social Context* (Belmont, Calif.: Wadsworth, 1981), pp. 151-58; Gail Gehrig, *American Civil Religion: An Assessment* (Storrs, Conn.: Society for the Scientific Study of Religion, 1981).
[11] Princeton Religion Research Center, *Religion in America 1982*, pp. 31-32. In 1982 35 per cent claimed to be born again; 45 per cent had encouraged someone to believe in Jesus Christ; 37 per cent held a literal view of the Bible.
[12] *Ibid.*, pp. 33-35, 91, 101-13, 119-28.

sect; it was absorbed into the Church because charismatics were among the Church's most faithful members.[13] Most charismatic groups draw members from across denominational boundaries and thus serve as mediating bodies in their emphasis upon the Holy Spirit and personal religious experience.[14]

The "electronic church," which consists of religious radio and television broadcasts, stations, and networks, also crosses denominational boundaries. Supported mainly by audience contributions, this successful multimillion-dollar business has been the envy of denominational leaders who fear money is siphoned away from their own programs to the mass-media "pastors" who cannot truly serve as pastors. The "empire" arose partly because time donated for religion in the mass media was narrowly channeled to groups associated with the conciliar movement; fundamentalists and evangelicals successfully countered this bias with a free-enterprise spirit. Critics often fail to recognize that the greatest budget item of the "electronic church" usually is purchase of station time. The extent to which broadcast services are a substitute for church participation, except among the infirm and elderly, is not fully known, but we do know that there is a positive correlation between watching religious programs on television and church attendance.[15]

Most religious mass-media production is part of the parachurch movement, consisting of organizations, alongside and separate from denominational structures, which are established to accomplish specific goals through the financial support of individual donors. These groups serve a variety of purposes, including the sending and support of foreign missionaries, evangelism, education for social justice, reducing languages to writing for Bible translation, rehabilitation of prisoners, child welfare, right-to-life efforts, and a wide range of social-service ministries. Some of their finances come from church members who, unhappy with a "unified budget" or certain causes included in it, desire to support specific ministries. The parachurch movement has flourished; many old organizations have gained strength, and new ones have come into existence. It is clearly an instance of the free-enterprise system in religion. It would seem, although there is no solid empirical evidence, that more of these parachurch organizations are related to the evangelical movement than to its theological competitors, although ministries like the American Bible Society, Voice of Calvary, Bread for the World, Young Life, World Vision, and Prison Fellowship have a very broad and diverse constituency of

[13] See Joseph H. Fichter, *The Catholic Cult of the Paraclete* (New York: Sheed and Ward, 1975).

[14] See Margaret Poloma, *The Charismatic Movement* (Boston: Twayne Publishers, 1982), and Meredith B. McGuire, *Pentecostal Catholics: Power, Charisma, and Order in a Religious Movement* (Philadephia: Temple University Press, 1982).

[15] Princeton Religion Research Center, *Religion in America 1982*, p. 103. See also Jeffrey K. Hadden and Charles E. Swann, *Prime Time Preachers* (Reading, Mass.: Addison-Wesley, 1981).

supporters.[16] In general they support American values. Of course, as beneficiaries of religious, political, and socioeconomic freedom at home and of American military and diplomatic power and protection abroad, they can hardly be expected to attack the societal arrangements which permitted their inception and nourished their prosperity; their support of democracy, capitalism, and the "free world" is easy to justify theoretically, theologically, and pragmatically. They desire to improve and correct, rather than to overthrow, the American political and socioeconomic system.

The Natural History of Religious Institutions

The five-stage model of the life cycle in the church (pp. 118-25) has been verified by both theoretical studies and real-life examples. The histories of Bethany Fellowship, Koinonia Farm, the Hutterites, Mayeem Kareem Kibbutz, and St. Julian's Community all support its validity;[17] and John Douhan has used it as a tool to help American Baptist congregations identify their developmental position so they can plan for maximum efficiency. Anabaptists (the Amish, Hutterites, and Mennonites) have survived over four and a half centuries, apparently avoiding disintegration because of a shared value system, stereotyping and labeling by both outsiders and themselves, formation of in- and out-groups, written documents precisely stating their doctrines, functional consequences of persecution and conflict, and strong social organization.[18]

O'Dea has noted various dilemmas which occur as a church passes through its life cycle.[19] (1) The *dilemma of mixed motivations* occurs when the focused, single-minded motives of early members become more diffused among the second and later generations. The clergy become more "worldly" and the laity more passive or lukewarm in commitment. (2) The *symbolic dilemma* is evident when worship rituals become objectified and routine, resonance between symbols and members' attitudes and feelings dissipates, and embodiment of the spiritual in profane vehicles contributes to loss of a sense of ultimacy. The perception of sacredness in ritual is lost by rote repetition. Alienation of some members occurs; the symbolic dilemma may even give rise to protest, sometimes as extreme

[16] Ralph D. Winter, "Protestant Mission Societies and the 'Other Protestant Schism,'" in *American Denominational Organization,* Ross P. Scherer, ed. (Pasadena: William Carey Library, 1980), pp. 194-224, documents the increasing dominance of independent organizations among the more than 600 Protestant foreign mission societies in North America.

[17] James W. Treece, Jr., "Theories on Religious Communal Development," *Social Compass,* 18, no. 1 (1971), 85-100.

[18] Ruth Shonle Cavan, "From Social Movement to Organized Society: The Case of the Anabaptists," *Journal of Voluntary Action Research,* 6 (Summer-Fall 1977), 105-11.

[19] Thomas F. O'Dea and Janet O'Dea Aviad, *The Sociology of Religion,* 2nd ed. (Englewood Cliffs, N.J.: Prentice-Hall, 1983), pp. 56-64.

as the iconoclasm of the left wing of the Reformation. (3) As the original charismatic leaders are replaced by bureaucratic offices, the *dilemma of administrative order* arises. Structures and procedural precedents developed under one set of conditions become unwieldy under new circumstances. Officers gain a vested interest in keeping the structure unchanged and may become alienated from rank-and-file members, as in the anticlericalism and conflicts between bishops and the Curia in Roman Catholic history. (4) While the message of the group, which was originally stated in terms relevant to the daily activities and concerns of early followers, must be protected against interpretations which conflict with its central thrust, it must also be adapted over time to changing social contexts and new converts. This demands continual redefinition of dogma, control of heresy, and efforts to prevent rituals and symbols from becoming quasi-magical substitutes for genuine worship. This *dilemma of delimitation* paradoxically relativizes the religious and ethical message even as it concretizes it, posing the risk of translating ethical insights into rigid rules that are inconsistent with the spirit originally behind them. (5) When a religious group becomes dominant in a society, the *dilemma of power* emerges. Personal commitment by an act of faith, which is invariably accompanied by the possibility of doubt, is gradually supplanted by the validation of consensus, support from societal authority, and compromise with cultural values, so the religious views seem self-evident. Religious leaders then begin to rely upon social consensus or even legal authority to buttress or compel membership. Intolerance or even persecution emerges because heretics and unbelievers seem to weaken consensus and pose a threat to society. "The alliance of religion and secular power creates a situation in which apparent religiosity often conceals a deeper cynicism and a growing unbelief."[20]

These five dilemmas are inherent in the life cycle of a church. As institutionalization occurs, religious values, emotions, and organizational structures run the risk of becoming routine. This is the root cause of much religious protest and conflict and is clearly related to the rise and development of new sects.

A strong church-growth movement developed during the 1960's and 1970's, its roots going back to McGavran's work in India and the U.S.[21] Periodicals like *Church Growth: America* and the *Global Church Growth Bulletin*, conferences and workshops for clergy and other church workers, and the Institute of Church Growth at Fuller Theological Seminary have stimulated the movement. Critics say that it stresses the wrong priorities, emphasizes quantity at the expense of quality, gives no attention to social

---

[20] *Ibid.,* p. 63.
[21] Donald A. McGavran, *The Bridges of God: A Study in the Strategy of Missions* (New York: Friendship Press, 1955), and *Understanding Church Growth,* rev. ed. (Grand Rapids: Eerdmans, 1980).

justice, and focuses upon segregated homogeneous units of people instead of integration of all ethnic groups, races, and social classes in the church. They argue that decreasing numbers in a church increase its power because those who remain are more faithful to Jesus Christ.[22]

Church-growth advocates respond that they are misrepresented. They point out that there is a vital interconnection between quality and quantity, and that their mandate under the Great Commission of Jesus Christ (Matt. 28:18-20) calls for "all that is involved in bringing men and women who do not have a personal relationship to Jesus Christ into fellowship with him and into responsible church membership."[23] They also point out that declining size usually reduces the quality of a church's ministries, that spiritual nourishment to improve the quality of people's lives and service can and must follow their conversion to Christ, that concern for the poor and oppressed is a part of the biblical mandate for growth, that Christian outreach must begin where people are, and that this can occur only by recognizing the variations in lifestyle, interests, needs, vocabularies, and other characteristics in human society, and therefore allowing for homogeneous cells and congregations within larger Christian celebrations and festivals.[24]

Dean Kelley, a National Council of Churches executive, concluded that churches which are growing provide people with meaning and identity through strict standards for membership,[25] but research in several denominations has suggested that variations in growth have more complex social and religious roots.[26] Kelley's summary response reiterates the need to return to "serious discipleship":

> If the mainline churches could muster sufficient seriousness about what they profess to believe, they might cease to be blown from pillar to post by every breeze of cultural climate, every shift in demography or other "contextual" factors. They might even begin to affect some of the circumstances around them, to influence the cultural climate themselves, as their forebears did. They might, in fact, cease to be a dependent and become an independent variable.[27]

---

[22] Robert K. Hudnut, *Church Growth Is Not the Point* (New York: Harper and Row, 1975).

[23] C. Peter Wagner, *Your Church Can Grow* (Glendale, Calif.: Regal Books, 1976), p. 12.

[24] C. Peter Wagner, Professor of Church Growth at Fuller Theological Seminary, is perhaps the most sophisticated theorist in the movement. His books include *Our Kind of People: The Ethical Dimensions of Church Growth in America* (Atlanta: John Knox Press, 1979), *Your Spiritual Gifts Can Help Your Church Grow* (Glendale, Calif.: Regal Books, 1979), and *Church Growth and the Whole Gospel: A Biblical Mandate* (San Francisco: Harper and Row, 1981). In *Hey, That's Our Church!* (Nashville: Abingdon, 1975) Lyle E. Schaller presents related pragmatic evidence and guidelines for action based upon extensive consultation, case studies, and observation.

[25] Dean M. Kelley, *Why Conservative Churches Are Growing*, rev. ed. (New York: Harper and Row, 1977).

[26] Dean R. Hoge and David A. Roozen, eds., *Understanding Church Growth and Decline 1950-1978* (New York: Pilgrim Press, 1979).

[27] Dean M. Kelley, "Commentary: Is Religion a Dependent Variable?" in Hoge and Roozen, *Understanding Church Growth*, p. 343.

Analysis of membership distribution by counties for 35 denominations in 1952 and 1971 confirmed that there was a mid-century revival of joining mainline denominations but no great change in their relative distributions or the aggregate patterns; in general stability is more evident than change. (It should be noted that the use of percentages instead of simple figures representing persons added tends to bias conclusions. The 40 per cent growth in the ten-million-member United Methodist Church from 1940 to 1969 included far more additions than the 90 per cent growth of the more conservative Wesleyan Church with 80,000 members.[28]) Considerable stability also is apparent in comparisons of the twenty largest denominations in the 1890 Census, the 1926 Census of Religious Bodies, and recent editions of the *Yearbook of American and Canadian Churches* when adaptations are made for mergers, splits, and name changes.

Social Concern and the Church

A persistent stereotype of the involvement of Christians in social issues is that theological liberals in the heritage of the social gospel have been actively involved in social reform movements, while the conservatives have resisted all change and focused all effort upon evangelism to convert individuals. While the general tendencies were in those directions, such a picture distorts reality. For example, fundamentalists early in this century were deeply involved in the prohibition movement to outlaw alcoholic beverages as well as in the rescue mission movement and other ministries to the underprivileged, while many—perhaps a majority—of the laity among the liberals strongly upheld the political and economic status quo. But with the fundamentalist-modernist controversies came the "Great Reversal" by which evangelicals departed from an earlier explicit involvement in many social concerns and liberals drifted away from attention to individual conversion and spiritual nurture.[29]

Especially among evangelicals, this "Great Reversal" has been modified considerably in recent years. The 1973 Chicago Declaration of Evangelical Social Concern made socially concerned evangelical Christians more aware of each other and led eventually to the formation of such parachurch groups as the Evangelical Women's Caucus and Evangelicals for Social Action. Publications like *Sojourners, The Other Side*, and *Radix* critiqued various theoretical and theological positions on social issues, disseminated information, publicized action programs, shared how-to-do-it techniques, created support groups for social ministries, and stimulated parachurch ministries to meet educational, economic, housing, health,

---

[28] William M. Newman and Peter L. Halvorson, *Patterns in Pluralism: A Portrait of American Religion 1952-1971* (Washington, D.C.: Glenmary Research Center, 1980), pp. 7-8.

[29] David O. Moberg, *The Great Reversal: Evangelism and Social Concern*, rev. ed. (Philadelphia: Lippincott, 1977).

social, and other human needs at home and abroad. The discrepancy of shunning social ministries in America while sponsoring them on foreign mission fields was reduced as countless evangelical churches became sponsors of day-care nurseries, volunteer visiting ministries, food and clothing banks for the poor, and Christian day schools for those unhappy with public schools because of their long-distance busing of children or their allegedly secular-humanist educational philosophy. A survey of evangelical leaders which was published in 1982 found that, in comparison with a decade earlier, 70 per cent had a greater belief in the Christian's social responsibility; only 2 per cent were less concerned about social issues.[30]

Social Ministries

Some imply that there is a distinct dividing line between social concern and evangelistic ministry to individual persons and families, but that boundary is largely artificial. Whenever religious groups are concerned about quality of life and the whole person, their spiritual, social, pastoral, educational, inspirational, therapeutic, and other ministries overlap. To be sure, fundamentalist Christians sometimes have claimed that conversion does not constitute merely a first significant turning point but, rather, resolves all human problems, while some liberals have assumed that re-forming the social order is the only need because it will produce the changed environment which will make people whatever they should become, but these extremes of "evangelism" and "social concern" are increasingly rare.[31] Although it is difficult to document, churches generally appear to be moving toward a better balance of diverse ministries. As they minister to personal needs, they are thereby involved in social ministries to meet collective needs as well. These social ministries may take the form of counseling hotlines, recreational services, family-support programs, help to single parents, senior-citizen centers, camping, day care for children and infirm adults, telephone reassurance circles, food assistance for the needy, or any of dozens of other specialized activities. Responses from 254 congregations in nine member denominations of the Greater Milwaukee Conference on Religion and Urban Affairs in 1983 found that 99 per cent were directly or indirectly involved with providing money, goods, and services for the needy. Over $1,600,000 in cash and goods was distributed and about 500,000 hours of volunteer service were donated in 1982. If representative of the entire religious community, this can be projected to annual contributions of at least $5,000,000 in the four-county area.[32] Similar ministries are found in every major community.

---

[30] J. Randall Petersen, "Evangelical Leaders Poll—Part 2," *Evangelical Newsletter,* 9, no. 2 (Jan. 22, 1982), 4.

[31] See Moberg, *The Great Reversal.*

[32] Mary Beth Murphy, "More Church Aid to Needy Backed," *Milwaukee Sentinel,* July 2, 1983, part 1, p. 7.

National polls reveal that involvement in charitable activities, such as helping the poor, sick, or elderly, is higher among evangelicals (42 per cent) than non-evangelicals (30 per cent), among persons with high spiritual commitment (46 per cent) than those with low levels (22 per cent), among those who have attended church or synagogue within the past seven days (44 per cent) than those who have not attended for over six months (19 per cent), and among those who attend more than once a week (54 per cent) than among adults as a whole (32 per cent).[33]

Although various liberal denominations may make more pronouncements and their leaders may be more outspoken, it is possible that evangelicals are just as socially involved as are liberals, if not more so. Contrary to common opinion, there is no direct correlation between level of social involvement and position on the theological spectrum. The "non-religious" Moral Majority, for example, with its ultra-conservative positions includes Catholics, Jews, and religious liberals as well as fundamentalists. It is patently incorrect to equate its social and political views only with those of theological conservatives, as well as to assume that the latter unanimously support it. Many evangelical Christians now cooperate with theological liberals, Catholics, Jews, and others in specific programs aimed at social reforms or other matters of social concern. This is evident in the parachurch activities of Bread for the World, anti-abortion efforts, and the anti-nuclear-warfare movement, to mention but a few examples.

Meanwhile, efforts of the World Council of Churches (WCC) and National Council of Churches (NCC) to deal with sociopolitical issues by supporting certain political implications of liberation theology have produced much dissatisfaction. The Salvation Army withdrew from the WCC when its philosophy of service and non-support for violent aggression seemed contradicted by WCC support of certain national movements in Africa. An original *Reader's Digest* article and CBS's "60 Minutes" alleged that the NCC and WCC were financially supporting Marxist guerrilla activities and propaganda aimed at the violent overthrow of existing governments in southern Africa, the Mideast, and Latin America and were co-sponsoring pro-Communist activities related to liberation struggles.[34] Other critics wondered why the NCC and bodies such as the United Presbyterian Church selectively condemned repression and human-rights violations in "rightist-controlled" countries like Chile, El Salvador, South Korea, South Africa, Taiwan, Thailand, the Philippines, and Guatemala, but were silent about well-publicized reports of repression and violations of human rights in such "leftist" states as Afghanistan, Cambodia, Vietnam, Ethiopia, Uganda, Zaire, Zimbabwe, Nicaragua, Cuba, East Germany, the Soviet Union, and Poland. These critics con-

---

[33] Princeton Religion Research Center, *Religion in America 1982*, pp. 76, 176-77.

[34] Rael Jean Isaac, "Do You Know Where Your Church Offerings Go?" *Reader's Digest*, 122, no. 729 (Jan. 1983), 120-25. CBS televised the broadcast "The Gospel According to Whom?" on January 23, 1983.

tended that people were turning away from political and social action by churches, seeking instead a greater emphasis on spiritual direction, and that this in part explained the decline of the heaviest supporters of the WCC and NCC while denominations like the Southern Baptist Convention, Assemblies of God, and Seventh-day Adventists were increasing.[35]

Leaders of the NCC and WCC responded to these allegations by arguing that only small expenditures had gone to the criticized ventures, that these were expressions of the commitment to economic, social, and political justice, that some details presented were erroneous, and that the reports ought to have been more balanced, including their side of the issues and not only evidence contrary to it. Michael Novak reminded them that they had not complained when "right-wing" causes like the Pentagon, major corporations, and Oral Roberts were skewered by "60 Minutes," so they ought not to complain when they themselves were humiliated by investigative reporting: "Maybe now they know what it feels like to be held accountable to the public, to have their internal judgments second-guessed, their motives doubted, and their activities unsympathetically scrutinized."[36] This controversy illustrates the tendency of the political and the religious right wings to coalesce in opposition to the left. At times it is difficult to discern whether religious or socioeconomic and political values take first priority in religious social ethics.

Charitable Giving

Benevolent contributions also reflect social concern. Over two-thirds (69 per cent) of families and single adults contributed to religious organizations in 1978. The proportion of income given varied directly with age and to a lesser degree inversely with education. People involved in volunteer work and regular churchgoers were much more likely than others to give a tenth or more of their incomes.[37] A 1973 survey similarly showed that people in the lowest income brackets gave the highest percentage of total income to religious organizations. It concluded that, beyond the tax incentives and other economic and demographic influences on giving, there remains an altruistic tendency expressed through various forms of philanthropy: giving money, donating time to organizations, and spending time to help individuals.[38]

More than two-thirds of U.S. income-tax payers do not itemize their

35 James J. Cochran, "Editorial: Selective Condemnation," *The Presbyterian Layman*, 16, no. 3 (May-June 1983), 12.

36 Michael Novak, "The Self-Righteousness of the National Council," *The Presbyterian Layman*, 16, no. 3 (May-June 1983), 9 (reprinted from *The National Review*).

37 Princeton Religion Research Center, *Religion in America 1981* (Princeton, N.J.: The Gallup Organization, 1981), pp. 69-72.

38 James N. Morgan, Richard F. Dye, and Judith H. Hybels, "Results from Two National Surveys of Philanthropic Activity," in Commission on Private Philanthropy and Public Needs, *Research Papers, Vol. I, History, Trends, and Current Magnitudes* (Washington, D.C.: U.S. Dept. of the Treasury, 1977), pp. 157-223.

charitable contributions, and others with low incomes do not file at all, so much charitable giving is not included in the research data. Another problem for the researcher is that clear divisions between religious and other philanthropic contributions are difficult to make because much individual giving is interpreted as "religious" when it goes to an organization such as a church-supported hospital, or is channeled by the church to a health, welfare, social-service, or educational agency.

To prevent fiscal abuses in parachurch organizations, the Evangelical Council for Financial Accountability was formed in 1979. It is an association of evangelical non-profit organizations that requires of members the highest standards of financial accountability and disclosure to government, donors, and the public along with a clearly defined statement of faith consistent with evangelical Christianity.

Religion and Prejudice

The results of research on religion and ethnic prejudice continue to be confusing (pp. 446-48). A survey of dozens of empirical research projects on the subject shows that the average church member is more prejudiced than the average non-member. It is noted, however, that it is "the casual, nontheologically motivated member [who] is prejudiced. *The highly committed religious person is—along with the nonreligious person—one of the least prejudiced members of our society.*"[39] This curvilinear relationship suggests that persons who are at the religious extremes—the highly committed and the nonbelievers—have value systems that are independent of the norms of their society. A high degree of commitment helps believers to transcend cultural traditions so that they are able to evaluate them according to a consistent value standard that is not itself a mere product of environmental circumstances and experiences.

This does not prove that churches have either failed or succeeded in promoting tolerance, for a wide range of definitions has been used, the influence of a religious institution is very difficult to determine, and it is impossible to ascertain the amount of prejudice which would prevail among respective sub-groups if religion had never existed. The more prejudiced groups among church members in most studies are fundamentalists, members of conservative Protestant denominations, those who are indiscriminately pro-church (in general agreement with the church's teachings), and those with an extrinsic or consensual religiosity. The less prejudiced members have a committed or intrinsic religiosity, are from moderate Protestant denominations, and claim that religion is a positive influence on their racial attitudes.[40]

[39] Richard L. Gorsuch and Daniel Aleshire, "Christian Faith and Ethnic Prejudice: A Review and Interpretation of Research," *Journal for the Scientific Study of Religion*, 13, no. 3 (Sept. 1974), 287 (italics in original).
[40] *Ibid.*, pp. 281-307.

These findings are buttressed by results of a national survey of United Church of Christ members in which attitudes on civil-rights issues were a major topic. One of the most prominent findings was that those who ranked high on an index of devotional orientation also were highly in favor of civil rights for and social acceptance of blacks. Only devotionalism reversed the patterns of social conditioning, apparently by enabling people to be "inner-worldly ascetics" who are in the world but not of it because they have a set of values which transcend their social circumstances. This surprised the researchers: "Prior to the study we would have been very hesitant to come out in favor of 'devotionalism' as an indication of how one can be in the world but not of it. Like other liberal Protestants we too were fearful of devotionalism becoming 'escapism.' But the data simply cannot be denied."[41]

The association of fundamentalism with high levels of prejudice appears to be inconsistent with such findings. However, when people are socialized into a religious group which maintains strong boundaries against outside "heretical" doctrines and people and teaches how to combat and correct their errors, this inevitably enhances intolerance and prejudice toward those out-groups, which is easily transferred to all out-groups, including the ones distinguished by ethnicity. "Religious particularism" seems to require militant opposition and triumphantly viewing one's own religion as alone correct.[42] Nevertheless, the indicators and measures of prejudice used in research must be examined with care; sometimes prejudice is defined as merely having distinctive beliefs or assuming that all religious views are not equally valid.

Theodicies

Traditionally, the church offers social support, comfort, and other help to people who suffer from illness, bereavement, natural disaster, family problems, crime, financial loss, injustice, and other difficulties or deprivations. Believers need help in understanding why their loving God allows these and other evils to exist. Theodicies are developed to explain that such experiences are not meaningless but are part of a transcendent system of justice and order. The resolutions provided include what Max Weber termed a "theodicy of disprivilege" or a "theodicy of escape," by which the socially and economically disadvantaged are told that true riches are in heaven and count for all eternity; in the eternal kingdom the last shall be first and the first last. On the other hand, a "theodicy of good fortune" appeals to people of wealth and high social status; they

[41] Thomas C. Campbell and Yoshio Fukuyama, *The Fragmented Layman: An Empirical Study of Lay Attitudes* (Philadelphia: Pilgrim Press, 1970), p. 224.

[42] Cf. Meredith B. McGuire, *Religion: The Social Context* (Belmont, Calif.: Wadsworth, 1981), pp. 162-64, and H. Paul Chalfant, Robert E. Beckley, and C. Eddie Palmer, *Religion in Contemporary Society* (Palo Alto, Calif.: Mayfield Publishing Co., 1981), pp. 413-42.

are led to feel that they deserve their good fortune.[43] It is not surprising that the preaching, teaching, and Bible interpretations which satisfy the needs of people who are materially prosperous and politically powerful often are unappealing or even repulsive to the disadvantaged and powerless classes of society, and vice versa.[44]

One of the issues addressed by religious theodicies is death. In the context of Christian faith it is not the end of personal existence but a transition to a glorious afterlife. Jews, Muslims, Hindus, and Buddhists have different interpretations of death. These divergent beliefs inevitably influence personal and social attitudes and behavior. Some have argued that Christian teachings about God's final judgment instill or increase the fear of death, but Leming's survey of relevant research found only three studies demonstrating higher levels of fear of death among the more religious people and ten in which factors like religious commitment, devotionalism, orthodoxy, and belief in an afterlife were significantly related to reduced anxiety concerning death.[45]

Pastoral-care ministries to dying people too often have rigidly accepted Kübler-Ross's five stages of dying (denial, anger, bargaining, depression, acceptance) as a process that all must complete. This is manipulative, isolates the dying from other people, and cuts them off from care they should receive. Based upon philosophical and religious convictions of body-soul dualism and reincarnation that are alien to Christianity, the stages do not correlate well with Christian faith and experience.[46] To complement the work of the pastor, which influences people's faith, values, and feelings about death and dying, many churches also have related diaconal activities and supportive group ministries such as widowed-persons services.

Structural Changes in American Religion

The rate of change in religious structures is related to the level of organization, the sub-groups within congregations changing most rapidly, congregations next, then state and regional associations, with denomi-

---

[43] Hans H. Gerth and C. Wright Mills, *From Max Weber: Essays in Sociology* (New York: Oxford University Press, 1946), pp. 271-76.

[44] This "homogeneous unit principle" is an excellent topic for further research through participant observation, case studies, interviews, content analysis of religious literature, and other methods.

[45] Michael R. Leming, *The Relationship Between Religiosity and the Fear of Death*, Ph.D. dissertation, University of Utah, 1975. See also David O. Moberg, "Spiritual Well-Being of the Dying," in *Aging and the Human Condition*, Gari Lesnoff-Caravaglia, ed. (New York: Human Sciences Press, 1981), pp. 139-55.

[46] George Kuykendall, "Care for the Dying: A Kübler-Ross Critique," *Theology Today*, 38, no. 1 (April 1981), 37-48. Cf. Elisabeth Kübler-Ross, *On Death and Dying* (New York: Macmillan, 1969), and *Death: The Final Stage of Growth* (Englewood Cliffs, N.J.: Prentice-Hall, 1975).

nations and interdenominational associations the slowest of all. The formation of new denominations and other religious bodies, together with the elimination of others through death and merger, has characterized all of American history. From 1890 to 1906, for example, 61 new denominations were added (13 by division of existing bodies) and 20 disappeared (4 by change in classification, 4 by consolidation with others, and 12 by extinction).[47] Comparison of any edition of the *Yearbook of American and Canadian Churches* with that of ten years earlier will reveal many changes, and reading religious news will reveal still more.

New Religious Movements

During the 1970's and early 1980's much attention was given to the new religious movements popularly labeled "cults." Many had exotic origins, novel lifestyles, intense loyalty from members, charismatic leadership, social conspicuity, international operations, and a following drawn disproportionately from better-educated, middle-class youth.[48] Because of their zealous evangelism and fund raising, allegations that several of them engage in kidnapping, brainwashing, and other unethical manipulations, and counter-attempts to deprogram the presumed victims, they have received so much popular attention that it appears as if the movement is unprecedented in American history. In fact, however, it represents a continuation of the formation of new religious groups that is as old as human history. Furthermore, the new groups are not nearly as large and strong as implied by popular mass-media accounts. Of the approximately 75 that anti-cultists emphasize, "the two most famous—the Hare Krishna and the Unification Church—number less than 5,000. . . . An estimated 150,000 individuals are involved in the so-called cults at any one time. Each of these groups experiences a large overturn in membership."[49] If, however, one includes all people who at some time have taken instruction in Transcendental Meditation, participated in various psychic groups, attended conferences or workshops of the human-potential movement, believed in astrological horoscopes and signs of the zodiac, or had their palms read and fortunes told, the number touched by the cults may range into the tens of millions.

The motivations which people have for joining the new religious movements and the processes by which they join vary considerably from one group to another, as do the theoretical perspectives which may be used

---

[47] Bureau of the Census, *Census of Religious Bodies: 1906* (Washington, D.C.: Government Printing Office, 1910), part I, pp. 14-16.

[48] Bryan R. Wilson, ed., *The Social Impact of New Religious Movements* (New York: Rose of Sharon Press, 1981), p. v.

[49] J. Gordon Melton and Robert L. Moore, *The Cult Experience* (New York: Pilgrim Press, 1982), p. 125.

to interpret them.[50] One of the most studied groups is the Unification Church, which Lofland labels "Doomsday Cult" and the "Divine Precepts group." Because its members, who are commonly called "Moonies" after its founder, Sun Myung Moon, consider their beliefs too "mind blowing" to reveal all at once, there is at first a "complete muting or denial of the religion and millenarian aspects" with only a gradual and progressive revelation of the ideology through five quasi-temporal stages:[51]

1. *Picking-up* is a casual contact in a public place—giving rides to hitchhikers, exhibiting displays on a campus, infiltrating religious gatherings, or approaching young adults in urban areas to which drifting youth gravitate. It usually involves an invitation to a dinner, a lecture, or both.

2. *Hooking* of the dinner and lecture guests involves elaborate promotion tactics. Each prospect is assigned a "buddy" who stays at his or her side, learning the prospect's background, opinions, and personal interests. Then the buddy writes these "hooks" down so that everyone in the center knows how best to follow up on the person. The guest is showered with compliments, service, attention, and a feeling of importance as many of the fifty or more orderly, talkative, smiling youth going about their various chores stop by, exuding friendliness and solicitude. An emotional emphasis predominates. No mention is made of the founder, but an entertaining lecture deals with the principles of sharing, loving each other, working for the good of humanity, and community activity that unites The Family. A slide presentation attractively shows The Farm; prospects are invited to a weekend workshop in the country.

3. *Encapsulating* follows at the workshop and subsequent periods. The ideology is progressively unfolded in a controlled setting at which doubts and hesitations can surface and be rebutted while affective bonds are forged without interference from outsiders. A cheerful quality pervades as the five principles of winning a convert are put into practice: (a) the prospect's attention is fully absorbed—a buddy watches over the "spiritual child" at all waking moments; (b) there is a focus on activities in which the group participates as a whole: eating, garden work, exercising, lectures, games, cheers, chants, dancing, praying, singing, and so on; (c) there is an exclusive input of the ideology—no newspapers, radio, television, or telephone for outside contacts; (d) the prospective member is kept in a state of fatigue through a full schedule of lectures and other activities, a Spartan diet, controlled sleep periods, and mild sexual excitement through frequent patting and hugging; and (e) the ideology is carefully and systematically unfolded until the potential convert comes to a logical, comprehensive cognition.

---

[50] See James T. Richardson, ed., *Conversion Careers: In and Out of the New Religions* (Beverly Hills, Calif.: Sage Publications, 1978).

[51] John Lofland, "'Becoming a World Saver' Revisited," in Richardson, *Conversion Careers*, pp. 10-23 (quotation from p. 11).

4. *Loving* is the most coercive power of all. Everything done moves the potential convert to the point of feeling loved and the desire to "melt together" into the enveloping embrace of the collectivity. Members of the commune consciously use "love bombing" as a strategy for promoting "blissed out harmony and unity."

5. *Committing* is the final phase. The blissed-out prospects are invited to stay at The Farm for a week-long workshop; if they stay, they are then invited for an even longer period during which they are gradually drawn into full participation by working, street peddling, and believing. Doubts are labeled "acts of Satan," and the dire consequences of leaving the movement are stressed. If any do re-enter the outside world, shock is a typical reaction, making return to the group all the more attractive.

This analytic description of the typical sequence of experiences in join-ing the Unification Church has obvious parallels in the evangelistic efforts of many other religious groups, new and old. Some of its techniques also are used in the "deprogramming" which concerned parents have em-ployed to bring their allegedly brainwashed children out of sects and cults to which they have been converted. Such anti-cult efforts sometimes have violated civil liberties by the use of deception, kidnapping, sleep depri-vation, and activities which themselves are tantamount to brainwashing.[52] Among those deprogrammed have been converts to fundamentalist sects and Roman Catholicism. There is growing intellectual and legal consensus that it is not right theologically, intellectually, and morally to assume that an adult in our pluralistic, democratic society who voluntarily changes religion has been brainwashed and hence ought to be forced back into the parental religion.

The Ecumenical Movement

In the late 1960's there were nearly 1,000 local councils of churches in America, but under tensions related to the crises of civil rights, poverty, the Vietnam War, and urban problems many died or were replaced by new agencies with different names and operational styles. The *1983 Year-book of American and Canadian Churches* lists 228 regional and local ecumenical agencies in the 50 states, the District of Columbia, and Puerto Rico. Under half (99) include "Council" in the name, 38 are labeled "Ministry" or "Ministries," 18 are "Conferences," and there is a wide variety of other titles.

William B. Cate, President-Director of the Council of Greater Seattle, has identified four characteristics of the local ecumenical movement in the early 1980's. (1) It is not a new inter-church institution but a network

---

[52] Cf. Anson D. Shupe, Jr., Roger Spielmann, and Sam Stigall, "Deprogramming: The New Exorcism," in Richardson, *Conversion Careers*, pp. 145-60, and Thomas Robbins, "'Brainwashing' and Religious Freedom," *The Nation*, 224, no. 17 (April 30, 1977), 518.

or system of relationships among congregations and denominational structures which aims to facilitate dialogue and common action in areas of common concern, enabling people to interact in joint mission. (2) Its heart is a renewed sense of spiritual oneness as an inner, personal relationship to God and to brothers and sisters in the faith. Unity is viewed as a movement of the Holy Spirit, not an outer, institutional form, so ecumenical worship at points of witness like world peace, human rights, or concern for the poor entails prayer to God for relief of human suffering, produces changes in participants, and leads to change in society. (3) It emphasizes action around issues of peace and justice, effectively challenging institutionalized injustices like redlining, school segregation, the arms race, and gaps in human services, and dealing with their systemic causes. (4) Its theological focus is on the church and how it ministers in the community as an agent in God's kingdom. It no longer conceives of itself in terms of simple inter-church cooperation but, viewing the conciliar movement as in direct line with councils of earlier centuries, dialogues about how to unite in mission to God's world. Catholic-Protestant ecumenical cooperation is strongly evident in many communities, but evangelical Protestants generally remain aloof except for occasional cooperation on specific issues.[53]

Theological conservatives generally view the ecumenical movement with suspicion. Their priorities are oriented more toward the ultimate fate of persons than toward proximate conditions in their earthly lives. They believe desirable change in society begins by first changing persons, not by giving primary attention to social structures. They deplore what they consider to be the watering down of biblical doctrine in order to accommodate beliefs or practices of groups in the movement which they believe are in error. They recognize that a latent consequence of cooperation is imparting legitimacy to the other partners as equivalent to themselves and fear that this could happen on the level of basic views about salvation, not only the societal issues around which cooperation occurs. They prefer to cooperate only with those who have similar "spiritual" values, and they fear the long-term effects of building bureaucratic structures.

Nevertheless, evangelicals are involved in cooperative ventures with others of similar faith, especially through agencies of the National Association of Evangelicals and numerous parachurch associations like the Lausanne Committee on World Evangelization, the Billy Graham Evangelistic Association, the Evangelical Press Association, Campus Crusade for Christ, and the Evangelical Foreign Missions Association, to mention but a few. Additional special-purpose cooperative enterprises have emerged among fundamentalist defenders of creationism, a doctrinaire interpretation of the Bible's creation accounts which most evangelicals view as

[53] William B. Cate, "Whatever Happened to Ecumenism?" *MPL Journal* (Minister's Personal Library), 4, no. 1 (Spring 1983), 3-5.

much narrower than is necessitated by accepting the biblical record as God's Word. Perhaps the most sophisticated of these is the Institute for Creation Research, but the Creation Research Society, the Institute for Research on Origins, the Bible-Science Association, and many other agencies are also diligently working toward the goal of having creationism taught alongside evolution in public schools as an alternative scientific explanation of pre-history.

Tensions are obvious within the ecumenical movement. As indicated earlier, there has been considerable opposition against some of its social-justice activities, but a more basic problem is what Garrett labels a "fundamental contradiction" in the structure of the movement, that is, the impasse between denominationalism and ecumenism. The goals of the movement presuppose a homogeneous social structure capable of disciplined concerted action, but it lacks the necessary institutional framework and supportive social environment. As "a confederated alliance of autonomous denominations," only its most modest goals can be attained. It also suffers from identity confusion in relationship to denominations, serving variously as an undeclared super-church, as a quasi-denomination (first among equals), and as a specialized service agency. Hence, although it has the ability to develop ministry from the perspective of the church-at-large while denominations necessarily conceive of ministry in terms of their more limited institutional perspectives, the ecumenical movement's structure as a mere federation of *"autonomous bodies which vehemently refuse to relinquish their hegemonic claims to power"* is a flaw which hampers both the NCC and the WCC.[54]

> When measured against the backdrop of American religious experience, the stated aims of contemporary ecumenism were *more* fully *realized during* the decades surrounding the *1820s than* the *1970s*. For after the second great awakening . . . [Protestants] collaborated in developing a remarkable variety of interfaith ministries. . . . Denominational structures were minimally developed by contemporary standards, and denominational leaders were largely confined to the functions of dealing with sacerdotal matters and the practical administration required for supporting *local* churches and ministers. . . . They were wholly unprepared to supervise the sundry projects initiated by radical and evangelical religious visionaries.[55]

One attempt to overcome some of these limitations is the Consultation on Church Union (COCU), founded in 1962 "to attempt, under God, a more inclusive expression of the oneness of the church of Christ than any of the participating churches can suppose itself to be." Aiming to become Churches of Christ Uniting into a "truly catholic, truly evangelical, truly reformed" Christian church, its nine Protestant denominations are care-

---

[54] William R. Garrett, "Interplay and Rivalry Between Denominational and Ecumenical Organization," in Scherer, *American Denominational Organization,* pp. 346-62.

[55] *Ibid.,* p. 348 (italics in original).

fully working toward an institutional and doctrinal framework for cooperation and eventual merger.[56] Initial enthusiasm for COCU has waned.
Most of the laity are more concerned with their local church than with
denominational affairs. Moreover, in the wake of the anti-institutional
movements of the 1970's, skepticism as to the values of large-scale bureaucratic structures remains, and denominational autonomy erects a barrier as well.

Thus, whether we are in an era of increasing or declining ecumenism
is problematic. On the local level cooperation of congregations and individuals from diverse Catholic, Protestant, Orthodox, and often Jewish
groups appears to be increasing, at least in specific action-oriented, conciliar, and parachurch ministries. On the national level, the NCC has lost
relative strength in Protestantism over the past two decades. Internation-
ally, the WCC is facing much stress. At the same time, the National
Interfaith Coalition on Aging has succeeded in drawing together fundamentalist, evangelical, and mainline Protestants, Catholics, Orthodox
Christians, and Jews to promote its aim of stimulating ministries with,
for, and by the aging and elderly, and parachurch agencies like the American Bible Society, World Vision, and Bread for the World function "ecumenically" to accomplish their goals.

Cooperative ventures among the major faiths are evident in nearly every
large community. Interfaith rallies, projects, and dialogue help to overcome past legacies of hostility and suspicion, but we are far from complete
consensus and peace on most social issues.

Religious Conflict

The issues of inter- and intra-faith conflict are similar to those of the
past, yet modifications continually occur. Opposition to having Catholics
in public offices has subsided since John F. Kennedy became the first
Catholic President of the U.S., but we have yet to see an Eastern Orthodox, Jew, Buddhist, Hindu, or Moslem in that position, and many religious bodies are divided over whether it is advisable even to consider a
woman, black, or other minority person for that office. There also are
disagreements within and between the religious groups on almost every
other public-policy issue. Some of the more prominent points of disagreement are the federal defense budget, nuclear armaments, equal rights
for women, social-welfare policies, capital punishment, religion in public
schools, tax funds for private education, sex education, and abortion.

---

[56] COCU's 1982 members are the African Methodist Episcopal Church, the African Methodist Episcopal Zion Church, the Christian Methodist Episcopal Church, the Christian
Church (Disciples of Christ), the Episcopal Church, the Presbyterian Church in the U.S.,
the United Church of Christ, the United Methodist Church, and the United Presbyterian
Church.

CONCLUSION

Differences also emerge with respect to international affairs. In this area an interesting turnabout has occurred vis-à-vis Latin America. Roman Catholics once were strongly allied with the vested interests of most Central and South American nations, the small minority of Protestants struggling on the fringes of the social, political, and economic power structures. By the early 1980's the support of liberation theology by leading Catholics made many priests and bishops allies of the peasants and working class in opposition to powerful landholders and politicians, while Protestants, struggling for recognition, focused on gradual change through converting individuals. In 1982 the rise of General Efraín Ríos Montt, a Pentecostal military leader, to the presidency of Guatemala, where about one-third of the population are Protestants, helped to solidify Protestant support for the government, but it probably also increased Catholic opposition. He was deposed by a military coup in August 1983.

In the Middle East the conflict of Israel with neighboring states, its involvements in Lebanon, and the problems of Palestinians have contributed to tensions in American religious groups. Most Jews fully support the military actions and other policies of Israel. So do most fundamentalists, who expect the great Battle of Armageddon (Rev. 16:16) to occur soon at Israel's Mound of Megiddo between the supporters of Jehovah (Yahweh) and their opponents from Syria and the U.S.S.R., together with allies of each side. Most Catholics and Protestants, however, are less supportive of Israel, many of them feeling that Israel has violated human rights by its militarism, colonization of the West Bank and border territories in the name of "self-defense," and refusal (to this date) to negotiate with the Palestine Liberation Organization.[57] Whenever they criticize Israel's domestic or foreign policy, some Jews accuse them of anti-Semitism.

Jewish-Christian tensions also relate to Christian evangelism. Effectiveness in winning converts has led to skirmishes between Jews for Jesus and the Jewish establishment in many communities. Jews castigate groups like the Messianic Jewish Alliance of America, which believes and teaches that Jesus Christ is Yeshua, the Jewish Messiah, and whose worship adapts Christian content to Jewish language, rituals, and festivals. Sometimes Jews also have been critical of evangelistic crusades directed toward the conversion of non-Christians. The reason for this criticism is that, proceeding on the misapprehension that any person baptized into a Christian heritage is automatically a "Christian," they mistakenly assume that Jews are the primary target of crusades. Evangelicals and fundamentalists, however, insist that even someone baptized into a Christian heritage must be born again, becoming Christian in the true sense only by a per-

---

[57] For examples of divergent perspectives on these issues see the pro-Israel *Dispatch From Jerusalem*, which is published by Bridges for Peace (P.O. Box 33145, Tulsa, OK 74135), and *The Link*, which attempts to impartially analyze the values, religions, culture, history, economics, and politics of the Middle East. *The Link* is published by Americans for Middle East Understanding (Room 771, 475 Riverside Drive, New York, N.Y. 10115).

sonal faith commitment to Jesus Christ. Most of their evangelistic targets in America hence have a Christian heritage, although Jews and others are included as well. This creates tension with sacramentalist Christian groups, too, who accuse them of proselyting.

Beginning in 1973 many fundamentalist groups published "Christian Yellow Pages" (CYP) for their communities. These directories of businesses owned or operated by born-again Christians aim to identify persons and agencies that can be fully trusted because they share the same faith. They enable Christians to help each other economically instead of siphoning resources out to non-Christians, "secular humanists," and "syncretists" who sometimes are charged with being part of an anti-Christ system. Critics claim that the CYP constitutes an act of aggression against a pluralistic society, that people of other religious persuasions are just as fair and upright in their business dealings, that the CYP amounts to exploitation of religion for material gain, and that it represents a modern form of anti-Semitism. In Portland, Oregon, where the CYP began, the Anti-Defamation League of B'nai B'rith boycotted businesses that advertised in it and threatened a discrimination lawsuit against it.[58] Ironically, one of the books featured in 1977 by the Jewish Book Club was *The Jewish Yellow Pages*,[59] and many religious groups provide similar listings by soliciting advertising for synagogue or parish newsletters, diocesan newspapers, denominational magazines, and similar religious publications. These are functional equivalents of the CYP, implying a special affinity with the advertiser.

Prominent conflicts within several Protestant denominations have centered on the ownership of church property when congregations seceded from a denomination or split into two factions. Several mainline bodies tightened their policies of denominational ownership to avoid losing wealth invested in local churches. Court cases were decided on both sides, depending on the specifics involved.

An analysis of the issues and protagonists of 153 conflict incidents within Catholicism suggests that there was continuity, yet differences, between the 1960's and 1970's. Conflicts in the 1960's represented a mobilization stage; they were more highly intra-organizational, more authority-related, and more highly focused on priests and the local Ordinary. During the implementation and extension stage of the 1970's there were a greater variety of issues, increased emphasis on matters relating to the laity, women, and society, increased salience of conflicts that involved other hierarchical levels, and extra-ecclesial protagonists.[60]

---

[58] "Christian Directory Faces Suit," *Capital Journal* (Salem, Ore.), June 6, 1977, p. 6C.
[59] Its successor is Mae Shafter Rockland, *The New Jewish Yellow Pages* (Englewood, N.J.: SBS Publishing, 1981). However, the later volume focuses upon explicitly Jewish decorations, entertainment, food, educational materials, gifts, services, and religious articles.
[60] John Seidler, "Changing Issues Within Catholicism," paper presented at the annual meeting of the Association for the Sociology of Religion, Toronto, August 23, 1981.

As indicated in Chapter 13, conflict is not always destructive; it can be very wholesome, helping to clarify values, goals, and objectives. How religious leaders can best manage conflict situations is a subject that deserves much more attention than it typically is given in theological education, as well as in sociological research.[61]

Research Methods and Religion

Contradictory generalizations about various aspects of religion are widespread. One source of them is the diversity of religious beliefs and behavior, alongside the tendency to extend conclusions about one or a few groups to all people. Besides that problem, the definitions, indicators, or measures of religion used in research may vary widely. Much social-science research has used only one simple criterion, such as Protestant, Catholic, or Jewish preference, identification with a denomination, church membership or attendance, or agreement with but one or a few selected beliefs. Even sophisticated combinations of several such criteria have pragmatic, logical, theological, and scientific limitations, so it is always wise to look for the precise definitions and indicators used in any study and to identify their strengths and limitations.

Religious phenomena are so complex that it is easy to find evidence in support of preconceptions, whatever they may be. Those who believe that religion is merely an imaginary reification or hypostatization find evidence that religious phenomena are natural consequences of social, psychological, genetic, biochemical, or other such factors without any supernatural basis whatever. Believers with a solid faith in their own religion regard whatever supports it as eternally and empirically true, tending to view religion as an independent variable that causes other events and ultimately explains everything. People at both extremes collect evidence to support their pre-judgments. Case studies of specific instances or incidents have been variously used to illustrate that religion contributes to the well-being and to the ill-being of people and society. Phenomenological and ethnomethodological investigations, although intended to be open, are pervaded with subjective interpretations which emerge from the tendency to selectively notice certain kinds of data, unconsciously bracketing contrary interpretations, and from the impossibility of ever being able to control all ideological perspectives. The effort to collect objective empirical facts through surveys and other "scientific" methods is similarly slanted (consciously or unconsciously) by the researcher's selection of questions, response categories, and respondents. In addition, there may be a halo effect—respondents may reveal themselves in a more religiously favorable

---

[61] The strategies presented in Speed Leas and Paul Kittlaus, *Church Fights: Managing Conflict in the Local Church* (Philadelphia: Westminster Press, 1973), provide an excellent foundation for such work.

light than fits their actual beliefs and conduct. There always are great or small discrepancies between professed ideals and actual conduct.[62] (Skeptics capitalize upon these discrepancies to charge Christian believers with "hypocrisy," but the Christians reply that they are still on their pilgrimage toward perfection, growing toward "the measure of the stature of the fulness of Christ"—Eph. 4:13.) The same findings in research hence may be used as arguments for or against any given religion, and opposite impressions may be conveyed by simple insertion of an adjective ("only" or "a surprising" with the same statistic obviously slants the message communicated).

With the increasing sophistication of sociology of religion during the 1950's and 1960's came growing attention to the multidimensionality of its subject matter. Glock's five dimensions of religiosity (pp. 418-19) stimulated much reflection and research. Fichter noted omission of the communal dimension, which theologians label *koinonia*—the association of people with each other in a religious group.[63] Other studies listed as many as eleven dimensions, adding such categories as devotionalism, dogmatism, instrumentalism, intrinsic-extrinsic involvement, salience, and ultimate concern.[64] Glock's sweeping statement that "within one or another of these dimensions all of the many and diverse manifestations of religiosity prescribed by the different religions of the world can be ordered"[65] was evaluated in the context of Christianity with the conclusion that he omitted a spiritual component related to the realm of faith, revelation, illumination, and insight. This component cuts across all the dimensions, infusing them with a supernatural quality pertaining to ultimate commitment or concern.[66] Many sociologists subsequently have begun to analyze this spiritual component with promising results.[67]

The consequential is perhaps the most difficult of Glock's five dimen-

---

[62] See Irwin Deutscher, *What We Say/What We Do: Sentiments and Acts* (Glenview, Ill.: Scott, Foresman and Co., 1973), and David O. Moberg, "Presidential Address: Virtues for the Sociology of Religion," *Sociological Analysis,* 39, no. 1 (Spring 1978), 1-18.

[63] Joseph H. Fichter, "Sociological Measurement of Religiosity," *Review of Religious Research,* 10, no. 3 (Spring 1969), 169-77.

[64] Joseph E. Faulkner and Gordon F. DeJong, "Religiosity in 5-D: An Empirical Analysis," *Social Forces,* 45, no. 2 (Dec. 1966), 246-54; Morton B. King and Richard A. Hunt, "Measuring the Religious Variable: Amended Findings," *Journal for the Scientific Study of Religion,* 8, no. 2 (Fall 1969), 321-23; Morton B. King and Richard A. Hunt, *Measuring Religious Dimensions* (Dallas: Southern Methodist University Press, 1972); Jerry D. Cardwell, *The Social Context of Religiosity* (Washington, D.C.: University Press of America, 1980).

[65] Charles Y. Glock, "On the Study of Religious Commitment," *Religious Education,* 57 (July-Aug. 1962), Research Supplement, p. S-98.

[66] David O. Moberg, "The Encounter of Scientific and Religious Values Pertinent to Man's Spiritual Nature," *Sociological Analysis,* 28, no. 1 (Spring 1967), 22-33. Cf. Luigi Sturzo, *The True Life: Sociology of the Supernatural,* trans. Barbara Barclay Carter (London: Geoffrey Bles, 1947).

[67] Contributions by 27 authors from nine nations are found in David O. Moberg, ed., *Spiritual Well-Being: Sociological Perspectives* (Washington, D.C.: University Press of America, 1979).

sions to analyze. A review of 185 articles which treat religion in some way as an independent variable, loosely defined as a cause of other variables (i.e., of dependent variables), found that only 5 come close to meeting the scientific canons for proving causal relationship, though 16 more meet somewhat relaxed criteria. The other 164 either report negative findings or employ insufficient controls to produce valid conclusions.[68] Furthermore, "although religions prescribe much of how their adherents ought to think and act in everyday life, it is not entirely clear the extent to which religious consequences are *a part* of religious commitment or simply *follow from it.*"[69]

Not only are there numerous dimensions of religiosity, but there also are large numbers of indicators for each of them, all of which can be combined in varying patterns by individual persons. Even with sophisticated computer technology, it is impossible simultaneously to "get a handle" on all religious dimensions, components, and indicators (although every expansion is enlightening), so reductionism is inevitable in the scientific study of religion. In addition, different religious groups emphasize varying combinations of religious expression, application, and involvement. What one considers important another treats as secondary or even irrelevant, so divergent styles, models, or patterns of religiosity are evident among the various religions as well as within their branches. Thus fundamentalist Protestants stress correct beliefs, traditional Catholics proper ritual observance, charismatic Christians emotional feelings and expressions of the moving of the Holy Spirit, and Unitarian Universalists the sharing of information about current issues.

The "official" criteria for "correct" expressions of religiosity also diverge from the nonofficial popular or folk religion of the people. The larger a religious body is, the greater is the likelihood that its members have diverse interpretations of their beliefs, even when using the same words from a creed. Christians' perceptions of God, Jesus Christ, faith, living the Christian life, baptism, and every other religious concept vary from person to person. Some groups allow a broad range of interpretations, while others are more conservative, permitting open expression of only a more narrow range. This may be one reason for denominational switching, at least within Protestantism; when people move to a new community, the local church of another denomination may come closer to the styles, beliefs, and perspectives of their former church than one of the same denomination. They feel more at home by switching labels in order to retain similar definitions and customs.

Awareness of such complexities and of the strengths and limitations of

---

[68] Gary D. Bouma, "Assessing the Impact of Religion: A Critical Review," *Sociological Analysis*, 31, no. 4 (Winter 1970), 172-79. The 185 articles reviewed appeared in 10 major sociological journals during the 1960's.

[69] Rodney Stark and Charles Y. Glock, *American Piety: The Nature of Religious Commitment* (Berkeley: University of California Press, 1970), p. 16.

each method of investigation can help to overcome the weaknesses in research on religion as well as to prevent the sweeping over-generalizations which purport to present "the whole truth" about whatever is studied. Triangulation is helpful when investigating any specific subject related to religion. It involves the use of multiple methods and techniques of research, study of numerous and diverse samples of the people and groups under investigation, application of several theoretical orientations, utilization of the perspectives and tools of many disciplines, and interpretations of findings by scholars of diverse professional orientations and ideological commitments. Applied to any topic, it typically reveals that religion functions diversely and often is simultaneously an independent, dependent, and intervening variable. The paradigm for the analysis of a religious group in the appendix illustrates that one can begin such research at an elementary level even without having explicit training in the social sciences.

A Mosaic in Constant Flux

We have seen that in some respects American religion is continuously changing, whether from the perspective of the statistics of church membership, participation, and distribution, the natural life cycle of religious agencies and institutions, the evidences and expressions of social concern in and by churches, the local, national, and international religious structures, the nature and forms of religious conflict, the research techniques used to improve our understanding of religious phenomena, or any of the additional topics discussed in this book. Fads and fashions come and go in the study of religion as well as in the activities of religious bodies and the interests of people, yet in their midst is a remarkable continuity of religious beliefs, behavior, and institutional structures.

Refinement of our understanding occurs with each additional piece of research, yet the basic elements change only very gradually and usually more in relatively trivial details than in crucial respects, remaining as a foundation for more detailed understanding. That foundation is sketched in this book; pieces of more detailed research on most of its topics are suggested by the footnotes and especially the annotated references at the ends of chapters.

While every analogy is defective, American religion is like a mosaic with changing parts.[70] The many pieces shift positions as environmental breezes blow, yet the overall pattern remains very similar from one configuration to another. Occasionally a new piece is added or an old one taken away, yet this addition or deletion only gradually modifies the basic

---

[70] See Phillip E. Hammond and Benton Johnson, eds., *American Mosaic: Social Patterns of Religion in the United States* (New York: Random House, 1970).

shapes and relationships. Both continuity and change characterize the church as a social institution and the larger religious phenomena of which it is a part.

Selected References

Anderson, Charles H., *White Protestant Americans: From National Origins to Religious Group.* Englewood Cliffs, N.J.: Prentice-Hall, 1970. The past and present status of the major white Protestant groups in America, which increasingly perceive that they are distinct from others.

Barker, Eileen, ed., *New Religious Movements: A Perspective for Understanding Society.* New York: Edwin Mellen Press, 1982. Studies of new religions, mostly in America, to improve understanding of the people, social processes, and societies involved.

Bromley, David G., and James T. Richardson, eds., *The Brainwashing/Deprogramming Controversy: Sociological, Psychological, Legal and Historical Perspectives.* New York: Edwin Mellen Press, 1982. Descriptions and interpretations of anti-cult activities and their implications for social conflict and religious liberty.

Carroll, Jackson W., Douglas W. Johnson, and Martin E. Marty, *Religion in America: 1950 to the Present.* San Francisco: Harper and Row, 1979. A summary of trends with tentative projections into the future.

Ducey, Michael H., *Sunday Morning: Aspects of Urban Ritual.* New York: Free Press, 1977. A study of ritual and change in four Christian churches in the Lincoln Park area of Chicago.

Eister, Allan W., ed., *Changing Perspectives in the Scientific Study of Religion.* New York: John Wiley and Sons, 1974. Significant essays on the renewed interest in the study of religion, its societal functions, liminality, belief and unbelief, the symbolization process, and the investigation of religious commitment.

Enroth, Ronald, *The Lure of the Cults.* Chappaqua, N.Y.: Christian Herald Books, 1980. A sociologist's discussion of the nature and allure of new religious movements, including Christian values for their appraisal and suggestions for parents and church workers whose youth have joined them.

Enroth, Ronald, *Youth, Brainwashing, and the Extremist Cults.* Grand Rapids: Zondervan, 1977. A sociologist's case histories of converts to seven new religious groups and commentaries on cult commitment with evaluations from a Christian perspective.

Fenn, Richard, *Toward A Theory of Secularization.* Storrs, Conn.: Society for the Scientific Study of Religion, 1978. Relationships between the secularization process and civil religion, new religious movements, and legal problems of defining religion.

Fichter, Joseph H., *The Catholic Cult of the Paraclete.* New York: Sheed and Ward, 1975. Research on the Catholic charismatic movement, including results of surveys.

Gerlach, Luther P., and Virginia H. Hine, *People, Power, Change: Movements of Social Transformation.* Indianapolis: Bobbs-Merrill Co., 1970. An analysis based upon three years of anthropological research into the Pentecostal and the Black Power movements.

Goldstein, Sidney, and Calvin Goldschneider, *Jewish Americans: Three Generations in a Jewish Community.* Englewood Cliffs, N.J.: Prentice-Hall, 1968. Conclusions about generation change based on a sample of almost 1,500 Jewish families.

Hadden, Jeffrey K., and Charles E. Swann, *Prime Time Preachers.* Reading,

Mass.: Addison-Wesley, 1981. A sociological analysis of religious-television producers.

Harwood, Alan, *Rx: Spiritist as Needed: A Study of a Puerto Rican Community Mental Health Resource*. New York: John Wiley and Sons, 1977. The subculture of Spiritism and its methods of treating mental illness.

Heilman, Samuel C., *Synagogue Life: A Study in Symbolic Interaction*. Chicago: University of Chicago Press, 1976. A sociological study of the activities and functions of an Orthodox synagogue based on a year of research.

Horowitz, Irving Louis, ed., *Science, Sin and Scholarship: The Politics of Reverend Moon and the Unification Church*. Cambridge, Mass.: MIT Press, 1978. A collection of papers critical of the "Moonies," their numerous spin-off organizations, and especially the International Conferences on the Unity of the Sciences.

Hunter, James Davison, *American Evangelicalism: Conservative Religion and the Quandary of Modernity*. New Brunswick, N.J.: Rutgers University Press, 1983. A sociological interpretation of evangelicals and their confrontation with societal changes related to modernization.

Kanter, Rosabeth Moss, ed., *Communes: Creating and Managing the Collective Life*. New York: Harper and Row, 1973. Forty-five articles on present and past communal groups, mostly in America.

Kauffman, J. Howard, and Leland Harder, *Anabaptists Four Centuries Later: A Profile of Five Mennonite and Brethren in Christ Denominations*. Scottdale, Pa.: Herald Press, 1975. A survey using numerous innovative measures.

Kephart, William M., *Extraordinary Groups: The Sociology of Unconventional Life-Styles*. New York: St. Martin's Press, 1976. Seven religious cultural groups in America.

Kersten, Lawrence L., *The Lutheran Ethic: The Impact of Religion on Laymen and Clergy*. Detroit: Wayne State University Press, 1970. Survey findings on religious commitment, church participation, religion and politics, civil liberties, morality, and other beliefs and attitudes.

LaBarre, Weston, *They Shall Take Up Serpents: Psychology of the Southern Snake-Handling Cult*. New York: Schocken Books, 1969. Anthropological study of the cult, its symbolism, and its people.

Lederach, Paul M., *Mennonite Youth: Report of Mennonite Youth Research*. Scottdale, Pa.: Herald Press, 1971. Findings of a sample of 1,232 youth in the Mennonite Church with comparisons to similar studies in the Evangelical Covenant Church and Southern Baptist Convention.

Lindt-Gollin, Gillian, *Moravians in Two Worlds: A Study of Changing Communities*. New York: Columbia University Press, 1967. A sociological study of the religious beliefs and practices, polity, family structure, and economy of Moravians in Europe and America.

Liu, William T., and Nathaniel J. Pallone, eds., *Catholics/U.S.A.: Perspectives on Social Change*. New York: John Wiley and Sons, 1970. Social-science studies related to "the massive social changes" that have occurred in the American church.

Moberg, David O., "Evaluation Research on Religion," in Eister, *Changing Perspectives* (above), pp. 335-53. A summary of evaluation studies with an extensive bibliography.

Moberg, David O., "Why Should Anyone Go to Church? A Sociological View," in *Why Sunday Mass?* rev. ed., ed. Karen Hurley. Cincinnati: St. Anthony Messenger Press, 1980, pp. 57-88. An interpretation of why people quit attending, functions and dysfunctions of church attendance, and the role of personal commitment.

Nordquist, Ted A., *Ananda Cooperative Village: A Study in the Beliefs, Values, and Attitudes of a New Age Religious Community*. Uppsala, Sweden: Religionshistoriska institutionen, University of Uppsala, 1978. An in-depth study of a rural California community of the Self-Realization Fellowship.

Obenhaus, Victor, *The Church and Faith in Mid-America*. Philadelphia: Westminster Press, 1963. Survey research in five towns of a typical Midwestern Corn-Belt county.

Poloma, Margaret, *The Charismatic Movement: Is There a New Pentecost?* Boston: Twayne Publishers, 1982. A sociologist's description and explanation of the ideology, history, emerging institutions, and impact of the charismatic movement based upon personal participation, extensive observation, interviews, and other research.

Raboteau, Albert J., *Slave Religion: The "Invisible Institution" in the Antebellum South*. New York: Oxford University Press, 1978. An excellent historical study which helps explain many distinctive features of the contemporary Black church in America.

Roof, Wade Clark, *Community and Commitment: Religious Plausibility in a Liberal Protestant Church*. New York: Elsevier, 1978. An empirical study of Episcopalians.

Schroeder, W. Widick, Victor Obenhaus, Larry A. Jones, and Thomas Sweetser, S.J., *Suburban Religion: Churches and Synagogues in the American Experience*. Chicago: Center for the Scientific Study of Religion, 1974. Research findings and interpretations.

Sobel, B. Z., *Hebrew Christianity: The Thirteenth Tribe*. New York: John Wiley and Sons, 1974. A sociological study of the origin and development of the Hebrew-Christian movement.

Southard, Samuel, *Religious Inquiry: An Introduction to the Why and How*. Nashville: Abingdon, 1976. An introduction to research methods for churches at the grassroots level.

Strommen, Merton P., ed., *Research on Religious Development*. New York: Hawthorn Books, 1971. A huge compendium summarizing research findings on various aspects of religious maturation and growth from childhood to old age.

Strommen, Merton P., Milo L. Brekke, Ralph C. Underwager, and Arthur L. Johnson, *A Study of Generations*. Minneapolis: Augsburg Publishing House, 1972. Results of a two-year study of 5,000 Lutherans aged 15 to 65 on 78 dimensions of beliefs, values, aspirations, and actions.

Wagner, C. Peter, *Our Kind of People: The Ethical Dimensions of Church Growth in America*. Atlanta: John Knox Press, 1979. A defense of the homogeneous-unit principle of church growth with much supporting sociological data.

Wallis, Roy, ed., *Millennialism and Charisma*. Belfast, Northern Ireland: The Queen's University, 1982. Essays on the linkage of millennial beliefs with charismatic authority in several new religious and quasi-religious movements.

Whitworth, John McKelvie, *God's Blueprints: A Sociological Study of Three Utopian Sects*. Boston: Routledge and Kegan Paul, 1975. Research on the Shakers, Oneida Community, and Society of Brothers (Bruderhof).

Williams, Peter W., *Popular Religion in America: Symbolic Change and the Modernization Process in Historical Perspective*. Englewood Cliffs, N.J.: Prentice-Hall, 1980. Popular and folk religions in modern society.

Wilson, Bryan, ed., *The Social Impact of New Religious Movements*. New York: Rose of Sharon Press, 1981. Essays and case studies from a working conference on the social context of the new religions, negative reactions against them, and the relative-deprivation thesis.

Wuthnow, Robert, ed., *The Religious Dimension: New Directions in Quantitative Research*. New York: Academic Press, 1979. A rich collection of 17 essays on research attainments and needs in the areas of measuring religious commitment, correlates of commitment, and religion and social change.

Zaretsky, Irving I., and Mark P. Leone, eds., *Religious Movements in Contemporary America*. Princeton, N.J.: Princeton University Press, 1975. Essays and research reports on phenomena related to new religious movements.

Zuck, Roy B., and Gene A. Getz, *Christian Youth—An In-Depth Study*. Chicago: Moody Press, 1968. The report of the National Sunday School Association survey of evangelical youth.

🏛 Chapter **20**

Sociology and the Church's Future

A major purpose of this book has been to indicate that all organized religion, regardless of its doctrines and creeds, rituals and ceremonies, organizational structure, and type of leadership, exists in and with reference to society. It functions in a social setting and is profoundly influenced by its environment in nearly every aspect of its ministry. Even the most subjective aspects of personal religion are influenced by group experiences, for the basic religious attitudes, concepts, and objectives, as well as the language in which they are couched, are learned in social situations. Man is never religious alone—even when he is alone. **As is true of other aspects of collective behavior, organized religion precedes** and in a sense transcends the contemporary individual.

Diverse as organized religion in America is, all of it can be treated justifiably from the perspective of elements common to it by virtue of its position as part of an overarching society. Dominated by Protestant Christianity with Roman Catholicism in a strong second place, American religion is much less fragmented than appears at first glance to be the case. Foremost among its shared elements are the sociological characteristics of social norms, social processes, and social structures and functions which we have examined. These features are involved in the formation, development, behavior, and decline of religious groups. Understanding the relationships between these groups, their connections with the rest of society, their social setting, and the social aspects of personal religion is of tremendous importance to successful achievement of the church's mission; every local church and denominational body is profoundly influenced by them.

Whether a church succeeds or fails in accomplishing its purposes depends to a great extent upon its social milieu. Every church reflects the surrounding community of which it is a part. When a community is prosperous, its churches generally are prosperous and vice versa, as we have seen. Non-material aspects of success and failure also are closely correlated with community characteristics and pressures and the church's responses to them. In order for any church to fulfill its functions effectively it is therefore of vital importance for its leaders to understand its social environment, the way in which its organization and activities are shaped and influenced by that environment, and the needs of mankind created and modified by characteristics and trends of their surrounding world. Needless to say, these features of social life are not automatically a part of man's knowledge. They do not become evident merely through casual observation of and normal participation in society. Extensive study of social structures and processes, including penetrating research related to the church's place and participation in them, is needed to call attention to matters which ordinarily would not claim the attention of church officials but which are essential to successful accomplishment of church objectives. Such knowledge has always been important, but it is especially necessary in the modern world.

The Church in a Changing World

When the lives and work of each generation were like stereotyped repetitions of preceding generations, tradition may have been a satisfactory guide. But today, with social change proceeding more rapidly than ever before in history and in many respects at an ever-increasing rate, it is particularly important that churches continually analyze their role in society, engage in research to clarify how they may best attain their goals, and adjust their programs to meet the spiritual needs of contemporary men. Flexibility must be juxtaposed with the stabilizing influence of conservatism if the church is to maintain itself in a changing world.

At many points in our examination, we have treated the church as if it were static and changeless, but this has been only for the purpose of analysis. From its earliest origins in pre-historic antiquity, organized religion has been a dynamic institution continually in flux. Its changes were relatively slow in the distant past, but in the great technological and social mobility of contemporary American society it is involved in a perpetual process of adaptation.

Integrated with a fluid society, every local church must be fluid. This is apparent in shifting schedules for activities, changing persons in membership, diversification of programs, and transitions in leadership. These adjustments may be observed in every congregation and parish as members move away and others arrive, as children grow into adulthood and old members die, and as economic means of livelihood are modified with industrial and commercial developments in a dynamic society. No local church is exactly the same in its membership composition from one decade to the next. Even if it consists of the same persons, they become more mature and change with their changing environment. Regular participants may believe a church to remain unchanged, but the migrant member who returns after a decade observes numerous modifications.

Few churches are able to retain successfully an unmodified program of activities over long periods of time. Social change cuts across every aspect of the work of the church. Differential rates of adaptation to societal changes create many of the problems and misunderstandings found within denominational bodies, as well as within local churches and between the major religious groupings of America. The successful religious group is involved in a continuous process of development, even though its members and leaders may be unconscious of that fact and as a result may permit it to drift aimlessly as environmental pressures lead to haphazard modification of one element of its organization and activities after another.

The static, structural view of the church is therefore like a snapshot, taken at a given moment in time, which arrests motion and may falsely convey the appearance of lifelessness. The dynamic picture of the church may be likened to a motion picture and a sound-track which record changes as they occur. Both the static or structural and dynamic or functional perspectives are essential to the sociological analysis required for adequate understanding of the contemporary church.

The conditions of modern civilization have made American institutions compete with each other to a much greater extent than they do in agrarian and primitive societies, where all institutions tend to reinforce each other. In this competitive struggle for power and influence the church must understand much better than ever before its continually changing social environment and the impact of that environment upon the lives of people if it is to cope successfully with the tremendous challenges it faces. If the church is merely another social institution, not significantly different in its objectives and activities from others in society, its services are not particularly needed to meet the challenges of the present age.

Is the Church Unique?

As we have seen, the same types of social forces which influence other institutions affect the church. The emergence, development, and decline of the church as a social institution are conditioned by and result from a host of social factors. These include population mobility, demographic changes within the community, social class distinctions, ethnic segregation, racial prejudice, social disorganization, and various other aspects of social life and change.

Conflict within the church arises out of struggles for power, personality clashes, differential acceptance of change, and other social and psychological factors, as well as out of ideological struggles. Relationships of the church with other agencies, organizations, and institutions of society reflect the same kind of struggle for survival, analogous efforts to gain and maintain power, and attempts to increase influence over persons and groups which are parallel to those of other institutions. Just as in other groups, cooperation and opposition in their numerous and diverse forms are commingled in the flow of human interaction that is the essence of institutional behavior.

The church's composite functions comprise a unique set of roles in society, yet most specific items are not unique to the church. Other institutions also help socialize the individual, promote social solidarity, foster stability in society, establish personal status, nourish social fellowship, support morality, exercise social control, meet social welfare and philanthropic needs, and provide esthetic, recreational, economic, educational, and other services. Furthermore, the professed goals of church activity for individuals and groups are often unmet, as is true of other institutions, and many church activities have detrimental side-effects. Because it is not as unique as many would like to think, its influence on individuals as well as on the family, government, business, education, and social welfare is difficult to separate from the influence of other social forces.

Similarly, many characteristics of other professions also apply to the clergy and the other specialized personnel of the church. To be sure, there are differences in the relative importance and intensity of these common traits. Yet the clergy are similar to others in that background influences draw them into the ministry, considerations of social status affect their work, numerous social controls exert pressure upon them, and they experience many special problems related to their occupational roles.

Profoundly influenced by urbanization, growth of the suburbs, industrialization, commercialism, pervasive secularism, the ideological struggle against Communism, a highly mobile and increasingly educated population, and other basic features of contemporary culture, the church in many ways bears the image of American society. It continues its attempts, however, to influence that society as well. Motivated by sanctions it believes to be supernatural and professing to be the conscience of society and the light of the world, the church believes that its religious education, social action programs, and evangelism wholesomely affect all other institutions from the family to world government. The full scope of its influence is unknown, but we have summarized the incomplete, imperfect evidence that is available to discover that unintended, often unnoticed, deleterious as well as wholesome effects grow out of the faith and action of American religions.

The church is a part of society; even when it pulls apart from society and tries to be separate, it cannot fully succeed in freeing itself from the web of economic, political, linguistic, and other social relationships of its culture and from the complex patterns of past cultural conditioning which its individual members have experienced. To establish what it considers to be ethically pure relationships with no tainting from "unclean" sources is impossible as long as society itself is not completely pure.

In its efforts to influence people and groups, the church often becomes a power group competing with other institutions for influence in society, funds, personnel, and other benefits. Its competitive techniques are similar to those used in business, government, and schools. At times local churches lose their competitive struggle for survival as populations shift or as they fail to make satisfactory adjustments to changes in the economic, ethnic, or institutional characteristics of the people and communities they serve. Leaders in them, lacking sociological insights, may not recognize when social forces are primarily responsible for these changes and may unjustly blame them on lack of spirituality among their people or on other imaginary causes. Yet, even when local churches disintegrate, the church as a major social institution lives on. New congregations replace those that die; new sects succeed disbanded denominations. For man, it seems, must satisfy certain religious needs, and he can do this only through some form of, or substitute for, organized religion.

General processes of social interaction and structural characteristics of human groups and institutions are of great significance to the church. Social science descriptions of these processes and structures are abstractions from reality of the same basic nature as the descriptions of physical and biological structures and functions in other sciences. Although values which dominate churches may differ from those dominant in other institutions, man's interaction in the church is not intrinsically different from his interaction in other social situations. Supernatural sanctions may be applied by the believer to every domain of life; they are not limited to organized religion.

The uniqueness of the church does not lie, then, in its social characteristics. Its social functions, structures, and processes are shared with other social institutions. The ideological values, philosophical rationalizations, and theological postulates which are typically emphasized in the church generally make it a distinct institution which is different from others. Yet even here the distinctness is not as great as might appear at first sight to be the case. The church appeals to divine authority as its basis, but so have many totalitarian governments. Supernatural sanctions for institutional behavior have also been applied to the family, the arts and sciences, and even the economic order. It is only by an act of faith that modern man can accept the tenet that the church is a special institution ordained by God and established in a unique manner. Even this concept is not easy to apply to local churches, for they obviously are organized and maintained by interacting men.

The greatest unique opportunity before organized religion today lies in man's desire to have an adequate philosophy of the nature of the universe, the meaning of life, and his destiny, to achieve a satisfying personal **relationship with the great First Cause of that universe, the Creator, and** to find associated values which can guide his daily conduct. If this challenge is not met by America's religions, it is possible that the void may be filled by pseudo-religions analogous to European fascism of the 1930's or even Soviet Communism. Since science cannot provide the basic values necessary for successful social interaction, the church has an opportunity to provide them and the accompanying individual attitudes toward self and others that are essential for the cooperative enterprises which comprise society.

To meet this challenge the church needs not only its basic tenets related to faith in a transcendent God, but also an understanding of the kind of world in which contemporary man lives, the changes occurring in that world, and the limitations imposed by the institutional organization, activities, norms, facilities, and personnel of the church. It must appreciate its unique role in the midst of a highly complex civilization. The **sociology of religion can make an impressive contribution to such understanding.**

The Sociology of Religion

Scientific examination of the organization and processes of group life in the church focuses upon that which is typical of a large number of cases and that which is repetitive, enabling prediction and increased rational control as knowledge grows. Specific events are influenced by the larger processes common to all of man's social behavior. These processes of interaction in the church involve human beings who also interact in other social situations. They therefore are not limited in scope to the church alone. The sociology of religion is but part of the larger social science called sociology. New findings from other areas of that discipline are relevant to man's social interaction in the church, and new findings in the sociology of religion similarly are relevant to other branches of the social sciences. Neither in practice nor in theory can one who is concerned with the sociology of American religion ignore the rest of man's life in modern society.

Goal-directed cooperation and conflict are basic to the existence of social institutions. In the struggle of individuals, of churches, of other religious organizations, and of other institutions to survive and to increase their power, the general cultural environment is both a container of the church and an all-pervading influence permeating its inmost being. How to resolve the dilemma of being in the world, permeated by the world and immersed in it, and yet of being distinct from it—as the ideals of most American religions advocate—is a major problem of social ethics confronting the contemporary theologian. The sociologist can indicate the nature of the problem, but its solution lies outside the immediate scope of his scientific work.

In nearly every major subject area we have examined, it has been apparent that a great deal more remains unknown than is known about the American church as a social institution. Only research can expand the horizons of our limited knowledge. Such research is reciprocally linked with the development of clear concepts, systematic theories, and reliable scientific instruments which will enable the detection and understanding of unplanned and typically unobserved consequences of the structure and activities of the church. Many of these unrecognized consequences currently counteract and negate the wholesome contributions of organized religion. Developments in other branches of sociology undoubtedly can contribute to such achievement, but without specialists who can devote their time and energy freely to sociological analysis of religion and the church, few of its benefits will flow to organized religion.

Scientific research in the sociology of religion must be related to relevant historical studies, psychological experiments, cross-cultural analyses, philosophical evaluations, and theological interpretations. Above all, it must be combined with basic sociological theory, testing hypotheses which are linked with that body of theory in order to develop reliable, systematized knowledge, which can then be used by those who wish to further the objectives of the church. Such work requires pioneering personnel who are trained in scientific methodology and who, for many types of studies, also have a sympathetic understanding of the beliefs and values of the groups they analyze. It requires cooperation from laymen and professional leaders in the church. It must be nourished with an atmosphere of liberty which permits discovery of the truth, whether that truth be pleasant or painful.

Unless research foundations, academic institutions, and religious bodies are willing to support basic research on religion which may not appear to have any immediate practical results, the sociology of religion will continue to lag behind the problems and opportunities confronting the church in this dynamic century. Other branches of social science and related disciplines will also suffer if sociological study of religion lags, for it calls attention to many insights and principles that tend to be overlooked when studying social structures and processes which are generally but wrongly considered to be purely secular or non-religious.

To succeed in accomplishing its purposes in the modern world, the church must plan systematically for the future. Ideally this includes the application of social research methodology to analyze and interpret its structure and functions in relation to the entire changing society of which it is a part. As it does this, many of the latent ill effects (dysfunctions) of organized religion can be avoided and its contributions to individuals and society (functions) can be promoted more effectively; both the ends and means of church organization and processes need careful scientific evaluation guided by the normative goals of the church.

When church work is based upon solidly established findings of the behavioral sciences as well as upon superempirical religious values and motivations, organized religion can attain its objectives much more efficiently than is typically the case at present when tradition, speculation, and guesswork dominate. It is therefore to the advantage of churchmen as well as of social scientists to work toward rapid development of the sociology of religion. Increasing recognition of this fact, accompanying support of religious research, growing pressures upon and within the church, and expanding needs and resources in society make it likely that major advances in the sociological understanding of religion will occur in the near future.

Selected References

Caplow, Theodore, et al., *All Faithful People: Change and Continuity in Middletown's Religion.* Minneapolis: University of Minnesota Press, 1983. The report of a team of social scientists who returned to Middletown (Muncie. Ind.) to gauge the changes that have occurred since the studies by Robert and Helen Lynd in the 1920's and 1930's.

Chalfant, H. Paul, Robert E. Beckley, and C. Eddie Palmer, *Religion in Contemporary Society.* Palo Alto, Calif.: Mayfield Publishing Co., 1981. A textbook in the sociology of American religion; includes a chapter on theories and one on fundamentalism.

Cutler, Donald R., ed., *The Religious Situation: 1968.* Boston: Beacon Press, 1968. A comprehensive collection of papers on the experience and expression of religion, definitions of the religious dimensions, and social indicators of the religious situation.

Cutler, Donald R., ed., *The Religious Situation: 1969.* Boston: Beacon Press, 1969. Commentaries on the world religious situation besides papers on topics in the 1968 edition.

Douglass, H. Paul, and Edmund deS. Brunner, *The Protestant Church as a Social Institution.* New York: Russell and Russell, 1972 (Institute of Social and Religious Research, 1935). A valuable summary of major findings and interpretations from 48 major research projects from 1922 to 1934; still a provocative and suggestive source of hypotheses and base for comparison studies.

Fallding, Harold, *The Sociology of Religion*. Toronto: McGraw-Hill Ryerson, 1974. An analysis of eight theoretical and pragmatic sociological issues centered on "an explanation of the unity and diversity in religion."

Faulkner, Joseph E., ed., *Religion's Influence in Contemporary Society*. Columbus: Charles E. Merrill Publishing Co., 1972. Readings to introduce major thrusts in recent sociology of religion.

Greeley, Andrew M., *Religion: A Secular Theory*. New York: Free Press, 1982. A stimulating presentation of 99 theses related to the social science theory that "the driving force of religion . . . is experiential, imaginative, symbolical, and narrational, not propositional."

Hargrove, Barbara W., *The Sociology of Religion: Classical and Contemporary Approaches*. Arlington Heights, Ill.: AHM Publishing Corp., 1979. An introductory survey of the sociology of religion which revises and updates *Reformation of the Holy* (Philadelphia: F. A. Davis Co., 1971).

Johnstone, Ronald L., *Religion in Society: A Sociology of Religion*, rev. ed. Englewood Cliffs, N.J.: Prentice-Hall, 1983. A textbook which includes four chapters on religion in society and four on religion in America.

Lenski, Gerhard, *The Religious Factor*. Westport, Conn.: Greenwood Press, 1977 (Doubleday and Co., 1961). An influential study blending statistical data and sociological theory which reveals religion to be a more significant variable than socioeconomic status in many areas of modern metropolitan life.

McGuire, Meredith B., *Religion: The Social Context*. Belmont, Calif.: Wadsworth Publishing Co., 1981. An introduction to the sociology of religion centered on key issues and including "extended applications" on such topics as women's religion, emerging religious movements, black religion, and secularization of health and healing.

McNamara, Patrick H., ed., *Religion American Style*. New York: Harper and Row, 1974. Essays on relationships between religion and society, American religious organization, religion and social conflict, and religion and contemporary change.

Newman, William M., ed., *The Social Meanings of Religion: An Integrated Anthology*. Chicago: Rand McNally College Publishing Co., 1974. Empirical and theoretical essays in the sociology of religion.

Wach, Joachim, *Sociology of Religion*. Chicago: Phoenix Books, 1962 (University of Chicago Press, 1944). A historical-theoretical analysis which aims to bridge the gap between theology and the social sciences.

Wilson, Bryan, *Religion in Sociological Perspective*. Oxford: Oxford University Press, 1982. Essays on basic theories and perspectives by a British sociologist.

Wilson, John, *Religion in American Society: The Effective Presence*. Englewood Cliffs, N.J.: Prentice-Hall, 1978. A smoothly written introduction to the sociology of religion which recognizes the importance of beliefs but is marred by biases against evangelism and evangelicalism, multitudinous typos, and other flaws.

Winter, J. Alan, *Continuities in the Sociology of Religion: Creed, Congregation, and Community*. New York: Harper and Row, 1977. The cultural aspects of religion as manifested in a creed and social organizational aspects manifested in a congregation and community.

Yinger, J. Milton, *The Scientific Study of Religion*. New York: Macmillan, 1970. A seminal investigation of many theoretical issues in the sociology of religion; emphasizes that religions are embedded in their societies and can be studied scientifically with appropriate theoretical and methodological tools. (Successor of *Religion, Society, and the Individual*, 1957.)

The most important periodicals for the sociological study of American religion are *Sociological Analysis, Journal for the Scientific Study of Religion, Review of Religious Research, Archives de Sciences Sociales des Religions, Social Compass*, and *Annual Review of the Social Sciences of Religion*. Occasional articles also appear in *Current Sociology* and a wide range of other sociological journals, most of which are indexed in *Sociological Abstracts*. Sociological articles on American religion also are scattered in periodicals from disciplines which are indexed in *Religion Index One: Periodicals, Religion Index Two: Multi-Author Works, Social Sciences Index*, and other indexes to current literature. Much current news about religion is reported in *Christian Century, Christianity Today, Evangelical Newsletter*, and other publications.

Comprehensive bibliographies which can help one locate elusive materials include the bilingual (English and Spanish) *Sociology of Religion and Theology: A Bibliography* published by Instituto de Fe y Secularidad (Madrid: Editorial Cuadernos para el Diálogo, S. A., 1975; Vol. B, 1978); Morris I. Berkowitz and J. Edmund Johnson, *Social Scientific Studies of Religion: A Bibliography* (Pittsburgh: University of Pittsburgh Press, 1967); Hervé Carrier, S.J., and Emile Pin, S.J., *Sociology of Christianity: International Bibliography* (Rome: Gregorian University Press, 1964), and Hervé Carrier, S.J., Emile Pin, S.J., and Alfred Fasola-Bologna, *Sociology of Christianity: International Bibliography Supplement 1962–1966* (Rome: Gregorian University Press, 1968).

Appendix: A Paradigm for the Analysis of a Religious Group

This model for the study of a specific religious group draws upon materials and perspectives scattered throughout this text, applying the methodological perspectives summarized in Chapter 19. Its use is not limited to social scientists and religious leaders; it can be used by "lay persons" too. It is deceptively simple; to develop an in-depth analysis of any one of its topics is likely to take a considerable amount of time and study. Even so, it will be incomplete. Although this model covers many subjects, others may be equally or more important in the context of specific needs for institutional self-study, evaluation, and planning or for student research. Many denominations have developed instruments for use by their congregations and agencies; most of them include schedules and forms to complete and other details which complement this introductory tool.

I. History
    A. How did the group originate?
    B. What have been its relationships to its parental sect(s) or denomination(s)?
    C. In which interfaith and interdenominational activities and groups has it participated? Are there any which it opposed or avoided?
    D. Describe its growth and development, including major events, turning points, trends, and the part played by significant leaders.

II. Norms
    A. What are the official and unofficial values of the group (theological, ethical, moral, philosophical, social, and socio-political beliefs and attitudes)?
    B. How are they worked out in practice? What are the specific attitudes on such matters as divorce and remarriage, sexual morality, dietary customs, use of tobacco and alcohol, recreational behavior, Sabbath observance, social ethics, social ministries, etc.?
    C. Are there discrepancies between stated values and actions? If so, how do members and leaders explain them? Are their accounts satisfactory?
    D. To what extent, in what ways, and with what results does the group attempt to enforce its norms?

III. Structure and Leadership
    A. What form(s) of church polity does the group have? Is the form "pure"?

   B. What is the relative distribution of power between the clergy and laity, men and women, denominational and local leaders, officers and employees, etc.?
   C. Trace the flow of authority in various domains of activity.
   D. Describe the lay and professional leaders: How are they selected? What are the minimal qualifications for each position or role? Are the leaders a representative cross-section of the membership by age, sex, socio-economic status, ethnicity, spirituality, etc.?
   E. Where does it best fit in terms of Troeltsch's classification of religious bodies—church, sect, or mysticism (or an adaptation thereof)?
   F. How does the group relate to denominational, interdenominational, ecumenical, and other agencies? (Compare local, regional, state, national, and international levels of cooperation and conflict.)

IV. Constituency
   A. What are the official qualifications for membership, and how strictly are they applied to individual cases?
   B. How large is present membership, and what trends are evident?
   C. What is the membership composition in terms of age, sex, social class, ethnicity, education, etc.? Is it a "homogeneous unit," or are there two or more such units within it? Are all given equitable attention?
   D. How do non-member constituents relate to the group?
   E. Can its leaders estimate how many members fall into each of Fichter's six types of parishioners (saint, nuclear, modal, marginal, dormant, spiritually dead)?
   F. What socio-psychological needs appear to be met by participation in the various activities of this group?

 V. Social Processes
   A. Describe the weekly, monthly, quarterly or seasonal, and annual cycles of "religious" activities and programs. How many and what types of people participate in each of them? Are the activities and programs "evenly distributed"? What roles are played (who does what, for whom, how, when, and with what effects)?
   B. Do the same for each of the groups, services, and ministries sponsored.
   C. Estimate the relative importance of each of Glock's five dimensions of religiosity as well as social communion and the spiritual component. To what extent is spiritual well-being of people a conscious goal?
   D. Are there any indications of cliques, internal conflicts, or divisions? If so, describe them and analyze the manifest and latent causes and the consequences.
   E. What subjective interpretations of their participation are given by group members? Was their own recruitment into the group a reflection of these?

VI. Location and Facilities
   A. Where does the group conduct its various activities? How central are these places to current participants? Are they easily located by newcomers and other target individuals? Are they convenient to both private and public transportation?
   B. How do its locations relate to other institutions of the community of

which it is a part? Consider shopping areas, other businesses and industries, churches. Natural and artificial barriers (lakes, streams, freeways, railroads, parks, telephone zones, and the like) should also be taken into account.

C. Locate the members by categories (families, couples, singles; students, employers, employees, retirees, etc.) on a large map of the community, ideally by both residence and place of work or school. What do the resulting distributions suggest?

D. Are facilities suitable for their respective uses? Consider size, space needed for each program element, acoustics, accessibility to the infirm, furnishings, lighting, ventilation, etc.

VII. Predicted Future

A. What stages of the life cycle (pp. 118–24) has the group already completed, where is it now, and what can be expected from current trends? If conclusions are undesirable, can the trends be reversed? How?

B. Is there a trend toward increased secularization or sanctification in this group? What evidence supports your conclusion?

C. What do the members expect to change over the next year and the next decade? Are their expectations a self-fulfilling prophecy?

Index

Subject entries followed by *n.* refer to footnotes. Most religious bodies are listed under major denominational categories; thus for "African Methodist Episcopal Church" look under "Methodists, African M. Episcopal."

Anarchism, 297
Anders, Sarah Frances, 353
Anderson, Charles H., 540
Anderson, Dewey, 302, 305
Anderson, Robert, 404
Anderson, Robert T., 197
Anderson, W. A., 393
Andrews, F. Emerson, 154, 155, 156
Anglicans, 78, 80, 102, 126, 177, 221, 252, 264 (see also Episcopal Church)
Anglo-Catholics, 257
Animism, 8, 227
Annulment, 363-64
Anomie (normlessness), 112, 461, 470, 471
Anthony, Dick, 72
Anthropology, 24, 158, 224n., 239, 511
Anthropomorphism, 161, 430
Anti-Catholicism, 286, 300-316, 329, 331, 447-48, 455
(See also Catholic-Protestant relations, conflict)
Anti-clericalism, 153, 519
Anti-Defamation League, 264, 327, 535
Anti-democracy, 304
Anti-intellectualism, 289, 332, 440 (see also Intellectualism)
Antinomianism, 290, 292
Anti-Protestantism, 303, 311, 312
Anti-Saloon League, 375
Anti-Semitism, 300, 311, 317-23, 329, 445, 469, 480, 493, 504, 534, 535
    Christian sources of, 286, 318-20, 326, 329, 447
    effects of, 264, 322-23, 411
    and interfaith marriage, 356
    Jewish, 323
    opposition to, 264, 265, 324, 327
    theories of, 320-21
Antitheses, false, 345
Antonovsky, Aaron, 322
Anxiety, 40, 163, 463, 467, 470, 474, 527
Apologetics, 120, 182, 190
Apostates, 413, 420
Apostles of discord, 447-48
Apostolic churches, 31
Apostolic succession, 61, 91, 96
April Fool's Day, 69
Arabian states, 374
Arbitration, 268
Argentina, 221, 311, 374
Argyle, Michael, 441, 520
Armageddon, 534
Armenian churches, 30
Arminianism, 59
Armistice Day, 69
Army, 396 (see also Chaplains, military; War; etc.)
Arnold, Charles Harvey, 282
Art, 68, 130, 136, 166, 169, 518
Arthur, Paul, 510
Artificial insemination, 359
Asbell, Bernard, 501
Asceticism, 58, 74, 526
Assagioli, Roberto, 464
Assemblies of God, 32, 120, 458, 514, 524
Assimilation, 268, 428
    into a church, 67, 402-3, 438
    of immigrants, 455-58
    of Jews, 279, 297, 322, 323, 392, 411, 412
    of sects, 59, 274

Association for a United Church, 260n.
Association for the Sociology of Religion, 13
Association of Christian Scholars, 202
Associations, 21, 23
Astrology, 528
Atheism, 202, 287, 325, 472
Atheists, 33, 319
Attwater, Donald, 264
Augur, Helen, 427
Authoritarianism, 312, 320, 367, 447, 463, 469, 491n.
Authority, 548
    types, 84, 95-98, 495
    (See also Legitimation)
Automation, 2
Automobile, 42, 85, 120, 260, 367, 391
Avato, Rose M., 151, 453
Aviad, Janet O'Dea, 158, 518
Avoidance, sectarian, 82, 116 (see also Withdrawal)
Awakening, spiritual (see Conversion)
Awana, 166

Babbie, Earl, 420
Babcock, Charlotte G., 465
Baber, Ray, 356
Baccalaureate services, 197, 244
Bach, Marcus, 276
Bachelet, V., 97
Bachmann, E. Theodore, 45, 238
Backsliding, 410, 436, 438, 441, 478, 484 (see also Leakage; Members, types of, dormant)
Bahai, 30, 112
Bahr, Howard M., 356
Bailey, Faith Coxe, 124
Bailey, Thomas A., 226, 235
Bain, Read, 337
Bainbridge, William S., 98
Bainton, Roland H., 274, 358
Baker, David W., 212
Baker, Roy S., 45
Bakke, E. Wight, 171
Bales, R. F., 130
Ballard, Guy, 96
Ban, Joseph D., 102
Bankers, 415 (see also Businessmen)
Banning, W., 66
Baptism, 492
    adult, 79, 85-86
    attitudes toward, 58, 247, 384
    believers, 36, 102, 351
    Catholic, 36, 309, 406
    and church school, 216
    functions of, 85-86, 140, 431, 436
    infant, 69, 74, 101, 226n., 254, 351
    (See also Life-cycle rituals; Ordinances; Sacraments)
Baptist Joint Committee on Public Affairs, 29
Baptists, 31, 32, 33, 34, 80, 83, 131, 301, 514
    American B. Association, 32
    American (Northern) B. Churches, 32, 37, 126, 146, 216, 276, 277, 404-5, 518
    attitudes of, 59, 177, 342, 384-85, 454
    behavior of, 177, 201, 390, 393
    black, 34-35, 396, 449, 452
    change from sect to church, 79, 83, 87, 101-2, 105, 257
    conflict among, 272, 276, 378, 404-5
    Conservative B. Association, 276

INDEX **583**

Menendez, Albert J., 329
Menges, Robert J., 511
Menninger, Karl A., 446, 462
Mennonite Central Committee, 155
Mennonites, 31, 56, 59, 76, 79, 81, 85, 91, 112, 208, 367, 433, 462, 518, 541 (*see also* Amish; Hutterites)
Mennonite World Conference, 255
Mental experiment, 129
Mental health, 329, 446, 467, 479, 480, 490
  dysfunctional church effects on, 165, 179, 366
  sects and, 88, 125
Mental illness, 179, 460-69, 498
  and conversion, 109, 424
  religion in causation of, 181-82, 271, 365, 400, 462-64, 480
  religion a preventive of, 139, 164, 446, 464-67, 479
  religion in treatment of, 139, 164, 467-69, 479, 541
  (*See also* Neurosis)
Mergers of churches, 122, 260 (*see also* Church union; Denominations, merger of)
Merriam, Thornton, 172
Merton, Robert K., 58, 90, 118, 129, 158, 178, 340, 413, 439
Messianic Jewish Alliance, 534
Messianic movements, 117, 479
Messianism, Jewish, 56, 117, 296, 297, 324, 494
Messinger, Sheldon L., 121
Methodist Layman's Union, 453
Methodists, 31, 32, 33, 34, 35, 59, 79, 81, 83, 86, 105, 146, 201, 213, 252, 254, 255, 256, 258, 376, 378, 396
  African M. Episcopal Church, 31, 32, 449, 533
  African M. Episcopal Zion Church, 32, 449, 533
  change from sect to church, 87, 102-3, 257
  characteristics of, 353, 361n., 384, 390, 391, 393, 401, 409, 422, 458, 459
  Christian M. Episcopal Church, 533
  clergy, 484, 503-4, 505
  conflict among, 91, 275, 286
  Evangelical M. Church, 256
  Free, 91
  M. Episcopal Church, 102, 285
  Primitive M. Church, 256
  Southern M. Church, 256
  United M. Church, 17, 32, 34, 35, 256, 521, 533
  Virginia Conference, 254
  Wesleyan, 31, 83, 91, 101
  World M. Council, 255
Methodist Youth Council, 504
Metz, Donald L., 299
Mexicans, 389, 457
Mexico, 457
Meyer, Alan S., 471
Meyers, Jerome K., 461
Meyersohn, Rolf, 354
Mezuzah, 18
Michigan, 197, 472
Mickey, Paul A., 299
Microcosm, sect as, 112, 117
Middle axiom, 178
Middle class, 112, 172, 180, 192, 215
  influence in Catholicism, 55, 173, 280, 308
  influence in Judaism, 55-56, 72, 296, 322, 412
  lower-, 228, 408
  Protestantism, 146, 218, 256, 296, 458

upper-, 223, 256, 459
  (*See also* Social class)
Middle East, 523, 534
Middle range, theories of, 338
Middleton, Robert G., 493
Middleton, Russell, 362, 419
Middleton, Warren C., 473
Middletown, 65, 344, 551
Midwest, 103, 215, 542
Migration:
  and church growth, 44, 214
  and conflict, 298, 463
  Negro, 115, 453
  and religion, 28, 106-8, 218, 392
  rural-urban, 44, 107-8, 110, 117
  (*See also* Mobility; Rural migrants)
Military service, attitudes toward, 120, 475 (*see also* Conscientious objectors)
Mill, John Stuart, 140
Millennialism, 87, 91, 282, 542
Millennium, 67, 283, 319
Miller, Daniel R., 361
Miller, Delbert C., 58
Miller, Lois Mattox, 177
Miller, Norman, 494
Miller, T. Franklin, 210
Miller, William Lee, 63, 175, 468
Millerism, 272
Mills, C. Wright, 58, 76, 86, 432, 527
Mills, John Orme, 26
Milwaukee, Wis., 522
Mind, 42, 183, 423, 467-68
Minister (*see* Clergy)
Minneapolis, Minn., 466, 473
Minnesota, 197, 386
Minnesota Poll, 509
Minorities, 45, 99, 327, 368, 388-89, 471, 533 (*see also* Ethnic groups; *etc.*)
Minority group, 116, 311
  every American church as, 374
Miracles, 281, 331, 469
Misnagdim, 278
Missionary, 141, 151, 454, 457
  background of, 223, 224, 225
  Catholic, 54, 221, 225
  duties of, 151, 224-25, 235
  influence of, 235, 374, 454, 483
  Mormon, 103, 388
  persecution of, 141, 306
  prestige of, 400, 503
  Protestant, 54, 221, 224, 225, 309, 481-82
  roles of, 224-25, 235
  types of, 151, 224-25, 400
  (*See also* Faith missions; Foreign missions)
Missionary Church, 256
Missionary programs, 155, 207, 208, 209-39
Missionary societies, 91, 214, 399, 450
  antipathy to, 91
Missionary stations, 233-34
Mission Covenant Youth, 428, 432
Missions (*see* Foreign missions; Home missions)
Missions of Christians to Jews, 324
Missouri, 84, 149, 245, 484, 486, 497
Mitosis, of Protestantism, 275-76
Mixed marriages (*see* Marriage, intermarriage)
Mixter, Russell L., 347
Miyamoto, S. Frank, 458

596

Smith-Hinds, William L., 347, 381
Smohalla cult, 454
Snake-handling, 373, 462, 475, 541
Snavely, Guy E., 199
Snyder, Charles R., 471
Snyder, Richard C., 235
Sobel, B. Z., 542
Social change, 165, 167, 385, 488, 513-43, 545-46, 551, 552
  and church effectiveness, 138, 184
  church reactions to, 144, 288, 326, 509
  church resistance to, 179, 334, 344, (see also Conservatism)
  and revivals, 443
  a source of sects, 111-13
Social class, 52, 66-67, 149, 446, 458-60, 479
  and Catholic-Protestant tensions, 312-13, 328
  and church joining, 47, 251, 255, 258, 291, 404
  and clergy, 415, 482, 503, 504
  conflict, 86, 297, 344
  and conversion, 432, 440
  and crime, 471
  and denominational policies, 147-48, 263
  and educational aspirations, 394-95
  and ethics, 390
  and family problems, 363-64, 365
  and fertility, 360
  influence on church, 175, 176, 179, 547
  and lay leadership, 132, 415
  and mental illness, 461
  and missions, 223, 235
  and mixed marriage, 356
  in parochial schools, 306
  politics and, 376, 460
  and religious attitudes, 385, 392, 526-27
  of religious bodies, 173, 458-59, 460
  and religious participation, 244, 263, 354, 387, 395, 396, 397, 458-60
  and sainthood, 406-7
  as a source of sects, 104, 113, 458
  (See also Lower classes; Middle class; Social mobility; Social stratification; Upper class)
Social climbing, 47, 228, 410 (see also Status-seeking)
Social cohesion, 469-70 (see also Solidarity)
Social concern, 246, 299, 380, 420, 480, 517, 521-27
  (see also Ethics, social; Social gospel; Social justice)
Social consciousness, 218, 292
Social control:
  in Catholic-Protestant tensions, 314
  churches as, agents of, 112, 135, 137, 138-43, 158, 162, 175, 184, 205, 368, 414, 450, 547
  in churches and sects, 85, 94, 128, 180, 389
  over clergy, 501-3
  foreign missions and, 229, 237
  internalized, 361
  over migrants, 107, 456
  techniques of, 139-42
Social crises, 111, 119, 165 (see also Depression; Social disorganization)
Social deviancy and marital adjustment, 357
Social differentiation, 65, 113, 138 (see also Social class)
Social disorganization, 107, 108-11, 456, 547
Social distance, 345, 409, 415
Social equilibrium, 163
Social ethics (see Ethics, social; Social concern; Social gospel)

Social evils, 104
Social fictions, 26, 71
Social gospel, 144-47, 158, 172, 175, 199, 200, 260, 283, 289-90, 343n., 375, 441, 521
  new, 263
Social identification, 132, 321, 346
Social integration, 81, 120, 128, 137, 156, 232, 306, 345, 440, 460, 492-93, 548 (see also Integration, racial)
Social interaction, 4, 7, 9, 10, 20, 101, 133, 146, 163, 312, 346, 548, 549
Socialism, 109, 143, 144, 297, 308
  Christian, 103, 145
Socialization, 20, 146, 398, 423
  church and, 131-32, 368
  into a church, 67, 439
  conversion and, 424, 426, 431
Social justice, 371, 451, 478, 509, 517, 524, 531, 532
  (see also Social concern)
Social location, 431
Social mobility, 47, 56, 65, 100, 101, 102, 138, 218, 228, 237, 255, 306, 356, 404, 414, 433, 451, 459
Social outcasts, 228
Social problems, church and, 190, 349, 445-80, 502
  (see also specific problems)
Social processes, 5, 8, 241-348, 544 (see also Cooperation; Conflict; etc.)
Social psychology, 71, 115, 398, 479
  and missions, 228-29
  of religion, 25, 90, 186, 383-480, 444
Social reform, 125
  church and, 102, 137, 143-49, 380, 406, 441, 474, 489, 494, 502
Social research (see Research)
Social responsibility, 111
Social science, 148, 183, 237, 287, 338, 340, 347, 439, 487, 491, 505, 548, 549-51 (see also Research; Sociology; etc.)
Social scientists, 13, 93, 125, 160, 173, 225, 332, 380, 406, 479
Social security, 139, 180, 506
Social solidarity, 236, 242, 432, 458 (see also Solidarity)
  church function of, 134-36, 156, 175, 321, 345, 547
Social stability, 334
  church as agent of, 51, 136-38, 547
  and sects, 108, 111
Social stratification, 97, 404, 458-60 (see also Social class)
Social system, 127, 128
Social welfare, 130, 533
  and churches, 65, 104, 114, 148, 149, 153, 184, 378, 445
  by churches, 133, 175, 244, 366, 454, 482, 494, 525, 547
  church influence on policies, 146, 178, 359, 375
  (See also Social work; Welfare agencies)
Social well-being, and religion, 153, 477
Social work:
  church and, 150, 152, 244, 349
  in churches, 94, 366, 481
  (See also Social welfare; Welfare agencies)
Social workers, 164, 184
  and clergy, 152-53, 476, 483, 491
  as missionaries, 225

Sterilization, 308, 359, 378
Stern, Bernard, J., 228
Stewardship, 358, 372, 393
Stewart, Jack, 132
Stewart, Omer C., 455
Stigall, Sam, 530
Stipe, Claude E., 239
Stokes, Anson Phelps, 381, 451
Stolz, Karl R., 498
Stone, Carol Larson, 466
Stouffer, Samuel A., 360, 466
Stranger, 224, 269
Stratman, Bernard F., 444
Stritch, Samuel Cardinal, 160
Strommen, Merton P., 511, 542
Stroup, Herbert, 96
Strunk, Orlo, Jr., 468, 485
Studd, C. T., 226
Student religious movements, 200, 259
Students (see College students)
Stuntz, Hugh, 236
Sturzo, Luigi, 537
Sub-cultures, 103, 184, 451
Subjective meanings, 233, 243, (see also Meaning)
   in religion, 12, 25, 53, 71, 228, 256, 367, 398, 406,
      474, 536, 544
Sublimation, 165, 400, 485
Sub-organizations of church, 83, 84, 124, 213-14,
      401-2, 408, 409, 450
   competition of, 269
   leadership of, 415, 416, 417, 490
   (See also Choir; Sunday school; etc.)
Subsidiarity, 371
Suburban churches, 46-47, 217-18, 276, 418, 542
   church attendance in, 395-96
   comity standards for, 252
   growth of, 253-54
Suburban Judaism, 47, 56, 72, 322
Suburbs, 45, 56, 192, 214, 276, 547
Suffering, 163, 165, 289
Suggestibility, 119, 441, 467
Sugrue, Thomas, 311, 316, 456
Suicide, 469-70
Sullenger, T. Earl, 254
Sullivan, Teresa A., 208
Summer Institute of Linguistics, 237
Sumner, William G., 21, 23
Sunday, Billy, 92, 442
Sunday evening service, 46
Sunday observance, 86, 167, 342, 540
Sunday school, 84, 190, 191, 192-93, 194, 195, 197,
      204, 367
   associations, 191, 245, 262
   attendance, 362, 428
   black, 449
   Buddhist, 231, 457-58
   for Catholics, 194
   and character, 131, 390
   and church growth, 253, 401, 402, 404
   and church vitality, 218
   contests, 166
   and conversion, 432
   cooperative, 245, 250
   decision day, 427, 430
   dropping out of, 362, 438
   educational materials, 283, 319, 448, 449
   enrollment, 32, 192, 214, 217

   and evangelism, 442
   Jewish, 192
   lessons, 189
   rejection of, 91
   teachers and officers, 139, 192, 362, 399, 416,
      438, 483
   World Convention, 191
   (See also Church school; Religious education;
      etc.)
Superiority, feelings of, 116 (see also Ethnocentrism)
Supernatural, 163, 175, 332, 403, 537
   sanctions, 64, 176, 547, 548-49
Supernaturalism, 367, 536
Superstition, 70, 236, 309, 334, 335, 339, 341, 351
Supreme Court (U.S.), 196, 303, 377
Sussman, Marvin B., 381
Sustenance rites, 69-70, 353-54
Sutherland, Edwin H., 479
Sutherland, Robert L., 14, 114
Sutker, Solomon, 97
Swamis, 79
Swann, Charles E., 517, 540
Swanson, Guy E., 361, 367
Swatos, William, Jr., 126
Sweden, 56, 428, 455n.
Swedenborgians, 80, 92
Swedes, American, 57, 106
Sweet, William Warren, 93, 146, 197, 198, 213, 257,
      325, 444, 486
Sweetser, Thomas, 542
Swift, Arthur L., Jr., 151, 332, 477, 502
Symbolic interactionism, v
Symbolism, 166, 168, 325, 372, 454, 459
Symbols, 470, 518
   American, 72
   churches as, 449
   of churches, 1-2, 53, 58, 103
   clergy as, 488, 489, 492
   economic, 70
   linguistic, 18, 52, 243, 372
   religious, 1-2, 52, 68-71, 97, 101, 111, 120, 121,
      134, 186, 384, 470, 515
   saints as, 406
Symington, T. A., 467
Symonds, Percival M., 435, 469
Synagogue, 36, 56, 203, 296, 317, 494, 541
   departure from, 323-24
   Jewish-Christian, 323-24
Synagogue Council of America, 264
Syncretism, 65, 82, 228, 230-31, 239, 433, 443, 454-55
   in Catholicism, 230, 238, 457
Syracuse, N. Y., 387
Syria, 534

Taba, Hilda, 466
Taber, Marcius E., 283
Tabernacle, Jewish, 218
Taboos, 85, 91, 116, 120, 141, 223, 384, 390, 429
Taft, Donald R., 446, 472
Tagiuri, R., 317
Taiping Rebellion, 235
Taiwan, 523
Talmud, 295, 359
Taoism, 30, 92
Tapp, Robert B., 196
Tappert, Theodore G., 254
Taves, Marvin J., 386